LITERARY INTENTION, LITERARY INTERPRETATION, AND READERS

LITERARY INTENTION, LITERARY INTERPRETATION, AND READERS

John Maynard

broadview press

Dedicated to three generations of students who relentlessly thrashed these issues out with me.

In memory of exceptional mentors:

Reuben Brower; Jerome Hamilton Buckley
Socratic critic; Dialectical historian

Library and Archives Canada Cataloguing in Publication

Maynard, John, 1941-
Literary intention, literary interpretation, and readers / John Maynard.

Includes bibliographical references and index.
ISBN 978-1-55111-897-0

1. Intention in literature. 2. Hermeneutics. 3. Reader-response criticism. 4. Authors and readers. 5. Literature–Explication.
I. Title.

PN81.M477 2008 801'.95 C2008-906348-1

Broadview Press is an independent, international publishing house, incorporated in 1985. Broadview believes in shared ownership, both with its employees and with the general public; since the year 2000 Broadview shares have traded publicly on the Toronto Venture Exchange under the symbol BDP.

We welcome comments and suggestions regarding any aspect of our publications—please feel free to contact us at the addresses below or at broadview@broadviewpress.com.

North America
PO Box 1243, Peterborough, Ontario, Canada K9J 7H5
2215 Kenmore Ave., Buffalo, NY, USA 14207
Tel: (705) 743-8990; Fax: (705) 743-8353
email: customerservice@broadviewpress.com

UK, Ireland, and continental Europe
NBN International, Estover Road, Plymouth, UK PL6 7PY
Tel: 44 (0) 1752 202300; Fax: 44 (0) 1752 202330
email: enquiries@nbninternational.com

Australia and New Zealand
UNIREPS, University of New South Wales
Sydney, NSW, Australia 2052
Tel: 61 2 9664 0999; Fax: 61 2 9664 5420
email: info.press@unsw.edu.au

www.broadviewpress.com

This text is printed on paper containing 100% post-consumer fibre.

FSC
Mixed Sources
Cert no. SW-COC-000952
© 1996 FSC

PRINTED IN CANADA

Using 820 lb. of Rolland Enviro100 Print instead of virgin fibres paper reduces your ecological footprint of :

Tree(s) : 7
Solid waste : 201 kg
Water : 19 004 L
Suspended particles in the water : 1,3 kg
Air emissions : 441 kg
Natural gas : 29 m^3

CONTENTS

ACKNOWLEDGEMENTS

My greatest debt in this work, as my dedication records, is to the many students, over many more years than I care to enumerate, who have agonized with me over these difficult and fundamental issues of interpretation. Their inventiveness with examples and their persistence in finding new arguments or new challenges to old ones have been a source of amazement to me, and also an inspiration and encouragement. Their interest persuaded me that these old problems are ever new in each interested reader. I am most grateful to them and sorry that most of them will never come to know it. Over the same long period, friends and relations, Sundeep Bisla, Susi Dathe, Virginia Franklin, Susanna Gaertner, Ursula Krammer, Gail Krupa, Alex Maynard, Florence Maynard, Jane Silverman, Saudamini Siegrist, Herb Sussman, and Warwick Slinn, all did the great kindness of listening to my often inchoate thoughts as this project twisted and evolved. My co-editor, Adrienne Munich, has kept my brain agile as we worked out intellectually, discussing so many papers over so many years. My companion, Joan Arkin, has been both a patient listener and a warm and constant support.

Paola Bottalla, Andrea Garbuglia, Mary Ellis Gibson, the late Frederick Karl, and Stephen Souris were generous with good ideas as I presented parts of this work. I am likewise very grateful for the many good suggestions made by the readers of my manuscript for Broadview.

I have been most fortunate in finding such a supportive and helpful publisher. Julia Gaunce and Marjorie Mather guided my work through final revisions with sensitive authority. Tara Lowes has been a genial and most helpful production editor and Piper-Lee Blackey has been tremondously cordial in seeing the work through the press. Finally, I especially thank Martin Boyne for the most penetrating and intelligent line editing I have ever been fortunate enough to experience.

SECTION ONE*

INTRODUCTION

I offer these essays, rethinking some of the grounds of literary interpretation from the point of view of readers, to readers everywhere. This in no way excludes that odd class (from a sociological perspective) of professional readers, to which I belong: literary students of the academies in the English-studying world. But I have approached basic questions here in what I hope is a style accessible to all readers who would like to think about what we do when we read a text and then have an opinion about it, which we may think, say or write—or perhaps sing, dance or perform. I especially welcome such readers who may come to see that my argument broadly if none too saliently incites their empowerment against the professional readers of our time, as in all times, who would seek to channel and regulate their responses to literature. I do not thereby wish to encourage foolish, mindless or, for that matter, heartless response to literature—though I rather think we professionals will always tend to fail in the heartless direction just as the unprofessional reader, who knows what he or she likes, may sometimes give up the business, which we are paid to encourage, of thinking hard about literature.

I do not mean that I have pulled any punches or taken the reader only into the vestibule of thinking about the premises of literature and its reading, though I have often carried on my engagements with the hardest issues and heaviest hitters in the footnotes and two appendices, where they may be ignored by some and relished by others. But I have chosen a broad view over intricate ones, wanting as I do to raise the big issues of

*Notes appear at the end of the section. Substantive notes are bolded.

reading and interpretation of our time as I see them. In this, I bring to the investigation of the possible premises of reading a broad working acquaintance with issues both of literary interpretation and of historical study. My work has been regularly in both fields, and my interest in theoretical issues, often pursued here in their own right, has emerged experientially from working with literature and literary history for over forty years.

In that time I have seen the pendulum of interest, increasingly following a beat of fashionableness which seems increasingly hard to keep from dominating the work of each generation, swing from historical to practical to theoretical study. And now a newer historical study is of course back in force almost as decisively as the older historical study was in my graduate-student days (Harvard being slow to catch on to the New Criticism of those days and its turn from history to interpretation). To write now about major issues in theory may seem an inconsiderate bucking of the trend of the day. Literary theory, so hotly pursued in the late 1970s and early 1980s that it was given the pet name "theory," has been followed by fewer and fewer people as it has seemed increasingly to occupy itself with its own vocabulary, its own set of approved gestures, its elegant pursuit of fine points sometimes shading into aridity and irrelevance.

In the English-speaking world, where predominant concerns had been with the binary of interpretation versus contextual, historical study, theory began especially as a reconsideration of the premises of interpretation. There was, perhaps, a hope that theory could finally oversee the enterprise of interpretation, putting literary study, as the early works of Jonathan Culler importing structuralist theory from France often suggested, on a footing of science-like security.[1] When this failed to emerge—the footing only sliding to other temporary standing places around a great quicksand of more and more theory—it was likely that someone would mount an argument claiming the irrelevance of theory. In the upshot that moment has been at least symbolically encoded in the essay of Steven Knapp and Walter Benn Michaels denying there are any consequences to theory.[2] And, as I read our history, such a conclusion led to the massive reloading of the guns of historical study. Some continued to follow theory as a prestigious special art with its increasingly large and dispersed family of terms of art. Most moved to research, seeking archival backing for renewed historical readings of texts, often without too manifest an interest in the reading or interpretation itself.

It was one of the byproducts of theory—one that is often especially deplored—that its failure to find a definitive and authoritative new set of rules for interpretation to replace the earlier ones of the New Criticism—hegemonic in the United States but also powerfully established in the more moralizing but equally interpretive Leavisite tradition elsewhere in the English reading world—led to a moment, let us say around 1980, when interpretation seemed to be an open field. By this I do not mean that one couldn't choose one's school: Lacanian, Marxist, historical, New Critical, Leavisite, structuralist, deconstructionist; that had always been possible, though the schools were certainly changing. But it seemed that theory was opening up a new pragmatic world in which none of these could feel entirely comfortable beginning interpretation by positioning their methods as intrinsically correct. As in other moments of especially generative ferment in cultures—for instance classical Athens, Hellenistic Egypt, pre-Christian Rome, the Italian Renaissance, Paris of the later half of the nineteenth century, or New York of the later twentieth century (to compare what was great to what was obviously a more niche renascence), variety of causes, highly active proponents of diverse beliefs, great enthusiasms opened doors to relativism as well as to eclecticism. In such a ferment, the better arguments might be allowed to surface in a general context of persuasion rather than be tested, compartmentally, against the orthodoxies and premises of the particular school of interpretation.

There even appeared a loose set of theoreticians/interpreters who took this pragmatic view. They were broadly labeled reader-response or reader critics, though the subject itself has sometimes come to be called by the broader term, reader theory. All of them shifted the place of interpretation from study of the author or analysis of the text to the reader. To the startled historical or New Critical orthodox, they also seemed as a class to throw the judgment on how to read to the readers. Instead of asking what he or she meant in writing the work, or asking what it, the work, means, they asked the receiver's question, what does this mean to me, or more directly, what do I mean in my reading of this work by this person. As in English and American law, the grounds of interpretation were not to be defined by law but rather left to the individual jurors. Appearing quite early in the story, David Bleich was their most Whitmanian figure, in fact very much encouraging the reader to read her way.[3] Norman Holland encouraged personal readings, from the hip of psychosexual response, but also attempted to frame and display them within his version of psychoanalytic theory.[4] Wolfgang Iser, representative of a German school from Konstanz which came to interest in readers from phenomenological philosophy's intense concern with the way the mind processes what it comes to know, was, more typically, a fairly well-organized prophet. Although seeming to offer a liberating system, he nonetheless controlled its tendencies to splinter into infinite parties of individual readers. Readers were given some space of freedom within a larger prescriptive formula for how reading takes place. Having started a movement, he would leave it to move on to more general theories of what he called literary anthropology, a throwback to traditional aesthetic theory, just at a time when the entire issue of the nature of aesthetics was being thrown into question.

Stanley Fish, of course, was its strongest thinker and most pyrotechnic debater. Yet he too seemed to offer more flexibility than he intended. His system of reading for what the text does (to the reader), rather than what it means, left Fish in charge of what it did: Fish, as Jonathan Culler would brightly conclude, reading as a Fishian critic. Fish then morphed into a theory Moses who led his literary followers into the desert with his tremendous assurance that readings were determined not by individual choice or by reasoning over premises of interpretation but by pre-established communities into which readers fell willy-nilly. He led them into the desert only to leave them there—as he went on to a second war in legal interpretation, while himself continuing his professional community's highly informed specialized historical work in literature. The philosopher of deconstruction, Jacques Derrida, never even identifying or being identified with the very loosely connected movement, was, in his broad advocacy of open-ended reading over all settled premises of reading, probably its greatest stimulator. Paul de Man, no reader-responser and also identified as major deconstructor, also wrote widely on reading. His contribution was also to open texts to many possible interpretations, though his particular contribution was to insist that all of them were wrong.

My aim in the essays below is to try to recapture that utopian moment of reader freedom and variety, explore some of its major issues, and appraise its value. Its achievement of a glimpse of utopia was from the beginning surrounded by the irony that few even among advocates of reader response wished to allow readers freedom from their own systems or empower their interpretations. And I say utopian rather than ground-breaking as I would like to, because I doubt that there will ever be long periods when can expect to live without setting ourselves rules for reading and interpretation.[5] Perhaps we cannot long stand such light, though I write and argue in hope that we may. Indeed I write at a time when the proponents of orthodox reading—Western as well as Eastern—are once again resorting to violence before the letter to try to enforce their interpretations of holy writings on others. Certainly the utopian moment of 1980 passed almost as soon as it arrived, passed virtually unnoticed and unlamented, passed at least in what Jonathan Culler liked to call the Institution of literature with a tacit sense of relief. Our occupation as a place of special competence available only to initiates seemed threatened just there for a moment. Having seen there were no rules governing interpretation, Knapp and Michaels led a major retreat into history, in which we now seem in danger of losing all interpretation to elegant contextual readings that can be done only by learned, researching specialists. I am certainly a party to this work, and I can with justice claim I was there before it had a new label, and a part of me rejoices in the triumph of such fine historical study—even as it sees the excesses of too enthusiastic, too totalizing, Foucauldian approaches, to cite an example of excellent historical work that has also led to excess. But good or bad, historical study, which may be happily pursued for its own sake, cannot evacuate the world of literature of its readers' interests in texts and their interpretation. We can even look at the history of interpretation (as I in fact will here for its recent life), but that interest doesn't justify walking away from what people—real readers, including real students and, one hopes, real professors—do and will keep wishing to do: read and interpret.

If the moment I recall and re-explore in the still central study of interpretation is utopian, I don't believe its premises are entirely so. And I write to suggest that they should be recalled as the only ones to direct our currently confused game of interpretation. They suggest a system that will please no party, because no party is endowed by it, neither the idealist one that finds a line of great spirits emerging directly out of religion (Milton the greatest in English tradition) but more broadly present in Shakespeare and Romanticism, Yeats and modernism, nor that opposed one that would place material conditions first, interpretation of them and their texts second. Or any other school whatsoever. I would argue that the interpretive turn, in which the pragmatic interpretation itself replaced any quest for guiding premises to control interpretation,[6] is a fundamental fact of our time which we literary thinkers, unlike the philosophers, have tended to run from rather than learn. If it may seem threatening to science, which may wish to discover some premises beneath its different work of exploration, or dangerous to the law, which may feel social cohesion requires widely agreed-upon premises to bulwark its interpretations, it can only benefit literary interpretation, where better readings must stand on their own merits as convincing approaches to the work rather than on the authority of premise or party.

Not only utopian, but bourgeois utopian? Not at all: the field of interpretation is open; let the most engaged and engaging Marxist reading win what adherents it may; but not for its premises as ideology received before interpretation, but for its power as a way of engaging with literature. To open reading and interpretation to competitive free play in no way privileges a hermeneutics of consciousness based on a privileged, highly capitalized subject. But it does forbid giving power over interpretation to any privileged party, left, right, or center.

Nor should we be afraid to talk about individual consciousness as part of the process of interpretation. Like behaviorists in psychology studying thinking apart from thought, anti-subjectivists in literary studies rather absurdly pursue the study of what are intrinsically subjective phenomena, writing and reading, by ignoring the experience of thinking and feeling. Thinking, writing, and reading are always done by somebody; they are done in a way that, still mysteriously to questers after artificial intelligence, mixes memory, desire, and ideologies. The mix is individual, unique, and constantly changing; it is aware of itself, hence conscious. We cannot study reading by eliminating the individual, conscious reader, aware of what she is experiencing as she reads and interprets. Organic intellectual, traditional intellectual, proletariat, bourgeois, whatever ideology she promotes or class position she represents, she cannot but be a subjective, individual, and conscious reader. Indeed, reading itself is intrinsic to subjectivity: it promotes and abets the development of a mind in dialogue with itself. Reading, even the memorizing out loud of a sacred text central to his culture of a medieval monk or young Taliban, gives him, as a byproduct of his absolute conformity to the ideology of his culture, an inner version of that text, his own subjective formation. My grandmother was raised in a Nova Scotian Victorian culture of oral reading. When she reacted to something, she often would recite poems she had learned by heart, Poe's "Raven" or "Casabianca" of Felicia Hemans ("The boy stood on the burning deck"). They were as much a part of her inner world as "The Charge of the Light Brigade" was to the annoying but individual Mr. Ramsay in Woolf's *To the Lighthouse*.

I will be arguing against simplistic views of authors that make them fully in control of the possible meanings for their readers of texts they produce; I will also oppose equally simplistic views that make authors mere creations of their times.[7] Similarly, I will neither wish to reify the reader into a totally independent master of meaning, a Descartes by the fire with a book in the silence of his isolated hut, nor wish to run to the opposite extreme and argue for a reader totally controlled by his society, without interest, agency, individuality. In both cases I side-step the old chestnut of determinism in the form we now hear it—of the individual determined by society; authors and readers may ultimately be Lucretian atoms cued here and there by the infinite atoms of society, history, culture, past culture, bodily and material conditions. In the final count this might be true but who is counting such infinity of causes.

Not only utopian, but anti-historical? Not at all. First, and of course, let historical studies of history, culture, societies, flourish; let rich studies of the broad cultural text show the power of their interpretive moves to engage with the thus embedded literary text, as the most fanciful and most productive brave New Historical worlds of interpretation did: but not through a hegemonic power given by some intentionalist premise that this is the only kind of meaning possible to the text or that any historical view is not itself just one of many possible interpretations—issues I will explore fully in my central chapter on literary intention. Hermeneutics, not historicity, is the ark of our foundation;[8] our refrain must be not "always historicize," but "always interpret." This utopian hermeneutics is without its independent rules. In the conundrum "it is all history, it is all interpretation," I suggest we take the second: no history without a prior act of interpretation. Yes, you can as easily reverse it, chicken for egg, but the result of reversal is the danger of reification and limiting of your interpretive approach to that particular reading of history. As you read history so shall you read all else. The possibility of other interpretations—of history as well as of texts—seems foreclosed. When we start with interpretation, granting that our interpretation then controls our view of history and our reading of texts within the history, we keep open and before us the possibility of other interpretations, other histories, other interpretations of texts—even those in historical contexts. Starting with history locks us into our premises: history then becomes not critique of our historically constructed moment but its reification. I stress strongly, to avoid any misunderstandings: I am not against historical studies in literary work, only against privileging historically based approaches in what should remain the free-for-all, no holds barred, of interpretation.

To return to the utopian moment of the interpretive turn, to an open sense of readers forced to try to persuade each other of their readings, may seem naive to the New Historian or student of Cultural Studies engaged in massive projects reading the texts of an age. But interpretation always seems naive to historians; and their green shades and blinders have always sought to limit the freedom of new approaches, open discussion. To turn again to interpretation, no holds barred or prescribed, is also an act of maturity: for the nonprofessional reader, to attempt to communicate the joy or anxiety or dismay provoked by literature; for the professional student, to see how persuasive, how useful to others, the approaches developed in the cunning and secrecy of her special art are when they must be compared with other approaches to literature. Do we have anything to show of ourselves to others, professional and nonprofessional readers alike, or only to our professional acolytes of the coming generation of place seekers?

I thus begin with a full revisit to what I take to be the central issue in contemporary historical work: a central issue in the entire history of hermeneutics but mainly submerged in the turn back to history. I mean that of literary intention or, as it is also called, intentionality. Declarations of freedom from intention, deaths of authors in general, were foundational to deconstruction (Roland Barthes's "The Death of the Author"), historicism (Michel Foucault's "What is an Author?") and reader theory alike.[9] In this, the newer directions of the late 1970s—at least in their Anglophone manifestations—rather unthinkingly accepted the fundamental premise of their universal opponent, modern formalism (New Criticism or Leavisism). As so often in postmodernism there was really a slide from modern to postmodern while a revolution was hotly proclaimed. Barthes might retain a certain attraction to a readerly text, a text that he defined as determined by its historical codes; and Derrida might posit intention as a transcendental reality somehow there but never attainable in his world of ever-opening interpretations;[10] but both essentially continued to cut interpretation loose from its bearings in intentionality. Fish, oddly, has been more ambivalent, seeming to say both that intentionality is merely an effect of interpretation and that it is a necessity.[11] His own period-based excellence and his pragmatic arguments have perhaps encouraged his students to run into new historicity without facing this central hermeneutic crux of intentionality. My contention is that in overlooking intention, relegating it to the old metaphysics of theory when it is in fact a central issue in the praxis of interpretation, the New Historical generation allow it to be their central blind spot, the issue that calls into question their histories in the central activity that they have believed distinguished their histories from earlier ones, their readings of texts. This has been a huge and central area of literary discussion—though one often wished away. I have rather called it to me, though this has led through a great thicket of complicated theoretical and practical arguments. I have tried to pursue the issue in its full complexity and articulation rather than performing some more comfortable task because I believe nothing can be more important to our work as servants to readers than thinking through these basic issues well.

The long section two (with many subsections) is foundational in reopening space for readers in other areas where they have been quietly closed off: where structuralism—now reduced from science of literature to the interpretive systems of narratology—finds intention coded in the text; or where a revived instinct for privileged, authorized interpretations resuscitates Hirsch's meaning/significance hierarchy in the name of contextual determination. Nor is my argument unaware of the ghosts and zombie authors always waiting in the shadows, or obviously present in the ordinary eponyms and metonymies of interpretive discussion (what is Maynard *trying to say* about intention?).

Briefer essays encounter other, salient, though less fundamental, issues in reader theory. These essays on four major reader theorists of the reader-response period (section three) assess the ambivalence toward reader empowerment and autonomy that made reader theory so quick to capitulate to the anti-theoretical thrust of the New Historicism. While its strongest advocates drifted away, reader theory by and large was reduced to the creditable but more specialized projects of history, reception history, and history of reading. My revisits to four major theorists examine the many ways in which discussion of reader response was, in an odd reversal, aimed at taming and controlling the new power given for an instant to the reader. My aim here, as in the longer study of literary intention, is to intrude on and interrupt this containing process. I look at Iser's attempts to have his free reader and control him too; my essay, which offended the theorist himself, essentially disallows his attempts to create a half-way house to reader control, while showing why his position, rightly understood as it was by Fish, seemed not only murky but dangerous. In contrast to Fish, I praise the wolf-bite hidden in Iser's theory, though for my troubles I have only succeeded in getting myself bitten.

Systems of proliferating signification deriving from deconstruction or other forms of intense postmodern skepticism have offered enticing but finally unhelpful paradigms for reading. Barthesian and Derridean deconstruction has tended to befriend the reader to the extent of opening room after room for interpretation, though endless interpretation can assuredly become a controlling system as much as one prescription for interpretation. By contrast, de Manian deconstruction has been directly hostile to all readers' interpretations (the more insight the more blindness) and attempted to stop the proliferation of readers and readings. De Man stems above all from New Criticism (not Nazism). New Criticism, in turn, has not been sufficiently recognized as the major interpretive engine of that broad twentieth-century aesthetics that reaches from aestheticism to modernism and even into the large side of postmodernism that continues to be inflected by the modernist triumph of craft and art (what else are we celebrating, if we celebrate it, in the postmodern commodity culture than the Wildean triumph of art over nature?). While I have strong allegiances to the de Manian school historically (I was among the last of the Reuben Brower nursery in which de Man was an early strong and independent seedling) and practically (we are all New Critics in the classroom or when we analyze a text to the extent that we still care about form; and I—probably like all of you my readers—do), yet I have had to reverse his attempt to place reader theory in his *galère* of blind approaches.[12] And I suggest that his aesthetic of unreadability is itself merely a rarefied (and somewhat mystified) version of the aesthetic tradition's reification of form as an interpretive mode in itself. And in de Man's system this is another blindness that, ignoring itself, leads inevitably to one stereotyped and repeated interpretive dead end. I do not share de Man's system of blindness multiplied erringly on all sides of me; I see rather partial truths, glasses half-full rather than half-empty. Having made the reversal, I am quite content to fence him in my garden of various useful insights, blind only when they claim hegemony. He may therefore stand for the larger tradition of New Criticism, which he led so well into his particularly exitless desert, my model of the hermeneutic mistake of trying to establish the text itself as a self-interpreting artefact. Humans, including even brilliant but hesitant interpreters like de Man, risk taking a position, making their mark for well or ill, in making an interpretation. None will stand forever (some may return on us as a haunting); none can be established, it is my argument, on the security of a base that precludes all others—as de Man in fact attempted to do—in advance of interpretation itself. So get you gone, de Man, though with blessings on your head.

A final resistance to reader theory among its friends I locate in a practice of what I call staged readings, in effect a system of reading hidden beneath apparently pragmatic instructions for ordering the project of interpretation. I find such a restraint built firmly into even the seemingly reader-friendly work of Robert Scholes, as his own structuralist interest in narrative slid most productively into his eclectic work of the 1980s. He pleased that age by advocating ideological reflection on texts once interpreted; fewer noticed, or perhaps they noted with relief, his assurance of correct procedure in interpretation itself. Here Scholes is, even more than Iser or de Man, example rather than central target. My point is more broadly to unmask ways in which so many critics hide a normative system of interpretation under a plan for staging interpretation. The gesture naturalizes what is in fact a decision to regulate readings; it deserves exposure and resistance.

My final colloquy in section three is with Fish again, here with his very influential and also much criticized concept of interpretive communities. Having shown a generation the power of conscious reading, of asking not what a text means but what it does, placing meaning in effect as action in the reader, Fish gives the appearance of having panicked. He never intended, he realized, to offer freedom. His reader had been only himself reading all along, a specially informed professional reader. Others might read differently but not as a matter of choice: they were simply automatous reading products of controlling communities. "It looks as if the text is about to be dislodged as a center of authority in favor of the reader." But the readings rendered by these other people (all others) "are, in effect, community property, and insofar as they [communities] at once enable and limit the operations of his [a reader's] consciousness he is too."[13] How much do they? how much don't they? is then my question. I try, once again, to cut the reader some slack without turning her from total automaton to totally autonomous.

This revisit to the near history of reader theory (near because it has of course been a permanent area of literary theory ever since Aristotle's concern with catharsis) has a direction that has been clearer here than it will be in the particular arguments of the individual chapters. Reader theory in its revival in the late 1970s through the mid-1980s offered a brief moment, what I have been calling a utopian moment, of theory turned against the theorists, literary criticism turned against the critics, opening thereby a chance for a variety of real readings, professional or merely interested. Even in its heyday, reader theory as theory acted as a drag on the tendency of its enthusiasts to distort it into a means to prescription and control. In the move back to history and away from theory it became a set of theory lost in the wilderness. Not that no one used it; in fact, it became part of most critics' repertoire. In the secondary schools, at least in the United States and Canada, it challenged the

New Criticism as a standard approach to reading (by this point my reader, I hope, sees some irony in this attempt to make an instrument skeptical of all readings into a variety of reading).[14] Its exponents continued to write and influence students. Its broad-reaching effect has been perhaps especially not an approach but a state of mind in approaching reading and interpretation. It encourages us to think about what we are doing: what kind of reading are we doing when we are doing this or that activity with texts? Perhaps the most permanent legacy of reader theory, which has not been universally welcomed by those who still hope to produce themselves as avatars of one new faith for literary study, is this self-reflexive reflex. Its theoretical point is that thinking about readers clarifies our sense of what it is we and others are doing when we do what we do as readers. That is the utopian realization I wish to recall. I find the study of reader theory to be a very useful way to introduce students to literary theory without having them blinded by the claims of one or another kind of interpretation. I have used it successfully from freshman seminars to doctoral ones; I equally recommend this self-conscious approach to reading to any nonprofessional readers who wish to develop their thinking about literary theory. I have similarly found it an excellent way to sort out the consequences, in interpretation, of that rich basket of theories left on our doorstop in the last thirty years. Show me what your theory does, I find it relatively easy to say to Culler, Iser, Michaels, Stephen Greenblatt, Terry Eagleton, Homi Bhabha, Fredric Jameson, and so many other lights I could cite, and I will tell you what it is.

Reader theory thus promotes thinking about interpretation and tends to shake the throne of any one interpretive approach that tries to set up as orthodoxy. But it is not a panacea for difficulties of interpretation. As my explorations of some reader theorists show, reader theory fails when it attempts to become a distinct practice of interpretation itself, when it offers itself as more than a clarifying device about texts (that is, as more than a way of finding various sites of reading or personas and figures of reading in the text). It fails to become a guide to the perplexed for correct interpretation, attempting to mark out a necessary place for all readers, in or out of the text.[15]

After the period of reader response and the utopian moment I recall, research and thinking about reading in no way stopped. It actually followed its own theoretical logic—toward individual readers—as well as the general trend into history in focusing on issues of the process and history of reading as well as the history of reception. On the whole this work exploring the nature of reading proceeded in an ever more unorganized and unconnected way. Since the time of reader response, we have had a trickle of useful works both on the process and history of reading (the latter more recently becoming a serious flow of studies of historical groups of readers, histories of reception, and histories of the book and print culture). There had of course already been a lively discussion, focused on pragmatic issues in childhood education, of the process of reading acquisition. To this has been added some inquiry into the physical and psychological process of reading during the development of the young person into maturity.[16] There has been further work on the physiology of adult reading.[17] And there is at least one inquiry into the effect of different kinds of reading on our physical and emotional states, reporting happily that "escapist" "trash" reading is the most beneficial and harm-free of narcotics.[18] The work on reading connected with Norman Holland had already come to focus, in a Freudian framework, on the ways in which psychological tendencies in the reader shaped the kinds of habitual stories the readers sought in works they read. This work has continued with further consideration of the ways in which such individual responses can develop into more comprehensive interpretation through discussion.[19] And Holland's later work brings together a variety of studies in the cognitive psychology of reading.[20]

The greatly renewed interest in history in the literary profession, which I find salutary as a general phenomenon but largely problematic in its effect on interpretation, has been helpful in stimulating work on history of readers. Studies as widely different in orientation as Roger Chartier's look at early uses of print and Gerald Bruns's look at the variety of hermeneutic activities in different periods and cultures inspired a new sense of the great variety of reading practices and interpretive methods in use in different periods of history.[21] And we have had a competent if very general general history of reading by Alberto Manguel.[22] Reception has moved on from the purely theoretical issue it seemed in Hans Robert Jauss, who was interested primarily in the changing aesthetic horizons that allowed works of genius to ascend in interest while bestsellers plunged with the sunset of their age.[23] More locally focused studies of reading and reception in individual periods of history have given us at least a patchwork of the ways in which works of literature, contemporary or past, have been received in individual time periods. Interest in the history of the book and more broadly all material conditions of texts have made the history of reading as a study of the conditions of reception an established topic in period works. The danger of such work is it may start imposing rigid taxonomies of reading onto all persons in an historical period, as if there were ever a Fishian community of the whole in which variety of response to writing was impossible. Its value has been to register difference, forcing theoreticians of readers to begin with variety rather than to commence imposing their own reading norms on all readers.

To the extent that theoretical work on readers continued, it tended, especially in the United States, to parallel the development of theory into issues of ethnic or sexual identity. There it found itself creating a great variety of classes of readers from those categories. There would be black readers, Chicano readers, women readers, gay readers, lesbian readers. This seemed perfectly to follow Fish's concept of communities of readers and it also implied, as his work did, that there is a great variety of reading approaches possible to different groups—quite different from the norming approach of his earlier readings of Milton and seventeenth-century literature.[24] In practice what emerged in the study of identities of readers was even more interesting: a tendency to ever greater elaboration of types and breakdown and fragmentation into ever more particular types.

An influential collection of essays trying to define the woman reader brings its reader to conclude that the woman reader is a sex that certainly is not one and may be a great variety of identities. It appears that there is no easy agreement on what defines a woman as reader, from the angry emasculated reader, forced to deny herself as she reads as a man in a man's literary culture, to the happily sympathetic sisterly reader. Such attempts to provide norms for women readers not only provoke more and more norms, suggesting none is alone correct, but also fragment. Classes such as the lesbian woman reader clearly don't fit the norms proposed for women in general but themselves become new sites of contention over reading identity.[25] The same proves true wherever we may look to develop a theory of reading around an identity group or community. What begins as a theoretical attempt to define a kind of reading ends turning us toward the variety of real readers. A more determinedly sociological approach such as that used by Janice Radway in her well-known study of a specific group of female readers of Harlequin-romance fiction who all bought from one lady supplier, *Reading the Romance*, creates a controversial profile of this small group of homemaker readers. But she finds the situation changed with a later generation of working women.[26] What initially looks like a study of the psychology of romance reading—she finds the first group using romance fiction to rationalize the apparent unromance of their marriages—actually becomes a contribution to the contingency of reading experiences: different readers at different times use fiction for different needs.

The burden of this considerable if ununified, unorganized work on readers since the heyday of reader-response discussion is, to put it bluntly and simply, moving toward a conclusion of so many readers, so many responses. That this is an unamiable conclusion to many professionals today may suggest why reader theory has not continued to have the play it did in theoretical circles twenty years ago. Are we brought down to the dregs of a democracy of readers? Is this the unwelcome wisdom that this branch of critical theory has to offer? Even one of the great instigators of reader theory, the semiologist and novelist Umberto Eco, blew a cry of warning in 1990 when he saw better where his style of thinking was taking others in the field of reader theory.[27] It is an offense to most professional readers to have this blunt fact before them. It has even seemed to me one good reason for the turn toward history in the 1980s that this conclusion, yawning up ahead in the ever-opening discussion of reader theory as it confounded all normative styles of reading, might thereby be put off indefinitely. History for most of its practitioners has been a place where readings could be professionalized and stabilized by specialized knowledge; for those interested specifically in reading, it offered the major research project, still very much in its infancy and greatly valuable in itself, of writing the detailed history of reading and reception. The first instinct has been to write that history in a Foucauldian mode, as a succession of fixed structures of reading, one age's reading *episteme* yielding to the different one of the next. Only when that research fully thickens its history into a variety of views on the reading of the age, manufactured by the variety of views of the historians, will we have to face the fact of the real variety of reading experience in every age.[28]

Only a few commentators have been willing to embrace the plurality offered by the development of reader theory. One is Michel de Certeau, whose lovely chapter on consumer reading in *The Practice of Everyday Life* champions the nonprofessional's astuteness in reading against the controlling or demeaning attitudes of the professional.[29] Another, from a very different viewpoint, has been the philosopher Richard Rorty, whose neo-pragmatic faith has been in the emergence of better opinion out of discussion. Focusing more on the practice of interpretation than the sociology of reading, he prefers, like this work, not to attempt to prescribe in advance the rules or norms for reading or interpretation.[30]

In the essays that follow, my own sympathy with these positions will be clear. My work, taking you back to the time of the major debates in reader theory, asks you to realize where that discussion has led us, why the sporadic work on readers since then has all been pointing toward the individual real reader as a person who, once admitted to literary discussion, cannot be easily dismissed or excluded. Real readers, like professional readers, can have great blind spots and, as anyone who has taught literary classes knows, can harbor great stupidities. But a greater stultification results from the attempt to limit damage by setting up prescribed models for reading or protocols for interpretation. Reading, to adopt Wittgenstein baldly, is a game of language for which it is impossible in advance to specify all the possibilities, or even a finite number of possibilities. To try to systematize reading is to be more than human, to specify the nature of emergent activity in advance. The machine cannot thus know itself; it can only try foolishly and damagingly to regiment itself, thus hiding some of its best tricks from itself.

Real readers, as I discuss in my brief, concluding section, far from falling into a few camps easily labeled by the programmatic critic (who may secretly or not so secretly wish them in some readers' gulag), are a delightfully democratic hoard. Imagine the very utopia itself, waiting at the end of my arguments, of the endless possibility of reading by real readers: even more like a carnival than a utopia. I wish this study had room to provide more than some notions and a slightly longer example, drawn from other work I have published, of where the study of real readers has been leading us. I hope the section will suggest where such inquiry into real readers may go. I end with a brief panoply of such real readers for what I hope will be my reader's delectation.

One final note, on taking a position: in a moment in publishing when we are inundated with ostensibly objective handbooks to all things literary, including topics in theory, I may seem out of fashion or even perverse in arguing a position throughout, especially in dealing with the old hot potato of intentionality. I respect the useful background information offered by these unpartisan introductions (my notes show I have sometimes benefited from them). And I believe that I in fact offer below the fullest discussion available on the subject of literary intention. But I am unreformed in thinking that major issues in critical theory are not dead subjects to be historicized, anthologized, summarized, and put on the shelf, and that they are best understood by continuing their controversial interrogation. I hope my work is the better introduction to this great subject in literary theory for its unwillingness to pull punches or withhold considered judgment. My readers may (certainly will) disagree in parts or in the whole. But their disagreements I trust will be honed against the edge of my engaged sharpening over this complex subject.

NOTES: SECTION ONE

1 Especially in his *Structuralist Poetics: Structuralism, Linguistics, and the Study of Literature* (Ithaca: Cornell UP, 1975).

2 "Against Theory," in W.J.T. Mitchell, *Against Theory: Literary Studies and the New Pragmatism* (Chicago: U of Chicago P, 1985), pp. 11–30; orig. pub. in *Critical Inquiry* (Summer 1982). See my discussion of their work in II.i, n. 20, below.

3 See his *Readings and Feelings: An Introduction to Subjective Criticism* (Urbana: NCTE, 1975) and *Subjective Criticism* (Baltimore: Johns Hopkins UP, 1978).

4 See especially, Norman N. Holland, *Five Readers Reading* (New Haven: Yale UP, 1975). Holland's once famous work has lost its place on the edge today though he continues to do interesting work, as I note below. Harold Bloom's work on anxiety made a similar move in the same decade in looking at authors as readers. It is worth citing Holland's importance in the history

of psychoanalytic criticism in moving from attempts to analyze the writer's work through biography to analysis of the reader. One can study readers, as Holland did, in a controlled, interrogative way not available in the study of writers through putting their writing on the couch. Lacanian work has generally been no exception to this, though the stress has been on direct analysis of the text; Shoshana Felman has interestingly used Lacan to place the reader the a position of understanding his own psyche by its reading of the subjective material of the text: not so different from Holland's interest in how material from texts selectively passes censors and is reworked in the reader's unconscious, then allowed to surface. See *Jacques Lacan and the Adventure of Insight: Psychoanalysis in Contemporary Culture* (Cambridge, MA: Harvard UP, 1987), pp. 19–25.

5 I use utopian in the common sense of attractive if impossible, not in the philosophical sense of creating an absolute. My utopia is only countless individual real readers reading with their own individual motivation; it is not, I repeat *not*, a transcendental Reader who occupies all possible reader positions.

6 David R. Hiley, Ronald Bohman, and David Shusterman, *The Interpretive Turn: Philosophy, Science, Culture* (Ithaca: Cornell UP, 1991). I discuss below, II.xix, n. 441, the strengths and problems of this turn as a version of pragmatism.

7 See II.vii, below.

8 Hermeneutics has been reduced in much recent thinking to a mere recovery of consciousness in writing and reading or to the historical grounding of interpretation practiced by the nineteenth-century hermeneutic tradition. I will be recovering it in the full sense of theory or practices of interpretation. See II.xviii, n. 11. Suzy Anger, *Victorian Interpretation* (Ithaca: Cornell UP, 2005), p. 5, has made the same point in her own recovery of hermeneutic discussion in Victorian England: whether under the name of hermeneutics, theory of interpretation, New Criticism's critique of "fallacies," Hirschian anti-intentionalism, reader response theory, or poststructuralist attacks on the author, the discussion of grounds of interpretation has followed the major issues introduced in traditional hermeneutic thinking, though often to very different conclusions.

9 See II.i, nn. 27 (Barthes) and 28 (Foucault), and III (reader theory).

10 See discussion of Derrida's skeptical but complex views on intention in Appendix 1.

11 See Appendix 2.

12 *Allegories of Reading: Figural Language in Rousseau, Nietzsche, Rilke, and Proust* (New Haven: Yale UP, 1979); the *galère* is displayed in his distinguished *Blindness and Insight: Essays in the Rhetoric of Contemporary Criticism* (1971; 2nd ed., Minneapolis: U of Minnesota P, 1983).

13 *Is There a Text in This Class? The Authority of Interpretive Communities* (Cambridge, MA: Harvard UP, 1980), p. 13.

14 The stress in the reader-response classroom, however, has been not so much on a particular kind of reading as in encouraging individuality in work on reading. The important revolution in the secondary school has changed pedagogy as the older teacher-controlled and normed readings in the New Critical classroom have been replaced by a somewhat "new-age" promotion of reading as individual unfolding and development. See Nicholas J. Karolides, ed., *Reader Response in Secondary and College Classrooms* (1992; rev. ed. Mahwah, NJ: Lawrence Erlbaum, 2000). As noted, Bleich, Holland, and especially Steig (see below) have promoted a similar development in the college classroom; the approach has been fairly widely developed with fairly wide suspicion that this may be an unprofessional development attending its spread. In their works for U.S. college teaching, the Bedford St. Martin's series of texts with appended samples of interpretive schools have canonized it as one of the eight master approaches of our time.

15 I should note my own failure from that period alongside my critiques of that of others, an attempt to apply an attractively high-tech idea of triangulation as a way of providing a calculus to reading Robert Browning's dramatic monologues, with their obvious problems of finding positions for reader and author: see "Browning, Donne, and the Dramatic Monologue," *John Donne Journal: Studies in the Age of Donne* 4 (1985): 253–67, and "Reading the Reader in Robert Browning's Dramatic Monologues," in Mary Ellis Gibson, ed., *Critical Essays on Robert Browning* (New York: G.K. Hall, 1992).

16 J. A. Appleyard, *Becoming a Reader: The Experience of Fiction from Childhood to Adulthood* (Cambridge: Cambridge UP, 1990). His study shows the difficulty of doing such work without comparative historical and cultural reference; it tends to reify reading growth in contemporary American culture into a norm for all reading experience.

17 Alan Kennedy, *The Psychology of Reading* (London: Methuen, 1984), offers a useful summary of a large amount of disparate work, which continues massively as special field studies, particularly on the always controversial topic of childhood reading acquisition.

18 Victor Nell, *Lost in a Book: The Psychology of Reading for Pleasure* (New Haven: Yale UP, 1988): a spirited but also experimentally backed defense of reading for pleasure as a psychological benefit.

19 See especially Michael Steig's records of his class work, *Stories of Reading: Subjectivity and Literary Understanding* (Baltimore: Johns Hopkins UP, 1989).

20 See *The Critical I* (New York: Columbia UP, 1992).

21 See Chartier, *The Cultural Uses of Print in Early Modern France* (Princeton: Princeton UP, 1987); *The Order of Books: Readers, Authors and Libraries*

in Europe Between the Fourteenth and the Eighteenth Centuries (Stanford: Stanford UP, 1994); *Forms and Meanings: Texts, Performances, and Audiences from Codex to Computer* (Philadelphia: U of Pennsylvania P, 1995); and also his edition of essays, *Pratiques de la lecture* (Marseilles: Rivage, 1985); Bruns, *Hermeneutics, & Ancient, Modern* (New Haven: Yale UP, 1992).

22 *A History of Reading* (New York: Penguin, 1996); see also Guglielmo Cavallo and Roger Chartier, eds., *A History of Reading in the West* (Amherst: U of Massachusetts P, 1999). For further references to work on history of reading, history of reception, and print culture, see IV, nn. 1 and 5, below.

23 See especially his *Toward an Aesthetic of Reception* (St. Paul: U of Minnesota P, 1982). Present work on reception is well anthologized in James L. Machor and Philip Goldstein, *Reception Study: From Literary Theory to Cultural Studies* (New York: Routledge, 2001). For further references on period works in reception, history of reading, and book history see IV, n. 2, below.

24 See his brilliant early studies, *Surprised by Sin: The Reader in* Paradise Lost (1967; Cambridge, MA: Harvard UP, 1998) and *Self-Consuming Artifacts: The Experience of Seventeenth-Century Literature* (Berkeley: U of California P, 1972).

25 Elizabeth A. Flynn and Patrocinio Swickart, eds., *Gender and Reading: Essays on Readers, Texts, and Contexts.* (Baltimore: Johns Hopkins UP, 1986). On emasculation see the founding work of Judith Fetterley, *The Resisting Reader: A Feminist Approach to American Fiction* (Bloomington: Indiana UP, 1978).

26 *Reading the Romance: Women, Patriarchy, and Popular Culture* (1984; rev. ed. Chapel Hill: U of North Carolina P, 1991). Ross Chambers's *Room for Maneuver: Reading (the) Oppositional (in) Narrative* (Chicago: Chicago UP, 1991) has more directly exposed the issues in identity reading as a part of the politics of reading; he ends a study that begins with reading in absolutist France with a look at the political/identity issues in *The Kiss of the Spider-Woman*.

27 *The Limits of Interpretation* (Bloomington: Indiana UP, 1990). Eco especially fears a critical agnosticism based on a combination of deconstructive thinking and reader theory. For an example of his earlier, more radical thinking about reading see *The Role of the Reader: Explorations in the Semiotics of Texts* (Bloomington: Indiana UP, 1979).

28 See the brief discussion and references on this emerging historical work in IV.i and IV.i, n. 5, below. An especially good example of work inquiring into the variety of reading practices in an age is Elizabeth McHenry's study of the particular case of African-American reading societies in ante-bellum America: see IV.i, n. 11.

29 (Berkeley: U of California P, 1984), pp. 165–76.

30 On Rorty see II.xix, n. 441, below. For Rorty's specific thought on interpretation see II.xvii, n. 396, and the dialogue in Umberto Eco, Richard

Rorty, Jonathan Culler, and Christine Brooke-Rose, *Interpretation and Overinterpretation* (Cambridge: Cambridge UP, 1992). Michael Warner has interestingly deconstructed the apparently unified and hegemonic concept of critical reading in also raising the issue of better study of nonprofessional, or other professional (as, for instance, religious professionals in various cultures), uncritical readers: see his interesting essay, "Uncritical Reading," in Jane Gallop, ed., *Polemic: Critical or Uncritical* (New York: Routledge, 2004), pp. 13–38.

SECTION TWO*

LITERARY INTENTION/ALITY

I. ONCE MORE WITH FEELING

> "Come, we shall have some fun now!" thought Alice. "I'm glad they've begun asking riddles—I believe I can guess that," she added aloud.
>
> "Do you mean that you think you can find out the answer to it?" said the March Hare.
>
> "Exactly so," said Alice.
>
> "Then you should say what you mean," the March Hare went on.
>
> "I do," Alice hastily replied; "at least—at least I mean what I say—that's the same thing, you know."
>
> "Not the same thing a bit!" said the Hatter. "Why, you might just as well say that 'I see what I eat' is the same thing as 'I eat what I see'!"

I thought of entitling this section "The Last Word on Literary Intentionality," but even I found that incredible. It is a, certainly nominated annually for *the*, central issue when one begins to consider interpretation, when one therefore thinks about readers interpreting. For the thought that the author may not be in charge is the one that opens up a space for the reader. "The birth of the reader," says Roland Barthes, "must be requited by the death of the author." "Either a text means what its author meant," says John Ellis, author of *Against Deconstruction*, "or we have textuality and free play."[1] As I discover when I teach courses on readers and reader theory, I find myself counting weeks until someone jumps into the intentional issue as it regularly confronts us in literary study.

*Notes appear at the end of the section. Substantive notes are bolded.

Did the author mean what he said or not? What right have we to have any interpretation but the one he, what? ... wished? assumed? had in mind? *intended*—that's the word! And we are off. Without regrets on my part and with great interest on theirs. The issue can take two three-hour classes and then, like a thunderstorm hanging around on a summer day, it keeps rumbling and grumbling throughout the rest of the term. A recent graduate seminar really could not get off the subject. Week after week every other discussion would regenenerate into the earlier one, with the usual suspects asserting the death of the author and the usually suspicious asserting his/her authority (but more often *his* authority). It is a subject, like welfare reform or balancing the national budget or cultural literacy, that seems to line people up, before any arguments, on the basis of temperament.[2] A student from Taiwan would have none of this American freedom with author's responsibilities. Two students who had chosen my class to come, in the academic context, out of the closet were equally concerned to out the reader and open endless spaces for readers' freedom of maneuver.

As I invite them into the professional discussion they find their temperamental inclinations replicated: heavy hitters like Wayne Booth or E.D. Hirsch champion the author's intention in tough, formal argument. Lithe David Bleich, agile Stanley Fish, offer alternative discourse, brightly extending freedom to individual readers or their communities in a style as flexible, sinuous, and open to reader co-writing as their theoretical formulations. Even among our usually even-tempered students, the issue seems so enmired in temperament and produces such tempers on all sides that I cannot help but reflect on the deep emotional hooks it must possess, perhaps the more so because it is a fuzzy concept. As my arguments will keep showing in a variety of areas, the idea of literary intention/intentionality is an unstable and imprecise one. Like many terms that accrue a great deal of ideological weight—freedom, leadership, enterprise, humanity—it does so by being many things to many people. It offers the kind of aura possessed by many other ideological keywords: security, integrity, or certainty; it tends to act as a talisman to ward off fears—especially those roused by the postmodern critical and literary scene—of anarchy, license, and the worst of evils to some of those in the academic literary world, deprofessionalization. The term itself sits uneasily between two philosophic ranges of discussion using intention/intentionality in different senses. Some philosophers (and psychologists) inquire into the nature of human planning of actions, intention in that sense. Many more others continue the use of intention from phenomenology as a way of speaking of the aboutness, in effect the meaning-fulness, of symbolic languages, especially in philosophy of mind.[3] Literary intention/intentionality borders on each but is really not quite either. It is concerned in a much more common sense way with motivation, wishing as it does to represent the author's motivated planning to say something.[4] It is concerned with aboutness not as a definition of meaningfulness in itself but, again in commonsense terms, as our usual desire to know what someone had to say, was talking about. While I will be writing about debates between literary intentionalists and literary anti-intentionalists, there is no assumption that these terms would line these customers up regularly on these, other, philosophical debates. One could say that everyone except perhaps a cock-eyed determinist believes it reasonable to discuss human motivation and planning as intentions. And no one denies that language has aboutness, though some might deny that that discussion is more than a tautology based on its own definitions of philosophical intentionality. It would be wrong, though it is sometimes done, to say that literary anti-intentionalists do not believe in human motivation (as, say, in a criminal justice system) or to say that they deny language can have aboutness, though this has sometimes seemed the inarticulate reasoning behind accusations that literary anti-intentionalism is preposterous because all statements have intention (are about something).

The debates over intention, whether in my class or in the professional literature, are perhaps so filled with feeling because disputants nonetheless slip into assertions from both these other areas of thinking. Literary intention is fought over as a place where human will and meaning might seem to come together. It is a vague area, as we shall see again and again, but loaded with distinct feelings. The feelings it arouses have something to do with our unique human possession (and perhaps someday that of our machines) of full systems of symbolic language. A grunt of a dog gobbling his dinner is his and no other creature's; our bodily cries in joy or pain belong only to us; they really possess specificity. But language, which we only borrowed in the first place, which we use in communities that claim back what they gave us, threatens us, some more than others. Literary intention wants to connect persons to their language in more than a car-for-hire way. Language may be by definition conventional, but intention wishes to connect it to the user as personal, special to us, as a kind of fingerprint. Our grammar, with its three persons, allows rental rights—we can assert and have inscribed in stone, "My name is Ozymandias, King of Kings"—though, as Shelley knew, we can't hold on to our words or take them with us. *Except* writers like Shelley, or monument and brass beating Shakespeare, the intentionalist will object!

But literary immortality comes at a price, indeed no less than mortality. The words remain but the man is ... nowhere. And those who criticize the intentional way of thinking tend to believe that the man lost control of the words not at his death but on their utterance or publication. They are, as publication lawyers say, in the public domain, but in these cases long before the financial copyrights expire. Intentionality wants to retain an intimacy with the person as opposed to the words. If we lived with a writer, we would know that we could not get that close to the writer writing. If we asked for a real meaning of the written words to set beside the words, we would only get more words, and so on until she threw us out of her study. But some people like to think that the real meaning is not so much in the words as in the writer's insides somewhere (the head, the gut, the heart?). Intentionality expresses the faith that we can, through her words, really get to know, become truly intimate with, her. The writing we style literary and subject to debates on literary interpretation, which we recognize as so much more than just plays, poems, novels, and essays, nonetheless shares with these stereotyped categories a quality of elusiveness: we like to read words that are different from those nice clear statements of fact (aboutnesses) that philosophers prefer.[5] We like "literary" words that almost by definition stand in a relation of distance and play from the writer. Yet do we then insist on breaching the barrier of language and distance and asserting that we can know not just the play of words but the intimate author's meaning (is it behind? inside? around? above?) the actual words? We desire what? That words should not be words but be Keats's living hand that writes, "see here it is—/I hold it towards you." But of course all we get is words.[6]

In our ordinary lives, words, usually spoken ("I'll kill you if you move!") but sometimes written ("Report without fail to jury duty") are often a form of action. As actions, though words, they connect to all the highly developed, half-unconscious/instinctual, half-conscious/reasoned responses we have to others' actions. In everyday life, our very survival depends on quick evaluation of intentions of others.[7] When we move from our action life to our life as readers, it is natural for us to bring those virtually instinctive reactions over to the quiet of our living room or study.[8] Indeed, we can perhaps understand the other instinctive reaction—of censorship—that dictators and tyrants everywhere exhibit when faced with works of literature that might actually encourage real-world action. At a conference of writers from many lands that my department once hosted, we discovered (no surprise once we thought about it) that there was an inverse relationship between the degree of repression of writers (mainly in the third world) and the acceptance of their works as having mainly aesthetic or entertainment value—as opposed to practical intentions/consequences (mainly in the first world). Anyone who has been at the site of a street happening kind of theater performance—there is a shooting, the police are called in, no one knows what will happen next—knows how important it seems to decide if we are dealing with a dangerous set of real life intentions or only Richard Schechner and his literary-dramatic intentions. In a summary of cognitive research in the 1980s and 1990s,[9] a psychologist notes how strongly and normally people are inclined to seek intentions in all kinds of artistic modes, literature, art, music, where the pragmatic reasons for such intentional thinking are no longer present—as they would be, of course, if we suddenly found, in bold print in a novel about a serial killer, our own name inscribed as that of victim-designate. No wonder that words easily resume for us in literary writing their native force as actions.[10] As we shall find, J.L. Austin's Speech Act theory—exploring how speech can be actions—has played a major part in the controversy over literary intention.[11]

In the large realm of words and their effects, another battle of temperaments emerges, indeed ever more clearly.[12] Those who wish to find the author in the words, somehow controlling our response and reception, seem manifestly bothered by the danger of plurality and uncertainty. More recent writers who defend reliance on author's intention routinely lament a critical scene of deconstruction and newfangledness that seems to them to endanger reason, communication, and civility.[13] Anti-intentionalists seem to thrive on variety, openendedness, complexity, and debate.[14]

With such reflections on the manifold messiness and emotionality of the issue, eventually the thought dawns on me, as it has sometimes on others,[15] that this may be a major non-issue in theory, an emotion-filled center of confusion in those confusing jockeyings for precedence among author, text, and reader that will not go away but that will not hold still to be solved either. Eventually I am tempted to tell the students that it is a paradox that can't be solved. One student, Marxist theorist in good earnest, used not paradox or neo-pragmatism but dialectic: this is a family affair, a quarrel among things that are really one; it is really just a matter of the perspective from which you look at the same thing; difference, in that happy Hegelian unity, is not real, just apparent.

A nice imaginary solution for a real problem, for make no mistake about the potency of the issue: it does not go away in students' or critics' ways of thinking about what they are doing when they read and interpret and it doesn't go away as a way of setting values on interpretive activity and priorities. Those who think this a period issue (circa 1946-1976) will bump into it where it is least expected, as recently in the issues between deconstructors—followers of philosopher Jacques Derrida or the critic Paul de Man—and New Historicists—who have returned to history in a new mode for inspiration in literary studies. "We feel impelled," wrote Alastair Fowler back in 1972, "to revolutionize the terms of a problem whose solution has become so intricate that it eludes our comprehension as easily as its own simplification. We want to move on, have done."[16] Graham Hough called it, also years ago, not a dead issue but a "ruined site."[17] Another commentator calls it an "essentially contested" concept open to endless rational debate but no resolution.[18] Stanley Fish called it "a vexed topic that usually brings out the worst in everyone."[19] I even assign Steven Knapp and Walter Benn Michaels's *tour de force* essay wishing away the whole debate from a neo-pragmatist viewpoint, as if no arguments in fact ever hinge on it; but they most evidently did and still do. Knapp and Michaels represent the issue as a foundationalist, ultimate one that has and needs no solution, but in fact, far from being above the fray, they resolve it in favor of intentionality.[20] Steven Mailloux, a writer on what he has called rhetorical hermeneutics, concurs in dismissing the issue as foundationalist, specifically connecting his position to the philosopher Richard Rorty's dismissal of epistemological issues (issues of foundations of knowing, not meaning or interpretation); only *he* settles the question wholly on behalf of readers, whose varied interpretations over the history of a work's reception are what he believes we study.[21]

Another commentator, less hopeful of dismissing the issue, calls his essay, "Why Intentionalism Won't Go Away."[22] As the exasperated Fowler continued, "the classic problem of intentionality moves too, as ineluctable as meaning, as inseparable as human nature. Criticism at every turn challenges our policy towards intention"—not our way of writing any more, but prophetic enough of the conundrum's legacy. Indeed, its complexity seems to grow with succeeding generations. An editor of a 1992 anthology of essays on the subject exclaims, "it seemed to me that almost immediately one got into very deep waters, not only in aesthetics, but in the philosophy of language, in the philosophy of mind, even in ontology."[23] And of course, as Terry Eagleton has reminded us, we will find it written very large in the history of interpretation, as a central issue, again perhaps *the* central issue, in hermeneutics or legal interpretation.[24] Indeed, E.D. Hirsch candidly remarked that when he began work he had not been aware of the connections between his independent thinking on this subject and the continuous tradition of hermeneutic theory in Germany.[25] Yes, Wimsatt and Beardsley exposed the Intentional Fallacy to daylight, lo so many years ago.[26] And Barthes, French critic,[27] and French historian and philosopher Michel Foucault[28] have proclaimed the problematization and subsequent death of the author.[29] But if authorial intention is now a phantom, it is one that walks the streets boldly at noon, that bursts into the 8 a.m. class. Undead, zombie and revenant, it continues as perhaps it always will, despite the attempts I shall make here to drive a stake through its heart, to leave its hoary toothmarks everywhere in literary discussion. (Its friends naturally prefer to speak of the return or resurrection of the author, but the terms, loaded with movie associations or religious mystery, nonetheless give away the ghastly irrational currents under these revivifications.)

* * *

The issues of authority that get tied up with the issue of the author's authoring are especially obvious if we start from the tradition of religious hermeneutics (interpretive theory and instructions for interpretation of religious groups). If God wrote the Bible through his prophets, storytellers, and apostles, then it matters tremendously that we ascribe His meaning to the text and not just some (other) reader's meaning. *Everything*—conduct, morals, eternal salvation, may we eat kid's meat seethed in its mother's milk, will there be marriage as we know it in heaven—depends on figuring out not just possible meanings but God's own meaning. The wars of truth, in so many ages of Western religious tradition, have been wars about this issue of authoritative interpretation. If only God taught Interpretation 101 and could show us all how to find the true meaning pumped into the text by its Omnipotent Author! But alas we have not that Course but courses; we are mere readers—and so many of us with so many opinions—and not the Reader.

All the players are already lined up in that first great hermeneutic action in the West: those on the side of authority who insist on the possibility of finding that so-needed right interpretation—and of course offer themselves as the true authority on the True Authority. The associated experts who bring special knowledge and scholarship just to make sure that the right reading doesn't lose its way. The obvious fact that experts nonetheless disagree, though all agree they should not and only do so because of the obvious deficiencies of the others. The awful battles that ensue, each bearing the banner of the Author's authority into battle. (On the side the unbelievers, skeptical, higher critical, wolves picking out the weakest of the faithful, offering a host of writers and cultures as author or authoress instead of the Host.) And eventually, the move to liberalism and some peace. Theories emerge that allow God's intentions to be progressively revealed to each generation, as the generation understands the Bible, much as the United States Constitution is, in liberal law theory, unfolding with its reception. Theories emerge that allow God to allow different meanings, found in good earnest and good conscience, to different believers. It's beginning to look a lot like Chanukah/Christmas, twenty-first century: we all may find the Author in his book in our own ways.

There are of course strong mutterings, and occasional serious violence in both the West and the Muslim world, but the new liberal society, half freed from its traditions and their quest for permanent authority, holds—for now. But the situation still bothers many people, and those who care about the religious text are most likely to be heard muttering under their breaths as the clergyman in the old joke: yes we all read God's word in our own, diverse ways, you all in yours, and I in His.

The situation in the associated world of secular reading, that seemingly permanent institution of English studies that only took over the business of interpretation in higher education from religious studies something over a century ago, is parallel. There is the acceptance of newfangled, way-out, modish, interpretations—formalist, Freudian, Marxist, myth and symbol, phenomenological, structuralist (which comes with debate over whether that is an interpretation), Lacanian, deconstructive (of many kinds), feminist (of so many kinds), Neo-Marxist, New Historical, queer, postcolonial, ecocritical, and on and on—but also a lingering sense that there is a beginning that might put an end to the endless process of interpretation: and that is the author's, the true meaning, the one that was there with the author in the beginning. And the compromise is usually similar: you read the text in your way, I in the author's. If Wimsatt and Beardsley, in one generation, and Barthes and Foucault in the next, succeeded in winning the publicity battles, they never have managed in fact to silence an opposition. E.D. Hirsch's *Validity in Interpretation* (1967), strongly and vigorously argued, took on the intentional fallacy orthodoxy of New Criticism and sponsored a major debate in *New Literary History* and elsewhere in which the intentionalists seemed to predominate, even as the pronouncements of Foucault were about to carry that day. And there have been more recent avowed intentionalists, philosophers of aesthetics close to the position of Knapp and Michaels as well as other philosophers and critics—as we will see—who have attempted to arm J.L. Austin's Speech Act philosophy for their purposes.[30]

The return of intention has however been heard most loudly, if we are not fooled by its claims to be beyond the usual literary work of theory and interpretation, in the form of historical definition of the cultural moment of the text's creation. I will be arguing that cultural context is a disguised form of intention that must be subjected to the same criticisms as authorial intention when it is offered as a master guide to interpretation. After the opening of interpretive possibility there has been the ominous return of history, albeit in hip guises of New Historicism and Cultural Studies.[31] But the underlying implication for interpretation has been stern: close thy modern (postmodern) interpretation; open thy history—and find the correct historical text (necessarily a context)—and with it the correct meaning.[32] Knapp and Michaels, those self-appointed anti-foundationalist writers, found a way out of neopragmatism, which would have opened the way to freely competing interpretations, and into history as a new, if very complex, foundation of interpretation.[33]

The return of intention, whether in the assertions of theorists or in the working assumptions of New Historicists and practitioners of Cultural Studies, usually takes the form of a suspiciously compromised formation: a distinction that claims a major difference, the drawing of a line somewhere. God is not mocked; the authority of the author or his age must not be set at naught. The compromise has, in the formulation Hirsch created, had the distinction of coming into our general literary vocabulary: meaning, what the author intended me to know, is one thing; significance, what it may mean to you and you at such and such a time following your interests in such and such subjects is another.[34] So binaries—opposed pairs about the same subject—are still being formed in the Derridean universe, right before our eyes, in this case staying together as a poorly matched, unequally endowed couple for a long, unhappy marriage. And binaries still grow, if not improve with the years. So another solemn theorist, anxious to preserve some authority, worried about deconstruction, suspicious of new approaches, but not wanting to swear off the modern critical world, Wendell Harris, expands from a binary describing the product to one embracing the activity: the quest for what the author and/or his cultural moment intended is interpretation; all else, if not deluge, is merely criticism, having your say rather than letting the author have his.[35]

They tell us this is only a matter of definition, getting a little clarity between two kinds of activities. I can't trust such a statement in such a temperamental area of discussion. We have learned to be suspicious of binaries, even if we aren't ready ourselves to blame the world's ills on grand theory's binary of Western, male logocentric domination over others' speech. Mere intellectual distinctions can have great consequences. When they start distinguishing true Germans from other German-speaking present residents (or functional American families—with family values—from dysfunctional families) you know there are problems up ahead. Indeed, the deconstruction of these binaries of interpretation is helpful. The first term, it shows, is being privileged in the binary. It is even being privileged, as Derrida would have told us, because it is closer to a privileged origin, the (potentially) spoken word of the author—an analogy between text and spoken word often leaned on in arguments to sustain the binary. If we take meaning as author's intention out of its privileged position and treat it as just another kind of significance or criticism, the loss of mystifying aura is clarifying.[36] Now we have an area of criticism that is far less political and patriarchal, offering not the privilege of authority but some useful kinds of information: a criticism that tells us about the author's times and life, about the language, desires, social structures of the time, about the possible modes of reception of the work in the author's purview: useful information but no longer analogous to the Word of the Author in the areas of interpretation/criticism in which we all fall afoul of each other.

Taking it this way, I have no desire in this revisit to this old argument to try to make the maverick case that there are no areas in which we can use information about the author or about her age and culture. Private writings of an author, biographical interpretation of her life and concerns, knowledge of customs and beliefs of her milieu, may all provide rich clues toward an interpretation of a work. They are, however, clues—suggestive rather than definitive—subject to promotion or refusal depending on how well they fit our interpretation of the work (historical interpretations are only other interpretations).[37] I also would not wish to be mistaken for offering to ban all thinking about intention just because it often runs to authoritarian extremes. In a question he posed to Jacques Derrida about *his* intentions in answering the American Speech Act philosopher John Searle, Derrida's editor Gerald Graff asked if Derrida had fallen into the position of identifying intentional arguments with absolute claims that "they don't [necessarily] entail."[38] Derrida's immediate answer was, in effect, to flip the coin: *his* position should not be taken to imply an assertion of unlimited undecidability—as his critics and the press so often have taken it.[39] Derrida then argued that Searle in fact *is* absolute in his intentional claims. But Graff's question deserves a more direct answer. My own response is to stress that I in no way wish to argue, in this broad argument on intention, that we cannot, more, that we do not, come to pragmatic decisions on meaning and interpretation based on information about the biographical/historical context and intention (for these are in practice indistinguishable—we know intention, a thing supposed to be in the mind, only from its outward evidence). We do so all the time. And we may remain content with our decisions (Hemingway was infected by machismo, so his stories are attacks on woman) until someone or something challenges them. Once the interpretation is in play, so to speak (Hemingway can demonstrate a remarkable insight into a woman's point of view, even seem to inhabit her consciousness), then I would argue, and this will be the point of all my discussion here, arguments from intention are not privileged. They are in fact rather weak ones, much given to entrapment in a vicious hermeneutics that only too easily finds what it seeks in the text because it is already persuaded of a kind of objectivity in its premise (isn't Hemingway well known to be sexist?).

The situation is a particular case of one that holds in all interpretation and to which I shall keep recurring in the discussion that follows. Much of what we do in interpreting texts of all sorts is totally non-controversial, a matter of noting information about content which is incontestable in the simple sense that summaries will not be contested by real readers. Norman Holland, who has thought more about obvious issues in texts that seem barely subject to interpretation than most theorists, who tend to leave this subject alone or to the linguists, recorded a set of protocols about a number of persons reporting their responses to a screening of the movie *The Story of O*. He piquantly remarks: "Everybody saw sadomasochism, whips, panties, leather, René and Sir Stephen. Everybody agreed that René's name was not Algernon. These perceptions were fairly fixed."[40] Likewise, we all agree Hemingway wrote stories about World War I. We all know that Bloom and Stephen take a pee together near the end of *Ulysses*. We don't need to defend our attainment of such interpretive insights; they may come from the most common meaning of the words (had I written pea instead of pee, or pe—the seventeenth letter of the Hebrew alphabet from the Hebrew word for mouth—everything would be in confusion), from our sense of the textual context (they had been drinking; the result is natural), from our received sense of the writer and his intentions (likely that Joyce would want to shock with urinary bluntness as he notoriously does with excremental). If our position, assumed to be that of everyone, certainly including the author, is once challenged, the arguments from intention will only prevail if we all believe that they are more powerful than others. My aim is not what Beardsley and Wimsatt seem to have wished in attacking the intentional fallacy, to exclude all discussion of intention—as mental act, as biographical context, or as social, cultural, historical context, but to deprivilege it. As I have suggested, these areas of study may offer many productive suggestions for possible interpretations. But they should never privilege an interpretation. Were its advocates merely pragmatic, as I certainly am in my own large commitments to historical work, there would be little to say. It is not I (nor indeed Derrida himself) who place users of intentional arguments in the position of the "all" of Graff's "all or nothing." As we see with the present generation of New Historicists (who have become more and more like old historicists each year), arguments from intentionality can quickly become assertions of an "all."[41] Why this is does not fit into my investigations here and could be better answered from the other side. Certainly a dislike of uncertainty or plurality continues to be a motive. But as with biographically based intentional arguments more prominent thirty or forty years ago, there is also the cultural investment (of time, special acquisitions, special knowledge) and the determination to obtain adequate cultural dividends (in the way of expertise, self-assurance, and professional rewards) from the cultural capital at risk. We can build a literary profession on this kind of expertise; and we may easily fool our constituents. But I write to try to ensure that we do not fool ourselves. I don't assert that historical information should be taboo, a fallacy to be eschewed. But I will assert in this discussion that there is an accumulated weight of arguments that forbids us from assuming that we can resolve important interpretive disputes by prioritizing one interpretation (our own, of course) and giving to it the aura of a special author's authority.

I invested my professional youth in becoming the published expert on the poet Robert Browning's youth; and a great deal of that work centered on issues connected to his first published poem, the mysterious Romantic monologue *Pauline*. But I confess I never enter a class on the poem with any assurance that I have any special claim to the correct interpretation of any passage or word, though I know a great deal more about the poem's milieu and context than my students. I do know that my expertise could have a political impact: I might sweep all but the most brave students out of my information-filled and learnedly pompous path.[42] But a strong mind could stand up to me and defeat me on a dispute over a matter of interpretation; the saddest event might be a timid but intelligent student (imagined with or without a sad tear in one eye) turning from this game as a rigged one. He or she would rather not play, if this is the way it is played. I write to fortify such independent readers from deserting the field, and to suggest to other experts that they avoid tilting the playing field. Do history, yes of course, but don't use history and biography to channel interpretation into your single, learned, and expert groove.

As in so many aspects of reader theory, the arguments here appear in a variety of topics, in effect windows one opens and considers somewhat separately. I don't know of, and pretty much don't believe there is likely to be found, a unified field theory of intention that could bring these into one. The issue I will want to raise will be the usefulness of the term itself in the interpretation of literature. Intentionalists find it a reassuring bedrock guiding interpretation to a proper home. Anti-intentionalists think the term is not useful. They find that its ideological aura covers up an actual vacancy so that its only function seems to be to get in the way of realistic discussion of interpretive issues, in general as theory and in particular as interpretations of works and groups of works. As a proponent of this view, I will be mainly having to argue the non-utility and non-practicality of literary intention as a practice of referring issues of meaning and interpretation back to the author. I will first wish to show that it is illusory to think of authors as in fact in full control of their texts. Then a number of chapters on intentionality in the text will show that it is not possible to think of texts as hardwired to their authors in the form suggested by literary intentionalists. Finally, I will suggest how impractical and indecisive it is to pursue the ideology of literary intentions through a quest for biographical and historical recovery. My agenda in advocating these positions is not to discourage work that considers the goals and statements of writers about their work, nor to inhibit historical and biographical work on writers and their periods. My desire to deprivilege appeals to intention in issues of interpretation does not make me a literary anarchist or an enemy to the literary profession (though I will be pleased to seem a friend of the nonprofessional or learning reader). I believe I am reasonable in discouraging rule-giving or self-privileging discourses of interpretation based on an ideology of intention.

My own larger argument can only be that in every window one opens, one finds good reason to be skeptical of a privileged interpretive mode based directly on author's intention or on more disguised forms of cultural intentionality. I ask my reader to bear with me as I rove widely, I hope not too confusingly, from theory to particulars of actual practice. The questions focused on here are not purely theoretical; my attention is rather turned to the effect of theoretical belief (as in the special privileges claimed for interpretations argued from author's intentions) on practice and also on the critique that practice, the actual problems of doing criticism based on author's intention, or even the problems in imagining a coherent author's intention usable by criticism, can make of theory. I am drawn to such a problem as literary intentionality just because it is susceptible to neither a purely practical nor a purely theoretical solution. A merely practical approach through investigation of some literary or speech examples in detail, for instance a study of a novelist and her novel or a look at certain kinds of communication, is soon lost in its blindness to other possibilities. This was true of both the older historical/biographical work and the New Criticism. But purely theoretical takes on the issue are equally easily blinded in their purity, single-minded logic, and obliviousness to practical issues in criticism. They take us away from the issue itself as it appears in our work of literary interpretation and try to eloign us to a different discipline.[43] In the ensuing arguments my own affinity (and debt) to the neo-pragmatic positions of Richard Rorty in philosophy and Stanley Fish in reader theory and literary hermeneutics will be clear enough. A literary philosophy that attempts to clear away all prolegomena to interpretation and broadly parallels Rorty's work in evacuating epistemology as a governing system in philosophy is the only one I wholeheartedly welcome and pursue. But unlike Fish, who is unclear on the subject,[44] unlike some of his followers who wish to disregard intentionality as not relevant to interpretive practice, I consider the issue to be a very real one, not only in the sense that it does not go away but also in the sense in which any argument can have reality: it matters in a great number of arguments over interpretation; it can't be wished away or ignored. I also grant, even as I try to, that the issue of intention cannot be definitively settled. And that is why the best position, as I see it that against intentionality, has to be persuasively restated in each generation. I believe this is best done by bringing together as comprehensive a range of thinking on the subject from as many perspectives as possible.

* * *

The issue of literary intention, again like that summer afternoon thunderstorm, has thus been rumbling around the world of literary discussion, coming and going, coming on again, sometimes focusing here, sometimes there. To summarize briefly the complicated career of literary intention that

I have been introducing: the older biographical and historical scholarship, stemming from German hermeneutical refocusing of literary study in the nineteenth century,[45] implicitly sought to stabilize literary meaning by attempts at knowing the inner life of the writer, following the work, so to speak, from the inside. Generations of late nineteenth- and twentieth-century literary historical work offered a grid of biographical and contextual information for guiding the reading of a work, trying "to understand the works from the life."[46] Modernist criticism, in reaction, turned from biography, intellectual history, and scholarly information to demand focus on the work. Views on intention, in the early and so influential I.A. Richards as well as in Wimsatt and Beardsley's brief but obviously critically positioned paper on the intentional fallacy, enabled their rejection of biographical/historical readings in favor of focus on interpretation of the writer's words themselves. As I will note when I look at intention in the text in a set of subsections below, their and New Critics' disgruntlement with intention was over the use of external information to guide interpretation; they often were quite happy, as indeed Richards, Wimsatt, and Beardsley generally were, to conclude that the text itself revealed the author's intention. Indeed, the apparent major controversy between New Critics and the outspoken and highly logical advocate of intention, E.D. Hirsch, in retrospect seems most odd. Generally eschewing biographical intention, he seems really to agree with New Critics, who certainly taught only *the* correct interpretation in their classes and writing, that the right interpretation is generally found in the text.[47]

The next generation of criticism in English was of course seeded from abroad, and the strong pronouncements of the exceptionally lively critic Roland Barthes and the exceptionally provocative historian Michel Foucault on the death of the author and/or the dispersion of the author function were far less accommodating to such a conception.[48] To Barthes the text speaks not of its author but only of how plural it is, how fitted with possible meanings to its reader; to Foucault the age rather than any individual author speaks through the text. In this anti-intentional stress on the variety of possible responses to a work, they were joined by deconstructionists, followers of the philosopher Jacques Derrida and the American Paul de Man. Neither left fully decisive views on intention, but both pulled away the throne of universal interpretive authority from which it could rule interpretation.[49] They were joined by German and American reader or reader-response critics, many of whom explicitly attacked the idea of author's intention or declared it, as Stanley Fish usually did, essentially a vacant category.[50] Barthes had declared the death of the author coincident with the birth of the reader and some reader critics became advocates of reader positions that would not submit passively to claims for authorial authority.[51] While German hermeneutics reversed course in the twentieth century and insisted on readers' sitedness rather than on authorial sites, the historical study of reception of literature provided new masses of evidence of constant changes in interpretive practice and definitions of authorial intentions.

The issue of intention keeps, however, being rejoined, sometimes at more complex, sometimes perhaps only more novel, levels. The turn to history, both in New Historicism and Cultural Studies, brought back a concern for intention, now more often implicit, as a tethering of interpretation to historical recreation of milieu (habitat) and text (discourse) of the society of the writer. Historical specificity rather than interpretive acumen or freedom became the watchword of the generation at the fin-de-siècle. At the same time, neo-conservative critics sometimes have explicitly hitched their pitches for cultural unity and humanist authority to a number of renewed or even new arguments for intention. Contextual knowledge—sometimes seen as solid history against Foucauldian Newspeak, sometimes half-sympathetically connected with New Historicism—and even biography would secure interpretations. Or it was possible to try to deny, as early Hirsch and Knapp and Michaels had, that a text could be conceived of without thinking of a real author, or at least the conception of an author. Meanwhile, the philosopher J.L. Austin and his followers' theories of speech acts were rejigged from their original application to pragmatic speech uses to interpretation of literary texts with the aim of guaranteeing that the text was the author's and nothing but the author's. In this work, metaphors and other tropes bearing change were declared univocal of the author. On the other side, the strongest philosophical competition to deconstruction in literary studies, the neo-pragmatism associated with the brilliant work of Richard Rorty, proved in its so-called interpretive turn a powerful destabilizer of authoritative authorship—though three of its most prominent (or at least prominently self-proclaiming) literary adapters, Fish, Knapp, and Michaels, somehow managed to endorse literary intention.

I need for a moment, on top of this so sedimented history, to locate myself where I am to be found, as if through some kind of plate shift, cropping up on a number of strata. A literary historian and old New Critic by training, I have been an NYU biographer in my day as well as a close analyzer of texts; then I have been broadly interested in adapting Foucault's thinking on history to literary history. For the last twenty years I have also used reader theory, meaning a broader interest in issues relating to readers than that suggested by the historically located term reader response—as I am in this study—as a place to explore structuralism, deconstruction, reception history, and hermeneutic theory. And, as I have indicated, I have found myself very comfortable with the conception of thinking, offered in Rorty's kind of neo-pragmatism, as an emergent search for better usable approaches. I continue to practice or be involved as an editor in work in biography and New (and also old) Historicism and respect the focus of these disciplines, which I also consider different from that of literary interpretation, though the disciplines may generate new ideas for interpreting specific works. My attempt here to explain why I find arguments for intention as a way of stabilizing reading of texts both unpersuasive and unattractive accompanies my commitment to encouraging vigorous, independent, and original reading of any texts readers wish to call literature. I devote so much space to the many ways this subject has been encroached upon and appropriated by so many of the literary tendencies of my time because I believe it has been and continues to be a potential place of literary stultification. Wherever a literary approach or movement has struck out to capture author's intention, it has seemed to me to be engaged in an illegitimate attempt to close down other approaches to reading and interpretation and to aggrandize and perpetuate itself as a kind of new dogma. It is generally a move to clear other players off the board; hence my own recurrent metaphor below of hoping to preserve a level playing field. I hope I am even-handedly annoying in this enterprise, worrying both currently stylish New Historians and conservative preservers of culture alike, nipping at the heels of very fine critics such as Fish, de Man, and Robert Scholes when they seem to me to fudge or smudge this central literary discussion. In an age without definitive religious or social ideology it is natural that some thinkers should gravitate to some obscure place of authority. What more natural obscure place than this idea of author's intention?

What more natural and yet what more obscure and vague—which is itself natural in blindly attractive ideological markers? Indeed, writers on intention regularly stop to ask whimsically what the concept can really mean in its apparent clarity and actual obscurity. What do they intend about intention, these intentionalists? And the answer is, as with other ideological formations, a great variety of things. For those who still look to the biographical figure of the author—a thinning band but speaking for a recurrent human need to know the writer behind the work—intention is about motives or desires, intention in the commonly used sense of reasons for action. As the detective in detective fiction at least tries to understand the criminal mind, this intentionalist tries to nail down the reasons that explain the writer-perpetrator's perpetration. It seems an open and shut case; Sherlock has only to examine the evidence with special insight; interpretation is being looked into, thank you very much, by authoritative experts, authorities on the author. Now who wouldn't want to be stimulated by the display of forensic evidence and clues (I myself have even handled relics—rings and hair clippings—of the Brownings and come back to tell about it)? But I will show why we can put no interpretive authority in the mystery tales of such scholarly sleuthing, indeed why the project of figuring other people out, of getting inside other people, is incoherent and self-limiting. This is a relatively easy task with our current generation.

A much more formidable task is getting the same generation, honey-mad on New Historical research and Foucauldian webs of diffused power, to see the implicit intentionality in the complicated skeins of explanation they cast in their broad readings of history. Having reprocessed authors into mere corks and set them out to float with the tide of the seas of historical discourse, Foucault and his followers move themselves into the position of masters of the video game of history, in which texts and their interpretations can be knowingly inserted—and controlled and delimited, and ultimately desiccated. This kind of history has become the major hideout in which those who would foreclose interpretive debate have recently tried to create a new hegemony. I will demonstrate that this disguised intentionality, of a period or episteme or parts thereof, cannot serve as the masterkey to all interpretations.

More metaphysical concepts of intention inhere in attempts by diverse critical groups, early and late, to define an all-weather intention not tied to the vagaries and uncertainties of research, archival availability, and subjective penetration. Somehow, really in various hows, they argue that the text is all we know and all we need to know. The author speaks not *ex cathedra* (from his investigable writing seat at home) but *ex libris*, from his very productions. Of course he does, and why should he not: isn't that what authors do? Speak to us from out of their mummified or tobacco-stained text, telling us what they had in mind, giving us indeed their minds' remains for our day's light. When I started teaching, we all taught that way: there was one true interpretation—what T.S. Eliot intended and we, major analysts in a bull market of interpretation, could reliably dispense or kindly lead young readers to. The text was one grand, *intended* unity with exciting moments of (also intended and crafty) ambiguity. Other faiths similarly worshipped at the temple of author's intention in the text. So-called Chicago critics found the big determining idea in genre choice that led readers to the (author's) determinate reading. Their scion, rhetorical critic Wayne Booth, found all texts (give or take a few troubled productions of troubled modernists like Joyce) implicating an implied author, the author as found in the work clearly telling us how to take her ironies and metaphors. And a slew of conservative critics, united mainly by their dislike of postmodernism as an anti-humanist and de-centering project of infinite jest and play, have revived intention in the text as a place of assurance and end to games. Why should they not? They have naturally wished to instruct youth on the values of great traditions and find their bully pulpits, even their good book(s), taken away. And in their place polysemy, plurality, multivoicedness, plurivocality, dissemination, deferral, difference, binaries, aporias, indeterminacy ... all kinds of fun and games—at which young(er) people generally excel (their professors).

There had traditionally been no love lost between such humanist critics, preserving and propounding, in Arnoldian vein, the great traditions (and from a distance those different versions of the tradition, some secular, some religious—Matthew Arnold, T.S. Eliot, F.R. Leavis, Irving Babbitt, and Yvor Winters—do begin to coalesce as traditional intellectuals) and the analytic tradition in Anglo-American philosophy. That other culture had preferred science to poetry and had seen its main mission, from Bertrand Russell to A.J. Ayer, as that of radically purifying the language of the tribe, purging it of tropical splendor, making it safe for clear, mathematical thinking. Literature departments did not reach out to philosophy departments, or if they did it was to departments in the University of Paris, Heidelberg, or Konstanz, where Continental philosophy still seemed to ask questions, granted also questions about limitations to meaning, convenable to the interests of many critics. In their anxiety to re-stabilize meaning in classic texts, conservative critics however now reached out to a branch of the Anglo-American tradition which had been trying to bring analytical philosophical clarity into everyday language use under the umbrella of Speech Act theory. The Englishman J.L. Austin and his co-philosophers John Searle in the United States and Paul Grice in England (later in the U.S.) seemed to offer ways to certify meanings in advance, thus assuring that the interpretation that the speaker and hence by extension the writer put into his language, using one or another speech act ("I now pronounce you man and wife"), was the same one that the listener or reader got out. Users of language, by their accounts, were under a rule of good communication (what Grice once called a Cooperative Principle) that made them create such a clarity in what they were writing that misapprehension was impossible.

To this keynote application of philosophy, textual intentionalists might join other arguments, attempting to wish away the play of word meanings that had so impressed Jacques Derrida or the play of tropes that had so struck Paul de Man. Or traditional ideas of genre as a tradition-controlled set of clear tales or structure as a natural, determining mold of meaning might be adduced. Or context, in or both in and outside the text, might be brought in to assure us that there is no question what the author intended. In the emotion-charged subject there always seems a further penumbra of metaphysics. Although our normal experience of conversation suggests that we often mistake meaning, frequently speak at cross purposes, often perpetrate misunderstanding, and regularly need further clarification and restatement, we hope we do not speak and listen in vain. We trust human communication is nonetheless possible; we do try to cooperate in language. Meaning, we trust, can't escape us; our words are still our words when they leave our lips. And so a kind of higher law of copyright seems often invoked with those in fact much further alienated words we write; no evidence can seem to shake the faith of some that the author retains meaning right in the words in perpetuity. So arguments on local issues of language, all those subjects of interpretation we generally quarrel about throughout the long day of our reading experience, always seem to persuade these intentionalists that authors' will will be done.

There is also a more subtle trap here for the innocent anti-intentionalist, which has not gone unsprung, though its irony has perhaps escaped even some of its perpetrators (as irony in fact will escape authors and still appear as irony to us). This is an odd higher faith in intention as a metaphysical necessity, which has been expressed implicitly by Stanley Fish. In his formulations, we in effect call author's intended meaning whatever meaning we find, because intention is a quality we must (are programmed to, cannot live without having to) ascribe to meanings we give to language. So there is no quarrel about whether true meaning is intended or not, only a regular issue about what is the true meaning. As I have noted, this is neo-pragmatism with a difference, and it is further aggravated in students of Fish's, Knapp and Michaels, in their notorious dismissal of theory.[52] In their view we really are programmed only to meaning as intended meaning (their proof being that we would not find meaning if the waves wrote a good poem in the sand, a metaphysical assertion masquerading as a thought experiment; obviously we would, as real pragmatists, read it and try to provide the meaning its non-author could not be said to have provided). Such faith does not even seem to allow for interpretive discussion; criticism can go out the window along with theory while we contemplate the meaningful intendedness of all documents we know to be humanly created. An intention is an intention is an intention. Others are tempted to retreat to an even simpler formulation. If intention only means aboutness, as it does to the philosphers,[53] then all texts have intention, are saying something about something. I will show, if I have not already persuaded you, at some length why we cannot have assurance of an author's deliberate, definite, determinate meaning from her text. A philosopher—William Irwin—who indeed leans in the direction of intention nonetheless imposes a properly philosophical, logical, and helpful clarification. Theory of interpretation—hermeneutic theory—he suggests comes in two varieties, normative and descriptive. Even staunch intentionalists like himself, he grants, may be arguing how they believe interpretation should take place (norms of interpretation), not how it does take place (descriptions of interpretation).[54] Amen! Only I can't seem to find any flavor of intentionalist in sight but normative. They tell us not what interpreters do but what they should do; and they use the ideology of intention to force interpreters to do their will. This study will hold such claims, in every area of discussion, up to the complex realities of interpretation—interpretation of authors' lives and historical sites as well as their texts.

One final procedural note. Because intention strikes me as a kind of ghost of assurance vigorously but hopelessly summoned up in these many invocations to its many ghastly incarnations, I am necessarily arguing limits: not that we can't often have a comfortable sense that we and the author are on the same page, but that where we most need that assurance, when a matter comes up for debate, it is nowhere to be found. I must show again and again that the assurance being sought is illusory, that in reading and discussing texts we will have to rely not on the talisman of authorial certainty but on our mother wits, our own ability to find what meaning we can by connecting the text to whatever we know, our savvy in framing arguments that persuade us and others of the perspicacity of our readings, even our ability to change and maybe grow in our reading as we hear others' interpretations. Interpretation is a jungle and those are the laws of the jungle. I can only show again and again that the jungle is always there when the going gets rough, that claims to know the author's single, correct, and reassuring reading of the work always run into problems. Therefore I will need again and again to push approaches, from the real world of the author to the virtual world of the text, a bit further, to show where the jungle of uncertainty reclaims its own. I will always seem vulnerable to the case where there seems only clearing and bright sky. In that world, the author could have meant no other; we can read no other. My argument will always take the form of, yes, in many cases there seems no issue (to us, anyway; to the next generation of readers an issue may seem just there to press). But it is precisely where the going gets rough that intention, useless machete in hand, gets hopelessly encircled by jungle, bogged down, a failure. And it is only the hard places, the hard interpretations, that raised the whole discussion in the first place. If there had seemed no fissures, no fault lines, no aporias, no disagreements, no controversies, no lines drawn and parties pried, there would have been no issue of authorial intention, just happy readers all agreeing about what simple authors wrote. It may make you think of the model of easy communication—a pragmatic (practical, real world) text, let's say a manual for a new gadget or assembly kit. You may think again as you try, in total frustration, to figure out what the company intended!

* * *

I will begin by looking at issues of the author's own control of her language. Most of the arguments are familiar; indeed, I would tend to suspect anyone who offers an original argument, for he or she might be likely, or tempted, to focus attention narrowly on a special case and offer it as a comprehensive proof. The matter of whether and in what way we can be said to mean what we say or write is so central to human experience that it must call forth our most global conceptual frameworks of human language and psychology. As I have been bold (and foolish) enough to choose a subject that opens endlessly into virtually every subject of literary theory and many major subjects of philosophy, psychology, and history (for which I hope to be forgiven as I have forgiven other bold, foolhardy souls who have tried to paint one or another big picture), I hope I may also be forgiven for briefly comprehensive notice of the main topics. The big picture rather than the elegantly elaborated detail by which we critics, imitating philosophers, say more and more about less and less, determines the major issues here.

Before I begin the subject in earnest, I recall its central concern with difficulties in human communication and, consequently, its inevitably polemical nature. If I shout "fire" in a crowded theater, leading to general mayhem and some real bodily injury, perhaps even mortalities, I am certain to be called to account for my shout, as it emerges that there was in fact no fire. It is a matter of serious moral, and indeed I imagine in most societies, legal, concern, a matter for the real police, not just the thought police. It will evoke strong expression about responsibility for intention just because it has been a matter of such consequence. But if my temperamentally conservative critics will call for me to be hanged forthwith, more thoughtful judges will want to look precisely at the relation between the tragic eventualities and my words, which proved fairly easily interpretable by most of the theatergoers whose obvious intentions in replicating my cry is not at question. They (the theatergoers) are indeed likely to be judged innocent of any moral failure or crime on the grounds of intention, though a more strict accounting might ask them to admit the terrible effect of their words and also to render account of the ease with which they passed on a mere rumor. But their intention was to warn of a real fire they believed to have themselves been warned of by me. Similarly, the mass interpretation of all these yells of fire as about a referent, namely a real fire in the theater, will not likely be criticized. It is not the only possible interpretation of my utterance, but a likely one; though we must add, in the hypothetical case (as I hope I don't in fact go around yelling fire in theaters or books), it proves to be wrong.

Now most further scrupulous investigation of this serious incident of intention and interpretation will certainly focus on asking what in fact I did intend. And we can think of many scenarios in which I give a somewhat satisfactory explanation, though most will nonetheless leave me rather convicted of imprudence or too sublime absent-mindedness to my real-world situation. I intended not fire, the burning stuff, but fire, the order: as I was pleasantly but, in my usual hearty, loud manner, telling my theater companion to ask me any question she liked about my dubious past. Or I was remarking, with my usual naive enthusiasm, on the fire portrayed in the faded ceiling frescoes; or I was suddenly struck by an excellent topic for my discussion of intentionality—fire, by Jove! And on and on. All these are in the daylight world of intentionality, where I am presumedly able to account for what I had in mind and my companion, embarrassed and annoyed, can nonetheless account for the misunderstanding by explaining the context, though they are compromised somewhat by the nuttiness of a nutty (and somewhat dangerously on the loose) professor. All raise interesting questions about intention and interpretation, including difference between oral and written language.[55]

But here let me focus on the more troublesome ones that those more deeply inquiring judges will at least wish to hear. They have to do with what some arguments over intentionality refuse absolutely to allow: that we may speak or write what we do not wholly, or at all, intend. Here are some examples: I am a strange professor in a strange land; I am having health problems but also language problems: I need water, which I shout to my companion but say the wrong word, which I associate with the word for water from the English grammar I have been studying. My intention was to say water but the words got in the way. Don't they often, even to native speakers or writers? Or, I noticed that my companion was wearing her very sexy slip, the one we privately call the Freudian slip; I meant to exclaim fine but out came fire. Don't we often slip? Or I am an even nuttier professor; when I saw someone with red hair like my inflamatory great aunt Pinkie's somehow it came out: "fire." Or, I had a secret life in the CIA where I underwent a training program on Pavlovian principles stolen from the KGB. Every time I said a word that didn't have security clearance I was given a hotfoot and had to say fire. Unfortunately, it leads to these little problems now that I am in civilian life, if, as happened that evening, I am drawn into a discussion of high-tech surveillance equipment. A, I assure you, penultimate example (because all games become tedious): my companion and I, my gossip in a complex Jamesian mode, love to play a little game ourselves. One of us says a common word, like water or fire, the other tries to guess what family member's conduct this week could be so described and why. My little trick this week was that niece Jane lost her job again, I am sorry to say for the usual cause, firewater: so fired for fire water. As I wonder if I am not being clever enough, it turns out the unclever denizens of our box area have totally failed to guess my meaning, poor literalists.

II. INDIVIDUAL PSYCHOLOGICAL UNCERTAINTIES

> "How do I know what I mean until I hear what I say?"
>
> Old joke.

> Constituting and dislocating it at the same time, writing is other than the subject, in whatever sense the latter is understood. Writing can never be thought under the category of the subject.
>
> Jacques Derrida, *Of Grammatology*

Enough examples. Note that a number would seem cases where I said what I intended to in the sense that I, as new to English, intended to say water (but said fire). This is where a precisian, like Hirsch, will hold to the intention is intention is intention line. But the only point of this discussion of intention seems to me the light (or firelight) it sheds on interpretation. And from the point of view of an author/speaker being able to say what he meant to say, as opposed to voicing what he wished to voice, they are all misfirings. (I as foreign professor did intend to voice the word fire, and did, but I intended—meant to say—the concept water, and did not.) Note also that the examples are simple, oral ones, a point I will hold against other arguments. But in this case these may be forgiven as the simplest, one-word, cases of misfirings. Complex written discourse obviously allows much more room for authors failing to control, or as is even more often, to offer a univocal discourse.[56]

The point of all these examples, taking the simplest communication system—face to face—is not that we and writers don't have intentions with language, but the simple one, that what we intend to send is often not what is received. Of course, unless the theater has already cleared out in a panic, unless the other person at the bar has already knocked out some of our teeth, there is usually opportunity in conversation to get some clarity. Successful couples will tell you that this can be a very hard job; unsuccessful ones gave up trying to get across what they meant a long time ago. This and the sections that immediately follow will look at the many and much more complicating circumstances in written communication to explain why it is not possible to refer places of difficulty, confusion, and reader controversy, in written texts, back to the biographical writer and his milieu.[57]

The subject needs of course to be located in the even grander topic of meaning, one that has produced a really great range of analyses in the long histories of philosophy and psychology and the shorter one of linguistics as well as in studies of rhetoric and literature; indeed, it has often brought out the interdisciplinary aspirations of thinkers in all of these fields. Nor has there emerged any consensus anywhere. A great variety of approaches, from promulgation of the system of Platonic ideas to statistical study of the language potential of apes, have been developed to explain what we should mean by meaning.[58] Even as we move to replicate intelligence in machines, we are totally in disarray as to what it would mean to say that they meant something. This may not hold back that project as much as one would think; we human machines have of course been meaning for a long time without any clarity in what that amounts to. Some wise persons have stood back and at least noted that the word "mean" has many use meanings.[59] Perhaps it helps here, without trying to settle the big questions, to note that meaning is often located in different places. And for these differences there are at least practical explanations. Those who wrangle over whether meaning is hard-wired in the brain, exists as a language below language (a kind of mentalese), is a matter of a great number of conditioned reflexes, is a result of a very complicated learning process on the part of the young child, or, to go back a bit in time as we often are doing in literary study, is the result of external things writing ideas on the mind, is the principle of reason placed by God within us, is indeed the activity of a little man within us, is the odd result of atoms bouncing endlessly from matter to matter, is a reflection of those eternal Ideas in the caves of our minds—all these have at least one major position in common. All such positions in the dispute over meaning, however different, generally locate meaning in the individual. Their disputes assume a site of one person, sitting by himself, meaning or being meaned somewhere in the head region. Other disputes are different; they are theories of discourses of a time period, of social constructions, of cultural determinism, of social identities interpellated into individuals and ideological meanings of communities, of a public discussion in a public sphere, of rational debate, of the best that has been thought and said, of clericies or traditional intellectuals, of priest or monarch set over others by God, of philosopher kings, of rhetoric and legal decisions. Here the unifying theme is shared meaning, whether seen as actually worked up by dialogue or imposed by some on others or inculcated in all by society or some principle operating in a culture or across all cultures. The specific site is two or more people communicating; and of course it is a place that in theory allows for clarification, for question and answer, for dialogue, for catechism or further inculcation. Meaning is in the society or emerges from social interaction; even if it originates in someone, it is subject to development, clarification, refinement as it comes into a community.

Another set of assertions on meaning is about the words themselves. Meaning is in words as used in language games; it is in words used as actions to do things; it is in words with clear referents that match the world with logical precision; it is in the metaphorical bringing together of domains of thinking; it is the deeper, universal structure of meaning behind all local sentences, a kind of universal grammar; it is a relation of signifier to signified; it is in a chain of signifieds never fixed; it is in the root meanings lurking behind words; it is the denotations or the connotations of words; it is in a book of word meanings or an encyclopedia of word applications; it is in the speech of Adam naming the creatures; it is in the stable Word of God himself. In all these approaches, meaning is in or behind the words themselves; we don't mean; it means, they (the words) mean. The site is words, spoken and heard, but even more, written and read. Imagine a philosopher thinking about meaning in words; he hears a sentence in the college common room that he wants to explore; he isolates it, takes it back to his rooms; he writes it down. It is about the words, not his relation to the original speaker, a colleague he rather despises. Imagine a poet reading his poem against the American-British invasion of Iraq to an audience on the eve of invasion. There is apparent dialogue, everyone is at the same point in time and shares points made as already meaningful to them: not so different from two people in an actual dialogue discussing a proposal by one of them, say, about how to get to St. Mark's Church for the reading. But now there is a question-and-answer session about the poem itself. Whatever interesting things the poet says, there is not quite a social development of meaning; we all have the poem in our mind; we all have opinions of what the words mean. We both, poet and audience, discuss what the words, not being developed or changed, frozen as they were written and read to us, mean. Imagine, finally, a reader of the poem one hundred years later; there are only words before him and other words he perhaps can find from that time.

Finally, there is a set of opinions about the receivers of meaning. Actively there as a partner in a face-to-face development of meaning, passively there as the ones on whom that poet's words fall, they are now the center of attention. Such a focus yields disciplines of theory of reception, reader theory, reader-response, study of the common reader, sociology of readers and reading, sociology of art and aesthetics, practice and theory of rhetoric. Here the site is, in the first instance, the individual, hearing a performance, more often reading a scroll, codex, or book. No longer in a dialogue with a speaker, not endowed with an extractor of meaning from words, the reader becomes the place where meaning is created. It may also be the place, in a performance rather than solitary reading of a text, where the individual is brought into dialogue with other audience members (why did they laugh at that point in the play? what will John Simon have to say?) or made part of an argument among readers (upstairs in the parlor or downstairs in the kitchen, in the classroom, in the book club, around the fire in tent or hut, in reviews and critical articles). Of course, those who attempt to write histories of readers may wish to take them in groups, to posit communities of readers who tend to read the same way, moments or ages of reception of works from other times; at the extreme they may attempt to generalize them into great types of different epochs, cultures, or religions, or even into stories of the changing technology of reading.

My point is that the enormous discussion of the issue of meaning can at least be sorted out a bit by seeing meaning as not a monolith; it is protean, occupying all these different places differently. When we look for meaning, we need to begin with the function being looked at, to consider the appropriate site of meaning and kinds of meaning available at that site. In my subject, the discussion of meanings of texts, it may be tempting to try to get back to the meaning with the writer as she sat alone or was located in her society; or to think that we can have a clarifying dialogue with the work as produced; or to imagine the words will be sufficiently clear to interpret themselves. But each avenue we will attempt to go down will only lead us back to the site of reading, the person trying to make sense of the text, completed and passed to him/her out of the writer's sphere and filled with words leading down a variety of possible routes of meaning. If reading may of course be greatly determined by the reader's presuppositions or those of her culture or reading method, the process of generalization should not lead us to forget that it is only enacted in the site of reading, of meaning-making, by the individual reader.[60]

D.H. Lawrence famously told us to trust the tale not the teller—certainly good advice in his case where much metaphysical commentary by him sits cheek to jowl with the works in the library. But my point is more complex than just that the writer will say things about his work that we can hardly trust.[61] It is that the conditions of human authorship are so complicated inside and outside of the writer that we should not expect to be able to find a clear set of intentions to match the production of the work. Even if we could do the unimaginable, lift up the top of the writer's head during writing and find that which is going on in there (what would it be, some clear text of electrode reports or synapse energy flurries to supercede the unclarities of the actual text?); or sift through every external evidence of the context of writing, from the detritus of her breakfast correlated to the agitation of the handwriting that morning out and out to all her relations with all aspects of her society and its history (what a massive biography this would be!). Even if we could do these impossibles, we would find not clear describable intentions but only the complexities and confusions in mind or external life and social/cultural siting that produce places of difficulty (and often of great interest) in the writing.[62] Anyone who writes knows writing is mysterious, not something a little man inside us plans out and dictates to us, whatever planning may have taken place before we sit down to write. Words seem to have a will of their own; they take us places we didn't know we were going; they cut us off from goals we thought easy; they lead us into traps and sudden releases. To conceive that the author really has a clean script within before he writes out his messy manuscript is to falsify the art of writing—which is what we literary types profess to be studying—in the interests of a foolishly consistent idea of some simple idea, some super-clear intention of the author.[63]

Even proponents of intention have been willing for a while now to grant some of the obvious problems in finding intention in the biographical author (as opposed to in the text—the subject of a later series of subsections). Easy to set the goal: "the interpreter must put himself both objectively and subjectively in the position of the author."[64] Hard to obtain full command of an author's outer life, far less the inner. The hope to do so grows out of our desire to connect language to a person, thus not to acknowledge its difference and alienation from us. In our own case, we know we experience some kind of connection between how we are as we write and what we write. This makes us imagine the same event taking place with others. But the philosopher who enters the world of psychology points out that we don't really know anything about that other person's inside.[65] What we know is actions, which might conceivably tell us something if we were there at the moment of writing and saw the writer do something—pick up a dart and throw it at the president's picture on the wall while writing an "Ode to the Chief"—but would itself be subject to the usual need to interpret and to possible misrecognitions.[66] Mainly, we would judge inside realities by outside words, which only brings us back around to where we started, the hope to figure out a definitive meaning of words by attaining a more intimate connection to the writer. We might feel we were getting somewhere if we could stop the writer and have a dialogue immediately;[67] generally we don't have this advantage and in any event we would have to interpret even these perhaps unusually focused words. And, as writers on intention have often pointed out, so I will not belabor here, comments from other times in the writer's life are all subject to our human transience and mutability.

The overall problem of not being able to get inside the head of a writer (why did he write a screenplay about getting inside John Malkovich anyway? how can we get inside *his* head and find out?) has been noted. Likewise, the unreliability of all kinds of records and writing about the writing have been generally acknowledged, though it is easy for anyone to face a crisis in skeptical faith when confronted with the actual clarifications by the author in diary entries by Virginia Woolf, introductions to *Lyrical Ballads* or Henry James's New York edition, letters explaining Inscape to a few friends or discussing metaphors of isotopes of carbon, coal, and diamond in relation to character in the novel, and on and on. These are wonderful writings and well worth homage or pilgrimage, often greatly suggestive (also sometimes greatly misleading if not downright tall-tale telling), but not locations where intentions can be found at home ready to declare their presence. Worse are of course other forms of evidence, like the recollections of Robert Browning's valet or Ben Jonson's report on Shakespeare's mode of composition. I won't say, would they had all blotted them all; they are fun to read but obviously no authorities. (I will leave until a later subsection wondering why, if you rightly won't trust such close testimonies of the day you will trust your broad-sweeping recreations today of that day's discourse as sufficient to secure the text.)

Then there are often granted the ordinary difficulties, when one thinks of an author as realizing intentions, of any kind of good intentions: carrying them through. No one really can doubt that a shadow can fall between their desire toward their production and their realization. If we listen to writers themselves—which advocates of paying attention to their statements might begin with—we may even conclude that this is pretty normal; the elusive words never quite capture the promise of the idea or the promise of the writer's talent. Clear intentions may badly fail; they fire off target—Robert Browning said he wrote his wonderful monologue, "The Bishop Orders His Tomb," as his contribution to the Oxford Movement controversy in the Anglican Church, but the connection is so oblique that no one then or since would have guessed it; the bishop's Renaissance vanity hardly reminds us of Pusey or Newman. Or they are plain duds: to stick with Robert for an instant, his *Sordello* was to have been his grand epic of the development of mind but it never went off in his time and has only made a dent in a few consciousnesses other than Ezra Pound's since. Or they may be contradicted by their results. D.H. Lawrence, to switch genres and centuries, wanted to work against the hopelessness of what he called those writers among the ruins of his time—such as Conrad—and ended up sifting through the personal ruins of *Sons and Lovers*. The point hardly needs examples; like all of us, writers take aim and often miss, regularly reach beyond their grasp. On the way to reach some goal, accidents, too, may happen. Words may come out wrong (Hamlet's brilliant "sullied" perhaps for "solid"—solid flesh should melt seems the logical but less interesting direction), visitors from Pornock may disturb, mental illness may descend, as it did on Ruskin's *Praeterita*, characters may get forgotten and never properly developed (whatever happened to John Reed, Jane Eyre's early antagonist? what did Lady Macbeth do with her unspecified number of offspring?), death may leave *Drood* a mystery.[68]

Writing, with a pen or a fine machine, seems such a decisive act (signing into law, signing our *will*, signing our checks) that we associate it with the daytime world of our ego, with our total control over our writing. Alas, it is not so. Although I am uncomfortable with global assertions that texts are written through a writer by his/her culture and episteme,[69] I have no difficulty in understanding that much of what we say or write comes through us with varying degrees of conscious control. We tell a story that was told us; we repeat in our somewhat altered terms what our professional group or class is currently saying; we pick up scraps of language we have read recently; we fall into traditional patterns of phrasing and commonplaces of ideas. We may think we are always individual and original; how easily we hear the conventionality and unoriginality of others—whether in board room, department meeting, or bar.[70] We even repeat ourselves and imagine ourselves original. The mind is part of a sensory system and responds to stimuli; our writing may be punctuated, and fragmented, by flashes of sensation as we write. Our mood changes with weather or love cycles or digestion—and interruptions of loved ones or students—and our writing moves with them. The writer at work is no single train of thought bound to come in its station on time but a complex, highly diffused processor receiving constant bombardments of bits of feeling and bits of language. Something[71] selects and makes a way, as new words chosen prompt other associated ideas. Our computer programs that suggest a choice of words to us with such annoying rapidity are a very simplistic and mechanical version of this process of association and suggestion. A better metaphor would be how our physical system pulls out of the stomach float of such varied chemicals and nutrients the substances needed for our nurture. Writing is a mysterious and exceptionally complicated process that deserves to be better studied if we could find a way to do it. Again, the myth that it is done by a little man in the brain who knows exactly what he intends to say and steps up and says it, in language uniquely his and in no way influenced or tilted into multi-voicedness, contradiction, equivocation by his world of language is unhelpful.[72] No one who writes, as my epigraph says, has failed to be surprised and interested by what has gotten written. The good writer is more often not the one who tries to dominate language but the person who listens into its diverse potential for the writing situation at hand and orchestrates it well. Who the writer of that text is at that time may very much depend on the words used rather than on any predetermined character possessing a predetermined intention.[73]

That old troubler of things human, time, also seizes our sense of control over writing from us, seizes it while using even our writers' selves as his instrument. This may seem so obvious as to appear banal. Banal, but not unimportant: as has been remarked, we not only never step into the same river twice (certainly a banal remark) but more interestingly are never the same person stepping into that river. Especially, of course, that river of time. We are changed at each moment, whether we talk of physiology of the brain (which I won't) or of the sense that we are made by our experience and thus constantly are different, have different memories, see things differently.[74] A writer at work on a text works in that river of time and cannot help but create a text that follows changing interests, indeed interests often changed by the progression of his thinking in creating the work. (I am inserting this little section on time two weeks after I completed what comes before and after because I have come to the lower section on revision and realized I missed an obvious point; so I insert it now, thus doubtless complicating the direction of my original intentions in this section.)[75] Thinking and composition are fluid, ever-mutating things where the whim-like and willful side of our intentions can allow frequent changes of intention from second to second, in this like conversation unless we resolve to follow an especially rigorous, mathematical kind of progression; but the process of writing—some stages of planning, writing, and reviewing—allowing, *encouraging* recursion and revision, adds to this possible flux of intention the superimposition of later intention on former, often creating a text that is a palimpsest of intentions so thickly layered that, in regard to intention, it may easily be unreadable.[76] I will look below (have already done so, as I write this you will say, but you would not know this from the apparent intention of my conventional use of this phrase if I had not told you—it is in subsection II.vi) at more institutionalized forms of revision, usually over longer spans of time, where the older author claims the right to adjust what his younger self wrote.

Derrida's observation (other epigraph) is golden. We are obviously, when we think of it that way, other than our writing (do you suspect that the whole story of a night at the theater concerned me not at all?). Having so far deconstructed the conscious writer at work, let me explore other ways how, in our most common understandings of the subject, the writer cannot be simply equivalent to the writing.[77] Both Hirsch and Harris find ways to avoid facing the obvious challenge of broadly accepted Freudian thinking about the psychology of language to arguments that insist on author's control. Hirsch says that wherever the thought comes from, the language itself is uttered in a conscious act of intention.[78] Obviously this doesn't apply to much borderline psychological activity, where the conscious control is lacking: we all talk in our sleep, I suppose, and the woman who moans her lover's name into her husband's ear could hardly be said consciously to intend her revelation. Some psychotic states are, almost by definition, states of failed conscious control over language.[79] The more common Freudian perception is of course that some of the unconscious intention manifests itself in apparently conscious language. I am falling asleep over a student paper (not one of my many brilliant students' papers) and find myself writing something else than I should have (awkward comes out as awful; say more comes out as say no more). A twilight zone of pedagogy! We all nod or daydream and something else than we might more consciously intend comes out.

Those are borderline cases in which conscious and unconscious sources of intention seem to be shading into each other. They suggest that we all know that there is more than one source of intention within us.[80] The condition of contemporary life has been to have divided aims but also to live with an awareness that we are necessarily divided in our aims. We know that we want—thy neighbor's wife, all the ivory that a worshipping people can bring us, the high-cholesterol tortilla chips—what we know we should not intend to want; we love some kinds of honor still, but desire calls incessantly for food. Freud is sure our divided natures will out somehow in language, not just in dreams or psychotic phenomena. The slip will show it, the pun will reveal it, the metaphor will unfold our doubleness for all our attempts to speak from only one of the registers of our nature.[81] An unpalatable truth to many, a useful attack on hypocrisy and ignorance to others. My point is only that such a view of the psyche and its language can hardly be turned away when we look at intentionality. We are divided; we speak our division whether we like it or not.

Now Harris, like Hirsch behind him, grants that there can be a Freudian level of meaning, but he throws it over from the author to the interpreter, and in so doing makes it a secondary level of criticism: not meaning, but interpretation. For him it is Freud and the Freudians, a form of criticism, that makes Freudian double meanings.[82] But I think we can distinguish here between large Freudian interpretations, explanations of the psyche of the author or characters about which Freudian analysts, looking at literature, tend to disagree, and the phenomenon of division in psyche and speech, which now seems to exist for us at the level of a truth universally acknowledged. And if so, then we at least look, as we all do in conversation or in reading, for the double, or triple, or quadruple, voiced-ness that constitutes us as complex human beings. The widow in the old joke who tells her children, now don't say anything about the minister's long nose, then proceeds, when that austere man arrives for tea, to offer him some butter on his nose, is too well known to all of us as a fact to dispute such slips. Piagetian child psychologist Lois Bloom has demonstrated how our first use of language emerges from our desires or needs, which reach out for useful language as for a toy. In maturity our many desires easily become merged or confused as they become frozen in language. We didn't mean to say the confusion we really meant.[83] An author may of course catch some of these and weed them out; but we also all know that it is precisely what we cannot see about ourselves that we often reveal most clearly to other people in more complex ways. Correct the slip about the butter and we still have a widow focusing on a man's nose in an obsessive way that speaks to us, in ways we are all familiar with in life and literature, of her divided concerns—social correctness, libidinal interest.

Julia Kristeva's essentially Lacanian Freudian thinking has added for its readers another area of explanation for authors' psychological division.[84] Without rehashing her system or the bodily chora underlying our grammatical speech, far less adding to the host of explanations of Lacan's magisterial but muddy explanations of different psychic developmental levels, imaginary and symbolic (semiotic and symbolic in Kristeva's version), we may find in such theories a concern with different centers of the language we speak or write. We progress in our development to abstract, symbolic language through a language closer to our body and lacking the grammar of our subjectivity. But these levels of more bodily-connected language are not so much abandoned as incorporated, somewhat suppressed, in our adult language. Whenever we stray from the path of adult symbolic language that acknowledges our inability to seize and possess our desire, the language of desire speaks more directly—as a rhythm of the body, as direct images of the desired object, as a disturbance of grammatical structures. Symbolist poetry, the language of profoundly upset persons (and who isn't from time to time?), the language of great passion or grief (which is repeating what I just said)—all may show us on the edge of our earlier linguistic selves; full-fledged psychotic states take some over that edge. Literature, of course, always risks deeper sources of language, in rhythm, use of tropes, fracturing of usual modes of discourse, and can be expected to voice especially often the division built into our infolded personalities.[85] Lacan's system, like its father system in Freud, may rise or fall with its practical use in psychology, may be in or out following the faddish interests of literary fashion. In this sense it is a system of interpretation that some will take and some will leave. But as Freud rightly said, most of his insights were already there as just that in the poets;[86] and our more systematic theorists of psychology only remind us—whatever we think of their explanatory systems—of the multi-voicedness of our natures,[87] a fact we all also acknowledge when we muse on the problem of making a computer that really would imitate our use of language rather than insist on its single-voiced commands.

We do not need to subscribe to one or another psychological theory about an author's psychic life to feel that a text may be the product of some kind of large division.[88] The classic case is perhaps still Milton's God, whom poet-critics as eminent as Blake, Shelley, and Empson have agreed in finding confusing because of the author's unclear allegiance to/defiance of the power that reigns in his mythic universe and in his psyche. The mere idea evokes similar psychic ambivalences in this critic's head, as he hears the echoes of Professor-*Vater* Douglas Bush fulminating against Empson for mis-reading Milton. But we don't have to join the devil's party and risk driving a father's ghost to walk to grant that such division may create a work that seems at war with itself, divided in its effects. A different father figure, the genial and Falstaffian Harold Bloom, began his long and productive career decidedly on the devil's side and of course proposed a universal conflict between generations of writers, each son distorting or remaking himself in struggle with or obedience to his chosen father. Not we women writers, say Sharon Olds or Adrienne Rich, to whom Bloom might answer, "alright, all *sisters*, but therefore no conflict, no deeper emotions trammeling conscious intentions?" Ever since she was early identified as a candidate for psychoanalysis as the neurotic woman of genius, sister Charlotte Brontë has had one or another psychological motivation loaded on her portrayal of the love/struggle between Jane and Rochester in *Jane Eyre* to explain it by its biographical genesis. She was in a struggle for control of her destiny with her gunslinging, tyrannical father-parson; she was acting out her passion for/anger at Belgian M. Heger and his preference for Madame Heger; she was in a Bloomian conflict with godfather Byron; she was trying to get to her preference for sisters and sister surrogates over all men whatever, or most simply, she was writing out her governess daydreams in all their attraction/repulsion.[89] When we are done exploring all these plausible entrances to Charlotte's psyche, we may not be persuaded of any of these entirely. But it will be hard to deny that we cannot easily imagine Brontë working like the Company accountant in *The Heart of Darkness*, all starched collar and clear, objective direction in that hot, down-under world of the human in mating mode.

III. IDEOLOGICAL AND DISCURSIVE UNCERTAINTIES

One fashionable critique of psychological systems has been that which encapsulates them within a system of social control of language and discourse. I will look later at the extreme of this view, which would substitute the age, the language of the time, and so on for authorship entirely. Here I want to think about the ways in which the author's enmeshment in language and discourse that comes from outside him or her—indeed is given to the child as the social gift of language—compromises the idea of a single author's intention that can be read by a privileged author-centered mode of interpretation. One way of thinking about this very broad issue is that written under the fairly recently hot term of ideology. Although, as Terry Eagleton has argued in his useful and comprehensive look at the term, we may sometimes speak of ideology as a set of beliefs we speak only as a party line, knowing they are not credible to us,[90] most often there is an implication that we are ourselves caught up in the ideology we speak. In the first case, that of an hypocrisy by which we show our subservience to some social system of thinking, whether in the hope of gain or because of fear of sanctions, we have a more complicated version of the difference between intended voicing and intended meaning. Like the professor from abroad who confuses fire and water, we intend to say it but we don't mean it. The perfect hypocrite will offer us thus a conundrum for interpretation. And it arises more often than we may think. Not just the conforming writer, emerging from years of prison to recant on his life all he said about freedom; but we also suspect the woman writer under patriarchy—Victorian Mrs. Ellis, highly successful writer on women's household duties—who seems too goody-goody for any two-shoed woman. Or the case of the well-paid minister who has overcome the modern crisis of faith and tells us how. Robert Browning made a permanently intriguing poem of the Catholic churchman,

Bishop Blougram, who seems for once to let down the guard of his public hypocrisy in a private audience with journalist Gigadibs—or is he the sincere believer trying to make a special argument? The thought that there may be many such people, saying with clear intention what they don't mean, indeed infects the whole thinking about intention. We begin to wonder about everyone; society controls us all to some extent; we are not Cartesian gentlemen alone in the integrity of our thoughts. Who really intends what he or she says? The possibility that all Indians in the tribes we know may lie actually makes us add a double voice to all utterance. We reserve the possibility of finding that he really was a Russian spy not an art critic; he really wrote to support the Occupation. We reserve judgment; we could be being made a fool of by someone who will tell us, when the revolution has succeeded, that he was of the revolutionary party all along, just not in a position to speak.

Indeed we naturally look for double-voicedness when persons write about subjects controversial in their society. We look back to find give-aways in the feminist critic who turns out to have been a home and family ideologue all along. The assumption is that very few are consummate actors; that most will show edges where their other position peeks out at us from behind the hypocritical cover, where the facepaint cracks to reveal skin beneath. We look for revealing places that talk against the ideology formally espoused; we are fascinated by the possibility of code language. In Communist East Germany, a friend who knows tells me, they would begin articles with the boiler plate of what was expected by way of submission, then become freer as they got into their subject: the bosses never wanted to read much or asked for more than the token of obeisance. Did Oscar Wilde, we like to ask, write for two audiences: the public that were more a threat than even he knew, gay friends who were coming to consciousness of their minority identities? Did E.M. Forster, terrified by the fate of his predecessor, hide his deviance far deeper in his text?[91]

These are of course cases of ideology as writing by those fortunate who know what they mean and therefore clearly don't write what they mean. Can we interpret their meaning as other than what they mean? Obviously they mean both, either clandestinely or at some level of encoded revelation. But what of most of us who are part of ideology in a more naive and existential way? We are, as Marxist sociologist Louis Althusser puts it, interpellated (rigorously called) by the dominant systems of our time; they name us and form part of our sense of self.[92] But then they constitute us as believing something and thinking it real that is not real but a desire.[93] I am a patriot who will support the military missions of my country under all circumstances; I am a pacifist who will always oppose military action. The effect is not merely an ideology we speak, and intend, without knowing why. It is usually incoherence.[94] If we are programmed by our identity to wave some kind of flag, we may find ourselves waving it even when other things we are saying seem to go in the other direction. "My country right or wrong" isn't just chauvinistic, it is incoherent: it speaks with a double voice it doesn't acknowledge; it tells us morality and patriotism may be at odds; it tells us they can't be for the speaker. What does he, or chauvinistic she, intend? These simple cases are hard to refute. The temptation with more complicated examples is to ascribe the othering of the discourse to the critic, not the author. So Fredric Jameson's idea of a political unconscious that speaks in a text what the author doesn't know is seen as a neo-Marxist interpretation, an addition of meaning by the critic.[95] But his point is that the author, working in the ideology of his time, necessarily embodies the contradictions of that way of thinking. As Pierre Macherey somewhat similarly has argued, the ideology a writer speaks may especially alert us to what his text knows but he can't acknowledge.[96] Mrs. Gaskell can tell us the responsibilities of the Victorian good mother; she doesn't consciously know but nonetheless does speak the slow suicide that it may involve. Writing an ideology may bring out against it a personal revelation of revulsion, in the form of a Freudian kind of dissonance. Or it may merely leave the unstated premises or contradictions exposed in a way that others, not pressured by the ideology in which the writer functions, can immediately sense. America, land of the free, home of the brave: which a drug pusher in the ghetto may still believe as he cowardly sells slavery, which a soldier in Iraq may have believed as he humiliated and tortured. But when he speaks of his patriotism we will hear the contradictions he lives but doesn't face. We will probably call it irony, the unconscious irony that is so different from the double voice we may ascribe to a single intention of an author who sees two sides of the same subject. Here, rather, the subject displays two sides of an issue he can't sufficiently bring into single focus.[97] Along with writers, we find ourselves enmired in a world that a good Marxist thinker—Antonio Gramsci, for instance—rightly finds "strangely composite": filled with contradictions.[98] We are all in some conflicted relation between the beliefs of the powers that be—which certainly serve their interest but may partly serve ours too—and our recognition of common humanity and its different logic and requirements.

When we consider the kinds of complicated discussions or discourses that we find in literature dealing with major subjects—discipline and punishment, sexualities, the country and the city, colonialism and post-colonialism, the body in language, Renaissance self-fashioning, modernism and post-modernism, uneven developments in women's equality, mimicry and hybridity in colonial/postcolonial discourse—we find that writers are unlikely to be able to unscramble the twisted skein of conflicting positions that they have inherited and that they attempt to darn or reweave. If Foucault seemed at first to offer broad clarifying schemes of great power, the epistemes or larger organizing principles of the discourse of any age, his followers (humbly including myself) have tended to find in the actual literature since the Renaissance a much more involved and multifaceted web: discourses, or major variations on a discourse, intertwined, rather than one discourse. So Mary Poovey stressed uneven developments and contradictions in thinking about women in the nineteenth century; in the same field a writer on Victorian attitudes to illness has stressed the rich and muddily complex interactions of theory, ideology, and point of view in Victorian discussion and revels, very attractively for her readers, in exposing "ideological quagmires" where intersecting and competing ways of looking at a phenomenon create texts that are only too interpretable.[99]

Presumably there may exist cultures that are so univocal and sheltered from conflicts that a writer merely replicates the integral positions of the society. To say this already sounds patronizing or Rousseauist, in the old sense of a simplifying view of original states (that has itself been so much complicated by more recent views of Rousseau's own complexity). Maybe somewhere in the darkest heart of the dark ages the West began to approach such simplicity, but I doubt it, since even there a rich heritage from earlier times offered many voices, many views to the next writer. The apparent simplicity of pre-Renaissance and Renaissance syncretic bundling of authorities of the past actually produces a very complex discourse of differing voices half amalgamated together. Looking at the Renaissance West in its most expansive, assertive facet, discovery and colonization, Stephen Greenblatt yet finds the texts of Columbus and other explorer/colonizers filled with "slips, cracks, and mistakes," with "ideological parapraxes" that are "particularly recurrent." With "rival discourses ... locked in an uneasy embrace," scholars "must concern ourselves with the half-hidden stress points in the offical structures, the contradictory and incompatible frames, the tensions, ideological negotiations, and rifts that are often plastered over in later accounts." Texts notoriously "create complex intertwinings of potentially competing discourses, systems that are perilously close to explosion or collapse."[100] I quote at length because Greenblatt's metaphors offer such a fine stockpile for thinking about the interweaving of beliefs, opinions, points of view, observations in complex discourses.

Only a complete ideologue would complain of the vision of author's control of intention that such a view of complex discourse offers. Most of us know this intuitively when we come to read literature. We look not for simple answers (the cookbook and Wikipedia web pages are for that) but for an unfolding of complex issues in their very complexity. A good writer offers his own attempt to reweave what is already a great mass of colors and strands from the past sources of his culture and the complexity of current ideologies and practices. We look for a new perspective but assume that it is the perspective of the roving eye, the moving intellect. Whitman's "well, then, I contradict myself" speaks for all writers who take on a great intellectual or human scene. In criticism of the past twenty-five years Mikhail Bakhtin has been our greatest discovery out of modernism just because he celebrates, as an aesthetic richness, the complexity introduced in a text by a writer who accepts the complexity of his world and intellectual past. Perhaps himself creating too simplistic views of monological writers coming out of closed societies or poets seeking to express self-sealed closed universes, he of course canonizes a writer like Dostoevski who writes not a single intention but the dialogic intertwining of diverse voices and points of view.[101] And of course his brilliant theoretical explorations attempt to charter the diverse ways in which writers swim in their societies' always already socially and politically inflected and divided language—its heteroglossia.[102] Barthes's memorable view of all texts as intertexts, as palimpsests of cultural writings and overwritings, makes much the same point.[103] We are born into language, write within its given formulations—which is not to say we cannot add to the *langue* by our *parole*. It is no surprise that writers also regularly display various forms of diversity in unity in their discourse. Not a genius but a singularly single-minded, closed-minded person could enter the house of discourse and find only one room.

IV. DELIBERATE UNCERTAINTIES

The issue of intention in irony, over which there has been a great deal of agonizing, suggests how hard it is to lay down internationally recognized borderlines between the three states of intentional meaning, uncertain intentions, and, what I now want to look at, intended uncertainty. It is not hard to conceptualize an act that is undertaken with a clear awareness, amounting to a semantic, moral, and even legal intention, that the consequences will be unforeseen. I shoot an arrow in the air (my neighbors in the big city are more likely to shoot a gun) and leave it to chance on what, or whom, it shall land. I yell "fire" in a crowded theater to see whether people can sense that I am just making a literary allusion to that oft-quoted scene of panic or whether I smell real fire. Morally and legally culpable, I hope I—or those neighbors—shall be found for irresponsible action not taking account of possible consequences. But I didn't intend the arrow to break the window, the cry to start a riot; I intended to leave it to chance. A nice critic—as opposed to the reasonable one who will have me restrained from using arrows or attending theaters forthwith—will have to inquire about my intention in relation to the reception situation. Was my arrow launched in vacant country or a dense urban world? How many people and what level of sophistication were there at the theater that night? A rehearsal, with only five people, all my friends: then Maynard was just up to his silly pranks again to get attention. Depending on the situation, my intended uncertain effect can shade over to virtually certain effect.

So especially with irony, which has struck most commentators as offering an especial problem of intention. The writer or speaker manifests an indirect relation to the subject at hand. The intention may be quite clear to the ironizer: "What a lovely buoyant hairdo, I just love the in-your-face effect you manage." As with any utterance, the person to whom it is directed may or may not perceive the intention, though here the statistical likelihood for a fight is high.[104] But a more subtle intended irony may misfire to some recipients: "I love the way you go over all the old arguments about intention, taking us right through it all once again": "Thank you, I thought that was what we needed at this point." But the third case, that the speaker/author looks for a space to express his/her own unwillingness to take a position is always possible; indeed, it is a major motivation for the wide range of effects we call irony. We shoot our arrow of one or another distancing device and see where it may land as a way of suspending judgment while having some say on the matter at hand; perhaps we also look for a space to explore the subject, to put it in play, to ask our listener/reader to think about its complexity as a way of asking ourselves to do so as well. Suspend taking an attitude and think for a while instead; get some distance on this matter; look at it from different points of view. It is a civilized if also sometimes dangerously delaying tactic.[105] My friend heard of my little escapade at the theater and should have disowned me; but, being my friend, wished to suspend judgment when I jauntily inquired if he knew of the event. "That was quite a *coup de théâtre*!" By which he allowed himself to mean either "you literally brought the house down" or "those people certainly behaved hysterically and histrionically." I can take it either way, but it will be difficult to argue that my friend had a clear intention. Barthes interestingly sees in this much of the special force of Flaubert's irony to provoke and interest readers by the "salutory discomfort" of his failure to take a clear perspective: "*one never knows if he is responsible for what he writes.*"[106] The author who works so subtly with irony will find he/she cannot reclaim control by any extra-textual assertion. We will not allow the thrust of the irony to be dictated to us by an authorial act of willful repossession.[107]

You may wish to object at this point (intentionalists often have) that there is an intention here. It is the intention not to take a position (yet?). In this sense the intention is to be indecisive; but I have to answer that it produces in its effect an indecisive intention, one that we can't read.[108] It is no consolation to me in trying to figure out if my friend is with me or against me in the little crisis I have brought on myself by my behavior at the theater to conclude that he isn't being clear; he may mean one view or the other; I may conclude that he does mean one or the other. What he knows in his heart of hearts to be a deliberately uncommitted gesture leaves me, and all other interpreters, with an intention that cannot be clearly read. We may claim in our interpretations that we know where my friend really takes his stand, but by not taking a stand he leaves all such claims about intention as a privileged argument in interpretation unfoundable.

The same is true of many other ways in which speakers or writers can be said to be deliberately unclear about their intentions. In each case you can say, well then, their intention is to be unclear; but the effect for interpretation is unclear intentions, intentions that no one can claim to read definitively. We know such verbal acts mainly by their effects. They are manifold in literature, where the writer feels the privilege of essayist, novelist, poet, or playwright to explore complicated subjects without rushing to business-world simple conclusions and recommendations for action. In literature we enjoy such effects as open-minded and mind-opening; in real life they may seem polite but, where a decision is required, they may seem the very annoying tactics of the time servers, the place holders, the "own-ass minders," in sum the politicians in all walks of life who wish not to nail down a matter for fear they should be nailed. A full catalog of deliberate unclarities could open up an entire taxonomy of literary effects.[109] I will just suggest a few other major types, here seen from the point of view of the author's attitude, which we cannot know from the effects alone, which by their nature leave us in controversy. For instance, the author may feel ambivalence, to make a fine distinction not quite the distance and irresolution behind the irony we have been looking at but a desire to embrace two or more positions or objects that may be mutually exclusive but both attractive. Such a position, as William Empson famously demonstrated, may lead an author to very complex forms of ambiguous expression, the word itself in its roots suggesting the driving around or leading (us) around (*ambi agere* in Latin) that they enact. There may be effectively double intentions expressed. When William Carlos Williams says in his poem, "This Is Just to Say," "I have eaten / the plums / that were in / the icebox / and which / you were probably / saving / for breakfast / Forgive me / they were delicious / so sweet / and so cold," we may think he is apologizing for his trespass; or maybe he is boasting; or taunting; or provoking; or just teasing: perhaps all at once. And of course what he, the poet, intends in making such a multi-intentional speech speak is another level of multi-possibilities: to express all of the above? to encourage us to be so arrogant/sly/regressive/transgressive/playful? to raise, in a domestic plum cup, serious interpersonal questions? to propose male-female desire/power issues? What did he have in mind?[110]

As I will discuss in more detail below in looking at problems in trying to read intention in texts, tropes and figures may allow the author to present two alternatives simultaneously, while still driving us as readers to try to choose between them: metaphors most obviously, though puns and many other kinds of play may work similarly—what a fiery performance I put on the other night at the theater! The author's use of grammatical ambiguities and slidings, shifts of register from assertion to rhetorical question—how *can* we tell dancer from dance? what's the difference?—have a similar effect on the reader. We may think we know what Yeats or Archie Bunker really intended, but are de Man or Archie's wife wrong in thinking it might be intended the other way? I realize I am crediting Archie here with more than usual subtlety, with intending to perplex his wife rather than just being flippant. Of course I don't know and you don't either. Or the author, as Erving Goffman noted, may use any number of other tricks to "ambiguate" language: puns, riddles, trick endings, and witty proliferation of frames that Goffman explores so fully.[111] The author who deliberately chooses the techniques of ambiguity makes himself indistinguishable from the accidental ambiguist.

Or the author may express his ambivalence in the form of larger kinds of textual open spaces, for instance by using multiple centers or focalizers for the author/audience: a Shaw play in which no one finally gets the last word, in which all seem Shavian sewing machines, as Shaw appeared to Yeats in a dream, going on endlessly with their potent arguments; or a famous case such as *The Turn of the Screw*, where James seems deliberately to have opened up so many possible routes of interpretation into a deliberately unresolved mystery. But such a situation is frequent in literature. Long before the central focus of New Critics on this aspect of literature, the presence of many characters, possibly many narrators, many subjects, made readers argue over where the author could be said to be spoken from. And we are all familiar with the kind of conclusion that says the author is dispersed, like Orpheus, in pieces all over the text, a little of him or her in each character or point of view. Long before Bakhtin's useful special use of dialogism, readers naturally spoke of complex works of literature as dramatic, allowing many voices and points of view, allowing thus in a broad way for an author to explore lives and problems about which he could not make up his mind. Where we are deeply involved in an issue—as we have been with *A Doll's House* for instance—it is not easy to keep in mind that Ibsen really may have wanted to tell us not to take a position and ascribe it to him. Or not.

An unclear author may be unclear in the way that normally seems grounds for criticism, as vague, self-contradictory, messily uncertain.[112] But if these sound negative, we often find in their effects in literature richness and freedom that offer attactions to weigh against the kinds of unclarities that *both* Yvor

Winters and F.R. Leavis could inveigh against. If they could find Shelley's symbols and metaphors messy (and Empson is highly critical of Wordsworth on the same grounds), most readers have tolerated his perplexing tropes for their strong emotional or visual effects: "Like a star of Heaven, / In the broad daylight / Thou art unseen, but yet I hear thy shrill delight, / Keen as are the arrows / Of that silver sphere, / Whose intense lamp narrows / In the white dawn clear / Until we hardly see—we feel that it is there": only an ideologue of clarity as a virtue fails to respond to such a skylark—in one way or another. Mystic writers similarly must stretch language to the edge of intelligibility to give readers some sense of what cannot be rendered as making sense: "I saw eternity the other night," writes Vaughan in "The World" so matter-of-factly that we all think we know what this is until we try to interpret. Then the unclarity will be clear, but not the direction of our response: unclarity of this sort opens up large possibilities for readers reporting different experiences and, if they wish, attributing them to some author's intention glimpsed through his/her vagueness. But the author has made it impossible to try to adjudicate among them by such an appeal. A final example is a kind of messiness one comes to easily with authority or years: the global statement, which looks like a comprehensive judgment, but really hides the author's wish not to admit the perplexity of things that threatens otherwise to overwhelm. How many history teachers have begun a class with the resounding, the Holy Roman Empire was neither holy, nor Roman, nor an empire, in order gloriously to stave off the fact that they had no idea what that complex stretch of history in fact was about. Similarly, selective clarity, that Valhalla of little minds, whether the soundbite attack in the real world or the extended academic nit-pick, allows the speaker/author to hide messy thinking behind apparent clarity, weakening the opponent but leaving us to speculate on what, if anything, is intended other than the joys of battle themselves. We may well prefer a more directly unclear, messy expression.

Finally, let me look at a paradoxical case of deliberate uncertainty, the author's addition of simplifying interpretive explanations as afterthoughts to creation in his prefaces, notes, or postscripts—what Gérard Genette has exhaustively explored under the term paratext.[113] Here the apparent aim is clarity about intention rather than diversity, and the case is sometimes, and naively I think, cited as an obvious proof of intentionality.[114] But when the author uses the bully pulpit of preface to give us a strong clear signal, the effect is always to produce only more diversity. As part of the offered work, if it is considered at all, which is of course the choice of the reader, it must be considered as an addition to, not a comment on, the text; and this will complicate/enrich the text. A Shavian explanation, say, of the Marxist economic logic of *Major Barbara*, can only add another complexity to a play filled with dissonance between patriarchal images of father's power and assertions of female or younger generational freedom, and celebrating the triumphant power of guns and capitalism and deploring the state of the populace. The author might then, seeing what he had done, wish to explain his explanation. If so, his fore-preface, also thus part of the text we critics confront, would only give us more reasons to sing out in different tunes, or sing of difference/dissonance itself.

Intentionalists, in their respect for authority, seem to presume that authors desire the control they wish to give them. But an author may have an opinion on her own degree of control whether wishing it to be total, partial, or non-existent. Michael Hancher, comparing reading of wills and poems, interrogates the idea of intention. It may be a general motive, the feeling driving the pen; it may be a very specific aim, as it often is in wills, where the letter seems especially important in some sections. It may refer to the aim of writing what the writer hopes to accomplish.[115] And we could add the intention deliberately to mislead as to intentions.

Or more generally, an author may actually say that he intends to leave the decision to the reader.[116] Such a position seems by its nature genial and welcoming, an invitation to make of her production what the reader wishes or take what he needs. A wise author will indeed know that she cannot control future uses of the text and, until the relatively recent invention of toilet paper, might be glad if it at least evaded the jakes. The conscious intention may be even not to have any intention as to what the text means, to avoid that hubbub entirely. Such global non-intentions may (or may not) be matched with the effects of uncertainty we just examined. Though vague (we can't know if such expressions of non-intention are sincere or part of a selling process), the possibility that authors may abdicate control over their work from its inception further complicates and weakens the case for intention. While critics may imagine an enraged phantom of the author rising from her grave to tell us that was not it at all, we may also find real authors—as I have indeed seen a number at readings or PEN events—shrugging their shoulders and saying they weren't really sure what they wanted to say: they let it come out and leave it to the reader to figure out what it means.

V. PERFORMATIVE MULTI-INTENTIONS

One other way in which the author may, deliberately or unconsciously, be motivated by at least a double intention can be given the still fashionable name of performativity. Here I mean the difference of which we are all at some times aware between what a speaker or author seems to be intent upon saying, his or her subject matter, and the communication built into the act of communication itself. As we have been seeing in the last two sections, literary intention as a concept often weds, or falls between, two fairly distinct philosophical ideas of intentionality: the content—aboutness—of a statement and the intention—motivation—behind the statement. What is written and where it is coming from are inquired after as one thing: the literary intention. But they often turn out to be in unstable, wavering, or even apparently contradictory relation. Literary intention then seems to be an idea that registers the many places of confusion between content and motivation.[117]

The commonest case of dissonance between what a statement is about and what its speaker is going about is perhaps those people who don't even write their own speech/text and who may thus seem especially likely to be motivated by a sense of the effect of their performance rather than their ideas: of course, you guessed it, politicians. If we may normally think of the role of speaker/writer and the speech/writing itself as merging into one, a wise speech filled with wisdom, with politicians and big men (or women) everywhere we are by contrast hypernaturally aware of the independent meaning of the performance. He talked Communist theory but meant I am the boss. She talked fiscal responsibility and tax reduction but meant re-elect me. The dean talked about academic leadership by professors but intended to justify his far more than academic salary by making himself into a symbol of faculty aspirations. These may seem cases of pure hypocrisy, the skillful—or blatant—use of one kind of speech act for an intended effect on a specific audience.[118] But usually there is a double intention: to say something important that makes us feel important. In this form most speech and authorship has at least an additional intention of boosting our egos or letting us feel big (a little bigger).

In works of literature this is likely to be present as a career performance, the author finding his or her role in doing the work he or she does. This, it should be noted too, is a strange position, more often developing out of a tradition than from simple personal intention: the mastery is often mastery and innovation (as more mastery) in a tradition. But there is likely to be some dissonance between tradition and the talented individual working within it. To the extent that the poet plays a role in an historically established tradition, he is creating a complex speech act, imitating a kind of speech act (the poet performing as lovelorn shepherd in pastoral, for example) while also adding his twist on the tradition (Colin Clout and sensible English rustics) and perhaps personal social opinions (statements about Ireland or England's queen). "All genres," Todorov interestingly asserts, "stem from speech acts."[119] But the speech act itself is greatly complicated by its promotion of a generic tradition. There are fissures and differences within tradition. In the mix of roles and speech acts it is hard to find the poet.[120]

This second, generally unacknowledged, intention is to be, in effect, the excellent actor of the subjects or ideas expressed. T.S. Eliot's *The Waste Land* may seem about personal and social loss and incoherence; yet we also experience it, indeed specifically experience its qualities as a modern poem, as Eliot's masterwork of control of cultural tradition, the web of the great web master. If Eliot wanted both to make a public confession of frailty and also to become a powerful someone by writing the poem, his divided intentions will be written into a division between its stated expressions and its performative effect.[121] No wonder that critics have been divided as to whether the poem is a deeply felt expression of torment (which I believe it certainly is) or one of the last power stands for the WASP male (which I believe it certainly is too). Aren't these interpretations incompatible? I think no: we can think of a work as being both confessional and masterful; but if we try to defend one or the other view of the poem by saying this is what the author really intended we have a problem. Well then, Eliot intended them both: and perhaps many other things too, but the pretense that we can find in the author's intentions some quiet, well-lit place where the complexities of interpretive criticism can be simplified and settled once and for all is reduced to mere fragments.

The issue of performativity has of course been explored at more local levels in applications of Speech Act theory to literature or in the early Stanley Fish's general exhortation to critics to explore what writing does (to us readers) rather than what it says. I shall return below to question theories that see in this aspect of language an assurance that we can know the author's intention from its apparently intended effect.[122] But the play on how a work means and what it means, both of which don't seem easily to go away, rather suggests the division in the intention itself that I am looking at here. If all writers writing are involved to some degree in a career performance of mastery, they may also have more specific personal goals, conscious or unconscious, in their writing.[123] If we write a love letter we may intend to talk about our mistress's eyes, or her career, but, as all readers of the Western love tradition know, we will be more likely to vent (the song says "celebrate") our love. Our need to perform such an act, for reasons God knows, may be manifestly in conflict with our subject, those peerless peepers, her most recent raise, or even a palpable rhetorical aim—seducing our coy one. Lovers, Shakespeare knew, are like madmen; certainly writing lovers are as incoherent in their intentions.

Tennyson in *In Memoriam* or Virginia Woolf in *To the Lighthouse* may have had an intention of remembering important people in their lives; yet the intention also seems to have been to work out their grief and move on: we know this in briefer works as the odd way in which elegies—Milton on King, Shelley on Keats—seem to start out remembering and celebrating the lost person but usually shift quickly to the author's preoccupation, in the face of mortality, with his or herself. Sophomore students wonder about this oddly confused motivation that seems behind works presented as great; we critics learn to try to read one side or the other and ascribe it to a single intention of the author. One can't deny Tennyson's needy affection for Hallam or the fact that, having grieved him well, he went on by careful revision of his grief-inseminated poem to become poet laureate. We may wish to say Milton and Shelley only looked for a chance to talk about mortality, but then why did these deaths seem at the time important enough to them to hang their best work on them? In all such cases of mixed intention involved in the need to write, the performance will offer different readers different perspectives on two or a variety of possible author's intentions. If I can imagine some mixture of intentions in an author performing the act of writing, could give imaginary percentages for each—say 40 per cent grief over Hallam and 60 per cent need to show his excellence in mastery of his craft—I cannot in fact know what they really were, or even if there aren't other percentages to be given to other motivations. Indeed, we can always ascribe some general kind of persuasive motivation, as well. *In Memoriam* reassured a generation fearful of loss of faith before the reality of death. This may (or may not) be considered an additional intention of the poet, further clouding his overall intent.[124] And remember, these intentions of performance have to be then recalculated against the "purer" intentions of propositional meaning: for instance, that Tennyson meant to say Hallam was like a nineteenth-century Christ, not that he needed to make the comparison to relieve his grief or establish himself as a new poetic prophet. The philosopher, attempting to establish clear distinctions and lay down conventions in ordinary language use, will separate out intentions for a meaning (the performative or in later Austin the illocutionary force) and the intention in the meaning (the constative or in later Austin locutionary); to a reader seeking to discover what an author really meant, both are present and the result is necessarily confusing.

Generally when a writer sings out of personal need—and there must be some element of this in all writing—when he or she sings because he or she must, then intentions are likely to lack integration. *Jane Eyre* may seem to many biographers to have been written out of Charlotte Brontë's sense of woman's weak position in her century, an intention to lament and grieve: and we have a large body of interpretation based on the assumption that this was indeed a correct reading of the author's intention. Yet the work, as others have seen, celebrates the power of Jane and her author to speak out loud and clear, to assert herself forcefully. No Helen burning within, Jane will get it out and she and her author will become empowered in the process.[125] When we begin to seek out intention by shrinking the author, division continues, with the text appearing now as a site not just of performance but of multiple acting out. And this will be in as many directions as our many psychoanalytic discourses direct us. Sylvia Plath's "Lady Lazarus" is not a poem that can easily be distanced as the speech of a mere New Critical persona. The artistic brilliance of the poem, the blatant feminist themes—hate of control, repressed anger—are objectively there, but so, we feel, is an author asking for our empathy, acting out and claiming our horrified involvement to the point where we withdraw from her and judge this suicide-act lady, even as we recall how really good she was at it and how strongly that final act brought her before her public.[126] Or we find, or project onto the psychiatrists in the poem our finding: bodily hysteria speaking through Nazi lampshade and swaddled (Lazarus-like) dead flesh. Or we see the vampire acting out her anger—or is it her sexual frustration?—on men who try to help, a modern Bertha in her attic. We can be pretty sure that Plath has put a great deal of her life before us for us to understand by whatever analytical tools of psychology we have. The trouble is the acting out itself is overdetermined, rent through by the many plausible psychological pictures of her that we can paint. The actor in the text, whether performing or acting out, destabilizes rather than solidifies our view of the text.

VI. LIMITS ON THE AUTHOR'S CONTROL

Even if we posit an author fully in control of his or her intention and posit this as a single intention—though I think I have suggested how unlikely this is in any but the simplest communication—there are still many cases in which the author is not able effectively to assert control over the text as it leaves the intending mind (if, with only some philosophers, we believe in such a thing) and proceeds, by some, or some changing, technology into reception. Here it is the author who shoots the arrow into the stream of history but can have no certain knowledge of where it will go and what shape it will be in. Writing, Derrida has famously pointed out, is able to make certain discriminations of meaning—French *différence* and the nonce *différance*—that are not heard. But the concept of intention forces one to conceptualize literature as if it were usually a spoken utterance, which in fact it rarely is in the publication and reception of literature.[127] Poetic contests, extemporaneous creations, and brilliant improvisations are rare forms of literature, and even these are perhaps more often reworkings of prior shticks/stichs than more spontaneous productions.[128] The exception that immediately comes to mind is oral literature, with the seeming full presence of a singer presenting work to us directly. In oral presentation the material production is pretty much still present wholly within the intending person (though a contingent gust of wind could certainly imperil even this). And accents, pronunciation disorders, and low volume levels can of course greatly disturb ordinary audition. In any case, the appearance of originary intended meaning, before us directly in immediacy and with every nuance, yields to the normal fact of performance: the bard in the Greek hilltop or the Anglo-Saxon mead hall is not presenting a first, authoritative meaning but remembering and interpreting, if it is his own work, what was intended months or years before. He too is a critic of his own work, trying to recover an intended meaning that is no longer present to him. I would not say I have not learned something about *The Waste Land* by hearing the aged and somewhat obese Eliot, dressed in a tuxedo, intone in Memorial Hall; but this was not the man who wrote that tortured poem, and his tortured youth, whatever it had been, was clearly no more before him as he read than it was before us.

Perhaps the form of presentation in which the intention of the writer is before us is one in which the division of intentions is usually more interesting than the unity: the recovery of drafts and manuscripts shows us a writer finding a direction in certain areas, but these documents also remind us how much division in the prior subtexts lies hidden in the final text. A keystroke record from a word processor—better yet a recording of all the starts and stops and corrections on a dictating machine—would offer some insights into what the author found he or she meant but also many roads not decisively taken but also not totally lost in the final draft.[129] We may argue authoritative interpretive approaches from either direction.

The case has mainly been that technologies since the invention of writing have increased the possibilities of reception by substantially reducing the ways in which the earlier face-to-face speech allowed the author to control the text as he presented it. Print, whether old-fashioned Gutenberg or the great highway of the internet, of course leaves out all gesture;[130] and it has generally no reliable way of indicating voicings that in oral speech render intention in a number of ways: stress (I *tell you and keep telling you that I can't use italics every time I want to emphasize a word*—and I can't use it to show where the accent goes in the word), emotional states and tone of voice (to say I intend to shout this one in hysterical agitation will make you laugh or frown, not experience the hysteria I can manifest first hand; in the good movie of *Sense and Sensibility* the sensitive hero is attacked for not putting enough feeling into his rendering of Cowper's "Castaway," but how should he know from the cold print how much feeling was appropriate to Cowper's fear, in non-mad times of his madness?), speed (we have no musical notations *andante, molto presto con spirito* to guide us as to pace), intonation (Joseph Brodsky read his Russian poetry with tremendous waving of arms, shouting, chanting; who would know that from the text? also, maybe this is just the normal way they read poetry, heavy or light, in Soviet poetry readings, a triumphant assertion of the resisting power of the poet to speak out), give-aways to point of view, irony or sarcasm, or joking.[131] The sociologist Goffman speaks of framing "directionals" in direct communication: "the most common regulation is the head nod, the equivalent of the verbal *mm-hmm*, other regulators include eye contacts, slight movements forward, small postural shifts, eyebrow raises and a whole host of small nonverbal acts."[132] Cognitive psychologists speak of information "given off" as opposed to given in direct face-to-face communication and find nonverbal communication significantly registered by their recipients in experimental takes.[133]

Anyone who has talked with actors or their directors knows that they are heavily involved in interpretation from the minute they begin to study a text. Even if their intention is mainly practical rather than interpretive, they must give their interpretations of all that is not observed in the text but must be decided in re-vocalizing the text. Directors at the National Theatre in London always emphasize the need to work out stress in every line. A useful exercise was to try the sentence again and again, stressing each word in turn, until one seemed superior. The performance is usually judged by the way other sound effects are restored—as well they should be since so much of the dramatic communication is created in the performance, the emotional affect of the character, the pacing and timing, the kind of delivery, and timbre of the voice. In modern times reading in the closet was closer to such dramatic revoicing than it is generally today, when the whisper of the lips in reading (I remember silently admiring my Victorian-educated grandmother thus whispering her way through mystery after mystery) is repressed as a sign of half-literacy (which it is not). "To read without uttering the words aloud or at least mumbling them is a 'modern' experience, unknown for millennia. In earlier times, the reader interiorized the text; he made his voice the body of the other; he was its actor."[134] Those of us who learned to teach in the New Critical classroom can attest that the power of the close critical method had much to do with restoring the power of this older voiced dramatic reading by dramatically performing the text—much as the director's practical workshop at beginning rehearsals must. We may think, perhaps more than the bolder director who usually sets out to create his version of somebody's novel, even if he calls it *Bram Stoker's Dracula*, that we are restoring the author's voice or the voices he heard; but the text certainly doesn't give them to us.

There is a final point to be made, which I could dwell on under the subject of rereading but will mention only briefly here.[135] If we think of intention as something that comes to the author like speech, with all its apparent directness but also with its spontaneity, then we must notice that writing has offered the reader a power denied all but the listener with total recall: that is, we can rescroll in scroll, print, or computer; we can examine the way in which utterances, arriving and disappearing like passengers in a railway station, actually connect, or fail to connect together. In this way the stream of acts of intention is muddied by our ability to reverse its direction and flow it all together. Here the technology has made our sense of intention—what did the author mean by this strange book?—far more global than the successive acts of intention that make up any communication: they become intentionettes and they may fall together badly in the final intention of the whole that we seek.[136]

Other limits to the author's control of the text come not from limits to what can be inscribed in any technology but from the fragility of the various barks to which his testament for eternity is entrusted. Even the initial embarking can present a considerable hazard to the author's intentions with the text. Publishing is by its very nature a negotiation between the author and the general society into which the work is published. Sometimes, as with Aristotle or Shakespeare, the author seems not to have been really the agent of the publication, students in the first case writing down the lectures, pirates or friends in the second bringing out the plays in different versions. In the positivist era of textual editing earlier in the twentieth century, editors tried to identify strictly one version of the published text as that chosen and controlled by the author. But even in this ethos, room had to be made for other possible sites of control of the text: for instance, plausible errors by the scribe or typesetter not caught by the author. Without a manuscript to check against, corrections back to the author's presumed intentions can only be guesses and will usually create controversial cruxes where experts can't agree.

And sometimes the better readings, for which we may fight with all our weapons of enthusiasm and scorn, may in fact be improvements over the author's own lesser choices; thus scrupulous scholarship is used to justify what is in fact competing authorship. Even with a manuscript to refer to, we may find that failure of control begins as early as the author's own hand—a confusing inkblot, an impossible, scribbled addition, a clutch in the keys, a blip on the tape, a blooper segment on the diskette, or a Freudian slip of stylus, pen, mouth, or hand. And there are of course errors of reproduction, copyist's fatigue giving us a number of manuscripts, all with the aura of original works but some different from others; or, in an age of mechanical reproduction, broken bits of type in fast-running steam presses: errors perhaps susceptible to careful sorting out, perhaps overlooked or not soluble. Despite the attraction of the ideal of author's control in higher (textual) as in lower criticism, the truth is that the author never has one-hundred-percent control even of the first published text. What was in his mind may not appear exactly in his first writing; drafts can introduce new errors or complications of earlier clarities, a layering of one intention on another one that all writers know: the final published form is usually a result of much copying, and all writers also know that copying will introduce errors.

The world anxiously awaits the author's intent; but usually it also insists upon intruding on his wish for sole control; we authors usually buy publication at the price of sharing our precious power of control socially with others. Peer reviewers, we academic types all know, as the culprits or their victims—and we are generally both Hydes and Jekylls in our careers—insist on the *droit du seigneur* of publishing: inserting their seminal ideas in our virgin text. Editors and copyeditors, too, will have their insertions, infusions, and bleedings, their pounds or little slices of our textual flesh, and tell us they do it for our sake, know what is best for us to intend better than we can. We like to think censorship, political, moral, sexual, is an aberration; but in the history of publishing it is more nearly the norm, and the author's intentions are made to speak in a civil tongue, to suit the Lord Chamberlain, to please the Pope or the little popes of Boston or Dublin, Beijing or Teheran. Joyce's *Portrait* was derailed because the very printers decided to censor it. Prudes and pirates work together to tear many works out of the author's control entirely, with first publication in a messy and totally un-authorized issue.

The fear of censorship and even of criticism could even be added to the set of divided intentions within the author surveyed above: if the author knows that he or she must conform to certain societal expectations he will write a text other than he intends. Hirsch will of course say this compromise is what he does then intend; but the reader who wishes to determine the author's intention from the text will usually find the divided aims lead to a controversial interpretive field. If Oscar Wilde really meant "bunburying" to speak of the joys of the homosexual closet, he certainly left us unclear as to what he meant to say, since he was forced not to say entirely what he meant to say, but allowed enough room to maneuver to leave us with both possibilities. "Well then, he intended both." Sorry, it isn't that simple: we are left having to decide which or how much of each. A similar puzzle offers whenever the author kisses the rod but leaves earlier intentions lying around for editors to find. What shall we do with the original edition of *Sons and Lovers* when we know Lawrence's text was censored down by Garnett? Arguably Lawrence's final intention for that edition was to let Garnett share control of his intention; yet Cambridge's editors have followed his penultimate intentions and published the deletions. We are coming in such cases to be more comfortable with a sense of different versions of a work not as less and more controlled in some hierarchy of ultimate authorial control but as merely different moments in which still shots were taken of fluctuating intentions.

Even without the help of editors and censors, authors of course muddy their own texts by jumping in, sons of the child who fathered their text, where even fool textual editors would fear to tread. They actually sit down with former versions of their masterpieces, written in the pride and power of their passionate youths, and rewrite them, graybeard and aged rheum falling down over the page. Men and writers improve with the years? Dubious, but some do, some don't; all doubtless change and the layering of author old and young, crafty or impulsive, coupled with changes in the general culture and language out of which he or she writes, can make a text that speaks more than one tongue, more than one stream of intentions. Again, under the pressure of our discovery of the variety of texts for which a case can be made, whether the various performance texts of Shakespeare or the different, published and unpublished, versions of Wordsworth's *Prelude* or Browning's differently published versions of his dramatic romances and lyrics, we have come to accept the idea of a text as a fluid, changing set of states rather than as a single, controlled entity surrounded by rejected variants. What this means however is that in some sense, like all of us, the author never really entirely knew his own mind. The author is our *frère*, a "continually innovating medium" as the editors of the Ohio Browning began to discover when they set out, somewhat naively, to take all the textual variants seriously: like ourselves, like America, always remaking itself because always a welter of confused intentions warring for a control that will never last. Because always in process, the author can hardly ever be univocal. As editor and interpreter of himself, the innovating author functions like a reader; he finds the figure in the carpet, the meaning in the mass, that suits his present interests and concerns; like a reader, he makes his interpretation; more even than a reader can, he rewrites to suit his interpretation. The confusion in a palimpsest of intentions in a much rewritten final text embodying the author's testamentary control is, however, only a more vivid case of the necessary layering of intentions in any text that undergoes revision—as what text does not?[137]

Now consider with me for a moment all the hazards that a text is heir to if it escapes major changes at the hands of its editors, publishers, or creators. (Note I don't use the word mutilation, which would imply that the original text is the best; that is a matter of our—readers' or editors as readers'—judgment based on our own criteria for best; editors or authors often have good notions of revision, for instance Pound's famous deletions from *The Waste Land* manuscript.) Fire in Alexandria's great library did away with so many authors' intentions that we shall never even be able to quarrel over! Acid paper, careless misshelving ("lost in collection" is lost! sometimes forever), zealots' depredations, careless reproductions (and even the most careful ones are unlikely to be error free), Sapphic fragmentation into mummies' wrappings, the invisible worm, these and so many other entropic forces mutate texts even before, like all bright things, they pass entirely away, obscuring the aims of their authors. Nor can we assume, as we write or read texts, that editors are always re-constructive; many have been like church restorers of the nineteenth century (or indeed those anti-aging experts of our bodily parchment) who remake to restore, whether by inserting a few commas to settle cruxes left unclear by the author or by amalgamating various states of the text into a jerry-rigged work that never was.[138] O Common Reader, if any such there be who may chance upon this text, do not put your trust in us men and women of learning; we too are only mortal readers with our own needs to seem important and our envy of the great and creative: we will have our will with the text, as any Reader such as yourself will, even in that science of editing—no settled science in fact but a site of our battles over texts as long as society allows editors a place in its allocation of resources.

Again, I have no wish to make the obscurantist argument that because some texts are so changed all texts necessarily become obscured. But the history of some of our oldest texts, those of classical antiquity or of biblical times, tells us that authors' control cannot be certain after the work is sent out on the waters of time. And not just lesser authors, either. The Author of the greatest story looks down at his work only in versions: "various Hebrew recensions, Aramaic Targums, the Samaritan Pentateuch, Masoretic texts, the Septuagint, Origen's *Hexapla*, the odd variety of Latin translations of which Augustine complained, the Vulgate, the vernacular versions that accompany the proliferation and modernizations of Christianity, and so on."[139] Not just all-important texts are likely to suffer the indignity, the making different and making new, of translation. Indeed, inevitably, as time goes by, all must do so if they are to be read at all. A similar process of necessary translation will occur more subtly as a text is reclassified in the changing and rather relentless pigeonholes of future times. We read as literature what was written as prayer, history, testimony to God's way with the author, or a political cudgel. Unless we confine ourselves to rare-book rooms or facsimiles (themselves almost but not quite the originals), we read in new material frames from the first ones—themselves not entirely and sometimes not at all chosen by the author.[140] The reorientation remains virtually as a change in the work itself, whatever historical knowledge we bring to bear on it. From wrong to wrong we proceed if we disaggregate only to alienate them further in special departments of comparative religion, historiography, history of religion, or political science. No one can really restore that lost framing.[141]

VII. CULTURAL DETERMINISM AS DISGUISED INTENTIONALITY

In this section I fear I am going to sound like an unpleasant and gloom-saying bear in a boom market. I refer to the market for historical studies in literary studies. I remember back in the inflationary times for New Criticism and then in the high-flying theory 1970s there were only a few visionaries among us who believed in the coming bull market for history. And we kept our belief even in the face of what then seemed the obvious difficulties of connecting two things essentially different in nature: interpretation and history. We all know the history of this market; we hardly need the sociologist of culture, Pierre Bourdieu, to show us how a new generation, finding prestige and places, brought in a wave of more speculative activity—New Historians with Foucauldian universalizers—and literature was part of one big episteme/period. And their stock shot up. Then came close at their heels a newer wave of cultural historians bent on new growth areas with high PEs (philosophical exemptions from textual analysis). Now I admit those were heady, wonderful times as the charts kept booming up—and there really were some Intels and Microsofts and Amazon.coms among them. If it was all one big textual muddle then some brilliant folk might have some inspired ideas, as indeed was true of Stephen Greenblatt or Andrew Ross. But the turn to history began to exhibit irrational exuberance, as these things will: everyone wanted a share, everyone rushed in. There was no small cap area underutilized; IPOs (idiosyncratic post out-of-the way subjects) were being issued everywhere. It was no longer fancy episteme gadgets or new texts of history: just grab whatever piece of history you can get while the market roars. As John Kucich has remarked, graduate students found the possession of one small subject an irresistible attraction in their actually steadily depressed area.[142] As a journal editor, I see seven such articles, picking out one unexplored area of history, for every one doing any of the other major tasks we traditionally perform. Who needs theory? Graham and Derrida had their day; just do it.

I confess I have always liked out-of-the-way, tasty bits of history (especially in my own Victorian period), liked them when the prices were ridiculously low. Historical knowledge is good; let it grow. The problem is when it becomes a short cut for what we need to do best, that habit of careful regard to fundamentals of interpretation that is one of our major professional *raisons d'être*.

There is perhaps no more fundamental issue in theory of interpretation—in the theory otherwise called hermeneutics—than the old chestnut I have been so bold-facedly pursuing, of intention. One sees the rise of historical positivism in the development in nineteenth-century thought of an intention-based hermeneutics. The demise of that positivist system of interpretation, the replacement of Schleiermacher and Dilthey with Nietzsche and Heidegger,[143] or nearer our realm, of the biographical-moral criticism of Arnold or Leslie Stephen by the textually oriented work of Empson or Wimsatt, seemed to accompany the historical skepticism of the twentieth century. Certainly by late in the century, say the 1970s and early 1980s, there seemed to be a consensus that the intentional issues in literature had been settled. If the newer criticisms, structuralism and post-structuralism/deconstruction, set themselves widely apart in the United States from the old New Criticism, or in England from Leavisism, they nonetheless reaffirmed rather than critiqued the old Wimsatt and Beardsley dictum, that intentionality is an interpretive fallacy. Arguments—actually rather bare-boned, as we have seen—by those New Critics were supplemented by that new thinking by Foucault and Barthes in which texts were further cut loose from their moorings in author's intention by declarations of the death of the author before the living reader and the non-individuality of textuality itself—a product of culture rather than of a Cartesian individual first cause.

The issue of intentionality went around, however, only to come around in disguised form with the emergence of a new history. And here it was of course Foucault's insistence that intentionality cannot be located in the individual author rather than Barthes's concern to release the text from readerly controls that implicitly prevailed.[144] New Historicism and American Cultural Studies, the former especially influenced by Foucault's shift of agency in history off the individual and to a large societal textuality, both began to spin a web of cultural determinism to replace author determination. If texts were written intertextually by an entire epoch, then the epoch could be made to stand in for the author as prior authority.[145] And this in turn seemed to offer a new security in interpretation. If New Historical approaches could show us the warp and woof of the cultural age on which a text was constructed, then they could also serve as a surrogate author, a place of intention. Historical texts of the age, rather than the biography and private writings of the author, could serve as reliable stabilizers of the interpretation. Welcome history, goodbye wars of reading.

Finally, theory, that multi-faceted investigation of the premises of literary study, was suddenly declared no longer exciting. It was, rather, to be put back on the shelf as inconsequential. Steven Knapp and Walter Benn Michaels, *enfants terribles* of the turn against theory and toward history, argued that no theory could guide interpretation. Their prime example was intentionality. Presenting themselves as neo-pragmatists neutral to anything but the effective force of arguments, they in fact argued strongly in favor of intentionality as a necessary and fundamental fact of interpretation. If Richard Rorty objected in the name of a clearer pragmatism,[146] their essay nonetheless carried the day—not by defeating anti-intentionalism but by declaring the issue both irrelevant and metaphysically determined. If intention was an irrelevant but necessary part of all reflection on literature, then the path was cleared for New Historical work offering itself as the only game in town, the only market in which to invest. Stanley Fish's own version of neo-pragmatism, especially his concept of communities of interpretation, similarly encouraged history-based interpretation by almost a sleight of hand. If the idea of communities accepts a pragmatic concept of meaning determined only by the differing approaches and presuppositions of groups of readers, his theory reserved a simple, particular community for serious critics, the professionally informed readers—who turn out to be especially informed about the correct historical interpretation.[147]

And this is where I feel the need to play the bear. As long as the turn to history was content to play a game, in which one grand textuality—canonical texts, uncanonical texts, texts of historical record, texts of other kinds—was interpreted by the finely sharpened tools of Anglo-American textual close criticism, there was no problem. But there was no claim to interpretive supremacy in looking at texts, merely to a broader kind of interpretive field of operation. The brilliant early work of Stephen Greenblatt even included specific disavowals of hermeneutic positivism in which he granted his own interpretive positionality:

> if cultural poetics is conscious of its status as interpretation, this consciousness must extend to acceptance of the impossibility of fully reconstructing and reentering the culture of the sixteenth century, of leaving behind one's own situations; it is everywhere evident in this book that the questions I ask of my material and indeed the very nature of this material are shaped by the questions I ask myself.[148]

But the growth in history, the turn away from theory, especially this central theory issue of intention, the need to answer criticisms of excessive historical presentism,[149] has tended to open a hidden route back to nineteenth-century positivism. Increasingly we have been told that the new historical work offers not another kind of interpretation but a canonical interpretive mode. This can only be asserted if those initial theoretical premises of the new history are ignored, the premises of both Hayden White and Derrida, that history is not available to us as fact, only as narration or text. We all knew that, but from the late 1980s on we seemed in the process of wishing to cancel, to forget, that knowledge. The current buzz words of the new study of culture, the newest history, show a turn against those textualist origins: we hear "historical specificity" valorized, as if particularity, the rehearsal of some new treasures from some new archival obscurity, cancelled the multi-determinations of textuality. Another author notes the current "unremitting commitment to the historic situatedness of texts."[150] We hear "subjectivity" talked down on all sides as if we, all subjects of our writing on these issues, could nonetheless efface textuality by effacing the receivers of texts. There is no one home inside human robo-computers so there is no problem about reading the so various and multivalent texts of history.

I am obliged here, and in subsection xviii below (subtitled "Babes in the Woods of Historicity"), to critique the simplicities that allow the re-emergence of intentionality in this historical disguise, essentially as the view that the meaning of a text can rightly be known only by knowing the historical site out of which it emerged. Let me repeat that I have no wish to deny the use of historical work, which I do a lot of, in opening new possibilities to interpretation, or in offering interpretation of broader subjects than individual texts—the normal business of Cultural Studies. Nor am I unsympathetic to the diverse field of critical endeavor, usually historically based, that goes under the catch-term of Marxist criticism, from Georg Lukàcs, Pierre Macherey, or Raymond Williams to Fredric Jameson and Terry Eagleton. These and other less brilliant, sometimes more scientistic critics have generally been clear that they are interested not in fitting literature into an historical picture but in exploring how their particular awareness of economic and class issues can leverage interpretations that give us insight into how material conditions affect human life—whether overtly or by the critic's divination and unfolding of the text.[151] But the hope to locate and freeze interpretive validity (to use the term of that last great intentional intentionalist, E.D. Hirsch) in an historical specificity (whatever that could be but another text!) where the text is said to do specific cultural work or (in England) labour, is countered by most of the same arguments that have carried weight against more specific concepts of intentionality based on biographical knowledge of the author.[152]

One thing one eventually learns in literary theory—after the first blush of hope for mounting a metacriticism that establishes the truth has faded from more experienced cheeks—is that theory offers in fact not truth but perspective—which is not in itself to be scorned. The corollary is that any corner of theory can offer a temporarily rather commanding view on any other. So, to take the case I am raising, the turn back to history in New Historicism and Cultural Studies has offered a powerful reading of reading, in which both readers and authors are caught up in the wave of a culture and swept along in their presentation/interpretation. In such a vision of cultural determination, no mere petty bourgeois beliefs in the independence of authors and readers can stand against the all-controlling force of culture. In this view we are born into a culture that makes us what we are and what we see and think; to try to escape ourselves is silly and impossible.

But then the reversal of theory fortune is always possible and likely, and it takes the form of a reversal of perspective. A cat (out-of-favor reader theory or hermeneutics) can always look back at a king (New Historicism and Cultural Studies riding high in the twenty-first century) and see the great one from its perspective. Reader perspective on cultural history begins by questioning the implicit pretensions of this historical discipline to a positive knowledge of the past; even in its especially textualized and nuanced version of history, the updated study of history almost necessarily leads the newer historians to claims to see the past as it was.[153] The lenses are finer than former kinds of political or cultural history, but they are nonetheless aimed at taking a view of what they consider the historical reality. By contrast, reader theory would insist that even such often fine and sensitive work can offer only successive, subjective readings of the great mass of historical evidence of all kinds. It would point out that the newer histories' awareness of other people's subjective readings of their world or history calls into question their own procedures. What is true of others in other times is presumably also true of the historians: they can only read the past through lenses given them by their own point of view or that of their times. With less need to solve beforehand, for other people, the old issue of whether individuals are controlled by culture or able to occupy diverse independent positions within it, reader theory is more insistent that all views, including views of the past, are located in a cultural or individual position, that they represent readings or points of view. Indeed, it has sponsored a burgeoning co-subject of study, reception theory or study (see section IV), that has already widely explored the diversity of readings of different ages—though it, too, can fall into a positivist assurance that it knows the reader and reading of the past.

In their readings of the text of the past, in which they move easily from the "text" of history to the texts of traditional literary study, the newer historians have tended, in their growing though mainly implicit cultural determinism, to suggest that the text can be stabilized in its meaning by its relation to the historical text. This sleight of hand, usually not intended as more than a testimony of faith in their recovery of the past, has the consequence in thinking about interpretation of re-establishing the old view, as a senior member of my first department once put it, that "history is the ark of our foundation": that is, we must ground all interpretation in history. He of course then meant the older context and background history which F.R. Leavis stigmatized in its time as "the arbitrary odds and ends of fact, assumption, and more or less historical summary,"[154] and which is now in such ill favor. Surely it had its uses in giving us some sense of what would be unlikely interpretations: that planes would more likely refer to trees than bombers in literature before the twentieth century, and so on. Nor would I, a fellow traveler in my historical work, wish to denigrate the subtle work that shows us, to cite an area I have worked in, how frequently Victorian medical or religious views of sexuality and the body were cited, enacted, or reacted to in the novels of the period. Yet the danger of such work, appearing with all the recommendation of special erudition and research, is that it tends to reify an interpretation into a fact of (new) history. It was easier to see the older history as merely an external, corrective shell to interpretation. Context, almost by definition, was a broad scatter-shot set of historical observations among which an interpreter could pick and choose. In its naivete, it did not attempt to be a full-fledged interpretation itself. Its wisdom was in its sense of the extensiveness, indeed extendability, of "context." Context opens up wider and wider, in time beginning to connect everything in the world, including everything in the work. It has no center that can hold, but its circumference holds more and more.[155]

The temptation now is that we believe that our historical reads, where history and text are so closely intertwined, are exclusive and correct. This reifying tendency has been aggravated, as I note above, by all the economic and ego-enriching forces that drive claims to professional expertise. If we have studied a good deal about an historical topic, we come to have various investments in our claims to be expert witnesses to the age, all goading us to want to say that ours is not an (even perhaps interesting) interpretation but *the* interpretation. This has been further promoted, in the case of New Historicism and Cultural Studies, by the need to fend off criticism that described the projects as merely literary, fanciful interpretations of little texts of history by those trained not in historical study but in the arts. What is brave and new about these critical traditions—their practitioners' willingness to take playful risks in trying on contemporary issues in the literary or historical texts of earlier times and in the mutual cross-fertilization of literary and historical interpretive moves—attracts critiques of that playfulness that ironically constrain its practitioners to assert the historical truth of their views. What began as an opening to new interpretations based on experiment with partial and idiosyncratic viewpoints, pleasant interpretive romps through history and literature alike, attempts to import current concerns—multiculturalism, postcolonial, or queer issues, and even issues of counterhistory, resistance, and oppositional tactics—into a past that had seemed closed to them, ends as the usual historical special interest, barring nonprofessional applicants from privileged positions in the enterprise of interpretation.[156]

To call an historical read correct would suggest a form of intentionality, now no longer the intention of the author conceived as a conscious, willing being, as he is in Hirsch's thinking on the subject, but the intention of the age flowing through the writer and his writing technology. I looked above at cultural influences on the writer as ways in which the individual writer can be said to be divided in his intentions, in effect between outside and inside. The case here is rather that we are asked to think of writers as controlled by the outside forces around them, which are thought of as always already inside them, aliens making their thought from the beginning. If this were the case we could have faith not in the coming end of history but in the end of interpretation. We would only need to refine our new history to the point where our understanding of the age provided an explanation of the necessary intention of the work. This would be true even where the work was seen as displaying the fissures and encountering positions of a fissured, encountering age. Here I hope I may be permitted the broad reflection that the great grandfather of all such thinking, Vico, made no such assumption about culture controlling people. His famous dictum was that society was made by men, presumably men who had some purpose in their individual activities. And the great father of such thinking, Karl Marx, who certainly did revolutionize thinking in the West to look for the origins of thought in material conditions of society and history, never seems to wish to look at cultural phenomena as merely the products of a determining history.[157] His main life's work—not as an activist but as a writer and intellectual—obviously testifies to his belief in the power of individual insight to change the minds of others and the thinking of the time.

The issue of social construction and social control has been a disturbing one at the heart of the New Historical project, raising issues of agency and causation that have refused to disappear.[158] The earlier Foucault, of *Discipline and Punish*, who was so influential on the initial New Historical work, set an agenda about power and the individual. Works such as Greenblatt's *Renaissance Self-Fashioning* early turned New Historians' interest to the ways in which the individual was constructed within the society. To some extent this seemed to go against the grain of some historians' own postmodern interests in diversity, cultural fissures, and opposition.[159] These thematic interests, which inspired some of the later work of Greenblatt himself,[160] seem to sit uncomfortably with the methodological imperative of historical specificity. Even where the text studied may represent a subversive position in the broader society, it is read into a web of other texts that locate it within its historical moment. The opening of early Renaissance society provoked by early capitalism or intersections with non-Western culture offered a scene of much cultural readjustment and confusion and inspired some of the best work, in Renaissance studies, as conflicting old and new roles for women or constructions of new sexual identities did in nineteenth-century historical work. However these topical issues of diversity, also perhaps encouraged by Foucault's theorizations of power in his later work on sexuality as more diffuse, did not disturb the essential premise of cultural embedding of texts. I want to look here directly at the premises of that embedding, which still carry the initial sense of individuals and their texts made and contained by their cultures, so that even diversity, often so well recognized in New Historical work, is contained by and in the larger culture.[161]

Let me sort out briefly some of the reasons why we can no more be assured of the meaning of a work by knowing the text of history that flows in and around it than we can by hearing from the author his or her stated intentions. First, as the best New Historical work recognizes but the rank and file often forget, there is no reason to have a firm belief in the coherence of the culture, any more than we can have a firm belief in the coherence of the author subject. As an analytic philosopher carefully put it, "cultures and communities are more or less disunified coalitions of more or less diversified groups of more or less disunified individuals."[162] Coherence is something historians may seek to impose upon the enormous complexity of the historical records in order to see certain strands more clearly. This is as true of the newer histories as of the older, and even when the unifying topic is cultural intersections or resistance areas. If we explore, as the later Foucault has done, the complex web of sexual discourse in the West, we are certainly giving a certain prominence to these areas of experience and discussion over others equally plausible. Despite the sexy subject, the day comes—especially if we understand Foucault's anaphrodisiac thesis about sexuality as a self-breeding discourse, not a projection of desire—when our fickle attention turns to some new topic: cesspools and sewers in London, say, or pre-computer cybertechnologies, or colonizer-colonized confrontations. And of course within his topic Foucault has necessarily emphasized certain issues at the expense of others, for instance women's and children's rights to sexual autonomy.[163] I choose Foucault as an example because he, if anyone since Oswald Spengler and H.G. Wells, has sought to render history as a coherence, in his case as a set of succeeding global modes of thought, epistemes by which the thought procedures of a time may be looked at as a single vast totality. Those who have been most attracted by his work, myself included, have found that history offers more often uneven developments of emerging thought processes, conflicting discourses in competition with each other, rather than great systemic wholes.[164] Yet even with less global agendas, New Historians are necessarily led to identify patterns in the web of social texts and to imply systems and coherences. It is not that this is different from what critics do with individual texts, accumulate instances and thematize; it is rather that the result is offered as a determining cultural reality instead of as one possible interpretation.

Even if we try to look at culture, in the underlying biological metaphor, as an organism that functions apart from its individual agents (we human beings), it is clearly an entity that is not only too large and complex for us to wrap simplifying historical conceptions around it but also one that seems to have diverse sensory and active appendages that function independently and often contradictorily.[165] Wherever we look for one set of influences as a dominant force in a culture, for instance the flow of Western free-market theories into Russia in the 1990s, we also find other antennae of the culture receiving quite different messages, for instance those of national socialism, seemingly dead since Hitler. Feminist thinking seemed almost hegemonic in the late-twentieth-century United States until the swell of family-values voices, stemming from religious and social-conservative traditions, threatened for a while to drown it out. Cultures, as we know, veer from one set of representative actions to another in quick succession or simultaneously. England calls in conservative Churchill, finally, to put down Hitler and all extreme twentieth-century ideologies only to send him down decisively at war's end in the first national attempt at English socialism. De Gaulle finds himself leading France out of Northern Africa, Nixon takes the United States out of Vietnam and into China, the isolationist younger Bush determines on an adventurist world policy. History has, we know, many cunning passages; any way we try to conceptualize our societies, we find them unsimple, riven into intellectual and political camps, social classes, gender, sexual, or ethnic identity groups, cultural enclaves.[166] Louis Althusser may find a coordinating set of state institutions shaping a single human type in the culture.[167] Cultural theoretician John Frow finds instead varieties of valuing regimes taking often polar positions on the same phenomenon—for example, urban graffiti as so differently seen and prized by the popular partitioners and the people at city hall.[168] Even Raymond Williams's conception of history as a mixture of dominant, residual, and emergent sedimentation, useful as it is, has perhaps too much the sound of teleology; we might better say that an age's parts are going in all directions at once. Unless we remain true believers in a Marxist historical progress, we are not going to know which way history was bound to proceed until we process a period in hindsight; our interpretive story of that history will determine what trends we see as going or as coming.

Nor is this merely a model of diversity founded on the special case of cultural confusion presented by pluralistic, multicultural societies such as the United States, Brazil, or Australia. Even highly stabilized, apparently unchanging societies offer a great diversity of perspectives, often built into the different class or subcultural positions of the society. In even the most tyrannical autocracy, court politics, intrigue, and king's or queen's favorites create diversity and contention. In cultures most dominated by a single system of belief, different positions occupied by different individuals, those for instance of priest and slave, create largely different views and actions. As communities create a set of defining values they also create the shadows in their midst of their opposites.[169] Repressive communism dominates China today, but then so does one of the most rabid efflorescences of capitalism ever seen. Islam has seemed a monolith to the Orientalizing vision of the West; those who know the culture well know it as tremendously diverse beneath its umbrella of single religion and tradition,[170] hence our difficulty in assessing the risk of extremist activity in any particular area. No one writing out of such a culture is merely controlled by a single integral position; diversity and conflict always occupy the site of the subject even if one imagines the subject not his- or herself contributing individual conflict to the stew. Religious persons may choose to believe that there is somewhere a plan to the mighty mazes of culture and society in which we live; historians and sociologists may dream of finding a plan comprehensive enough to serve the purpose; meanwhile we run blind between hedges, with no idea of what awaits us at the next opening. If we are to think of ourselves as mere pawns in the play of the maze, we may at least have the consolation of finding the maze itself incoherent, no sign of one single maker's Daedalian intention behind its twists and breaks.

If we wish to think of a culture as a text that then flows into the text of a writer in the culture—and this is often the way such cultural determinism of writers and readers is conceptualized—we will also need to interrogate the idea of a cultural text. Cultural historians of all stripes like to insist that the text of culture is more than just words; it is visual representations, rituals, structures of the society, buildings and monuments and so on. But then the very fluidity of this idea of cultural "text" undercuts the implication that the text can simply flow into and out of the individual writer. Working with words, he or she must meld together impressions from various cultural locations and media, and this conflation can in itself cause fissures in the text created. Baudelaire writes with visual nostalgia for the old Paris being laid over by new boulevards, but he uses the poetic language of *avant garde* shock and discontinuity. His urban culture's visual conservativeness and linguistic progressiveness clash interestingly in his text, as they will in much modern urban poetry that follows. The diverse languages in which culture dictates its text to us are likely to make our text a multi-faceted or multi-stranded one rather than open up a single determining interpretive explanation.

That each text within the text of culture is likely to be already a collection of diverse voices and points of view makes it unlikely that our repetitions in our texts will speak one coherent language. Such multi-voiced, dialogic texts are, as Bakhtin argued, the natural consequence of socially mixed, heteroglossic language everywhere in history. Yeats celebrates the Anglo-Irishry in "The Tower"; but as these Anglo-Irish are a culture mixing at least the apparent opposites of rapacious exploitation (dear Mrs. French, who had the insolent farmer's ears clipped off and delivered to her in a little covered dish) and noble artistic values, it is no surprise that his poem on the culture speaks with forked tongue, and also no surprise that some readers find him celebrating his caste, others deprecating it.[71] This may offer an attractive case for the New Historian looking at moments of cultural cleavage, and it may well lead her to interesting parallels elsewhere in Irish culture. But the very instability means these will in no way resolve the critical issue that the poem presents—which is of course my interest here. The culture's text is generally already developed as a palimpsest of different meanings accreted at different moments in the culture, through either historical action or the influx of some new influence. Think only of the possible layers of meaning around the use of "liberal" in the contemporary United States: a writer writing that word out of this culture necessarily picks up implications as diverse as socially generous, progressive minded, and mindless advocate of welfare-state spending, not to mention its nineteenth-century meaning of advocating laissez faire. Because culture brings together so many changing values and directions under its surviving terms and symbols, these latter are normally sites of conflicting aims and points of view. The writer who lets culture flow through his or her work creates a text equally as full of contradictions. Fine to explore broadly the complexity of such places of conflict in the culture, but this labor will offer no determining interpretation of any individual text we approach.

This is especially the case where writers embody constructions of the society in which the complex pressures of ideological commitment are at play. As noted above, ideology often speaks a double language, saying one thing while meaning another: the assertion that we must control our borders, for instance, has conscious or unconscious promises of racial division within our borders. Ideology also drives contradictory statements that revel in their mixed intentions: Big Brother (or in the family ideology Big Daddy) is only doing this (harm to us) for our own good. The vision of all writers' texts as driven by a cultural operator really in charge actually suggests that all texts are kinds of ideology, something we write because we have been programmed to do so by the culture. But if this were the case—which I am about to doubt—it would also mean that most texts would end up bearing the marks of ideology's hidden or directly contradictory meanings. Far from finding a stabilizing source of intended meaning in the driving culture, we will only find intentions divided at their source. Such awareness of contradictions, hidden spaces, secrets in the text because hidden in the culture, informs much of the best work in the new histories and best shows their somewhat repressed genealogy as Marxist criticism, where contradiction in the social world is of course a major theme. But it is just in this success that it most contradicts the premises of a coherent cultural text behind individual texts; at its best it realizes the contradiction in its own aims and exposes aporias (again reminding us of the play in New Historicism and Cultural Studies between utopian hopes to write history about relations without causation and the normal fall into stories of causation). At its best it may open new possible approaches to texts, but it does not verify or authenticate any.

A New Historicist approach to T.S. Eliot, for instance, argues, against the grain of much prior aesthetically oriented modernist criticism of the modernist text, that it is precisely what Eliot seems to intend to say little about that connects him to the cultural text of his time: he is, in this view, which I neither endorse nor discard, homosocial, ethnophobic, homophobic, and gynophobic.[172] His stated intention, say to work over the fallen gods of a great tradition he inherits as *disjecta membra*, conflicts with the underlying need to deplore, as other elements of his culture did more directly, the emerging others that threatened hegemonic male culture: Greek businessmen, also homosexual threats; neurotic women, also sexual threats with their gramophones that allow them to march to their own sexual music, and so on. If this is persuasive then it asserts the cultural text, as more directly Marxist critics like Macherey or Jameson have, as a text that hides in the manifest text, as one that may give the last word to a cultural reading, if you choose to accept it, but which does so by premising a text that is always already polyvocal, speaking a text of author's intention beside and in conflict with a text of culture's aims. If cultures have unconsciousnesses just as authors do, they similarly confuse whatever "conscious" intentions may seem manifest.

I have been following an "even if" argument here; but it is my own belief that the common contemporary view of all thinking as always already determined by the culture or society in which we are born and given language is only plausible when both culture and the individual are simplified into unreal counters of reductive thinking.[173] Culture is so diverse that it is a mistake to conceptualize it as an operative force; if we are born into it and given our possibilities within it, it is still more correct to think of it as a great chemical vat of possible nutrients (or poisons), from which we draw to make up our intellectual bodies, than as a mechanical arm pushing us into its forms. It is similarly a rationalistic simplicity to think of the individual as prevented from original thinking by the theoretical limits imposed by his or her containment in a culture. Even relatively uncosmopolitan cultures contain a great mass of information, present and past, and allow diverse speculation on the future. Cosmopolitan cultures such as our own or the empires of past times contain endless windows, through records and other texts, or through conquest or hybridizing exchange, into other cultures.[174]

We have one of those arguments in which all theory may be in favor of a kind of determinism; but, due to the incredible diversity of possibilities leading at each moment to other worlds of diversity, all experience must be against it. In Voltaire's *Micromégas*, the giant is surprised to find that the little folk he studies are studying him in return: "cet atome m'a mesuré"; we atoms of our enormous cultures also measure them in return; we come to our conclusions, we come to a certain sense of our relation to our culture; we even make critiques of it, as Marx did, offering our view of where it is going as a reason for our altering its direction. "There is nothing compelling about the intellectual consensus at any given time."[175] Is this freedom? In any theory of intelligence there comes a point where action based on representation and understanding of the environment gives the appearance of freedom. Is the bee who follows his fellow's dance to the flower free? The flower, the colleague bee, the dance are all given in his world. But his "learning"—here genetic rather than cultural—gives him a program to follow as an individual. But he can't choose not to, you may object. On the contrary, he can, if we chase him away, presumably a cultural learning. We are told how to deal with bees: avoid them or kill them—a cultural learning—but have also learned to innovate, so we move the flower away so as not to be disturbed—by the bee, or by our moral principles about speciesist arrogance, also learned. We may be following a maze of learned programs but the appearance is of some kind of control in our hands, not merely in the culture's.[176] And there is always the possibility that our learning allows us to learn more on our own, as in fact much of our cultural learning involves trying something—like a bee sting—and then getting cultural advice about it. I don't think I need to belabor this point as it is the commonest human experience.[177]

To grant that a great deal of what we are is the result of our production by our culture should not allow a reductive view of the individual that erases his or her ability to maneuver within the enormous array of options made available by culture and language. Anyone who deals regularly with the huge analytical capacities and relative inflexibility of a personal computer knows the difference between flexible choice between options, as humans have, and inflexible programmed routings (yes, improving over time). Culture and language are not prison houses but huge playgrounds—as Ludwig Wittgenstein realized in his later work on language games—with lots and lots of options. If cultural systems may have conservative tendencies that maintain them somewhat against outside change, they also evidence growth and change that can be registered in the culture only through the insights of individuals.[178] Just as all of us experience daily little events of learning that extend our cultural knowledge to another stage (even if we find others, as in this ageless discussion, have been there before), so the culture as a whole finds its way into its future by the little learning steps of individuals.

All this suggesting an interplay between culture and the individual seems commonplace enough and perhaps would not be worth arguing here if it were not that the assumption of a kind of general cultural determinism has proved so seductive.[179] I have begun with the hardest issue on which to persuade the already persuaded, the importance of individual choice and learning in the matrix of culture. The other half of my argument is easier and also obvious enough, when one thinks in this direction; hence I will not overdo it. The reader will probably have already questioned the view of humans in culture that the argument above implies. Humans are, as my bee example might have suggested, also in nature; if I am stung by a bee I may learn something about bees and contribute it to the cultural lore of bees. But I may also be motivated, in my pain, to give my discussion of intentions a sudden tragic turn, which no degree of information about my culture can explain. My physical, biological history gives me a unique source of intentions quite apart, though often in direct conflict with, my culture—which, finding me facing the enormous pain of the bee sting only gives its usual answer: be happy, don't worry, enjoy! The same is of course true of accidents of history, of which great numbers intrude on culture every day. Our Western history, where we are more free to imagine the autonomy of culture just because of our military and economic success in relation to the rest of the world, has for a long time now been intruding on the cultures of that rest of the world in many ways, brutal or subtle. And our history of expansion has in fact, even though we may not have wanted to acknowledge it, also been a history of intrusion on our culture,[180] which has become ever more complex and cosmopolitan. In the twenty-first century the chickens of the cultures we have scorned or overlooked have been coming to roost most emphatically in our own home.

Finally, there is a set of motivations within us which are not subject to the same kinds of cultural constructions as our conscious ideas or half-conscious ideologies. I refer to the area of our experience having to do with emotions and depth psychology. Even if we conjure up the most monologic and totally controlling culture imaginable, a kind of zero degree of cosmopolitanism and innovation, an age deader than the Dead Ages, where patriarchal and matriarchal wisdom combine to deaden all possibility of other thinking or acting, still there will be some maverick, with an itch in his or her pants, a liking for a brawl, a positive capacity not to fit in and not to please the elders. And this psychological, perhaps genetic, resistance place, this more than Shindler Shindler, will open up subversive spaces in the culture. Were there homosexuals before the construction of the term and the various cultural positions that have been created under that term? Yes, though not with those identities. Are there usually such other positions being created out of alternative what? ... genetic dispositions? ... developmental propensities—a debated point? Presumably yes. Do other kinds of genetic or developmental propensities of the individual disturb the hegemonic tendencies of the cultural web? You bet: try to understand criminality without it; or sexual variations or offenses; or alcoholism; or character types who make great changes and are called genius or scourge. The answer from the cultural determinist party is the emasculated Marxist one we hear: yes, but in the last analysis cultural patterns, instead of the old conditions of production, will prevail. Don't cultural patterns make the nineteenth-century neurotic types Freud finds? Haven't they created an upswing of narcissistic borderline types in our more indulgent society? Maybe: hard matters I can't presume to solve here for the professionals who haven't agreed. Again I might lose the argument at some level where culture has become a kind of God of last resort, a kind of nature of things that makes us all. But this is not what is meant when the term is used to explain cultural products, say writers' work. At that level, individual neurotic compulsions, sudden events, out-of-the-way reading, or falling in love all will keep the clear waters of culture from flowing through a writer's pen unmuddied.

Arguments on intention are so controversial because they quickly open out into arguments on human nature; and I am sorry to report a fuzz: I find neither rational man/woman lucid in his/her intentions, nor subservient man/woman, open like Wordsworth's London to all external influences, nor genetic man/woman programmed by his/her genome. All this is a nuanced way of arguing for that out-of-favor term, subjectivity.[181] Our subjectivity is diverse and messy, a combination of reason, cultural knowledge of various sorts, individual learning, neurotic (or psychotic) needs and urgings, strong feelings of many sorts. It is messy, nothing like a Cartesian rational man, and certainly gendered diversely too. But it does exist. We are no mere puppets of culture, strings to be pulled, or computer game figures programmed for certain responses and behaviors. I argue neither for rational men inside men nor for souls behind minds and bodies, only for a complexity managed by some kind of self-consciousness, including consciousness of what is experienced but not directly known within. The salient point about self-aware complexity is that it seems to generate its own symbol systems in response to those it takes in (as by reading), and it is relatively unpredictable. If not somewhat free, it gives a good imitation of it.

In all the cases I have been looking at, the effect is the same as that which I have already discussed from the point of view of the intention of the individual author. There I found the author's integral meaning troubled and conflicted by cultural patterns flowing into her/his intentions in a variety of ways. Here, looking at the matter from the view of cultural intentions flowing through the writer, I find the quirks, kinks, and queer spaces of the individual to be distorting, bifurcating, and multiplying the intentions of the culture—which I have argued are usually already polyvocal. My conclusion is the same in both cases; while we may learn useful things about the possible interpretations of a piece of writing by looking at the culture or by looking at the individual's stated aims, we cannot have an assurance from either direction that our constructions represent a privileged interpretive position of intention.[182] We may usefully occupy our scholarly and critical faculties in spining our own webs within the greater webs of author's life, culture's texts and structures,[183] or even the work's initial reception, which can be too easily privileged as the historically specific place of true meaning;[184] or we may spin our web of intention directly on the work, using whatever information we have from our first three webs, but using them with humility as merely more selective interpretation, rhetorically useful perhaps but just for that reason to be used modestly without the paid arrogance of the expert witness. (Expert witnesses in court, they tell me, receive $1500 a day; who would want to pretend to a definitive interpretation that we all know to be impossible, for less?) Historical work is interesting in itself, as history, and it may suggest avenues for interpretation; but it cannot replace hard work in and on the text. In the last analysis, we will trust the text (as *we* read it), not the (old or new) historian.

Perhaps the problem I have been addressing here was raised when the first wave of New Historians, instead of being content to read thickly the cultural texts of the past with a new eye for detail and nuance, justified their work, usually being done in English departments, by turning it back on the traditional literary texts.[185] They thus opened the way for claims of historical specificity as an interpretive method, which in turn led to dismissal of other reading approaches as untouchable because they were not justified by a genealogy of cultural embedment and causation—the hidden, but intentional, requirement. In the process, the place of meaning, necessarily in the individual reader, was oddly displaced. The tendency was to reduce texts to one set of the great variety of possible meanings that they might be given, the usual upshot of any ambitious new critical move. Not only were we to avoid any of the aesthetic pleasures of texts, an indulgent practice ascribed to the New Criticism (even as New Historians borrowed close analysis and its pleasure for their historical escapades); meaning was to be held strictly to the "cultural work" or "cultural labour" of a text in its moment of production, that much vaunted place of historical specificity.[186] Indeed, meaning, which is about interpretation, was eliminated in favor of historical description. The parallel to biographical intentionality is clear enough: it is as if we were told—as we always were by the traditional school of intentionalists—that we must restrict our meaning in reading the text to those motivations that caused the writing in the first place;[187] only here the motivations are derived from the broad cultural scene—as organized and interpreted by the New Historian—rather than by the biographical evidence as organized and interpreted by the biographer.

VIII. INTENTION IN THE TEXT

> Critics are like medical students: they always think a writer is suffering from the very disease they happen to be studying at the time.
>
> Milorad Pavic, *Dictionary of the Khazars: a Lexicon Novel*

The arguments adduced so far, far flung as they have been—though I hope not far fetched—have had in common a look at the problem of intentionality as about an effect of a cause. The implicit question has been, can we imagine the creator of the text, whether conceived as Cartesian individual or cultural tendency, having sufficient control over the text to guarantee that the intention, if obtainable, represents a privileged, indeed correct, meaning? The answer has been a variety of negatives, all indicating that a literary text, a thing dissociated from any simple, face-to-face communication, has much too complex a genesis to represent any single, identifiable aim of its creator, or its creator's age. It is an end result so overdetermined, by personal psychological, ideological, and cultural forces, that it is hardly surprising that different readers have always found complex and quite diverse patterns in its rich carpet. Eventually I will want to ask the pragmatic question, can we ever know such an intention with assurance? But I wish here and in the next few sections to pause for a while on that mysterious entity, subject of all actual acts of interpretation, the text. The overall question here will be whether the text itself, based on the little we have learned about texts after so much fighting over their interpretation since the beginnings of culture, can be thought of as a wise child that knows its mother, can be thought of as a pigeon which has its home inscribed in its heart, can be said, as theologians used to say of nature, to speak volubly the name of its creator.[188] Or to come down from theology to law, is it right to say that intent is in the statute?[189] Or can ordinary defenders of author's authority in literary interpretation, who find themselves annoyed by the problems of ascertaining biographical or cultural proof, resort to claims of intention manifest in the text itself?[190]

Here I should warn my reader that I intend to Wimsatt-and-Beardsley Wimsatt and Beardsley. If those gentlemen were determined to put a stop to biographers and historians who offered what they called "external evidence" to solve a question about a text where they felt only "internal evidence" would do, they at least had little problem with the view that a text itself was the best evidence of what the author intended. How is the critic "to find out what the poet tried to do? If the poet succeeded in doing it, then the poem itself shows what he was trying to do."[191] Let the New Critic do his business well, without silly static from the biographer, and without interference from the critic/reader's personal quirks and biases, and *the* interpretation shall come to light soon enough.[192] Empson, wise father of New Criticism, knew better. Interpretive criticism since the New Critics has been largely aware of the naïveté of a view that finds one meaning—call it the author's intended meaning for dignity's sake—and only one meaning, in a text. Oddly, what Beardsley called the Intentionalist Backlash, perhaps stung by his and Wimsatt's arguments against biographical and contextual interpretation, has tended to occupy just the position of single meaning in the text that those arch-anti-intentionalists warmed toward. Hirsch was especially concerned to establish a determinant meaning to guard against a democracy of meanings, which he believed a true threat because of his acknowledgement of a text's open interpretability.[193] Unlike Hirsch, who insisted on priviliging author's intention because he found the text otherwise so variable, his conservative followers have tended to place their bets mainly on determinant meaning in the text as the guarantee that author's intended meaning shall not perish from critical studies. The battle for intention then becomes one against textual multi-determination. What seemed hardly an issue in a world where everyone felt there was only one right (usually unified and organic) interpretation of a text, has now become one of the two major issues (historical context the other) in the seemingly endless intention debate. And it has drawn in energies from the long-raging battles between interpretive theories stemming from newer positions such as reader theory, reception history, deconstruction,[194] postcolonial, multicultural, identity, gender, and sexual studies on the one hand, and more tradtional interpretive positions on the other.[195] The latter have often found author's intention in the text to be their Holy Grail, their piece of the Rock. I will be wholly and necessarily broadly and sketchily concerned with that entire critical history of trying to read intention in the text in the following set of subsections. I also warn my reader that I will be serving up a cocktail of modern critical schools—Speech Act theory, structuralism, deconstruction, and various identity hermeneutics (feminism, queer theory, ethnic studies)—within a master discourse of pragmatic reader-oriented hermeneutics.

Reader-oriented hermeneutics? Meaning we readers argue it out—as we have always done since the beginning of culture (of course, hearers and observers of performance culture as well as reader culture), except when some appointed or self-nominated experts have temporarily laid down a set of rules giving themselves a special privilege—and let the most persuasive interpretation carry the day.[196] The idea of fighting over texts since the beginnings of culture reminded me that I never did know what those ape-men jumping at, what were they ... metal markers? meant in Stanley Kubrick's *2001*, and here it has come and gone. Let me say, without any knowledge of what Kubrick intended, that they were beginning the long fight over interpretation that has actually distinguished ape men from the apes.[197] This I know is not a promising image (even if it is not your interpretation of that scene—and I am willing to grunt, hop up and down, and scratch my chest to say that I am right about my reading) with which to begin to ask whether texts have their author's names written within them, beyond the title page or running headers. But I think we would be foolish not to mind that image. We have all been howling over meanings of texts for ever so long; and what can this mean, sensibly speaking, but that I am true but all men (and women, sorry) are liars. Or, if you don't like this reflection, let us say instead that we are all out in the dark. We do not agree; interpretation would not be the ape-men playground that it is if the apes or houyhnhnms had really inherited the planet. It is what we do professionally, we critics, to argue over interpretation and not agree; it is what everyone does when they read the latest book or go to the latest movie. And what do they do when they are sure they have persuaded themselves, if no one else, of their interpretation? They give the author's name to it in some form, name of a person, name of an age, name of a society and culture. It is a habit of us ape-men to respect authority overmuch, especially when we can hide under its wing and thereby take on authority ourselves. Best, the author is dead but we keep him/her alive as a counter in our game of authority, as they used to say communist bureaucrats liked to keep their stiffening leader this side of the mausoleum so they could still pronounce in his name.

We do not of course learn; we are always hot on the trail of our next interpretation (as I write this I am preparing to expound on the true Victorianism of the movie of *Possession* for a select group of my friends—which interpretation I shall certainly dignify by ascribing to A.S. Byatt—one of us Victorianists herself). But if we pause a while from our interpretive learning to be wise, that is, if we look back, we shall see our attics filled up with our cast-off former critical flights: so much interpretation, all of it ascribed to author or authority so-and-so, none of it surviving as authoritative. Is it only that Pierre Bourdieu is right: these incessant reinterpretations are merely career moves of other critics, curse them, trying to gain symbolic capital so they can push us on into early retirement, only to be themselves attacked by the next swarm of new somethingorothers?[198] Comforting to know that we were first and right all along, the only impartial critics not caught up in the prestige-accumulating mill; except, were we? or did we come into the scene of interpretation when it was always already grinding away?

I wish to avoid seeming to argue from mere general skepticism about agreement. The argument that no religion can be right since all the rest are then wrong, I confess, has always had a certain weight with me; but tell that to God (or is it Allah) at judgment day. In interpretation, the difficulties of coming to general agreement are obvious and must carry their weight. This does not allow us to conclude that all texts must be received controversially. We can well imagine texts where disagreement will be unlikely and also where we can rather assume the author stands with all of us. If I write, "the batter hit the ball," almost all of you will follow ordinary English grammar determined by word position and presume I meant that the batter hit the ball, not "*the batter* hit the ball"—as an emphatic answer to an implied question, "what did the ball hit?" And, knowing something of American cultural history you will provide a referential context in baseball and not imagine a lump of wet dough hitting a cheese ball in some inane TV cooking show. Such a case does not in fact offer one-hundred-percent certainty, especially as we move away from the moment of writing or any knowledge of the writer of the sort possessed by his friends. As Bakhtin has emphasized, cultural knowledge quickly is lost to later readers,[199] so a day may come when there is considerable disagreement over what seem to us the most obvious details (what kind of batter—would an English professor in this century have been more into cricket than baseball? what is a cheese ball anyway? on what occasions would grammatical reversals be likely? is there some hidden, Maynard's bawdy, meaning in all this about hits and balls?—after all, the man did write books on something they called sexuality in those ignorant times). The skeptical perspective can throw doubt on any particular interpretation of the most obvious matter; and one can always imagine new contexts of utterance that would utterly change our views: "In a fit of his final delirium, Maynard cast his eyes to heaven, then uttered 'The batter hit the ball'; I, Marlow, knew then the horror: no answering cheers emerged from the profound depths, green stadium of wilderness, surrounding us as at an ultimate but inconclusive tournament." But if we can rack our brains to imagine skeptical retakes, we can also imagine a comfortable agreement on the original utterance, connected to a sense of the author's intended support for this view, rather than subversive trickery or doublemindedness over the most practical of statements.

The trouble with this good commonsense view, that there are issues of interpretation on which reasonable persons can agree to agree, is that it is only reassuring.[200] That some statements should not be subject to skeptical nonsense, as the old boys at the club would say, is fair enough, but it leaves us absolutely nowhere better off when we confront the kinds of interpretive problems where we could use such assurance. There we have already a controversy, reasonable people don't agree, and they all presume they know what the author intended. Harris demonstrates this problem very well, just where he is most intent on arguing from simpler interpretive problems, where assurance is possible, up to more complex ones, where it may not be.[201] To say that we have keys to meaning in grammar, in dictionary meanings accepted by most, and in contexts provided by the work is acceptable enough—it will work up to a certain probability in certain cases. Yet there is always the borderline one crosses into controversy and uncertainty. For Harris the glass is half full; I have to say that a half-full glass is not full: it leaves fifty-percent uncertainty. Drawing on Speech Act theory to suggest that context in a text can give us assurance as to intended meaning just as it can in a spoken utterance to which we are present, an argument by analogy that I have already criticized extensively above, Harris goes on to admit that such a contextual (he calls it ecological) reading is less precise the more general the interpretive issue being considered. "Macro-illocutionary force"—the theme intended—or "macro-perlocutionary intent"—the moral urged upon the reader—is even for him hard to be sure about. Intention, he follows Charles Altieri in saying, is best for sentence-level interpretations, whereas rounder terms such as purpose of a part of a work or project of the whole seem better for more extensive objects of interpretation.[202] But this is just a careful way of saying, as with so many nostrums and gadgets offered to us that work well, offer plenty of help, but not for us, not for our case, that the approach is not useful for any of the many interpretive issues on which we tend to disagree. It helps us establish that, when Mr. Ramsay says in *To the Lighthouse*, "But it won't we fine," that he is speaking about the weather and his judgment that the family won't be able to go to the lighthouse and we can be pretty well assured that that was what Virginia Woolf intended (had in mind as we say) when she wrote it. But it won't tell us whether she intended such macro-interpretive meanings as, Ramsay is a scientific realist who should gain more respect from the children and women around him for his meteorological acumen; or, Ramsay is a sadist who takes pleasure in wishing rain in advance on his children's marine parade; or, Ramsay is pleased no one can go to the lighthouse because of his egotistical investment in his own inability to get from Q to R in his philosophical investigations, and so on: all that we really wish to have some certainty about that we could ascribe to Woolf.

I choose one of many possible areas where one can construct an argument for obtaining relative certainty in ascribing intention, namely context (within the text), here the whole scene of summer place, planned trip to the lighthouse, and doubtful English weather making it clear Ramsay is not saying that the wedding cake for Paul and Minta won't be fine according to his late Victorian culinary taste. I imagine that for many critics who don't think about these issues, everyday context seems sufficient, especially because we are so used to fast decisions about context in our own everyday oral perplexities: for instance the question faced by a professor from a student of Stanley Fish's, "Is there a text in this class?" (does she mean actual text or new theory about texts?).[203] In fact, even in oral life, context never totally can determine meaning. As Willard Quine has argued, we can't be precise about even the meaning of one word merely from knowing its context. A word in another language repeatedly associated in reality with rabbits might mean rabbit, or rabbitness, or the space to the left of a rabbit. Similarly, work on people deaf from birth has had to accept the limitation that context alone cannot specify meaning.[204]

I could as well look at claims that we know pretty well the meanings of words, for instance (to return to that famous case) the special meanings of that "sullied" (actually "sallied" in the Second Quarto), if that is indeed the word

Shakespeare intended Hamlet to say (some editors prefer to read the Second Quarto's I.ii.129 with the Folio as "solid," too solid flesh should melt), and note that the idea of "soiled" or "defiled" that it evokes doesn't take us to some secure place where we might want to go in determining intention: did the Bard intend to imply that Hamlet was a Puritan? a melancholy-humored type? a pathological sexual obsessive? a prince acutely sensitive to hints of racial difference coming in from the new world which made him identify with the "other" oppressed? Or I could follow claims that even hard diction, such as Gerard Manley Hopkins is notorious for, can often be worked out by a good mixture of grammatical analysis and logic.[205] *Perhaps* I can persuade you, and all other reasonable people who agree with us, that the exclamation mark after "Buckle" in "The Windhover" indicates that Hopkins intended us to think of the speaker as calling for a buckling to happen: "Brute beauty and valor and act, oh, air, pride, plume, here / Buckle!" Having had his heart stirred in hiding for a bird, he asks that its qualities buckle to him, as an odist usually asks for some quality to come, to be present. But if we *might* agree on the grammar (and indeed, we may not),[206] we still won't agree on any one of those other macro issues that have made this poem, with its dedication "To Christ our Lord" a billion times told more dangerous, as well as lovely, for the critic than its syntax might suggest: the uncertain meanings of buckle itself, even if he is calling for it to happen, whatever it is (coming together or breaking apart, for starters); the location of buckling: in the poet as persona or here on the page of verse, rove over and enjambed, which the word "buckle" pulls tight—or explodes? the interpretation of chevalier: bird, savior, or what? the reasons for the billion times lovelier and more dangerous fire resulting from the buckling? the big questions of nature, man, and the possible figure of salvation.[207] Of course we use the usual tools we have for making meaning and establishing identity with our high flying author; our "sheer plod" will certainly help; yet the danger and beauty are not so easily buckled down in the works we most admire. To show why they are not would be to undertake to unveil the entire mystery of language and literature. I can only remind the reader in the sections that follow of the many ways in which, if some aspects of a text's language can be stabilized and laid out for general agreement, others are necessarily destabilizing and controversial.

IX. INTENDED INITIAL RECEPTION AS A GUIDE TO INTENTION

As a special case to assert that we can know the author's intention clearly, it has been suggested that intention can be judged by the structures and cues in the text that suggest its intended initial reception.[208] The argument here is not the historical one, that a fuller knowledge of the actual original reception can give us a good idea of where the author was likely to be—an argument I considered in section vii. It is rather a special version—generally tarted up and trotted out—in arguments over intention, of the old structuralist notion of coding.[209] In this view, the text presents to us, whether by direct intention of the author or by the nature of the structures the author has chosen, a code we may read to know what is generally intended. It would be, in that sense, "self-declaring."[210] I would not deny the usefulness of such information in developing an interpretation, and in some cases it seems plausible to ascribe the specific effect to a deliberate intention of the author. Much of reader criticism of the more conservative sort did just this in trying to find, as the name of a well-known anthology put it, the reader in the text: that is, the ways in which a text seems to command a certain kind of reading. Unfortunately, the development of reader theory has tended to put most of these in question. For instance, take the case of a text that offers an interpretation inscribed within it. Few readers will ignore such a central statement, but on what authority do we privilege it? Is it expressed by the narrator? Then we may call in an implied author, creation of our own interpretation of the text, to set the narrator in the wrong. Is it spoken by a character in novel or drama? Then we may say this is another case of Edmund's speech on nature in *King Lear*: a devil's advocate. And so on. Reader theorists who have tried to specify the reader as created by the text—Gerald Prince in his well-known idea of the narratee as whatever specific characteristics the receiver in the text is given in the text, Peter Rabinowitz in his concept of a narrative audience—have both found that such a creation does not define the actual reader's position.[211] The reader created by and in the text is always different from any actual readers. As creations of the text, readers in texts are, like the text generally, subject to the reader's own interpretation. In Prince's formulation a reader may agree (or not) with the narratee's perspective, but in Rabinowitz's notion of an authorial audience the perspective is bound to be different from that of the narrative audience. (Narrative audiences, reading Goldilocks's story, believe in talking bears; authorial audiences do not.)

In all these cases we shall be well into the whirling hermeneutic circle: we know what the meaning of such a reception cue must be because we think we know what the author had in mind; we use the cue to justify our sense of what the author had in mind. This is not to say that we should not formulate a coherent interpretation as a kind of geodesic dome, all inter-supporting; only that the author is then only a designation, a mythic place of coherence and origination that we use to justify our own creation. More specific cues to reception, for instance indications that a play was intended to be performed at the Royal Haymarket Theatre on a certain day, are interesting but not likely to yield too much information. Alfred Harbage had a widely influential theory that Shakespeare's Globe Theatre was a place of democracy as opposed to the aristocratic theater of the chamber performances; but it would take a bold intentionalist to move from our knowledge of Shakespeare's intended venue for *Julius Caesar* at the newly opened Globe in 1599 to an assertion that Brutus speaks with the author for those groundlings tired of Tudor hegemony and always already ready to establish a commonwealth. Of course Shaw, wanting to be better than Shakespeare in some clear way, wrote his long stage directions covering all subjects. But if they don't agree with our reading of the play we shall certainly find a way, as noted above, to dismiss that section as the work of the other Shaw, Shaw the intellectual ideologue rather than Shaw the instinctive playwright. More likely they will lead, by our disagreement, to a sense of Shaw's habitually dialectically divided intentions.

All such framing materials—Gérard Genette's paratext, again—will be subject to the same play of interpretation. Even a title, as well as the more obvious case of the preface or framing epigram, does not freeze the meaning of what lies within but only adds more possibility for play of meanings.[212] If we find even the title of a work seemingly out of touch with our reading of it, we will certainly find a way to fit the title to our size, whatever cartwheels this may cause the author to spin in his/her grave. If we find Stephen Daedalus to be a fraud and fool, we will not hesitate to ironize the "artist" of the title where our neighbor will insist that Joyce "meant" us to focus on the "young," with faith that the boy will grow—into the "ineluctable modality" of his next (he needs admit) none too impressive, too self-conscious appearance. Well, he was *still* young in *Ulysses*, he will rejoin. If titles can't stand against our will to interpret, studies by bibliographers and students of material conditions of publication will hardly stop us in our tracks, much as we may admire their cultural history of endpapers, bindings, typefaces, or modes of website publication. These things, as the best work in this area shows us, are themselves all signs with meanings attached—but therefore not settled, stable, essential meanings: rather more meaning subject to interpretation, even if we can connect them directly to the author rather than to the printer, agent, bookbinder, reseller, or purchaser. They thicken rather than clarify the plot of interpretation.

A text that seems especially fully coded to a particular reception is in fact rather rare.[213] Special examples would be a masque intended for performance before a king and thus inscribing with great assiduity its sense of agreement with that Leviathan spectator, perhaps by a very clearly defined allegorical system. But then we are likely to speculate on the author's perhaps only hypocritical conformity to the political demands of the reception, leaving us looking for subversive maneuvers hidden deep in the text. A *roman à clef* can certainly be read, once we find the key, as very specifically coded by the author. But by what logic do we assume that that is the sole intention of the author in the text? Perhaps the notoriety of scandal publication served to attract attention for a serious political satire or critique, as it perhaps did for Thomas Love Peacock in *Nightmare Alley* or W.H. Mallock in his *New Republic*. Most often, the clearer the reception called for in the text the more trivial the area of the text to which it gives us some possibly special access. *Carpe diem* poems encapsulate, of course, their seductive ambitions, which are clear enough. But it is a poor sophomore (I have had a few) who reduces Marlowe's part in "The Passionate Shepherd to His Love" or Marvell's "To His Coy Mistress" to a (seduction) routine. The works gloriously exceed the apparent initial intention—which should be a practical lesson as well for would-be seducer sophomores. When James Thomson tells us in his wonderful "City of Dreadful Night" that he writes not for the young and hopeful but only for those as disillusioned as he, he writes eloquently but tells us little we don't know immediately from the subject and laments of the text, that the author has suffered disillusion and heartbreak enough.

X. SPEECH ACT THINKING AS A WAY OF ESTABLISHING INTENTIONS

In order not to give my reader the impression that this is a mere philosophical discourse on intentionality, I have postponed until we have substantially entered the subject a consideration of more philosophical arguments over literary intention. For those who have looked at literary intention from a philosophical point of view, it has been properly classed not as an issue of the confusingly same-named philosophical intentionality—an issue in the nature of mind and other phenomena displaying aboutness,[214] but as an issue in theory of meaning.[215] What does it mean to say that something means such and such? In this form literary intentionality wishes to locate meaning not in the utterance/writing or hearer/reader but in the speaker/author. We should begin—and perhaps also end—by saying that there is no clear answer to this issue of meaning offered to us as any kind of consensus of contemporary philosophers. If the comparatively metaphysical tradition of continental philosophy has issued in the skeptical questioning of all kinds of origination and authority of presence in the work of Jacques Derrida, Anglo-American continuers of the analytic project of Russell and young Wittgenstein have found a clear theory of meaning elusive in the world of W.V. Quine and the later Wittgenstein, with its own skepticism about determining systems aimed at limiting possible meanings to utterances. A sampling of serious views offered by the 1990s *Cambridge Dictionary of Philosophy*, for instance, shows the philosophical world in especial (or is it typical?) disarray on the theory of meaning. The article on the subject summarizes eight different primary theories of meaning, each occupied by many sub-positions and most incompatible with each other. Only one, "ideational or mentalist theories, according to which meanings are ideas or other psychological phenomena in people's minds," seems promising for the literary intentionalist's desire to refer meaning back to a mental state.[216]

E.D. Hirsch's spirited defense of literary intentionality against the orthodox New Critical pronouncements of Wimsatt and Beardsley began with premises most thinkers would not now be comfortable with (though Wimsatt and Beardsley themselves probably did not disagree): namely that there must be a determinate meaning to every utterance/writing and that there must be only one. He then located that meaning in the intention, the conscious intention, of the author. The most damaging critique of this view finds its power from the general uncertainty about theory of meaning. We have no reason to assume that there is only a single meaning.[217] More specific criticisms have been offered for the attempt to locate meaning in the speaker/author's intention, most cogently, as I have been and will be throughout this discussion, by citing the endless cases of possible multiple meanings that must be overcome to maintain the position. Though it begins as an apparently commonsense view based on our habit of inquiring from speakers present before us what they do mean when we run into ambiguity or multiple meanings, it reveals its impracticality soon enough.[218] A parallel critique notes, as I have been and will keep doing, that decisions on meaning are always made in fact by hearers/readers, even when they bring in additional information about the author's meaning, life, or context. Finally, locating meaning in a speaker/author's intention seems not only to violate our normal practice as hearers/readers of determining meaning from the utterance/text but also seems to threaten an infinite regression. If meaning is in the intention, argues Max Black, then that can only be known by a statement about the intention, which must in turn be understood by another statement about the intention, in an infinite regress.[219] Black sensibly proposes that we think of intention as defining meaning only by a tautology, where we have decided in advance to call whatever meaning we find the author's intention—a point I return to in my final subsection (II.xix).

There has, however, been one segment of contemporary philosophy that has sometimes worked with concepts of meaning as intention (in our literary sense as often also in the philosophers' more special sense of aboutness). Speech Act theory is a branch of Anglo-American analytic philosophy that has attempted to continue the project of early Wittgenstein or Russell of clarifying meaning but, following the later Wittgenstein's own lead, has moved from concern with mathematical philosophy into the study of everyday, ordinary language.[220] Given the direction of this thinking toward clarifying meaning, as well as its considerable intrinsic interest as clear thinking about uses of language, it is not surprising that attempts have been made to arm it to defend the location of meaning in speaker/author's intention.[221] I have already drawn upon the interesting tradition of thinking about language that begins with J.L. Austin's *How to do Things with Words* and has found useful elaboration and modification in John R. Searle's work on the subject in order to think about the way intentions can be said to be divided between performative and propositional or declarative ends.[222] It has been a major project of this thinking to distinguish utterances that do things (explicit performatives or utterances with illocutionary force—"I sentence you to five years hard labor on Speech Act theory"), from those that say things (locutionary statements—"he worked five years hard on Speech Act theory"); however, it has also, in its development, tended to see that Austin's clear categories were not so clear: when we state things there is always some performance.[223] In literature, if I represent a world, say Shakespeare creating *The Tempest*, I am soon aware that, like my character Prospero, I have the power to do something with this locution—even to move the Globe to further financial success and win happy retirement for its playwright-shareholder. While Austin tried to keep out such imaginary utterances as merely parasitical copies of real ones, literary criticism has especially focused on the interesting ways in which we do things as we find words for our imaginations.[224]

The application of speech act thinking to the intentional debate tends to move back in the other direction, toward Austin's original sense that utterances can be more clearly understood if we understand precisely the intention from which they emerge. Austin's thinking, that of an ordinary language philosopher emerging from analytic philosophy, was based especially on thinking about language in communication systems, especially ordinary interchanges in real life, mainly oral. He was thus able to call attention to a dimension of language overlooked in much purely analytical analysis of meaning. We do things, exert illocutionary force, and may actually explicitly perform something when we use words, as in the notorious case of the marriage performative, with which Austin had some trouble. Austin's overall point, whatever his knowledge of the wedding ceremony, was that much of what we call meaning can be made more clear by seeing it as an intention similar to an action. From this rather clear view of certain kinds of speech acts (the Queen of Hearts says "Off with his head" and we know what is intended) it is tempting to move in two directions. The first would be to say, as in moral theory, we judge intentions by the result (called the perlocutionary consequence in Speech Act theory): by the fruits of the speech act you shall know what the speaker intended. This has generally seemed a problem, however, because it is clear that some speech acts may fail through the speaker's ineptness, failure to be heard, or confusions. I may shout fire, to return to that burned-over example—this time it really is a fire—but no one in the theater hears me correctly because a loud noise like heavy wind escaping occurs just at that moment on stage as Caliban appears. Or we may ask the gruff lady bus driver in our polite way if she can drop us off at the next corner—her yes occurring about the same moment she shoots by that spot. (There are many amateur eccentric logicians walking outside of Alice's wonderland.) These examples embody in a nutshell the problem with this use of speech acts: if unquestionably intended speech acts may fail, then we are really admitting from the start that there are occasions (some? many?) on which we shall fail to figure out intentions (at all? correctly?). Pragmatically that would mean we are admitting that we can not be sure of intentions, as listeners, far less as readers.

The second strategy, much more likely to be in fact taken, is to declare that, even though speech acts may fail, we cannot fail to derive the intention from the speech if we only scrutinize it closely using speech act thinking. This was in many ways the point to Austin's new way of thinking about language (always more interested in illocutionary force than in perlocutionary consequences), and in simple oral acts it is clearly effective as a way of describing ways of understanding meaning as intentions. If the Connecticut state trooper tells us to pull over, it is very much in our practical interest not to have to debate about what he has in mind but to move from the statement to his intention for us to stop, not speed away. We can imagine coming to different conclusions about what he intends—he wants us to "pull-over," show off our new sweater, or pull (the wool understood) over his eyes by telling him we were not speeding and he will let us off—but these seem rather too fanciful. We know what he means in a way that allows pragmatic context-related meaning (our interpretation) and his intention practically to coalesce. This is the happy model that defenders of a privileged author's intention like. And this case, unlike many, many others, is backed up by the well-known convention at least in the United States.[225] But it is utopian in trying to found a whole view of intention and interpretation on rather specially clear cases. Look for instance at this apparently similar case: a friend working in a boutique is held up by a robber flourishing a gun and making the following speech act: "Lie down with your face to the floor and you won't get hurt." Clear enough instructions with a clear enough intention, like the policeman's: do this act. But she imagined this was not his intention: the speech act wanted her in a position where he could kill her without looking in her eyes as he did it. She refused and lived. Maybe she would have lived anyway: maybe the robber really didn't have his intention clear; maybe he said what they all say, what robbers, he thought, were supposed to say. The speech act approach, in most of the more complicated situations looked at above, does not necessarily give a clear knowledge of intention.[226]

Quite early in the discussion of application of speech act thinking to the special problems of literature, Wolfgang Iser made an excellent critique of the line of reasoning that would say we can know the intention of the text as clearly as we can that of the state trooper.[227] He pointed out that the nature of textual reception very often precludes the very conditions that make speech act approaches seem useful for oral communication. Austin himself acknowledged that "written utterances are not tethered to their origin in the way spoken ones are."[228] What we generally lack in literature is context. If the trooper sends a fax through his car computer to ours saying in bold caps PULL OVER, that text is clear enough: we have him in our rear-view mirror; though it is a text, we have a clear context. The same is still somewhat true if we hear from the postman who fell on our unshoveled steps yesterday via a pompous letter from his lawyer today; we are no practical fools, even if we do read Speech Act philosophy for a living: here comes trouble. But the literary text by its very nature usually has no such clear context. And it of course precludes the interrogation eliciting further speech acts providing further context that normally is our easiest way to understanding real acts of speech. As with speeches in Plato's *Phaedrus*, "you would imagine that they had intelligence, but if you want to know anything and put a question to one of them the speaker always gives one unvarying answer."[229]

Iser's career-long insistence on the aesthetics of textual reception drives his approach here, but it also keeps him from slurring over the difficulties inherent in evaluating intentions behind imaginary works as a way of prioritizing one interpretation.[230] It may be clear enough when a state trooper in a novel stops a character and commands him to pull over that the context is what we are used to in real life. But to say that there are speech acts in literature that may thus be understood by a context clearly provided in the work does not demonstrate that many utterances, and very often the ones most interesting to interpretation, have such a clear context.[231] If the novel imitates the real world in such details, as a speech act itself it gives us few clues to the author's intentions. When we look into *it* as a speech act we are sorry to find that it is a deliberate lie: I will tell you what is in fact not true—as even Defoe's titles boast to us. We, unlike Plato, can get over the lying of poets—or novelists or dramatists or storytellers: all those who deal in fictions. Their speech acts are, the philosophers tell us, made with "intention to pretend, without intention to deceive."[232] But knowing this much leaves Speech Act theorists worrying about the truth status of real toads in imaginary gardens, for instance the location of Baker Street in the Sherlock Holmes tales or the problem of consistency in the differing locations of Watson's old wounds. It leaves us tiptoeing out to pursue instead our usual hard investigations: what kind of narrator, as opposed to the real voice of Arthur Conan Doyle, is speaking to us in each story? What does our view of this narrator do for us in our interpretation of the story? What does our reading of the story lead us to conclude about the narrator? We may talk of an implied author who stands, like Caliban's Quiet, behind the narrator, but these wise are still, and as always, saying nothing. We will create an implied author, as we always do when we do this, after our image of the story as a whole.

Even in less overtly fictional writing, where we think we hear an author directly, we learn that these speech acts don't function nearly so regularly, nearly so civilly, I dare say, as polite conversation in philosophical Oxford common rooms or Berkeley living rooms.[233] We do not know from the text what context there is even for familiar essays such as those of Addison and Steele or Charles Lamb. We hear a talking voice that sounds like someone on easy, conversational terms with us, but we do not know whether Lamb is writing on roast pig—to take a familiar example—because he wishes to warn us about reductive habits of mind, or because he wishes to amuse us, or because he wishes in a disguised way to warn us about multicultural difference in approaches. To decide these matters we would need to know what the work of literature, even in this seeming conversational form, does not offer (and will not offer the historian either): the real Lamb conversing with us in a real situation in which he has just had to deal with our (we are some workmen coming to repair his house) insistence on doing it the hard way, or he has told us we seem glum (we are friends dipping into the laudanum again) and he knows just the nonsense story to cheer us up, or he has just observed that we have come in our time machine with, to him, unusual looking friends of non-English ethnic background, and he expresses his surprise at our tales of a multicultural English future.

The reader of real letters will see that such real speech acts tend to provide a running context in which what we know of Virginia Woolf's relation to Vita Sackville-West last week lets us understand the elusive intentions of the next. But if individual letters by Clarissa in Samuel Richardson's novel can equally be understood in relation to Clarissa's earlier statements and actions, we are contrastingly totally at sea—in the normal welter of conflicting interpretations—in determining what Richardson intended us to make of her letters: is she a Christian saint? a piteous victim? a victim to be blamed, a model gentlewoman pushed to the extreme? the first consciousness of feminine resistance to patriarchal society? a surrogate male? and on and on. To ask his intentions is to ask all those questions we could equally well put by asking what interpretation we like best. The best answers we can give take us back to those global performatives: creative writers are probably trying to demonstrate their ability to create interesting or believable imaginative worlds. But this, perhaps generally true enough, leaves us only able to recognize the world as indeed imaginary. Someone intends to tell a story, recite a poem and is doing it; but what it is intended to mean is not given a context sufficient to help us. Despite a generation of grumbling against the fatuousness of the New Critics in not seeing a poet as a man speaking to men, we have not seen fit to throw away their useful term "persona" for the speaker of the poem, whose speech acts may themselves be so wild and interesting and unlikely to speak from the poet as a person. Certainly sophomore English goes better if we don't get into Marvell's seductions and problems of Puritan biography but rather invite his neophyte readers to hear a persona from a great tradition of poetry's speakers: "Had we but world enough, and time ..." Like his mistress, we may try to figure out his speech so we can figure him out, but neither she nor we will be easily privy to his creator, who also says, join with me in imagining a speaker.[234] Prefatory statements, such as Coleridge's "explanation" of "Kubla Khan" by the circumstances (context) of its writing, are notoriously unhelpful or problematic; further, they seem to disappear into the work itself as collateral tale-telling by the writer.[235] Perhaps as much critical debate has been elicited by Shakespeare's dedication of the sonnets to Mr. W.H. than by any other part of that work, which it very much seems a part of. Anyone who has ever dedicated a book to friend, family, or lover knows how little the mixed feelings behind the dedication speak of the actual context and motivation of the work, although the conventional appearance is that the work was somehow intended to bear witness to the qualities the dedicatee has demonstrated to receive such honor.

Readers wishing to go further into the details of the debate over Speech Act theory in literature are invited to read Appendix 1: More on Speech Act Theory and Intention, which other readers, less fascinated with the much debated subject, may shun without more than a passing twinge of stricken conscience.

XI. WORDS GETTING IN THE WAY

Having looked first at readings of the text sometimes offered as especially cogent in establishing an intentionalist position, I will now offer a broader survey keyed to different levels of critical analysis, to demonstrate more generally the impossibility of establishing, from a text, an authoritative intended meaning. We are necessarily on our own, adrift among choices whenever we attempt to assign meaning to a set of words, cut off by the nature of language from the author's intention. Let me begin at the micro level, where agreement on intended meaning might seem more generally possible. Look first at word meanings themselves. The very fact that we now usually speak of words being defined by a context means we have accepted a different view of word meaning than that implied in the traditional distinction between denotation and connotation. In effect, connotation has eaten up denotation, that is we no longer think of words as fixable by one primary meaning, the denotation, and then shading off into secondary meanings.[236] Our computer does, but it is still, on that issue, an idiot, though on other matters it may be an idiot savant. If you are among those who like to fulminate against deconstruction, you can blame demotion of denotation on the influence of that baneful philosophy and its reconstruction of Ferdinand de Saussure, seminal structural linguist, as a seminal theorist of endless dissemination of meaning based on mere difference. But more likely the very Western quest for artificial intelligence, so that we may really talk with Hal, which has proved so elusive just because words do not function like mathematical symbols representing one and only one intended meaning, has made us all realize the tricky nature of the words we use. Or a world unified by new communication networks finds the only barrier to global talk is the old one, the immense difficulty of translation. No system of one-to-one equivalences based on primary, denotative meanings is going to obviate the need for translation as an interpretive art based on a continuous process of interpretation (of the originating text) and original composition (in the target language).

At some point in a literary student's education he or she has perhaps necessarily faced the slipperiness of language. And here it is the other great branch of linguistics, historical linguistics, that opens up a world of difference. As we move from a short dictionary that seems to denote the main meaning (of the moment) to the *Oxford English Dictionary* with its records of historical varieties of meaning for each word, we begin to realize that language has never functioned according to the *Académie française* rational concept of denotation settled and authorized by the entire culture. We find that words are always moving from one meaning to another by all kinds of interesting associative processes. The word "individual" that could mean "indivisible, unitary" in the Renaissance now can mean many things, but not that.[237] "Gay" had a frequent sexual implication in the nineteenth century as in ours, only about females in the sex trade rather than males who preferred males (and increasingly females who prefer females too). What we first find as historical change in meanings over time eventually strikes us as generally true of words: they are always carrying a range of uses. The radically historical nature of the *OED* exposed, despite the editors' reliance on a classical range of written source texts, what was there all along: that words really had many uses. As Umberto Eco has pointed out,[238] we have moved from a dictionary model (a diction-ary, a model of proper choice of words) to an encyclopedia model of word meaning, a listing of all the ways the words have been used. We may not allow any fool malaprop to add new words or meanings at will, but we also grant that the language is not a set of permanent, precise dictionary definitions but an encyclopedic range of uses established with some regularity of recurrence.[239] One has only to recall the furor over Webster's Third International back in 1961, a revised dictionary based on principles of not what men say they should do with words but what they actually do, to recognize a paradigm shift in our society's thinking. So not any fool; but if a brilliant man—Wittgenstein—posits a private word—"bububu"—to mean, "if it does not rain I shall go out for a walk," in order to demonstrate the necessarily social nature of language for words to have meaning, we may soon overturn this or any such limit at the next meeting of the Wittgenstein Club, where this may become a word with a public meaning to all and also rather open to a variety of associations and meanings.[240] William Safire and our many other pundits on diction owe their popularity to the very fluidity in thinking about word meaning that many of them seem to exist to deplore.

The point of this quick retake on language is that it is hard to resist the view that the words of a text, once written, enter a public domain of many possible meanings. Even if an author writes in the belief that she has control of the exact meaning of the word, in most cases this is false. Unless the writer—a logician[241] or a mathematician, say—offers very rigorous definitions as he goes along, or works—perhaps he is a lawyer or a computer programmer—within an established closed system of special meanings, the words will be open to a variety of meanings. The intentionalist may well yearn, such is the usual temperament of intentionalists, to be assured of one and only one determinant meaning, but this will not be given where most needed. Yes, we may be able to limit them in simple cases, cases of the "can you pass the salt" variety—aha, by "can" this polite dinner guest means "will you," not "are you able." But, again, it is not the easy cases we puzzle over or quarrel about.[242] "A red fox stain covers Blue Hill": Robert Lowell says of "Skunk Hour," "The red fox stain was merely meant to describe the rusty reddish color of autumn on Blue Hill, a Maine mountain near where we were living."[243] I have not found many readers, in teaching the poem to many classes of good undergraduates, who don't find other meanings in the acrid word "stain." Lowell was a marvelously flexible reader of poetry, so I am sure he knew this and would have understood how the metaphorical context, the red fox, adds different kinds of feral implications for different readers. But look even at the dictionary definitions of "stain" in a current and not very extensive conventional set of definitions (in the U.S. Webster's Collegiate): a soiled or discolored spot; a natural spot of color contrasting with the ground; a taint of guilt; a stigma; a preparation used in staining; a dye or mixture of dyes used in microscopy. The only one that sounds *outré* is the last and, given the poem's obsessions with an "ill" season, with the sobbing of the speaker's own "ill-spirit," it begins to have some resonance once one thinks of it. Skunks and foxes go together here as emblems of the exacerbated spirit, and this in turn allows the sense of stain as moral problem, as stigma. Once the word is in play, as we all know when we read or teach complicated works of literature even if we may seem to forget it when we think of author's intentions or read, with transient shame at our fancifully poetic minds in face of the straightforward assertions of what a sober poet "really" intended, it is bound to carom and bounce a good deal. The plausible idea, implicit or explicit in so many normative systems of reading based on stages of reading, that there is a basic, safe level of reading where we merely get the words right, merely decode the language, do normal philology, before we go on to the speculations of interpretation, seems bound to founder on the slippery tendency of even individual words. Certainly for any vital reader, such a mystified invocation of a rite of reading as a place of authority would seem the triumph of hope over experience.[244]

Now, add to these more or less commonsense reflections on connotations a dash of popular deconstruction just to add a bit of spice. Unlimited semiosis, says Eco, not sure whether he approves or not. A system in which each signifier (word in use) is interpreted by a signified (meaning in play); but then, since there is no transcendental signified (the tableness in the sky somewhere of Plato, the word with God from the beginning), that signified becomes in turn a signifier only temporarily stopped by its signified, with which it never has a direct and perfect connection, and on and on.[245] Charles Sanders Peirce, whose isolated speculations in the Victorian period have become gnostic lore to both analytic philosophy and deconstruction, similarly sees an unending chain of possible meanings (which is not the same as saying all meanings are possible, not at least until the chain reaches infinity); each sign (word here) can only be understood by an interpretant (another word) with a similar relation to the first sign's object (whatever it may be thought of as referring to—a nebulous idea since, once named, it is merely another interpretant). The interpretant in turn becomes a sign that demands another interpretant, and on and on.[246] In the nightmare of the anti-deconstructionist this quickly looks like the following, where w is the original word to be interpreted and w1 the first signified or interpretant, which yields its own signified or interpretant w2, and so on: w} w1} w2} w3} w4} w5} w6} w7} w8} w9 etc.: to an alarming extent! But a little nervous reflection shows that this is only a small part of it; for each w yields not really a directional series of substitutions, of differences, of unlimited semiosis in a direction, but in fact creates a ring around itself, so that it is surrounded by its any number of w1,2,3,4 etc. And each succeeding w1 etc. forms its own planetary system (w1.1,w1.2 etc.). So it might better be visualized as in the figure below:

w2.2 w2.3
w2.1 {w2} w2.4
w2.6 w2.5

w3.2 w3.3
w3.1 {w3} w3.4
w3.6 w3.5

w1.2 w1.3
w1.1 {w1} w1.4
w1.6 w1.5

{w}

w4.2 w4.3
w4.1 {w4} w4.4
w4.6 w4.5

w6.2 w6.3
w6.1 {w6} w6.4
w6.6 w6.5

w5.2 w5.3
w5.1 {w5} w5.4
w5.6 w5.5

... and so on.

But of course that is just a simple planetary system in two dimensions whereas it should be in three; and as the w1s are surrounded by w1.1s, and they by w1.1.1s and so on, the space becomes ever more crowded. The nightmare is less the familiar one of an infinite stretch of galaxies but a more claustrophobic horror familiar to genealogists of large families, as each signified or interpretant begotten also begins to beget and, however much space one designates, it all gets eaten up. That *is* scary, but I play these silly games of diagrams only to suggest a kind of limit. There is wiggle room for much interpretation here but no justification for conservatives' fear of global anarchy. When we read "stain" in Lowell we don't easily manufacture enough quite distinct meanings to make such a big family genealogy, far less a "galaxy" of meanings. When we go high up in the numbers, where great-great-grandchildren of meaning are begetting great-great-great-grandchildren of meaning, we begin to notice that six degrees of separation can also create alienation. The route that takes us from stain to stigma, from stigma to stigmata, from stigmata to crucifixion, from crucifixion to apocalypse and from there to eternity is easily recognized as a fallacy of extension in practical interpretation. When we wander too far from the first generation we get lost in interpretive space and easily shoot away from any interpretation that might make sense to other people; one could well make a kind of law that further removes are less trustworthy, just as we all have played the game of whisper where the word, passed on from mouth to ear to mouth becomes increasingly less trustworthy as a (here phonetic) interpreter of the first cause. So unlimited semiosis is more a recipe for hysteria than for any hazard in actual interpreting. Yet the model does suggest that there is no easy way to limit the first or second order of planets around our sun (word-being-interpreted) to one planet favored by the author. Whatever his or her feelings about the "joyous affirmation of the play of a world of signs without fault, without truth, and without origin, which is offered to an active interpretation,"[247] about a "galaxy of signifiers" where meanings "extend as far as the eye can reach,"[248] about how "certain forces of association unite—at diverse distances, with different strengths and according to disparate paths—the words 'actually present' in a discourse with all the other words in a lexical system,"[249] this much even an earth-bound, pre-deconstructive (or post-deconstructive) interpreter should agree to, which is my business here—with apologies to those virtuosi who might prefer an elaborated deconstructionist systemization.[250]

In order to maintain some sense of discipline in this seadrift of language, more science-leaning, sober-pated semanticists try with far less theory enthusiasm to distinguish kinds of meanings. One approach is to try to preserve a world of abstract meanings (denotations) separate from a world of reference (referents)—things the words refer to.[251] But if this division may seem to protect traditional definitions of a word from a burgeoning set of applications, its firewall is soon overcome by flames on both sides. A variety of definitions still means that a word can present an alarmingly large set of options to a reader. Or linguists may try to distinguish firmly between various meanings of a single word—polysemy—and true homonymy, words sounding the same and usually spelled the same but not the same word: the first are close semantically or derive from the same roots, we are told. But there is port the city and port the drink, looking like very different words despite a tortured common etymology.[252] Are there not very often such diverse meanings in officially polysemic words that we would better think of polysemes as effectively divorced and set up as bachelor/bachelorette homonyms? Add to this those simpler family divisions that lay waste hopes for clear one-on-one word meanings: words that can occupy two grammatical positions: go fish! Out in the realish world of referents (things words refer to), isn't the encyclopedic range of so many words, which take us such distances, effectively a range of different meanings? A favorite problem is a place like London, which means such different things to the restaurateur, the country wife, the financial reporter, the art maven—and on and on.[253] Or consider the word "home" and how differently it means for Manhattanites, Hobbits, and the homeless under Waterloo Bridge.[254] No French accents on these ever-expanding differences but the same breakdown of binaries and prevalence of polysemy as in the heady cross-channel work: and we haven't even brought in what no solid German scholar would omit, those portmanteau words—like the chunnel that seems here to be allowing a polysemy express from London to Paris or, bigger crossing, from the linguistics department to the English department. If not unlimited semiosis, at least polysemy with no preordained end.[255]

While most literary critics have been reacting on these issues, positively or negatively, to French deconstruction rather than semantic linguistics, the old literary problems raised by verbal polysemy have also been much occupying a set of hard-hat academics, linguists, psychologists, and their portmanteau psycholinguists, neuroscientists, and computer scientists. Their studies of ambiguity, which have especially focused on lexical (word) ambiguity, have been very differently focused from New Critics' celebrations of an aesthetics of tension and open possibility or postmodernist critics' rejoicing in pure indeterminacy. They have, rather, the practical end of trying to create computers or other devices in Artificial Intelligence that can deal with the ambiguities of human language. Is there a problem with ambiguity? "You bet," is their answer: "all words carry with them more information than a person requires for comprehension of any particular message ... far from being unusual in language, ambiguity is widespread.... It appears that much less is given explicitly in a linguistic message than we need for full understanding."[256] Although they have disagreed in their theories of how the mind processes words with many meanings (some seeing a context limiting the number of meanings accessed, more seeing the brain accessing all possible meanings at once—and positions in between) these researchers agree that human or machine interpreters of natural language are regularly faced with a welter of possible meanings for many words, even such simple words as "go"—sixty-three meanings in Webster's pocket dictionary alone—or "over" provide a computer-boggling range of choices. And here the visual metaphor is not a planetary system but a wheel of associated meanings, "a radially-structured lexical network."[257] Other researchers similarly see some kind of web or net of closely or less closely related uses. Rather than dictionary-precise meaning, they tend to find "nodes" of other words activated by one word, so that even for them meaning seems a collection of other words rather than one concept.[258] We think "bank" (of a river) if we find "fish" in the sentence and may in turn think of fishing. We think "bank" (for money) if we hear of tellers, and this may make us think of windows.[259] Here again Paris and the cognitive psychology department don't seem so far apart. Researchers conclude that words have a way of resisting fixed meanings, even that there can never be a finite lexicon for a word as the number of "meanings is truly indefinitely extendable."[260] "In short," concludes another, "polysemy is everywhere."[261]

The goal of such research is to learn not how ambiguous words are but to find out how we humans cope with them and how our machines, which at this writing still have trouble knowing whether I said Boston or Bangor to them (i.e., still at the level of phonetic ambiguity in train reservations), can learn to disambiguate. Interestingly, no one talks about how the machine should try to figure out the mindset or larger goals of the human (or other machine?) who is using words. They do, however, write a great deal about using context for disambiguation. Here again, it is not the nebulous ideas about determining the context of the speaker-writer that is usually discussed.[262] Obviously we use that context in ordinary speech a great deal to decide whether we are being encouraged by the boss to take a window (of opportunity) or to take the open window to the end of all opportunities. But researchers, especially looking toward AI, are thinking of processing of text by itself, much as we do in reading. The context is thus the relation of words to other words. No doubt, in a great number of uninteresting because uncontroversial cases of potential word ambiguity, context conquers all. Apparently our minds work by trying all possible meanings, then choosing one that fits.[263] In their world of cases, a CIA inspector checking for bugs is not looking for roaches. In our common world of literature, when Keats's speaker in "Ode to a Nightingale" says he feels like he "emptied some dull opiate to the drains," we discard drain pipes easily for the rarer meaning of the draining of the last drops (not in fact in my American Heritage Dictionary) because we know what he is (imagining himself) having done. But sometimes, and these are the times we may wish to fight over what might have been intended, the word leaves us unclear.[264] The explanation of the operator's intrusion is only rendered tersely, "to get the bugs out." Which bugs?

Later in the poem, Keats's speaker considers another change of state, now in response to a Nightingale, not that possible opiate: "To thy high requiem become a sod." We think we know where we are, in our context in the poem, in that bower, beyond the garden, with thoughts of "easeful Death": plenty of context. But when the text becomes complicated, one difficult word may serve to divide it strikingly and leave us with only too many contexts. A sod in the garden, clear enough, but the odist become a sod? Such a simple three-letter Anglo-Saxonish word. But what is he? a chunk of grass? That must not be what sod means in this context. We run to the dictionary and find "turf": no, same grass idea; "native land": hardly; "bugger" (from Sodomite): not likely with a nightingale and probably an anachronism. So back to turf, but no turf we know of: a part of nature? but is this really a poem about nature? some kind of insensitive thing, like a dumb clod? but grass isn't entirely senseless; it lives and responds to light or feet. Something actually dead? no, same problem with sod; something under sod, so he is the object of the nightingale's mourning song? promising; a sod, merely sentient combining a sense of being over-mastered and being mourned for.

Well, *I* like that; but would I dare wish it on Keats out in the garden in Hampstead? Can I stop the play of even this simple little word? And you, who have your own view of this troubling little word, let alone more troubling big words, will you? Context is like this in literature; it works fine until—like our brain-imitating computer, or any other necessary machine—it suddenly doesn't work. Then we are back in the hopper, up language creek without our useful paddle. In practice we may decide on an interpretation of the whole that justifies one reading of that troublesome word; the hermeneutic circle we have in play becomes our preferred context; or we may, in a Keatsian mood, resolve to enjoy the possibilities without a restless move to judgment. We may even wish to call *this*—the production of ambiguity in us—the author's real intention; but that is merely one interpretation among others. It won't pay the rent any better to say we know this is the author's; and someone else may prefer their own interpretation as disambiguation or even say the ambiguity persists, but that just proves the author had no clear intention.

Having considered such technical expert testimony from literary theorists and psycholinguists, I end with the sober judgment of John Marshall, the revered fourth U.S. Supreme Court Justice. Among his many decisions over thirty-five years in the Court, he ruled very simply on the character of language: that no word conveys to the mind, in all situations, one single definite idea.[265] Judgment rendered, court dismissed.

XII. SYNTAX, GRAMMAR, LOGIC GETTING IN THE WAY

> The "inhuman" is not some kind of mystery, or some kind of secret; the inhuman is: linguistic structures, the play of linguistic tensions, linguistic events that occur, possibilities that are inherent in language—independently of any intent or any drive or any wish or any desire we might have.
>
> Paul de Man, *The Resistance to Theory.*

And of course the case is so much more complicated where we are looking at clusters of words rather than single ones, as we generally do in interpretation. The "red fox stain" on Blue Hill of Lowell's poem begins to suggest many more planetary systems as we factor in the color tension, the foxiness of the stain, the idea of a stained fox staining the pure Maryian or cerulean of the Hill, and so on. When we start looking at texts at the level of sentences and statements we face other large areas where multiple interpretations, now in the form of paraphrasing sentences rather than individual word interpretants, are possible, and where it seems therefore extremely hard to determine which, if any specific one, the author may have intended. Again, I can only apologize for not being able to do anything more than point toward what is another major focus of practical interpretation. William Empson's classic but still fresh *Seven Types of Ambiguity* moved freely among uncertainties focused on individual words to problems of "double grammar [in Shakespeare's sonnets]," "two apparently connected meanings ... given simultaneously," "alternative meanings combine," "fortunate confusion," "what is said is contradictory or irrelevant," "full contradiction" including "confusions in negation and opposition." Empson ranges widely, sometimes ascribing these larger than verbal effects to the author's confusion in writing, sometimes to the reader's confusion in reading. But when the issue is not play in the meaning of a word, most of these and other such examples have to do with difficulties in syntax, in grammar, in logic, or in the difficulty inherent in the concepts being presented.[266] Indeed, Empson explains his interest in his classic study of difficulties in practical interpretation as an exploration of degrees of "logical or grammatical disorder."[267] Literary works, poetry especially, are often packed so fully with action in language that the connections of words become difficult or dubious. Empson proved father to a generation of critics, the New Critics, fascinated with effects of ambiguity in writing. If he has been criticized for an unscientific, miscellaneous approach to the topic (and here which of us literary types can escape whipping?),[268] his broad insights have been sustained by linguistic and psychological researchers into ambiguity. Syntactic or structural ambiguity (as opposed to lexical ambiguity, looked at just above) is built into the way natural language works as a system of ordering words.[269] "Ambiguity is ubiquitous in language," assert two researchers; "ambiguity arises at every level of language processing ... Ambiguity is a fundamental problem of language comprehension," agrees another.[270] "Natural language is known for the ambiguity of its expressions," affirms another.[271]

Words are put together by conventions of grammar which are fairly well hard-wired over extended periods of time.[272] But within these firm but spacious boundaries there is a great deal of room for variety of order and expression. Here we find numerous structures that seem far less firmly wired, able to be modified or substituted for. As a legal commentator on wills noted in the nineteenth century, "The convention on which usage of language rests, is not a single or a fixed one, but is the aggregate of an innumerable number of lesser conventions, which intersect and conflict with each other, and are continually shifting and changing from year to year."[273] Writers especially, but all of us in speaking and writing, can take many routes in ordering our words; and the great variety of structures can easily lead us into intractable problems in trying to make our meaning clear; they offer to writers a commensurate amount of room for nuance, double-voicedness, and ambiguity.[274]

At the level of individual sentence structure (syntax) there are a host of uncertainties that can be locked in to present diverging paths to interpreters, especially in unchanging, unresponding written texts. The mere location of an adverb can open a real aporia—Bill said that Mary left yesterday—which would not be there if "yesterday" were moved closer to the beginning of the sentence.[275] The layout of phrases and clauses in sentences can cause a garden path divergence, leaving us, like Alice, wondering which answer can be right: "He hit the man with the umbrella": which man did he hit and what did he hit him with?[276] A common problem we in writing find (we in the writing business, or find as we write?), though we hope we don't fall into: "At the pancake supper there will be men flipping the flapjacks and costumed waitresses."[277] Refeence obscurity, especially in pronouns, can leave us wondering whether she is really the cat or the queen. Number or scopal ambiguity (ambiguity about the scope of reference in verbs where quantity is an issue) can dizzy us when we hear "Three girls mailed four letters." Segmentation alternatives in compound words (*chimneysweeper* with moveable s; *record*: a disk or a high score; *record*: make a record; *reserve*: serve again; *reserve*: put on hold: not very common ambiguities in hybrid English) can start us down quite different paths.[278]

Then, in different ways in different languages, parts of speech ambiguity can throw us into duck-rabbit dilemmas. Nouns and verbs can trip over themselves directly—"They saw her duck"—or more subtly: "The shooting of the hunters was terrible."[279] Various forms of condensation or truncation can pose other problems: relative pronouns omitted, as in the news story of the burning gusher, "which had killed nine men and destroyed oil statisticians estimated in value up to $200,000." We don't know whether to grieve or wonder how inexpensive statisticians used to be! News headlines (no, not new shedlines), like lines of poetry, are notorious: "Trade Shows Increase," "French Army Cooks Women," and more recently, "Prostitutes Appeal to Pope," "Teacher Strikes Idle Kids," or "Miners Refuse to Work After Death."[280]

My astute reader will note that the funnier ones are also not so hard to disambiguate. But the good reader of literature comes to many syntactic cruxes that are worth fighting over. The best close study of ambiguity in literature since Empson, that of Soon Peng Su, keys her linguistic examples to the many places of difficulty in Hopkins's poems, though she could as well have used Shakespeare's sonnets, Browning's *Sordello*, Emily Dickinson, George Meredith's *Modern Love*, Pound, T.S. Eliot, or Dylan Thomas (not to mention novelists such as Joyce, Faulkner, or Pynchon). Stanley Fish famously resolved such disputes over cruxes of ambiguity by suggesting that they should be allowed to work both ways.[281] And on any individual passage some readers may agree; but some may not. We have little problem agreeing in the case of a joke based on *double-entendre*, or a pun. But when we read Robert Frost's poem about mid-summer unpromise, "The Oven Bird," and are told, "The bird would cease and be as other birds / But that he knows in singing not to sing," we stop, puzzle, interpret, and argue over the condensation. But—because—he knows how not to sing? that is, knows the secret of a diminished season after the promise of spring? Or but—except for the fact that—he knows how not to sing, that is, is a loud mid-summer bird, as the beginning of this sonnet told us. As the sonnet concludes, "the question that he frames in all but words" ("what to make of a diminished thing") is either his wise insight into condensation itself ("a diminished thing") or merely an impoverished mid-season song leaving us with the question. The flip-flopping "all but words" (almost words or words about diminishment, "all but") continues the syntactic double routing. The teasing contraction of the syntax invites us to identify with the bird, place the bird into a general viewpoint on the changing seasons (a diminished bird in a diminished season), or argue that both are present. Which is Frost's? one? the other? both together? some other? I have never taught a class that didn't fall into interesting conflict over the nebulous, gnomic syntactical play of the last four lines. Ambiguity, Su notes, really begins when two readers disagree. And that may include disagreement over taking a text as ambiguous. Note I don't say as intended to be ambiguous. That is what you can't decide if you disagree about how you take it.

Such self-contradicting qualities of language, rather than disappearing with more textual context, may actually become more evident. Plots of novels may seem to tell us that the hero was finding his way in life and also coming to a dead end (Lawrence's *Sons and Lovers*), is weighed in the scale and found wanting and remains the most desired object of her society (Austen's Emma). Poems may both celebrate the coming of civilization and deplore its conclusion (Tennyson's *Idylls of the King*), or excoriate bad wit and taste and celebrate its own excess (Pope's *Dunciad*)—not to mention works justifying God and the devil in the same epic. Logical wires cross easily in shorter works leaving us having to choose one, the other, both, or neither. Katherine Mansfield's wonderful story "The Garden Party" seems to celebrate the class system of her childhood New Zealand while it officially critiques it. "A Game of Chess" in Eliot's *The Waste Land* glamorizes and vents disgust at women at once. Yeats makes old age in "Sailing to Byzantium" a place of tremendous energy ("perne in a gyre") only to leave generation A in a boring and artificial rest-home environment. Good students work through these apparent paradoxes and find something deeply important in them. But by then they have stopped trying to guess what divided intentions created the final mix. The same is true of works of paradox. *Alice in Wonderland* pleases everyone with its word-thought games playing on logic, but it has not left anyone agreeing on what it could be said to be meant to mean. If we all might agree it was intended to be playful (and we won't, because some people will prove it is about pedophilic obsession and point to those nude photos), the image of a playful avuncular author will not do duty to describe how it is playful, which we will have to work out on our own. First-time readers of Joyce's *Ulysses* may well charge, as they find hard-enough stream-of-consciousness presentation superseded by a welter of other overall styles, including the fantasy in Nighttown, that the author's clear intention was to confuse them by such global changes in the rules. But the effect is to remove the author even further from us as an especially inscrutable arranger, peeling his nails in indifference to us. When we read Nabokov's "Invitation to a Beheading"[282] or Borges's stories, we do know the author was very clever to play such games, but all those games only create more ambiguity. He intended it. But what *did* he intend? Noam Chomsky claimed to prove the autonomy of syntax by the sentence "Colourless green ideas sleep furiously." What it proves, two researchers comment, is that we will try to interpret anything presented as if it is interpretable language.[283] But the degree of agreement on the interpretation of "Jabberwocky" is low.

If psychologists and linguists give us lots of space to play in finding ambiguity in syntax, most of Empson's and most of literary readers' perplexities, when not about individual word meanings, come from unclarities about information or conceptions. One can debate, and there have been unuseful debates, as to whether these should be termed ambiguities, as Empson called a great variety of effects of unclarity, or vagueness. Unclarity is perhaps the best term, as it suggests a simple focus is lacking that leaves matters finally nebulous. Simple cases are terms that are, almost by definition, highly subjective, for instance descriptions of longness and shortness. Those are intrinsically vague concepts which we cannot help but process subjectively. The same is true of those true subjectivities, sense impressions.[284] Our friends who are oenophiles work long and hard to establish an objective language of the nose, tongue, and palate, but normal uncoded users of language such as authors must leave it to us to reconstitute what they tell us of smell, taste, touch, not to mention sight experiences, by our own impressions. Readers of Wolfgang Iser's books on reading will recognize this recoding as a version of his well-known gap-filling procedure.[285] And here the clinicians follow the critic, calling this work "pragmatic inference processing."[286] A reader figures out that the account of John, unemployed, who went to the bank with a gun, may be about bank robbery. The researchers' hope is that, while the reader holds onto his supposition, such matters will be clarified by the text. But Su, wiser to literature, sees in reading many gaps never resolved and left subjectively filled in differently by different readers. In this, she can say that texts always have much built-in indeterminacy.[287] A great deal is underspecified in the text itself.

The general situation is much clearer in drama, where we are aware that someone, director or actor, will have to make a great number of decisions not only about the *mise en scène* but also about the looks and attitudes of the actors, relative emphases, and so much more. In all forms of literature what is perhaps most important—the implications of the whole, indeed our central interpretive move—may be only an implication we draw. Just as local speech acts may not say directly "pass the salt," much literature doesn't speak directly any meaning at all. But "Can you pass the salt?" is at least governed by a convention; in drawing out meanings from literature we are filling out the biggest gaps on our own. Literature often accentuates this process by leaving major matters totally unclear or unremarked, an openness that sucks us into the breach.[288] We may be told "so much depends upon a red wheel barrow" and left there depending and debating. Novels like *Vanity Fair*, where the narrator admits to not knowing important facts of the cases he recounts and knowing others he dare not, *pro pudore*, share with us, or like Ford's *The Good Soldier*, where the narrator is himself still trying to fill in the gaps in his life, have a tonic effect upon us readers. Perhaps they bring our powers into play more than equally self-conscious postmodern works that dazzle and overwhelm us with their paradoxes, intricacies, and perplexities.

Finally, as Empson also well shows us, unclarities often arise from the inherent imprecision of ideas and conceptions. George Meredith is a difficult novelist to read not because of complicated narrative modes but because his rather direct narrator usually has a great deal to say that is rather complicated. Ditto with Melville and sometimes Norman Mailer. Chapman is not a metaphysical poet of complicated wit and conceit but a poet with very abstract, complicated things to say. In such cases each reader is more put upon to try to figure out what the meanings are and is unlikely to attain the exact view that another reader does. Abstract nouns are by their nature places of unclarity with no easy referents in sight.[289] We all know this even in everyday politics where we know someone else's ideas of freedom or liberty are not likely to correspond to ours. Readers of Shelley's poetry know how nebulous his abstractions, especially as the end of a simile, can seem. "Conceptual meaning," a psychologist assures us, "is inherently unclear or indistinct. It relies on mental nebulosities such as prototypes, schemata, abstract concepts, and perceptual sets. It exists in minds."[290] Abstract, conceptual, obscure, difficult writing, whether one labels it ambiguous or gives it a category all its own—metaphysical, intellectual, abstruse—necessarily works, like more local ambiguity or like other forms of openness, to ambiguate the text, leaving readers much room for their own abstract interpretations.

To try to be less nebulous myself in this look at nebulosity, let me end this section by giving one example of the practical difficulties hard texts present to us (and we all thought literary theory was hard work!). I will then, in an unusual spirit of homage, leave the reader to resort to Empson, who has presented so many examples so well and with such great invention, for more cases. Mine is from the *bête noire* of Victorian interpretation, Dante Gabriel Rossetti, whose sonnet sequence *The House of Life* begins with a well-known sonnet on "The Sonnet":

> A sonnet is a moment's monument—
> Memorial from the Soul's eternity
> To one dead deathless hour. Look that it be,
> Whether for lustral rite or dire portent,
> Of its own arduous fulness reverent.

Here the combination of abstract, Latinate language, the condensation required by the tight and brief sonnet form, and the sensuality so often found in Rossetti (repeated "m"s and "l"s and the various "ess" and "ous" endings) give the lines a slow, clotted quality. What seems like clear and, if I may, authoritative assertion—"A sonnet is ... Look that it be"—is quickly lost in too plenteous and sweeping options. A sonnet is a monument to a moment or a momentary monument: the grammar really allows both and chooses neither for us. It is a memorial from the soul's eternity to an hour, that seems clear; but what is a soul's eternity? the undying soul enmeshed in the world? or is it a glimpse of some other world—the soul's eternity—where hours are somehow counted up? And what are we to make of the oxymoron in the third line: dead because gone, deathless because still in the soul? Or is it a memorial (funeral) for an hour, now dead, that once seemed alive—deathless? The odd "whether" clause seems almost deliberately set to make the awkward construction "be ... Of fulness reverent" even harder to follow so we are, like the recruit in the army told for the first time to clean the latrine, confronted with an urgent order we can't understand. With "lustral rite," "dire portent," and "reverent" we may go scooting to our dictionaries to find special meanings—but without any great clarification.

Roman ceremonial purification after the census doesn't add much here, though we, unlike Rossetti's Victorian readers, may not have recalled (or known) it. Dire portents we know of, omens or prodigies. Both seem calculated to raise great shadows of important avenues of meaning for the sonnet without giving us more than a sense of their murky presence. Even if we reduce them to "purifications or warnings" we can't quite see any logical connection to usual subjects of the sonnet. "Reverent," put in the punch position at the end of this heavy command, bearing importance from its religious associations, is most confusing. We could understand "toward" instead of "of" as a controlling preposition, reverent toward its own arduous fulness: self-satisfied with its own difficult bombast, if we want to be mean. But how is it reverent of? perhaps redolent of. Having just argued that words keep producing new meanings I can hardly object if Rossetti found a new sense of reverent to use here; I am just sorry he didn't share it with us. And of course there are minor problems besides: for instance, on second study that "arduous fulness" is trickier than it seems: hard to get full? full of hardness?

hard-worked fullness? Perhaps we will choose the third, as it seems to fit our experience of the poem so far, the author laboring to pack it full of meanings that we labor without great success to unpack.

The point, of course, is not that we can't find our way through the hard passages and create a meaning; we can then easily declare it to be the author's. But as so often when we read hard texts, whether such poetry, or Faulkner's or Pynchon's novels, or contested lines in Shakespeare's plays, the difficulty is exactly in working through the too many choices offered by syntax, grammar, or logic, usually, as here, larded on top of words susceptible to multiple interpretations. If we set our critical task as going back from such multiple situations and declaring what the author had in mind we will never be able to make any one interpretation. Of course, we could declare, as the New Critics often implied and, as noted above, Stanley Fish famously argued, that clever authors wrote excellent texts to give us just this workout among multiple choices. But again, the fallacy there is just the same as that in forcing one choice we make upon the author's intention: we guess the author's intention among four choices: he meant a, he meant b, he meant a + b, he meant neither a nor b; but any one of these, including all of the above, is merely our opinion. Nothing is added to the truth of our assertion by declaring the author our secret sharer. Much the same could be said about translations. Did C.K. Scott Moncrieff, in his Edwardian richness and elegance and reticence, get Proust right in English? Or did Lydia Davis with her sparser, wittier clip or did Ian Patterson with his blunter approach (*Finding Time Again*)? Was Beckett more Beckett in his translations of his own work into English, his native language, or in the original French? Translations may claim, as Proust did in translating Ruskin, to capture the spirit of the original, but if all practitioners (and reviewers of translations) believe in the possibility of a copy that is, in another time and language, a true copy of the original, all theory—at least in our time—must be against it.[291]

XIII. TROPES AND FIGURES GETTING IN THE WAY

Paul de Man and his followers have reminded us of the special problems for interpretation offered by the astounding variety of figures of speech that writers, all writers but especially writers of what they believe to be artistic or expressive work, use. In the traditional discussions of rhetoric from the Greeks to Nietzsche, these were considered to be tools for achieving persuasive eloquence (*elocutio* with a broader meaning than mere eloquence), for adding fullness of matter and speech to an argument.[292] As such, these so-called rhetorical figures, outlined or enumerated in guides for the orator (or later, for the writer), may have seemed, as they were often called, ornaments.[293] Cognitive semanticists, looking at the way people actually use metaphors, have found that they are anything but decorative: they are central to how we think and express ourselves.[294] In literary writing, their potency in adding and also in subtracting possible meanings, which has made them the center of de Manian deconstructive thinking, makes them anything but dull sites of authorial clarification. Just where we find these signs of literary artistry, we find ourselves especially left to our own devices.[295] The author who uses rhetorical figures to add power to his or her meaning does not so much further clarify an intention as stimulate the reader by offering a variety of possible meanings.

One should speak here really of both a constructive and deconstructive function. The best-known trope, the still and always mysterious metaphor, as the term's etymology suggests, brings change; it brings change by adding as well as subtracting possible meaning. When Pound writes "Your mind and you are our Sargasso Sea," he adds many possible meanings to the "mind and you" that we have barely met at the beginning of his unflattering, perhaps sexist "Portrait d'une Femme." Whatever associations we may have with the floating weed, with any sea itself—senses possibly of density, of floating lack of direction, of enormity—open up possibilities of interpretation of this person whom the poem seems to wish on us as a kind of institution, "our Sargasso Sea." At the same time the metaphor subtracts in the sense of making it harder to settle on any one specific meaning. One should see these as places in a text where the author especially has attracted our interest and even emotional involvement—the traditional idea of why the orator used such terms in adding eloquence to his argument—but has done so by getting us more involved, that is throwing more of the decision as to meaning onto us. Indeed, as one philosopher observes, "the producer of metaphor" does not know what he is saying ("the meaning" of what he is saying). "For the metaphorical term he uses has an extension [what it applies or points to] he typically cannot elucidate at the time of utterance."[296]

I find another philosopher, Donald Davidson's, hardheaded analytical clarification of how a metaphor functions in fact most helpful. By insisting on the literal sense of metaphorical statements as a starting point, he can clarify the responsibility for meaning. A metaphor is normally false on a literal level (her mind is not a Sargasso sea).[297] That has the effect of making the hearer or reader have to think what it might mean since it can't be a literal statement. Davidson then sees that what it may mean cannot be then defined definitively from the text. In this clarifying view, there is no second-level hidden meaning that metaphor conveys from author to us. Rather, it makes us work on possible meanings: "What we attempt in paraphrasing a metaphor cannot be to give its meaning, for that lies on the surface; rather we attempt to evoke what the metaphor brings to our attention." There is "no definite cognition content that its author wishes to convey and that the interpreter must grasp if he gets the message."[298] In this conceptualization there are also no defined borders to interpreters' meanings: "When we try to say what a metaphor 'means,' we soon realize there is no end to what we want to mention ... You might list a great many, but you could not finish since the idea of finishing would have no clear application."[299] It is conventional wisdom to say that the context in the work we are reading helps control the open-ended power of metaphor. If it sometimes does, letting us know that Pound's poem concerns a certain independent woman in touch with the currents of his London, it also offers more room for speculation as our mind connects the garbagy, seaweed-filled calm sea to all the trophies we find she has been accumulating about the town over many years.[300] Davidson finds that similes, those metaphors where the comparison is laid out for us in full, by contrast, generally begin with literal meanings that seem true. He doesn't pursue this but one could say that similes usually offer striking connections between things we might not have thought to connect, and hence provoke us in the same way to provide possible meanings—often the effect of what New Critics called imagery generally. When Burns writes, "O my luve's like a red, red rose," he adds many possible meanings of red, red rose to whatever may be established of a "luve": redness, beauty, roseness, and so on, but also makes the total effect less univocal. How indeed *is* his love like a rose? Let me find and count the ways, says the reader. Metaphorical language, including similes and images, whether in ordinary or more intense literary use, throws the decision for meaning-making onto the reader, out from the author.[301]

While de Man has overstated the view that it is the nature of such language to make any reading impossible by creating a kind of black hole of meaning in the text,[302] he has been right in encouraging us, as Nietzsche did, to retain a sense of the power of such places in a text, a power perhaps too easily overlooked in our general tendency not to want to separate artistic or expressive texts from others. The point, as the traditional theoreticians of rhetoric knew, is rather the opposite: that all language, to the extent it is made vivid, contains such "eloquent," that is specially artful, effects. If the writer wished to be very clear about her or his chosen meaning, the opposite approach would be natural: to use as logical, detailed, and, if possible, mathematical an exposition as possible. In scientific or mathematical work, in special work such as legal writing, the dangers of tropes and figures have been propagated by philosophers and logicians from Hobbes and Locke to Russell or Carnap; and the writer generally tries—though rarely successfully—to keep out all but the most established (dead) metaphorical language. But just as the lecturer who wants to keep his class from dozing off must throw some questions at them, the writer of such scientific or legal language must throw us some control, some sense of our determination of the meaning, by adding this potent "decoration." At a deeper level, unacknowledged or hidden metaphorical action may be strongly working in non-fiction historical or scientific writing, as well as more directly ideological expression, as a hidden force and complicator of our response.[303] Linguists and psychologists studying ambiguity have similarly taken metaphor and figurative language as a major place of possible confusion in communication.[304]

There has been a traditional distinction drawn between tropes, such as metaphors, similes, or metonymies, as turns or play on meaning in a word or words,[305] and figures, in a narrower sense, as artful arrangements of word sequence, though this has been a distinction never definitively articulated and often violated by the use of trope *or* figure to cover all varieties of such eloquence. The differences registered have in fact little bearing on the effect of the many rhetorical figures on possible meaning, which tend to function in broadly similar ways as tropes to open possibilities of meaning and throw their resolution on the reader. To take a simple but very effective example of a figural word placement, look at the use of repetition (*repetitio*) in Wallace Stevens's "The Snow Man." The poem ends by asking us to focus on the snow man, mind of winter whom we join in the cold scene of snow, January sun, and junipers shagged with ice: "the listener, who listens in the snow, / And, nothing himself, beholds / Nothing that is not there and the nothing that is." The peculiar and very striking form of repetition here, for which I am at a loss for a more specific name, in which a word is repeated with different meaning (nothing himself, nothing, the nothing) or different grammatical form (listener, listens) obviously adds sonority as well as monotony to the description of the winter day. We can say as well that the double listen makes us listen up, underlines the effect of trying to hear with the ears of a snow man; but of course it also takes away the possibility of listening to anything by the very repetition which tends to white out the meaning of the term, turning it into a mere mantra: listen, listen. The ritual-like repetitions of nothing at even intervals certainly bring home that unfact of nothingness. But here again the figure of repetition also undoes its emphasis by boggling our mind with a trinity of three distinct nothings and a tour de force of different kinds of nothingness: the snow man who is nothing, who therefore sees nothing but also is thus especially well equipped to see the nothingness of things in the winter scene. By adding self-conscious effects that come between the reader and the meaning, figures, like tropes, necessarily multiply the possibilities of meaning while also undermining our certainty of what the author may have intended.

Here again I can only give a few small examples of what is a mighty tributary to our Mississippi of literary interpretation. We can rarely speak of interpretive issues without falling into problems with how to evaluate a trope or figure, as de

Man's famous Archie Bunker rhetorical question made clear.[306] It makes quite a difference how we take his remark on difference, so his rhetorical question (what's the difference? on the issue of shoe laces threaded over or under), far from controlling his wife-reader, seems calculated, as I noted above, to give her enough interpretive rope (or laces) to hang herself. Figures and tropes seem necessarily to open up a great space of play—a trope I prefer to that of the black hole above (and here I follow an *occultatio* that in fact stealthily brings in that antithetical characterization of tropes and figures even as I seem to wish it away)—in the text that brings us into necessary debates over meaning. Whatever direction we may be giving our game of interpretation, these somewhat wild cards allow us to call our hands more emphatically. You can say of course that the dealer was nonetheless the author, and we do tend to thank authors for such good hands; but the author who gives us more wild cards merely gives us the opportunity to come up with more various winning hands, and what configuration we will give them is correspondingly less in the author's control.[307]

There has been a danger of redundancy in the structure of my argument which I have tried to face by avoiding overlap and repetition. In the earlier sections looking at the ways in which an author can be said not to control his or her text, I have been looking from the point of view of the author; here I imagine a text without an author present and ask in what ways the text speaks of its author's intention and in what ways it refuses to do so. I only briefly mentioned unclarities of intention through tropes and figures in the author section since I wanted to look at them here as effects faced by readers of texts. There I gave more space to the large special area in rhetoric of irony because that seemed an especially author-oriented way of thinking about a text.[308] We are used to talking of irony as something the author does, the irony of irony being that the author does this, asserts his or her authority, by precisely opening up questions about the intention. Here I would only remind my reader that the whole range of effects often lumped under the term irony follow other figures in throwing decision-making from the author, who may be manipulating us cruelly but who is not there to tell us what the right answer finally is, to the reader.[309] It is especially natural for us, faced with difficult decisions about seemingly strange or contradictory texts, to try to imagine an intended meaning to settle the issue. Yet, to the extent the issue is a hard one and eminently debatable, we will find ourselves cut off from the author and on our own. Irony exists in the eyes of the beholder, a broad point that criticism often misses. If you write on the margin here something like "nice work, Maynard, you just evaded another long discussion of that hard mystery, irony," and I take out the library copy and read you on me, what am I to make of it? To the extent you haven't penned merely an insult or a slur, that is you have attained an ironic distance from what you are writing about me, I am genuinely perplexed as to whether to report you for writing in library books or call you brother/sister/friend, noble and just.

Two further points are worth repeating here as they pertain to our reading of all rhetorical figures. First, I have no wish or need to argue that all effects that one could label as examples of irony offer us equal difficulty in coming to agreement on intention. Irony shades over into mockery and derision and in another direction it becomes directly persuasive, rhetorical in the Madison Avenue pejorative sense.[310] We all have a pretty good sense of when we are being made fun of or mocked (come to think of it, I think I will report you to the library authorities) and we are used to the pressures of persuasive irony—those lovely little innuendos we all love to listen to in TV ads as to sweet music, don't we! (like this bit of anti-Madison Avenue irony). But even if the intention can be rather obvious, the point is that the figure has the effect of introducing some level of play about intention, it brings us into play, it even opens possibilities of resistance and rejection (what's wrong with Madison Avenue innuendos; they *are* more fun to listen to than the programs they support). One reader may conclude that Swift's famous observation about seeing a man flayed showed Swift's indignation at man's inhumanity to man; but then there will come the reader to confound the first by insisting that the whole distant observation on how it changed the man for the worse in fact shows Swift's distance and indifference—a savage heart of stone—much as he may want to suggest to us his heart-of-gold hidden involvement. To the extent that satire attains ironic distance from its subject, it opens the possibility of conflicting interpretations. The tool easily turns in the hands of its new receiver-user.[311] The second point I have already made: distancing irony, like other figures, may indicate that the author's intention was exactly not to be clear, to sit back like a god paring his nails while we sweat over his text. But, again, we can't know this, as the diversity of opinion over irony about Stephen Dedalus in *A Portrait of the Artist* has certainly demonstrated (is the novel satirical, celebratory, or something in between?). A large amount of modern and postmodern literature leaves us similarly embattled by a trope or attitude so hard to read. But it is wrong to see this as merely the effect of post-1900 distance or post-1950 game playing. In all periods of literature this is the usual work of this slippery trope which—like so many other tropic uses of language—so easily drops out of the author's hands and lands in ours.

XIV. VOICE GETS IN THE WAY TOO

No practice in the New Criticism, and to some extent in the parallel but more moralistic Leavisite criticism in England, offered more assurance of a stability in literature's meaning than what they called voice or tone. Arguably no aspect of the New Criticism remains more influential, at least in the literary interpretation classroom, than this belief that other aspects of a poem or narration, which may on the surface appear unresolvable—for instance tropic play or thematic ambiguity—can be definitely sorted out once the disposition of the speaker or narrator is ascertained. The New Critics famously released the literary work from naive critical assumptions that the speaker in a poem, the narrator in a story or novel, could be identified with the author's self and the work secured in meaning and intention by reference to the author's life and opinions elsewhere. Indeed, on this level of interpretation, of author's relation to the speaker or speakers of poems, novels, plays, even the more tempting case of voices of essays, no one seems now to want to try to deny the separation by art of the speaker/s as character/s or persona/e from the writer as living person.[312] On this level, we are all New Critics, knowingly or not. But the question I pose here is this: can we obtain certitude about the intention behind the text by simply seeking out a speaker's expressed disposition?

I would be the last person to say that focus on the voice or tone is not an appropriate move in interpretation. In my own teaching to sophomores, I have even updated the terms, finding "attitude" (even including the popular sense of "he's got an attitude") a better cue word than the now stuffy-sounding New Critical "tone." I recommend it. Classes in the current generation regularly respond with interest to the question, "what attitude is the narrator displaying?" while a question about tone may serve only to move the discussion off center to jazz and popular music.

When I started teaching, in the famous Harvard Humanities 6, I confess I was comfortable with the New Critical assumption that questions about tone had one, ascertainable answer. All I needed, in those innocent days of Socratic teaching, the then liberal alternative to expert and uninterrupted lecturing, was to get those students to agree with me about where the speaker/narrator was coming from and where she (but it was he then) wanted to go. I now begin with the question of attitude not because it will close down interpretation but just because it so centrally opens to every other interpretive question. Attitude, tone, voice: these are all subject to interpretation, not fixed realities standing outside our debates. Whatever conclusions we jump to about the poem as a whole we will bring to our ascription of voice. Sylvia Plath's "Lady Lazarus"—to take as example again that brilliantly tortured work—is a poem of feminist anger: we hear it in the sarcastic voice of the speaker. No, it is a poem, obviously, about suicide and despair. The voice is a product of hysteria: illogical (comparing herself to Jewish Holocaust victims!), desperate, preoccupied with its apparent disintegration into body parts. Wrong again, the attitude is triumphant: empowered over death and doctors by her fearlessness, the speaker is playful, ironic, flamboyantly in control. And on and on. In the universally operative hermeneutic circle we reach from our positions about the whole to articulate the voice we are determined to hear in it; we then seek out other material in the poem to confirm our views.

Of course the good instructor that I try to be also works the other way, giving the appearance of inductive rigor by starting out with trying to hear the voice in the work. I begin with vocalizing: how would you speak this? what qualities of real voice would you add to these words on the page? I note that words written in our writing system are largely unmarked for attitude or tone in any way that would bring these written Lazaruses properly to life. Even exclamation marks aren't subdivided into those used for mere emphasis, for "there, take that," or for "I know you will agree with me," or for "note this well," or for "wow, I am overwhelmed." Other tones and moods, sadness, elation, madness, suspicion—all the human emotions that artists or actors were traditionally taught as an alphabet of gestures—are essentially unmarked. I tell them how actors sometimes begin with words alone in their first read-through of a script, debating how they should put a voice to those dead words on the page. I encourage them to see how writing has alienated language from immediate presence of speech and ask them to try to repair that fall in their own attempts at reading a poem or narration aloud.

Later we can take this apart as a conception. At the high level, this is of course *the* deconstruction: at the center of Derrida's thinking in *Of Grammatology*. Why are we presuming some monistic clarity in speech itself that privileges it over writing? The condition of writing is no different from that of all interpretation: we will have to decide what the actor is voicing when she voices the script; and on this act of interpretation we may disagree too. When the student in class ventures an oral reading, far from having provided a present clarity that ends all discussion, she must decide what meanings she has orally imputed to the written work. At a less anti-Olympian and Derridean level, there are more practical problems. In voicing we may import the idealizing view that the written language must carry a clear emotive direction. As even the New Critics implicitly suggested, a possible interpretation of voice is that it is unclear, an indication of their favorite underlying situation, ambiguity. The narrator of Ford Madox Ford's *The Good Soldier*, for example, can't find his voice because he can't decide what he thinks about his years of being cuckolded by the man he so admired. The New Critics would generally not go further, as has often been remarked of their view of word meanings, and accept indeterminacy of voicing.[313] Still, it exists; for instance, once again in William Carlos Williams's well-known "This Is Just to Say": "I have eaten / the plums / that were in / the icebox / and which / you were probably / saving / for breakfast / Forgive me / they were delicious / so sweet

/ and so cold." How will we ever distinguish here the attitudes: childish glee, half-repressed matrimonial resentment, sadistic toying with another, macho self-aggrandizement? The question raised in such instances is not whether we say what we mean, but whether we know how we feel. That the language of emotion usually comes from a place of conflict—we want our will but perhaps don't want to lose our wife (yet)—or, to follow Lacan's psychology of our alienation from our desires, that it expresses our necessary absence from ourselves, means that the whole attempt to assign a clear interpretation of attitude may usually be unproductive. How much more so in a work of literature in which—to credit those New Critics—it still seems best to assume that the speaker who is apparently speaking straight from the heart is only a creation of an author, not *the* author.

A final complication, but an important one: as Derrida has forced us to ask, why do we presume that language needs a voice? American Sign language has no voice (I guess it shares with oral language the "voicing" of body language). Chinese ideograms can be voiced in many languages but are themselves a visual language, not needing voice; ditto Egyptian hieroglyphs. And before these written languages, which do connect each ideogram/hieroglyph to specific spoken words, there were (and still are in some pre-writing cultures) the pictographic languages that are sets of pure visual symbols, which command an object or idea but no specific voiced words (a picture of something in pants can mean men, gentlemen, guys, mens/boysroom, etc.). Ideograms and hieroglyphs perhaps trail such specific visual concepts from earlier pictographic languages of communication from which they have derived. Today Swedish educators are developing a new pictogram system of communication for learning-disabled persons; and scientists working with apes have developed hundreds of lexigrams, word symbols to the scientists but clearly pictograms to their subjects. Mathematical symbols of course represent the same concepts in different languages and with no particular words required in voicing (= is the same as or equals). And, to return to our reading system, reading specialists show us we learn to read in modern Western culture both with and without voicing. Written language in our alphabet system can go straight to the brain without the loop of even a speech impulse.[314] It then exists, like signs or pictograms, as a voiceless system of communication, though one always, as ideograms are to the reader but sign language is not to the signer, on the edge of voicing (with pictograms allowing multiple voicings). Reading fast, we suppress all or most of the voice in the brain. In the classroom we rightly start by encouraging students to reverse this process and give voice to what they read; they are commonly so unused to this—unless they are young actors in our Tisch School—that their productions seem totally incompetent. We work on this and by and large succeed, especially with poetry, with which most New

Critics liked to begin. It is an art that often bears with it traces of its origins in oral performance. Here, to choose a voice is to make an interpretation.

But voice is not always available as a central quality in literary works: not in the visual play of emblem poems, not in the interiority of much modern epic from Wordsworth's *Prelude* to Robert Browning's *Sordello* to Derek Walcott's *Omeros*; not in the word games of Wallace Stevens, Marianne Moore, James Merrill, or John Ashbery. Many modern poems, from *The Waste Land* on, have waged a war on the idea of lyric as coming from a stable or even single persona; the dramatic monologue, with its apparently coherent speaker character, has been itself rewritten as the mere display of a moniker for varied moods and ideas—something one finds, on revisits to them, even in some of the classic dramatic monologues of Browning or Tennyson.[315] If most of us have warmed to the Russian Formalists' idea of *skaz* as prose narration imitating racy oral first-person tales or made the inevitable comparisons of oral story and narratives,[316] we cannot deny that a good deal of the most interesting narrative creates a language out of many written forms—journalism, sociology, history, specialized discourses of all sorts, from cetology to cyborg studies—that are virtually unvoiceable. I was told when I visited Trieste that the local Joyce society literally read through *Ulysses*, aloud, over some sleepless nights. What a way to read (interpret) Joyce—or Melville or Henry James, or Pynchon! (exclamation here for benevolence mixed with disdain). Or Dickens, for that matter, whose narrators I always find are much more literary (imbued in traditions of written language) than I generally think of them as being. Dickens's characters may be bursting with life, his world filled with oral activity, but the writing of his various chroniclers are often far from anything anyone would even think to speak. (Yes, he loved to read to great crowds; but also, yes, he died doing it.) Our technology has allowed us to build great gazebos of our written language where we can create views of all things beyond any simple, voiceable attitudes. Having shown my students the need to find a voice in what they read, I show them that this is always a matter of dispute, a central place in interpretive conflict rather than a guide out of it for the perplexed. Toward the end of the course I try to suggest ways in which literature may take us into a literate world beyond the simple tones and attitudes that they, like the New Critics, so bravely set out to nail down. What is the attitude or tone of *Bleak House* or *Ulysses*? Voices—too many of them too fully nuanced, too vacillating and modulating, too comprehensive—get in the way of easy intentionalist answers.[317]

I look below at problems in attempts to determine intention based on genres of written works. In teaching I do find it helpful to amplify discussions of voice by connecting that work to discussion of speech acts as very basic genre types. We can focus our interpretation of a work by seeing what answers we obtain to a question about what kind of speech act is being used in the work. So Donne's "Batter my heart" is an unusual version of a prayer; that helps. The problem with this procedure as a way of securing interpretation of attitude is that even where we can agree on such a classification it in no way eliminates others. The work may seem to embody a number of speech acts depending on the interpretive emphasis. So Donne's sonnet may also appear to be a command, an attempt to have God have him on his (the speaker's) own terms; or a surrender, a giving into God's rape and battery. The point is then that the attribution of speech act goes hand-in-hand with judgments on attitude and voicing: one can't predetermine the other. If we think Donne's speaker is surrendering to God we will also hear a very different voice from a speaker commanding the deity or from one merely engaging in hyperbolic but otherwise generic prayer.[318]

Mikhail Bakhtin's rather similar concept of speech genres, which allows him to relate pragmatic speech to fictional uses, wants to define genre in large part by addressivity.[319] This brings his thinking especially close to issues in the work of reader theorists and leads him to the problem of the labile, unstable quality of address in fiction as well as poetry. For instance, apostrophe, the figure of address, can be merely a rhetorical figure, only serving to divert, really divide, the speaker's voice from one addressee to someone else. Wordsworth's turn to "Great God!" in "The World Is Too Much with Us" seems to convert preaching to his generation about their worldliness into a fervent prayer—or is it a curse invoking God's wrath? Coleridge in "Frost at Midnight" interrupts his long discussion with himself to address his sleeping infant: not a likely listener but sufficient to confuse us between a speech genre of solitary confession and that of blessing another. That is a problem for those who would circumscribe interpretation, not a problem with the poem, which I would say combines both addresses quite well, and perhaps others too, reverie and celebration of God's nature among them. Address in literature seems regularly multiple and fluid. We are rather surprised to find André Gide's Michel in *The Immoralist* placing his very private memoirs of his wars against his own personality in a frame of seeking counsel from his old friends. Has his attitude only been that of *épater les bourgeois* (friends) all along? Or, to take one final example, Renaissance poems ostensibly addressed to admired mistresses are often divided in address, and hence also in speech genre and tone, by their coterie circulation, mainly to admiring fellow males.[320]

XV. THEMATIC FOREGROUNDS ABOUNDING

When we are looking at the general irony of a work, we become aware that we are dealing with a macro issue of interpretation rather than merely a matter of figures of speech. At this level of interpretation even advocates of authorial intention in the work have begun to lose faith, as I have noted. I have never liked to call such broad interpretive moves by the common term still in use, themes. It carries such a flavor of bold moves by our high school selves to exhaust the theme of whales in *Moby-Dick* or, a little older, Elizabethan political beliefs in Shakespeare. But my talk of macro interpretive gestures and of broad interpretive moves will doubtless annoy in the opposite direction by its cumbersome pseudo-theoretical pretension,[321] so let me use the usual shorthand for what, I hope, may be much more sophisticated interpretive moves or thematic approaches to exploring broad issues in works of literature. Although Wolfgang Iser has not appreciated my appreciation, I have been struck by the way in which his system of reader theory allows a place for these most common gestures of grouping of aspects of a work and its interpretation.[322] He developed his model after Gombrich's work on visual ordering ("thematizing") as a foregrounding and backgrounding of different elements by the viewer. Iser's way of thinking of any interpretation as a foregrounding and grouping of certain elements of a work, which will then necessarily yield to some other thematic foregrounding and grouping, and so on, accounts nicely for the sense we all have—all of us at least who have been around long enough to find that Heraclitus had it right about the only constant being flowing change—of discovering *the* central issue important about a work in one reading or in one generation of criticism, only to find another unthought-of theme beginning to command our later attention. With each shift we see a different work, rather literally because we bring a new set of details forward to support our thematic focus. (Yes, this very much includes interpretations generated off of a New Historical matrix that only seems to occupy solid ground free of the interpretive flow!)

I cannot agree with Iser's premise, or hope, that somehow this dynamic process is all initiated by something in the text, presumably put there by a foreseeing author that then begins to work on and on, but presumably not without a plan, as we work the text up into an aesthetic object in our reading. This is a good example of the "a little for the author and a little for the reader" compromise on the issue of intentionality that Fish has rightly criticized.[323] Iser's approach would suggest that we all come into a text in one, author-prescribed, way, whereas in fact the themes we select seem especially motivated by our own extra-textual interests, whether these are our hobby horses as individuals or, what our current social construction hobby horse tells us may not be so different, the commanding hobby horses of our cultural moment. What allows us to do so many different things to texts as varying thematic foregroundings is nothing more or less than the diversity that almost all literary texts embody. Propositions about what makes a text literary, no longer much in favor in any case, usually themselves foregrounded, within a modernist aesthetic tradition, the self-conscious and single-minded artistry of the literary work as opposed to the imprecise workaday aims of the non-literary.[324] But there would be good empirical reasons to argue the opposite, that we begin to accept works within whatever classes of literariness we set up to the extent that they make interestingly dispersed observations on a diversity of matters. By contrast, the non-literary takes a narrower view, offering a focused report on some specific (maybe newsworthy) subject, a scientific treatment of some specific issue, an inquiry into some topic in the social sciences or history following a restrictive methodology. Essays on diverse issues, a history, such as Carlyle's *The French Revolution*, which may be poor in consistent methodology but is good in broad description of life and times, broad reflections on the social condition: such works are easily classed next to novels that essay life in their time, modernist poems that attempt psychological insights or reflect broadly on the human condition, epic visions of history and fate, tragic or comic views of the human condition.

The point, which I needn't, I think, labor or restrict to specific periods of literature, such as the representational traditions of the more recent West, is that what is literary seems to be in some way broadly observing. It gives us much diverse matter to reflect upon. Above all, it allows us to dwell now on this subject, now on that, as it spreads before us representations, reflections, or projections of the diversity of outer or inner worlds. A bibliography-making computer compiling the diversity of so-called thematic interpretations for each work studied would slowly move toward something like a filled space of thematics. So every graduate student dreads as she or he begins to look for something new to write a dissertation about. But as interpretation brings our own particular bundle of thematic interests and our own approach to them to the work itself, the diversity of interpretive themes seems, from a mere human point of view, virtually endless. So most graduate students find by the time another unique study has been rounded off and polished up.

It is easy to say that the author intended all our thematic interpretations: that is why we find Shakespeare such a big person, why Dickens or Balzac seem such titans. But the effect is as operative with writers we think of as far lesser in natural curiosity and range of subject: Hopkins, although obsessed with his relation to nature and to God, opens up worlds of interpretive subjects, from theology and nature—the obvious though almost infinitely extendible ones—to aesthetics, homosexuality and homosociality, class relations, colonialism and imperialism, and of course prosody, to name just a few. Katherine Mansfield, minor perhaps among "big" modernists such as Joyce or Woolf, opens to colonial issues, class warfare, Chekhovian comedy, Freudian psychological topics, and of course a great diversity of feminist concerns, and alas to the subject of sickness and mortality. I could go on to discuss a work that might seem to be narrowly focused on whales in classic American literature, or a poem merely recounting the story of the Fall, or a novel offering one day in the life of some Dubliners; but I need not and will not. The person who says that what text x is really about is y simply can't see the great woods of other interpretive subjects waiting behind the present trees on which he or she is focusing.

And of course we don't merely identify and catalog themes determinable from the richness of options offered us by works of literature.[325] We take a view on a theme, give it a theoretical approach or a specific spin, only to find that other showmen and showwomen (curse them!) have taken the text out for quite a different spin on the same theme. The argument does not degenerate into the stereotype its enemies might wish to offer: that any one can find anything he or she wishes in any text. People can, but there are many thematics that at least a majority of us would say are unlikely with particular texts. (Here I will offer no examples because I would then expect a brilliant treatise on just this subject to arrive in the mail with added instructions on how I can eat my own text. We do keep being surprised by what thematic approach to what text they will come up with next, and persuade us too!—at least for a time.) But the diversity of themes that will be found in just about any text we may choose to call literary is so great that it makes no practical difference whether we ascribe it to the author or not. What we have in practice is a series that seems to have no end, which we cannot look at all together any more than we can see Gombrich's inside-out cubes both ways at once or look at a picture in a gallery without sizing up one visual section or connection and then letting our eyes drop that strand to find another.

The critic who would stop the process by claiming that he or she has attained to privileged inside knowledge of what the author had in mind as a result of his or her especially sensitive or especially rigorous approach to the text is merely mistaking the working of the hermeneutic circle, in which detail is naturally pulled out into the foregrounded topic and made to support its claim to centrality, for the author's intention.[326] And he or she is trying to hold back a natural flood of interpretation with a flimsy levee, or (shall we say) trying to stop a roaring train filled with diverse persons following diverse exciting interests with a mere emergency flare, soon to be spent and disregarded entirely as the train roars on. (I look further at claims that study of history can provide a privileged set of themes in II.xviii, below.)

XVI. FOREGROUNDING FORMS ABOUNDING: GENRES AND STRUCTURES

The same is true, though perhaps less immediately apparent, of approaches to texts that would look for author's clear intention in the genre or structure of the text.[327] If the thematic critic who would rest his case on the author's intent often comes bearing down on us blown up big with special knowledge of the themes of the author's day, the genre critic or critic of artistic structure claims special knowledge either of the history of genres or of the universal categories of art. Although this latter is said to be a different enterprise of criticism, poetics rather than hermeneutics or interpretation, I would argue that both are essentially forms of interpretive thematics.[328] The historian of genres attempts to say that what is important to foreground in a certain work of art is the way in which it can be seen to participate by its form in certain kinds of literature—themselves either defined by someone of the time or created after the fact by comparison of readings of various works using such a foregrounding theme. The theorist of one or another universal poetics has come up with a system for defining the structure or form of works that is then used as a foregrounding theme to bring together evidence in the text that fits the system. Instead of reading to discover a social or psychological theme—the rise of the artisan class to self-consciousness in a popular poem from the earlier nineteenth century (perhaps a Corn Law poet), the demon lover as a projection of Kleinian mother figures in suicidal poets of the mid-twentieth century—we are asked to read eighteenth-century *vers de société* as a version of the familiar letter (genre); we are told to understand the odd details of Lewis Carroll's *Sylvie and Bruno* as another crystallization, in the tradition of Petronius or Rabelais, of the universal, archetypal Menippean satire (system of poetics).

Let me look briefly at the more obvious one, genre, first. In these foregroundings, labeling is especially common. Genre, the issuing of a brand name, gives focus to interpretation and tends to naturalize it. Any quality or qualities found in a work, thematic or formal, may of course sponsor a label. As always, I am happy to admit that there is a level on which the case for author's intention is obvious. Where a kind of literature has been named and widely accepted by readers and writers over time, genre may seem to have a contractual feel, equivalent to "a set of fore-understandings exterior to a text which enable us to understand the text."[329] In this traditional view, genre then determines what the author presents and what the reader reads, "so that every text is defined, projected, and in some way written within the limits of generic forms. It intervenes in reading too, to the extent that the initial interest of the reader is directed not at an as yet unknown text's achieved individuality, but toward a textual type or ideal ... *genre carves out the text*."[330] And of course this structure is raised on the old foundation of intention, as Manfred Frank summarized it: "According to the classical view ... a text reflects the unity of a central *vouloir-dire*, of an intention which determines the sense and arrangement of the expressions and qualifies them as 'functions' of a whole."[331] We may insist on a special kind of foregrounding if we are doing, once more, with I hope something more than anesthetized feelings, the history of the sonnet form from the English Renaissance to Elizabeth Barrett and George Meredith. If you tell me that I should not deny that Barrett knew she was writing in a specific formal tradition with a specific name, I will gladly agree. And so will everyone else; the case is another easy one for intention whether we read Barrett's letters to see if she refers to the term or whether we simply start out, having arrived from Uzbekistan with sufficient English but no sense of local cultural history, to compare the *Sonnets from the Portuguese* to the classic cases of the form. That is simple,[332] and even sophomores will not raise their hands with objections, though there is so much variety of form loosely cast under the name (and such a variety of matter) that they could very well do so, up to a point—as they certainly will with Meredith's extra-length sonnets.[333]

But let us wander just a bit further into the meandering mazes of genre history and we find no such clearly marked paths. The ode is a pretty well recognized form, but when one has read all the histories, as I guiltily confess I have, one comes out with rather conflicting ways of reporting what is there. It is a structure of verses? compare Ben Jonson, Cowley, Keats, and Coventry Patmore and try to say so. It is a gesture toward calling down godhead? well, I like that but that is rather like the theme of calling the god in lots of works, including odic interludes in novels.[334] It is a cry from the heart that embraces potential presence and potent absence? yes indeed, and so is the whole logocentric tradition according to Derrida. Or try the genre blithely called the novel. All definitions beginning "a prose work of a certain length dealing with characters in a real state of society ..." rapidly begin to leak once we fill them up with real novels. And so we will end up with statements like James's "impression of life" or some more glib formula of our own: a permanent site of revolution in human self-reflection, a site of discursive intersections (to trip it in the light Foucauldian fantastic, with which I am far from unsympathetic): something broad enough to keep down those penetrating sophomores with their ready artillery of exceptions to whatever rule we try.[335]

E.D. Hirsch, whose good book arguing in favor of intention got me started on all this a long time ago, still seems to offer the most useful general reflections on genres—even though it takes me to a very different view of the relation between genre and intention than his. He sees genre as essentially what I have been calling foregrounding, a picking out of any qualities that strike us for the sake of comparison between works: that is, genre is in the eyes of the beholder, it is any grouping; and in this surprisingly pragmatic view of genre, he is close to the similar approach to genre of neopragmatists, postmodernists, and deconstructionists—not his chosen playfellows.[336] Looked at this way, genre in fact becomes a catch-all term for whatever qualities we see in more than one work that allow us to name their resemblance, this "similarity between certain works."[337] Nor has there been consistent agreement over the range of reference of the terms genre and mode. For some, tragedy is a genre in all cases, whether drama or novel; for others, tragic is a mode, drama or novel a genre; for still others, including Aristotle himself, mode is the person or address system of a work (lyric, dramatic, epic), while tragedy is a genre.[338] Northrop Frye gloriously confused matters with his army of mythoi, modes, and genres.[339] Some like to think of genre as essentially a matter of form; yet there seems no way to exclude content and thematics from genre, as in the grand old one of pastoral itself or the also venerable pornography. Nor can genres be distributed rigidly between those based on content or discourse and those on form. A bildungsroman is a novel (form) about growing up (content). "Classification by content can be extended *ad infinitum*";[340] the only rule seems to be whatever can classify will classify for someone sometime.[341] New subgenres appear regularly, but, when scrutinized, can be raised to primary status, as in a system of magnification, and can then boast primary status and their own subgenres. Underlining the proliferation of genres, they also have a clear tendency to propagate by bonding, like organic chemicals, into ever more complex multi-genres, as Polonius well understood.[342]

Aware of the many faces of genre, I can find mountain castles (well almost, the Heights is kind of like a castle with its dogs and stone kitchen floor), open graves, and frequent stylistic aporia in *Wuthering Heights* and call it a version of a novel called gothic (not too original if I do); you, more original, can see it as operatic novel based on your sense of the high flights of melodramatic language that characters perform at each other in magnificent duets or sing to us in agonized solos about soul connections. And we can both allow this kind of not too representational novel into our view of the genre, though it might not fit Hazlitt's idea of the novel as about society. And others will of course find others. So when the going gets rough in determining genre the tough will either get going or have to accept a playing field of many genres packed into a single work. And if this latter is the case, we find our position in regard to multiple themes of genre very much the same as that with multiple themes in a work generally. Each one seems to fit; each one, we can persuade ourselves for a moment as we foreground it, is obviously what the author had in mind because it is obviously true. But then the author had them all in mind, or none: the author has created a work complex enough that we can name it as we wish, compare it to other works as we wish, but how will we know what the author had in mind?[343] We can find a reference to vampires in Emily's sister's *Jane Eyre* (to continue with the Brontës' work as gothic); did Charlotte Brontë intend to write a vampire novel? Well, not a vampire novel like the later *Varney, the Vampyre; or the Feast of Blood* or

Bram Stoker's *Dracula*; if we want to argue for other connections to vampires (Bertha's ancestry in a faraway place, though not exactly Transylvania; her undead, nightly wailings), we will have to make the case, as we do with any theme, from the text, not by positing the author's intention and then jumping over the hard business of amassing sufficient evidence.

In Memoriam speaks loudly of its connections to the great tradition of pastoral elegy, everyone will agree, and we will hardly imagine that young Tennyson, fresh from a rich education focused in the classics and setting out to deplore his friend's death, as Theocritus had Daphnis, as Milton had King, as Shelley had Keats, as Arnold would Clough, was unconscious of the tradition in which he worked. And busy historical scholarship, as Pater might say, has shown us the numerous echoes and appropriations of specifics of that tradition.[344] So much is clear. However, those who think genre is generally a stable direction from the author to the reader have not sufficiently understood the plurality of genre qualities that may appear in a work we label by the term for the general class.[345] Sonnet, yes, is rather unusually specific (and tells us therefore little other than the number of lines and some kind of rhyme scheme). Pastoral, even the more specific genre label of pastoral elegy, is much more diverse. Like most genre labels, it is a fuzzy class based on an unclear number of defining qualities.[346] And they have not meditated sufficiently on the historical phenomenon I like to call genre drift, as old wine is poured in new bottles and the characteristics identified by a name—here pastoral—progress and develop openendedly over time.[347] The clear fact of a poet's working in such an historical, established genre[348] will not settle the points about our reading of the poem over which we are likely to dispute: is *In Memoriam* a poem, for instance, to cite an issue that regularly perplexes my students as it does professional critics, that dares to speak the love that could not speak its name before it was spoken? Does it do so by an elaborate overlay of Greek love, shepherd for shepherd, coded for an elite of the Cambridge Apostles, who, like the later club of E.M. Forster and Maynard Keynes, or the group around Wilde, would know to add country matters to a poem professing love between men sometimes tricked out in shepherd's weeds or to annotate a phrase like "more than my brothers are to me" with Homeric companions/lovers Achilles and Patroclus.

An attractive interpretive direction. But I should not be able to persuade you by jumping from such a confection of genre and history to proclaim that this establishes the coded but explicit homosexual discourse of the poem. It is a perspective, an approach; if it proves heuristic in opening up the poem to further reading, it will have legs. But we might, on the other hand, find conclusive evidence that the tradition of pastoral was regularly coded to male-male relations in England or even that Tennyson well knew this, yet still deny that the poem must/should/can be read in this way. (After all, we don't eliminate the possibility of a pastoral homosexual meaning in the poem just because we rather think that Milton and Shelley were heterosexuals.) We don't know until we interpret the poem what qualities of pastoral it buys into; and we will have to try to persuade others by arguments other than "genre tells me so." My example is a special case of a more general one that Adena Rosmarin raises: if the author names a genre, as Fielding does in *Tom Jones*, will we use it as our best scheme for interpretation if we find another genre attribute more useful? Her answer is no.[349] This in turn is a special case ("intrinsic" versus "extrinsic" genres in Hirsch) of Hirsch's meaning versus significance.[350] In fact, we consider the one most useful to be the real meaning. Whether rooted in history or conceptualized by a current critic, genre classes are useful if they allow the reader or critic a "powerful practice,"[351] allowing us to see how a work participates in some parts of a class as well as how it does not.

Although the rather traditional, recently only sporadically cultivated subject of genres[352] seems quite a different activity from those still fashionable (if now of a certain age) theoretical areas of poetics and formalisms of all sorts—e.g., structuralism, narratology, theory of drama, the cases are really virtually identical, as the drift of such work, as in the thinking of Tzvetan Todorov or Northrop Frye, into genre creation or analysis suggests. The theorist, like the historian, identifies certain qualities which he or she believes the text to possess. The historian of genre may take the modest view suggested above, that this is merely one way of looking at the qualities of a work; in fact, he or she has been until recent times more likely to believe that categories such as epic, tragedy, and so on are universals, at least for the West—and he/she may have been wishing in noting this to raise the West's genres to an exemplary position as universal truths though not universally acknowledged.[353] The structuralist theorist often acts as if grand theory allows him or her to pronounce universal qualities of all art, which may then be labeled within the variables of any individual text; often, however, the theorist is quite aware of the posited, tentative nature of his or her own attempts to foreground a particular set of patterns in the working of texts. Jonathan Culler's early but penetrating analysis of the structuralist project both noted and exemplified the tension between universal aspirations and more modest particular achievements of a thematic nature.[354] He resists Paul Ricoeur's reduction of structuralism to mere arbitrary taxonomies of whatever subject is under study; using the model of linguistics, he argues that the structures chosen can be proven to be relevant ones by their function; the linguist looks for productive, repeating patterns in language, not just any pattern.[355] This argument from one particular field is of course not logically persuasive in other fields: it rather defines a project for asserting that structures in other fields are sufficiently universal to work in literary study as well. But the project in literature seems bifurcated from its beginnings in Culler's insistence that the structures, in the literary application, will define literary conventions. Although any language is of course conventional in its phonology, grammar, and many other qualities, these conventions are presumably subject to organizing structures that we may theorize as universal in all human languages. By contrast, conventions in literature seem to be cultural and subject to change with cultural change: what we normally mean by conventional, that is only conventional.

Culler well points out this problem when he sees one service of structuralist criticism to have been displaying the ways in which traditional kinds of literature naturalize their own conventions, as if these were also the universals Culler's own system seeks. He then naturally falls into a model of identification between reading and writing, as if our task is indeed to figure out the codes by which the works were written and thus presumably should be read. Interestingly, traditional genres seem a particularly good example: "If a theory of genres is to be more than a taxonomy it must attempt to explain what features are constitutive of functional categories which have governed the reading and writing of literature."[356] Reading falls in here "naturally" with writing as if the "governing" relation of the two were not one of the naturalizations that most needs to be questioned. When Culler concludes his authoritative summary of structuralist literary activity, he returns to the fundamental uncertainty as to whether this literary project is a study of nature or of culture. Most of the work, he acutely notes, has been a matter of applying language from linguistics, *langue* and *parole* and the like, to criticism; more direct attempts at a linguistics of literature, as in the literary work of Roman Jakobson, have not led to a universal system. Culler ends by restating his hope for such a system based on a vision of literature as a *langue* of conventions known in the competence of qualified readers, a project that first leads to odd stress on literary institutions as inculcators of conventions,[357] then becomes lost in his increasing focus on deconstruction. In the meantime he seems right about what the tradition of structuralist theory has achieved, which in many ways fits Ricoeur's taxonomic model: interesting ways of finding relations in literature on an essentially *ad hoc* basis.[358]

One of the thinkers broadly associated with structuralist rethinking of narratology, Gérard Genette, whose works have in fact had quite good staying power, ends what seemed when it first came out a bewildering strategic application of new, technical-sounding terms for describing narrative effects in Proust, with a very modest self-evaluation:

> The categories and procedures put forward here are certainly not faultless in my eyes: it has been a question, as it often is, of choosing between drawbacks.... The proliferation of concepts and terms will doubtless have annoyed more than one reader, and I do not

> expect "posterity" to retain too large a part of these propositions. This arsenal, like any other, will inevitably be out of date before many years have passed ... if the critic can dream of an achievement in the second degree, the poetician for his part knows that he labors in—let us say rather *at*—the ephemeral, a worker aware of becoming unworked.... all this technology—prolepses, analepses, the iterative, focalizations, paralipses, the metadiegetic, etc.—surely barbaric to the lovers of belles lettres, tomorrow will seem positively rustic, and will go to join other packaging, the detritus of Poetics.[359]

Detritus seems even *too* modest for what has proven a very useful work with inkhorn terms still in use today; but the sense of working terms is helpful, a way of seeing such focalizations—there it is, that useful term—of theory as a living, changing process of foregrounding different elements in texts that interest individuals or critical cultures at one moment or another. If all theorists were so modest there would be no need to even argue my case here; the foregrounding subjects of the poetician are his inventions by which he makes sense of the workings of the text, offers his theme, a description of the text. There is no need to justify them, arbitrary and finally ephemeral ways of describing some of the complexity of the text, by foisting them off on the author. If Genette, in his interesting look at what he calls anisochronies, decides to ratio the time of action in Proust to the length of narrative rendition of the action, and thus finds that Proust's text tremendously varies in time/length relations, he has discovered a useful physics of narration which gives us one way to speak about the narrative resourcefulness of Proust; but he does not need to posit that Proust himself possessed such a physics or intended, in this form, this explanation of his self-conscious artistry.

Yet the temptation is great to begin to think that something we see has been seen in the same way by the author;[360] and indeed Genette begins to succumb: he concludes from the higher proportion of length of narration over time of action in the later sections he studies, "It certainly seems that Proust wanted, and wanted from the beginning, this ever more abrupt rhythm, with a Beethovenian massiveness and brutality, which contrasts so sharply with the almost imperceptible fluidity of the early parts, as if to compare the temporal texture of the older events with that of the more recent ones—as if the narrator's memory, while the facts draw nearer, were becoming both more selective and more enormously enlarging."[361] It seems he wanted: maybe; or he found he had more reflections on his society from the later times and inadvertently created the Beethoven effect. As always, the vision we take on a text, even when we seem to cull out such very mathematical "facts," very much creates one way of thinking of it. If Genette wants to believe Proust shared his perception of this timing, he is of course welcome to; if he tried to persuade us that this "seeming" adds any power to his argument by bringing the author in as his critical *semblable,* he is not being his usual logical self. When we focus on the art of the works of art we study, we are naturally inclined to think we have come closer to sharing the study and writing desk of the author than the mere thematic critic who wants only to share the author's cultural times. We begin to glow with reflected cleverness, truly reflected because it is our own clever formulations of the author's strategies that we project onto the author and then bask in as they return to us. Aren't we clever to be in with the greatest artists of all time! When they tell us they were never so (consciously) clever, as they usually do when we try to talk to them about their art, we lash ourselves to the mast of our theories and refuse to hear.

The same confusion on the issue of intention, though ultimately more clarity than confusion, is present in the especially attractive and playful critical work of Roland Barthes.[362] If the theoretical critic thinks that his methodology is inevitable, a scientific realization of the nature of Literature that will then apply in all cases, he or she is also likely to assume that the author necessarily intends the system found in the work. Although Barthes memorably agreed with Michel Foucault's conclusion that the author, in modern critical thinking, is dead, he kept a living trace of author alive even in his later work, the work that has placed him historically on the edge between structuralism and deconstruction, *S/Z* and *The Pleasure of the Text.* He insists in both on constructing a binary, usually the readerly versus the writerly text, then only partly subverting it by making clear his preference for the writerly text, the text celebrated in the latter work as the place of fissures and rough breathings that offer not just ordinary pleasure of following the author but the extreme bliss, the reader's orgasm, of finding uncontrolled spaces in the text where the reader can really take his or her pleasure. In *S/Z,* where Barthes deliberately focuses on a perverse version of the classical, readerly text in Balzac's *Sarrasine,* he begins by proclaiming his, albeit somewhat reluctant, adherence to the notion that some texts are indeed readerly, produced within a closed system of meaning of their time. The "if" phrasing itself interestingly arrests the closure of his own assertion: "for if there are readerly texts, committed to the closure system of the West, produced according to the goals of this system, devoted to the law of the Signified, they must have a particular system of meaning."[363]

Barthes's critical *tour de force* in the structuralist analysis of *Sarrasine*—which comes to seem, after the first blush of joy in reading about joy in the later *The Pleasure of the Text* (1973 in French) to be in fact Barthes's most subversive work—is to use an apparently scientific approach to demonstrating the connotative workings of the text in a way that evidences the arbitrariness—that is mere topicality of thematics—of all critical activity. He offers himself as the reader of the connotations, the string of meanings that reinforce the representational denotation of the text as created by the author. The end of his sentence quoted above is "and that meaning is based on connotation." Barthes thus seems to be exploring all the meanings Balzac himself put into the text. Yet his model for meaning-making puts Barthes, the brilliant twentieth-century reader, clearly in control of the nineteenth-century author whose brilliance he appears to celebrate. This is most obvious in explications which become minor classics of critical speculation in themselves, bringing much more to Balzac's sensational little story than a mere exploration of the web of connotative meanings might allow. The stunning control however is in the methodology itself, which makes no attempt to ground itself either in an inductive analysis of what categories of art are used in the text or on a theoretical system defining necessary categories. Barthes notoriously creates his musical score of five codes (though by the time he scores it visually he has slipped in a sixth—antithesis—a bit mysteriously)[364] into which he sorts his various aperçus about language or actions of the text. Their global but entirely arbitrary nature—classifications of parts of a text which we might apply to any text yet which would admit easily to revision, division or addition—keeps him from the usual critical drive to rein in the text under universalizing interpretive topics of content or form. The free play of critical pleasure, often rising to critical bliss, is unimpeded by these loosest of all categories. Though so mysterious to a generation of his readers, they are merely Barthes's gesture toward system so that he could allow connotation to move freely into a space more like unlimited semiosis. Impossible to imagine that Balzac wrote with the categories in his mind as a way of organizing the suggestions of connotation; impossible to think that such loose categories could constrain us into a mode of seeing his text if he did. The heir to structuralist thinking thus in many ways detonates structuralism itself, mocking its pretense to science, in his best-known and perhaps greatest work.[365] The author's readerly text is run through his critical cuisinart and comes out riven and writerly—the chef-critic's text.

Deconstruction, heir to this freedom, can hardly reimpose binding categories of form on author and text.[366] So if Derrida becomes attracted to a way of thinking about interpretation, for instance to the metaphorical notion of a text as a crypt in which meaning lies dormant waiting for a special key to open it, as in Abraham and Torok's reading of the Wolf Man's meanings hidden in cross-language word play with his native Russian,[367] this does not produce a final interpretation which can be wished upon the author; rather it opens another route for the play of signification that can play, next day, in another way: it is one more example of how many ways we can find meaning in a text. We—and especially Derrida—often admit as much when we hit upon a meaning hidden in the etymology of a word. To set that additional, "root" meaning in play we need not prove the author worked by the lamp of an historical dictionary; nor does the attribution of a subversive etymological root necessarily cancel our sense of surface. Economic theory is no less about the large, anonymous outside forces of society when we have reminded ourselves that it possesses an encrypted reverse discourse of society as a home, a place of its root meaning of home economics. By contrast to the psychoanalysts whom he applauds, Derrida is not looking for the single meaning that can lead out of the crypt of possible meanings and into a psychic reification of the author underneath the text.

I have myself perhaps only effected a taxonomy in suggesting that critical observations about genre or structure of texts are no less arbitrarily chosen thematic subjects than observations about content and subject. And of course I cannot even begin to extend classifications into more detail. Any day we can invent new critical classes to register what we see in a work, the postmodern novel as the internet (matrix) novel, taking the traditional web of the social world of the novel into the websites and search engines of the new technology; this indeed may begin as a thematics of form, how the postmodern novel seems structured, and end as tomorrow's theme of content, the love on the internet novel, webs as lovenests. The first will hardly tempt us, when we study works written before the net opened up, to ascribe our clever structuring to the novelists; the second will tempt such attribution, especially where the case is obvious, that is a novel about late-night internet activity. And where the case is obvious it will not matter that reader and author seem on the same track. But as always I have to insist that just where it will matter, when the case is unclear, there will the old ghost raise its head out of the critical crypt of intentionality and try to tell its tale of authorial support for its invention: usually a gothic tale of monster critics trying to abduct the dear pure maid of author's intended meaning so they can set up their lurid whores of critic's thematics in her place. I advise the young critic coming of age not to worry about purity and genealogy—including its currently most fashionable incarnation as richly specific historical embedding in the works of New Historicism and Cultural Studies—in choosing an interpretation, but only to see which way of organizing the text is likely to bring mutual bliss in the encounter. If she chooses to write literary history, she will perform so much the better for having understood what in the text provokes her interest today.

I cannot be expected to anticipate all the ways in which special arguments will be made for our ability to read out of the text a clear author's intention. I trust that my method, to show that in any case other instances will always be found which will confound the apparent clarity of the attribution, will suggest how they would be answered. I will end this section, on the other side of the issue, reminding my reader how often a text is susceptible to an organizational pattern that suggests the very multiplicity of possible meanings. This too, my critic will quickly say, is only a pattern, and I agree; but it at least is turnabout fair play against the tendency of arguments for authorial control to adopt very simple examples to make their case. I will here not reach for the labyrinthine works of that old artificer Joyce or younger ones such as Borges, Pynchon, or Valenzuela. These are the usual cases, so famously complex that critics both admit that anything can be found in them and try to affirm that whatever is found was already anticipated by those super-persons of cunning authors.[368] Yes, it is clear to almost everyone that these authors intended to write complicated, perhaps often ambiguous or indeterminate texts; but that won't establish your particular reading of a text's ambiguity or indeterminacy as an authorized one, nor will it persuade another reader who sees a thread through the labyrinth that her unambiguous, determinate reading was prohibited by the author's will. And only a very impressionable student will be impressed by your approach to the complexity of these works if you walk around them talking about the author's love of complexity or about the modern/postmodern age as one of collective complexity. After the brave talk of author's biography (out of style) or parallel cultural moments (in style just now), there will still be the text to conquer.

Let me instead try some others, kinds of literature rather than specific works, inevitably producing multiple readings. Consider, as Karl Kroeber has, the traditional oral literature of storytelling. A conventional view might be that here, in the immediacy of oral communication, the relation of author (the fabricating teller) and audience (that crowd in the mead hall being made effortlessly to laugh, cry, or hold their breaths) would be secure. After all, isn't our idea of traditional societies that they do not have space for variation, so here, if anywhere, teller and audience are always already in synch? But in his interesting story of storytelling Karl Kroeber, drawing on anthropological archives, finds a very different scene of hearing. The story as the work that is always being retold and remade is a center of continuing difference, not static presence. As each teller remakes the tale, new events and contingencies are brought in forcing the audience to revaluate even the well known. With its stress on story events, storytelling provokes its audience, serving "as a continuing focus for the most probing moral questions we can devise, every retelling and rehearing being—and demanding from its audience a reevaluation."[369] So the Indian story "Why the Buzzard is Bald" confuses us because it is "constructed to arouse heterogeneous evaluations." It uses silences, repetitions, transformations in viewpoint, loose forms, segmentation, and inversion to permit polysemism, continuous reader "reshapings."[370] Kroeber finds the story aimed not at shaping a reader's interpretation but involved in a social negotiation to provoke thought, through provoking interpretation, on major, often moral, issues. Yes, you can say the storyteller thus provokes certain kinds of responses in shaping this open kind of art: but that fact about the author certainly won't tell us which interpretations the author wants us to choose. And we are of course free to not follow Kroeber's view of the story and read the text otherwise, for instance by a reductive subtext based on kinship patterns of the sort applied to this kind of text by structuralist anthropologist Claude Lévi-Strauss.

My second example of a kind of literature that seems most obviously to embody the author's intentions in the text is the one that perhaps comes most easily to mind: various versions of allegory.[371] We possess a kind of stereotype of this form, in which one can almost imagine no reason for the writing of the work. The writer and his audience are, in this model, bound so tightly by a convention which both accept, that the text merely enacts what is already totally known. We of course know such experiences from religious or secular rites: the wine stands for Christ's blood (in, say, the Anglican rite where it is most often taken as symbolic only), the wafer for his body; the symbols of the Eucharist become a little drama of our taking into ourselves the good of Christ. Where an allegorical story is written entirely within such a tradition, the historian can give us a pretty good idea of at least one set of intentions easily recognizable in the work.[372]

But here once again I must point out that arguments for intention generally fail because they are based on obvious cases and expect us naively to accept that all cases fit the models they create. They then sail into heavy seas the moment one posits more complicated, which is normally to say more usual, cases. Our culture is still close enough to, or still directly enough involved in, the symbolism of the Eucharist, to make the correspondences seem hard-wired to us. The same would be the case if we spoke of the Big Bear being led by the rock-and-roll music of Uncle Sam, here dressed like Billy Joel, into the sensuous world of capitalist gratification. Once we are outside of the immediate codes that exist almost as common sense in a culture at the moment of reading, problems arise. The fact that a code is being used becomes suddenly apparent rather than transparent. Soon arguments develop over the nature of the ancient code, which often appears more complicated than it first seems (are they contemplating Christ's goodness, his immortality, his saving of humankind, or his sacrifice, or what, when they think of the Eucharist? doubtless they disagree among themselves; does the Bear refer to just Russia? or to the former USSR? or to the Russian folk? is Uncle Sam the government? or the people? or just whom? and so on). And in the particular work, the elliptical external indication of the code's application, for instance Edmund Spenser's much contested Letter to Raleigh on the "generall end" of all the books of *The Faerie Queene*, usually seems to create diversity rather than end it.

In these harder cases the simple view is that the text will be self-defining; it will carry its key inside it like a little program that one can run with the text to render the correct correspondences. The reader "is not allowed to take up any attitude he chooses but is told by the author's devices of intentional control just how he shall interpret what is before him."[373] There are a number of problems with this view: first, we have to ask who shall interpret the author's interpretation? No explanation given in the text will not be subject to its own set of interpretive differences of opinion. Even when the author seems emphatically clear, telling us just what each character really represents, we are free to conclude that all this is done tongue in cheek or that it is in fact a part of the allegory, not its key. Or we may take the view that the author could not control, for any one of the many reasons given in my section on authors, the text he thought he had controlled. Although this argument may seem casuistic, as we can conceive of cases where the text seems to speak of a sincere author with a simple allegorical program, in fact the experience with interpretation is that disagreements normally do break out. And the reason for this opens to the larger difficulties in conceiving of a fully coded text.

An allegorical narrative or poem will necessarily be more than the code that it may carry within it; otherwise it would simply be that code. To the extent that other interests are included, it will be possible to find other subjects to foreground, which in turn may interfere with the code. "The allegorical representation leads toward a meaning," Paul de Man argues, "that diverges from the initial to the point of foreclosing its manifestation.... The two meanings fight each other with the blind power of stupidity."[374] We may begin accepting the view that Britomart, with a name like that, represents England; but as she also becomes not only a powerful but a vulnerable and lovely woman, her adventures can seem to cloud the allegorical application in a great number of its important details. It is typical of the arguments from the simplest case to argue that this is because Spenser writes during the breakdown of a full medieval system of correspondences, thus imagining a time of perfect cohesion between code and story. But wherever there is imaginative literature, as opposed to the pure codes of doctrinal writing, there will be an excess that feeds back different meanings into the code. In his careful rethinking of allegory as a process of reading, Sayre N. Greenfield in fact finds a broad dissonance or even deconstructive effect emerging from the independent life of the literary meaning to challenge the coherence of any posited allegorical level. In his elegant formulation, it is precisely the strangeness or incoherence of a literal account that drives readers to seek a different level of meaning. Allegorical readings try to constrain or recoup the diversity of the literal but generally cannot do a total job of it. Dissonance remains always potent to invite the next reader, or especially readers in a culture of different concerns and interests, to try another containing system. Whatever assurance all readers may have that they know what was intended, a student of allegorical reading finds that they keep disagreeing.[375] And because imaginative literature opens up non-doctrinal space, there will probably be disagreement even within the writer's time and culture—as there was in the medieval period despite our tendency to romanticize it into a time of a single, all-encompassing cosmic order—as to what interpretive moves are acceptable.[376]

The simplest case in allegory is not likely to arise in real interpretive arguments for a powerful reason: it is generally the kind of allegory that no critical readers take sufficient interest in to lead to debate. If, in our patronizing view of the past, we can imagine a simplest time filled with simplest readers, I think we will have trouble imagining a future time when anyone would care about the interpretive issues raised by arguments over intentionality when simple allegory will be of great interest. Even granting the cultural influence of New Critical valorization of ambiguity, it is striking that most modern enthusiasts for allegory—a rare enough breed—emphatically prefer texts where authors bring in lots of play outside of or around their more strictly coded areas. Rosamond Tuve tells us that "*good allegory never tells* in so many words" what its images mean; Isabel MacCaffrey holds that the best texts allow "the reader's resourcefulness its full scope"; and Walter Benjamin, whose lengthy study of German baroque drama qualifies him for this *galerie*, affirms "the basic characteristic of allegory is ambiguity, multiplicity of meaning."[377] Allegory is seen as valuable to the extent that the pattern of correspondences is either taken for granted—one of those simple systems that are merely a frame, not likely to be controversial in itself, for a richly elaborated tale—or made a subject of mystery around which the other aspects of the story or poem weave their major further complications. In the first case, we may all agree that we know what the author intended but also see nothing important here in interpretive debate: the important issues unfold in terms of the various subjects, formal or thematic, that we may wish to foreground in the embroidery of the tale. For instance, even Maureen Quilligan, who believes medieval allegorists can insert a controlling set of codes in the text, still sees the value of allegory not as a veiled truth, a puzzle to solve, but as a kind of reading that involves us in other activities, introspective self-analysis or ethical reflection.[378]

In the second case of allegory, where the codes are hard to ascertain or multiple (for instance the various forms of fourfold, multi-level interpretation where different kinds of allegory, in a broad rhetorical sense, were supposed to supplement the specific level designated as allegorical),[379] the reader will be especially tempted to try to identify his or her coded reading as the author's intended one; and we may well believe that the author did wish to make the reading a test in which true meanings are sorted out from others. Yet such an approach to authorship offers us precisely a text upon which we will not easily agree and in which various codings can reasonably be argued to be the author's. The attempt to read a text within fourfold (or other-fold) systems in fact offers not a closed system but a number of competing ways of organizing the material of the text that multiplies possibilities of variation and sites of ambiguation.[380] "The work's surplus of meaning," Paul Ricoeur observes, unhappily "negates all the reader's attempts to adhere to the text and to its instructions."[381] Once again we have a case where we can also conclude that the author intended all or none of the above (or only some of the above); but none of these conclusions about intention is more definitive than the individual allegorical readings.

I will look even more briefly at another major kind of literature, parody. Linda Hutcheon has assembled a very bright collection of examples from music, art, and photography, as well as literature.[382] And she makes an important and persuasive case for thinking about parody as comprising a variety of intertextual relations, serious echoes and resoundings, satirical reuses and spoofs, as well as burlesques. Her work thus opens possibilities for richer readings, especially of the wealth of twentieth-century literary interconnections. Texts talk through earlier texts not just to mock them, but often rather to pick up their qualities as ways of discussing contemporary issues.[383] She imposes a drag on this interesting sense of the varied play of parody, however, by adopting what she calls a pragmatic model of artistic communication. As in Wayne Booth's ideas of rhetoric, which she admires, a sender communicates an art work that intends certain effects/understanding in the hearer/viewer/reader. Our business as receivers is to infer from the text an encoding put thus by an encoder (a kind of implied encoder on the model of Booth's implied author).[384] Hers is a very clear statement of what I have been looking at generally in these subsections, the idea of intention found in the work itself. This model has its special attraction here because we tend to think of parodists, like joke tellers, as witty people who have a point to make which we hope to get, fear to miss. But if parody often seems especially to embody some highly conscious decisions of the artist (one does not put a moustache on the Mona Lisa without some premeditation), the fact of likely intentions does not change the position of the interpreter. We are faced with a work of art that may seem to us to be recasting work or works of the past.

Some issues may be obvious and unlikely to require interpretive argument—Joyce's *Ulysses* blatantly as well as most cleverly alludes to the classical epic, Eliot's *The Waste Land* restates, among so much, famous lines from *Antony and Cleopatra*. The rest, as anyone who has taught the poem to sophomores will agree, is not so easy. The way not to do it is to insist that all the texts registered in Eliot's notes register in each reading. Hutcheon is not encouraging us to go to the author to find what he *thinks* he encoded. There we would be in simple violation of Wimsatt and Beardsley as well as of Lawrence's injunction to trust the tale not the teller. Clever authors may think they have brought past works into their works but we may not find them there or may not find their presence important to our reading. The same should be said of our scholarly exercises in uncovering other texts we believe are echoed in the poem. Here we do not have to cite biography to make the comparative reading credible. It doesn't matter to our reading whether the author schemed to imitate a past writer with book open before her as she wrote or whether the cadence and some of the words stuck in her memory from a reading she wouldn't even be able to locate, perhaps from those broadly afloat in the culture (we don't have to know the location in Tennyson's *In Memoriam* to play at "'Tis better to have loved and loathed than never to have loathed at all").

The main point here is that all parodies are not equal. They are material in the text that we may make something out of in our reading. Just as Hutcheon releases us to think of parody as an effect that can be used in many ways, we may go further and think of it as a form to which "receivers" may respond in different ways, finding one effect important, another insignificant. We will not likely read *The Waste Land* without responding to its use of parody. But we will have to argue why some effects merit attention, some none. There is no authorized reading that will secure the right interpretation of what is a very volatile and productive relation between text and each so-called target text. Nor is there any particular merit in the philology of accumulating lists of possible targets.[385] Commenting on *The Waste Land*, Hutcheon suggests that just such philological work is the lesson to be inferred from Eliot's parody: The poet asks us ("trusts" us) to have the "willingness to work towards achieving such breadth and depth of culture as to make comprehension of the text possible."[386] This, I may remark, is certainly the way some of my students have responded to those notorious notes, as a very steep *gradus ad Parnassum* or *ad culturam*; and those of a masochist inclination have even kept at it for a while. It happens not to suit me, as I take *The Waste Land* as a poem that takes seriously personal and cultural dissociation and uprootedness, that is, it is a cry of pain not a plan for restoring monarchy, Elizabethan culture, and the rest. But of course I will have to argue that the blatant echo of Enobarbus's description of Cleopatra in the poem in a section evincing satirical repugnance for the *grandes dames* of Eliot's contemporary post-feminist England is not there to teach us to start brushing up our Shakespeare (now), but to suggest the felt sense of lost female magnificence in a merely grandiloquent world of female fashionableness—set in a disturbed homosocial, homophobic, gynophobic poetic vision.

Hutcheon goes on to arm Edward Said's reflections on the sitedness of works of literature in their origin of time and place—"historical, social, and ideological context."[387] But parody fits very poorly this extension of intentional thinking to the context of a work's appearance. Parody is necessarily about the relation between texts of different times: It tells us, as Hutcheon herself so well shows, how a work lives beyond its time and accrues meaning in its new contexts. A text exists as a fluidity of its incorporation (what for a while was called an intertext) brought to life, if at all, in present readers (reading Edward Said reading Orientalists reading Middle Eastern texts). Parodies are always floating between past and future, sometimes, as when there is parody of a much-parodied text such as Horace's "beatus ille," the tongue-in-cheek Second Epode in praise of country life—by a city slicker, allowing the reader to pull together texts from many times (Horace, Dryden, and looser romantic echoes such as those by Coleridge in "Frost at Midnight"). Hutcheon herself names this, with some apology, "trans-contextualizing." But we need to mark that "trans," as in the carrying over of metaphor, leaves the relations between contexts unstable and subject to reader interpretation.[388] Of course, if the reader chooses to see the parody effect as about difference of context, as comments on two or more ages, the contexts themselves will not exist objectively as a given to the interpretation but as something to be worked up in the process of interpretation. Inevitably, if we take *The Waste Land* to be contrasting the Elizabethan age to that of the 1920s, we will tend to project our ideas of both contexts into our reading. But interpretation of parody need not be an allegory of contexts of text and target text(s). Take Pound's allusion in "Mauberley" to Ovid's account of a hunting dog turned into stone along with its enemy: "Vacuos exercet in aera morsus" (Pound's Latin epigram): "Mouths biting empty air, / the still stone dogs, / Caught in metamorphosis, were / Left him as epilogues." I read this not as about the Augustan age and the modern but as extension and realization of Mauberley's "anaesthesis," the progressive conversion of his amorous and artistic aspirations into impercipient gorgonization.

"Is parody in the eye of the beholder?" Hutcheon asks at one point in her discussion[389] only to give a hasty no and present her theory of encoding. "Where else could it be?" I must respond. Its power and fascination is especially that it teases and provokes us to very decisive readerly action. First, to connect a work before us to whatever we can: to Leonardo's Mona Lisa, of course, but also to graffiti everywere with moustaches added, so we have a parody of street urchin burlesques, or perhaps to that large literature, focused on Pater's description, of Lisa as the ultimate and universal feminine, here so easily regendered, or to the ambivalent world, transgendered rather than trans-contextualized, of circus bearded ladies. But the real work of "reading"

Duchamps's painting begins when we ask what to make of it. Is it merely a modernist laugh at the mythic accretions of a great painting into an icon of conservative artistic (and gender) culture? Is it a modernist masculinist attack on the power of that eternal female nature, older than rocks or vampires? Is it a queer reading of that so iconic female, explaining its mystery as that of repressed sexual ambivalence? As always with parody, the work of interpretation is double, not just what we decide the new work is saying through the old but also what the old master itself was saying—for instance about sex and ambivalence. Hardly an exhaustive list but enough to suggest how much is left up to the reader, how little parody actually works as a puppet show in which the creator jerks us smartly around.[390]

The particular kinds of literature in which the author would seem to intend some specific and palpable operation on the reader are sufficiently legion that I could go on and on cutting off Hydra heads without exhausting the monster of sloppy thinking, Intention (why trot out that old chestnut Hydra here? because I intend my allegory of the Hydra to work on you reader, letting you imagine any number of further qualities of snake-monster Intention being slain here, as best he can, by Professor Hercules). Let me take as the final example the hard one you have no doubt anticipated, special friend of the structuralist codes as well, the mystery. When Hercule (Poirot here, not Maynard) shows poor Hastings, once again, alas, that he has been following the wrong set of leads all along, most of us, unless we are true buffs, must identify with that loveable but none too clever pragmatist: we too have followed the clues laid down to mislead the unwary Englishman and have missed the other pattern hidden more deeply in the carpet of Agatha Christie's imagination, a pattern open only to the genius of Poirot himself. The text of course definitively declares our Hast(y)ings's solution to the events incorrect. Now how will Houdini Maynard get himself out of this water chamber of obvious intentionality, one that would seem to apply to adventure stories and so many other sub-genres based on surprise and conclusive plots? The answer (here slipping off those wet handcuffs, reversing body position, and surfacing refreshed from the tank) is similar to that with simple allegory. We do not—marvel at my easy solution—doubt the tale has been solved by the implied author who made the plot clearly and definitively. If the route seemed hard when Hastings, the Chief Inspector, and we tried to work it out on our own, it has now become crystal clear, a rational explanation in expository Belgian English prose and, usually, a corroborating event (the murderer tries to exit and is detained by a waiting bobby). We have no more need to refer our conclusion to an authorial intention than we do when we conclude that a loaded gun, aimed at a victim's head and fired, has caused a murder. These are facts of the text not likely to produce arguments in which intention is appealed to.

Those who don't like mystery stories will remind us indeed of how really mindless this process of solution is, a kind of operation like a computer game in which the computer is always correct in the end—an "automatized"—some might say lobotomized—text.[391] Those who adore Poirot, in David Suchet's version or in text, will defend it by saying that clearly intended conundrum is not what makes this interesting art: it is a thousand things about that strange little man, how he plays against our Hastings or our dogged, down-in-the-mouth, Chief Inspector, about the fast art deco world he suits so ill, about the perspective on English conventionality allowed by the Enlightened vision of a man from a land where they order these things (greed and passion) better.[392] In other words, we will find as many different patterns, besides the one that we may be willing to abandon in face of the reason, as you English call it, and the facts. As in simpler allegory, the central business, on which we are not likely to need to speak of intentionality because the text claims such total agreement among all potential readers, is a useful structure to allow the better reader to ignore the aims of the better writer and, instead, enjoy playing in his or her own preferred way with the text.[393]

After writing this section I found a mystery writer, Laurie R. King, had put her intentions (yes intentions, I never said we couldn't learn from writers; I always learn a great deal from their statements of intention, which give me information and provide possible interpretive moves) more clearly than I could: "So why a mystery novel? Because it is a strong form that allows me to do what I wish with it. I love the genre, with its rigid structure and its immense freedom. On its bones I can hang a story about things that matter, about death and pain and the dark side of the human mind, about fear and triumph and joy and the price we pay for justice, about the full gamut of human response."[394] Wherever there is interest that makes the text worthy of literary discussion, potentially open to literary debate, there will be the same kinds of varied possible foregroundings that are found in any other kind of literature.

XVII. INTERPRETATION: SOME MORE PRAGMATIC ARGUMENTS

> The reader takes neither the position of the author nor an author's position. He invents in texts something different from what they "intended." He detaches them from their (lost or accessory) origin.
>
> Michel de Certeau, *The Practice of Everyday Life*.

As I pile them up, I am becoming so persuaded by my own arguments in this matter of intention, where I began by admitting that it was an issue that would always provoke new partisans and new debates, that I confess I am becoming nervous. I am especially coming to believe that interpretation has a rather arbitrary quality to it: that it is a matter of finding the pattern, providing the foregrounding, as I have argued above, that will suffice. But suffice for what? For whatever we have in mind proving at the time. Now this sounds so much like the kind of obscurantist argument, so often tarred with the general brush of the popular imagined monster deconstruction, that I have to ask, do I really mean it? I remind you and me that I do not mean that all interpretations are equally persuasive; some seem to marshal more detail of evidence from the text and do so in more exciting ways that seem to be discovering more and more, opening up new vistas to us also, as they go along; and these we, as editors or readers for journals, are happy to recommend for publication. Others seem poorly argued, by which we usually mean they have not a lot of interesting evidence from the text and they do not seem, as we say, to be going anywhere; and they don't. But I have to be candid and say that there are other kinds of added values at work. The interpretation that repeats what we already know about a work but does so in an elegant and thorough way may seem impressive just because we so fully agree with it already: what oft was already thought by us but now seems so very well expressed. Or there may be the interpretation that seems to open up new vistas just because it does: it builds upon a new way of organizing experience or form and shows us a received text in this new foregrounding light; and we are dazzled, at least until that mode of thinking, Freudian reading, 1930s old Marxist reading, old Leninist imperialist reading becomes passé—for a while—and something new, Lacanian reading, new Marxist Jamesonian, new the Empire strikes back to the metropolitan center seems to open up new vistas by foregrounding other parts of the text. And our friends, the currently still fashionable social constructionists, will not be slow to remind us that what seems new and fashionable is just that, views being adapted as the latest thing from Paris because the entire culture is already committed to that fashion system.

But I guess I do mean that interpretations are in one sense all the same, if not of equal value. That is they are, to return once again to that phrase—a dirty one to the Structuralists—mere taxonomies. There, I have dared to say it, as I realize I have been saying this all along. They are mere taxonomies, ways of ordering what is seen (from the Greek for arrangement, order). And what is not? Who isn't making mere taxonomies these days? I will not carry this over where it gets difficult, into the sciences, but merely note that thinkers on even scientific organizing schemes have often had to acknowledge that theories are not really proved because they are in accord with the nature of things, let us say the Intentions of the Great Maker, but because they are more concise, more elegant, or have greater heuristic value. The Ptolemaic system goes out,

Copernicus comes in, not because the epicycles of the former could not offer an adequate account of the data being interpreted—roughly speaking, the scientist's text—but because the new system was more economical and more elegant, at least in that time period of scientific interpretation.[395] Certainly in the area of artistic interpretation, I have not seen the evidence that would allow any interpretive system to claim better status than the universal and humble one of a mere taxonomy, merely a taxonomy but someone's nonetheless well-loved brain child (or pledge of allegiance to a favorite cause), dear as sin to the interpreter, no less dear in that in structure it is no different from ugly and unmodish interpretations that are shunned like death. It too is an intellectual creation, a mere ordering by foregrounding of some thematic or formal quality or qualities into some system, some schema (plural schemata), some framing device, some taxonomy.[396]

Critic S (for Special) wishes not to fall into this taxonomy of interpretation as mere taxonomies and does so by seeking to claim author's warrant for his or her taxonomy: these, he/she asserts, are the matters the author wished to stress in these orderings. The pragmatic argument against his or her exit from the circle is another argument that has been universally seen as something of a permanent scandal, normally by those who wish to establish what cannot, really by definition, be established. Here let me return to my opening comparison of the quest for interpretive truth with that for religious truth. The believer regularly declares scandalous the argument that most of the human race disagrees with the belief that he or she holds most dear. What does God care for pollsters or opinions of the majority? Yet that piece of simplistic enlightenment refuses to go away: if the religion of one's choice is such a clear truth, such a central truth, why isn't it obvious to others too? The answers are legion, often of the sort that declares others unfit by nature, or God's choice, or their sin, to attain the truth that is so obvious to the believer. But the fact of continuing difference remains, to the great number of quiet agnostics, professed or merely passively unimpressed by arguments of the religious, an impressive pragmatic reason for risking burning in one or another hell by not enrolling in one or another faith. It is the argument most scorned by the faithful, most beloved of the village atheist, idiot, or wise one, because it is both easy and obvious and also hard to bury. It keeps coming up out of the ground of faith wherever that is found.

The same scandalous pragmatic argument says that we in fact do not agree about interpretation, even if we subscribe to the (false, I believe) view that the author's intention would carry special weight. Behold, on any important debated matter we disagree. We keep changing the systems of ordering that we ascribe to the author (was Browning a new Christian seer? a happy realist untroubled by modern anxieties? a proto-modernist lost in the maze of formal structures—hang it all, there can be only one *Sordello,* says Pound—a Protestant democrat? an Hegelian self-master of endless new becomings? Was T.S. Eliot part of the lost—Waste Land—generation? a bulwark of conservative sanity against the vulgar modern tide? a master of concise, honest language? a Fascist, racist, sexist, anti-multicultural bore?). And we keep seeing different points of focus in the works, all intended by the author. Hang it all, we now have to *read* that masterwork *Sordello* as we once had to put down our *Areopagitica* and read *De Doctrina Christiana*; and my generation will have trouble getting the *Four Quartets* out of its ears, before those ears become dust in the rose garden, as the masterwork during our years of education, though it has now fallen, or is certainly toppling from its pedestal. A prior generation who read D.H. Lawrence fervently as the apostle of heterosex would be amazed to find the main action recently has been in exploring his homosexuality and his response to being cuckolded. Heraclitus, another scandalous arguer of the obvious, was right: all things change and this certainly included those rock-solid views of what the author really intended. If we have disagreed, and we do disagree, we can only anticipate that we will disagree in the future, as well. What is certain is that new, inventive interpretations that effectively challenge the old in ways you could not anticipate will keep arising.[397] You may of course hold to your faith, Critic S; but forgive us poor critical agnostics for not accepting your argument from privilege. If it doesn't persuade, or if it will not do so for any great length of time, then it lacks something as argument. It may or may not possess interest or eloquence; these will give it its real merit as it merits. But you can't make us believe it a better interpretation by claiming authority; we know it will not persuade the many and this in turn becomes a reason, despite the force of your claim when we first confront it, with all its new research and aura of expert witness, why we will not let ourselves be persuaded either. When you go on jury duty the lawyers sort out the jurors by asking, "You will hear testimony from expert witnesses who are called in because they have special knowledge of the matter at hand. Does this mean that you necessarily believe them?" The right answer, which seems not so hard for the juror off the street, is of course no; you have to see whether you are persuaded by what they say.

XVIII. YOU CAN'T PROPERLY GET THERE FROM HERE: BABES IN THE WOODS OF HISTORICITY

> We are incapable of knowing *Hamlet* exactly as Shakespeare knew it or exactly as other readers have known or will know it another time.
>
> Christine Brooke-Rose, "The Readerhood of Man."

> The words of a dead man
> Are modified in the guts of the living.
>
> W.H. Auden, "In Memory of W.B. Yeats"

My reader will note the hole I leave open immediately above: what if we *are* persuaded by the expert witness? doesn't this allow us, this once, to declare the agnostics silly and accept the true faith with an easy mind? And here, I am sorry to say, is where I must bring in another argument generally considered scandalous and unfair by the faithful of intentional interpretation: you can't get there from here. By which I mean the old chestnut, that even if you believe in author's intention as a special mode of knowledge, one and simple, which it should be clear I do not, it is, for practical reasons, impossible to have certainty of what it is. My discussion here of the impracticality of obtaining certainty on issues of interpretation from historical research will proceed mainly on the level of skeptical hermeneutics, what degree of privilege knowing allows. I don't rehearse here but should note the simpler practical issues I discussed above (II.ii). If we really wish to know what a writer intended in a moment of writing, we would have not only to know facts of the historical context but to be able to do what God or stream-of-consciousness novelists may, but biographers only wish they could: peep into the inner mental and emotional states of their subjects during specific moments of writing.[398] Biographers (I am one, reader, and know of what I speak) greatly envy the license of both God and novelists and sometimes do pretend to know what their subject was thinking as she was writing *To the Lighthouse*. They often signal their lapses into novelist imagination by questions: "Did she, as she sat in her study musing, recall her father's incessant pacing to and fro outside the window of their summer cottage in St. Ives reciting 'Some one had blundered.'" Often stolen from the work, such moments of course can never provide a solid wall on which to nail up intentional readings.

Despite such manifest impracticalities, people still have faith that biography or history are more solid than interpretation. A donor, that rare species, actually walked into our department some years ago and offered to donate his stepfather's hard-earned money for the rational study of literature, by which he meant the study of biography and source studies. He wished above all things to counter the tendencies all around to what he called trendy criticism and to restore literary study by resting it on the rock-solid foundation of facts from biography and source studies. No one in our Department wished to look a gift horse in the mouth nor did anyone deny the interest and value of studying biography and source studies; and indeed, despite an article in the *New York Times* to the contrary, we faithfully used his donation to publish such a journal with the title, of course, *Biography and Source Studies*.[399] But his argument, if not his credit rating, seemed shaky. This was clear enough in his own work for a PhD (for this donor was in fact, it turned out, one of us), which had been a study into certain possible sources for Conrad's Kurtz. Interesting, plausible, as facts in the large historical record about the writing of *Heart of Darkness*; but to my mind all wrong in the implication that this kind of biographical fact, if accepted as a fact, could offer a different kind of truth about the work than that promoted by "trendy criticism." The problem is that facts don't say anything in particular about the work until we put some kind of spin on them. What does it say about Conrad's great work to say that he probably read about certain German explorers in Africa? It doesn't even say Kurtz was German, despite his name, for we don't dispute that he is from some place rather like Belgium.

What we find is that even biography falls into territory our donor would stigmatize as trendy—indeed, that was where as a donor he came closest to wishing to prescribe what we could not accept: some criteria for distinguishing trendy goats from hard-fact sheep. For in truth all biography is trendy once it seeks to probe an author's intention. It requires interpretation of the facts to create a story that can be used to create an author with an intention. Similarly, in the world of historical interpretation, even our intentionalists cannot find a privileged interpretation; there are no authoritative interpretations of history, only histories by those claiming to be authorities. One exception proves this rule. This is the one authority ever claimed in history, that Higher One with a Higher Intention mentioned above, who authorizes providential history and allows the historian-prophet the same wide sweep of what is relevant and how it should be organized as the intentionalist literary critic. (It would open up a space of repeating regression here to challenge this view of history by questioning the grounds of the prophets' knowledge of Higher Intention; suffice it to say that it has been much challenged with most of the same arguments I am in the process of using here and much defended by many of the arguments I am countering here.)

For normal human interpreters there is an obvious circularity which nonetheless traps a great number of them in practice. They have a view of the work already, otherwise they would hardly be moved to seek more hard facts completing a picture of the author's intentions. They then use this view, without consciously realizing what they are doing, to shape and organize the materials of history that they confront in such a way that, prophets too, they naturally confirm their prophecies. Unfortunately the rest of us are not likely to be impressed by this logic, except perhaps by the confidence with which they assert it. If you believe that Conrad's work shares your own conservative faith in hard facts, you may, for example, create a view of Kurtz based on your historical facts about possible sources, which will insist on

Conrad's intention to imitate historical fact. But what if, as Achebe may believe,[400] Conrad was really intending, at some less than fully conscious level, to tell the tale of his and Western racism, even in its liberal form, and hard facts are hardly to the point?—or maybe they may even be made to serve his point: for instance that the source for Kurtz, German that he was, can be seen to embody this racism of the liberal West.

Not wise to argue with a donor, as our Development people warn us. The point here is that we never confront the hard facts of history without the mediation of some way of organizing them, some historical taxonomy if you will. Only a mad deconstructionist—the opposite to a mad believer in hard facts—would argue that there are no such things as hard facts, though trendy criticism is daily said to do just this.[401] What is argued is that the facts become a text, a set of things which we recover and consider as we do a text, and that there is no way of dealing with them in a way that would interest those interested in author's intention without interpreting them. We, not author or Creator, must organize and give meaning. The trendy, dangerous, scandalous perhaps, but inevitable conclusion is that readings of the author's life (in old biographical criticism) or of the historical context (in old historical terms), or of the texts/discourse of the age (in trendy New Historical criticism) can have no more—indeed no different—grounds for obtaining our assent than readings of the author's work. In both cases we organize the material as we necessarily or perversely wish to see it.[402]

There is a further kicker to the problems of the historian or broad-viewing biographer here: complex as any text of ours may be, any Browning's *Sordello* or Pound's *Cantos*, the text of history (as both those authors' epics of history knew, though Pound sometimes forgot what he knew) is much more complex. So rather than a clarifying and comforting view of some solid facts from the historian with which to face the confusion of interpretation of the literary work, we are faced with some outrageously broad summaries of an incredible amount of textual material. Though some historians have been slow to accept their responsibility here, the historian is even more dependent on her own contemporary ways of seeing and thinking for the way in which she organizes the "factual" materials.[403] Though we may think we can, through much study of a person or a period, come to know our subject as it knew itself, as we may think by much reading of an author we may come to know an author's intention, we are never able to put down the lenses of our own time through which we both select and organize those treacherous "facts" of the past. Douglas Bush may thank heaven, at the end of his fine history of seventeenth-century literature, that he was able to live a great deal of his own life, in that disastrous twentieth century, in the other world of his subject (another disastrous century?); but if he might dwell among the remnants and facts of the period, he could not in fact cease to approach it from his particular view of our age, that, all his students knew, of a convinced Christian Humanist with alliances not only to Irving Babbitt but also to Christian realists of his own century, such as Reinhold Niebuhr, intent in fact on facing the evils of the century from a Christian viewpoint. Consequently, though not without a fine sense of the play of difference on the issues embraced in this apparently simple taxonomic binary—Christian humanists and their enemies—and not without a wry sense of humor that included self-consciousness of his own organizing approach, the texts of the age were historically, and thus necessarily partially, read.

Easy to see the organizing, and limiting, principles of the old historians; indeed they often saw a battle for point of view as part of their aim, whether to celebrate an age when they believed their Christian values were still seriously in play or to find, as Whigs of democracy had, the seeds of a coming time. From a very different standpoint than Christian Humanism, Walter Benjamin formed his classic statement of the way in which present concerns control the past we possess: "every image of the past that is not recognized by the present as one of its concerns threatens to disappear irretrievably."[404] Our Newer Historians, despite regular homages to Benjamin, may more easily forget the necessary subjectivity of their reading of history as they work so close to the texts themselves that they may sometimes imagine they are making the age speak for itself rather than selecting what their approach to the texts leads them to.[405] In an interesting essay reacting to reader-response thinking as based on a system of thought that keeps alive the belief in the centering Cartesian subjectivity of the bourgeois individual, Walter Benn Michaels makes the since then well-worn turn of declaring the individual as merely a text among the others of history; we as interpreters cannot choose the kind of interpretation we do or, at the best, "the most we can say is that we can choose our interpretations but we can't choose our range of choices."[406] Such a critique would seem to inspire a career in which interpretation, and perhaps theory itself, is seen as a mere curiosity, a derivative of history, and in which the turn to history seems inevitable. But this is to miss the lesson in such a view for the historian, whose interpretations of history are no less constrained by his or her historical embedding. And this means that those New Historical projects, which seem to leave subjective interpretations far behind, are anything but objective readings from the text of the age being studied to the text of the age doing the interpretation. They too are formed in the subjectivity of our age (though I would continue to give more play to the subjectivity or eccentricity of the individual in the age than Michaels does) and motivated and limited by the "range of choices" of the age[407]—an issue much explored in post nineteenth-century hermeneutic theory, where arguments about historical sitedness and intention have been as prominent as they were in the earlier hermeneutics, though now these are generally disavowed.[408]

To take one obvious example among many, it hardly seems surprising that so much New Historical work has been spotlighting the intersections between European cultures and "other" cultures, European worlds and newer and older worlds elsewhere, whether in the studies of Renaissance awareness of the extra-European world or the nineteenth- and twentieth-century postcolonial or Orientalist/Occidentalist studies. In our multicultural, ever more communicating world, these are of course trendy themes—taxonomies—of our common subjectivity, and we naturally give them more space in our historical stories than the quest for religious peace or the history of parliamentary institutions—subjects that tremendously excited students of history in other ages. In all cases, the fundamental operation at work is the hermeneutic circle, or a major portion of it: we start with an hypothesis about the work in order to make an interpretation.[409] If we begin by deciding, with de Man or the New Critics, that a work is self-reflexive, then we will read it in a way that stresses its non-pragmatic, non-referential functions. If we begin by seeing it as a product of/comment on the gold standard (Walter Benn Michaels) or on the development of limited liability (Mary Poovey on *Our Mutual Friend*), then we will necessarily find a web of gold or anxiety over limited liability in the text. Stanley Fish, a hermeneuticist whose theories of communities of interpretation influenced the new turn to history in someone like Michaels, himself insists that interpretation from the historian's point of view is taking place in this New Historicist work: "In the end you cannot 'defy categorization,' you can only categorize in a different way."[410]

The use of biography or history to define the author's intention or, to put it in more complicated New Historicist terms, to uncover a flow of discourse in which the apparent subjectivity of the author can be located and given an implicit intentionality, makes an additional demand on the interpreter's contemporary theoretical self-definition: in order to go from factual information and its interpretation in the life and/or times of the author to definition of intention, one must import some system for understanding the subjectivity of the individual who writes. If the author is declared dead, he or she is still not without a pen or computer and there must be some way of explaining how the writing took place. In defining the difference between definitions of subjectivity in old historical work and the new, one can say that in the former there is some assumption that the author, like the critic, held positions which he or she attempted to maintain as truths. In the latter, as we have become used to it in Foucauldian work, there is more a sense of a subjectivity being shaped in a flow of discourse in which it participates but which it does not really control.[411] In order to make my arguments earlier about the nature of the author's intention I had to try to spell out somewhat my own premises about the nature of the author, in which I was rather between Cartesian and post-Cartesian assumptions about individual subjectivity, with a large additional concern with the multiplicity and psychologically layered nature of subjectivity.[412] In the end, all specific interpretations of intention will similarly depend on some notion of how human nature works—even if the mere idea of "human nature" seems anathema to you as a form of essentialism: in that case that is your anti-humanist view of human nature.

If you believe that a set of ideas on improving farming found in your research in a great heap of dusty county-seat newspapers of a certain time and also in handbooks written for the up-to-date farmer are likely to have molded the thinking of anyone of that time, you will be able to ascribe an intention to, say, the Talbothays farm section of *Tess of the d'Urbervilles* that allows you to assert your interpretation as a privileged one. (If you think this and don't imagine that the individual might have a different view from reading his Bible on the harvest, or Vergil's *Georgics*, or hearing what his dad told him in the fields, or from mere unexplained crazy cantankerousness—he always was that way and will always be that way—then you are likely to be a New Historicist.) In this case you aren't showing much respect for the individual genius of the author and his rights, but you are creating a web of intention that gives you special rights as an historical interpreter. But my point is only that you should grant that the whole thing depends on your particular view of the relation of the individual to ideas of a time; you should also grant that this view is probably, to turn your own system back on you, related to recent reading you have been doing on this topic, which very likely includes views of "Tintern Abbey" as really intended to hide the fact of homeless people existing in the wreck. Despite your wish to create an historical system that guarantees the rightness of your interpretation, as that which the author had to believe, you have actually grounded the entire great machinery, milking and distribution systems and all, on a mere act of interpretation—in the hopper for argument along with all the rest. Perhaps you thought you were evading the siren call of theory for unmetaphysical, factual certainty; in fact, you have tried to make metaphysics of your moment of reception of history.[413]

If, on the other hand, as a free thinker and founding member of the atheists' club you have determined from certain statements in his letters that Hardy was a fellow soul (despite other places where he proclaims he is only a poor agnostic treated as if a hardened atheist, like yourself), you may wish to see the Talbothays section as a deliberate statement, consciously arrived at, of the natural way of human life, which errs when, angel-like (and like Hardy's character Angel), it tries, of course ineffectually, to be better than its natural self; and you will likely foreground the deliberate naturalism of Hardy's treatment.

Fine. But when you argue with your New Historicist colleague, who sees the entire section as a statement of the changing conceptions of the business and technology of milk farming and its distribution, then coming under increasing rationalization and national surveillance during this transitional period in farm discourse, you will find that your premises about the force of individual reason have been themselves instrumental in leading you to your conclusions about Hardy's conscious intentions. What you wanted to see as a clear and simple case of he believed and he wrote—and you who know what he believed, know what he wrote about—begins to look more complicated, a case of your interpreting Hardy's human nature in much the same way you would wish to interpret his life. And well you may if you wish; but don't think I, mere harmless agnostic, will be impressed, above the quality of your argument itself, by appeals to author's clear and rational intention. I won't be.

The far reach of this discussion is that one cannot theoretically distinguish a reading of a work based on our own interests and discourses of today from a reading of a work based on careful historical work, including work on the text's initial reception;[414] both are readings from today, one of one text of the older period, the other of many texts, biographical and/or historical, of the older period. This again, I need to repeat, is not to deny the use of philological work, even if it is philology done from a contemporary point of view, and all kinds of useful diggings, which I enjoy doing and enjoy reading about. Historical work, as we have just affirmed, offers fertile ideas for interpretation, a way of generating interpretations out of interrogations of the author's immediate context, his or her age, or preceding age or ages. It may also be itself the goal: to place a work in relation to its age, the result of many, many interpretive decisions; or the work as interpreted by the historian may play a subordinate, piece-of-the-puzzle part in a broad historical account, diachronic or synchronic in plot. In all these historical enterprises, interpretation is a prerequisite to historical assertion even if it, in turn, may offer schemes to the interpreter. The intentionalist who really enters the fun house of history will come to realize that there is not *an* historical understanding of the author and her times but various interpretations which themselves change with changing present times. It is not that we cannot know the past—our good research can turn up endless points of information and these can sometimes be helpful in clarifying the meaning of a word or providing information about an historical or social reference. Anti-intentionalists don't deliberately ignore such clarifications. The problem in broader interpretation is rather that there is no end to knowing: we produce a hopelessly full screen of possible historical understandings, all arguable, none canonical.[415]

But I would go farther out on a limb here, having gone so far, and try to maintain that in practice the usual distinction drawn between historically specific interpretations and so-called modern, newfangled ones cannot be upheld.[416] Let me begin here with a simple example so we will not become tired together thrashing out what I don't mean. In my youth I saw, I think it was at the Old Vic when it was still doing service as national theater location, a version of *As You Like It* in a form that many did not like: the majestic solitudes of the forest of Arden were invaded by heavy characters, the rockers of that British time of rockers and mods (the Beatles being the apogee of the latter) on Harleys. I didn't mind; you may. It obviously hasn't become a classic performance. The first point is I don't wish to argue that such a modernizing interpretation was not anachronistic; by the banks of the Avon, when it ran deep and clear in Sweet William's time there were assuredly no chromy bikes. I even think the director must have known this. But on the other hand the values the director wished, I guess, to bring on the stage (who am I to assume I know what the director intended?) by using the modern symbolism of the rocker and his bike are hardly alien to Shakespeare's world: *Romeo and Juliet* shows us the potential violence he found lurking in hostile young spirits in his day, as it lurked in west side stories of all sorts in ours.

My main point is—surprise—a rather classic one: while the moderns may keep introducing new technology and new terms which will appear as local anachronisms in their interpretations of works, the larger foregroundings in interpretation will not show anything really new under the sun.[417] The former need hardly concern us as the critic who does not limit himself to a search for author's intention will be happy to back away from interpreting plastic, in Akenside's "plastic arm" (dating from 1744) as about synthetic polymer; the anti-intentionalist is not ignorant of word shifts and the history of technology, though she may also point out that our use of the term unavoidably adds specificity and a resonance in our reading to the vaguer eighteenth-century term.[418] The more profoundly scandalous point, scandalous to those who traffic in the trendy as much as to those who try to keep spaces of authorial intention safe from the latest intellectual commodities, goes to the heart of most debates on intention. For Hirsch's famous distinction between meaning and significance has been a fundamental binary that maintains many of the major rifts between traditional scholars and interpreters, or between New Historicists and deconstructionists, and most especially between mainstream literary studies and special areas of interpretation, such as Marxist or Freudian approaches.[419] As I observed above, the typical move of the historically centered critic is to damn with faint praise; over there, outside the privileged circle of intentionalist work, there are interesting purveyors of significances of all sorts, crying "come buy, come buy," and their wares are indeed interesting (with a yawn), versions of trendy and newfangled approaches and theories that, bless us, show how busy the modern mind is. Let them enjoy themselves, out there where we know what they are not, not meanings intended by the author or his or her time. On the other side there has often been equal contentment with this division. We are the exciting intellectuals, who put everything we see in relation to the most exciting ideas of our own time; our interpretation of play or novel makes it for our time, gives it relevance and intellectual force that the work itself cannot expect to have; after all, a fine writer, but from a dark, interestingly dark (here a yawn) period.

The assumption on both sides is that if the author were alive he would not recognize the interpretation that gets classified as significance rather than (author's) meaning (too crazy modern, says one group; too much a man—or woman—of the time, says the other). Both the traditional and the modern commentator sponsor a stultifying reduction of a person in an age to a concept of the typical—and typically very limited—rather than maverick, unusual, dare I say original.[420] More important here, I think both groups overrate the technical detail and underrate the universality of the discourses of the new—if I may so lump all those new ways of thinking that have been applied to literature, a great many when we look at them rather falling under the old two-master-thinkers-of-the-nineteenth-century-in-the-twentieth-century categories: the big ideas are not that hard to identify, and both Freud and Marx saw their work in a continuum of earlier thinking.[421] Having wrestled with his lectures, I am not one to say that Lacan, or Macherey or Jameson for that matter, are sweet Arnoldian humanists who purge their literary work of technicalities that no earlier writer would have imagined as he or she sat writing *Hamlet* or *Wuthering Heights*. But to the extent that these seemingly modern and alien ways of thinking are used to open up interpretations of texts from earlier periods, they are not converting the text into a personal code for their technical positions but finding in the text orderings that fit their larger paradigms. As such, and if well argued, they could be understood by writers of any time, even if the writer would also find the groupings and foregroundings rather uninteresting or implausible. New psychological readings don't depend on new psyches, much as Freud may have stressed the neuroses of his time and a more contemporary psychoanalytic critic may emphasize our narcissistic problems. It is still possible that Hamlet, even then, loved his mother not wisely and too well. Marxist readings are often explicitly devoted to finding what the text importantly doesn't acknowledge, for instance and famously the laborers at Penshurst; but this is no less a reading of what the text might really mean; doesn't New Historicism do the same, provide additional relevant insight in calling attention to the homeless people in the ruins of Tintern Abbey? Marxism or New Historicism did not discover something new, never seen before, in laboring people and poverty. Who ever, except a March Mad freshman or mad in all winds professor, tries true anachronism—Hamlet was able to plan his actions by internet connections with the ghost of his father; Ben Jonson's speaker was defying globalization by taking on the International Monetary Fund in his celebration of local products; or even, "Lines Composed a Few Miles Above Tintern Abbey" is an attack on the work of Oxfam at home and abroad. Anti-intentionalists do have their trendy heads screwed on!

Let us perform a thought experiment where an earlier time speaks to us. George Eliot's Casaubon was not alone in seeking an interpretive mythology of all mythologies; Milton is of course much concerned with rationalizing the relation of pagan deities to biblical and rabbinical accounts of devils in *Paradise Lost*. Either one, brought back from the crypt and asked to interpret the mingled classical and Christian references of *The Waste Land* might naturally tend to stress the ways in which the ruins should be reassembled within one coordinating story of Christian history in which devils mislead fallen mortals. We might find their theology arid going and their project retrograde and could hardly resist the impulse to violate their historically specific minds by thrusting James Frazer in their faces (perhaps with a sudden insight that he was not so different from them after all), but we would have no trouble following the direction of their interpretation. We might say, oh no, we know Mr. Eliot didn't intend this—with then a sense that he just might have intended this also since he certainly recalls it in his text as a coherent way of thinking about what we have lost—but we would find it hard to deny that their interpretation was coherent. Classical man—Tereus and Teresias—and modern man—the young man carbuncular and the river maidens—alike suffer the torments of a world dominated by their false devils rather than by the beliefs of religion. Rudely forced, no doubt, but a meaning found in the text by a process of selection and ordering, not some alien piece of theology existing only below or above the text.

The same is true when we force—or modestly fit—earlier texts to our modern conceptualizations. To the extent that our argument is that we know something the text could not possibly have known, we are not even engaging in interpretation; we are just vaunting our superiority. But even readings that find a political or Freudian unconscious behind the text are actually telling us something about the text that organizes and foregrounds its materials. If we tell Ben Jonson (to use a case from Williams rather than Jameson) that he did not tell us much about the exploitative relations of gentry to Penshurst laborers, he may respond that that is hardly a matter for poetry. We may go to the Met to see Breughel's peasants taking lunch under a tree during harvest if we want to know about them! But he will hardly say that we have no point if we insist on the unseen hands providing our consumer poet the unshowy goods that he receives as his due as poet. Yes they are having to work—if that is what you moderns mean by being exploited—as peasants do, as we all do in our places. He did not foreground such a matter, but if we do have this interest in country folk he can see that we would find them strangely absent, an indication of his different way of thinking about the social orders. In the same way, having dared to assert that Charlotte Brontë anticipated many of Freud's ideas about the unconscious, Oedipal conflict, sibling rivalry, incest anxiety and the rest, I sometimes imagine Brontë calling me to task. But my answer would be obvious: that I do find such insights in her work, not just in my book of Freud, and I do admit that the knowledge of Freud let me see what was, obviously enough since I have found it, there in her work. Here the consolation is that Freud himself ascribed prior understanding of his various positions to the poets and indeed used literary interpretations as a prime way of organizing his thoughts about the real people he saw, in this much more conscious than many historians or other scientists of the ways in which fictions are used to organize real life. Brontë herself might shake her head and declare she still preferred her own talk about the stormy sisterhood of passions to these elaborate parallels from the Greek dramatists; but she would hardly deny that a mode of organizing her work had been found.[422]

Older, more classically Freudian interpretations of literature have been labeled as extrinsic criticism in that they seemed to offer a new truth based on an arcane system of symbol equivalences. The letter hidden in broad daylight in Poe's now so overdetermined "The Purloined Letter" is in fact, Marie Bonaparte argued long before Lacan and Derrida came to the text, a symbol for what is most generally missing, the female penis, a symbol of what all the men in this so homosocial text are still always looking for.[423] Absurd, the anti-Freudian responds; out of date, the Lacanian chimes in; insightful, somewhat, but how blind to its own one-sided distortion of the text, the de Manian sighs. But can we say that this is merely imposed on the text? Once we understand this particular version of Freudianism that speaks of masculinity as fear of castration, we hear this as an assertion of what the text is about, not some additional significance layered onto its main meaning; it becomes a competing explanation, a meaning. This does not mean that every such Freudian interpretation is going to be persuasive (this one so far has not proven to be). It will in fact be unpersuasive as an interpretation to the extent it still seems merely added on arbitrarily rather than gaining power as a way of organizing what is in the text.

Criticism based on one or another construction of subject positions—gender, sexual preference, class, or culture—has of course been another major area in which seemingly modernized interpretations fall. There has been a great deal of new and highly interesting theorizing, especially in areas of feminism, queer studies, and multicultural studies, that has leveraged new interpretive moves. So I don't mean to be taken as arguing that there is nothing new under the sun, although I would argue that these approaches would be comprehensible to writers of other ages, even though some—as some people in our age—might find them antipathetic. In the case of queer studies we even have the interesting problem, still largely unsolved, of whether the love that could not speak its name was known, if unnamed, or named only in Latin and Greek, in certain earlier periods, especially the nineteenth century. If we find in Charlotte Brontë's *Villette* a triangle female erotic relation between older, disciplining Madame Beck, younger acting-out Ginevra Fanshawe, and located between such women, one-time cross-dressing character-narrator, Lucy Snowe, are we bringing something Brontë could not possibly have known to her text? The answer would seem to me to be no, that at some level of her psyche she could know such a matter. If interviewed, she might deny it, but we would be comfortable saying she had repressed such knowledge and nonetheless was aware at a less conscious level of the desire we claim she presented (the issue here is not whether we are right in our reading of the text, whatever that would mean, but whether we believe ourselves to be working with a mere significance that we import and do not imagine Brontë could have any connection to).[424]

In the case of feminist moves, it has been said that various readings bring a new political consciousness back into writing not concerned with these issues.[425] It is true that if we are simply doing evaluative criticism it may be possible to critique a work, say, for showing no consciousness of the rights of half the human race without also shaping our interpretation based on that insight. Evaluative criticism, to the extent it merely judges works by certain criteria, may really appear an external criticism, bringing our values into confrontation with those in the work. But even here interpretation raises its hungry head: aren't we assuming some interpretation of the work, say that Housman's "To an Athlete Dying Young" excludes a world of women athletes, when we judge it from a feminist view as wrongly doing so? (And we may thus also be excluding other interpretations, for instance that the poem is about a world in which male-male love cannot grow to fulfillment anyway—indeed cannot even speak its name.) Once we use our insights into some aspect of feminist politics or feminist theory to explore the work, we are, I think, necessarily not just confronting old and new but making claims about the work which we consider valid for it. We don't in fact know if the writer would agree with us, but we believe all right-thinking people, if sufficiently persuaded by an argument that has already persuaded us, will agree with this meaning of the text and we naturally enlist the author among such folk.

In an earlier reader-oriented feminist work,[426] Judith Fetterley conceives of the woman reader as necessarily resisting a masculine bias built into most classic American works. Her idea of reading against the male chauvinist grain, put forward without a sense of the possible deconstruction of any one position in a text and also with a somewhat essentialist view of gender differences before the generation of the philosopher Judith Butler, would seem almost to accept its own status as feminist criticism imposed from the present on an uncomprehending and resisting past. But in the actual act of interpretation, the drawn battle between author and critic that her conceptualization of her project seems to demand breaks down. Her look at Henry James's *The Bostonians* begins by citing all the male critics who have made a canonical tradition of interpreting this work about a triangle between the traditional Southern man, Ransom, and the feminist woman, Olive, who both desire to possess nubile Verena, as the defeat of dangerous and anti-social lesbianism by the natural rites of heterosexual marriage. Whereas elsewhere she tends to set up such a traditional chauvinist interpretation as built into both the work and the author's intention, here she more correctly sees this as one view, and offers a different view, namely that the text offers a vision of male power as sexual sadism, female resistance as needing to work outside the realm of sexuality, where the male is more powerful. Not an attractive queer reading for the present; my point is only that it is offered as a plausible view of what James might have known, not as the resistance from outside that her original conception demands.

Deconstruction has allowed us to deal more easily with such fissured texts, where an intense drama of values may allow us to read the text against itself. If we carry this back to intentions of the author, we then have to say something along the lines of the unclearly divided consciousness of the author I posited in my earlier discussion of the author. It is quite possible to say that most persons of James's time would have been unsympathetic to a reading that found Ransom's will to marriage the problem of the work; yet it is also undeniable that the reading is not imposed on the work as an alien awareness but merely takes a possible position on what is there. It is indeed a position that Fetterley can rightly imagine James, out of his own complexities and perhaps torments over straight sexuality, feeling sympathy with; and one that a considerable minority of his time—which, after all, was a time, like our own, of important feminist self-consciousness, as the intellectual portraits of Olive and Verena show in this text—would have also found attractive. But given these alternatives, we can hardly pretend to know which James listened to most acutely. We have to resolve the mixture in the text as our own meaning. I can follow this with a briefer, more obvious example. Grant the possiblity that all scholarship shows that the Wife of Bath followed and was received within a tradition of satire of independent women; yet any interpretation that validates her view of her story will hardly hesitate to say that that interpretation, a foregrounding of those values and their forceful expression, is in the text, not superimposed on it by a different modern perspective. If the issue is displaced to a discussion of possible intentions, we will always have the answer to the canonical tradition of an anti-feminist Chaucer taking his stand with the male writing of his time in a putative subversive side of Chaucer himself that could be of the Wife's party without knowing it. Whichever side we prefer, or some other approach entirely, the (I am arguing here bogus) issue of intention will always be resolved as a corollary to the interpretive decision, not the other way around.

It is our normal experience of interpretation that it both works with what is there and seems to add something of its own; but if the value added is merely extraneous information, which can often take the form, in historical work, of trivial and irrelevant information, and in non-historical work, of simple-minded anachronistic importations, we easily dismiss that section of the argument. Similarly, the more whimsical and arbitrary the organizing system, as in those enticing numerological systems popular in some medieval and early Renaissance studies forty years ago, the more likely we are to find the interpretation a failure, precisely as a mere external order imposed as a kind of arbitrary allegory on the text. What is usefully added is rather a plausible frame, a set of organizing principles for selecting and presenting what is to be foregrounded. Good interpretation will always give us the impression that something new and valuable is being elicited from the text itself.

A brilliant interpreter of Browning presented a conference paper to high acclaim in which he found parallel versions of older fear of the Inquisition and newer, Freudian, ideas of paranoia, in the poem "How it Strikes a Contemporary."[27] The poet who reports all to God but is being himself reported on by a man of the town was suddenly displayed to us in a new light. Yet it wasn't that there was definitive new news about Browning's allusions to the Inquisition in the poem (a better subject for a note or query), or that Browning necessarily anticipated Freud; it was only that the viewpoints allowed a sudden revisit to this celebrated celebration of the poetic nature as a much more sinister and suspicious business altogether—and this was interesting. I don't know if Browning thought about the poem in this way as he was writing it; I don't know if he thought about the more conventional views of the poem as about poets as God's spies (spies now taking on a new resonance from the interpretation). Both seem not importations but in some strange way meanings carried in the work in potential that could be organized by interpretive conceptualizations. Neither, the standard nor the new, though the first has usually had an aura about it of being the view intended by the author, can be said to be in a different category as sub-textual, extrinsic, hermetic. We don't have to like both of them equally, but it won't do to create two clubs and blackball the ones we don't like from the meaning club while saying they are perfectly acceptable, in their way, for the significance club.

You begin to see, I hope, that this binary of meaning/significance is truly a distinction without a difference and needs not deconstruction but retirement. It is a genteel way of privileging our kind of interpretation and consigning those we don't like to second-class status. I can at least well imagine the writers themselves, excellent folk as I believe they generally are (live ones I have met have not been the sanest people but they have certainly been clever and open to new ideas), asking us to take one more walk around the rose garden as they hear out fully our newfangled interpretations and then deciding that they had indeed meant such a thing, maybe. Maybe they would be just being polite; we often take their works so much more seriously than they did. But just maybe they understand that works mean many things, they come from mysterious places in the psyche and the society of the writer, and they may, more or less acutely, be said to "intend" many meanings at once. I hereby retire the word significance in this special meaning and offer it a gold watch and a lifetime membership in the meaning club across the street. But that club, come to think of it, had better have a name change: the univeral, Everyone is Doing It and Always Has Been Interpretation Club.[428] Literature continues to find readers, to provoke interest, because we make it live again in giving it meanings; dead men's or women's words, to follow Auden, are modified in the guts of the living. That is what must keep happening if they are to provide their nourishment, both imaginative and critical.[429]

XIX. BRIEF CONCLUSION TO A LONG DISCOURSE

> By its very nature available to a plural reading, the text becomes a cultural weapon, a private hunting reserve, the pretext for a law that legitimizes as "literal" the interpretation given by *socially* authorized professionals and intellectuals (*clercs*).
>
> Moreover, if the reader's expression of his freedom through the text is tolerated among intellectuals (*clercs*) (only somone like Barthes can take this liberty), it is on the other hand denied students (who are scornfully driven or cleverly coaxed back to the meaning "accepted" by their teachers) or the public (who are carefully told "what is to be thought" and whose interventions are considered negligible and quickly silenced).
>
> Michel de Certeau, *The Practice of Everyday Life*

> Re-vision—the act of looking back, of seeing with fresh eyes, of entering an old text from a new critical direction—is for us more than a chapter in cultural history: it is an act of survival.
>
> Adrienne Rich, "When We Dead Awaken: Writing as Re-Vision"

My reader may wonder what *I* could possibly have intended in playing author at such length against authors. After all, it is long since both Foucault and Barthes agreed on this as on little else, that the author was dead. Have I then fought here with a phantom, phantom of the *opera* of all *auctores*? Perhaps I have, but it is a phantom of more than my making and it still boldly walks the streets of interpretation at noon—or in the otherwise commonsensical 8:30 a.m. class. The ghost of intention that survives the wreck of the author survives because we don't think hard enough about who makes meaning, author or reader, and tend muddily to split the difference rather than think the matter out clearly. We may say authors believe they make meaning, readers that they do; and conclude with Portia-like portions, that they both do. In fact the assertions tend to be more dialectical: authors believe they make meaning that is verified by the reader; readers, on the other hand, tend to think that they make meanings that are verified as realizations of the author's intentions. As I have attempted to demonstrate, authors cannot control the meanings that readers will find in their work. Whatever ideal conceptions we may possess of what meaning is—something from the beginning with the author, something immanent in the text—we find it only exists in the possession of successive readers.[430] Whenever the point is obvious—*Othello* is a play about jealousy—we can say that the author has been verified by us readers. But the minute we come into controversial terrain—*Othello* is really about race relations, or about Western civilization and its others, or about male homosociality suppressing women—we find that the only game in town is that of readers against readers.

And in this normal interpretive focus on contested issues, each reading's claim to realization of the author's intention is merely a trope of interpretation, a ritual appeal to authority as a rhetorical move (appeals to authority constitute of course a central set of rhetorical acts). We like to authorize and dignify our interpretation by crediting it back to the author both because it may help persuade others and because it may also help us persuade ourselves. Thereby we try to hide from ourselves the necessary instability of our particular foregrounding of the work.[431] Those who appeal to intention show a protective concern for authority; naturally so, for it is their own authority that they actually seek to protect, and in doing so they confirm their appropriation of the author, which they exemplify especially by ascribing their views to his intention. It has become fashionable recently to mount moralistic retro-arguments against anti-intentionalism by associating it with anarchy and relativism presumed to contaminate theoretical positions of the past thirty years and sometimes, in addition, with personal attacks on the morality of a Paul de Man or Hans Robert Jauss based on their wartime lives (and I hereby swear I was born in 1941 and did not collaborate, or even much cooperate, during the war years, nor vote for Bush). But there is a serious moral problem built into the very workings of intentionalist interpretation. Because, as I hope I have now shown, intentionalist demonstrations are necessarily so shrouded in obscurities, their ultimate sources of authority so private and mysterious, they allow closed or unargued interpretive positions that finally ask us to trust the expert, the knowing one, the insider, the one at the source of power. I prefer that my students and I trust our own ability to argue openly over the meaning of the text and to face forthrightly the possible insecurities that our procedure may open. Our abilities develop in facing such difficulties; they atrophy in opening to obscurantist authorities of all stripes.

Jonathan Culler makes a cogent point in reply to a broader attack by Richard Rorty on all readings that try to generate a system of privileged codes that certify their interpretations, as it were, from the outside: "The pragmatist's conviction that all the old problems and distractions can be swept away, installing us in a happy monism, where, as Rorty puts it, 'all anybody ever does with anything is use it,' has the virtue of simplicity but the difficulty of neglecting the sorts of problems that Umberto Eco and many others have wrestled with." Culler caricatures Rorty as offering the "pragmatist's injunction not to worry but simply to enjoy interpretation."[432] But this misses Rorty's general point about the mistake in pre-privileging interpretive theories. And it would miss the more modest one about that most common form of authority in interpretation that I have been developing. The aim is not to discourage tough thinking and vigorous debate in favor of mere enjoyment—though that is certainly a reasonable goal of reading too.[433] It is to ensure that the games of interpretation, tough or gentle, are played out on a level playing field where no interesting argument/way of organizing the text can be dismissed in advance. Intention, as I have been arguing implicitly throughout this discussion, seems to me the place where foundationalism has still been hiding out. It is for hermeneutics—taken broadly as the ongoing controversy over interpretation[434]—the place of idealism, the location of residual hopes for grounding interpretive acts, for avoiding the flux of real interpretations by real readers at varying times and places. Barbara Herrnstein Smith has written persuasively about the need in evaluative criticism to go beyond trying to find firm and permanent grounds for valuing art; she argues that we must begin by acknowledging, in a pragmatic move, that judgments of value keep changing.[435] This pragmatic move on evaluation has been difficult for those invested in canons or particular favorite works. But the idea that interpretation is also fully contingent has been even less attractive, so much so that even some prominent self-identified pragmatist literary critics have clung to the place of authorization, intention, where, as I have been arguing, new versions of grounding for interpretation are let in, in effect, through the back door.[436]

It is perhaps the necessary hidden grounding of even the pragmatist to declare that all grounded arguments will not hold.[437] I have wished, in the sphere of hermeneutics, to argue vigorously against that old place of grounding, intention, as in the much larger issue of epistemology Rorty has argued against grounding for knowledge of nature. We should understand instead an ongoing competition for successive interpretive arguments, a pragmatic hermeneutics that accepts the inevitability of changing interpretations while it insists on the role of the individual interpreter in forging the approachs of the future out of the competitive arguments in play today.[438] But the pragmatist argument against foundationalist arguments must not be a dogma; it can only have merit as argument or arguments attempting, as I have been doing, to assert the failure of arguments in favor of a foundationalist position.[439] The consequence is that there is always the possibility of some new belief. It is at best only a weak rhetorical argument to declare that there is no longer any use for arguments on first principles. There will be such arguments and when the anti-foundationalist cannot persuade others of their failure, as I hope I have persuaded in the case of intentional arguments presently in play, a new foundationalism will become endowed with force.[440] Neopragmatism would then seem to have been a philosophical holding pattern that kept winning by default until some new critical religion lurched toward academe and was born.[441] But if debate on first principles—on theory—will inevitably take place, as I have tried to engage some of those on interpretation here, I will assert that there is *no* room for readings of texts that justify themselves by the certitude with which their proposers hold their premises; and there is even less room for those that base their claims not on the power of the reading to make the text live for others but on reinserting the text in the author's, or author's culture's, intending womb: as if its end were indeed in its beginning and not in its ability to provoke, ignite, incite, delight, and certainly move to strong argument, its readers. Those guardians of the arts who see their work as restraining, rewombing or entombing the work, preserving it immaculate in its author or its time from the corruptions to which all vital reception is heir, will always be with us.[442] I feel them moving in from the shadows even as I begin to end this paean, once more with feeling, to the persuasive art of reader's interpretation. If we want the house of the arts to be more than a mausoleum, we must be vigilant in keeping them at bay.

The rewards for not allowing the neo-historicist paradigm to dominate our relation to literary texts, I think, are substantial. Live texts, texts that remain in play rather than in the mausoleum, are texts that can make a difference in our personal, cultural, and political lives. Only the most hard-hatted cultural constructionist would debate the first: that we do imagine ourselves to have inner lives, even if much of that personal life of ideas about ourselves and our world comes from the outside into us. Texts are part of that process, and our ability to receive them as still in play allows us to stir up and restructure our inner lives; and that may lead us to stir up and restructure the world around us. As I have often had occasion to oppose the hermeneutic naïveté of historicisms that believe a text can be frozen in its historical period, if one just approaches the bigger text of the entire period in the right way, I may seem in strange company in talking of texts and cultural lives.[443] But live texts function vigorously and importantly as places of cultural and political conflict, reinterpretation, adjustment and readjustment. Received as live texts, open to proposals for new meanings from any direction, they allow us to participate in the "floating, ungrounded, conversations" of our time,[444] conversations about our reading and about its connections to everything else. No society complicated enough to reflect widely on a variety of texts functions as a simplistic single community of interpretation. The contemporary debate over interpretation is part of the process by which cultural difference is enacted and cultural change, onto new conversations, new arguments, takes place.[445]

The naïveté of historicism can be precisely in its not recognizing that our seizures of the past are part of this play, a special arena in which we test our fictions of reality against texts of other periods. Small wonder that our generation has found in history, say of the Renaissance, its own favorite themes, sexuality, self-construction, multiculturalism and colonialism, gay and queer studies. And rightly so; these are areas of the past that we are better able to open up than earlier historians. Whether in the specialist realm of such historical reinterpretation or in the open marketplace of current discussion of ourselves and our world—our constructions that also construct us—the live text offers a center for debate and thinking.[446] Indeed, it *is* normally the center in an age when there is no settled metaphysics but only theories, of society, psychology, language, valued as heuristic measures exactly in their exploration of live texts. My intention—which hereby leaves me and becomes yours to give meaning to as you may or can—has been to keep the debate alive by ensuring that texts are, also, not drained of life and filled with the intentionalist's embalming fluid.

An assumption underlying this work is that arguments about interpretation—and in my case theory of interpretation—matter because they may thus live and participate in our ongoing cultural debate by actually persuading. I have not been persuaded by the direction of thinking, following Fish's ideas of communities of interpretation, which concludes that interpretations are mere party performances of different communities in a system in which individuals are unable to be persuaded by argument to different or new positions. And if I had been, it would prove I should not have been. Such an extension of pragmatism turns it into mere fatalism; those who believe it should logically relapse into silence, not New Historicism. (See the discussion of

Fish's theory of communities in III.v, below.) I would hardly argue against the force of appeals to intention in arguments if I did not believe that my audience could possibly be persuaded of my position. It is not necessary to accept a model of rational man to accept persuasion as a vehicle for change in opinions; rhetoricians have long known that persuasion is a process that may draw on many aspects of the person who is being persuaded, and the process could even be considered one of ideological indoctrination, whether that is conceived as an appeal to interest or as a more irrational development of social conditioning or psychological interpellation. I have done all I could, while making my moves around the multiplex of arguments over intention, also to move you by laughter, by pathos, by appeal to authority against authority, by exhaustive and perhaps exhausting treatment of my subject, even by performative buffoonery, to lead you to my views on intentionality; I have tried to show you that it is in your interest as a reader to keep your options open in interpretation; I have repeated my mantra against intention until it penetrated deep into your cerebellum; and I have certainly called you back to your culture's inculcated sense of individual freedom, the open road of interpretation, against the closed ways of authority and expert testimony. All this I have done, believing it possible to persuade you. And perhaps you are persuaded; and if you are, you will agree that I can have no idea what you have been persuaded of. That is business I leave to you, my reader.

There is a final defense of intentionality—pragmatic but I think rather desperate—and I mention it here only to be clear that I have dismissed it. This takes the sophisticated form of admitting much or all that a critic of the concept such as myself can offer; but then reinviting the term in as a necessary fiction. The harmless version of this is merely a matter of a way of speaking: we refer to our interpretation of Jones's work as Jones's view as a shorthand, as the good astronomers since Galileo have still spoken of the sun rising and setting.[447] Jones stands for, merely, what we currently think the work means. His name becomes a kind of metonymy of what meaning we find in his work. It works as well for Jones, who we know to be the real author of *From Here to Eternity*, as it does for Homer, who we know to be a metonymy not only for texts but a farrago of actual authors.[448] In commercial conditions of authorship the name may even be deliberately produced as a branding that identifies and sells the work, with both author and the publishing/advertising world collaborating to give the impression that naming or signature denominate some essence of the work.[449] In extreme commercial conditions, we could even imagine the licensing of the author's name to works only generally approved by him, as designers' names are licensed in perfumes and accessories.[450] This idea of a brand name as meaning seems possible in the easy and uninteresting case that there is only one game in town, one meaning asserted so we easily include the author in our party of the whole. But the minute there are two, or more than two, versions of meaning contested among readers, all doing so in the name of an author, we are reminded again that the author's name as a site of intention is only a fiction, and not really a comfortable one.[451] It will not pay the rent; it will not separate sheep from goats or men from boys. We must argue the reader's position—*our* reader's position—on its own merits without appeal to a Big Brother author of our invention.[452]

The stronger, and I think pernicious, version is to conclude that intention is a necessary way of thinking—in this view we can't think of communication without thinking in terms of agency, a sender to send and a receiver to receive. It may seem natural to speak of agency, to suggest that this science of reading, like the natural sciences, is a science of tracing causality, as if the explanation of an effect—the reading of the text—lies in an author as cause.[453] We need to remember that the proper science here is that very inexact, rather subjective, and highly contested one of hermeneutics. The agent in sciences of interpretation is the interpreter; her goal is not to figure out the creator of the text (that is a specialized goal for the biographer or historian) but to find out what this text means to us and to test it in attempts to persuade others by reference to the text.[454] In doing so, she provides a context for reading but may not privilege any particular context on causal or metaphysics-masking-as-causal grounds. Well, do we then need the idea of an author with an intention to talk about a text? Is this a necessary illusion that can't be discarded, so talk about it has no consequences, another version of the skeptical theory of no consequences to theory raised by Fish, Knapp and Michaels?[455] Are we forced by the nature of texts to create a stand-in for a speaker, with texts a mere parasitical version of real, face-to-face, communication? If we look at this shibbolethic myth directly and courageously, in fact it vanishes, evaporates by light of day, this ghost of intentionality, ghost of a ghost. No, we have already proven that we don't need intentionality to talk about literature. We have now, for a long time, been talking of our reading as "the text says," "the story says," as "the poem says"; we have spoken of "it speaks," "it performs," "it enacts," for all these years. Perhaps with Kristeva we have been talking not of the "person subject of writing" but of the "ambivalence of writing."[456] Now perhaps the day has come when we can drop even the unnecessary fiction of the personification of the text, that strangely passive agent always capable of such double or triple talk about itself. Perhaps we will say "I read the text as" or "What the text means to me is." We may find we have been talking reader interpretation all this time without knowing it. In any event, we have long done without the name of the author in our talk about literature. The apparently harmless claim that we necessarily imagine an author as the site, indeed projection, of our interpretation is in practice malign. It allows individual interpretations to vaunt themselves as authoritative and privileged readings.[457]

I hope this essay may have laid the ghost of the author, his or her intention, forever. In this brief farewell I would ask the reader tempted to fall back into an intentional state of mind to recall what I consider my single best point, a clarifying standard that eliminates much of the needless fluff of argument and pontification that keeps up belief in these ghosts. This is that we only come into real issues about intention when we are already in a place where such rhetoric might seem to help an argument. Intention is not proven by all the obvious ways in which we assume an author would agree with all readers about his or her text.[458] It is always open for the eccentric individual, or one of Stanley Fish's eccentric communities of mutually perplexed interpreters, to call a textual hawk a handsaw. "'The question is,' said Alice, 'whether you *can* make words mean so many different things.' 'The question is,' said Humpty Dumpty, 'which is to be master—that's all.'" Humpty may have the right question but it doesn't mean that we will accept any Humpty Dumpty interpretation that a would-be master egghead puts forth. To oppose the use of intention is not to release the text to be anything at all one may fancy it to be. The prophylactic against real absurdities is not to bring in guesses about what the author intended but to observe the failure of absurd approaches to persuade others. In such cases it seems indeed true that the author, even if these people are not exactly founts of commonsense wisdom and right thinking, if asked, would probably agree with the rest of us. No one bothers, however; absurd views fail quite sufficiently without appeals to authority. When we come into real interpretive battlefields, where there is much to be said for two or more positions and where there are reasonable proponents on all sides, then alone do we hear appeals to intention. And of course it is just there, as I have been arguing, where the complications of the text predict that we can never discover an uncomplicated author who will make all clear.

I will end with a parable: a scientific colleague at my university publishes a paper in a major journal devoted to a certain kind of cultural studies approach to political and social issues that has been approved by the distinguished board of editors. He then reveals that he intended the article as a hoax to prove that a Cultural Studies approach to the rigors of science is bosh. The world is amused and considers the journal and its particular kind of discourse discredited (that he appealed to the wish of the editors to find their beliefs corroborated by a convert from the world of hard science will not be part of my discussion here, though it may have had real consequences that add a further spin to the story). There is good grounds to argue that the author (a genial as well as very smart person), in preparing the paper to pass muster in a certain discourse group, has only too well imitated (parodied) its thinking and style, thus making it possible to argue that as he wrote the work he became an unwilling scribe to the new discourse; he came to scoff and stayed to join, despite himself, thus becoming one of my fissured and self-perplexed authors. I don't wish to take a position on the issue, only to point out that if so many professionals were taken in by the hoax then it may be the author was too, or at least left a text open to different perspectives, some serious, some ironic. Irony is in the eye of the beholder; none of us will cede to the author our judgment on this issue but will rather read and decide for ourselves.[459] Imagine if the author, in quest of even more media attention, should later proclaim that his first charge of hoax was only intended to show how no one reads for his- or herself, that all merely follow the proclamations of authority figures; the text was dead serious. Who now will you believe? He could change again next week.[460] At some point, and this is the point I hope you my reader have now arrived at, you will determine that you will stop listening to assertions about what the author intended, even those made by the author as self-promoter, and interpret the work for yourself.

Let Christina Rossetti tell you for me that meaning isn't about truth hidden in the author;[461] it is about the grand old problems of good interpretation, parts and their relation to the whole:

A Sketch

The blindest buzzard that I know
    Does not wear wings to spread and stir,
    Nor does my special mole wear fur
And grub among the roots below;
    He sports a tail indeed, but then
    It's to a coat; he's man with men;
        His quill is cut to a pen.

In other points our friend's a mole,
    A buzzard, beyond scope of speech:
    He sees not what's within his reach,
Misreads the part, ignores the whole.
    Misreads the part so reads in vain,
    Ignores the whole tho' patent plain,
        Misreads both parts again.

My blindest buzzard that I know,
    My special mole, when will you see?
    Oh no, you must not look at me,
There's nothing hid for me to show.
    I might show facts as plain as day;
    But since your eyes are blind, you'd say:
        Where? What? and turn away.

NOTES: SECTION TWO

1 *Roland Barthes by Roland Barthes* (New York: Hill and Wang, 1977), p. 55; Ellis: (Princeton: Princeton UP, 1989), p. 119: cited by Michael Hardin, *Playing the Reader: The Homoerotics of Self-Reflexive Fiction* (New York: Peter Lang, 2000), p. 9. Hardin sees the severing of the author from the text as a basic shift in power: "The shift to 'the text' is a feat executed by the critical reader to claim authority over a creative text": p. 7.

2 I have found Robert Crosman's "Do Readers Make Meaning?", a lightly presented little essay that my students confront in an anthology of readings on reading early in the course, very useful in its recasting of the battles over intention in political terms: those, like E.D. Hirsch, who insist on author's intention as *the* meaning are arguing for a need of central authority, in Hirsch's case for a source of authority in a "cognitive discipline of interpretation," *Aims of Interpretation* (Chicago: Chicago UP, 1987), p. 7; those who allow diverse meanings accept the possibility of diversity, plurality, even democracy. If this is the underlying battle joined over intention, one can understand why that battle is forever being fought again within the competitive hierarchies of academic literary study. For Crosman's article see Susan R. Suleiman and Inge Crosman, *The Reader in the Text: Essays on Audience and Interpretation* (Princeton: Princeton UP, 1980), pp. 149–64. Crosman builds on Michel Foucault's observations on the ideology of author function in the famous essay, "What is an Author?": see n. 28, below.

3 I begin my discussion here using the term "literary intentionality" or "literary intention," though not always hereafter, to allow thorough cataloguers to avoid placing this study under the two other, also much contested, discourses using intention/intentionality, both in the area of philosophical discussion rather than literary theory. The less well known of these is the simplest of the three in its direct connection to the common use of the term: the study of human intentions and planning in actions. Two of not too many studies of this broad issue are G.E. Anscombe's *Intention* (Ithaca: Cornell UP, 1963) and Michael Bratman's *Intention, Plans, and Practical Reason* (Cambridge: Harvard UP, 1987). Bratman wrote the brief entry on this subject for the *Cambridge Dictionary of Philosophy*. As in so many fields begun in philosophy, the experimental psychologists have been laying claim to this discussion with special interests in how we generally conceptualize and evaluate intention, how perceptions of intention develop in children and animals, and how intentionality is used in explanations of behavior and attributions of responsibility/liability. See the broad discussion in Bertram F. Malle, Louis J. Moses, and Dare A. Baldwin, eds., *Intentions and Intentionality: Foundations of Social Cognition* (Cambridge:

MIT P, 2001); as the title suggests, many of the articles look at the social relations involved in intentions, not just the reason to be given for an action. This combined philosophical/psychological discussion obviously bears somewhat on any approach to literary intentions as that is displayed in interpretive work, especially in the issue of motivation for writing that I explore in section II.v, below. A.J. Close, "*Don Quixote* and the Intentionalist Fallacy," in David Newton-DeMolina, ed., *On Literary Intention* (Edinburgh: Edinburgh UP, 1976), pp. 174–93, even attempted, as have a number of writers since, to reduce the question of literary intentionality to clear statements of purpose without any consideration for any broader "mental aims" of the author. I explore the difficulties in his attempts to define purpose through literature seen as speech acts in Appendix 1. This way of thinking of broad purposes in speeches/writing should have more play in studies of rhetoric. See II.v, n. 118.

Far more common in twentieth-century philosophical discussion is the special use of intentionality as a technical term to refer to aboutness, that is to something that is about something else. Originally a scholastic term translated from the work in Arabic of Avicenna and distinguishing first intention (attention to things themselves) from second intention (attention to conceptions of things), it was revived by Franz Brentano in the nineteenth century as a way of identifying mental phenomena (that have intentionality). It was adopted by Husserl and other phenomenologists, and also by Jacques Derrida, who retains the term but, at the end of the phenomenological line, denies that it can be established. In phenomenological use, intention does not refer to an author's meaning before writing but to the possibility of an expression bearing one, restricted, meaning. The term was also resuscitated in later twentieth-century analytic philosophy as part of the ongoing attempt to reflect on mental activity. William Lyons, *Approaches to Intentionality* (Oxford: Oxford UP, 1995), esp. pp. 3, 21, 65, 79, 160, 163, 193–94, provides a helpful summary of the complex range of applications of philosophical intentionality, which amount to no less than thinking about the nature of intelligence, though consciousness is not a condition (a thermostat is often said to have intentionality). Lyons offers a taxonomy of intention in language, pp. 212–19. It has been easy for literary theorists to blur this discussion into the question of literary intention, as I note below. Daniel C. Dennett's influential *The Intentional Stance* (Cambridge: MIT P, 1989) argues that intentionality is known by its susceptibility to predictions about the action of the intentional thing, but his interest is not in the planning itself. Similarly, Donald Davidson's work on making sense out of others' behavior on the principle of charity—that they are likely to have reasons for what they do—has been used to apply to speech situations. See Raymond Gibbs, *Intentions in the Experience of Meaning* (Cambridge: Cambridge UP, 1999), p. 72 and Appendix 1.

John R. Searle's theory of intentionality supposes an intentional state (of mind) with an intentional object (outside it). In a theory such as his that still maintains a category of mind, intentionality is in effect reproduced (or extended) by a speech act (asserting a belief—a proposition—or a desire about an object). See his *Intentionality: An Essay in the Philosophy of Mind* (Cambridge: Cambridge UP, 1983). In this form it is, as I explain below, not so far from a concept of meaning based on author's intention in the much more diffuse senses in which I will be discussing it here. Cognitive psychologists sometimes speak of mental intentions or intentional states, meaning pre-verbal states with aboutness—for instance, a child's awareness of ice cream before the word comes to him or his awareness of his missing his mother. See, for instance, Lois Bloom, "Meaning and Expression," in Willis F. Overton and David S. Palermo, eds., *The Nature and Ontogenesis of Meaning* (Hillsdale, NJ: Lawrence Erlbaum, 1994), pp. 226–30. Bloom calls these also "private and personal mental meanings" before language. To add to the confusion, analytic philosophical discussions of intentionality (sense 2) often distinguish between intension, the conceptual meaning of a term logically in it, and extension, its application by denotation (in the special sense of things an expression points to).

Because of the widespread use of this term in literary discussion, it has seemed to me too late to leave the field to students of philosophy or psychology studying actions or to our not too friendly analytic philosopher friends in the pursuit of meaning and choose another term. Their difference is written into the history of reader theory very clearly in the early work of Roman Ingarden. Like his follower, Wolfgang Iser, Ingarden works out of the philosophical tradition of phenomenology and defines the art object as an "intersubjective intentional object": *The Cognition of the Literary Work of Art* (Evanston, IL: Northwestern UP, 1973), p. 14 (in translation). His aesthetic theory stresses the independence of this intentional (phenomenological philosophy) object from any need to determine intentions (in the literary sense) of the author. The work, he insists, has an "ontically heteronomous mode of existence," independent of both author and reader who intend it: *The Literary Work of Art: An Investigation on the Borderlines of Ontology, Logic, and Theory of Literature* (Evanston, IL: Northwestern UP, 1973), p. 362. In a recent work, Jeff Mitscherling, Tanya DiTommaso, and Aref Nayed, *The Author's Intention* (Lanham, MD: Lexington Books, 2004), though professing respect for Ingarden, attempt to offer a different phenomenology of literary work based on the reader's ability to re-experience the author's pre-linguistic intention, understood as emotion or inspiration, an inspired conflation of phenomenological intentionality and literary intention that takes them into deep waters of the metaphysics of light and even into mystical apprehension of the logos behind the work à la St. John (pp. 94–97, 99).

I am using interchangeably the noun "intention" (as in my title) with the also commonly used noun "intentionality." With intentionality I risk the additional possibility of confusion with different projects in philosophy because the "-ity" ending suggests the issue is a problem that we all must grapple with. By contrast to both these terms in use today, if we return to the seminal article, by W.K. Wimsatt and M.C. Beardsley, "The Intentional Fallacy," in W.K. Wimsatt's *The Verbal Icon: Studies in the Meaning of Poetry* (New York: Farrar Straus & Giroux, 1954), pp. 3–20 (first pub. in *Sewanee Review* 54 [1946]: 468–88), we find their term, never much followed though sometimes still appearing, especially in legal discussion, is "intentionalism" (p. 17). But this suggests some kind of dangerous cause or deep belief that they need to stamp out and stamp, as they did, as a mere mistake. The date even rather recalls a general cultural tendency to limit dangerous "isms." Gibbs chooses to use "communicative intention" to distinguish this from other kinds of intention, but that seems clumsy.

While acknowledging that both terms are commonly used to cover the same range of meaning, Malle, Moses, and Baldwin, in their "Introduction: The Significance of Intentionality," to their collection of essays, p. 3, propose to distinguish intention from intentionality in issues of action by limiting intention to the agent and taking intentionality as what is located in the event. This might be useful in literary study but I have not seen it distinguished clearly in this way. The primary use in literary study is to indicate a mode of interpretation, based on a belief in literary intention/intentionality: perhaps again a consequence of the confusion between, and attempt to join, thinking about the author as agent in an action and trying to define the text as an intention of consciousness. My discussion in the sections that follow will move from the first, author as intending agent, to the second, text as displaying intentionality.

4 Dennett's theory of an "intentional stance"—see his essay, "True Believers: The Intentional Strategy and Why It Works," in his *The Intentional Stance*, pp. 13–35, esp. p. 27—tries to define intentional thinking (thinking about something) as capable of being read in the conduct of the person—which is not the same as reading writing as motivated conduct. Imagine a jealous spouse reading a writer's work to see if the spouse had cheating on his or her mind; that would be an intentional stance to literature.

5 Of course, most philosophers find some secondary place for these "parasitic" uses of language, for statements about imaginary facts. See discussion in Appendix 1.

6 The complexities of this example, including uncertainties as to the author or addressee of the text, have been much discussed. See the useful summary by Gerald Graff, "Determinacy/Indeterminacy," in Frank Lentricchia and Thomas McLaughlin, eds., *Critical Terms for Literary Study* (rev. ed., Chicago: U of Chicago P, 1995), pp. 172–74.

7 Children seem to recapitulate this evolutionary priority in beginning by giving intentional explanations of all phenomena: Terrance Brown, "Affective Dimensions of Meaning," in Overton and Palermo, eds., p. 177.

8 Often called, after Dennett's work, the intentional stance. See n. 4, above.

9 Gibbs's *Intentions in the Experience of Meaning*, chs. 2–7. Gibbs's somewhat odd work is helpful in its broad summary of research on people's concern with intention in daily life (on which there is a good deal of thinking in philosophy of motivation and intentions) and in approaches to art. He offers interesting material, pp. 136–42, on cultures that refuse to seek intentions as a way to explain meaning even in ordinary oral discourse (esp. p. 140), yet he never acknowledges that the rest of his material is thus culturally biased by its Western, mainly American, research base. When he takes on, as he does massively, the issue of literary intention, he uses the research experience as a kind of essentializing argument. He is a good enough student of the debates over meaning to keep showing how often meaning is detached from intention; yet he regularly implies that because people tend to think, consciously or unconsciously, in intentional ways, that this is a good argument why they should approach interpretation in this way. He eventually compromises on a position he found in a piece by Jerrold Levinson—in Gary Iseminger, ed., *Intention and Interpretation* (Philadelphia: Temple UP, 1992), pp. 221–56—in which he proposes that we all work with the presumed human bias for intentional thinking by looking for a hypothetical intention compatible with historical facts (pp. 262–64, 294, 305, 328). But the hypothetical intention is merely an interpretation we foster on the author (see n. 30, below); I will explore at length below problems with "simple facts" of composition/publication in assuring us of intentions. In general, Gibbs displays the same human propensity that he believes natural indeed to the species, to see the human origin of most art. Of course; nor is there any doubt that most artists are up to something. The question is whether speculations about intentions take precedence or are even much help in interpretation, not how we feel about human intentions. In the end, Gibbs is reduced to the weak assertion that intentions are at least "relevant" (p. 268) to interpretation.

10 Similarly, a linguist who tries to enumerate the various uses of the English word "meaning" finds most of the ten uses including some sense of what was intended or what value was placed on it: John Lyons, *Semantics: I and II* (Cambridge: Cambridge UP, 1977), pp. 1–3.

11 See II.x, below, and Appendix 1.

12 Göran Hermerén, "Allusions and Intentions," in Iseminger, ed., p. 218, notes that discussions of intention are often "disguised normative" disputes over fundamental issues of values in literature and criticism.

13 For some more recent examples of many see nn. 30 and 35, below, and the pro-intention essays in Iseminger, ed.

14 Fairly recent examples, of many, are essays by Joseph Margolis and Richard Shusterman in Iseminger, ed., and Arabella Lyon, *Intentions: Negotiated, Contested, and Ignored* (University Park: Pennsylvania State UP, 1998). On Richard Rorty's views see II.xvii, n. 396 and II.xix, n. 441, below, and n. 20 immediately below.

15 See discussion of Knapp and Michaels, immediately below.

16 "Intention Floreat," in Newton-DeMolina, ed., p. 242.

17 "An Eighth Type of Ambiguity," in Newton-DeMolina, ed., p. 224.

18 Suresh Raval, "Intention and Contemporary Literary Theory," *The Journal of Aesthetics and Art Criticism* 38 (Spring 1980): 261.

19 *Doing What Comes Naturally: Change, Rhetoric, and the Practice of Theory in Literary and Legal Studies* (Durham: Duke UP, 1989), p. 116. On Fish and intention, see Appendix 2.

20 "Against Theory," in W.J.T. Mitchell, ed., *Against Theory: Literary Studies and the New Pragmatism* (Chicago: U of Chicago, 1985), pp. 11–30. The argument mounted in that (in)famous essay is that theoretical positions on interpretation never control actual interpretive activity, which proceeds apart from theory—a position with which I am broadly in sympathy. But their essay in fact very much attempts to govern practice by a theoretical argument that supports, without citing it, historical interpretation. This is most clearly operative in their most important specific argument, which very much depends upon their attempt to close permanently the issue of intentionality. They wish to say that the debate over whether meaning is in the author or lies somewhere else is an unreal one; if it is, then there is no theory, just an unreal question producing imaginary alternative theories of correct interpretation. But their desire to dismiss theoretical issues turning on intentionality leads them not to argue what they pretend to advance, that intentional issues are unreal, but to take one side on the issue of intentionality. As if there had not been a long and continuing debate on the issue, they simply decide in favor of intentionality under the guise of indifference. Their argument is a simple one: they begin by asserting that it is impossible to think of meaning without thinking of an intentional being who has made the meaning (shades of arguments from creation for the existence of God); the grounds of this argument are not really given but they are obviously essentialist: we are such creatures as have to attribute an author

to all productions that we believe to have meaning. In fact, as I will here, it is possible to give many reasons why this is far from an essentialist and self-evident truth. Their most dramatic example, that of someone seeing the waves of the ocean writing Wordsworth's "A Slumber did my Spirit Seal," is a bad one because it shifts attention from the real issue, whether meaning is necessarily connected to a meaning maker, and onto the question of whether waves can make marks like words, which we all naturally doubt. As I argue below (see II.viii, n. 188), many cases of monkeys typing Shakespeare, of computers or robots writing, of cameras taking pictures, of found art, have raised these questions of authorless meaning repeatedly as live ones without obvious answer. Even an advocate of intention as a natural way of thinking such as Gibbs (pp. 73–75), grants that people often respond to non-human sentences, like those created by the psychoanalyst program ELIZA, as meaningful. We may have a bias to look for an intender behind meaning, but we respond to meaning as meaning wherever found. The direction of their argument, especially in light of Michaels's practice as a leading New Historian, must be taken not as being neutral on theory but as being typically intentionalist: to make the way clear for interpretive work that finds meaning in the author or his times and hence claims privilege in interpreting the work—exactly the kind of privilege the argument seems to argue against. One needs to observe, as with the work of Wimsatt and Beardsley, how partial and uncomprehensive, here really proclaiming by fiat what is not actually established, such well-nigh notorious arguments on intentionality are. It is also surprising to see how much weight is put on the dubious old chestnut of unauthored writing, and without any apparent sense of the rich discussion by surrealist and other avant-garde twentieth-century artists and writers in automatic writing, group writing, found or ready-made art—a major issue, for instance, in Barthes's by then famous proclamation of the death of the author. Unless they take Duchamp's, Yeats's, or Barthes's special fervor for ordinary madness, it is surprising that Knapp and Michaels can write as if unauthored meaning was an obviously mad impossibility.

There were two especially cogent ripostes to their argument in later issues of *Critical Inquiry*: Adena Rosmarin, "On the Theory of 'Against Theory,'" in Mitchell, ed., p. 83, finds that their work argues by begging the question by switching it from the real issue of where meaning lies into the silly argument about who or what creates language. In a self-styled "more pragmatist than thou" argument, Richard Rorty, "Philosophy without Principles," in Mitchell, ed., pp. 133–34, criticizes their argument for attempting to decide on what should be left undecided, though he does not exactly see that they are in fact deciding for intention. He does deny their argument, rightly insisting on the possible meaningfulness of many linguistic items apparently not produced by any author's intention. His argument is that "Linguisticality" is given not by the author but by anyone who wishes to impute it. Rorty's position on interpretive activity as recontextualizing leads him instinctively to oppose writers like Hirsch or Searle on issues of intentionality. See Richard Rorty, "The Pragmatist's Progress," in Stefan Collini, ed., *Interpretation and Overinterpretation* (Cambridge: Cambridge UP, 1992), pp. 89–108, esp. p. 93, and "Inquiry as Recontextualization: An Anti-Dualist Account of Interpretation," in David R. Hiley, James F. Bohman, and Richard Shusterman, eds., *The Interpretive Turn: Philosophy, Science, Culture* (Ithaca: Cornell UP, 1991), pp. 59–80, esp. p. 67. Since then, another neo-pragmatist, Richard Shusterman, has twice responded to their take on intention, in both cases accepting their premise about language having intention (but he seems to mean here something closer to the philosophical idea of intention as aboutness) but arguing that intention may inhere in the reader in cases where language seems authorless, thus discrediting author's intention. See Iseminger, ed., pp. 65–75, 167–82. Shusterman's observations on Knapp and Michaels's very unpragmatic "necessitarianism" are helpful in questioning the use of pragmatic-like arguments by them to constrain interpretation (p. 172). Reed Way Dasenbrock, *Truth and Consequences: Intentions, Conventions, and the New Thematics* (University Park: Pennsylvania State UP, 2001), p. 155, cutely noted that intention hardly seems the common assumption Knapp and Michaels take it as obvious that it is—many critics never claim their interpretations are based on it.

Knapp and Michaels returned to this issue with essentially the same take on intention in "Against Theory 2: Hermeneutics and Deconstruction," *Critical Inquiry* 14 (1987): 49–69, in which they argue against (especially) Hans Georg Gadamer and Derrida. As in their first article, they reject conventional verbal meaning as an acceptable alternative to author's meaning, especially so as in these thinkers it allows more than one reading of a text, whereas they believe there is only one, the author's intended meaning. Later, in an exchange with John Searle who disagreed with their position, "Literary Theory and its Discontents," *New Literary History* 25 (1994): 649–50, and Michaels, "The Shape of the Signifier," *Critical Inquiry* 27 (2001): 266–83, the position is even more clearly intentionalist. Real meaning that we argue over in interpretation comes from someone who creates signs. Writing on Earth or Mars that is merely marks can be interpreted any which way. The pragmatist mask is no longer bothered with, as Michaels can see no process of interpretive struggle within a non-definitive frame; he merely sees the danger of "as many meanings as readers" (283). More recently, Jorge J.E. Gracia has rehearsed many of the examples of texts without authors (esp. the warhorse of a monkey—who now should be promoted to a computer).

Despite all commonsense evidence that we take a text as something to read and interpret wherever we find it (the monkey writes a *Hamlet* in an imaginary world where no Shakespeare ever existed), he follows Knapp and Michaels by closing all discussion by fiat: "texts do need historical authors, for texts without authors are texts without history and texts without history are texts without meaning; that is, they are not texts": "A Theory of the Author," in William Irwin, ed., *The Death and Resurrection of the Author?* (Westport, CT: Greenwood P, 2002), pp. 179–80; orig. pub. in Gracia's *Texts: Ontological Status, Identity, Author, Audience* (Albany: SUNY P, 1996).

21 "The way to answer the realist/idealist question 'Is meaning created by the text or the reader or by both?' is simply not to ask it": Mailloux, *Rhetorical Power* (Ithaca: Cornell UP, 1989), p. 14. See further discussion in Mailloux, "Interpretation and Rhetorical Hermeneutics," in James L. Machor and Philip Goldstein, eds., *Reception Study: From Literary Theory to Cultural Studies* (New York: Routledge, 2001), pp. 52–55 (rpt. from his *Reception Histories: Rhetoric, Pragmatism and American Cultural Politics* [Ithaca: Cornell UP, 1998]). The position I argue for here is very close to that which Mailloux wishes merely to assume. And my argument is, as Mailloux would argue it has to be, rhetorical, a citing of reasons that seem powerful to me in hopes that they will seem powerful to you. Unlike Mailloux, or Knapp and Michaels for that matter, Richard Rorty has not affirmed anti-formalism by fiat but by careful and extensive critique of the Western epistemological tradition. Neopragmatism isn't about proceeding without clarifying and justifying one's position. Knapp and Michaels chose an intentionalist New Historicism; Mailloux prefers reader-based rhetorical history. None of them is obviously justified by denying the importance of major questions about literary theory. If this has been, at least for Mailloux, a rhetorical strategy (overcoming by dismissing), it has not been a winning one; the winning strategy has been historicist and covertly intentionalist, not about history of rhetorical interpretations but about history of discourses in which interpretation can be situated—though interest in reception has been growing: see section IV, below.

22 Denis Dutton, in Anthony J. Cascardi, ed., *Literature and the Question of Philosophy* (Baltimore: Johns Hopkins UP, 1987).

23 Iseminger in Iseminger, ed., p. ix.

24 Terry Eagleton, *Literary Theory: An Introduction* (Minneapolis: U of Minnesota P, 1983), pp. 68–74; Eagleton correctly stresses the centrality of intentionality in hermeneutics; in Eagleton's story of hermeneutics, the issue of intention is the main one that divides nineteenth-century historical hermeneutics, which attempts to promulgate rules to recover original meaning, from the positions of twentieth-century thinkers such as Martin Heidegger or Gadamer who insist on the sitedness of the interpreter.

Eagleton's critique of Gadamer's classicist bias seems to me to call attention away from the centrality of this issue in the Marxist and social criticism he sponsors. Peter Szondi has similarly underlined intention as an issue in his history of the eighteenth-century predecessors, in a variety of secular fields, of classic German hermeneutics: *Introduction to Literary Hermeneutics*, trans. Martha Woodmansee (Cambridge: Cambridge UP, 1995). Because I will often, like Eagleton and Hirsch, place issues of intentionality and issues of reading theory broadly in the area of hermeneutics, I need here to note that hermeneutics is a discussion, usually an argument, about the grounds for and procedures of interpretation. Although I frequently find it asserted to be, it is not a belief that interpretation must explore the consciousness of the author. That is merely one position, often associated with nineteenth-century romantic hermeneutics, nor is it a belief that the recovery of an author's milieu and worldview is the foundation of interpretation: that is merely one position, especially associated with the German historian W.T. Dilthey, and often revived today. Hermeneutics does not have a position on intentionality; it is a major part of the debate itself. As good a critic as Annabel Patterson can speak of "Foucaultian analysis" as "resolutely anti-hermeneuticist," in the sense that it denied the search for "meanings that originating authors had hidden in their writings": "Intention," in Lentriccia and McLaughlin, eds., p. 144; that is a hermeneutic position, not anti-hermeneutics. See II.xviii, n. 408, below, on hermeneutic theories.

On relations between legal and literary interpretation see the collection of essays, Sanford Levinson and Steven Mailloux, eds., *Interpreting Law and Literature* (Evanston, IL: Northwestern UP, 1988). Because of the presence of a masterful but often elusive founding text as ultimate authority, legal discussion in the United States has had issues of intentionality before it from the beginning. Major traditions of interpretation, from formalists' belief in the plain meaning or words of the text, to original intentionalists' attempts to recover founders' meanings, to the liberal evolutionists of various stripes still predominant in law schools but not in the Supreme Court: all begin with a very self-conscious position on intentionality. Legal intentionalists can summon a great array of authoritative figures upon which to rest cases or do biographical or sociological research in historical reconstruction: the authoring framers themselves, the constitutional assembly as a group, or all the ratifying conventions of the states. Further recourse can be had to the general values and conceptions of the time in order to try to nail down exactly what any of these groups meant. In light of such rich possibilities for special pleas on special evidence, it is no wonder Justice Brennan once characterized intentional arguments as "little more than arrogance cloaked as humility": quoted in Gibbs, p. 280.

Evolutionists of many varieties at least accept the idea of changing interpretations with changing values and mores, that is, that the Constitution must be interpreted by our present values and points of view in ways that might never have occurred to the founders. Formalists, who believe in the possibility of a plain or clear meaning in the text itself, deny the need to seek out original intentions and tend not to accept the possibility of evolving and changing interpretations over time. The essays in Levinson and Mailloux's volume offer a tremendously vigorous workout on different arguments on intention: virtually every essay considering the theory and practice of constitutional interpretation directly faces or ultimately finds it has to face the issue of intention. In legal thinking the association of authority in intention with authority itself is of course manifest. Most naked is the adage about the Unites States Supreme Court's Authority: "We are not final because we are infallible, but we are infallible because we are final": quoted by Michael Hancher, "Dead Letters: Wills and Poems," in Levinson and Mailloux, eds., p. 113 (a truth made clear enough in George W. Bush's election). Behind such real authority it is also easier to understand the connections to various forms of power than in the more gloved hand of literary institutions. Stanley Fish argues that legal arguments are all part of politics, as politics itself is always in a web of traditions of interpretation: "Fish versus Fiss," in *Doing What Comes Naturally*, pp. 120–40. Fish would argue that the same is in fact true about literary studies.

25 In his *Validity in Interpretation* (New Haven: Yale UP, 1967), Hirsch speaks of the science of hermeneutics as having become "vestigial" (p. 210) and notes that the problem in hermeneutics that he addresses has been "neglected in recent years" (p. viii).

26 A rereading of that classic essay—much referred to but I think little read—mainly impresses one now with the thinness of the debate actually engaged, with a relative failure to see what a central issue in interpretation the authors had stumbled on in their effort to provide some theoretical justification for New Critical preference for texts over context and biography. Intentionalism, to revert to their word, which appears in the guise of Livingston Lowes's study, in his *The Road to Xanadu*, of the reading behind Coleridge's "Rime of the Ancient Mariner," an unnamed critic's historical work on Donne and the new astronomy, and Mr. Eliot's footnotes to *The Waste Land*, is seen not as a place of orthodox interpretations that limits critical flexibility but as an annoyance, parallel to the affective fallacy of too personal judgment, that gets in the way of the goal of criticism, finding "the meaning of the poem" (p. 10). Nothing in the essay suggests that finding "the meaning," from semantics, syntax, grammar, and knowledge of the language (p. 10) is a perilous or even very difficult task; in that faith they would even seem to be

professing a faith in author's intention as *the* meaning of a text, only insisting that it is to be found in the author's text, not in his or her biography (see the unclarity on just this issue in W.K. Wimsatt, "Genesis: A Fallacy Revisited," in Newton-DeMolina, ed., pp. 135–36); certainly nothing suggests that in the end there could be more than one meaning, about which sound exegetical critics—other kinds are not even mentioned—could disagree: an impression conveyed even more strongly in Beardsley's arguments in his *The Possibility of Criticism* (Detroit: Wayne State UP, 1970), consolidated and reprinted in Iseminger, ed., pp. 24–40, though he does argue that the single meaning is not necessarily the author's (pp. 25–26). Meaning as interpretation seems indeed not the goal of exegesis; the goal is rather an aesthetic declaration of form in a context of aesthetic autonomy—a conclusion continued by Beardsley's later preoccupation with aesthetic issues within a New Critical context. But to ensure the happy progress of exegesis those fallacy-bound historical and biographical critics must be stopped from stirring up new interpretive ideas with their fallacious arguments from history. The authors are able to place their opponents in history; they see their intentions as those of the romanticism that New Critics usually opposed, concerned as they saw it with elevating and then throbbing in unison with "great souls" and with "intuitive expressive" aesthetics (p. 6), but they show no sense that they themselves might also be placing their own work in a niche of their own historical moment. In their dislike of arguments from history, they especially seem to have erected a considerable firewall against seeing the necessary interplay between interpretation and history. The "way of poetic analysis and exegesis" is to be kept totally separate from that of "biographical or genetic inquiry" (p. 18) as if the two were not necessarily always mutually infected, our interpretation driving our historical interests and our conception of our relative place in history driving our interpretations.

Even the positive statements of what criticism does seem woefully shrunken. Although the romantic biographical tradition is ridiculed for moving from "What did an author set out to do?" to "How far did he succeed in carrying it out?", this is not because of what strikes us, the narrowness of this judicial role assigned to criticism; it is only because the grounds of judgment are based on the wrong, external, evidence. Apparently the true critic, the exegetical critic, using the correct, internal, evidence, fulfills the same judicial goal: he goes to the heart of the rules the poet (p. 14) has adopted in the work and can then judge to what degree they are fulfilled. (The authors do not carry this reasoning to the point of seeing the logical problems, so common in fact in the kind of genre and formal qualities criticism that their project implies, of forcing a work into a procrustean bed and then declaring its general messiness—the result of their own hewing and chopping to make it fit!) Patterson, in Lentricchia and McLaughlin, eds., pp. 141–43, notes this disinterest in hermeneutics more positively than I do, as a focus on evaluative aesthetics, but I don't find the authors indifferent to the issue of meaning as writers in another age might have been, just somewhat ignorant of the issues raised by the search for meaning. The impression one comes away with is that they don't really get it about interpretation, that they would not imagine a case where critics' different preoccupations and worldviews could yield well-stated, persuasive, and very disparate views of the same work. Interpretation, as opposed to "analysis and exegesis" (their terms), might seem to be to them merely the end result of judgmental errors coming from the other, affective, too personal, kind of critical thinking that they also brand as fallacious.

Lest this seem a too condescending note on the progenitors of the position I am defending (they would say perversely and as a result of my false judgment placed in hock to the affective fallacy), I do approve their somewhat influential approach to autobiographical materials—e.g., Eliot's famous notes—closely associated with a text: that is, treat them not as external evidence pretending to authority but as subsidiary (of course that subsidiary *is* a problem) parts of the text itself (p. 16). And I also highly commend their scandalous willingness to face the issue of meanings changing over time—so-called anachronistic meanings—an issue I will look at in section II.xvii, below. Finally, one can only applaud the rhetorical finesse demonstrated in succeeding in placing such a light and short article among the few universally acknowledged critical statements of the Anglo-American tradition.

27 Roland Barthes's essay, "The Death of the Author," *Image—Music—Text* (New York: Hill and Wang, 1977), certainly competes with Wimsatt and Beardsley's for number one place in the countdown of all-time anti-intentional favorites; and, like it, it seems surprisingly undeveloped when revisited, though it is certainly bright and dramatic. Its overall framework is Marxist and historical: the author was established as an "author"ity during the time of "capitalist ideology," but those days are over and the author may safely be declared dead as a historical phenomenon. The tone reminds us of the historical site of Barthes's own authorship, a year before the climax of the utopian hopes of 1968. The essay, as Michael North, "Authorship and Autography," *PMLA* 116 (2001): 1378, has reminded us, was originally published in 1967 in an avant-garde random art-box publication, *Aspen*, with the work of such people as John Cage and Robert Rauschenberg. The heady politics gives way very quickly to a more literary attack on ascribing meaning to authors. Whereas Barthes famously ends proclaiming the death of the author as the cost for the birth of the reader, he is in fact especially concerned with enunciating his own theory of authorship. Truly seen, authors are not

originators but "mixers," people whose originality consists only in blending different past writings. As scriptors rather than authors, they rather selflessly and monkishly quote the past.

Art is thus a web of intertexts, each new scriptor tapping into the cultural heritage: each "a tissue of quotations drawn from the innumerable centers of culture" (p. 146). It is perhaps wrong to call this a text taking a position against intention, as it is enacting rather a repositioning and renaming of the author; once rebaptised scriptor and given a set of scriptorial attributes, this mixer figure is as central to the act of reading as the author had been in intentional theories of meaning. With the author thus not really dead but redefined, the reader can be positioned—as in traditional intentionalist critical theory—as one who is ready to receive the author. Only now that the author is an intertextual mixer, a maker-new of many cultural pasts, the reader is not a student of the biography or milieu of the author, nor is he the traditional critic who ferrets out the author's privileged meaning and conveys it authoritatively to the public; rather he is an expert on intertexts, a disentangler: "In the multiplicity of writing, everything is to be *disentangled*, nothing *deciphered*" (p. 147). We can easily recognize the kind of non-criticism Barthes hails as much like his own subtle unweaving of a text into its many strands. But the striking thing in this essay is that the system of author communicating through a text to a reader is still preserved; only the authorial situation has been redefined, and with it the reader. The new author as scriptor is used to justify a particular critical practice: the trademark move of intentionalism. As North, p. 1383, notes, Barthes is attracted to a writing that really lacks an author entirely, as in Barthes's examples of surrealist interest in automatic writing, group writing, and, in the visual arts, found or ready-made (Duchamp) art; but these are analogies to his normative idea of the scriptoral origin of writing; they are additional more random scriptings, and they only enforce a Barthesian critical practice: "the structure can be followed, 'run' (like the thread of a stocking) at every point and at every level, but there is nothing beneath: the space of writing is to be ranged over, not pierced; writing ceaselessly posits meaning ceaselessly to evaporate it, carrying out a systematic exemption of meaning" (p. 147). Far from allowing the birth of the reader as free agent, for instance to make a feminist or political interpretation of a work of literature that seems not to raise such issues, this definition of scriptor and the text he/she/it produces drives the reader into a formalist and aestheticizing position. Barthes's later work, moving into deconstructive approaches, in effect contradicts this famous statement by leaving more space for play. The writerly text as defined in his famously intensive study of one text, *S/Z*, superseded the more traditional readerly text and, despite its name, allowed the reader to eschew bondage to the author.

28 Michel Foucault's "What is an Author?" *Aesthetics, Method, and Epistemology*, ed. James D. Faubion (New York: New York Press, 1998), pp. 205–22, is an essay only somewhat less well known than Barthes's, which it indeed follows in time (a lecture of February 22, 1969) and in many of its prominent themes. Like Barthes, Foucault is quick to see authorship as an ideological preoccupation of the age of capitalism and private property and, also like Barthes, he predicts its demise. Although he claims not to perform here a "sociological analysis of the author's persona," his instinctive, and brilliant, historical orientation makes his essay at least a prolegomena to the subject. He is especially good at identifying the ideology at work in the use of the author, offering a useful detachment of "author function" from the biographical author and showing us how differently this function is constructed in different ages. His taxonomy of four ways (p. 216; he suggests four need not be definitive) in which the author function works in our discussion of texts effectively deconstructs author function, which is constructed in each of the cases, from mere maker of a text—he does not use Barthes's scriptor but the effect is the same. With Barthes, he shares a central belief that the author function has been constructed not as a place of generative meanings but as a site that limits signification and the circulation of discourse (p. 221). This seems an effective way of indicating the ideological pressure behind the recourse to intentionality—which creates an author function to control reading. His explanation of how intentionality works is as lucid as Fish's will be without Fish's ultimate hesitations: "these aspects of an individual which we designate as making him an author are only a projection, in more or less psychologizing terms, of the operations we force texts to undergo, the connections we make, the traits we establish as pertinent, the continuities we recognize, or the exclusions we practice" (pp. 213–14). See n. 30, below, on some attempts by philosophers to answer his conclusions abut the repressive function of author constructs—unsuccessfully, I conclude.

To those, like myself, who have benefited greatly from the broader notion of discourse and episteme that Foucault put so effectively in circulation (even while we worried over its tendency to excessive globalizing), Foucault's work has obviously allowed for an important new kind of intellectual history that captures not just individual authors but an age. (His *Archaeology of Knowledge,* also appearing in 1969 in France, makes this view of authorship central to his project.) However, Foucault's historicism, which has been generally so influential in literary history, threatens to create its own limits on signification and circulation of discourse. His project, "to arrive at an analysis which can account for the constitution of the subject," seems to offer not just a panopticon to observe subjects but a factory to mass produce them on historical frames: "Truth and Power," *Power/Knowledge: Selected*

Interviews and Other Writings, 1972–77 (New York: Pantheon, 1980), p. 117. Inviting us to define how an author function works in texts of any age, he also opens the possibility of historical closure, in which a set of historical assertions about the nature of authorship in an age could replace author's intention by historical determinism. His somewhat nebulous taxonomy suggests a history that might impute author functions to texts and then read them by the presumed ideologies that the author functions embody. We can easily move back here into what is only a more elaborate intentionalism, with historical author function replacing biographical author. Paul A. Bové, "Discourse," in Lentricchia and McLaughlin, eds., pp. 50–65, makes a strong case for throwing out the interpretive hermeneutic baby with the Old Historical bathwater and re-rendering literary studies as studies of how discourse creates subjects. This opens the way to a positivist's historical knowledge that disallows any disagreements over texts' meanings, as these would have to be a re-opening of the discarded and banned interpretive debates. Much as I respect Foucault's insights, I cannot hail this brave new world of his enthusiasts. See my broader critique of history as implied intentionality, II.vii, below.

In his interesting and philosophically informed study, *The Death and Return of the Author* (Edinburgh: Edinburgh UP, 1998), pp. 20–115, Seán Burke argues that both Barthes and Foucault gesture at banishing the author only to find she inevitably returns in their work—for instance in Barthes's awareness of himself as author in *Roland Barthes by Roland Barthes* or in Foucault's discussion of founding thinkers. Burke's larger concerns are with the attempts of both writers to deny human subjectivity—a point with which I am much in sympathy (see II.vii, below). He shows that the author as human being cannot so easily be dismissed (I would also agree and indeed I am much in favor of literary biography as an art separate from interpretation). But his point doesn't really confront both authors' wish to unsettle the place of authority in interpretation of texts. Intention and authorial subjectivity are different subjects; we may agree that authors have subjectivity (those I have known always appear to) without therefore asserting their authority over their texts. The more blatant argument, that both writers obviously function as authors themselves, is less impressive; given Barthes's focus on intertexts, Foucault's on social text, both could argue they do not see themselves as authors in a traditional sense.

29 Jacques Derrida's extensive controversy with John Searle over Speech Act theory often raises issues of philosophical intention that border on or touch issues of literary intention, with Derrida opposing Searle's use of Speech Act theory to define stable speech acts based on intentional systems of meaning: published as "Signature Event Context," "Limited Inc," and an Afterword in *Limited Inc* (Evanston, IL: Northwestern, 1988)—discussed in Appendix 1.

30 Newton-DeMolina's collection of essays offers a useful anthology of earlier thinking, including Wimsatt and Beardsley's original essay and generous selections from Hirsch. Most of these essays critique Wimsatt and Beardsley's thesis and continue even in attacking them in their primary focus on the uses of internal and external evidence, though a few begin the discussion of Speech Act theory that emerges in later intentionalist commentary. Much of this debate is continued in the Iseminger collection of 1992, which includes a reprint of some of Hirsch's argument and Joseph Margolis, "Robust Relativism," pp. 41–50 from 1980, as well as a later essay by Beardsley, "The Authority of the Text," pp. 24–40, responding to Hirsch's "intentionalist backlash," p. 24. Irwin, ed., *The Death and Resurrection of the Author?* offers essays since (and including) those by Barthes and Foucault responding to the death-of-author question, many by philosophers.

The vigor of Hirsch's individual arguments in favor of author's intention as the secure way of securing "determinate" meaning still command attention. The strength of his argument, unlike that of many who argue for intention, is his ready acceptance of a variety of interpretations, though one, he insists, must be attached to the author's will. Hirsch's second Appendix on Gadamer and his later (1972) very lucid explanation of hermeneutic tradition located intentionality, as Eagleton and others do, at the center of the hermeneutic controversy: "Three Dimensions of Hermeneutics," in Newton-DeMolina, ed., pp. 194–209. As with many strongly held positions, Hirsch's carries major consequences for him: the objective, "scientific" status of literary criticism; the critic's ethical responsibility to maintain the "true" determinant meaning against other only interesting significances. See the interesting evaluation of Hirsch in Raval, 266–67. Hirsch's identification of professional correctness with our ability to produce one determinate author's meaning came under a good deal of criticism. See, among many, the tight argument against his premises in Lutz Danneberg and Hans-Harald Müller, "On Justifying the Choice of Interpretive Theories," *The Journal of Aesthetics and Art Criticism* 43 (Autumn 1984): 7–16. They, Crosman, Barbara Herrnstein Smith, "Actions, Fictions, and the Ethics of Interpretation," *Centrum* 3 (1975) 117–20, and, most recently, Mitscherling, DiTommaso, and Nayed, pp. 81–88, in a useful analysis of Hirsch's arguments, all question the ethical argument Hirsch mounts from Kant's practical imperative, that author intention must be considered *the* meaning as a way of taking other people (authors) as ends in themselves, not instruments. The alternative danger, that critics should use their conceptions of author's intentions as a way of denying other readers' right to be ends in themselves seems a greater ethical, and indeed, as Crosman argues, political danger. Even Dasenbrock, pp. 162–64, grants that intentionalism can be used to justify an arbitrary impostion of will, as in the "originalism" of Bork.

Hirsch impressively continued to rethink his position. In a 1983 essay, "Past Intentions and Present Meanings," *Essays in Criticism* 33 (April 1983), developed more fully in "Transhistorical Intentions and the Persistence of Allegory," *New Literary History* 25 (Summer 1994): 549–67, he modified his concept of authorial intention in a major way. First, he stressed that intention should be taken not as about specific mental states in the actual author but merely as about possible positions of anyone at the time of writing. Then, drawing an analogy with the conservative evolutionist theory in constitutional hermeneutics associated with United States Chief Justice John Marshall, he opened a very large place for acceptable interpretation that develops, from the view of the present state of consciousness of readers, the original ideas. Here, he realizes, authorial meaning threatens to become merely another reader's significance, and on the whole he is not opposed to this. Where the author allowed broad development, really wished to talk to future readers as he believes classics do, Hirsch now believes there can be much latitude in interpretation. Indeed, the exception is only named references that cannot be made into something else, which really amounts mainly to issues we would not debate. See my discussion, below, II.xviii, nn. 20, 21. Hirsch's developing engagement with hermeneutic theory is impressive, though it leaves him here virtually of the devil's anti-intentionalist, "radical historicist" (his own former excoriation) party without knowing it. He even hails Foucault as a fellow traveler, who at least believes in a simple "author function," though it may be occupied by the reader ("Transhistorical Intentions," p. 550).

Hirsch's belief in single, determinant meaning continued to find serious supporters, for instance John Reichert, *Making Sense of Literature* (Chicago: U of Chicago P, 1977), e.g., ch. 3, "Writers and Readers," P.D. Juhl, *Interpretation: An Essay in the Philosophy of Literary Criticism* (Princeton: Princeton UP, 1980), and more recently William Irwin, whose *Intentionalist Interpretation: A Philosophical Explanation and Defense* (Westport, CT: Greenwood, 1999), is explicitly a tribute to Hirsch. Irwin's philosophical clarity, which is impressive, is sometimes a benefit, sometimes a weakness. He out-Hirsches Hirsch by returning to a strict binary of meaning/significance and critiquing later Hirsch for not keeping the faith; and he rests his case on the weak ethical imperative for preferring an intentional meaning. His philosopher's fear of relativism keeps him far from accepting an open conflict over interpretation to which his lucidity might seem to bring him. Instead he offers an "urauthor" as a revised place of Hirsch's meaning—a mental idea of an author to whom we *must* look for meaning (cf. the discussion of Knapp and Michaels above, n. 20). Although the idea of an author may be filled in or supplemented by biographical or historical information, the formulation seems patently to allow readers to support whatever interpretation they come to by cloaking it in the authority of the urauthor (cf. also discussion of Stanley Fish in Appendix 2). Irwin is weakest in dealing with the complexity of real interpretive situations, whether in literature, history, or the law. Irwin is following Gracia in imagining what Gracia calls a "pseudo-historical author," as with the urauthor a constructed amalgam of what the reader imagines the author to be from the text and what she knows of the historical author. See Irwin, ed., *The Death and Resurrection of the Author?*, pp. 180–81. Both acknowledge that they are indebted to Alexander Nehamas, "Writer, Text, Work, Author," repub. in Irwin, ed., pp. 95–115, whose idea of author as construct is similar: "a plausible historical variant of the writer": pp. 101, 109. Like Irwin, Gracia and Nehamas give us no reason why this concept of the author is different from merely someone's interpretation pinned onto the author; to the extent the concept is reinforced by some real details of the author's life or time the concept becomes merely an intentional reading. The combination of interpretive invention plus a little knowledge seems too often a dangerous and easy way to pretend to interpreter's assurance. Essays by Nickolas Pappas and Robert Stecker, in the same volume (pp. 117–28, 129–40), similarly question how the construct can be other than the "repressive" (i.e., improperly exercising control by confusing interpretation with author's intention) use of the author that Foucault opposed. Ironically, what they propose as a way of using the idea of the author to stabilize meaning is exactly what Foucault opposed and exposed.

31 I should be clear that I have long admired much of this diverse work as contributions to their proper fields, social and cultural history. Indeed, I have done such work, am co-editor of a journal (*Victorian Literature and Culture*) closely associated with such work, and even an author of a biography focused on a poet (Robert Browning's) social, cultural, and intellectual world. My concern here is with its use in issues of interpretation and then only when it presumes to do more than just present one way of looking at a text.

32 Mary Louise Pratt's early review essay of influential anthologies on reader-response criticism makes the connections with great—and quite unusual—clarity: "Interpretive Strategies/Strategic Interpretations: On Anglo-American Reader Response Criticism," *Boundary 2*, 11 (1982–83), esp. 203–10. She identifies reader-response criticism as a theory area that has been standoffish toward the new swing to history that at that time she still mainly exemplified by the theory of Louis Althusser and British Marxists Raymond Williams and Terry Eagleton. Although her argument is political—we should prefer talking about the production of literature, with the social issues it raises, to the mere aesthetic consumption of literature, which she equates with reader-response work—her argument then perspicuously becomes one about interpretation.

Reader response has taken down the Berlin wall of the affective fallacy, allowing critics to talk about response to literature. But it has not been similarly willing to take down the intentional fallacy. If it did, Pratt argues, we could look at the production of texts as a full study of historical sitedness.

Despite the attractive appeal to symmetry in wall bashing, such an argument leaves Pratt somewhat naively in the midst of enormous interpretive problems, which I will attempt to explore in the course of this essay. She seems to want to say that the production has a symmetry with the consumption; but then she realizes that this would limit interpretation, as an intentional view will, to a meaning embodied somehow in the production, so that she ultimately waffles and allows further production of meaning(s) by the readers. The major problems of diachronicity of reception and of the necessary acts of interpretation made in writing the history of production do not yet appear in this essay. But her essay is impressive in facing rather than ignoring the issue of intentionality in the turn to history.

33 Like Mailloux also, they seem to have leveraged neopragmatism in order to dismiss philosophical (here hermeneutic) discussion (pragmatism *is* a philosophical discussion) in favor of history (in Mailloux's case, history of readers and rhetoric); they thus reverse Rorty's own use of history (of philosophy) to gain a handle on the failure of epistemology. Anti-foundationalism is not the end of philosophy and the beginning of history; it would logically produce a skeptical hermeneutics (see my discussion, II.xix).

34 Hirsch's deep insight as a theorist is evident in his preoccupation with this distinction as a proposal for hierarchizing and thus harmonizing different meanings. If disparate interpretations had of course always been a central issue in hermeneutics, there had not been sufficient focus on this problem in the American and English context, where old historicism assumed a determinate author's meaning but New Criticism, as in Wimsatt and Beardsley, also preserved the idea of determinate meaning, located in the text—and thus easily associated with an author's intention as well. Irwin, *Intentionalist Interpretation*, properly follows Hirsch in locating the entire discussion of intentionality in the broader European debate on hermeneutics.

35 *Interpretive Acts: In Search of Meaning* (Oxford: Clarendon, 1988); *Literary Meaning: Reclaiming the Study of Literature* (New York: NYU Press, 1996). In the first book, Harris calls his approach ecological criticism, as if he wanted to parallel the school of critical green environmentalists under that name by nurserying authors and rescuing the breed from the extinction Barthes already announced. His second book more boldly proclaims the return of intention (pp. 124–25) and the demise of structuralism, deconstruction, neopragmatism, and most reader theory (all labeled as hermeticism). Like G.K. Chesterton's Man who was Thursday, he inhabits a world threatening to disintegrate into

total non-communication and solipsism and finds the only reassurance is the moly of author's intention. As the last of the red hot anti-intentionalists I hereby reassure him (speech act, reassuring, with perlocutionary intent of calming—which I fear may not be fulfilled) that these interpretive issues do not affect normal social interaction and relation. In this work Harris offers a lexicon of binaries equivalent to Hirsch's well-known meaning and significance (p. 141). He often prefers "symptomatic" for significance. This later book argues less from Speech Act theory than the first, though Grice is still offered in evidence (see my discussion in Appendix 1), more on (very) traditional Diltheyan hermeneutics (see my discussion, II.xviii, n. 408, below). John Shawcross, *Intentionality and the New Traditionalism: Some Liminal Means to Literary Revisionism* (University Park: Pennsylvania State UP, 1991), similarly feels a calling to save the author and his craft from readers' purported indifference, especially to issues of genre—as if genres only existed in authors' minds. Patrick Swinden, *Literature and the Philosophy of Intention* (New York: St. Martin's P, 1999), rearms intention as a "flanking manoeuvre" against the challenge to "humane values" in current theory (p. x). More impressive because broader in thinking is Dasenbrock, who adds a moral brief for intention to what is mainly an argument against Fish and Foucault, both of whom he sees sponsoring a simplistic view of meaning as the creation of an agency-less community—a critique I find in itself often quite cogent and always interesting.

36 I am mainly characterizing the aura of intention as political and patriarchal in nature. Visitors to patriarchal regimes will know that power has its human face, the loving, good, father/brother authority. So occasionally the anti-intentionalist is characterized as lacking personal respect for the author, being unwilling to meet him in an I/Thou relation (see n. 30 above on Hirsch's ethical argument). Nöel Carroll, for instance, speaks of needing to have an "authentic conversation" with the author: "Art, Intention and Conversation," in Iseminger, ed., pp. 123–24, justifying even recourse to biographical knowledge. I have never met an author who didn't turn readers who wanted to have conversations with their texts to the texts themselves. Swinden similarly casts his intentionalist views in moral terms; he writes of the "writer's responsibility for his work," which he fears has been attenuated by writers' own attempts to divest themselves of the "purposiveness" of use of words (pp. xi, 3). Dasenbrock's moral argument, p. 80, is about understanding others as "different from ourselves"; he argues that Derrida does just this when it is a matter of defending the writing of his friend Paul de Man (pp. 85–106) or his copyright. This is *ad hominem* with a thrust but also mistakenly assumes that the anti-intentionalist homogenizes what he reads with what he is, more than the intentionalist does. Both may; neither has to.

37 I have no desire either, as perhaps Wimsatt and Beardsley did, to deny other obvious uses of literary historical work in interpretation, mainly those dealing with what are essentially historical issues—did Jane Austen know about the feminist discourse her work is said to subversively encode? did Tennyson ever speak of the love that could not speak its name directly in *In Memoriam*? above all, is the allusion to the work of another writer found in the text possible or plausible? Frank Cioffi, "Intention and Interpretation in Criticism," in Newton-DeMolina, p. 58, speaks of such work as providing a "kind of sieve" that excludes certain possibilities. These are always in fact critiques of interpretations that have themselves been built on prior historical assertions or assumptions so that here historical work purifies itself. In writing biography I found that my new fund of knowledge about a writer (Robert Browning) produced more such limiting critiques of others' biographically inspired interpretations than new suggestions for interpretation.

38 Derrida, pp. 114–15.

39 Derrida, pp. 115–31; on p. 121 Derrida does address the question more directly, arguing that there is a *telos* of—an assumption of direction toward—plenitude in the intentional thinking of Searle.

40 *The Critical I* (New York: Columbia UP, 1992), p. 21. Holland proceeds to propose a system in which "codes" control (in the reader) tight, "not otherwise," responses, for instance those in word voicing or grammar, whereas "canons" are looser, variable cultural systems (pp. 32–40). But there are of course also endless pragmatic contextual responses which are not definable as hardwired but which appear so because we will not disagree over them.

41 See, for instance, the discussion of Suzy Anger's Introduction to the collection *Knowing the Past*, in II.xviii, n. 415, below.

42 Gibbs, pp. 200–01, cites research he and Kerry Pfaff did that offered different students different profiles about an author before they all read the same work; the work tended to be judged within the frames provided by the varying author profiles. I justify biographical work in relation to interpretation mainly negatively: it may not provide the correct interpretive frame but it may at least shake up the stultified accepted ones that have dominated approaches to works.

43 Fish makes this point clearly in regard to yet another field: his second one, the law. Law should "be self-declaring and not in need of piecing out by some supplementary discourse, for were it necessary for the law to have recourse to some supplementary discourse at crucial points, that discourse would be in the business of specifying what the law is, and consequently its autonomy would have been compromised indirectly": *There's No Such thing as Free Speech ... And It's a Good Thing Too* (New York: Oxford UP, 1994), p. 141.

44 Though most of his work finds ways to minimize its traditional force, I find Fish himself is unclear on the issue of intentionality. See Appendix 2.

45 On the different generations of hermeneutical thinking on intention see II.xviii, n. 408.

46 Hans-Georg Gadamer, *Truth and Method* (New York: Seabury, 1975), p. 56.

47 A fact obscured by the anecdotal focus on Hirsch's take on Wordsworth's "A Slumber Did My Spirit Seal," one of his few biographical contextual readings.

48 See nn. 27–28 on both, above.

49 On Derrida's lengthy but conflicted views on intention, see Appendix 1; on de Man, see III.iii, below.

50 Again, on Fish on intention, see Appendix 2.

51 For instance, the work of David Bleich and Norman Holland and the work developing in the late 1970s and into the 1990s on reading as a woman. See Judith Fetterley, *The Resisting Reader: A Feminist Approach to American Fiction* (Bloomington: Indiana UP, 1978), Elizabeth A. Flynn and Patrocinio P. Schweickart, eds. *Gender and Reading: Essays on Readers, Texts, and Contexts* (Baltimore: Johns Hopkins UP, 1986), and essays on gender and identity in Andrew Bennett, ed., *Readers and Reading* (London: Longman, 1995). In Section III, I critique the work of Iser, de Man, Scholes, and Fish, all males, as attempting, by contrast, to corral the reader into one or another prescribed position.

52 See n. 20, above.

53 See above, n. 3.

54 Irwin, *Intentionalist Interpretation*, ch. 1 and throughout. He critiques Knapp and Michaels for asserting their normative views as a matter of descriptive fact (p. 50).

55 As fairly simple oral speech acts, they are explained by context as problems in pragmatics, not semantics (meaning); as ambiguities introduced by play of language, they are explained as problems in rhetorical (tropic) ambiguity. Both are discussed further below. (See below II.ix, n. 6 and II.x, for the major differences between interpretion of oral and written language and II.xiii on tropes.) The philosopher Donald Davidson, in a book I did not read until this section was written, interestingly draws on the same analogy of a fire in a theater to emphasize the potential for misunderstanding between an apparent literal meaning and a speaker's ulterior purpose. He imagines an actor in a theater trying unsuccessfully to persuade his audience that he isn't acting, there really is a fire. His point is that there is no way to *say* one's true intention—which is always determined by an act of interpretation—even if the actor used Frege's invention of the assertion sign (a capital H without its

second post). To use it might only lead to more applause at his representation of sincere fears of fire: "Communication and Convention," *Inquiries into Truth and Interpretation* (Oxford: Clarendon, 1984), p. 270.

56 I will not rest my argument on the rather decisive but recently rare case of joint authorship. How much more complicated to the point of impossibility becomes the hunt for the real author behind the work when we find, as with the wonderful poems of Michael Field, that the gentleman in question is in fact two ladies, niece and aunt, writing seamlessly. Yes, they were both lesbians and in love with each other but distinctly different generations. How much more complicated the cases with work written down from oral sources, where the "author" may have lived hundreds of years. Gibbs, p. 218, cites Brecht's work with Elizabeth Hauptmann or the easier case of Pound and Eliot, as well as work in fixing dramatic texts in rehearsal or the more common collaboration in academic papers.

57 Gibbs, pp. 45, 123, 135, 177–78, stresses how much oral communication works out intentions (for the practical purpose of knowing where the other person is coming from) by interactive means, questioning, feedback, establishing common grounds, testing assumptions—none really available in attempts to determine intention in written work. All former students will recall, all professors know, the difference that settles in at an exam when we answer a question by limiting the exam-takers to the text: those awful words, "read the question!"

58 See Appendix 1.

59 C.K. Ogden and I.A. Richards, *The Meaning of Meaning* (1923; rpt. New York: Harcourt Brace, 1956), pp. 185–208. Lyons, *Approaches to Intentionality*, pp. 1–3. Ogden and Richards consider only oral cases and find 14 or 16 versions of meaning, depending on whether we count (they do) complications in meaning due to symbol situations.

60 See my discussion of Fish's theory of communities of reading and its problems in III.v and my own discussion of reception in section IV, both below.

61 Gibbs, p. 14, for instance, notes that Georgia O'Keefe rejected sexual interpretations of her work. Viewers who experience the sensuous thrill of her paintings are not likely to be deterred from their meanings (an odd case for Gibbs to cite on the other side of the issue of intention). Even Harris, *Literary Meaning*, pp. 93–94, easily grants Lawrence's point.

62 This apparently so plausible goal was of course the aim of much biographical and historical criticism in the nineteenth century. It was the large project of hermeneutics from about 1800 on in the work of Friedrich Schleiermacher, with his stress on working into the spirit of the author as well as the more historically oriented Wilhelm Dilthey. See II.xviii, n. 408, below. Gibbs reminds us, pp. 58, 91, that even if we seize on some evidence and call it an intention for the work it is also subject to multiple interpretation, as are

characterizations of ordinary actions. He (Spenser) wrote to clarify the Irish issue, or to castigate the Irish, or to encourage a tougher policy in Elizabethan Ireland. Similarly, attributions of intention can imply more or less. She (Woolf) wrote to express her experience of madness through Septimus, or to ask for sympathy for the mentally ill against those doctors, or to stave off further illness.

63 Swinden's intelligent approach tries to follow changing intentions both as realized in characters as represented and in the text as a whole. He believes he finds them in the language. But his exploration of forms of intention—purpose, motive, preintention, intention in doing—suggests how difficult it would be to specify actual intentions of an author.

64 Friedrich Schleiermacher, "Compendium of 1819," in Heinz Kimmerle, ed., *Hermeneutics: The Handwritten Manuscripts* (Missoula: U of Montana P, 1977), p. 113.

65 See Lyons for a very full discussion of various approaches to judging others' meanings. The practical means we have developed to figure out other people's meanings generally apply to behavior, not to writing. Even committed intentionalists now seem ready to disavow a psychologism of seeking out inner intentions. Swinden, pp. 27–35, follows Gilbert Ryle's thinking on mind similarly to deny the idea of a prior intention of a little man within the man or ghost in the machine. Such as it is, intention inheres in the action itself. He thus argues intention only from the language itself, using Speech Act theory, on which see II.x, below and Appendix 1. Another similar view, argued as from Wittgenstein with only a few oracular quotes from him, is Colin Lyas, "Wittgensteinian Intentions," in Iseminger, ed., pp. 132–51. His discussion of the dependence of word meanings on language, not mere will of the user—pp. 144–45, the famous bububu case, see *Philosophical Investigations* (New York: Macmillan, 1953), p. 18—would seem to say just the opposite, that words in play are in play apart from the author. Lyas's point then becomes the weak one, that one cannot outlaw speaking of intention.

66 Which is exactly what we do in biography: face endless data that all need to be interpreted to have any meaning. We here surely may read the work in the hope of interpreting the intentions; this becomes a specialist reading, the biographer's attempt to fathom some of the personal issues behind the text. Only a hasty and foolish biographer claims that his biographical conclusions about intentions can serve as a guide to reading the work. It is one, very widely interpretive, approach, I might almost say wildly interpretive, as it adds to all the guesses it makes about motivations behind the tale its so many interpretations of the life. We biographers may claim an expert's knowledge of life and works explained by some key or other to the person: don't trust us. The more we are expert the more we have an overall take on

the writer, the more we become Shandyans with our particular hobby horses to ride through every work of the writer. The kinds of intentions biographers deal with are almost certain to be those that fall under the category of broad motivations. These have not been much considered in literary discussions of intention as, when they are clear enough not just to be interpretive moves, they are likely to be blatant, of the sort we identify with rhetoric rather than literature: Samuel Smiles went down to Leeds to give an address to the working men to persuade them of the need for learning to read. For an excellent discussion of intention in the field of rhetoric, see Lyon, *Intentions Negotiated, Contested, and Ignored*. See also II.v, below, esp. n. 118.

67 Gibbs, pp. 135, 178, but cf. 123, tries to argue that writing should also be seen as a feedback dialogue with readers: sometimes; one thinks of Thackeray including reader comment preferring Becky to Amelia in *Vanity Fair* but, as here, it is generally the writer who gets feedback from the reader, not reader from writer. The text keeps giving that same answer to our questions.

68 Mitscherling, DiTommaso, and Nayed agreeably (for philosophers very agreeably) compare the experience of writing fiction with a "firm intent" in mind to "shopping for food staples when we are hungry. If you haven't eaten all day and you set out to the store to buy milk, eggs, and bread, you're liable to return home with chocolate chip cookies, potato chips and a half-pound bag of M&M's" (p. 108); they also offer a good example from Mark Twain of an author's experience of changes on the way in writing (p. 109).

69 See my discussion of Foucault, II.i, n. 28, and section II.vii, below.

70 Gibbs, p. 64–65, records cognitive research into speech, showing that even there words and word patterns are regularly picked up from others, so that there is finally "a very complex relation between intentions and what is actually said."

71 Our I or ego of course; but a more mysterious something than we generally like to think about. Is there a thought system, a language of thought (LOT), beneath our thought system of language, as Jerry Fodor likes to suggest? Or is writing and speaking the process of thinking itself? For Fodor, see *The Language of Thought* (Cambridge, MA: Harvard UP, 1975).

72 Gibbs, pp. 56, 163, 228, finds all of these present regularly even in speech. Who has not thrilled to Whitman's big embracing of even his contradictions?

73 Again Gibbs, who gives a rich selection of evidence against his own position for intention, records research that shows speakers often occupy a variety of positions from which they seem to talk: so I write to you as authoritative professor and brother reader—what are you to make of me? J. Hillis Miller similarly finds Jacques Derrida, in his thinking about speech acts, asserting that the word comes before any self: in the sense that "the

self is multitudinous and variable, permeable, remade from moment to moment by speech acts": *Speech Acts in Literature* (Stanford: Stanford UP, 2001), p. 61. Miller speculates himself that even the medium—letter, telegram, email—defines the role the writer assumes: p. 194.

74 W.V. Quine, *Word and Object* (Cambridge: MIT Press, 1960), pp. 42–46, sees our experience of a word as made up of all the prior experiences we have had of it, but even this creates too coherent a machine of the mind. If, to use his traditional example, we understood "bachelor" in our unique way as the sum of all the unmarried men we have known, we might also forget some of them, choose to repress the one that remarried mom and treated her so badly, give extra weight to memories of the best man to our own wedding, and keep revising these as we always are revising memories over time. On Quine's thinking see also I.xvii, n. 396 and Appendix I below.

75 Michael Krausz, "Intention and Interpretation: Hirsch and Margolis," in Iseminger, ed., p. 152, makes a similar point: the author as an entity is not stable over time. Gibbs, pp. 61–62, notes that even in speech, research in cognitive psychology shows speakers changing intentions in mid-stream. The subject of language is a vacillating, changeable one.

76 Paul Whitney and Matthew B. Clark, "Disambiguation and Cognitive Control," in David S. Gorfein, ed., *Resolving Semantic Ambiguity* (New York: Springer-Verlag, 1989), p. 250, see major opportunities for complication or confusion in each of the stages.

77 Michael Ryan, "Narcissus Autobiographer," *ELH* 43 (1976): 204–05, argues that even in autobiography the self of the writer is necessarily an "alterity ... at once parallel to and radically different from the consciousness." Having summoned up that philosopher here, I should note that Derrida is comfortable, as John Searle is not, with the view that some statements can arise from our unconscious or take on meaning by provoking a response in our unconscious. More broadly, statements are never fully conscious to themselves in the philosophical sense of intention as aboutness: literally they do not fully know what they are about, *Limited Inc*: pp. 73–76. See Appendix 1. Dutton, p. 197, notes that arguments against intention are sometimes based on the difficulty of knowing what is intended, sometimes dispute the coherence of an intender: both Freud and Derrida in different ways question the unity of the source of intention—what Dutton calls a "metaphysical" objection.

78 Hirsch, pp. 51–57. With his usual acuity Hirsch tried to wish away all such concerns with the complexity of the author's life and mind, conscious and unconscious. He doesn't seem to face squarely the division of possible intention that such states of biography and mind imply, making intention inevitably complex and unclear. And such abstraction to some specific intention manifest in the work leads him away from all biographical/historical situation

of intention. Irwin sees him, like himself, Nehamas, and Gracia, as really offering an author construct, not a real author: *Intentional Interpretation*, pp. 28–29. Irwin's discussion of unconscious intention (pp. 41–42) seems also to miss the multiplicity of intention introduced. He later tries to remedy this by breaking a work up into many mental intentions (p. 64), some of which the author is aware, some not. Here intention falls back into the philosophical use of the term, in effect a being about something. This in turn cuts off the text from the author, again requiring a mere conceptual author construct.

79 See the discussion of Julia Kristeva's work on language and madness, below.

80 After writing this I found a thought in Culler suggesting a different kind of psychological bifurcation, that of unconscious mastery, where, as in driving, we do something without that time consciously willing it. (Malle, Moses, and Baldwin, in their Introduction, use the same example along with eating, but seem to prefer to think of these as conscious.) Applied to my concerns: if driver (of his pen) Dickens falls into a routine he has used so often that it is virtually automatic, he could very easily fall into writing that contradicts the conscious point he has in mind. See Jane P. Tompkins, ed., *Reader-Response Criticism* (Baltimore: Johns Hopkins UP, 1985), p. 106. On other unconscious actions and speech see n. 88, below.

81 See Freud's well-known *Jokes and their Relation to the Unconscious*, trans. James Strachey (New York: Norton, 1960). *The Interpretation of Dreams* (New York: Basic Books, 1956) proposes a view into the psyche through dream analysis: what Freud famously finds there is a system of motivation. The desires of our dream thoughts are simplified into the manifest dream content, what we dream. The linguist Roman Jakobson and Lacan both followed Freud himself in seeing these representations as functioning in complicated literary ways by condensation or displacement (all three disagree which are metaphorical, which metonymic, and how). To find the intention (dream thought) behind a dreamer, we can only multiply possible meanings as we try imagining ways in which the dream thoughts have been converted into the manifest dream content by figures of speech. Unconscious motivation in a writer presumably produces similar overdetermination of possible meanings if we try to work our way back through the work's manifest content to the original desires as the motivations and intentions.

See also the interesting essays in Jonathan Culler, ed., *On Puns: The Foundation of Letters* (Oxford: Basil Blackwell, 1988) for more recent essays on intentional and unintentional play in our words. Malle, Moses, and Baldwin in their Introduction, p. 4, insist that intention as motivation is not merely a desire but a desire put in action. I would agree but add that desire in action often complicates the original desire. We want expensive, dangerous *pâté de foie gras* but settle for chopped liver.

82 Harris, *Interpretive Acts*, p. 138.

83 Her essay, "Meaning and Expression," in Overton and Palermo, eds., pp. 215–35, offers a brief summary of her work. See also *The Transition from Infancy to Language: Acquiring the Power of Expression* (Cambridge: Cambridge UP, 1993). Bloom calls the pre-language states "mental meanings" or "mental intentional states": p. 224. Students of literature might have a bias in favor of language allowing the states rather than the other way around; but her information is persuasive. Indeed, don't we all generally sense that we are hungry before we actually say, "I'm hungry"—though, yes, we may decide we are hungry because dinner time has arrived or even actually feel hunger because we know the time for eating has arrived.

84 See her *Revolution in Poetic Language* (New York: Columbia UP, 1984). Lacan's most lucid explainer, Shoshana Felman, delineates ways in which his practice follows all Freudian analysis in reading a division in the patient's discourse: in "the practice of psychoanalysis, 'reading' refers to the analyst's activity of interpreting, and the emphasis is on the displacement operated by the interpreting; the analyst is called upon to interpret the excess in the patient's discourse ... the analytic meaning is then a displacement of the meaning of the patient's discourse, since it consists in giving what has been pronounced *another reading*. The analytic reading is thus essentially the reading of a difference that inhabits language, a kind of mapping in the subject's discourse of its points of disagreement with, or difference from, itself": *Jacques Lacan and the Adventure of Insight: Psychoanalysis in Contemporary Culture* (Cambridge: Harvard UP, 1987), p. 21. Felman goes on to define Lacan's difference in also finding self-division in the reader. Raval, 270, makes a broadly similar point about Lacanian thinking as an interrogation of a unified subject speaking (or writing).

85 Lacan's emphasis on language as the place from which human self-division speaks has been recognized as obviously approaching his thinking to the broader project of deconstruction of the subject in Derrida and others: man's "nature is woven by effects in which is to be found the [divided] structure of language of which he becomes the materials": Lacan, *Ecrits: A Selection* (New York: Norton, 1977), p. 284; "*no* intention can *ever* be fully conscious, or actually present to itself": Derrida, *Limited Inc*, p. 73 . On the broader project of deconstruction of the subject, see Leo Bersani, *A Future for Astyanax* (Boston: Little Brown, 1976).

86 As well as in some of the thinking of predecessors in psychology in his age. See Lancelot Law Whyte, *The Unconscious Before Freud* (New York: Basic Books, 1960) and, for the period near to Freud, also Rick Rylance, *Victorian Psychology and British Culture 1850–1880* (New York: Oxford UP, 2000) and Sally Shuttleworth, *Charlotte Brontë and Victorian Psychology* (Cambridge: Cambridge UP, 1996).

87 Including our differing sense of our selves over time. Paul A. Roth, "Interpretation as explanation," in David R. Hiley, James F. Bohman, and Richard Shusterman, eds. *The Interpretive Turn: Philosophy, Science, Culture* (Ithaca: Cornell UP, 1991), pp. 179–96, interestingly suggests that psychoanalysis itself could be seen not as a quest by analysis for some deeper "real" meaning of the self ("unacknowledged but intentional contents of actions of an agent," p. 182) but as a reconceptualization of the experience itself over the course of the interpretive process of the analysis.

88 Gibbs, pp. 26, 30, 32–33, reports on more specific actions done unconsciously and thus unintentionally from work in cognitive psychology and philosophy of intentions and motives. These include neuroses but also panic reactions and different-level intentions.

89 See my "Charlotte Brontë on the Couch," in *Charlotte Brontë and Sexuality* (Cambridge: Cambridge UP, 1984), ch. II.

90 *Ideology: An Introduction* (London: Verso, 1991); see his taxonomy of types of ideology, from mere hypocrisy through rationalization to total belief, in "What is Ideology," pp. 1–31. See also Raymond Williams, *Keywords: A Vocabulary of Culture and Society* (1976; Hammersmith: Fontana Press, 1983), pp. 153–57. This activity falls more broadly under intentions hard to get at because of deliberate deceit, which may indeed be the case where a writer hides a political or ideological postion she actually holds from powers of her place and time. Gibbs, pp. 153–60, presents surprising evidence on how regularly deceit is the intention in everyday speech. We are a race of liars, we human race, and writers especially are generally dealing in the non true. Sincerity as a value opens further room for deceit—as anyone who studies the self-presentations of writers knows. Gibbs wishes to exclude such aims from "communicative intentions" (p. 7), but anyone who wants to think about writers' intentions will find that hard to do. Hitler's *Mein Kampf* was not just intended to communicate the story of his life and vision; it had something to do with the *Kampf* itself.

91 Dasenbrock, p. 139, notes similar issues of ideology repressing homosexual expression raised in Emily Dickinson criticism. Slavoj Žižek calls attention to postmodern cynicism in the form suggested by Peter Sloterdijk: "they know very well what they are doing , but still, they are doing it": *The Sublime Object of Ideology* (London: Verso, 1989), p. 29. Lacan recovers the ideology in postmodern life as a more fundamental avoidance of the Lacanian Real of our desire by the creation of a social reality—itself an ideology cynicism can't see through.

92 Louis Althusser, "Ideology and Ideological State Apparatuses," in *Lenin and Philosophy*, trans. Ben Brewster (New York: Monthly Review Press, 1971), pp. 127–86.

93 Althusser, *For Marx*, trans. Ben Brewster (New York: Random House, 1970), pp. 233–34.

94 Kenneth S. Abraham, "Statutory Interpretation and Literary Theory: Some Common Concerns of an Unlikely Pair," in Levinson and Mailloux, p. 148, notes similarly a confusion in conscious intention: we may intend to say p but are not aware of the implicature that makes us also saying q. We are caught in a web where we say what we mean and also what we don't mean—as indeed so often happens in family quarrels—a point also made by Beardsley, in Iseminger, ed., p. 27.

95 Jameson, *The Political Unconscious: Narrative as a Socially Symbolic Act* (Ithaca: Cornell UP, 1981).

96 Macherey, *A Theory of Literary Production*, trans. Geoffrey Wall (1978; London: Routledge, 1985). For him, ideological representations display their conflict of meanings.

97 It does not follow that the author's command of irony will make his or her presentation and intentions certain to the reader, as I will observe immediately below in looking at irony as a means to deliberate uncertainty and again when we look at textual uncertainties (II.xiii).

98 *Selections from the Prison Notebooks*, trans. Q. Hoare and G.N. Smith (New York: International, 1971), p. 324. See also Eagleton, *Ideology*, pp. 46–47.

99 *Uneven Developments: The Ideological Work of Gender in Mid-Victorian England* (Chicago: U of Chicago P, 1988); Athena Vrettos, *Somatic Fictions: Imagining Illness in Victorian Culture* (Stanford: Stanford UP, 1995): see especially her introductory chapter where she theorizes this vision of discourses. Amanda Anderson, *Tainted Souls and Painted Faces* (Ithaca: Cornell UP, 1993) offers a similarly nuanced approach to issues of agency and character in discussions of cultural discourses. See also my own introductory chapter to *Victorian Discourses on Sexuality and Religion* (Cambridge: Cambridge UP, 1993), where I also adjust Foucault. For a broad discussion of the uses of discourse see Sara Mills, *Discourse* (New York: Routledge, 1997).

100 "Columbus Runs Aground," in Paola Bottalla and Michela Calderaro, eds., *Counting and Recounting: Measuring Inner and Outer Space in the Renaissance* (Trieste: Edizioni La Mongolfiera, 1995), p. 24.

101 *Dostoevsky's Poetics* (Minneapolis: U of Minnesota P, 1984).

102 On heteroglossia see esp. M.M. Bakhtin, "Discourse in the Novel," *The Dialogic Imagination: Four Essays* (Austin: U of Texas P, 1981), pp. 259–422. With his interest in the social origins of language, Bakhtin frequently uses a critical language of intention, in his case close to the philosophical sense of the term, a control exerted over language by consciousness, but his stress is especially on how language is always already "shot through with intentions and accents" (p. 293) that resist a writer's attempt fully to appropriate them

to his intention; and he valorizes the novel, whose heteroglossia embodies the welter of mixed intentions in a society's language in use. Bakhtin's views on poetry seem limited just because he seems to believe that such work can be defined as a simple, clear intention of an author. The fertility of his approach to the novel is especially in his acceptance of the text as a place not reducible to a simple author's intention—even if he will attribute the diversity of *Crime and Punishment* to a biographical entity, Dostoevski. For further discussion of Bakhtin on intention see II.xiv, n. 318.

Jauss has noted (see Machor and Goldstein, eds., p. 15) that Bakhtin thought through literature from the perspective of author and production, not reception, and consequently he did not face hermeneutical questions. Bakhtin's late work on speech genres, however, is concerned with address in texts (see below, II.xvi, n. 352 and discussion in text).

103 See II.i, n.27. Derrida has famously also developed an explanation, at the level of philosophy of language, of ideological double-voicedness. In his thinking, language is fractured against itself from its moment of enunciation. Although utterances may appear to create hierarchies in binary oppositions, they necessarily speak both sides of the opposition. Deconstruction isn't merely something one does to texts; it is the uncovering of the plurality already there from the moment of writing. See Appendix 1.

104 Linda Hutcheon, *Irony's Edge: The Theory and Politics of Irony* (New York: Routledge, 1994), looks at irony in confrontational and political situations, where irony is often intended and often taken as mockery and jeering and may prove risky to the subject, a moment of possible insult or political reaction. I look below, II.xiii, at problems of judging such irony in the more distant communication systems of writing and from the reader's point of view. Here I explore the uncertainty often introduced by irony, in person or in writing, from the speaker/writer's point of view. On the various types of literary irony see II.xiii, n. 110.

105 Richard Rorty, *Contingency, Irony and Solidarity* (Cambridge: Cambridge UP, 1989), esp. p. 87, sees open-ended irony as just such a place of possible distance and danger. We may think beyond our own current beliefs, yet this must remain a private, not publicly acknowledged, awareness (see also II.xiii, n. 309).

106 Roland Barthes, *S/Z*, trans. Richard Miller (New York: Hill and Wang, 1974), p. 120. Conversely, Barthes dismisses irony when it is used to assign ownership to a discourse. See the discussion in Hutcheon, p. 120, who quotes this point. In her chapter on "Intention and Interpretation," Hutcheon's attempt to solve the problem of intention by trying to forge a total intention made up of the author's *or* the reader's perception of intention seems a mere willed solution to a problem of uncertainties in intention that doesn't go away, so

another imaginary solution to a real problem. Barthes generally is uncomfortable with irony as asserting a stereotype that destroys multivalency by affirming the power of one discourse over another. I return to the issue of irony, there to the greater complexities of reading irony, in II.xiii, below.

107 See the discussion of irony in Daniel O. Nathan, "Irony, Metaphor, and the Problem of Intention," in Iseminger, ed., pp. 183–96. Nathan notes that inadvertant ironies continue to seem ironic even if the author disavows them. Irwin, *Intentionalist Interpretation*, p. 66, n. 28, states Nathan's argument but then tries to close it by an appeal to intention: this misses Nathan's point.

108 Paul de Man's earlier reflections on irony look at the way the speaker doubles himself in irony, reflecting on himself (Baudelaire's image of a man slipping on a banana and then standing outside himself to laugh is his example). Ironic consciousness, like that of the philosopher, is a deliberate division of the self: Paul de Man, "The Rhetoric of Temporality," in Wlad Godzich, ed., *Blindness and Insight: Essays in the Rhetoric of Contemporary Criticism* (1971; Minneapolis: U of Minnesota P, 1983), p. 211. (On de Man's later discussion of irony see II.xiii, n. 309, below.) The effect of taking a position above oneself in an unstable irony is of course treated historically as romantic irony.

109 Erving Goffman's classic sociological analysis of real communication systems, *Frame Analysis* (Cambridge: Harvard UP, 1974), more benignly than I, sees most person-to-person interchanges as based on complicated game playing, what he calls the trial performance—in his system characterized by sudden changes in frame, each indicating a different conversational game.

110 Gibbs, pp. 34, 53, 157, sees such complexes, even in ordinary speech, as the result of a nesting together of overt and covert aims or of ostensive (here apologies) and intentional (he's not sorry at all) ones; or of equivocation used deliberately to hide intentions.

111 Goffman, p. 442. Gibbs, p. 56, notes how even speech acts, those last fortresses against ambiguity of many intentionalists, can express simultaneously a number of different acts: the operatic gangster who says, "this comedy will now stop," can be announcing that he quits, that he is leaving, or that we are about to leave our money or our lives behind (my example).

112 A very real problem in legal issues of intention—as a messy will can summon up all *Bleak House*.

113 *Paratexts* (Cambridge: Cambridge UP, 1997), orig. pub. in French as *Seuils*—thresholds. Genette's effective and often very bright catalogue is also often unclear on just the issue that I believe must remain in play: the authority of the paratext. I look at the particular case of titles in II.ix, below.

114 For instance, F.E. Sparshott, "Criticism and Performance," in Newton-DeMolina, ed., p. 107. Sparshott ends by admitting, "We have been reduced to babbling." William Bell, "Victorian Paratexts," *Victorian Literature and*

Culture, 27 (1999): 330, more subtly sees the paratext as a threshold to the material text, but I think incorrectly implies that this anchors interpretation.

115 "Dead Letters: Wills and Poems," in Levinson and Mailloux, eds., p. 112.

116 This case and that below have been brought forward as important ones in United States Constitutional debate, where the wisdom of the founders may be taken to be their awareness that they could not anticipate and close in advance all the cases that might arise. See the excellent discussion in Paul Brest, "The Misconceived Quest for the Original Understanding," in Levinson and Mailloux, eds., pp. 75, 82.

117 In their Introduction, Malle, Moses, and Baldwin helpfully distinguish between the intentionality we presume as "the property of actions" and the intention that is an "agent's mental state" before or as the action is done (p. 3). The complication with speech, and the much greater complication with written language, is that the action is the special one of statement about something. A mere cry of the body—"ouch"—is much easier to relate to motivation; of course, in a play or poem it takes on the opacity of language that represents something.

118 In Speech Act theory (see below, II.x and Appendix 1) this could be described as a locutionary (propositional) act with veiled ("if you agree please vote for me") or hidden ("I'm worth my salary as your faculty hero") illocutionary force (trying to accomplish something with words) and a perlocutionary consequence (having an effect), which may fail if we are not taken in. The philosophers, who came to this study of mixed meanings in an attempt to clarify individual, sentence-length speech acts, seem not much interested in such broad aims of discourse acts, though to us—heirs to the Sophists—they are a large part of persuasive rhetoric. John R. Searle, *Expression and Meaning: Studies in the Theory of Speech Acts* (Cambridge: Cambridge UP, 1979), pp. 30–37, examines single forms of indirect speech acts, where statements have an indirect illocutionary force usually thus veiled for purposes of politeness. P. F. Strawson grants that all speech acts are not conventional and they may not be picked up properly by their (in his case, oral) audience; but he excludes language that hides its intentions on the audience from his class of speech acts (his examples are showing off and insinuating, two of mine here): an arbitrary exclusion that preserves his and Austin's desire to pronounce all speech acts as speaking their intentions—a hope to avoid just the unclarity I wish to explore here: "Intention and Convention in Speech Acts," *The Philosophical Review* 73 (Oct. 1964): 452. Skinner (in Newton-DeMolina, ed., p. 215) speaks more broadly of "perlocutionary intention," which may indicate the motivation driving even literary work, whether a "simple desire to enlighten or amuse" or broad drives of "envy or resentment." His attempt to distinguish sharply between perlocutionary

intentions (behind the work) and illocutionary force (in the intention expressed in the work) seems simplistic: as I am arguing here, the force of many different motivations may be registered in our reading of a work. The same needs to be said of Alastair Fowler's attempt to make a hard and fast distinction between "practical intention" and "literary intention" ("Intention Floreat," also in Newton-DeMolina, p. 244). Although I critique her earlier speech-act work below (II.x), I recommend Mary Louise Pratt's "Ideology and Speech-Act Theory," *Poetics Today* 7 (1986): 59–72. Pratt there finds division as virtually a universal effect of speakers' "socially constituted position" (p. 64), which forces every speaker to perform one role or another, or both together, usually without integration. Pratt takes my case of the hypocrite speaker as the human condition of inauthenticity. I persist in distinguishing such role-playing from divisions caused by a speaker/writer's internal emotional needs. We are only sometimes social automata, as the brilliant satire of her characterizations suggests: they play as misanthropic portraits of our inauthenticity.

Michael Hancher has also noted a division between what he calls "active" intention and "final" or perlocutionary intention to achieve a desired effect. His concern is more with clearly planned intentions to persuade; I am especially interested in those more subtly embodied in the performance itself. See "Three Kinds of Intention," *Modern Language Notes* 87 (1972): 827–51. See also the useful discussion of rhetorical aims in intention in Lyon, who is more concerned than I or others who discuss literary intention and interpretation with issues of intention as planning. Her interesting study is unique in distinguishing clearly between literary (and rhetorical) and philosophical ideas of intention. She notes Charles Altieri's distinction between intention to do something by the text and intention in the text (an issue of meaning): see *Subjective Agency: A Theory of First-Person Expressivity and its Social Implications* (Cambridge, MA: Blackwell, 1994), p. 26. Despite my admiration for Lyon's work and its dynamic sense of the public reception of works of rhetorical force, I need to note that she seems to assume there is not a major issue in interpreting the rhetor's (persuader's) meaning as part of its negotiation. She also understates (p. 40) the degree of contestation of argumentation and ideology in literary studies of interpretive theory, especially in the political world of identity reader theory (concerned with issues such as reading as a woman or a member of a minority group).

119 Tzvetan Todorov, *Genres in Discourse* (Cambridge: Cambridge UP, 1990), p. 19. As an example of an eighth type of ambiguity, Graham Hough makes a similar point (in Newton-DeMolina, ed., p. 227) by using Donne's division in "Go and catch a falling star" between apparent satirical and personal aim on the one hand and his performance of a clever turn on a traditional theme

on the other. The issue of what kind of performance a text is obviously shades into that of assignment of genre.

120 Anthony Paré notes the same confusion of identity and hence of intention in pragmatic games of professional writing: "Genre and Identity: Individuals, Institutions, and Ideology," in Richard Coe, Lorelei Lingard, and Tatiana Teslenko, *The Rhetoric and Ideology of Genre* (Cresskill: Hampton Press, 2002), pp. 66–69.

121 P. Juhl wishes to distinguish intention here from motive of the whole: *Interpretation*, p. 24. But in practice the two aims function at the local level of language use so cannot be so simply separated and hierarchized.

122 The philosophers find a gap opening up between sentence meaning and situational aim (utterance meaning) and try to close it immediately. This is, as I am arguing here, much harder to do with extended literary work, where there is no simple conversational situation and where propositional statements (Austin's locutionary acts) almost always carry illocutionary force. Johann Köberl smartly calls the doubleness here that which results when "the illocutionary force of an utterance and its overt construction may not coincide": *The Indeterminacy of Beowulf* (New York: UP of America, 2002), p. 3. In addition, authors rarely respect the rules of conversation. If we accept Paul Grice's maxims as summarized by Mary Louise Pratt, *Toward a Speech Act Theory of Literary Discourse* (Bloomington: Indiana UP, 1977), p. 130, writers would have to change their spots, as Pratt, p. 144, notes: "Avoid ambiguity, avoid obscurity of expression, be orderly, be relevant, avoid unnecessary prolixity, make your contribution one that is true and as informative as is required"! I discuss her attempt to adopt Grice's system of violation of these maxims in Appendix 1, where, and also in II.x, I also look more broadly at problems in using Speech Act theory to stabilize interpretation.

123 Gibbs, p. 8 and in his discussion of speech acts, pp. 56–59, discusses well the presence of multiple intentions in speech.

124 Cf. Harris, *Literary Meaning*, pp. 100–02, who also sees the possibility of multiple divided intention.

125 I am here imagining possible intentions in the author; my examples necessarily return in circular route to our situation as readers imagining intentions from the text. There it is no surprise that these different guesses of Brontë's intentions follow the interests of generations of criticism: feminism of the 1970s reading in Brontë its own frustration over an unequal lot, that of the 1980s celebrating a sense of new power. We could go on to a lesbian or colonialist Brontë in succeeding periods. We generally, I am afraid, read our own intentions into the author.

126 J. Brooks Bouson, *The Empathic Reader: A Study of the Narcissistic Character and the Drama of the Self* (Amherst: U of Massachusetts P, 1989), offers

an approach to reader empathy/distance as an application of Heinz Kohut's object relations psychology.

127 I might add here that I am not in fact assuming that direct speech, face to face, necessarily conveys one clear intention to the listener. I have argued above that intentions are often bifurcated from their inception and I will note below, in the look at arguments from the text, Derrida's assertions about the general dividedness of language that underlies his attack on Western logocentrism as a privileging of the spoken word. (Derrida could see differences in both speech's attempt to approach writing and writing's to approach speech: "A purely phonetic writing," he insists however, "is impossible and has never finished reducing the nonphonetic": *Of Grammatology* [Baltimore: Johns Hopkins UP, 1974], p. 88.) My argument does look here at the ways in which voice can offer, at a practical level, more clues to an author's intention than technologies for recording words. And of course, as I discuss below, direct speech allows interrogation and dialogue where written texts have nothing more to say for themselves.

128 Robert Browning, the creator of the great musical improviser, Abt Vobler, has left only an improvised "You Ought to Sit on a Safety Valve" (a challenge to rhyme). But it was itself written and I know it only as a written reception.

129 Short of that, or scrutiny of various variorum editions, Barry Wallenstein and Robert Burr offer a rich selection of versions of well known poems: *Visions and Revisions: The Poet's Process* (1971; rpt. Peterborough, ON: Broadview, 2002).

130 Norman Holland remarked on hearing tapes from interviews he did with his *Five Readers Reading* (New Haven: Yale UP, 1975): "On hearing a tape for the first time, I never failed to be shocked at what had been lost by way of facial expression, gesture, stance, manner, and the like": p. 45.

131 Communicators by email—and only a few peace-loving diehards aren't—will know how often its efficiency is cancelled by the time wasted on silly misunderstandings that are avoided in the telephone communication that email tries to replace. Interestingly, computer culture has sought, pretty much for the first time in this long technological development, to reverse the increasing alienation by the desperate remedy of emoticons—those versions of smiley faces, :) or winking communicators, ;-). Roger Chartier has noted earlier technologies, "forms and processes designed to submit the written word to the requirements of performance," in sixteenth- and seventeenth-century France, where reading was often thought of as read speech: in Bennett, ed., p. 138. See also his fuller discussion in "Leisure and Sociability: Reading Aloud in Early Modern Europe," in S. Zimmermann and R.F.E. Weissman, eds., *Urban Life in the Renaissance* (Newark: U of

Delaware P, 1989). Kate Field, *Pen Photographs of Dickens' Speeches*, developed an unusual technology for marking rising and falling vocal patterns: cited in Gerald Curtis, "Shared Lines," in Carol Christ and John O. Jordan, eds., *Victorian Literature and the Victorian Visual Imagination* (Berkeley: U of California P, 1995), p. 31. Goffman, p. 228, cleverly exposes the limits of ordinary orthographic equivalents of signals in direct communication.

132 Goffman, p. 214. Our later age will be quick to add what Goffman doubtless knew, that these directionals are also a language and are learned in different cultures. A Greek teacher explained to us that his father, a modern Greek, communicated the ultimate patriarchal prohibition by nodding his head, but just once and ending with his nose far up in the air.

133 Gibbs, pp. 82–88. Gibbs includes body language and distance, touch, use of time as message, and manipulation of objects—as the Harvard graduate dean who showed us negotiators of the teaching fellows' union that he had brought his great ax from the country to have it sharpened—as he denied our request for a raise.

134 Michel de Certeau, "Reading as Poaching," in Bennett, ed., p. 160; orig. in *The Practice of Everyday Life*. Alberto Manguel cites conflicting evidence on oral reading in antiquity, generally concluding that silent reading was unusual before the Middle Ages: *A History of Reading* (New York: Penguin, 1996), pp. 41–53. See also the accessible account by Mary Carruthers, *The Book of Memory: A Study of Memory in Medieval Culture* (Cambridge: Cambridge UP, 1990), esp. pp. 156–88, which offers a nuanced view of levels of oral reading in antiquity and the Middle Ages. The issue has been much discussed in the specialized literature.

135 See Matei Calinescu's study of *Rereading* (New Haven: Yale UP, 1993), a work that loses its good points about circularity in reading in a plethora of exemplary readings.

136 Critics in the first generation of reader-response criticism, such as Wolfgang Iser and Stanley Fish, excitingly attempted to restore some of the force of the ongoing march of oral performance to written response to a text, Iser by his connected segments of intentions (pieces of meaning in the philosophical sense of intentions) that ask us to fill in the blanks, Fish by his word-by-word processing of what the text *does* to us. Yet studies of eye movement in reading show that on a local level that is not how we read but rather we dart back and forth to figure out the sentence; and no reader can be forced to proceed in linear non-recursive fashion; nor would the Anglo-Saxon around the mead house fire have the same "read" if he had heard the oral performance before.

137 It is worth noting how far textual practice has thus brought us from the idealist assumptions prevalent when Hirsch wrote, where authors' changes

were assumed somehow to fulfill an initial intention, a way of thinking only possible if we saw the text as the outer manifestation of a Real Thing, the author's inner intention. Hirsch was, as always, sharp in his thinking, offering the apparently opposite case of Arnold repudiating "Empedocles on Etna" as an argument that he clearly had an intention controlling the first work which he could thus repudiate; in fact Arnold vacillated, cannibalized and published fragments, and revised.

138 Even the seemingly most mechanical aspects of editing can open up major aporias in the goal of maintaining the author's intentions. Do we normalize idiosyncratic or archaic spelling—certainly not what was originally intended? Do we offer helpful interpretations of hard passages in notes—maybe contradicted by someone else's reading of the author's meaning? Do we arrange works (e.g., poems) in order of writing, first publication, or author's final ordering—often mutually exclusive with major differences of effect?

139 Gerald Bruns, "Intention, Authority, and Meaning," *Critical Inquiry* 7 (1980): 299.

140 See Jerome J. McGann's groundbreaking bibliographical studies, *The Textual Condition* (Princeton: Princeton UP, 1993) and *Black Riders: The Visible Language of Modernism* (Princeton: Princeton UP, 1993).

141 Bruns, p. 303. I discuss the equally inevitable reframing as systems of interpretation and ideologies change with time in II.xviii.

142 "Confessions of a Convert: Strategies for Teaching Theory," in Dianne Sadoff and William E. Cain, eds., *Teaching Contemporary Theory to Undergraduates* (New York: MLA, 1994), pp. 45–56.

143 See II.xviii, n. 408, below. I have chosen generally to maintain the reader and author/intentionality mode of our contemporary Anglo-American discussion, though as a broad discussion it might well have been placed from the first within the field, already existing for centuries, of hermeneutics; when Hirsch began his discussion of intentionality, he reconnected to a great tradition in literary theory as to a rediscovered knowledge. The development of an independent tradition of hermeneutics in English under other names can perhaps be ascribed to the virtual demise of interest in traditional German thinking outside of German departments in the period after World War II. Hermeneutics is also sometimes still identified with a specific concern with historical reconstruction or reconstruction of consciousness, when in fact it indicates general discussion of interpretive approaches. I note below that a brilliant practitioner of hermeneutics in English, Gerald Bruns, makes little or no connection to the reader discussion. For Suzy Anger's useful rediscovery of the Victorian English tradition of hermeneutics see II.xviii, n. 415.

144 Dasenbrock, pp. 110–14, correctly sees Foucault as providing a major armament for what he calls "the social turn," but he sees this too simply as an

outgrowth of an anti-intentionalism shared with him by Derrida, as well as Barthes. But Foucault's "author-function" is not anti-intentionalist, merely anti-individual. His sense of an age writing a text (whereas Barthes, the literary critic rather than the historian, thinks more of the ages writing it) reestablishes a new kind of intention, historical rather than individual, for his age. On Foucault, see II.i, n. 28, above.

145 The interrelation of ideas of author's intention with knowledge of context, background, or milieu has of course been present in all discussions of intention, which were traditionally sited in the broad area of biography—inner intentions need in any case to be motivated or registered in the outer world. Cf. "The meaningfulness of action has been variously situated in actors' intention, rules constitutive of their behavior, background practices that provide the context within which action is intelligible": Joseph Rouse, "Interpretation in Natural and Human Science," in Hiley, Bohman, and Shusterman, eds., p. 42. In this traditional view, however, the author as subject is still the location of intention.

146 See the fuller account of their essay and responses to it in II.i, n. 20, above. The turn to history seems made possible through a less than thoroughgoing neo-pragmatism which fails to apply its skepticism fully to historical hermeneutics and historiography. It seems to assume that Rorty's use of history (of epistemology) as an argument in philosophy suggests that philosophy tells us to turn from other tasks to history. See II.xix, n. 435, below, where I note that Barbara Herrnstein Smith, in a different move to pragmatism in evaluative criticism, avoided privileging history as a new foundationalism.

147 See my discussion of Fish in III.ii and v, below.

148 *Renaissance Self-Fashioning: From More to Shakespeare* (Chicago: U of Chicago P, 1980), pp. 4–5. Claire Colebrook, *New Literary Histories* (Manchester: Manchester UP, 1997), provides a probing but generally sympathetic description and evaluation of New Historical theory and practice with useful comparisons to other seminal thinking on history in Foucault and de Certeau and on the task of cultural description in Clifford Geertz, Althusser, Bourdieu, and others. She sees a number of recurrent theoretical problems that perhaps explain the reluctance of New Historians to theorize this undertheorized discipline. These are especially the problematic concepts of discourse formations or culture as ways to avoid the text and context oppositions of old historians; culture, as in Geertz, as a place of continual exchange and connection of everything with everything; texts as productions in a cultural field doing work rather than offering meanings to interpret; and especially the relation of the New Historian to his subject—that central hermeneutical problem since at least the turn of the twentieth century. She is generous to New Historicist interest in oppositional positions

and the cultural domain as a contradictory site. Ralph Cohen, "Generating Literary Histories," in Jeffrey N. Cox and Larry J. Reynolds, eds., *New Historical Literary Study* (Princeton: Princeton UP, 1993), p. 45, fundamentally agrees with René Wellek that "the new literary history promises only a return to the old one" (p. 50); yet he grants that Greenblatt has looked at an unstable, fissured text of history in a playful way (p. 45).

149 An ironic development to the extent that criticism from old-guard historians and historiographers encouraged the new historians to reify their works as true history and hence to move from presentism to pastism and positivism. See Carolyn Williams, "Victorian Studies and Cultural Studies," *Victorian Literature and Culture* 27 (1999): 355–64. This was a major topic in a number of contributions to the forum on Victorian Studies and Cultural Studies in this issue. It is interesting to observe even a would-be container and critic of New Historicism waffling on the issue of needing to locate in "the realms of particularity and contingency something of the specialness of literature": George Levine, "Introduction" to his *Aesthetics and Ideology* (New Brunswick: Rutgers UP, 1994), p. 4. How aesthetics can bind itself to historical contingency alone is hard to fathom unless we can all read in time machines!

150 Bell, p. 330. Colebrook similarly iterates the importance of the mantra of historical specificity to New Historicism.

151 Marxist theory has in fact been less deterministic in its view of the relation of societal values and systems to individuals; enlightenment does exist in the saving few of revolutionaries, Marxist economists, and organic intellectuals, and it may be extended—a point also made by Dasenbrock, pp. 120–30, who prefers Althusser and Marx to Foucault in their less total social determination. Nor have Marxist critics like Pierre Macherey or Fredric Jameson, to choose among the best, been interested in creating a causal web of intention in which to read a text. Macherey works from the unspoken in the text to what is useful in the social structure to make it speak. Of course, the weak side of this project can be reductionistic explanations of works by the orthodoxies of one theory—most often of history—or another. Nor has openness to varieties of interpretation been a watchword of Marxist critics, who have generally been as intolerant of each other as they are of most other approaches to literature. Jameson's "always historicize," though it has become the categorical slogan of a generation of historical scholars, seems much inferior to E.M. Forster's more universal "only connect," which allows for a range of critical activity. From within its critical world, Tony Bennett has interestingly criticized Marxist criticism for its usual focus on the conditions of production rather than reception of a text: "Texts in History: The Determinations of Readings and their Texts," in Machor and Goldstein, eds., esp. pp. 65–73.

152 The new buzz/keyword of "historical specificity" may be unpacked as a concealing term for the positivism lurking in New Historicism: it implies that there is a specific, therefore naively "real," history to which we may have access away from all interpretation. Here I find myself in agreement with my genial colleague Denis Donoghue, with whom I am not always in agreement; he remarks, in his golden-tongued way, "I assert, provoked by the opposite claim now more commonly heard, that a work of literature is accompanied by the circumstances and forces of its production, pressed upon by them, but it is not determined by them": *The Practice of Reading* (New Haven: Yale UP, 1998), p. 74.

To talk about a text only as a thing that performs work or labour at the time of its production is to attempt to freeze it essentially away from interpretation; the interpretation is the historical story of the text's production among other texts and there is no other story to tell about the text. Of course, in practice New Historicists don't agree any more than practitioners of other schools of literature so what we are given are varying interpretations of the text and the other texts of the culture to which it is compared. But the ideal, however naive, would be to arrest interpretation before it began.

The political scientist Quentin Skinner parallels (indeed predates) this thinking of texts as actions in the context of their time, the context in his cases being usually political ideas of a period. He attempts to stabilize the meaning of the textual action by a system of interpretation based on our ability to "uptake" the "illocutionary intentions" of authors—a very broad, almost metaphorical use of speech acts as what authors wished to do in politics by their writing (see II.x and Appendix 1 for a critique of the use of speech acts to assure us of the meaning of words). Skinner thus reduces texts to one ascertainable meaning as action in its time. Such a system, based on prior historical certainty about what could be said in a period, virtually guarantees that all new thinking about the meaning of a text, or about the ideas and ideologies of a period, cannot take place. For a summary of Skinner's thought, see James Tully, ed., *Meaning and Context: Quentin Skinner and his Critics* (Princeton: Princeton UP, 1988), esp. ch.3. See also the cogent critique of this historical-action limitation of meaning by Charles Taylor, ch.13.

Older historians might have talked about the author's intentions in relation to his social and cultural context. The respect for Foucault as founding historiographer of New Historicism has perhaps blinded its practitioners to its return to intentionality in its talk of historically specific work. Seán Burke observes that specificity as a goal would naturally mean "authorial specificity": "retracing of the work to its author is a working-back to historical, cultural and political embeddedness": p. 202.

153 See my discussion of Suzy Anger's edition of essays, *Knowing the Past*, in II.xviii, n. 415, below. Turns of theory usually revisit earlier versions of the same turns. If we call this newer perspective a form of hermeneutics in at least its contribution to interpretation, using history to control interpretation, then the reader move is a version of Heidegger's view of historical interpretation as necessarily situated as opposed to the more positivist hermeneutics of Wilhelm Dilthey, who struggled to make decisive interpretation of the past seem possible and also stressed understanding in relation to the entire web of the cultural context. See again the fuller discussion in II.xviii, n. 408, below.

The parallels come out, somewhat despite the authors' attempts to sidestep them, in what is perhaps the closest thing to an official theoretical statement by two of the self-defined practical and anti-theoretical practitioners of New Historicism: the "Introduction" to Catherine Gallagher and Stephen Greenblatt's *Practicing New Historicism* (Chicago: U of Chicago P, 2000). They acknowledge that in practice they never feel they can put off "all our historically conditioned" feelings and beliefs (p. 17); yet they insist that they know the culture they study better than it knew itself (p. 8)—anything but an admission of historical sitedness. As I note in II.xviii below, this assurance has allowed much New Historical work to reflect, often without reflection, the interests of the historians' moment. Yet Gallagher and Greenblatt are not at all ready to grant that they are merely bringing new perspectives from their time onto an earlier age. Following the interest in thick description of Clifford Geertz's anthropological work, they see their business as showing how cultural texts come out of the "life-world" of their cultures (p. 13). They are thus able to find the relation between poetry and its cultural setting: it is "the key to particular historically embedded social and psychological formations" (p. 7). Behind this assurance is the structure of the older hermeneutics. Herder is cited with approval here and throughout the essay for his belief in the study of a culture, and Schleiermacher (p. 7) is cited as a fellow worker in the field even as he and Herder are critiqued for not sufficiently confronting the complications within this practice, especially boundary issues. Their claims to know a culture better than it knows itself are identified as "the core hermeneutical presumption" (p. 8)—which they ascribe to Geertz but we must presume to be a presumption of nineteenth-century hermeneutics. As might be expected, this project is connected to a turn against the anti-intentionalist position. This is presented as an attack on the aestheticist position of the New Criticism and what they characterize as its religious-like exaltation of the canonical text as "a sacred, self-enclosed, and self-justifying miracle" (pp. 11–13). One may well ask how this applies to other forms of non-historical interpretation. Despite the openness to variety in a culture (p. 17) and to the diversity of interpretive possibility in the archive of history (p. 15), which have given the historical work of Greenblatt and Gallagher its exciting and innovative interpretive edge, the theory here largely leaves the older hermeneutic project in place; small wonder that less individual and exploratory historians in their wake have moved back toward an implicit historical intentionalism and fetishizing of historical specificity.

154 Donoghue, p. 90; quoted from *Scrutiny*.

155 It only seems to stabilize interpretations; as it is further pursued it keeps suggesting new interpretations and destabilizing former ones. See the discussion of the concept of context in II.xvii, n. 396, below.

156 Gallagher and Greenblatt, "Introduction," interestingly continue to assert their own belief in the diversity of historical experience in a culture—counterhistories and resistance—and their sense of the broad possibilities of interpretation in the archive of history despite their framework of hermeneutical intentionality. The conflict between the two positions has perhaps been a productive tension in their own interesting work and perhaps explains their hesitation about offering a full theorization of their position. See II. vii, 153 above.

Throughout this section I am obviously in the complicated position of admiring the innovative work of the originators of New Historicism in opening new worlds of cultural study while deploring the impact of their fine work in tending to close down and marginalize other forms of interpretation.

157 See the collection of his and Engels's work on literature in Lee Baxandall and Stefan Morawski, eds., *Marx and Engels on Literature and Art* (St. Louis: Telos, 1973). I would grant, of course, that both Vico and Marx see history creating great cycles in which individual possibilities are largely inscribed but not totally excised. Useful as his concepts of interpellation (calling to identity) of the individual by state apparatuses (functions) are, Louis Althusser's Lacanian Marxism is closer to Foucault's thought—and has been influential in the same areas—in its tendency to take away agency from most people. His attempt to provide a (Lacanian) psychology for the process of ideological interpellation conflicts with the everyday psychological reality that people are called to new ideologies at different times in their lives. The student in the ghetto is called to his abject and rogue existence. Given a scholarship, he is called to a different status as token ethnic success; and he may be called again to the culture of CEOs of late capitalism. Even Althusser's postulate of maverick "bad subjects" who have to be put down by Repressive State Apparatuses tells us that the ideological control is not complete. At least there is room in Althusser for a Marxist elite and consciousness, where in Foucault it never seems possible for many other than Foucault to stand outside. The development of class consciousness exists, as Fredric Jameson has noted, outside normal interpellation ("class as such can never be a mode of interpellation"): *Postmodernism. Or, The Cultural Logic of Late Capital-*

ism (Durham: Duke UP, 1991), pp. 345–46. Here I agree with Dasenbrock's critique of Althusser (pp. 120–26) as well as of Pierre Bourdieu (pp. 231–34), whose concept of *habitus* he sees as denying agency also.

158 Lee Paterson, "Literary History," in Lentricchia and McLaughlin, eds., p. 261, critiques the tendency of Foucauldian work to elide individual agency and causality. Frank Lentricchia offers a broader, more penetrating analysis in which he sees Greenblatt's "hermeneutical savvy" inevitably in conflict with his historical project. Comparing New Historicism with the older historicism of Hippolyte Taine, he finds both necessarily replacing a romantic originary self with causation by history. Everywhere there is discomfort with this removal of agency from the individual, as in Greenblatt's own resistance to his story of social "self" fashioning; yet there remains commitment to causation: "In its newer phases historicism rejects the metaphysics of determinism while cunningly retaining (not without discomfort) a complicated commitment to the principle of causality, for without causal explanation there is no historicism, old or new": "Foucault's legacy—A New Historicism?", in H. Aram Veeser, ed., *The New Historicism* (New York: Routledge, 1989), p. 231. Lentricchia looks at issues of self rather than direct causation of texts, but the logic would be the same. I am not sure his assumption is true. What may seem a determinism necessary to all writing of history may be more a tendency, which could in theory be opposed by the historian, toward reification of coincidental relations into forces or cause; so it is possible to imagine a Foucauldian system of relations without agency, as Foucault indeed tried to, or a New Historicism or Cultural Studies, as their most Barthesian practitioners approach, that make no claims about causes, merely read the text of history alongside of literary texts. Unfortunately the tendency has been, except perhaps in a few originators such as Greenblatt himself, away from such utopian practice.

159 See Colebrook as cited in II. vii, n. 148 above.

160 For instance, *Shakespearean Negotiations: The Circulation of Social Energy in Renaissance England* (Oxford: Clarendon, 1988) or *Marvelous Possessions: The Wonder of the New World* (Oxford: Clarendon, 1988).

161 Alan Sinfield, "Cultural Materialism, Othello, and the Politics of Plausibility," *Faultlines: Cultural Materialism and the Politics of Dissident Reading* (Berkeley: U of California P, 1992), pp. 29–51, well articulates the problems in New Historicist tendency to create culture as a monolithic reality and critiques the supporting assumption that dissidence, even when acknowledged, is characteristically contained by cultures. He insists on the variety of historical functionings and ideologies and the realities of political power.

162 Samuel C. Wheeler III, "True Figures: Metaphor, Social Relations, and the Sorites," in Hiley, Bohman, and Shusterman, eds., p. 198. Wheeler, p. 208,

goes on to interrogate the concept of culture as "a masking term" that fits no reality, "referring to a loose assortment of coexisting, overlapping, and interacting groups and individuals."

163 See the critique of Foucault on the issue of women's rights by Margot Gayle Backus, "Discourse and Silence in the Victorian Family Cell: Problems of Subjectivity in *The History of Sexuality: Vol. I*," *Victorian Literature and Culture* 24 (1996): 159–74.

164 See II.i, n. 28, above. Though I feel the need to critique even these below, the explicitly Marxist Raymond Williams offers the well-known historical categories, dominant, residual, emergent, more useful than Foucault's global structures. Colebrook, pp. 56–59, in a more detailed and nuanced way than I can here, discusses Foucault's own attempts to critique and limit his system making. But even the latest work on sexuality in the ancient world and the uncompleted work on the early Middle Ages finds him in practice offering global systemizations of the ages he treats.

165 Dasenbrock, p. 158, criticizes this homogeneity as he finds it in Foucault and Walter Benn Michaels's work as creating by historical distance from real diversity "an epistemic happy family" that also does not allow for explanations of how change can occur. Colebrook, pp. 88–89, notes that even the identification of culture as a subject implies a number of unifying conceptions. Derrida similarly sees in the concept of the historically specific an implied idea of "history in general": Colebrook, pp. 94–95.

166 The tendency in identity thinking to conceive of a group as standing in for individuals in it has encouraged a way of thinking that reifies the group, once identified, and tends to presume uniformity among individuals. When interrogated, however, groups usually fragment into other diverse subgroups.

167 On Althusser see II. vii, n. 157 above.

168 In Machor and Goldstein, eds., p. 302. He is citing work by Susan Stewart on graffiti. See Frow's fuller study, *Cultural Studies and Cultural Value* (Oxford: Clarendon, 1995). Pierre Bourdieu of course offers a system of cultural capital but his evidence similarly shows varying valuations from different classes or groups—see especially his tables of aesthetic preferences in *Distinction* (Cambridge, MA: Harvard UP, 1984). Cultural capital is not universally fungible. Colebrook again tries to associate the work of Frow, de Certeau, and Bourdieu with the side of New Historicism more open to social diversity and resistance. I resist Colebrook's tendency to group all cultural study of the past thirty years together. That some historical work imports insights from de Certeau, Frow, or John Fiske into its exploration of history doesn't change its primary focus on locating literature in an historical text—text conceived from its etymology as an ultimately stable woven fabric.

I also resist her instinct to place reception study under New Historicism, though that work can certainly become positivistic at its worst, insisting it knows and can therefore limit the interpretive possibilities for a text in any historical specificity of its ongoing reception. On the play in cultural theory over hegemony and resistance see II. vii, n. 176, below.

169 A point well made by Kenneth J. Gergen, "The Communal Creation of Meaning," in Overton and Palermo, eds., p. 34: drawing not on Derrida and binaries but on Mikhail Bakhtin and ideas of centripetal/centrifugal cultural forces.

170 As even a standard Western expert (Orientalist?) such as Bernard Lewis, *The Middle East: 2000 Years of History from the Rise of Christianity to the Present Day* (London: Weidenfeld and Nichols, 1996), testifies. I was shown a burial mosque in Cairo with a number of doors leading to offices for teacher representatives of the various schools of interpretation—not a bad plan for an English department! Each could be called prince (sheik) of his point of view.

171 Dasenbrock notes, p. 145, how early Yeats seemed representative of the Irish nationalism of his time; later, his political poems show him perplexed between personal, national, and British responses. On Bakhtin see II.iii, n. 102, above and II.xiv, n. 319, below.

172 See Gregory S. Jay, "Postmodernism in *The Waste Land*: Woman, Mass Culture, and Others," in Kevin J.H. Dettmar, ed., *Rereading the New: A Backward Glance at Modernism* (Ann Arbor: U of Michigan P, 1992): not an especially radical or new view of T.S. Eliot, who in the older kinds of histories was often accused of hidden fascist tendencies. The advantage of this work is that the assertions are able to be less barnstorming, more specific, and in closer relation to the text—all ways in which I am happy to be a fellow traveler with this direction of historical work.

173 This again is a central issue in the broader concerns of New Historicism that have focused on the issue of agency and causality, a concern I have noted as centrally present in Foucault's meditations on webs of power in discourse or Greenblatt's early project, in *Renaissance Self-Fashioning*, to test how the individual was a product of society.

174 In the language of the older criticism—of history as context—Adena Rosmarin succinctly remarks, "'context' is itself a terminological tool, which serves a distinct but limited critical purpose: it tells us what is or was possible, not what is or was done.... in any given situation the so-called determining variables number themselves into indeterminacy": *The Power of Genre* (Minneapolis: U of Minnesota P, 1985), p. 15.

175 Dasenbrock, p. 43, summarizing Martha Nussbaum's critique of Stanley Fish: do we accept uncritically the current childrearing orthodoxies? etc.

Donald Davidson has similarly denied that people are divided in their thinking by their cultural communities: Davidson, "On the Very Idea of a Conceptual Scheme," *Inquiries into Truth and Interpretation* (Oxford: Clarendon, 1984), pp. 183–98.

176 This issue has been more directly and more interestingly addressed in a variety of sociologically oriented areas of study in (mass) communication studies, in the work of the Frankfurt School, and in British Cultural Studies, with its long involvement with issues of popular culture. There the debate has been going on between those who see a dominant ideology having its effect on the masses (effects model) and those who argue for audience control of inflow for its own uses (uses and gratifications approach). Theodor Adorno, Hockheimer, and, more broadly, New York intellectuals of the 1950s and 1960s tended to imply the extensive power of ideological control over audiences even as they deplored its existence, usually taken to be the result of capitalist economic hegemony in Western society. Raymond Williams was followed by the interesting voices of Michel de Certeau in France, Stuart Hall in England, and John Frow and John Fiske in Australia (and later elsewhere), all arguing for the relative power of audiences to appropriate and recode their cultural intake to their own uses and often to undertake subversive assertions of control against the controllers. See the useful summary and partial bibliography of these major disciplinary issues in Machor and Goldstein, eds., pp. 204–06. For de Certeau see *The Practice of Everyday Life* (Berkeley: U of California P, 1984); for Fiske see *Reading the Popular* (Boston: Unwin, 1989) and *Understanding Popular Culture* (Boston: Unwin, 1989). See also his brief statement, "Popular Culture," in Lentricchia and McLaughlin, eds., pp. 321–35, where he argues directly that popular culture interrupts dominant ideology. On Frow see text and n. 27, above. Machor and Goldstein offer examples in work by Janice Radway, Andrea Press, and Elizabeth Cole as well as Fiske. Wheeler, in Machor and Goldstein, eds., p. 209, usefully interrogates the term and concept "hegemony," finding it inconceivable that the oppressed in any culture would be able to participate fully in the hegemonic discourse of their oppressors: "Alleged hegemonies are themselves incoherent, and so less than totally determining of what we say."

177 Dasenbrock opposes the use of "conventionalism" in contemporary social and literary thinking to contemporary analytic philosophy's continued interest in adaptive thinking, nonce theories, and problem solving. See especially his chapter on "The Social Turn," pp. 107–30.

178 I note above, II. vii, n. 157, how reductive the useful and attractive work of Louis Althusser can be. Interpellation provides a term and hence a presumed mechanism by which the individual is literally called by the culture to ideological positions as part of his psychological maturation (a

Lacanian frame of symbolic law of the father). But if this may console us in explaining some of the irrational force behind others' adoption of their beliefs, it tends mechanically to minimize possibilities of growth or change, even for ourselves, as if ideologies were merely injected into people by those ideological state apparatuses (ISAs). Stuart Hall has argued that Althusser allows for individual mediation (see Machor and Goldstein, eds., p. 210) and obviously he would exempt himself, but his system is structured against it.

179 For instance, Walter Benn Michaels's influential article in Tompkins, "The Interpreter's Self: Peirce on the Cartesian 'Subject,'" pp. 185–200, which moves from a brilliant interrogation of Peirce's critique of Descartes's excessive belief in independent individual reason to much too simplistic conclusions about writing and reading being determined by the culture in which they are located. The question of intention seems to place me in a Hobbesian position as a party of one against all: it is a place where the most extreme believers in individual autonomy clash by night with the most extreme believers in cultural determinism. My view, always likely to get squashed in the middle, is that each position necessarily limits the totality of the other: individuals are indeed shaped by society and its discourses but make choices or express personal (psychological, even biological) idiosyncrasies that in turn have an effect on the society.

180 Both subjects are major topics in New Historical work (and of course central issues in postcolonial studies), though again containment by culture rather than abrupt dislocation and change has been the more usual treatment. Greenblatt's work here again is both typical, in seeing the need for recuperation, but also exemplary in acknowledging the force of historical contingency to in fact disrupt culture; he even offers the effect as wonder, a temporary response he excludes from the usual workings of culture: see *Marvelous Possessions.* Such radical contingency should, however, be seen not just as a place of response in wonder but an opening to radical change in action or in representation that leaves a dropped stitch in the web of culture.

181 The interplay between genetics, environment, and individual accident is the subject of the old and continuing nature–nurture debate. Studies especially of identical twins have suggested the genetic force behind many traits. But, as Steven Pinker has argued well, the admixtures among influences need to be teased out in individual cases. And all parties, as I am arguing, do not give enough space to subjectivity. See Pinker, "Why Nature and Nurture Won't Go Away," *Daedalus* (Fall 2004): 5–17, and his *The Blank Slate: The Modern Denial of Human Nature* (New York: Viking, 2002). A few other recent studies, of so many, are Matt Ridley, *Nature via Nurture: Genes, Experience, and What Makes Us Human* (London: Fourth Estate, 2003); Michael J. Meaney, "Nature, Nurture and the Disunity of Knowledge," *Annals of the New York*

Academy of Sciences 935 (2001): 50–61; Jay Joseph, *The Gene Illusion: Genetic Research in Psychiatry and Psychology* (New York: Algora, 2004); and Sesardic Neven, *Making Sense of Heritability* (Cambridge: Cambridge UP, 2005).

The subject, subjectivity, is at least beginning to be studied as more than a Cartesian error: see Ruth Robbins, *Subjectivity* (Basingstoke: Palgrave, 2005). The works of Greenblatt (*Renaissance Self-Fashioning*), Regenia Gagnier, (*Subjectivities: A History of Self-Representation in Britain, 1832–1920* [Oxford: Oxford UP, 1991]), and the collection of essays edited by Roy Porter (*Rewriting the Self: Histories from the Renaissance to the Present* [London: Routledge, 1997]), with varying degrees of disbelief in the subject, at least offer its history, though by and large as the creation of external discourses or contexts. Robbins uses Lacan to suggest how complicated the inner self is as a creation of forces of the unconscious under a tenuous authority of the language of the father. But I would add that the play of language within the conscious self allows a kind of freedom. Robbins adds, giving her view of Lacan, "although there is much pleasure to be derived from speech, its acquisition is also always a process in which there is a near-total surrender of perceived autonomy" (p. 15). In fact, the universal perception is rather of autonomy, of a place in which the individual can refigure life for herself and find a path for herself. Indeed, what else are we doing, was Lacan doing, writing these essays and books? To give up the idea of a self as immortal soul, the self inside the self, does not mean that the creation of body and language in the mystery of mind is not a formation capable of a degree of independence.

182 Annabel Patterson, "Intention," p. 139, posits that in a view dominated by cultural history, intention could be identified in the individual's departure from the cultural norm (as, for instance, innovation in a particular genre). But that melange of culture and individual direction, in theory the traditional concept of the man and the time, would be hopeless in practice. If the time, as I have been arguing, is never a monolith, then we would have no way of knowing where the cultural ends and the individual begins—which is what I believe is indeed the case.

183 Or author function in Foucault's use (see II.i, n. 28, above). Foucault, as I noted above, frees us from inquiry into the biographical author's intention only to remand us to the larger cultural intention as a replacement author (function).

184 The bright idea of determining intention from initial reception naturally occurs within historical work. I will try to dash that hope here. (I look below, II.ix, at the parallel attempt to judge, from the work alone, the reception intended for it by the author.) The hope is often implicitly, or even explicitly, there where, as in much New Historical work, the focus is on the web of circumstances at about the time of the first performance or issue of a work

(though this is different from the most typical New Historical focus on the production and cultural work of the text, which is in effect a causational interpretation, explaining the cultural work being done in the writing and offered by no contemporary reader, only by the New Historicist). The simple problems with using reception responses from close to the time as a *fil de labyrinthe* to lead us back to the author is that they are very hard to find and determine in any authoritative way. We have no Harris pollsters for Shakespeare's audience or for Faulkner's readers; what we do find varies a great deal for the same reason that a cultural moment is always already fragmented and in self-division; for instance, Robert Weimann's work in *Shakespeare and the Popular Tradition in the Theater: Studies in the Social Dimension of Dramatic Form and Function* (Baltimore: Johns Hopkins UP, 1978), pp. 185–92, 208–46, stresses the lack of any simple unity in Shakespeare's audience. Detailed reception studies are still mainly ahead of us, but it is perhaps a fair guess that the more we come to know about the details of any reception the more complex it will seem. A good recent study of one period, William St. Clair's *The Reading Nation in the Romantic Period* (Cambridge: Cambridge UP, 2004), p. 6, warns that reviews, which on first glance might seem convenient "surrogates" for reception in general, cannot be presumed to be "representative records" of the opinions of a text's "many other readers." Also, time goes by so quickly and time can change response utterly (which response to Wilde's *Importance*, the one before or after his trial the same year?)—a great pragmatic problem in historical work which I raise generally in II.xviii, below. And, finally, as I have been arguing here generally, we cannot make easy equations between authors and their diverse contemporaries. Jacques Leenhardt has properly criticized the simplicity of thinking such as Lucien Goldmann's that merely posits that writers and readers simply share a "world-vision": "Toward a Sociology of Reading," in Suleiman and Crosman, eds., p. 105. The same reductionistic assumptions about cultural unities are implied in Hans Robert Jauss's sweeping conceptions of horizons of reception. His theory of serious or aesthetic writers not writing to their horizons already demonstrates the permeability of the original horizon.

The more complex answer is along lines I will explore in II.xviii: it requires an act of interpretation on our part to determine what aspect of reception should be looked at and in what way, so we are caught in a web of our own point of view. This said, I do find such research especially valuable in helping us develop better fictions (in Hayden White's sense) of an historical period than we begin with. As a general approach Steven Mailloux, *Rhetorical Power*, is useful in restaging histories' specific acts of interpretation—though he sometimes moves to overly global historical stereotypes of an era's reading. Or Kate Flint's heavy but very well researched book, *The Woman Reader: 1837–1914* (Oxford: Oxford UP, 1993), fills in an important, almost vacant space. See section IV, below, and Machor and Goldstein, eds., for a broad overview of reception study. Let such knowledge grow, but not as a way of misarguing a case for a privileged, author's-age reading of a text. We study reception moments in history, not production meanings.

185 Colebrook, pp. 61–65, observes that Greenblatt's first effective difference from Foucault in the pathbreaking *Renaissance Self-Fashioning* was his thematization of power for study of representation and its interpretation.

186 Colebrook, pp. 207, 209, 212, argues that New Historicism, in its "examination of the text's labour," dispenses with other meanings than those evident in the historically specific production of the text. But texts manifestly have other meanings to their readers—often many very different ones to different readers at the same or different times—not just a textual function in their originating history. Note again that the production is not the same as the initial reception, so that we are being held to meanings that precede even those of the first actual readers, that is to the reading of the New Historicist herself.

187 I have looked at the multiplicity of possible meanings introduced by the personal performative element of a text in II.v, above; they add possible interpretations to a text rather than stabilize the meaning.

188 The theological argument from design, so dear for so many generations, to them so obviously true, so easy to expatiate on in details of the creation, including of course the tool and maker argument (or its variant the pot and the potter). In aesthetics, where artists were conceived of as godlike makers, with conscious control of all they did, it seemed similarly natural to speak of the work as speaking volubly of its maker.

Though it is surprising to find him using this argument at all, in his early work Paul de Man focuses on the essential issue in speaking of a built-in intended meaning in a text. The text is not a natural object but a created thing (he uses a chair as an example) that speaks its design, "the intentionality of the structure," which is not dependent on what the contingent chair maker happened to have in mind: "Form and Intent in the American New Criticism," *Blindness and Insight*, 2nd rev. ed. (Minneapolis: U of Minnesota P, 1983), p. 25. That we guess something has a purpose does not, however, determine its purpose, which must be the subject of its user's speculation or argument. One is tempted to counter with the story of the Africans unpacking missionaries' crosses and placing them not among religious objects but among miscellaneous ordinary wooden dry goods. But if we grant that a hammer will appear to most inspectors: 1) a made object and 2) probably made for some purpose, we still find that, as any workman knows, hammers serve any number of construction games, with no limit to the possible new games a versatile workman my discover (yes, I could say the same of chairs, but the hammer works even more easily). What we make of a hammer has little to do with some ghost of intention guessed in its design. The first hammer-like things were, indeed, natural objects (rocks) and became hammers of one sort or another only by design of the user (our reader). Barbara Herrnstein Smith, *Contingencies of Value: Alternative Perspectives for Critical Theory* (Cambridge, MA: Harvard UP, 1988), p. 33, remarks that our survival as a species has much to do with "our ability and inclination to reclassify objects." What we learn from the urinal is, after all, that what we make of something depends on the way in which we look at it.

I ask my reader's indulgence while I follow a need here to take apart the design argument a further step by imagining a possible art-like world that is not designed—so-called accidental art. This can be done in the usual case of art *objets trouvés* or of sounds that seem to speak to us, a raven that quoteth nevermore, sounds on the wind, traffic buzz recorded at a busy intersection, "noise as an articulated utterance": David Hoy, quoted in Fish, *There's No Such Thing as Free Speech*, p. 182. But let me offer a more imaginative example: photographs taken by a randomized robot, like that more directed one we saw on Mars. Now sharp students of the exciting field of culture of photography for whom the issue of photography as a socially motivated art form has been a hot one in our culture debates and who have even coined the term "pictorial intention"—Jennifer Green-Lewis, *Framing the Victorians* (Ithaca: Cornell UP, 1996), p. 110—will immediately object that the technology trails its human intentions egregiously, especially in its need to frame its structure around our visuality: yes, it is still a very human product. But this said, in random photographs within these structures its shots will call up our human need to order, classify, pontificate in ways that clearly do not relate to our sense of the robot's actual random choice of subjects and relation, and this not only as commentary about the world reported on as documentary but on the point of view (our robot will shoot at random heights and distances so one can't ascribe this to the technologist in the machine), symbolic connections, etc. Say it catches a mother and child together in what happens to be a balanced, framed shot: will we fail to make our interpretations of that meaningful connection? The point of the case is to say that though we, like those followers of William Paley in the eighteenth and nineteenth centuries, might be tempted to impute design even when it is not there, design need not be present for us to make interpretations.

Any artist would tell us, of course not. Artists have been interpreting the world without benefit of a belief in design since Paley fell out of favor. Henry James in *The Art of the Novel* (New York: Scribner's Sons, 1934), p. 63, spoke memorably of the very essence of his affair being "the imputing intelligence" to life as he interpreted it. Green-Lewis makes a similar point from another angle, beginning with photographic criticism's attempts to sort out objective "found" photography from art photography. Neither, she argues, can in practice be distinguished because "what a photograph means is likely to have some relation to what we do with it—the language ... with which we endow it—it is simply not useful to separate out different kinds of photographs from each other": "Landscape, Loss and Sexuality," *Victorian Studies* 39 (Spring 1996): 404. Finally, all the arguments I summoned in the prior subsection can be marshaled here to head off a view that works' classifications as art tell us of their age's intentions. (See Annabel Patterson, "Intention," p. 139). Think of that urinal. Gibbs, pp. 293, 304, asks us to recognize that Duchamp gave it meaning as he intended to, by giving it a title ("fountain") signing it (with a false name) and submitting it as a work of art. That is obvious. But *what* does it mean? Is it about the art hidden from us in the ordinary, about a urinal thrown in the public's face, about our real nature finally brought into high culture, about the public's gullibility? You will have to argue these points, not adjudicate from some lofty position high above the urinal where you know how it speaks the artist's meaning. Come to think of it, isn't its regular effect to provoke us to new uses for an old receptacle?

189 See Max Rudin, "Statutory Interpretation," reprinted in Levinson and Mailloux, eds, p. 40.

190 Harris's second argument, in *Literary Meaning*, pp. 93–94, 99–103, 107, seems virtually to abandon biographical intention for intention in the text. Cf. Umberto Eco, who hedges with "intention of the text": Collini, ed., *Interpretation and Overinterpretation*, p. 96. K.K. Ruthven muddily speaks of the distinction between "purposeful" intention in the author and "purposive" intention in the text: *Critical Assumptions* (Cambridge: Cambridge UP, 1979), p. 137.

The title of this section does not follow Malle, Moses, and Baldwin in using intentionality rather than intention to suggest what is in the text rather than in the maker. Their distinction, as I noted in II.i, above, is not generally observed for the good reason that the discussion of intentionality, as indeed I pursue it here, is about finding intention in the text. If we find it, we can say it carries intentionality.

191 Wimsatt and Beardsley, in Wimsatt, ed., *The Verbal Icon*, pp. 6, 14. So also Cleanth Brooks: the formalist critic "assumes that the relevant part of the author's intention is what he got actually into his work": "The Formalist Critic," *Kenyon Review* 13 (Winter 1951). Cf. a professed intentionalist who calls a signifier (in a text) a "sign of recoverable intentions": Shawcross, p. 8. The illogic of Wimsatt and Beardsley's claim should be obvious: presumably if he/she failed in achieving his/her aim, we have no clue in the

work to his/her intention. (It isn't to be determined by quality as the work may be a glorious failure of author's intentions.) But then we have no way of determining which texts fail to represent author's intentions and which succeed—really a major problem. The reverse argument, as tried by Herschel Parker, "Lost Authority, Non-Sense, Skewed Meanings, and Intentionless Meaning," in W.J.T. Mitchell, ed., *Against Theory: Literary Studies and the New Pragmatism* (Chicago: U of Chicago P, 1985), pp. 73–79, is that we can see the failure of intention in the illogicality and self-contradictoriness of texts themselves, which reveal the author's failure to gain control. But how are we to sort out the unintended confessions from the intended ambiguities and complications? This is not an argument I can feel comfortable using.

192 They are not entirely consistent in this, however, as we shall see in their views on the progressive emergence of meaning over time. Clearly one reason for their assurance about a single meaning emerging was their commitment to looking at one kind of meaning, that is an aesthetic unity. Beardsley, especially, was mainly interested in aesthetic issues at a time before their massive reconsideration in political terms. He declares that the primary purpose of literary interpretation is "to help readers approach literary works from the aesthetic point of view, that is, with an interest in actualizing their (artistic) goodness": *The Possibility of Criticism*, p. 34.

193 Krausz, in Iseminger, ed., p. 155, notes that "democracy of readings" is the explicit problem for Hirsch. He interestingly analyzes "Indeterminate" as "not fixed" rather than uncertain. In "Transhistorical Intentions," Hirsch, p. 551, even acknowledges "the potential polysemy of language," taking irony as an example which he indeed treats as I will below.

194 In his difficult and repeated meditations on speaking and writing, Jacques Derrida, for instance, has insisted that all realization in words necessarily divides whatever precedes it—thought, idea, conception—from itself. Once in language it cannot simply be itself—"it will strive or tend in vain to actualize or fulfill itself" because of language's susceptibility to different meanings, different interpretations, different contextualizations: *Limited Inc*, p. 56. His view of interpretation as recontextualization is shared by many, for instance the non-deconstructionist Krausz in Iseminger, ed., p. 158. See fuller discussion of Derrida on intention in Appendix 1, below.

195 Legal thinking has in the same way become increasingly skeptical of a plain-sense or plain-meaning formalism that evades issues of intentionalism by assuming that whatever the writer of a construct or a constitution intended will be plain and clear to its reader in the text.

196 An early version of a pragmatically oriented approach to the issue of intention is that of Joseph Margolis, "Robust Relativism." Margolis argues, as Crosman

did, that there is no need to seek one determinant meaning. His "relativism" suggests that judgments of relative plausibility of interpretations will depend on "preferred explanatory models in any given domain" (p. 44)—suggesting a changing context of preferred models as opposed to a final truth. Margolis cites Peirce but is not specifically neo-pragmatist. Richard Shusterman, "Interpretation, Intention, and Truth," also in Iseminger, ed., pp. 65–75, by contrast does work specifically in a neo-pragmatist tradition. And he finds Margolis trying to preserve a space of certitude within his relativism by making description a pre-interpretive activity (p. 70). See my discussion of staged readings in III.iv, below. There I discuss Robert Scholes's resistance to Stanley Fish's neo-pragmatist approach to interpretation by positing of stages. On neo-pragmatist approaches to literary theory and interpretation of Rorty, Fish, and others, see II.xvi, n. 357 and II.xix, n. 441 below.

I should be clear here that I am writing of pragmatism as a philosophical tradition and its development as an approach to literature. The area of linguistics called pragmatics borders on my concerns throughout these subsections looking at intention in the text. It purports to study meaning as it is received in actual communication, obviously a cognate to interest in readers in literary criticism. I do not draw much on that discussion, not because I don't welcome examination of reception in language but because I welcome it only too much and am uncomfortable with assumptions, built into the pragmatic-semantic binary, that a meaningful line can be drawn between meanings built into words—semantics—and the ways in which meanings are received. As I am arguing generally here, the text should not be conceived as having determinate meanings apart from the play of possible receptions.

197 Interpretations of Kubrick's film confirm this view: a group that gathered at the new watering hole, the website Message Board of the Internet Movie Database (IMDb) from April 30, 2004 to June 13, 2004 (and right on to your day of reading me for all I know) immediately began to quarrel over the meaning of the monoliths (or, argued one, sentinels, or obelisks, argued another): the monolith was put there (and the other two, on the moon and Jupiter too) by some E.T.; it represents change; it is aliens or magic; it is kind of like from God; it causes stronger apes to lose their rule at the watering hole to tool-bearing ones; it is a source/trigger for enlightenment; it should not be taken literally; it is a sentinel that merely monitors progress of the human race. YodaFan 465 of April 30, 15:03:12, more modest than the others or myself, confessed, "The monkeys confused the hell out of me."

There were also some moments of hermeneutic wisdom that suggested a possible working out of the ape and tiger when some future millennium approaches. While predictably one intentionalist recommended we all consult authority in the form of *The Making of Kubrick's 2001*, ed. Jerome Agel, and another suggested source study in Arthur C. Clarke's seminal short story, "The Sentinel," or his later book (1968) and sequels, another, identifying him/herself as orangerevolution (June 13, 7:55:33), asked, "Is it possible that Kubrick didn't know how to explain it either?" Whether with scholarly precision—or honesty—or not, erolallamani (April 30, 18:36:03) quoted the author to anti-authoritarian effect: "i would not think of quarreling with your interpretation nor offering any other, as I have found it always the best policy to allow the film to speak for itself. Stanley Kubrick." ow_dino (May 5, 14:33:50), confessing that he was opened up to space-age possibilities by a "good smoke" when he watched *2001* many years ago, un-concludes definitively: "What i want to say is, 2001's message varies in dependence with the person, who's watching." Bravo, ow_dino, the ape grows toward the star-child!

198 See *The Field of Cultural Production: Essays on Art and Literature*, ed. Randall Johnson (New York: Columbia UP, 1993), p. 60.

199 Bakhtin, "Discourse in the Novel," pp. 272, 276, 288. The historian may wish to run in here and say this is precisely why we need history to restore the context—but this misses Bakhtin's point. It *is* lost and can only be restored as controversial speculation over what is no longer known with assurance.

200 The problem is sometimes stated as a binary of objective versus subjective views of a text, as if some readers believed in the text, others only in what they themselves have to say. Doubtless there are, in practice, some of the former who believe so much in the text that they have nothing to say and more of the latter, who virtually ignore this text, merely using it as a pre-text for other observation. But it is a false binary (on which nonetheless a good deal of ink has been pumped) to oppose an Arnoldian believer in objective texts against a Paterian subjective critic. Pater is merely the better philosopher (and reader critic) in knowing that we only know our impressions of the text. See Donoghue's good summary of this issue, pp. 36–46; also Walter Benn Michaels in Tompkins, ed., pp. 185–88.

201 I use Harris as example in the text because he does argue for a built-in textual intention. A more subtle position, but one I think is still subject to the critique of inefficacy in an attempt to provide a guiding set of rules for interpretation, is offered in the thoughtful hermeneutic study by Paul B. Armstrong, *Conflicting Readings: Variety and Validity in Interpretation* (Chapel Hill: U of North Carolina P, 1990). Armstrong separates his position firmly from the one I oppose, in which determinate meanings can be rightly organized in the work of the hermeneutic circle into one correct, valid approach. But he also attempts to stake out a centrist position by positing his own straw men, theoreticians who find all interpretations equally valid (not, I think, the position of Fish, Rorty, Derrida or others he associates

with this "leftist" theoretical stance). In his *tertium quid*, a place that really doesn't exist between intention and non-intention, he generally bans intentional arguments but then offers a series of pragmatic arguments to guide interpretations. These (inclusiveness, intersubjectivity, and efficacy) are sensible enough but have the force merely of a debating coach's suggestions to the team. Next week there might be other points. They are categories of persuasion and as such cannot be fully specified or limited in advance.

However, he also wishes to posit a "resistance" of the text to interpretation, an "otherness" of the text that "constrains interpretation" (pp. 22–24), rewards or discourages certain moves (p. 25). This emerges as a kind of clandestine place of intention within his anti-intentionalist argument. I don't think there is a half-way house between authority and argument; all such authority, even the cautious sort that Armstrong tries to empower, begins to offer a fortification for not leaving open the open field of interpretation that Armstrong believes in as passionately as I (see his excellent observations on power and hermeneutics, pp. 136–37). Therefore I must reconvert his arguments to more pragmatic ones: more persuasive arguments may seem to have more effectively organized the text. They may do this by seeming to meet little resistance or by seeming to repress it effectively in the interest of a powerful interpretive move or in any number of other ways which may not be fully specified or limited in advance. In other ways, I should note, Armstrong opposes views that the text has interpretation coded into it, whether in opposing Jauss's idea of a text pre-coded for future readers (p. 38) or in the special case of what he calls "plurivocity" (p. 129)—a text coded presumably by a clever "aesthetic" author, to open itself to all readings.

202 Harris, pp. 45–49; he cites Altieri, pp. 41–44.

203 Fish himself seemed locked into this resolution by the oral nature of his famous example. He assures those who fear indeterminacy that context will always provide the local answer we need, as it finally did for his colleague, so not to worry: *Is There a Text in This Class?: The Authority of Interpretive Communities* (Cambridge, MA: Harvard UP, 1980), 305–21. Context instead only provides various arguments to those who interpret a text, normally a much more complicated set of information that can be worked up in so many ways and must be argued without benefit of clarifying questions like, "are you one of Fish's victims?" The situation is a simple version of a hermeneutic circle that can easily turn self-righteous, if not plain vicious. I look more closely at interpretation of oral versus written language in II.x, below.

204 W. V. Quine, "Translation and Meaning," *Word and Object*, pp. 26–79.

205 The belief that language is controlled by clear rules that constrain and channel the meaning of a text is sometimes called conventionalism. However, this is easily confused with another sense of conventionalism as a Fishian

belief that communities determine interpretation: indeed by Dasenbrock in his attack on both ways of thinking.

206 Of course the subject of one of Empson's most influential explorations in *Seven Types of Ambiguity* and a subject of controversy since. Buckle can be a statement of fact with an exclamatory stressing how very true it is. Empson sees the ambiguity as a fundamental division that cannot be healed. That view is impressive, has been influential, but can't be definitive.

207 Even the poetic context for the language used has been described as "overdetermined." Julia Saville, *A Queer Chivalry: The Homoerotic Asceticism of Gerard Manley Hopkins* (Charlottesville: Virginia UP, 2000), p. 2, sees the medieval language as arguably in either an English or a Catholic tradition of devotional literature. (She reads "buckle" in her interpretive context as an act of ascetic self-denial as poet and as imitator of Christ, thus a kind of breaking down of the poetic pride of the octave.)

208 Especially in Harris, *Interpretive Acts*, pp. 95–98; I will look at the issue of genre, on which Harris especially leans, in II.xvi, below. See also work by Jerrold Levinson, "Intention and Interpretation: A Last Look," in Iseminger, ed., pp. 224–33, who follows a proposal of William Tolhurst, "On What a Text Is and How It Means," *British Journal of Aesthetics* 19 (1979): 3–14. This approach by an "hypothesis of what a speaker-writer is attempting to communicate to an intended audience" (p. 225) is an amalgam of what I critique below, reading the text for an author's overall intended communication to an audience, and what I analyze in II.xviii, below, an historically contextual reading of the text. Since both he and Tolhurst do not pretend to be able to specify a particular first reception, the approach really amounts only to a combination of weak claims for "hypothetical" intention in the text and weak claims for an historically contextual reading. When they thus choose an appropriate audience (p. 227), they are really only performing an act of individual interpretation.

209 A reasonable presentation of that original case is made by George Watson, "The Literary Past," in Newton-DeMolina, ed., p. 164.

210 Derrida, *Limited Inc*, p. 3; Derrida of course denies that the text can declare either its appropriate codes or context.

211 See Gerald Prince, "Introduction to the Study of the Narratee," in Tompkins, ed., pp. 7–25, and Peter Rabinowitz, "'What's Hecuba to Us?' The Audience's Experience of Literary Borrowing," in Suleiman and Crosman, eds., pp. 241–63. Rabinowitz's fuller discussion of authorial audience appears in his *Before Reading: Narrative Conventions and the Politics of Interpretation* (Ithaca: Cornell UP, 1987). Rabinowitz argues that there is an authorial audience intended by the work but believes this is determined by politics (social context and ideology). His work oddly vacillates between insisting on

an authorized frame for reading (defined as that of the authorial audience) and exploring a politics that allows other frames. Although he forswears traditional concerns with authorial intention, he inevitably creates something similar to Hirsch's (author's) meaning versus (later readers') significance. In his attempt to specify author's intended audience, he argues that we (should) apply certain rules (conventions), yet his intelligent, nuanced discussion refuses to overlook the problems with this, essentially structuralist, approach to intended audience. Readers often don't apply such rules or apply "wrong rules" (p. 170), and the reasons are both political (they don't like the readings the rules produce) or practical (they can't determine—recover—the intended authorial audience). See II.xvi, n. 393, below.

212 On the variety and classes of titles, see also Alastair Fowler, *Kinds of Literature: An Introduction to the Theory of Genres and Modes* (Cambridge, MA: Harvard UP, 1982), pp. 92–98. Fowler's delightful survey demonstrates patterns among kinds of titles in an era but also that these require varied interpretation: the worlds of *Mansfield Park, Wuthering Heights*, and *Bleak House* stand in very different relations to their similar property titles—add *Heartbreak House* for full measure. See also John Hollander, *Vision and Resonance: Two Senses of Poetic Form* (New York: Oxford, 1975), ch. 10.

213 Comparison to direct oral communication makes the point in two ways. As Goffman, p. 441 notes, we not only share an immediate context with a speaker, thus letting us know where he is coming from because we are coming from there too, but also the speaker is able to microdirect the speech to the very specific people he knows us to be (see further discussion in the next chapter). Most literature is much more like an oral address to a large crowd to whom we may encode our talk only in obvious and superficial ways. Only letters to individuals or poems addressed to individuals—as they so often were before 1750—might seem promising ground for planting more specific markers of an individual audience. But then in these cases we bump into the second half of my point: *we* are not the recipients and are therefore virtually by definition unable reliably to identify the codes; if we know that a reference to Aunt Millie would evoke comic hats we would already be in on the joke from which we are usually barred. Anyone who has tried annotating letters will agree that most such meaning, for all our editorial hard work, will remain a truth veiled from us.

214 On this intentionality, see II.i, n. 3, above.

215 Those who seem persuaded that all language has intention, without any need to face the many issues I and others have raised around this knotty problem, may be suspected of confusing the two: suspects might be Knapp and Michaels, Gracia, Irwin, and Nehamas: see II.i, nn. 20, 30, above.

216 (Cambridge: Cambridge UP, 1995): article on Philosophy of Language by William G. Lycan; a parallel summary is offered in Brian Loar's article summarizing concepts of Meaning. Richard F. Kitchener, "Semantic Naturalism: The Problem of Meaning and Naturalistic Psychology," in Overton and Palermo, eds., pp. 279–93, offers a similarly complex taxonomy, four major categories with many subcategories. Of the four, only two, Conceptual Role Semantics and Intention-Based Semantics, concern mental meaning, and the first is not much advocated in that form.

Cognitive psychology, sometimes more specifically cognitive semantics, seems somewhat less perplexed on the subject, primarily because it thinks in terms of functions. Gibbs, p. 44, suggests four paradigms: encoding/decoding (meaning in the message), intentionalist (meaning in the speaker/writer), perspective-taking (meaning in the receiver), and dialogic (meaning in joint activity). His attempt to reconceive of reception of written material as joint activity does not seem to me persuasive. The essays in Overton and Palermo, eds., on meaning and its development in growing humans (and a few other primates) see the major division as between those who conceptualize meaning in a model of brain as computer and those who see it in an embodied mind, that is connected to the physical and emotional development of the species or individual (see Overton, "Contexts of Meaning: The Computational and the Embodied Mind," pp. 1–18). Another major issue concerns whether creation of meaning in language is developmental (as it appears in the work of Lois Bloom) or, to some extent, hard-wired and instinctual. Finally, is thinking itself always linguistic or generally pre-linguistic? Bloom, "Meaning and Expression," pp. 215–35, makes a strong case for the latter as she describes the development of infants' speech from desire to speak to finding rudimentary speech. Work on animals' use of symbols as a non-verbal language also suggests thinking finds symbols to express it. See Duane M. Rumbaugh and E. Sue Savage-Rumbaugh, "A Comparative Perspective on the Etiology of Meaning and Assaying Behavior for Meaning," and John D. Bonvillian and Francine G.P. Patterson, "Sign Language and the Development of Meaning in a Lowland Gorilla," in Charlotte Mandell and Allyssa McCabe, eds., *The Problem of Meaning: Behavioral and Cognitive Perspectives* (New York: Elsevier, 1997), pp. 147–219, esp. pp. 151, 203. By contrast, some computational models find meaning only in the language system itself.

See also my discussion of the locations of meaning in general thinking on this subject in II.ii, above.

217 Crosman's article makes this point effectively as the foundation of his critique of Hirsch. In their analytical discussion of Hirsch's positions, Mitscherling, DiTommaso, and Nayed divide Hirsch's argument into two parts and deny the validity of both of them. First, it is prudent to adopt author's intention as *the* meaning as this is the only generally accepted valid meaning; answer: it

is not generally accepted so not necessarily prudent (pp. 84–85). Second, the vocation of interpretation entails a moral obligation to respect the author's intention as *the* meaning; answer: many interpreters who would say they are professionally involved in interpretation do not feel an obligation to practice author's interpretation. On the ethical issue see also II.i, nn. 30, 36, above.

218 In controversial cases, arguments, negotiations, or responses to insults, we are also used to finding that somehow the new formulation says what was not said before, hence the common accusation, either continuing or ending a quarrel, "but that's not what you said before."

219 Max Black, "Meaning and Intention: An Examination of Grice's Views," *New Literary History* 4 (1973): 257–79. As the title indicates, Black is critiquing the philosopher Paul Grice, not E.D. Hirsch or other literary theorists, as an exponent of meaning as speaker's intention, although he also offers observations on literary applications of his arguments. Black offers a concise exposition of most of the arguments made against intention above.

220 For more on this history and a fuller discussion of this philosophical tendency see Appendix 1.

221 This line of defense of intention appears as early as 1972 in essays by A. J. Close, "*Don Quixote* and the Intentionalist Fallacy," and Quentin Skinner, "Motives, Intentions, and the Interpretation of Texts": both reprinted in Newton-DeMolina, ed., pp. 174–93, 210–21. In an answer, pp. 222–41, Hough pointed out that speaking of speech acts in literature (as of characters) is not the same as speaking of speech acts of absent authors and that speech act categories are too gross to be much help in literary analysis. The argument for intentionality from Speech Act theory has been reverted to most recently, and at fullest length, by Harris, *Interpretive Acts*, ch. 1. On Skinner see above, II.vii, n. 152.

222 J.L. Austin, *How to do Things with Words* (Oxford: Oxford UP, 1962); John R. Searle, *Speech Acts* (Cambridge: Cambridge UP, 1969) and his further work in *Expression and Meaning*. See also the parallel work in theory of conversational implication by Paul Grice, cited and discussed below in Appendix 1. For literary application see especially Mary Louise Pratt, *Toward a Speech Act Theory of Literary Discourse*; for my critique of Pratt, see also Appendix 1.

223 A point made by Searle, who sees locutionary utterances as also illocutionary ("2+2=4" is really a briefer form of "I believe 2+2=4"). J. Hillis Miller's revisit to Speech Act theory in Austin, Derrida, and de Man elegantly demonstrates how Austin's thinking already implicitly performs the kinds of deconstruction of the opposition of performatives and constatives that Derrida and de Man enact: see *Speech Acts in Literature*, chs. 1–3.

224 Jonathan Culler offers an excellent brief introduction to the positive uses of Speech Act theory in interpretation: "Performative Language," in *Literary Theory: A Very Short Introduction* (Oxford: Oxford UP, 1997), pp. 94–107. See also Miller's interpretive examples, where the undecidability of speech acts in literature opens irreconcilable interpretive possibilities and where the expression of feeling in speech acts may seem more often to create the feeling than feeling to originate the expression. His examples are especially from Proust (his ch. 5), though he returned to interpretive use of speech acts in a study of Henry James. See also my own discussion of speech acts in interpretive issues regarding voice in II.xiv, below.

225 Strawson, pp. 456–60, makes the point about convention, rather against the tendency of Austin's thinking about illocutionary speech acts.

226 Searle, *Expression and Meaning*, pp. 27–28, insists (or does he assert or express the belief?) that mere choice of verbs is not enough to identify a class of speech act: his taxonomy is based on broad types of illocutionary force, such as directives (asking, ordering) or commissives (committing the speaker). The point is there is no simple rule for evaluating the kind of speech act apart from interpretation of the entire statement. I summarize Davidson's general conclusion, that the ulterior purpose (intention in my sense) and the literal meaning of an utterance are independent, at the end of Appendix 1. I have already noted Gibbs's (p. 56) exploration of how one speech act can fit in a number of different classes depending on how we interpret the speech act. I discuss Searle's views in greater detail in Appendix 1.

227 Wolfgang Iser, *The Act of Reading: A Theory of Aesthetic Response* (Baltimore: Johns Hopkins UP, 1978), pp. 54–62.

228 Quoted in Stanley Cavell, *A Pitch of Philosophy: Autobiographical Exercises* (Cambridge, MA: Harvard UP, 1994), p. 119.

229 *The Dialogues of Plato* (Oxford: Clarendon, 1875), II, pp. 154–55 (Jowett's translation).

230 Monroe Beardsley, early advocate of anti-intentionality, similarly found it easy to insist that speech acts in literature are generally representational—in the world of art—not pragmatic. See his "Intentions and Interpretations: A Fallacy Revived," in the aptly named *The Aesthetic Point of View*, ed. Michael J. Wreen and Donald M. Cullen (Ithaca: Cornell UP, 1982). Noel Carroll, pp. 103–11, makes an interesting critique of Beardsley's view: he notes that a certain amount of what is classed as literature at different times may be of course non-fiction. Hence we might be able to take statements in some literature as true illocutionary utterances. But again the problem here is that we have no clear conversation-like context. We may be uncomfortable about saying the work has been aestheticized, but there is no question that it is alienated from its original use by its reclassification as literature

and also has been thrown open to interpretive dispute. Of course a simple statement, I inform you that Ireland is in a bad way, will not be disputed. It is a clear case where we read with the action of the author. But try to get into the irony or madness of the speech acts of a proposal for a solution to Ireland's problems and critics will manufacture as many Swifts as there are divergent interpretive moves before the amazing text.

231 Harris leans on such context-laden speeches within literature as examples parallel to the communication cases he primarily uses.

232 Searle, *Expression and Meaning*, pp. 58–75.

233 Miller interestingly analyzes Austin's world of philosophical examples as very much suggesting an ideology of law-abiding Western rational persons threatened by dangerous and irrational others: pp. 49–59.

234 John Reichert, "Do Poets Ever Mean What They Say?" *New Literary History* 13 (Autumn 1981): 53-68, discusses literature (poems again, in his cases) that offer the direct voice of an author giving us not fiction but opinions, maybe even wisdom, on life. Reichert perhaps too easily waves away New Critical answers that such poems are still to be seen as spoken by personas rather than as direct statements. But in any case, such poems, though offered as if bald statements of fact, are really opinions and world-creations and should be seen as disguised illocutionary speech acts in the implied form, I affirm that; or I conjure up a vision of things in which it is clear that (to use Reichert's example from Frost), "Nothing gold can stay." Like all speech acts, they may succeed (here in persuading or illuminating) or fail (in not persuading or not illuminating) individual readers. They will also be open to different interpretations of what the persuading/showing is all about: is it persuading whimsically? by evoking the whole heavy drama of the Fall? by enacting grieving? Here our interpretation of what the New Critics liked to call speaker's tone but my students understand best when I talk of speaker's attitude has generally to prefigure, or at the least go hand-in-hand with our assignment of a speech act. When I ask a student to identify a speech act, which I do regularly as a helpful classroom stimulus, I force her to decide what attitude the speaker has, what he is up to. We are back in the business of interpretation with no magic keys to author's meaning. Neither the first person, un-dramatic monologue form nor the illocutionary speech act brings us closer than in other kinds of literature to specifying the author's intention—which in any event, in trying to make sense of it all, might be multiple. See further discussion in II.xiv, below, in my look at the general difficulties of interpreting voice.

235 A point made by Wimsatt and Beardsley: see II.i, n. 26, above.

236 Here again, as with the word intentionality, I must apologize to the philosophers for using common terms in the common sense in an area where

special philosophic uses might apply. In common use, denotation refers to the explicit meaning of a word; in philosophy, especially analytic philosophy and logic, denotation has the special sense of the things that an expression applies to (points to), its extension. In common use, connotation indicates the suggestive or associative implications beyond the explicit sense of a word; in logic, connotation refers to all the attributes constituting the meaning of an expression, its intension.

The difference in meanings of denotation and connotation is so striking as to make my point in itself. Umberto Eco finds the difference between connotation and denotation only conventional, an imposed coding system: *A Theory of Semiotics* (Bloomington: Indiana UP, 1976), p. 56.

237 See the full discussion of the emergence of the modern meaning from competing, contradictory meanings in Peter Stallybrass, "Shakespeare, the Individual, and the Text," in Lawrence Grossberg, Cary Nelson, and Paula A. Treichler, eds., *Cultural Studies* (New York: Routledge, 1992), pp. 593–610. Stallybrass's inquiry, relying heavily on the *OED*, shows how easily that tool unfolds the unstable and often synchronically conflicting uses of words within its diachronic organization. The dictionary, conceived in the age of Darwin, in fact chronicles the struggle for survival over time not just among words but among variant meanings for surviving words.

238 *The Limits of Interpretation* (1990; Bloomington: Indiana UP, 1994), p. 143. Eco makes a very interesting case for an even broader encyclopedic view of interpretation, even as he shows profound concern that what he calls, usefully, "unlimited semiosis" should be delimited by contextual reading (e.g., p. 21; this is a collection of essays so he may express his own drift here without my attacking him for it). He even records his half-belief in the older idea of qualitatively different connotative and denotative meaning: "The first sense of the word [denotative] has to be kept in mind (or at least socially recorded by a dictionary) in order to make the second [connotative] sense acceptable" (pp. 29–30). The recourse to a dictionary as somehow producing some stable meaning against which the other can play is precisely what is not available in our current view of language.

The move to an historical and relative view of language as a changing practice of its speakers of course began before the *OED*, in the historical orientation of nineteenth-century thinkers about language, whose historical premises then underlay the work of the great dictionary itself.

239 Gibbs, p. 50, though arguing for humans' bias to think intentionally, grants there is no plain sense for all of what is called a literal reading, even in law or other special disciplines: "What we think of as literal depends on a variety of factors including culture, individuals, context, and the task. People often fail to acknowledge that certain knowledge and assumptions drive their

judgments of literalness for words, sentences, and texts": quoted from his own *The Poetics of Mind* (New York: Cambridge UP, 1994), p. 78.

240 A good example offered by Culler of the ways in which new words, or new meanings for old words, keep being added to the language: preposterous before being used, they are assimilated to the encyclopedia with each use: in Umberto Eco, *Interpretation and Overinterpretation* (Cambridge: Cambridge UP, 1992), p. 121. Anyone who spends time in different zones of our especially encyclopedic world of English will know of many examples of new words—"baps," for instance, fully accepted in one section (hamburger buns in England) but not another; or diverging strong meanings of common words: "pissed" in England (very drunk) versus "pissed" in the U.S. (very angry). A not brilliant but powerful man, Dwight Eisenhower, seems to have had his way with us in adding that once preposterous "finalized" at least to the American encyclopedia. Soon Peng Su, *Lexical Ambiguity in Poetry* (London: Longman, 1994), pp. 149–56, summarizes the many ways in which "lexical innovation" brings nonce words into the language, where some may catch on. Languages also provide for regular modes of creating nonce words, for instance compounds based on those already present (we may easily create camelcart by analogy with horsecart and dogcart if we need it—my silly example—or words formed by derivation: Hopkins's unfathering—p. 155). These can be especially open to a variety of possible meanings.

241 Hilary Putnam's "The Meaning of Meaning" highlights this point. He finds that generations of philosophers have insisted on necessary conditions in the extension of a term as its meaning when in fact meanings in use are fuzzy sets not requiring all possible denotations: a non-yellow lemon is still a lemon: in K. Gunderson, ed., *Language, Mind, and Knowledge* (Minneapolis: U of Minnesota P, 1975), pp. 131–93.

242 I need to keep underlining this point, essential to all my discussion of intention, that it is in hard cases, where we might need it, that intention fails, especially here before I lightly trip the deconstructive fantastic of polysemy and semiosis. Harris, *Literary Meaning*, pp. 25–27, 95, 129, bravely counters the dragon of deconstruction with context: words in use are usually constrained in their meaning by their use/context. And his point would be badly required if neophyte deconstructionists thought all words as used were easily open to all possible meanings.

243 Robert Lowell, "On 'Skunk Hour,'" in Thomas Parkinson, ed., *Robert Lowell: A Collection of Critical Essays* (Englewood Cliffs, NJ: Prentice-Hall, 1968), p. 134. Lowell notes that in looking at his work in relation to critics' interpretations, "I am not sure whether I can distinguish between intention and interpretation": p. 131. Lowell was responding to interpretations by Richard Wilbur and John Frederick Nims, which go much further than the

possibilities I suggest below—an allusion to the Spartan boy with the fox (Wilbur), Satan looking enviously at Adam and Eve (Nims).

244 See my critique of Robert Scholes's stages of reading approach in section III.iv, below. My critical reader may here counter that my faith in the historical approach of the *OED* shows that I assume meanings can be stabilized at least by time period if not by dictionary norms. See, for instance, Theodore Redpath, "The Meaning of a Poem," in Newton-DeMolina, ed., p. 23, who sees all order in the language system stabilizing the "meaning of the words." Of course, meanings change as well as propagate (my own examples are based on this), and much reading in literatures of other ages, or the formalization of this process in an *OED*, sensitizes us to possible earlier meaning. But, as with all historical work, these provide suggestive rather than definitive meanings. We look for new (older) meanings when we feel a problem in the text in the course of our interpretations; we accept an earlier meaning if, and only if, it fits our interpretation. The relative and unnormative view of word meaning embodied in the historical approach of the *OED* also opens the possibility of additions. If our interpretation finds a new meaning or nuance of meaning in a word, it can claim to open a revised meaning in that dictionary. The *OED*, after all, is not a definitive list of all possible meanings but a pragmatic encyclopedia of hitherto discovered actual uses, based in each case on an interpretive decision. So our new, proposed, meaning, which may even push back a modern meaning some hundreds of years into the past, may certainly claim admission to a revised *OED*.

245 The concept of a sign as a joining of signifier (sound or the material symbol) and signified (concept) is of course central to the thinking of Ferdinand de Saussure, who did in fact see meaning as only an arbitrary system of differences, though he did not focus as forcibly as deconstructionists have on the implications of this conception for our thinking about meaning. See his *Course in General Linguistics* (New York: Philosophical Library, 1959). In Derrida's thinking, the absence of the transcendental signified extends the domain of the play of signification indefinitely: "Structure, Sign, and Play in the Discourses of the Human Sciences," *Writing and Difference*, trans. Alan Bass (Chicago: U of Chicago P, 1978), p. 280. I note in Appendix 1 Derrida's more general insistence on the cleavage between speech or writing and the words produced. Famously, sound may create an aporia of two possible meanings (as indeed writing may do too—present *read* and past *read*, or the schoolboy favorite *wind* and *wind*. See discussion of homonymy and polysemy below). More broadly, the context of utterance is never iterable, so the context of reception is always an uprooting of the word, an assertion with which this entire essay agrees.

246 Charles Sanders Peirce, *Collected Papers,* ed. Charles Hartshorne and P. Weiss (Cambridge: Harvard UP, 1931), II, 169. Jonathan Culler, *On Deconstruction* (Ithaca: Cornell UP, 1982), pp. 188–89, and Eco, *The Limits of Interpretation,* pp. 34–42, 211–12, both suggest the degree of metaphysics that walks within this system, especially in Peirce's desire to have an object (what Peirce calls the Immediate Object behind which leers the Dynamic Object calling forth the sign); both read Peirce, and Culler reads Derrida, conservatively as not wishing merely to allow any and all interpretations without judgment or contextual evaluation. G.B. Madison insists that Peirce—quite differently from Derrida whom he, I think rightly, sees as insisting on the possibility of unlimited semiosis—grounds his chain of interpretants in the context of the pragmatic meaning, that is the effect of the word on a person in terms of habit and action (presumably in a specific place and time): *The Hermeneutics of Postmodernity: Figures and Themes* (Bloomington: Indiana UP, 1990), p. 113.

247 Derrida, "Structure, Sign, and Play," p. 292. Derrida is careful to insist that the risk of interpretation based on such semiosis should only be taken on "rigorously and prudently": *Dissemination,* trans. Barbara Johnson (Chicago: U of Chicago P, 1981), p. 130. I can't resist noting here a thought from Norman Holland's comparison of cognitive psychology's ways of thinking of interpretation: that, like Derrida, cognitive psychology finds no resting place of interpretation but interpretation all the way down, with "reality" always subjected to our frames of vision and paradigms, all interpretation justified by prior acts of interpretation: *The Critical I,* p. 158.

248 Roland Barthes, *S/Z,* trans. Richard Miller (New York: Hill and Wang, 1974), pp. 5–6.

249 Derrida, *Dissemination,* p. 130.

250 Obviously my quotations here out of context reduce the elegant argument of Derrida's philosophy of language. For those who haven't approached the complexity of Derrida's thinking on dissemination, Culler's lucid systemization in *On Deconstruction* is a good place to begin study, then the chapter "Question of Method," in Derrida's *Grammatology,* and "Plato's Pharmacy," *Dissemination,* pp. 61–171.

251 Robert Scholes's critique of deconstruction in *Textual Power* (New Haven: Yale UP, 1985), uses reference to mount a significant argument for limits to unlimited semiosis. Scholes insists on the term omitted in Saussure, reference, in any system of signs. Reference, the relation of words to things—Scholes's example is that new thing to the West, the kangaroo, which then demanded a sign—draws on the Anglo-American tradition of commonsense connections of signs to things; he argues that later Peirce also insisted on adding "objects" to signs and interpretants. But in such a reference system of word meanings, signs

may still have a planetary cluster of various reference meanings. Eco's useful concept of meanings as residing in an encyclopedia of all the actual uses of a term similarly tends to re-link words to reference (an encyclopedia is about words and their specific work histories in the real world, not just about their signifieds). Eco no doubt intends this as a broad but finally limiting guard rail to the possible proliferation of meanings, but as noted above, its open-endedness would always allow x+1 referents to any signifier. If a native sees a new kind of animal and chooses to say "gavagai," we have just registered a considerable expansion of possible meanings for that word that run from the animal itself, to its particular (pet) name, to that-animalness, to like-that-animal, house of that animal, and beyond (following W.V. Quine's thinking).

252 Su, pp. 33–35. Su in fact stresses the difficulty in distinguishing polysemy from homonymy. Homophones are spelled differently but sound the same; like homonyms they have different meanings and origins. Derrida's favorite homophone was of course the nonce creation of his own, *différance*. A homograph is spelled the same as another word but differs in meaning and origin and may differ in pronunciation (wind, wind).

253 Called by Noam Chomsky fuzzy sets: see discussion in Massimo Piattelli-Palmarini and Carlo Cecchetto, "The Problem of Meaning in Generative Grammar," in Mandell and McCabe, eds., p. 454. Lawrence Barsalous and Dorrit Billman, "Systematicity and Semantic Ambiguity," in David S. Gorfein, ed., *Resolving Semantic Ambiguity* (New York: Springer-Verlag, 1989), pp. 146–47, suggest how variable individuals' senses of word meanings are.

254 Or consider the often-cited case of "school," as a group of people, a learning process, an institution, or a building—leaving aside schools of fish and music: Anne-Marie Mineur and Paul Buitelaar, " A Compositional Treatment of Polysemous Arguments in Categorical Grammar," in Kees van Deemter and Stanley Peters, eds., *Semantic Ambiguity and Underspecification* (Stanford: CSLI Publications, 1996), pp. 130–31. Or the even simpler case of "room," a single entry for dictionaries but analyzed as at least four meanings by Greg B. Simpson, "Varieties of Ambiguity: What Are We Seeking," in Gorfein, ed., p. 15.

255 On polysemy as multiple lexical entries for the same word, see even the analytic philosopher, Earl R. Mac Cormac, *A Cognitive Theory of Metaphor* (Cambridge, MA: MIT UP, 1985), pp. 183, 185.

256 Greg B. Simpson and Curt Burgess, "Implications of Lexical Ambiguity Resolution for Word Recognition and Comprehension," in Steven L. Small, G.W. Cottrell, and M. Tanenhaus, eds., *Lexical Ambiguity Resolution* (San Mateo, CA: Morgan Kaufmann, 1988), pp. 276–77.

257 Claudia Brugman and George Lakoff, "Cognitive Topology and Lexical Networks," in Small, Cottrell, and Tanenhaus, eds., p. 480. They argue that

new meanings seem to develop out of natural-seeming extensions of the use of a word. On "go" see p. 179.

258 Robert R. Hoffman, "Some Ambiguities in the Study of Ambiguity," in Gorfein, ed., p. 210, offers a category of ways of thinking about word meanings in lexicons.

259 Domenico Parisi and Cristiano Castelfranchi, "Disambiguation in a Lexically Based Sentence Understanding System," in Small, Cottrell, and Tanenhaus, eds., p. 136. They speak of "an encyclopedia of world knowledge" rather than a dictionary. In their interestingly speculative article, Barsalou and Billman, in Gorfein, ed., conceptualize the psychology of word meanings as encyclopedic clusters of words associated around basic systems or culturally learned systems, again suggesting meaning embedded in use groups rather than stratified in precise definitions.

260 Georgia M. Green, "Ambiguity Resolution and Discourse Interpretation," in van Deemter and Peters, eds., p. 16. She sees new meanings accreting by a process of fossilization of nonce uses. In Steven L. Lytinen, "Are Vague Words Ambiguous" in Small, Cottrell, and Tanenhaus, eds., pp. 109–28, tries to deny ambiguity to polysemous words. But if some senses are obviously close enough for mere adjustment on the part of hearer or reader, some are not, and the gap can always widen, if you see my drift, which begins to be quite a different and potentially ambiguous sense from drift in a tide. Many developments of meaning are, as this is, metaphors that have fossilized, as Su notes, p. 136. I look at metaphors and other tropic effects below, II.xiii.

261 Mineur and Buitelaar, in van Deemter and Peters, eds., p. 129.

262 See for instance the chart of lexical access models in Andrea Bubka and David S. Gorfein, "Resolving Semantic Ambiguity: An Introduction," in Gorfein, ed., p. 5, where all versions resort only to textual context. I discuss more broadly my own difficulties with using context to determine meaning in II.viii, above.

263 Massimo Poesio, "Semantic Ambiguity and Perceived Ambiguity," in van Deemter and Peters, eds., p. 166.

264 See the useful analysis of how different contextual information resolves or does not resolve ambiguities in Su, p. 73, summarizing a Princeton dissertation of P. M. Gildea.

265 McCullough vs. Maryland: quoted in Levinson and Mailloux, p. 71.

266 William Empson, *Seven Types of Ambiguity* (1930; rev. New York: New Directions, 1947), pp. v–vi: examples from Empson's summaries.

267 Empson, p. 48. I should be clear again here that Empson himself often speaks as if the ambiguity could be referred to that in the author, itself a loose form of intentionality. This was often the direction of New Critical work in Empson's wake, where ambiguity was often treated as if it were a method by which

the author created an independent aesthetic whole; deconstructive work has of course brought practical work back to the effect of Empson's study, which is to stress confusion on the part of both reader and author—the text as a place of multiple, not necessarily resolvable alternatives. Elizabeth Freund can even claim that in Empson "ambiguity was a condition of the reader's response": *The Return of the Reader: Reader-Response Criticism* (London: Methuen, 1987), p. 48. Empson, having not had a chance to read Wimsatt and Beardsley on either intentional or affective fallacies, speaks loosely of both author and reader but demonstates superbly well the varieties of ambiguity in the areas of word, syntax, or logic; Empson distinguishes logical from what he calls ambiguities of "feeling," that is hazy emotional states.

His versions of ambiguity thus participate in both sides of the ambiguity/indeterminacy distinction as Gerald Graff and others have defined it: both ambiguity in the text (as in word ambiguity) and indeterminacy in the reader of the text: see "Determinacy/Indeterminacy," in Lentricchia and McLaughlin, eds., p. 165.

268 See the critique in Su, pp. 6–9. Su rightly finds Empson especially attuned to ambiguity as an effect in readers, which distinguishes his thinking from the more objectivist textualist work of most New Critics. It also drives the eclectic approach that Su criticizes: he sees ambiguity as complicated effects of language often working together in a work. Su prefers individually striking effects in her main exemplar, Hopkins. She offers more cogent critiques of other approaches to ambiguity in literature, e.g., the work of A. Kaplan and E. Kris and of S. Rimmon; see her pp. 9–15.

269 It is worth noting that the now-contested idea of linguistic deep structures proposed by Noam Chomsky and the concomitant ideas of hard-wiring of the brain proposed by Jerry Fodor never offered a system denying ambiguity at the surface level, despite the obvious values of permanence and deep semantic clarity built into the models. If meanings are deeply structured, they are less likely to become confused than if they are produced in culture and constantly changing: see discussion by Smith in Mandell and McCabe, eds., pp. 60–64.

270 P.A. Prather and David A. Swinney, "Lexical Processing and Ambiguity Resolution," in Small, Cottrell, and Tanenhaus, eds., p. 290; Simpson, "Varieties of Ambiguity," p. 14.

271 Van Deemter and Peters, "Introduction" to van Deemter and Peters, eds., p. xv.

272 I am still fighting with students on the battle lines of "like" and "as" used in verb clauses, a battle begun in public expression many years ago by Winston cigarettes, which were said to "taste good like a cigarette should." If that is the worst grammatical change in a lifetime, I am hardly in a whirlwind.

273 F. Vaughan Hughes, "On the Principles of Legal Interpretation, with Reference Especially to the Interpretation of Wills," quoted by Michael Hancher, "Dead Letters," in Levinson and Mailloux, eds., p. 105.

274 The look at attempts to use Speech Act theory to stabilize language in II.x, above, has already suggested that there are no rules that ensure clarity in statements. Here I suggest the likelihood of unclarity. Paul de Man would go further and assert that the necessary unclarity of tropes ensures, in its clash with the performatives of statements, the failure of statements generally. See III.iii, below, and Rodolphe Gasché's fuller statement of the development of this thinking in de Man's *Allegories of Reading* and *The Resistance to Theory*: *The Wild Card of Reading: On Paul de Man* (Cambridge, MA: Harvard UP, 1998), pp. 11–47, 114–48. The well-known example of the title of Keats's *Fall of Hyperion* that de Man offers, it should be noted, is a case of unreadability offered not just by tropes but also by grammar itself. De Man's first complication comes from trying to read the genitive of the title grammatically. Is it to be read as the fall (or downfall) of Hyperion, or Hyperion falling? De Man, who might seem to present grammatical elements as stable ones that are destabilized by his skeptical mode of reading, here rather sees the aporia of grammar as the first unreadability that opens up the greater one in tropes (is Keats referring to the failure of his earlier poem, *Hyperion*?). Another case, carefully discussed by Gasché, pp. 207–08, 211, is the conflicting meanings created by French *comme* and its two grammatically possible subjects in Baudelaire's "Correspondences"—explored by de Man in his *Rhetoric of Romanticism* (New York: Columbia UP, 1984), pp. 248–50. I cite both because stress on tropes and figures has tended to focus attention on those instances of ambiguities and less on grammatical and logical unclarities.

275 Parisi and Castelfranchi in Small, et al., eds., p. 133. They identify this as an ambiguity of space management procedure.

276 Su, p. 30.

277 Green in van Deemter and Peters, eds, p. 22.

278 See discussion in Geert Adriaens and Steven L. Small, "Word Expert Parsing Revisited in a Cognitive Science Perspective," in Small, Cottrell, and Tanenhaus, eds., pp. 32–35.

279 Poesio in van Deemter and Peters, eds., p. 164; Simpson, in Gorfein, ed., p. 13.

280 Examples in Green in van Deemter and Peters, eds., p. 23. Recent ones are from Bill Mason email, Headlines of 03, Jan. 10, 2004—all plausible enough that I am not much concerned with the degree of accuracy/invention of this email circular for my purposes.

281 "Interpreting the Variorum," in Tompkins, ed., pp. 164–72. Fish's unclarity on intention is at work here as in much of his work. See Appendix 2.

282 See Leona Toker, "Ambiguities in Vladimir Nabokov's *Invitation to a Beheading*," in Hans P. Braendlin, ed., *Ambiguities in Literature and Film* (Tallahassee: Florida State UP, 1982), pp. 95–103. Hardin draws on game theory to study the complicated game-playing of postmodern texts: see esp. pp. 1–34.

283 Mineur and Buitelaar, in van Deemter and Peters, eds., p. 126, quoting Chomsky's *Syntactic Structures* (1957).

284 On these subjective vaguenesses see Israel Scheffler, *Beyond the Letter: A Philosophical Inquiry into Ambiguity, Vagueness and Metaphor in Language* (London: Routledge & Kegan Paul, 1979), pp. 57–72. Scheffler, I should say, opposes the view that vagueness itself is a logical category. See also Su, p. 114.

285 See the fuller discussion of Iser in III.ii, below.

286 Jennifer K. Holbrook, Kurt P. Eiselt, Edward H. Matthei and R. Granger Jr., "(Almost) Never Letting Go: Inference Retention During Text Understanding," in Small, Cottrell, and Tanenhaus, eds., pp. 401–3.

287 Su, p. 113. The term indeterminacy has deconstructive overtones Su would not necessarily follow. As we saw in the discussion of word meaning, ideas of Derrida suggest indeterminacy as an unending process of substitution; similarly Paul de Man's ideas of tropic language suggest a final impossibility of interpretation (see discussion in II.xiii and III.iii, below). Gerald Graff, "Determinacy/Indeterminacy," in Lentricchia and McLaughlin, p. 165, draws on work of Timothy Bahti to suggest a radical difference between ambiguity and indeterminacy. Indeterminacy is a feature of all texts, ambiguity, in effect, just an attractive figure of speech. But certainly Empson is not thinking of ambiguity as a mere decoration put there by the author. Obviously, I am arguing for ambiguity as a property of texts. One can also ask if ambiguity/unclarity/indeterminacy always has to lead to interpretation interminable. A reader may resolve uncertainties for an interpretation she wishes to argue while still being willing to grant possible other readings based on ambiguity/unclarity/indeterminacy—a point I make in critique of de Man's interpretation of all texts as about their indeterminacy (III.iii, below).

288 Robert R. Hoffman, in his taxonomy of varieties of ambiguities, calls this "open meaning ... without any obvious resolution or completion": "Some Ambiguities in the Study of Ambiguity," in Gorfein, ed., p. 208.

289 Deidre Gentner and Ilene M. France, "The Verb Mutability Effect: Studies of the Combinatorial Semantics of Nouns and Verbs," in Small, Cottrell, and Tanenhaus, ed., p. 348, shows how verbs are changed to work around the perception of abstract nouns as easily creating semantic unclarities.

290 Hoffman, in Gorfein, ed., p. 207. See Su's discussion of obscurity, pp. 116–21. Her distinction between obscurity at the semantic level and at the pragmatic level (interpreter's meaning) seems, as so often with this distinction, one without a difference.

291 Walter Benjamin's famous essay on translation, "The Task of the Translator," *Illuminations*, trans. Harry Zohn (New York: Schocken, 1968), pp. 69–82, has seemed to please both idealist believers in metempsychosis by translation and skeptical poststructuralists; Derrida's system of dissemination in translation, which reads Benjamin as offering a messianic hope for some future unity of language meaning and critiques it on that basis (Babel lives), more clearly indicates the necessary production of difference—different expressions, different manners and meanings, in a different language: see his "Des Tours de Babel," in Joseph Graham, ed., *Difference in Translation* (Ithaca: Cornell UP, 1985), pp. 165–249. Tejaswini Niranjana, *Siting Translation: History, Post-Structuralism, and the Colonial Context* (Berkeley: U of California P, 1992), suggests how much translation is at play in any culturally oppositional situation. For a fuller discussion of the issue of copy and original in translation see Laura Mackay's study, "'Midway Between Poetry and Doctrine': Marcel Proust, Samuel Beckett and Translation as Poetics," Diss. New York University, 2000. All the arguments about textual resistance points in these sections suggest more broadly the impossibility of translation as a capturing of the intentions of an original.

292 Brian Vickers, *In Defence of Rhetoric* (Oxford: Clarendon, 1988), pp. 64, 459–61. Vickers makes a major point of following some traditional distinctions between trope and figure. I am speaking here of figures of rhetoric or rhetorical figures to cover both; I look at separate examples of both below.

293 Richard A. Lanham, *A Handlist of Rhetorical Terms* (2nd ed.; Berkeley: U of California P, 1991), by a contemporary rhetor, provides a useful if rather miscellaneous list of terms. Lanham is helpful in admitting throughout the redundancy of terms and also their illogical and opportunistic history. We have as yet no grand rhetoric for the structures of the mind, just a primitive botanist's lexicon of flowers (of rhetoric) observed and named.

294 I refer especially to work of George Lakoff and his associates, who have been developing a model of how much conceptual thinking develops out of ways we speak of simpler bodily experience. For them, as for Nietzsche, the world of language is filled with metaphorical concepts—for instance going somewhere as a metaphor for a host of goal-oriented pursuits: "we are going/getting somewhere now." Dead metaphors are very much alive and well in our thought processes. See Lakoff and Mark Johnson's *Metaphors We Live By* (Chicago: U of Chicago P, 1980) and Lakoff's more recent *Philosophy in the Flesh: The Embodied Mind and Its Challenge to Western Thought* (New York: Basic Books, 1999). That metaphors are so much in common use should not assure, rather should further upset and confound, the lineup of philosophers, from Aristotle, through Hobbes and Locke, and on to Russell and early Wittgenstein, who wished to create a language without play

for use in philosophy and science. See the useful historical summary of attitudes toward metaphor in Laurence D. Smith, "Historical and Philosophical Foundations of the Problem of Meaning," in Mandell and McCabe, eds., pp. 32–34.

295 Nathan, in Iseminger, ed., pp. 183–84, notes how such devices put pressure on intentionalist instincts to look to the real author for clarification just where they leave the text especially open to interpretation (and therefore leave the interpreter unlikely to trust the teller over the tale). The context is not the author but the rest of the text, which enters whatever hermeneutic circle we start up (p. 186).

296 Scheffler, pp. 129–30.

297 The non-applicable cases are trivial, mainly negations of metaphors, which are only comprehensible at all because of the positive idea: see Dan Fass, *Processing Metonymy and Metaphor* (Greenwich, CT: Ablex, 1997), p. 64.

298 "What Metaphors Mean," *Inquiries into Truth and Interpretation* (Oxford: Clarendon, 1984), pp. 245–64; quotation is from p. 262.

299 Davidson, p. 263. See also Samuel C. Wheeler III, "Metaphor According to Davidson and de Man," in Reed Way Dasenbrock, ed., *Redrawing the Lines* (Minneapolis: U of Minnesota P, 1989), pp. 116–39. Davidson's clarity has also helped focus the play of discussion in theory of metaphor. His opponents argue either that metaphors do not function this way or that all metaphors do not function this way. The variety of alternatives is well displayed in the record of the conference where Davidson presented his paper, in Sheldon Sacks, ed., *On Metaphor* (Chicago: U of Chicago P, 1978)—much of it originally vol. 5, no. 1 of *Critical Inquiry*—useful here to summarize the variety of thinking on metaphor because still widely available and consulted. Max Black, "How Metaphors Work: A Reply to Donald Davidson," pp. 181–92, argues that the focus (metaphorical tenor) may be untrue, but placed in the frame (the vehicle, its sentence context) it says "something" (p. 183), even means "something" (pp. 185, 190); that metaphors have a "cognitive content" and do "carry a message" (p. 187). See Black's earlier full study, *Models and Metaphors* (New York: Cornell UP, 1962). Similarly, Nelson Goodman, "Metaphors as Moonlighting," pp. 175–80, offers to solve most or all of Davidson's cases. Karsten Harries, "The Many Uses of Metaphor," pp. 165–72, splits the differences, finding that some metaphors bear meaning across their gaps, while others bar it (pp. 166–67). The assumption in those who oppose Davidson's open-ended structure is that all/some metaphors have a single determinable point (or, broadly speaking, meaning). One example given is AC/DC (Harries, p. 166): does it mean one thing? or does the metaphor keep opening meanings beyond the coded one of bisexual? A frequently given answer is that to the extent that a metaphor becomes widely known (dead) it ceases to seem untrue

as the word (here AC/DC) takes on that lexical meaning; tension is no longer present in the hearer/reader; exploration is less called for, unless a new use drives us to revaluate it as metaphor: for instance, if I say Stravinsky was AC/DC in a musical world split between twelve-tone and traditional tonics.

Interestingly for my broader argument, those who see single determinant meaning in a metaphor tend to appeal to a writer's intention, a competent reader judging the metaphor maker "as intending to mean" something (Black, pp. 183, 185–91); John R. Searle, "Metaphor," in *Expression and Meaning*, pp. 76–116, sees a metaphor as an utterer's meaning capable of being paraphrased, then verified: well criticized by Armin Burkhardt, "Searle on Metaphor," in Burkhardt, ed., pp. 303–35. The paraphrase of the utterer's intention would only be one of many possible interpretations. In contrast to Black and Searle, Davidson prefers, as I do, "standard sense," not the pretense to knowing intention. Wayne Booth, "Metaphor as Rhetoric: The Problem of Evaluation," pp. 47–70, follows the great tradition of metaphor as rhetoric of persuasion, not exploration. Metaphors are chosen to sway an audience by appeal to ethos (his example is a folksy metaphor in a Southern legal case), a view in line with his position in his major works, of meaning as something an author directs in his audience in relation to their specific shared context.

That volume summarizes much current thinking on metaphor. More broadly, traditional theories of metaphor imply more or less determinate meaning: substitution (Quintilian)—a metaphor sits in for some meaning (often single); comparison (Aristotle's)—a metaphor is based on an implied comparison (simile) which may be open or closed; tension or interaction—a metaphor holds I.A. Richards's tenor and vehicle in tension, which can suggest openness to a series of meanings, as the two interact. With further openness to a variety of meanings embodied in metaphor, other recent writers such as Paul Ricoeur, "The Metaphorical Process as Cognition, Imagination, and Feeling," in Sacks, ed., pp. 141–57—and see his major study, *The Rule of Metaphor: Multi-disciplinary Studies of the Creation of Meaning in Language* (Toronto: U of Toronto P, 1978)—have stressed the ways in which metaphors break down our ideas (or defamiliarize them, to use Russian formalist language) by forcing us to live through our senses as if metaphors take us back to an origin of language in pre-linguistic experience. Similar to Davidson's view, which is sometimes called controversion theory, is the deviance approach, which sees metaphors as violations of grammar.

There has been an enormous amount of work on metaphor from viewpoints of a variety of disciplines, each using their own special rhinestone-studded technical terms and some bedazzling their work and readers from other disciplines alike with elaborate charts. By even 1990, there were six thousand bibliographical entries from fields as diverse as philosophy, linguistics, cognitive psychology, anthropology, and sociology: see Sabine Maasen and Peter Weingart, *Metaphors and the Dynamics of Knowledge* (London: Routledge, 2000), p. 26. Mac Cormac clearly summarizes the various positions, but his attempt to develop a "conceptual theory of semantic anomaly" (p. 27) leaves him in a position close to Davidson's: metaphors create anomalies which lead to creative thinking (pp. 6, 34, 50). This and other versions of so-called domains interaction theory of many commentators (a more particularized version of tension or interaction theory—see above), especially in Lakoff and his associates, also see metaphors as opening up possible meanings by bringing over a concept from one domain (or discourse) to another, where it can suggest new thinking. See also Tim Murphy, *Nietzsche, Metaphor, Religion* (Albany: SUNY UP, 2001), p. 37—who offers a view similar to that of Maasen and Weingart and also somewhat similar to Eva Feder Kittay's concept—*Metaphor* (Oxford: Oxford UP, 1987)—of "semantic fields" in which the sides of metaphorical connection are contextually enmeshed.

300 An observation about context confirmed by an experiment on actual behavior of readers by Allyssa McCabe, "Narrative Threads of Metaphor," in Mandell and McCabe, eds., pp. 359–62: as many extensions of possible meaning occurred by connections with the context as between the tenor and vehicle of the metaphor alone.

301 Mark Turner, "Design for a Theory of Meaning," in Overton and Palermo, eds., pp. 105–6, follows Lakoff in stressing how broadly communication, including reasoning, is based on this area of play.

302 See my discussion in III.iii, below. Despite their different traditions, de Man and Davidson are not so far apart on the question of the instability of metaphor. Both deny that metaphors can be pinned down to certain meanings. But if de Man offers paralyzing indeterminacy, Davidson opens rather the possibility of endless productivity.

303 Hayden White's now classic studies of historical thinking have demonstrated how much tropes and narrative structures shape historical presentation. See *Metahistory: The Historical Imagination in Nineteenth-Century Europe* (Baltimore: Johns Hopkins UP, 1973), *The Content of the Form: Narrative Discourse and Historical Representation* (Baltimore: Johns Hopkins UP, 1987), as well as *Tropics of Discourse* (Baltimore: Johns Hopkins UP, 1978). Similar studies of the tropics of science, from Mary Hesse, *Models and Analogies in Science* (London: Sheed and Ward, 1963) to the wide arguments over Alan Sokol's hoax in *Social Text* (see II.xix, nn. 459–60, below), have been far more controversial. On metaphor in the social sciences, see Maasen and Weingart. An entire generation of feminist, multi-cultural, queer studies, and social/cultural historians have insisted broadly on the power of unexamined tropic

language. Much of this discussion of the power of metaphor in apparently non-metaphorical discourse has been influenced by Nietzsche's early work (mainly unpublished in his lifetime) on tropes. Both Sarah Kofman, *Nietzsche and Metaphor*, trans. Duncan Large (Stanford: Stanford UP, 1993) and Murphy argue that Nietzsche's mature work was founded on his early sense of language as built up from metaphors and of truth as a marshaling of metaphors: the famous declaration of truth as a "mobile army of metaphors," in "On Truth and Lies in an Extra-Moral Sense," *The Portable Nietzsche*, ed. Walter Kaufmann (New York: Viking, 1954). Philosophy itself, as well as other sciences, must open itself to metaphorical thinking which hides, in any event, beneath attempts at orderly conceptualization as a more archaic level of thinking based on sense experience and multiplicity. See Jacques Derrida, "White Mythology: Metaphor in the Text of Philosophy," *Margins of Philosophy*, trans. Alan Bass (Chicago: U of Chicago P, 1982), pp. 207–71, and Paul de Man, "The Epistemology of Metaphor," in Sacks, ed., pp. 11–28, for more recent deconstructive takes; also see the more conservative statement of logician W.V. Quine, "A Postscript on Metaphor," in Sacks, ed., pp. 159–60.

304 For instance, Dan Fass, "An Account of Coherence, Semantic Relations, Metonymy, and Lexical Ambiguity," in Small, Cottrell, and Tanenhaus, eds., pp. 151–77, and Su, pp. 131–43; also the long chapter by the philosopher Scheffler, pp. 79–130, who sees metaphor as a prime case of "deviational language behavior" (p. 1).

305 Metaphor has often been taken to stand in for all tropes as the master trope, though that threatens to efface the particular qualities of metaphors. Metonymy as a trope (as opposed to Roman Jakobson's broad mode of syntagmatic language use), a near thing substituting for another, seems less open to play—the crown for the government, hands for the factory workers have fairly clear meanings. But metonymies usually have some of the suggestive qualities of metaphor: crown makes us think of gems and riches, of personified power behind government, even of the uneasiness of the head that sleeps under the crown; hands (specifically a synecdoche) bring us into a world of possible meanings, men reduced to hands, handymen, work as in touch or touch and go. And these old examples are of course kinds of dead metonymies. Cf. the more suggestive "nerds" for high-tech workers or "9/11" for all that happened on and as a consequence of that fatal day.

While Jakobson made metonymy, controversially, a master trope, other writers have interestingly explored its centrality to kinds of reading. David Lodge stresses readings of fiction that appreciate the differing balance of contiguity relations (metonymy) and substitution ones (metaphor), the nineteenth-century novel generally overweighting the former, the twentieth-century the latter: *The Modes of Modern Writing: Metaphor, Metonymy, and the Typology of Modern Literature* (Ithaca: Cornell UP, 1977), esp. Part II. Elaine Freedgood, in an interesting new reading of nineteenth-century British fiction, demonstrates how metonymic reading leads us out from the specific references in the fiction to increasingly open readings of the novel in its world of things and places: *The Ideas in Things: Fugitive Meaning in the Victorian Novel* (Chicago: U Chicago P, 2006).

306 Clayton Koelb's de Manian study, looked at in the subsection on de Man (III.iii, below), *Inventions of Reading: Rhetoric and the Literary Imagination* (Ithaca: Cornell UP, 1988), esp. pp. 24–61, offers a useful further discussion of some special types of figures and tropes that necessarily detach the author from the text he thereby creates, although Koelb vacillates between attributing effects to a controlling author, seeing them as a property of texts, and throwing them to the reader's control. De Man was correct in insisting that all attempts to write texts on purely realist/representational or on purely symbolic/allegorical levels will fail because of the texts' necessary presentation of both representational and symbolic possibilities: "The Rhetoric of Temporality," *Blindness and Insight: Essays in the Rhetoric of Contemporary Criticism* (Minneapolis: U of Minnesota P, 1983), pp. 187–228. J. Hillis Miller similarly noted "the impossibility of distinguishing for certain between literal and figurative language in the text": *Theory Now and Then* (London: Harvester Wheatsheaf, 1991), p. 307. This uncertainty undercuts the only apparently clear distinction Jakobson made between metaphorical and metonymic language use. Michel Le Guern, *Sémantique de la métaphore et de la métonymie* (Paris: Larousse, 1973), tries to systemize this distinction as one between real reference (metonymy) and transfer of sense only (metaphor). But in creative work, where all reference is in fact imaginary, the two often refuse to stay in place.

307 Written before Gasché's study was published; but see his p. 7 for the similar idea. The wild cards in de Man's wild card of theory are doubtless tropes. Again, I prefer to think of them as giving us more room to create our interpretation than as short circuits, à la de Man, that prevent all interpretation.

308 See II.iv, above, on irony.

309 The general critical point, that all judgments on irony are a matter of interpretation, that there is no literal level on which we can all necessarily agree as to the perspective within which a statement calls to be read, has been well made by Stanley Fish, "Short People Got No Reason to Live: Reading Irony," *Doing What Comes Naturally: Change, Rhetoric, and the Practice of Theory in Literary and Legal Studies* (Durham: Duke UP, 1989), pp. 180–96. Fish refutes Wayne Booth's attempts to assert the stability of readings of irony in his *A Rhetoric of Irony* (Chicago: Chicago UP, 1974), where Booth used author's intention as a way of arguing that interpretations of irony become "firm as

a rock" because in irony, "we can know other minds clearly" (pp. 10, 16, 235). Claire Colebrook, *Irony: The New Critical Idiom* (London: Routledge, 2004), is on both sides of the issue. She can conceive of irony as a form of reading: "reading ironically means, in complex ways, not taking things at their word; it means looking beyond standard use and exchange to what this or that might really mean" (p. 4); she grants that "underlying or unifying intention is undecidable" (p. 12) in many cases. Yet she also tries to arm Speech Act theory to stabilize meaning after all (p. 168); she denies that statements can exist without possessing "a [i.e., one] truth toward which speech and language strive" (p. 177); and (see n. 310, below) she argues for stable historical contextual meaning in irony. Finally, she opposes Rorty's idea of irony as a place for thinking beyond our present commitments (see II.iv, n. 2, above) by insisting that irony must aim at a truth. I cannot fully endorse Fish's assurances to Booth that the play of interpretation over irony is nothing to worry about because the play in the professional discussion acts as a constraint on maverick interpretation in every age. Revolution, even Fish admits, is always possible. So non-change is always a call that the glass (of revolution) is half empty; contrary to what literary critics may think, the profession does not consist of lemmings all doing naturally what the major debaters have decided. If revolution were not possible, how else could so many of us have arrived at positions so diverse from Booth's authoritative views during the 1960s and 1970s? Dutton, in Cascardi, ed., pp. 200–204, like Booth, asserts that irony needs a reading controlled by author's intention but offers no secret as to how we ascertain that intention. That the decision is an important one for readers doesn't relieve them of the burden of making it. Paul de Man comments on irony much in the spirit of Fish, whom he compliments in his later discussion: see "The Rhetoric of Temporality," pp. 187–229 and "The Concept of Irony," in *Aesthetic Ideology* (Minneapolis: U of Minnesota P, 1996), pp. 163–85. The later essay, focused on Fichte and Schlegel, continues, despite some self-criticism, the earlier work of refusing to diminish the destabilizing effect of irony. Here he looks at theorizations of irony, aesthetic, psychological, or historical, that attempt to limit its power. Quite the contrary to Wayne Booth's view, irony is a destabilizing trope as interruptive to narrative certainty as metaphor is to thematic certainty. De Man would say it is a trope that creates undecidability ("permanent parabasis," p. 179—a term he takes from Schlegel). I would rephrase this: it is a trope that shifts decision to the reader.

310 Lanham associates with irony the following rhetorical terms: dissimulatio, drie mock (Puttenham's term), enantiosis, and illusio. Of these, dissimulatio (dissembling, concealment) suggests irony as deliberate unclarity, enantiosis (persuading by opposition or by opposing contraries) suggests irony as

persuasion, and drie mock (mockery) and illusio (mocking, jeering) suggest irony as direct mocking or using mocking to persuade. Colebrook, *Irony*, provides a useful, concise summary of the Western history of irony and a taxonomy of its types. She distinguishes broadly between irony as a trope and as a broad attitude or situation. Among historical versions she distinguishes especially Socratic irony (a broad point of view), romantic irony, satirical irony, and postmodern irony. That irony has traditionally broken into so many synecdochic parts suggests its general instability as a broad category for what in fact are widely varying reader positions.

Romantic irony adds a sense of self-cancellation of any fixed point of view in order to try to articulate what is impossible to articulate, what is actually ineffable. See discussion in Ernst Behler, *Klassische Ironie, romantische Ironie, tragische Ironie* (Darmstadt: Wissenschaftliche Buchgesellschaft, 1972), pp. 15–16. Studies of romantic irony in English include Anne K. Mellor, *English Romantic Irony* (Cambridge, MA: Harvard UP, 1980), Lilian R. Furst, *Fictions of Romantic Irony* (Cambridge, MA: Harvard UP, 1984), and Lloyd Bishop, *Romantic Irony in French Literature from Diderot to Beckett* (Nashville: Vanderbilt UP, 1989), esp. ch. 1. Colebrook, *Irony*, pp. 47–71, has tried to define romantic irony as lifting speaker and reader to a place above the body. But the point that needs to be made here is that that place is usually not a defined one as it might be in Socratic irony. It is thus not as easily distinguishable as she suggests from what she calls postmodern irony—irony with no clear viewpoint. Like Booth, she is attempting to contain the general problem of irony as a trope that throws decision to the reader and not back to the author by an historical schema that makes uncertain irony a deliberate postmodern authorial activity/madness. Her premise is that stable irony can be assured by intentions of great writers (Booth's position) and by a context of stable values from more stable historical times. My sections II.vii and II.xviii suggest the many problems with this idea. When we all agree about irony, the historical context seems to mirror our agreement; but the mirror shatters when the interpretive agreement breaks into different points of view. S. Sim also attempts to identify a specifically postmodern irony, which he uses as an emblem of its culture: *Irony and Crisis: A Critical History of Postmodern Culture* (London: Icon P, 2002). This view on irony runs into the usual problem of histories of postmodernism that have difficulty distinguishing it from pre-postmodernisms in modernism or, in the case of irony, Romanticism. Irony has been stably unstable for a long time.

311 Hutcheon explores well these complications of satirical personal and political ironies, including interesting examples from non-literary uses of language. See discussion in II.iv, above.

312 The subject is not therefore a simple one and I can only briefly rehearse some main topics here. In first-person narration we obviously have a created character, whose relation to the author may be a subject of biographer's speculation but this cannot let us evade interpretive responsibility for such creations in the text, characters to be figured out, just as others are. Nor are distinctions between reliable and unreliable first-person narrators, made to try to detain uncertainties in this work in a quarantine of one special narrative type—the demon unreliable narrator—likely to relieve us of our sense that all fictional creations slip and slide in our interpreting hands, may, finally, only seem more or less consistent and coherent to us. Drama offers only a variety of characters as locations of narrative: we try in vain to raise one to author status; and in a monologue the character simply becomes a first-person narrator. Third person not only does not presume identity with any part of the author but may disturbingly turn into active first person at any time, as Thackeray's narrator in *Vanity Fair* surprises us by his personal appearance on the narrative scene. Always pulled toward the positions of the characters, he/she morphs into free indirect discourse with great persistency in the history of the novel, only to leave the reader unclear as to who really is speaking or attitudinizing in any particular phase of the narration. Even in lyric poems or essays, how can we know to what extent the author has projected herself into her speaker? A lyric poem can be merely an effusion of a moment or a dramatic monologue in drag—how shall we know? An essay tries out ideas, points of view, and selves. Do you think you have met me in these chapters? Seymour Chatman, "The Structure of Narrative Transmission," in Roger Fowler, ed., *Style and Structure in Literature* (Oxford: Blackwell, 1975), pp. 213–57, offers a helpful introduction to these mainly narratological issues, especially useful as it does not insist on a full set of structural categories.

313 See the useful discussion by Gerald Graff, "Determinacy/Indeterminacy," in Lentricchia and McLaughlin, eds., pp. 163–76.

314 Garrett Stewart, *Reading Voices: Literature and the Phonotext* (Berkeley: U of California P, 1990), has interestingly explored the possible different or double meanings in written and audible versions of the same text. Pictograms, as in ancient Mesopotamia, were developed as early as 9000 BC. Chinese ideograms and ancient Egyptian hieroglyphs are not generally pictograms but contain some true pictograms that perhaps suggest the pre-development of these writings in a system of pictograms. Work on developing and using a pictogram system is done by the Institute for Remedial Teaching in Sweden. Research on use of lexigrams/pictograms to communicate with apes is taking place at the Georgia State Language center and at the Great Ape Trust of Iowa.

315 A subject explored in deconstructive studies of Browning's characters by E. Warwick Slinn, *Browning and the Fictions of Identity* (Totowa, NJ: Barnes and Noble, 1982) and Constance W. Hassett, *The Elusive Self in the Poetry of Robert Browning* (Athens: Ohio UP, 1982).

316 E.g., Pratt, *Toward a Speech Act Theory of Literary Discourse.*

317 Sianne Ngai's interesting *Ugly Feelings* (Cambridge, MA: Harvard UP, 2005) has pursued the New Critical interest in tone or attitude to a broader concept of the affect of the entire work—with appropriate characterization being euphoric, paranoid, or, in her cases, anxious or disgusted. Her revisit to New Criticism, Empson (who similarly sought to expand tone—to mood), Suzanne Langer, and even Heidegger offers a useful expansion of tone to a kind of descriptive term for the affect of a complex work with no single voice, though her global approach also opens the way back to a-formal impressionism so disliked by the New Critics. Bakhtin's ideas (see n. 319 below) would have been useful to her.

318 Hillis Miller interestingly probes the nature of such speech acts themselves. Just as even Austin admits that it is often impossible to conclude whether a given speech act is a performative, trying to do something, or a constative, stating a state of affairs (one of his "infelicities"), speech acts in literature are riven by what Miller calls a "perhaps." Any assertion by a persona or narrator may be taken as an achieved reality (constative) or an attempt to achieve (performative), which may or may not succeed (be felicitous). So, looked at from this point of view, Donne's sonnet may seem to be attempting to assert the nature of God's relation to man (a secure constative of a person of faith), but this statement of belief may be merely a prayer, a speech act that leaves his relation to God undetermined. The speaker seems to want to suggest that he knows the spiritual score but he may just as easily seem to fall into mere helpless (and masochistic) pleading. Depending on how we take the speech act itself we will interpret the position and voice of the speaker. See his *Speech Acts*, p. 184. The chapter on Proust attempts to show the uncertainty worked by speech acts in literature even when dealing with passages without clear and overt performatives.

319 *Speech Genres and Other Late Essays* (Austin: U of Texas P, 1986), esp. p. 95. Bakhtin's thinking about the novel suggests again (see II.iii, n. 102, above) that he is conflicted over issues of intention. In "Discourse in the Novel," for instance, he first speaks of a work fulfilling an author's intention only to then reveal the various complications, even aporias, that open up in his brilliant explorations of social voice. Literature moves away from the culture's authoritative, single, voice of ideology. Double voicings are allowed in by the author to subvert the culture's monologue.

The resultant dialogic discourse in a novel multiplies perspectives, social contexts, social strata. If he can describe the creation of such systems of hybridity from an author-active point of view, he nonetheless ends up offering a view of narrative of such complexity that the novel seems always already multi-voiced and impossible to read as a clear intention. Add to this his view that local uses of language are hopelessly lost to history in a relatively short time and we have, from a reader's view, a work effectively cut off from its creator.

320 My thinking here has been indebted to the much more profoundly and complexly pursued exploration of divided address and instability in speakers in Renaissance lyric of Heather Dubrow: "The Audiences of Early Modern Secular Lyric, or, This Poem May Be Monitored for Quality Control," paper delivered at NYU, April 14, 2005.

321 In cognitive psychology, where there are few such inhibitions, the researcher speaks of high-span and low-span (word and sentence meaning) readings; Whitney and Clark, "Disambiguation and Cognitive Control," in Gorfein, ed., pp. 239–51.

322 See Iser, *The Act of Reading*, pp. 92–103 and my fuller discussion in III.ii, below.

323 Again, see my summary of Fish's criticisms in III.ii, below.

324 Fowler, ch. I, usefully summarizes various definitions of literariness only to throw up his hands at the task of selecting any one set of criteria for the over-genre of literature, which, like other genres, changes from era to era and even from critic to critic. Notions of aesthetic fiction and poeticalness of language were of course popular during modernism. Postmodern criticism has tended to deconstruct all such definitions of the literary and the canons they promote by a hermeneutic of suspicion in which the assertion of literariness or aesthetic value is seen to hide interests or ideologies. The New Critical and also de Manian project of diminishing interest in thematics in favor of formalist concerns seems to have been unavailing in the past twenty-five years of identity, political, and sociological focuses in literary study: so much so that one of the most interesting recent topics has been thematic and historical treatment of issues of form.

325 I avoid calling these genres here, as thematic criticism may focus on single works and as I wish to explore the labeling effect in the next section. But obviously many thematic categories have become generic labels, such as, for Mansfield, Leon Edel's "psychological novels" or the Chekhovian short story.

326 E.g., Harris, *Literary Meaning*, p. 142.

327 Fowler, *Kinds of Literature*, ends his substantial discussion of historical genres in the West with a chapter on "Genre in Interpretation," in which he signs up with Hirsch for attribution of genre as a way of "constructing"

author's intention and thus regulating our interpretation. His assurance that historical work can assign such a clear formula for reading the text seems at odds with his practical sense in the rest of his study of the changing, highly diverse nature of genre in any period. His excursion into comparative reception of *Hamlet*, p. 262, only shows that "construction" of genre is part of the act of interpretation, not a fact before interpretation. In a complex case, which is the only kind we will argue over, our reading of the text determines which, of so many qualities, we pick out to define a genre.

For Hirsch's assertion that valid interpretation must be governed by valid inference about genre see *Validity*, p. 113. The idea that author's intention can be located in genre has been traced back as far as the work of Christian Wolff (1679–1764): see Kurt Mueller-Vollmer, ed., Introduction, *The Hermeneutics Reader* (New York: Continuum, 1985), pp. 4–5.

328 Adena Rosmarin, in her thoughtful discussion of theory of genre, finds it essentially "a kind of schema," a pragmatic ordering device, what I am calling a taxonomy: *The Power of Genre*, p. 21.

329 Frank Kermode, *The Genesis of Secrecy* (Cambridge, MA: Harvard UP, 1979), p. 162.

330 Denis Kambouchner, "The Theory of Accidents," *Glyph* 7 (Baltimore: Johns Hopkins UP, 1980): 157–58. In fairness to the author, I should note that his specific argument, within this view of genre, is that there are reading accidents which interrupt it.

331 "The Infinite Text," *Glyph* 7 (1980): 73.

332 Shawcross uses genre as his prime case for reading what he calls "author's text" rather than "reader's text"—a rough parallel to Hirsch's meaning/significance binary. In practice his cases are persuasive wherever the generic identity is clear enough and needs no recourse to the author's intention; wherever it is not the case, he seems to use intention to justify his own, controversial reading. I have no difficulty endorsing his assertion that a poet chooses consciously to write a villanelle (p. 24). I don't see why we need accept intentionality in interpretation to believe in author's craft as part of writing (p. 23). We know a villanelle directly from the form of the text.

333 See Rosalie L. Colie, *The Resources of Kind: Genre-Theory in the Renaissance* (Berkeley: U of California P, 1973), pp. 69–75, 103–9: the sonnet "proved extraordinarily open to the topics, styles, and tones of other literary genres": pp. 106–7.

334 See Karen Ruth Kligerman, "The Ravishing Word: Modern Narrative and the Romantic Ode," Diss. New York University, 1998.

335 See Robert Champigny, "Semantic Modes and Literary Genres," in Joseph P. Strelka, ed., *Theories of Literary Genre* (University Park: Pennsylvania State UP, 1978), p. 107, on the difficulty of writing histories of genres.

336 See the long discussion of genre in Hirsch, *Validity in Interpretation*, pp. 68–126; Hirsch would doubtless not welcome the ideas I father on him, as he is intent on using shared genre as a way of our determining further implications of meanings intended and "genre-bound" by the author. Yet his logical approach to genre as something we work our way to in a work, what he calls an "intrinsic genre" as opposed to given extrinsic concepts of genre, usefully demystifies the traditional views of genre as abstract universals of humankind or some great tradition within it. It thus allows him, in the section on historical genres (pp. 102–11), to accept mutation of genres, indeed the fitting of an appropriate intrinsic genre to each work; by contrast, he finds Northrop Frye's full schematic system inappropriate if used to reimpose qualities abstracted from a text as a "deeper and higher" meaning (p. 110). This is to my mind what most genre criticism tries to do in interpretation, including Hirsch when he rules that only one intrinsic genre will be found for each work, the one intended by the author. Irwin (*Intentionalist Interpretation*, pp. 43–46), who follows Hirsch explicitly on most issues, insists even more than he on the case-by-case openness of genre. Genre has been very much undertheorized in recent theory, perhaps from a feeling that Frye's universal theory of genre and myth, with its essentializing of a bewildering group of four narrative categories (romantic, tragic, etc.) and five modes (myth, romance, high mimetic, etc.), important as it had been in the rebirth of theory, had finally been going down a wrong road. Nonetheless, there has been, since Croce denied the validity of genre to art works (which he wished to see universally as unique), important thinking by critics of the standing of Mikhail Bakhtin, Hans Robert Jauss, Tzvetan Todorov, and Gérard Genette. David Duff, ed., *Modern Genre Theory* (Harlow: Longman, 2000), offers a useful collection.

Derrida's "La loi du genre/The Law of Genre," *Glyph* 7 (1980): 176–232, stands out as a well-known discussion by a major thinker. Derrida's piece, centering on interpretation of the generic self-presentation/non-presentation of Maurice Blanchot's *La Folie du jour*, is, even for Derrida, especially playful. He sees genre, which he compares to gender, as a law that calls to us but that we may refuse (if even that isn't too schematic a reduction of his play). He does question all sorts of limiting categorizations, whether called "genre, type, mode, form" (p. 210), which he sees as always playing "the role of order's principle: resemblance, analogy, identity and difference, taxonomic classification, organization and genealogical tree, order of reason, order of reasons" (p. 228). He even calls into question Genette's attempt to divide genre into modes (often taken to be natural forms) and genres (as historical thematics): a text may not seem to us to respect the categories or may even seem to wish to undo them (p. 209). Derrida's attempt, in his reading of

Blanchot, to locate genre indications in a threshold space (title or announcement in text) that is thus a fold or invagination at once inside and outside the texts seems to me unnecessary, as genre will necessarily be something the reader ultimately determines. He himself is clear that an announcement of genre may be rejected as a red herring or spoof (my Anglo-Saxon terms), so it seems unnecessary to create an ideal form—genre announcer—and then deconstruct it. Jean-François Lyotard, looking at genres of discourse, is less troubled by ideal possibilities. He sees genre as an arbitrary way of overriding difference between sentences. Any set of sentences can be inscribed into another genre of discourse so that the difference of sentences now becomes a series of potential differences in genres that could unite them; metadiscourses can be multiplied, in principle endlessly: *The Differend: Phrases in Dispute* (Minneapolis: U of Minnesota P, 1988), p. 138. Paul de Man only glancingly considers the issue when it comes up in practical criticism. Speaking of lyric, he finds all generic terms those of "resistance and nostalgia," a place of desired interpretive totality, which for de Man is never possible: *The Rhetoric of Romanticism*, p. 262.

The approach to genre that we find in Lyotard, that theorizer of postmodernism, as an unlimited series of games of classification where the critic pragmatically constitutes the class to suit her interests in the work, has been influential in what specialized studies have taken up genre in the last thirty years. Paul Hernadi, *Beyond Genre: New Directions in Literary Classification* (Ithaca: Cornell UP, 1972), competently summarized theories of genre up to his publication date, especially German ones and especially since 1800. He finds them focused mainly on the "holy trinity" of the traditional great genres: poetry (lyric), fiction (epic), and drama (dramatic); he suggests rather a "polycentric" multiple classification system, including subjects and "worlds" of writing (pp. 152–56). More recent studies include Thomas O. Beebee, *The Ideology of Genre: A Comparative Study of Generic Instability* (University Park: Pennsylvania State UP, 1994), Gary Saul Morson, *The Boundaries of Genre: Dostoevsky's Diary of a Writer and the Traditions of Literary Utopia* (Austin: U of Texas P, 1981), Rosmarin, *The Power of Genre* (explicitly deconstructionist and pragmatist), Jean-Marie Schaeffer, *Qu'est-ce qu'un genre littéraire?* (Paris: Seuil, 1989), Morris Weitz, *The Opening Mind: A Philosophical Study of Humanistic Concepts* (Chicago: Morris Weitz, 1977). Genre games (taxonomies of one or a set of qualities defining a genre) are not only endless, as in Wittgenstein's games of language generally, but also subject to loose systems of classification—fuzzy sets—in which members of a game, like members of a family, may be considered to possess only some of its possible characterizations (seen in any case as matters of definition, though the approach is useful in conceptualizing the drift of expansion—"perennially flexible, perennially debatable" of historical genres over time: Weitz, pp. 33, 103). Neopragmatic approaches, followed by the same theorists, add the spin, as I do here, that genre games will prevail or die out as they are persuasive to succeeding generations. A third alternative between such pragmatic approaches to genre, which I follow, and rigid taxonomies reified from partial practice and criticism into presumptive universals, which I critique, has been the utopian concept of a literature beyond all genre. This concept was especially developed in the Romantic period, as in the Schlegels, as an ideal for the fragmented, universal work that fits no traditional kinds of literature. Michael Beaujour argues that it found a location in views of the Bible as a universal or all-genred work or "*genus universum*": *Glyph* 7 (1980): 18. Other contributors to this volume note the Romantic ideal of mixing genres, including combining prose and poetry (p. 135) and cite texts by Nerval, Mallarmé, or Blanchot. The symposium from which these papers came was stimulated by Jean-Luc Nancy and Philippe Lacoue-Labarthe's work on *Absolu littéraire*. As the fact of the discussion shows, such works are already a kind of genre and will doubtless be assigned various sub-genre classes by their readers.

Despite such specialized work on genre theory in the last thirty years, it is striking that this central subject isn't given a place even in the second edition of Lentricchia and McLaughlin's much used edition of essays on critical terms.

337 Hernadi, p. 4.

338 See discussion in Gérard Genette, *The Architext: An Introduction* (Berkeley: U of California P, 1992), pp. 60–72. Genette unfolds the broad confusion over modes, prefers forms of enunciation, but denies grand genres or modes are more and more capacious, broader classes. On genre, see Shawcross, pp. 26–31; on mode, Colie, p. 7. Jean-Paul Richter added the view that lyric is past time, epic present, dramatic future: see Adrian Marino, "Towards a Definition of Literary Genres," in Strelka, ed., p. 44.

339 *Anatomy of Criticism* (Princeton: Princeton UP, 1957); his approach to genre is discussed well by Hernadi, pp. 131–51.

340 Adrian Marino "Towards a Definition of Literary Genres," in Strelka, ed., p. 41. Tzvetan Todorov, *Genres in Discourse* (Cambridge: Cambridge UP, 1990), pp. 10–11, usefully defines thematics as any discourse on subject or subjects, thus evading the tendency to think of genre as only for works defined as literary.

341 In the medieval age, before the norming forces of neoclassical categories were at work, an astounding variety of qualities, verse form, subject, theme, prose or poetry, religious or secular, presumed audience, etc., became the grounds for genre classes. See Johannes A. Huisman, "Generative Classification in Medieval Literature," in Strelka, ed., esp. pp. 129–44. Colie, pp. 11–12, suggests how diverse classical genres in fact were.

342 Fowler, *Kinds of Literature,* attempts to separate genre from subgenre as form and content classes respectively. But though sometimes helpful, this fails: subgenres of the sonnet are Shakespearian, etc.

343 Thomas Kent, *Interpretation and Genre: The Role of Generic Perception in the Study of Narrative Texts* (Lewisburg, PA: Bucknell UP, 1986), pp. 23–26, offers, more somberly, a case of critics finding different generic structures by which to interpret *Moby-Dick.* His exploration of how we use genre in interpretation too much reifies his nonetheless useful taxonomy of formulaic (obviously generic) and unpredictable works (supergenres); I would have to add that the emergence of reader differences, not some simply definable quality of a text, creates generic variety in a text. Wolfgang Iser's system of reading allows him to see judgments on genre as sometimes a processive *Gestalt*-like series of formations, though he is as usual unclear whether this is a reader action or programmed into the text: *The Implied Reader* (Baltimore: Johns Hopkins UP, 1974), p. 58. Beebee offers a different approach. Following interest in the 1990s in border crossings, boundary spaces, and hybridization, he explores genres as generally multiply at work in a text; more broadly, genres are differential systems known only by contrasts to and play against other genres, usually within a text: esp, pp. 28–29, 250, 268. His critique of Rosmarin, pp. 255–56, seems unjustified; both use genres as heuristics. Morson also explores generic boundaries and thresholds in a work.

344 See Christopher Ricks's magisterial annotation in his edition of *The Poems of Tennyson* (Berkeley: U of California P, 1987). On Tennyson and pastoral see Owen Schur, *Victorian Pastoral: Tennyson, Hardy, and the Subversion of Forms* (Columbus: Ohio State UP, 1989)—but not on *In Memoriam*; and the good article by Ian H. C. Kennedy, "In Memoriam and the Tradition of Pastoral Elegy," *Victorian Poetry* 15 (1977): 351–66, which sees Tennyson critiquing and revising the pastoral in *In Memoriam.* Neither explores the gay implications of the tradition.

345 See Marino, in Strelka, ed., p. 49.

346 Kent argues that simple, "formulaic" genres are regularly made more complex by mixing genres in a work or by changing ("deforming") it: p. 40.

347 Marino quotes Albert Thibaudet, "To write in accordance with one genre means to extend this genre": in Strelka, ed., p. 52. Todorov, p. 15, similarly answers the question of where new genres come from: "Quite simply from other genres." Cf. "it is hardly possible to give a static definition of genre which could embrace all genre manifestations: genre is moving": Yuri Tynianov, quoted by Teslenko in Richard Coe, Lorelei Lingärd, and Tatiana Teslenko, eds., *The Rhetoric and Ideology of Genre* (Cresskill, NJ: Hampton Press, 2002), p. 329. Teslenko cites Yuri Lotman's concept of genre formation at cultural boundaries: p. 337.

348 Historical genres are those established for some period as recognized classifications by numbers of people, who of course may include authors who may bring elements of the genre into their work. Anyone may propose a genre; the trick is getting others to believe your classification is a fact. Those who like to think in normative terms will not only look for ways to ground genre in universals, God, human nature, the nature of language or of voice or of tense (though such essentialistic thinking has been highly unfashionable in recent years) but also wish to limit the "club" of historical genres in some way: members must exist in more than one culture or period, comprise canonical works, some of which function as paradigmatic, and of course possess certain minimal conditions for classification. Of relatively recent useful critics on historical genres see Fowler, *Kinds of Literature* (though he believes genre provides the code needed to crack the work of literature, Fowler has an excellent sense of the variety and diverse development of genres), and David Fishelov, *Metaphors of Genre: The Role of Analogies in Genre Theory* (University Park: Pennsylvania State UP, 1993). Fishelov's study also offers a reasonable conservative taxonomy of historical genres and also a useful metatheoretical look at the metaphors underpinning various systems of classification. I have tried to apply my own open-ended view of genre to a literary historical account, so my reader may hold me to account: "The Bildungsroman," in Patrick Brantlinger and William B. Thesing, eds., *A Companion to the Victorian Novel* (Oxford: Blackwell, 2002), pp. 279–303. See also my approach to a thematic class, "Sex, Love, and Victorian Poetry," in Richard Cronin, Alison Chapman, and Antony H. Harrison, eds., *A Companion to Victorian Poetry* (Oxford: Blackwood, 2002), pp. 543–66. Far from being against history, I do history, only write here to put history in the bigger context of literary study (yes, bigger than history!—as history depends on interpretation of writing).

349 P. 29.

350 Hirsch, *Validity in Interpretation*, pp. 88–89.

351 Rosmarin, *The Power of Genre*, pp. 46–49.

352 A currently lively area, owing much to Bakhtin's interest in genre as social action, is in rhetorical studies, with a focus on genres of social communication. See Coe, Lingärd and Teslenko, eds., and Bakhtin's influential essay, "The Problem of Speech Genres," in *Speech Genres and Other Late Essays* (Austin: U of Texas P, 1986), pp. 60–102. (On Bakhtin see also II.iii, n.13 and II.xiv, n.7.) Georg Lukács's Marxist adaptation of Hegelian thinking about the relation of genre to historical epoch also represents a more global way of relating genre to social life. See discussion of his views of genre in Hernadi, pp. 114–31. Fredric Jameson elegantly updates the traditional interest in the social grounding of systems of genres in *The Political Unconscious*,

pp. 107–50. It is of course a big step from saying historical circumstances shape and adapt genres to positing the generic nature and then the meaning of a text on the basis of its general historical position. It offers helpful ideas as to possible genre and its use. The same has to be said of Hans Robert Jauss's concept of genre reception as an historical horizon: neither genre nor reception is an historical horizon; neither genre nor reception is ever a monolith. Nathan, p. 191, well critiques Hirsch's use of a similar conception. To posit a genre in the horizon (typical genre) of the day is to presume that the author might not have had something else, less typical, in mind. And even when a major historical genre is clearly present, it doesn't tell us how to interpret the work, only that it may have some place in our interpretation.

353 The tendency of neoclassical genre criticism from the seventeenth century on to prescribe norms for conformity to genres: see Marino's summary in Strelka, ed., p. 50. John Reichert, "More than Kin and less than Kind: The Limits of Genre Theory," in Strelka, ed., pp. 60–65, critiques the neo-Aristotelian Chicago School critics such as R. S. Crane for imposing on a work one and only one genre, and that rigidly defined, to limit interpretation to one set of effects the author is presumed to have intended in the genre: "the practical dangers of the assumption that genres can direct and restrict our mode of inquiry": p. 64. Reichert sensibly concludes, virtually a neopragmatist *avant la lettre*: a "question cannot be dismissed out of hand on the basis of a prior act of interpretation; it can only be rejected after due competition with other ways of making sense": p. 66. Colie, discussing Renaissance thinking and practice, elegantly indicates an earlier, much more flexible tradition in the innovation among, and mixing of, classical genres, especially in Scaliger.

354 Culler of course went on to produce his own, very cogent restatement of these issues in poststructuralist terms in his excellent *On Deconstruction*.

355 Jonathan Culler, *Structuralist Poetics: Structuralism, Linguistics and the Study of Literature* (Ithaca: Cornell UP, 1975), pp. 26–27: critiquing Ricoeur, "La structure, le mot, et l'événement," *Le Conflit des interprétations* (Paris: Seuil, 1969).

356 Culler, pp. 137–38.

357 Culler, pp. 257–65. His solution, the notion of literary competence as presented in the chapter of that name and the succeeding one on the problem of convention, pp. 113–60, again demonstrates the bifurcation between nature and culture in this thinking: as if language conventions of the sort displayed by structuralist linguistics were dependent on their being inculcated and maintained by an *Académie* of language use. As I remark in III.iii below, the structures Culler finds behind the surface play of literary interpretation of his time (in institutions) look very much like New Critical orthodoxies.

Dismissing a forerunner like Frye for creating only taxonomies, he turns around and creates his own. Vicki Mistacco's interesting attempt to understand a change in basic structures in the *nouveau roman* by adapting Cullerian conventions to new conventions, "The Theory and Practice of Reading Nouveaux Romans," in Suleiman and Crosman, eds., *The Reader in the Text*, pp. 371–400, displays in its almost inevitable confusions between assumptions about author's intentions and interpretative structures the problems with literary structures: they change as literature changes, but also we learn new interests as culture changes, bringing us back to early literature with different interests in different kinds of structures.

In an essay broadly stating his neopragmatist's faith, "The Pragmatist's Progress," in Eco, *Interpretation and Overinterpretation*, pp. 89–108, Richard Rorty states powerfully the position he identifies with Fish and himself, that no approach to a text can be more than a focus on some issue to which the critic wishes to give special weight. No rigorous method goes beyond this to reveal "something a given text is *really* about" (p. 102). But he generally grants that his capacious pragmatic view is also a kind of "monomania" by which he insists on reading all texts (p. 96). If there is no end to the making of taxonomies, he can at least offer a moral hope that criticism will use reading "not as a specimen reiterating a type, but as the occasion for changing a previously accepted taxonomy" (p. 107). For Rorty's classic statement of pragmatist interpretation, see "Nineteenth-Century Idealism and Twentieth-Century Textualism," *Consequences of Pragmatism* (Minneapolis: U of Minnesota P, 1982), pp. 139–59.

358 Fowler, *Kinds of Literature*, p. 49, interestingly sees this entire project merely as a new form of the old neoclassical idea of unchanging genres, now founded not on principles of taste or authority but on claims of a pseudoscience. Harris, *Literary Meaning*, p. 76, also sees Culler mediating a moderation in structuralism from a scientific study of linguistic absolutes to "a study of Poetics understood as the study of conventions."

359 Gérard Genette, *Narrative Discourse: An Essay in Method* (Ithaca: Cornell UP, 1980), p. 263.

360 Indeed the structuralist project, wishing to avoid assigning meaning to the individual text or the reader, is peculiarly prey to slipping into assignment to author rather than its preferred but vague ghost author-in-the-machine, "literature." Not without fighting the lapse, however. Mieke Bal notes how Genette even changed terms, from retrospection and anticipation to the more "barbaric" "technology" of analepsis and prolepsis in an effort to avoid "subjective phenomena": *Lethal Love: Feminist Literary Readings of Biblical Love Stories* (Bloomington: Indiana UP, 1987), p. 72.

361 Genette, pp. 86–93.

362 So attractive indeed, especially in its motion toward deconstructive play of interpretation, that it exerts considerable pressure on Culler's interesting work, looked at above, to abandon the project of finding a key to all conventions as a key to meaning and merely, as they say in New York, enjoy. "But pleasure," he notes after attractively rerendering Barthes, "is not the only value that a structuralist study of literature might serve. It is a concept that made its appearance rather late in structuralist discussions." And he goes on to rejustify structuralism on the grounds of its production of knowledge of man's nature as "*homo significans*: a creature who gives sense to things" (p. 264).

363 Barthes, *S/Z*, pp. 7–8.

364 Barthes, *S/Z*, p. 29. On p. 19 he declared "there will be no other codes throughout the story but these five."

365 Mieke Bal's feminist structuralist reading of the Bible, to take an attractive example, shows that clearly post-intentionalist interpretations can be made within a structuralist format. Bal uses a structuralist engine to open up different subject positions in her biblical texts but does so understanding that these are merely taxonomies, which then allow her to try out a new, feminist, view of such patriarchially received texts: see Bal, p. 132.

366 Hence the bite in M.H. Abrams's riposte to deconstruction that its "new meanings" are in fact very predictable, once stated: they too are formulas—taxonomies—that Abrams finds easy to anticipate: "How to do Things with Texts," *Critical Theory Since 1965*, ed. Hazard Adams and Leroy Searle (Tallahassee: Florida State UP, 1986), pp. 448–49. See also III.iii below on de Man's interpretations as also a predictable method of interpretation.

367 Nicholas Abraham and Maria Torok, *The Wolf Man's Magic Word: A Cryptonymy*, trans. Nicholas Rand with Foreword by Jacques Derrida (Minneapolis: U of Minnesota P, 1986).

368 For examples of reader-oriented exploration of such postmodern works, see Calinescu and the study of reading situations as versions of uncooperative game theory in Hardin.

369 Karl Kroeber, *Retelling/Rereading: the Fate of Storytelling in Modern Times* (New Brunswick, NJ: Rutgers UP, 1992), p. 34.

370 Kroeber, pp. 72–85.

371 Fowler, *Kinds of Literature*, p. 193, calls the allegory, taken as a broad effect, a mode working in many genres. But it is of course regularly considered a kind of genre: in their adjectival form (here "allegorical") genres all seem to morph into modes (taken in this sense).

372 George Watson, "The Literary Past," in Newton-DeMolina, ed., p. 165, goes much further, seeing historical comparative work on genre as revealing a clear, arguable intention—his case being Spenser's relation to prior Italian epic. But this avoids important questions: Are there more persuasive cases

that can be made for categorizing the work by other generic definitions? Is *The Faerie Queene* better understood as epic, as Christian allegory, or as postmodern games with conventions? What is the relation of the work to the historical genre?—a critical question that necessarily arises even where the work clearly speaks of its connection to an historical genre. Is Spenser's epic copying Tasso's or burlesquing it? That this is a convention and thus part of the organization we may wish to bring to a reading of the work may be obvious; that this fact leads us to a clear interpretation even within that context is not.

373 Angus Fletcher, *Allegory: The Theory of a Symbolic Mode* (Ithaca: Cornell UP, 1964), p. 323. Here and elsewhere in this section I am indebted to the very useful general references to discussions of allegory by Jane Garrison Bailey, "The Act of Reading Allegory: Filling the Gap between Narrative and Interpretive Strategies," MLA Conference, Dec. 28, 1995.

374 Paul de man, *Allegories of Reading: Figural Language in Rousseau, Nietzsche, Rilke, and Proust* (New Haven: Yale UP, 1979), pp. 75–76.

375 "One cannot study the history of allegorical interpretations without destroying one's faith in the stability of allegoresis's accomplishments": *The Ends of Allegory* (Newark: U of Delaware P, 1998), p. 155. Greenfield builds his system of readers reading allegory on Roman Jakobson's metonymy/metaphor distinction. The metonymies of the literal level are only partially stabilized by the metaphorical connections of allegorical reading. The allegorical level is put together from necessarily incomplete or sporadic metaphorical connections; hence it is normally completed by the ideology or system brought to the text by the reader: a reason why it may be less than convincing to someone with a different interest: see esp. chs. 1, 2 and pp. 86–89. Greenfield works with the vocabulary of allegory (a quality supposedly built into the text) and allegoresis (a system of second or multi-level interpretation). However, he finds the distinction one with no real difference. All readings are allegoreses; if we believe, as most such readers do, that our reading is found in the text, we will call it an allegory. Sayre's approach is helpful precisely in looking at allegorical reading. He draws on the earlier work of Jon Whitman, *Allegory: The Dynamics of an Ancient and Medieval Technique* (Oxford: Clarendon, 1987).

376 A careful reading of the real diversity of attitudes toward reading medieval allegorical texts in the medieval period is provided by Robert S. Sturges, *Medieval Interpretation: Models of Reading in Literary Narrative, 1100–1500* (Carbondale: Southern Illinois UP, 1991). There seems to have been even a fundamental disagreement as to whether a correspondence reading would be appropriate for anything but sacred writing; the world, it might be agreed, spoke of God, but a merely human writer might seem to overreach if he or

she claimed for an imaginary world the same unities as God could achieve. Aquinas considered only the Bible should be read on spiritual levels (p. 16); Sturges notes that the often cited "Epistle to Can Grande," possibly not even Dante's own work, fits fourfold interpretation to a text (the *Paradiso*) quite special in its essentially religious claims to continue inspired, prophetic writing (p. 37). Sturges offers a view of an unstable system of correspondences being increasingly eroded by a cultural and authorial sense of multiple meanings and a progressive dropping out of the spiritual codes in favor of the polysignification of the historical. The fact that critics vary as widely as D.W. Robertson, with his heavily coded readings, and Morton Bloomfield or Sturges himself, with their sense that secular literature was not generally written or read as scripture subject to full codings, in itself indicates that we cannot easily read the historical situation—how medieval people intended to read allegorically—or the texts themselves.

Despite my general sympathy with Sturges's moderate conclusions, I must note that his strategy, in which he attempts to resolve the contested issue of the nature of medieval allegory by making a set of (I should say attractive) readings of medieval texts based on an assumption of progressive historical abandonment of allegory, is circular; with a different view of allegory in the period he would make different readings leading to different conclusions about the nature of allegory. All of which is grist for my mill, which observes both positions to underline the fact that this issue is generally unresolved even in the Valhalla of coded allegory, the medieval period. John MacQueen, *Allegory* (London: Methuen, 1970), pp. 46–58, offers a brief view of medieval allegory.

Deborah L. Madsen, *Rereading Allegory: A Narrative Approach to Genre* (New York: St. Martin's, 1994), writes a much broader history of different views of allegory: Hellenic and Rabbinic "allegorism," or "fabulism," i.e., allegoresis; Christian allegory based on a sense of God's structuring fixed meanings into the (Biblical) text, history or world; "figural" allegory; and, from the Romantic period on, symbolic, individual allegory. Her ambitious study insists on not eliding modes of allegory, arbitrary metaphorical ("fabulism") connections and metonymic essential connections (as in Christian typology), with symbolism being a version of these intrinsic connections set loose from any clear metaphysical system but inspired in the author's romantic imagination. She finds most contemporary thinking about allegory (Benjamin, de Man, Jauss) based on "metaphoric fabulism," with a few others (Maureen Quilligan is her main citation) seeing mainly metonymic figuralism: see pp. 121–33. However, to know that some allegories in a period were written in assurance of their truth doesn't assure us about which ones or what truth they assert, which we must work out for ourselves in reading.

377 Rosamond Tuve, *Allegorical Imagery: Some Mediaeval Books and their Posterity* (Princeton: Princeton UP, 1966), p. 290; Isabel G. MacCaffrey, *Spenser's Allegory: The Anatomy of Imagination* (Princeton: Princeton UP, 1976), p. 45; Walter Benjamin, *Ursprung des deutschen Trauerspiels;* English as *The Origin of German Tragic Drama*, trans. John Osborne (London: Verso, 1985), p. 177.

378 *The Language of Allegory: Defining the Genre* (Ithaca: Cornell UP, 1979), p. 235. We must not miss "the radical significance of that much-dismissed literal surface": p. 29.

379 Commonly, three "spiritual" levels above the first, historical or literal level: allegory, anagoge, tropology. Sturges, p. 13, offers the following example: Jerusalem is, as history, a city; as allegory it is the church of Christ; as anagoge it is the heavenly city of God which is the mother of us all (our beginning and end); as tropology it is the soul of man (in a moral issue). On the question of limits to such approaches to medieval literature, see II. xvi, n. 376 above.

380 "To make any one of the four readings of a text (the literal, the allegorical, the moral, and the anagogical) subject to any other would be to misunderstand the nature of the division. While a hierarchy clearly exists among those readings, 'higher' and 'lower' levels do not cancel each other out but function individually and together at all times": Johann Köberl, *Indeterminacy of Beowulf* (Lanham, MD: U Press of America), p. 7.

381 *Time and Narrative*, vol. 3 (Chicago: U of Chicago P, 1988), p. 168. I would quarrel, however, with Walter Benjamin's seemingly similar formulation: that the "antinomies of the allegorical" are the fixed convention and unfixing interpretation (quoted in Jenny Sharpe, *Allegories of Empire* [Minneapolis: U of Minnesota P, 1993], pp. 143–44). This installs a frozen dialectic where I would argue that the form is always in play in the interpretation itself, so that each reading of an allegory proposed, for it, a new version of allegory.

382 *A Theory of Parody: The Teachings of Twentieth-Century Art Forms* (New York: Methuen, 1985).

383 Margaret A. Rose's later study, *Parody: Ancient, Modern, and Post-Modern* (Cambridge: Cambridge UP, 1993), though less full of interesting examples (she does discuss Robert Venturi's postmodern architecture) offers a methodical history of theories of parody. Like Hutcheon, Rose includes both comic and serious reused (intertexts) under her conception of parody, though she defines postmodernism as moving beyond comic or serious parody to a combination of the two: pp. 55 (on Bakhtin), 272, 282–83. She also grants that postmodernism is a rather floating term, allowing a variety of dates and artists. Her work is especially good, as is Hutcheon's, in suggesting how parody can take many forms from light allusion to the target text, to "an almost complete solidarity": p. 139.

384 Hutcheon, *A Theory of Parody*, pp. 84–85.

385 Indeed, plausible approaches to parody even suggest that it is really the pres-

ence of the target text in the parodying text that mainly matters. In this view, effective parody lets us experience enough of the target text even in its changed or distorted form to apprehend its values and forms. See Rose, esp. pp. 39–40, 122, 170: a persistent theme in this work. Rose's historical approach makes her less concerned than Hutcheon with promulgating her own theory. She uses reader reception in two sections yet also speaks of intertextual theorists such as Renate Lachmann as falling into the "intertextual trap of eliminating the author as the arbiter of meaning": p. 183.

386 Hutcheon, p. 98.

387 Hutcheon, p. 100: context is her word, not Said's.

388 See the discussion of the instability of metaphors, II.xiii, above.

389 P. 84.

390 From another, more historical view, Fredric Jameson has similarly called attention to the prominence of parody in modernism and postmodernism by attempting a genealogy that leaves parody stable until the postmodern moment, when the failure of direction in consumer capitalism turns parody into mere pastiche, a "blank" form of parody where a prior work is imitated without ironic, critical, or other particular intention: "Postmodernism, or the Cultural Logic of Late Capitalism," *New Left Review* 146 (July–August 1984): 59–92; reprt. as ch. I in *Postmodernism, or the Cultural Logic of Late Capitalism* (Durham: Duke UP, 1991), pp. 1–54. This may be a useful way of laying down a grand history of divide between those elusively intertwined periods, "modernism" and "postmodernism" but, like all grand histories, it homogenizes the necessary interpretive acts on which it must be based. As with all interpretations of parody, the decision as to whether a work is mere pastiche or "stable" parody must depend on a complex argument about its style and content in relation to putative targets (dip into the debate over Browning's Victorian parody/pastiche of Darwinian/natural theological? thinking in "Caliban upon Setebos" to experience this complex decision at first hand; my own opinion is that this work is already pastiche). Readers enthusiastic for, rather than critical of, the play of late capitalist culture will naturally mount strong arguments—as they have in the reading back of postmodernism into the modernism of Woolf and Joyce—why parodies, once received as stable, should be reinterpreted as playful and open-ended. As with irony, the decision will finally be in the hands of the reader, not the histories or biographies. I have already made clear my reasons for objecting to a historical system, whether coming from sociology or (often brilliant) Marxist economics, that constructs all readers as bound into a single modern or postmodern community. Rose, p. 221, notes Jameson's own unstable application of pastiche back to modern writers.

391 Kent, p. 78, a term he borrows from the Prague school.

392 Carl D. Malmgren, *Anatomy of Murder* (Bowling Green, OH: Bowling Green State UP, 2001), identifies the detective as the interpretant, p. 29, with whom the reader identifies; in fact, he is normally alien, cocaine addict, outsider, weird one, Belgian, and the story usually invites us to connect with it elsewhere (the familiar figures of Watson or Hastings).

393 Rabinowitz, *Before Reading*, p. 42, offers an interesting example, whose real interest he misses because of his attempt in this work to stabilize meanings of texts by his concept of an authorial audience, a frame which sorts out acceptable from unacceptable interpretations in advance. Rather against his own approach, he notes that some students in his class read Christie's *Mystery of the Blue Train* not as a mystery but as a romance choice of a young heiress, Katherine Grey—who eliminates the killer from her two possible mates, thus giving us a satisfying, sensible, Austenesque romance ending. Rabinowitz sees this as a product of an author's failing to provide enough clues to what the authorial audience should create itself as. Instead, I would agree that we should see it as a text that has greater interest because it can be interpreted, even simultaneously by the agile reader, in two (or more) frames at once. Rabinowitz's closely argued work elsewhere more consciously confronts the possible discrepancies between frames of reading. Generally he wishes to establish one intended frame, though his most interesting cases are where these can be argued. In fact, as the case here shows, they can always be argued; where no interesting argument emerges, there will be no need to appeal to an authorial audience as a form of intention. As I have already revealed, I love the BBC series of Christie/Poirot and read it as a tension between the art deco world, the traditional (Victorian/Edwardian) world, and the world of Continental difference/rationality; I have almost zero interest in the mystery being solved so especially sympathize with the other reading of Rabinowitz's students.

394 Laurie R. King, "Why a Mystery," 1996 Edgar Allan Poe Awards Supplement, *New York Times Magazine*, April 21, 1996, p. 2.

395 Here the reader expects and finds a reference to Thomas Kuhn, *The Structure of Scientific Revolutions*, 2nd ed. (Chicago: U of Chicago P, 1970). For a taste of the broader controversy over whether scientific interpretation is fundamentally different from that in the humanities see, for starters, Joseph Rouse, *Knowledge and Power: Towards a Political Philosophy of Science* (Ithaca: Cornell UP, 1987); Bruno Latour, *Science in Action* (Cambridge: Harvard UP, 1987); Charles Taylor, "Interpretation and the Sciences of Man," in his *Philosophy and the Human Sciences* (Cambridge: Cambridge UP, 1985), pp. 15–57; and of course the large body of commentary generated by the Sokal-*Social Text* affair. For a useful brief summary of arguments against Kuhn's relativism in scientific truth, see Dasenbrock, pp. 35–43. See

II.xviii, n. 11, on the specific issue of Diltheyan hermeneutics as a dualist version of knowledge versus Rorty's anti-essentialism.

396 Taxonomy has seemed an attractive term for an arbitrary classificatory system because it does not trail any essentialist literary interpretation with it. The structure obviously follows that of the traditional hermeneutic circle, where details are organized into a hypothesis which then commands the organization of further details. If biologists once used it with a sense of the permanence of their system, post-Darwinian science has become used to the nonce-ness and boundary shifting of classificatory systems. I use the term especially as one suggesting the arbitrariness underlying the pretense of systems of literary classification. As Gerald Edelman concludes, "Meaning simply refuses to be bound by a fixed set of terms in a specific coding system.... the mind is not a mirror of nature. Thought is not the manipulation of abstract symbols whose semantics are justified by unambiguous reference to things in the world": *Bright Air, Brilliant Fire: On the Matter of the Mind* (London: Penguin, 1994), p. 237. Harvey N. Quamen, "Unnatural Interbreeding: H.G. Wells's *A Modern Utopia* as Species and Genre," *Victorian Literature and Culture* 33 (2005): 67–84, looks interestingly at Wells's connections between biological and literary instabilities; literary types interbreed, Wells observed, as shamelessly as dogs.

Another similarly attractive term is schema/schemata from cognitive psychology. Schemata are used as a structure for organizing a reading by Mary Crawford and Roger Chaffin, "The Reader's Construction of Meaning: Cognitive Research on Gender and Comprehension," in Elizabeth A. Flynn and Patrocinio P. Schweickart, eds., *Gender and Reading: Essays on Readers, Texts, and Contexts* (Baltimore: Johns Hopkins UP, 1986), pp. 3–30: a system my students are as comfortable in using as they are in using taxonomies. Crawford and Chaffin acknowledge drawing on cognitive studies for the term as a description of the way the mind organizes information. Norman Holland, who has also looked in his work in the 1980s and 1990s to cognitive research for models of interpretation, similarly speaks of schemata, which he attempts to organize into his own taxonomy of kinds of schemata: *The Critical I*, pp. 32–40. Rosmarin, *The Power of Genre*, p. 14, uses the singular, schema, "thinking by sorting," which she finds in Gombrich's *Art and Illusion*. Erving Goffman's use of frames I find useful as a similarly open term, though he is almost comically unclear as to whether frames are contextual and thus essential and given or the framer's imposition. His analyses of frames clearly prefers the second, with his bewildering panoply of frame shifts, multiplications, telescopic movements to higher or lower powers of framing, often cited from his favorite theater of absurdity with its proto- (or really) postmodern refusal of grounding. By contrast, the common phrase "point of view" seems to privilege a spatial, visual positionality, as if we could know where indeed we or others stand definitively and finally.

Another term that can be used in this way, though it tends to confuse just because it has been associated with historical and intentional framing, is context. It has been used to somewhat the same purpose to suggest any organizing principle in an interpretation (whatever goes—"con"—with the text) by two major contemporary philosophers, Richard Rorty and Jacques Derrida. (Etymologically, our word comes from Latin *contextus*, the coherence or sequence of words, but at an earlier, more literal level what is woven together, thus whatever is woven with the text, to give it meaning.) This is clearest in Rorty, who sees all beliefs and desires that are active in any field of inquiry or explanation in humanities, social sciences, or science as a "contextualization," and a shift of them as a "recontextualization"; and in the postmodern context this may be in effect another language game done even "for the hell of it": see "Inquiry as Recontextualization: An Anti-Dualist Account of Interpretation," in Hiley, Bohman, and Shusterman, eds., p. 80. Pragmatists (who Rorty believes are united in this with deconstructionists) think "that anything can be anything if you put in the right context, and that 'right' just means the context that best serves somebody's purposes at a certain time and place." By contrast, "Metaphysicians think that there is a Right Context": "Response to Simon Critchley," in C. Mouffe, ed., *Deconstruction and Pragmatism* (London: Routledge, 1996), p. 43. In "Signature Event Context," in *Limited Inc*, Derrida examines directly the more traditional concepts of context, whether "real" and intentional or internal to the writing itself. In both cases his critique denies the possibility of determining the work by such contexts and argues instead that contexts endlessly multiply, thus preventing any one determination: "there are only contexts without any center or absolute anchoring": p. 12. Context for him is what is never determinable because always subject to further contexts. In his "Afterword" to *Limited Inc*, pressed to define more generally the context of "Signature Event Context," Derrida adds that he sees context as infinitely expanding: "the finiteness of a context is never secured or simple, there is an indefinite opening of every context, an essential nontotalization" (p. 137). The possible context is ultimately as large as the "entire 'real-history-of-the-world'" (p. 136). Deconstruction takes this potential context into account as it tries to be aware of each "recontextualizaton" (p. 136). The spelling out of a context is always political: "the question can be raised, not whether a politics is implied (it always is), but which politics is implied in this practice of contextualization ... I do not believe that any neutrality is possible in this area" (p. 136). Jonathan Culler similarly adds, "if we say that meaning is context-bound then we must say that context is endless": *Literary Theory: A Very Short Introduction* (Oxford: Oxford UP, 1997), p. 67. Similarly, Hillis Miller, commenting on Derrida on context, finds a "context in the sense of total circumstances is always overdetermined, always heterogeneous. It is uncontrollably diverse in itself. It stretches out to vaguer and more distant fringes....": *Speech Acts in Literature*, p. 100. The thinking of W. V. Quine can be usefully applied to the problem of context. As noted above (II.ix and II.ix, n. 17), Quine argued that a hypothetical visitor to a culture whose language was unknown to her could not determine meanings with any effectiveness by framing words by their context. The problem was that context is always overdetermined: a word spoken each time a rabbit appeared could mean rabbit, but could mean rabbitness or this is where we find rabbits. Context is sufficient to give *an* explanation but not to limit explanations. The same has been discovered in work with those deaf from birth, who cannot learn meanings simply from a context (on Quine's thinking more generally see also II.ii, n. 74, above).

My own argument is so much involved, like Derrida's, with delimiting the hegemony of traditional ideas of context (biographical, historical, sociological) that I avoid the confusion of the more global, and, I agree, more adequate concept by not using context when I mean taxonomy.

For a philosophical discussion of systems of classification see John Dupré, *The Disorder of Things: Metaphysical Foundations of the Disunity of Science* (Cambridge, MA: Harvard UP, 1993)—not at all opposed, despite the title, to Foucault's sense of the political motivations of systems: *The Order of Things: An Archaeology of the Human Sciences* (New York: Vintage, 1973).

397 "There are inventive interpretations that make us find in the text or the situation points and possibilities we would otherwise not have seen." David Couzens Hoy, "Interpreting the Law: Hermeneutical and Poststructuralist Perspective," in Levinson and Mailloux, eds., p. 338.

398 Ronald Dworkin has noted how difficult the project of United States Constitutional intentionalists really is: to recover the fleeting "mental states of each of the drafters of the Constitution": Levinson and Mailloux, eds., p. 49. Those philosophers, such as William Irwin, who have proposed that we think of intention in terms of an author construct ("urauthor" or Gracia's "pseudohistorical author"), do so in large part in despair of identifying the actual author's intention. See II.i, n. 30, above.

399 *New York Times*, City section, May 5, 1996, p. 6. The donor has now died but his project survives, an annual published by AMS Press and edited until his death by biographer Fred Karl.

400 Chinua Achebe's often cited "An Image of Africa," *Research in African Literatures*, 9 (1978), 1–15.

401 Harris, *Literary Meaning: Reclaiming the Study of Literature*, years after Derrida and company's frequent disclaimers on this issue, continues to see what he calls "hermeticism" disconnecting language from "reality": pp. 11, 74, 82.

402 Commenting on reconstructing intention in Constitutional law, of course a major political as well as interpretive issue, Mark Tushnet similarly observes: "The understanding we achieve is not the unique, correct image of the Framers' world. On the contrary our imaginative immersion is only one of a great many possible reconstructions of that segment of the past, a reconstruction shaped not only by the character of the past, but also by our own interests, concerns, and preconceptions. The imagination that we have used to adjust and readjust our understandings makes it impossible to claim that any one reconstitution is uniquely correct": "Following the Rules Laid Down: A Critique of Interpretivism and Neutral Principles," in Levinson and Mailloux, eds., p. 202. Hoy makes a similar point in his essay in the same collection, p. 321. Hoy also fully appreciates the relevance of hermeneutic thinking to issues of intention (see n. 408, below).

I will not take space to rehearse the reasons behind Lawrence's universally acknowledged truth about authors' direct statements about their work. We trust the fullness of the tale, as we see it, of course, over the random statements made by the teller outside the work at other times and places. That one is even in orthodox old biographical or historical work as a skeptical principle for research on a writer. All those Indians of all those tribes lie in new and interesting ways always. Which is not to say that what they say cannot be suggestive, helpful, provocative, and most certainly interesting.

403 History has been slowly becoming as self-aware and therefore as controversial a discipline as literary study; Hayden White's *Metahistory: The Historical Imagination in Nineteenth-Century Europe*, with its inscription from Bachelard, "One can study only what one has first dreamed about," seems still to mark a moment in awareness of the necessary interpretive moves in history—moves which, like those in literary interpretation, are necessarily narratives.

In an essay, "Whose History is It: Class, Cultural Democracy and Constructions of the Past," in their *Cultural Politics: Class, Gender, Race and the Postmodern World* (Oxford: Basil Blackwell, 1995), p. 117, Glenn Jordan and Chris Weedon offer the current view of the trendy historian: "Truth: Whether public or personal, history is always an interpretation of the past, constructed in the present on the basis of a selective range of source materials." The issue is of course part of a broader one of ideology which has threatened ingrained positivist attitudes not only in historical studies but in science; a quotation from a writer in *Social Text* is appropriate to this point: "there is no such thing as a category of the 'essentially descriptive'; that 'description' is never ideologically or cognitively neutral; that to 'describe' is to specify a locus of meaning, to construct an object of knowledge, and to produce a knowledge that shall be bound by an act of descriptive construction": Aijaz Ahmad, "Jameson's Rhetoric of Otherness and the 'National Allegory,'" *Social Text* 19 (Fall 1987): 6. In my more minimalist terms, all description, including historical "facts" and all kinds of historical specificities of the New Historicists, will place the facts within some interpretive taxonomy for categorization. Perhaps New Historicism makes such a mantra out of historical specificity itself as a way of not facing the problem of which specificity to focus on and what interpretation to give it. As so often used, the term is essentially incoherent.

Recent thinkers in historiography have generally distanced themselves, more or less, from positivist claims to objective knowledge of the past. For a few examples see R.G. Collingwood's now classic *The Idea of History* (Oxford: Oxford UP, 1945); J.A. Passmore's early "The Objectivity of History," *Philosophy* 33 (April 1958): 97–111; and the still influential E.H. Carr, *What is History?* (London: Penguin, 1961). More recent are Peter Novick, *That Noble Dream: The 'Objectivity Question' and the American Historical Profession* (Cambridge: Cambridge UP, 1988); Kenneth Cmiel, "After Objectivity: What Comes Next in History?" *American Literary History* 2 (Spring 1990): 170–81; and Alun Munslow, *Deconstructing History* (London: Routledge: 1997). Georg G. Iggers offers a history: *Historiography in the Twentieth Century: From Scientific Objectivity to the Postmodern Challenge* (Hanover, NH: Wesleyan UP, 1997). A number, including Carr and Novick, attempt to rescue ideas of objectivity within the new sense of subjective perspective and the sitedness of the historian, but even an advocate of objectivity such as Mark Bevir, "Objectivity in History," *History and Theory* 33 (Oct. 1994): 328–44, feels obliged to argue for "objectivity" as the result of comparison of "rival theories" or points of view: p. 332.

404 "Theses on the Philosophy of History," *Illuminations*, p. 255.

405 Worse, they may accept my point, in theory, but then, like so many of us intent on doing what we know to be questionable, go right back to doing it, building a system of historical interpretation that seems to obviate the necessity of choice and interpretation. Derrida's sense that the text moves out of its original context irretrievably puts the same perception in non-hermeneutic terms. See "Signature Event Context," in *Limited Inc*, p. 8. His term is the strong one, in translation of course, "rupture."

406 Walter Benn Michaels, "The Interpreter's Self: Peirce on the Cartesian 'Subject,'" in Tompkins, ed., p. 199.

407 Paul Armstrong, p. 105, has similarly critiqued New Historicist theory for attempting to elude the historians' own hermeneutic sitedness (his target is Steven Mailloux, "Rhetorical Hermeneutics," *Critical Inquiry* 11 [1985]: 620–41): "disagreements about the kind of coherence that internally unifies the text mirror themselves in the critics' hypotheses about the type of

context to which it belongs." See further discussion of this point by Mailloux in Machor and Goldstein, eds., pp. 51–56.

A more subtle critique follows lines Max Black opened up in suggesting applications of his argument against Paul Grice's use of intention in literary interpretation. In his argument, any attribution of intention will be justified by the use of another text (say of autobiographical revelation) which must in turn be given a meaning by another text demonstrating intention, with an obvious infinite regression (p. 276). Applied to broader historical work, this seems to have especial merit: if we interpret a text from the (intending) text of the age, we are then forced to justify our reading of that complicated text of the age by readings of more texts of the age. The result, actually a logical nightmare in which more and more obscure archival findings can seem to give authoritative status to less and less sensible interpretations, may seem like a self-supporting system: it will fly until someone else's opposite historical citations bring it down like lead. The application reminds us that there is no text of the age whose interpretation can settle interpretation of literary texts, only texts that lead on to other texts. Colebrook, *New Literary Histories*, pp. 56, 57, 84–86, and elsewhere, treats extensively and penetratingly the discussion within New Historicists (mainly Greenblatt) and in Foucault, Clifford Geertz, and others, of the sitedness of the historian or anthropologist. Greenblatt and Foucault both were aware of the issue, even agonized over it, but had trouble overcoming it. Geertz's solution, mere ethnographic subjective observation, would undercut historians' claims to knowledge. Colebrook sees Foucault's change of agenda, from archaeology to genealogy, partly caused by a recognition of his earlier sitedness and his appreciation of Nietzschean hermeneutics.

408 The full discussion of this point requires a book of its own, as it has been a central issue in hermeneutics as a German tradition. On the earlier German hermeneuticists, through Schleiermacher, I have found Peter Szondi's acute *Introduction to Literary Hermeneutics*, originally notes to a course on the subject published after his tragically early death, especially useful for his focus on the emergence of literary hermeneutics from historical and religious ones and his probing of the issue of intention in individual theorists. Suzy Anger, *Victorian Interpretation* (Ithaca: Cornell UP, 2005), provides a useful and well thought out account of the somewhat overlooked history of English hermeneutic thinking in the nineteenth century, where religious hermeneutics are closely intertwined with legal and literary. See also the standard English account, Richard E. Palmer, *Hermeneutics: Interpretation Theory in Schleiermacher, Dilthey, Heidegger and Gadamer* (Evanston, IL: Northwestern UP, 1969). The late nineteenth-century rationalist historiography of Wilhelm Dilthey aspired to scientific recovery of the past, in

much the way that the coterminal realism of that time aspired to objective representation, hence the term sometimes used for this thinking: "objective hermeneutics." Twentieth-century rethinking of historians' relation to the past of course includes the work of Heidegger (building in his *Sein und Zeit—Being and Time*—on Dilthey's later thinking), sometimes called the new hermeneutic or hermeneutic phenomenology or even philosophical hermeneutics, and that of Hans-Georg Gadamer in his *Truth and Method—Wahrheit und Methode* (German, 1960; English edn. ed. Garrett Barden and John Cumming [New York: Seabury, 1975]; later editions trans. and rev. by Joel Weinsheimer and Donald G. Marshall), as well as more local work of Hans Robert Jauss on reception—see esp. *Toward an Aesthetic of Reception* (Minneapolis: U of Minnesota P, 1982). Heidegger especially saw the author in effect self-destructing once the text was issued, leaving a discourse between the text and its ongoing reception. Texts are approached not from a neutral vantage point but from where we find ourselves and with the prior ways of apprehending, seeing, and conceiving with which we exist in our place in being and history. A past meaning cannot be reproduced in another time as the otherness of the time necessarily changes the meaning. All three have insisted on the subjective sitedness of all historical observation, as on an interpreter's necessary interaction with a text: our representation, again as in thinking about representation in the novel, is necessarily shaped by our present point of view (horizon). We bring a text not to life again, as a resuscitation of the author, but "to speech again," as our resiting and respeaking of the text—Gadamer, *Reason in the Age of Science* (Cambridge: MIT Press, 1981), p. 119. In American historiography, Hayden White has also extended this to speak of historians' products as "fictions"—that is, not deliberate lies but representations that necessarily embody a perspective of the historian and/or his time: see the "Introduction," *Metahistory*, pp. 1–42. White's work in asserting the necessity of interpretation from an interpreter's "meta" point of view interestingly grows out of study of predecessors, Hegel, Droysen, Nietzsche, Croce, whom he locates in historiography rather than hermeneutics. The parallel development of awareness of the sitedness of interpretation in the modern hermeneutics of Heidegger (in *Being and Time*, esp. paragraphs 31–32) or Gadamer is striking: as the new hermeneutics insists that interpretation of individual texts cannot find a secure ground in mere biographical knowledge of the author—because that is conditioned by our point of view—the newer historiography finds that interpretation of a past age cannot find a secure ground in mere "explanation" of the facts of the past apart from one's interpretive position. For a history of the shift to the newer hermeneutics see Palmer.

Hermeneutics as a way of thinking has been subjected to poststructuralist critique as a science seeking presence. But the new hermeneutics, despite

Heidegger's hope of a developing understanding, even unfolding, of texts in their ongoing reception, really establishes interpretation as a place where presence cannot be reached, only endless re-sitings. Gadamer's residual belief in classical values in a tradition received in each age and thus allowing those in the tradition some access to the past has also tended to veil the skeptical nature of the new hermeneutic tradition. Gergen, "The Communal Creation of Meaning," in Overton and Palmer, eds., p. 23, even sees this process as a way back to Romantic hermeneutics of identification: for the privileged in the tradition, the Heideggerian situation is suspended. Mitscherling, DiTommaso, and Nayed, pp. 94–99, somewhat similarly argue that Gadamer's skepticism has been overemphasized, that he is in any case not specifying a method of interpretation, and that he hopes tradition in language can—somewhat mystically, as they present it—lead the way to an intuitive interpretation. But certainly, as they acknowledge in their very argument, this has not been the influential force of Gadamer's hermeneutic thinking.

One can disavow the new hermeneutics but one cannot avoid entering into discussion of hermeneutics, which is theory of interpretation itself. Only those who are so sure they have the correct system of interpretation that they refuse to discuss other points of view will wish to deny the reality of the discussion; but this has sometimes been the case of the two leading interpretive systems of the past three decades, deconstruction and New Historicism/Cultural Studies. Hermeneutics is thus sometimes reduced to a science of Romantic or phenomenological consciousness (as in the work of Friedrich Schleiermacher on striving to enter into the spirit of the original writer by a spiritual reenactment of the creation) and then dismissed, as it is in Friedrich A. Kittler's interesting *Discourse Networks 1800/1900* (Stanford: Stanford UP, 1990), where Stefan George is represented as going beyond hermeneutics in his resistance to hermeneutics as personal presence as he found it in earlier nineteenth-century German hermeneuticists; he in fact only advocates a different, machine hermeneutics. Gerald L. Bruns's excellent study, *Hermeneutics Ancient & Modern* (New Haven: Yale UP, 1992), offers a revaluation of Gadamer's system as allowing a place for resistance in the text to appropriation, thus giving us the tragic experience of our failure of interpretation against the text—a kind of insight into our blindness that seems a de Manian riposte of hermeneutics. But if this is another, not especially new hermeneutic of modernism, Bruns's historical work seems especially important. It reestablishes a broader context for hermeneutic discussion in its eloquent exposition of the many, so varied ways in which different cultures at different times have seized upon a book, from the unending debate over meanings sponsored by Jewish Midrash to the merging of oneself into the sung text of a Sufi Muslim practice. These are communities of interpretation, each one rightly seen as built upon a hermeneutics of its own, with a very broad scope. Whatever the position of our moment should be, it is chastening to contemporary zeal to observe with Bruns the breadth of fine thinking about hermeneutics across cultures and across time. However, in his focus on restructuring Gadamer, he seems not to notice the wider world of contemporary hermeneutics, for my purposes especially the widespread Anglo-American-German discussion since about 1975, under the terms reader, reader-response, or reception—what has been, in effect, our hermeneutics and with strong specific genealogical liaisons to Heidegger and Gadamer through Jauss and Iser. Anger, p. 5, is certainly correct to insist, as I do here, that the study of theory of interpretation, whether named as hermeneutics or not, is essentially heir to the tradition of hermeneutic debate—though her project in nineteenth-century hermeneutics perhaps encourages her to diminish the break from intentionalist and naive historicist thinking in modern hermeneutics, whether in the Heideggerian tradition, New Criticism, or poststructuralism.

I would not wish to give the impression that relatively naive arguments from the view that history can locate an author's intention and thus control an interpretation have gone away. Harris, *Literary Meaning*, frames his intentionalist arguments with a claim to be thereby doing hermeneutics. While he cites Dilthey as authority for his concept of hermeneutic "understanding," he misleadingly mentions Gadamer and Heidegger (mainly, p. 13) as if they had not revolutionized the nineteenth-century science of historical reconstructive interpretation that he advocates. Hermeneutics is reduced from the study of interpretation to one theory of interpretation, intentionality. His view that their positions are only metaphysics misses the major practical problems in arming history for establishing intention that they point to and I attempt to suggest here. His "common sense" view that context can be easily limited for most works flies in the face of real historical complications; New Historicism has been opening only more and more contextual doors. By contrast, Irwin, an advocate of intentionalism on ethical grounds, offers a philosopher's awareness of the broad tradition of old and new hermeneutics in which the discussion is embedded. See *Intentionalist Interpretation*, esp. ch. 1. He interestingly discusses Gadamer (ch. 4) as attempting, largely unsuccessfully, to create a normative hermeneutics that can eschew relativism in the new hermeneutics; from a different perspective he could seem to be arguing that Gadamer is closer to Heidegger and even to relativism than his supporters *and* critics suggest. Like Harris, however, he does not appreciate the complications of historical determinations.

In discussion of the similarities and differences between scientific method and method in the humanities and social sciences, hermeneutics is sometimes used to distinguish interpretive scholarship from scientific research. This area of very hot contention is often located in distinctions made by Dilthey himself which carry with them implications of an intentionalist search for original meanings as the distinctive work of the "human" sciences. See, for example, discussion in essays in Hiley, Bohman, and Shusterman, eds., by Joseph Rouse, Richard Rorty, and Charles B. Guignon. Rorty, "Inquiry as Recontextualization: An Anti-Dualist Account of Interpretation," pp. 59–80, argues against the neo-Diltheyan dualist position of Charles Taylor; from his position, "anti-essentialist all the way," he offers "the suggestion that one might cease to see an interesting, Diltheyan, difference between the procedures of the physicist and the sociologist—or, more precisely, that one might find a context in which those differences become irrelevant" (p. 71). Science, like humanities and social science, keeps putting its concerns into new beliefs and desires, which he sees as an open-ended series of recontextualizations (an organizing approach, not at all specifically historical). Madison, p. 51, has argued, as I will in the next section, that Rorty's views of interpretation are close to those of post-Heideggerian hermeneutics generally.

As noted above, both Richard Rorty and Jacques Derrida use context in this way, without privileging the taxonomy of social or historical context that literary critics are likely to import. Context is simply something one puts with a text, of whatever order (see fuller discussion of "context," II.xvii, n. 2, above). Although Derrida regularly deplores hermeneutics as a system (in effect the older, nineteenth-century system) of strict determination of context, his theory of context is itself a hermeneutics in a post-Heideggerian mode. Derrida is clear that context is often relatively stable. But the apparent stability is only a result of the stability of the world vision that creates it at any moment, a "solid zone of implicit 'conventions' or 'contracts'" (p. 144).

409 It is unclear if the detail spawns the hypothesis or if the hypothesis is at work from the beginning of contact with the text. One could elevate the issue to a fundamental difference between inductive, empirical work and deductive, idealist work, as has often been done in comparing parallel variations of thinking in Anglo-American and Continental science. But most interpreters will believe they are beginning with the work and coming round the hermeneutic circle to the hypothesis; most will see others as not doing this but beginning with an hypothesis and forcing it on the work.

410 *There's No Such Thing as Free Speech*, p. 253.

411 The regular evasion in Foucault and in much of the New Historicist and American Cultural Studies work of traditional Marxist concerns with base and superstructure, historical reality and ideology (or representation) allows me to use a model here that seems to make all context and text one large

text, subject to the historian's choice of interpretive taxonomy and the resulting reification of the interpretation in the hermeneutic circle. But the Marxism of more traditional British Cultural Studies (say in the work of late Raymond Williams) or in other neo-Marxist positions which keep surfacing in the history of New Historicism and Cultural Studies in the United States would be subject to a similar analysis: base-superstructure theories, theories of interpellation by society of ideology into the individual, all tend to offer an intention in the contextual world to replace that of the author, which is merely determined by it. And all are also likely to bring a similar interpretation to the history and the text. Marxist systems of base and superstructure do, however, allow more or less independence for the individual (as Marx's own literary criticism shows); and interpretations of the material base may follow other interpretive systems than those applied to the superstructure, so that the work of interpretation proceeds by a more complicated two-phase engine, as it did in other older historical contextual work: history was understood in one way, the relation of history to text in another. Yet anyone familiar with Marxist criticism will grant that taxonomies used are usually quite similar for both. Even in the sophisticated work of Pierre Macherey or Fredric Jameson, the unconscious not recognized in the surface text is determined by the political sub-text (base) of the times as they read them.

412 See II.vii, above.

413 Even an old historian, George Watson, who saw historical work as offering immediate and unmediated access to author's intention, nonetheless admitted the necessary interpretive activity of the historian: "the historian, whether of literature or of anything else, is in no way committed to the view that everything about the past is of equal interest: in fact it is precisely the historian who is expected to show the greatest skill in sorting the important evidence from the insignificant. That is his trade": Newton-DeMolina, ed., p. 167. One pragmatic definition of New Historicism and Cultural Studies alike would be a great sea change in what the historian considers "important evidence"—which should make it clear that historical sortings out are always interpretations.

414 On the difficulties of trying to use initial reception to stabilize meaning as an intention, see II.vii, n. 184 above.

415 A point also made by Paul Brest, In Levinson and Mailloux, eds., p. 91. For a similar critique of the implications of New Historicism in interpretation see Wai-Chee Dimock, "Feminism, New Historicism and the Reader," *American Literature* 63 (1991): 601–22. Dimock critiques New Historicism's outlook for reifying "power relations within the literary *form* itself, as if power could inhere in a form and be ontological to that form, independent of the shifting contexts in which it figures, the varying uses to which it is put, and

the changing audiences it speaks to and for" (p. 621). Her critique of a reader frozen in time and thus essentialized by the historian's synchronic vision of the time is strengthened by awareness, from Raymond Williams, of the varied sedimentations, emergent, dominant, and residual, that keep history from ever being simply readable as one text commanding one interpretation (pp. 614–15).

Suzy Anger, in her "Introduction" to a useful set of essays on topics in Victorian culture and/or literature, *Knowing the Past* (Ithaca: Cornell UP, 2001), ranges over many of the issues I raise here from her special interest in Victorian hermeneutics. I am sorry to find that she rather tends to follow the rigid oppositional thinking of our donor between trendy and serious views of history depite her much fuller awareness of the historiographical issues. She sees a polar theoretical world of "objectivists" and "constructionists," the latter believing the past is shaped, broadly speaking, by the interests and politics of its historians (p. 7). Objectivists seek to "recuperate ... objectivity and intentionality" (p. 2). She identifies the skeptical constructionist view with deconstruction in general, Foucault's views of power, and Hayden White's conflations of history and other narratives. Somewhat surprisingly, as also in her generally more balanced and authoritative treatment of these issues in her later book on *Victorian Interpretation*, she tends to minimize the revolution in twentieth-century hermeneutics, finding the nineteenth century less concerned with objective knowledge and a post-Heideggerian such as Gadamer more concerned with it than seems correct to me. Her argument, that there is no reason "for giving up on understanding" (p. 12) because of skeptical historiography, itself embodies the "false dilemma" (p. 11) of thinking which she appears to critique. Her skeptics (e.g., Foucault) are not giving up on history but doing it with an awareness of the interest/power in all interpretations. Her argument should mediate between the objectivists and constructionists by saying that this weight of theory, which she does not directly oppose, should make us more wary as historians, more careful to try to be aware of our biases and presuppositions even as we know we can't fully overcome them. In my argument, Foucault and his followers in New Historicism have been too assured of their large views, not too timid to do history. The short answer to her question is we cannot know the Victorians but we can try to know them better from more points of view in more ways by self-critical work. In her terms, my argument, which is about the possible misuse of objectivist history in interpretation, is against naive objectivism that tries to substitute claims to really knowing the past for interpretive work and controversy.

416 Morse Peckham, "The Intentional? Fallacy?" in Newton-DeMolina, ed., p. 156, comes to a similar unitarian view: arguing that, since we can't

know an author's intention we necessarily offer interpretations in the form of "additional instructions," he also finds them all the same as kinds of interpretation—which is of course not to say that all will strike any reader as equally valid in a particular case.

417 The concept of anachronism has played a central role in discussions of intention, with charges of anachronism standard accusations by intentionalists (e.g., Harris, *Literary Meaning*, p. 143). Wimsatt and Beardsley first dared confront the issue of "meanings which if relevant to the original pattern should not be ruled out by a scruple about intention"; in his later revisit to the original essay, Wimsatt is much more explicit, indeed eloquently so (and oddly captures much of Bakhtin's historian's insight into the perishability of historical moments): "The search for the author's generative intention as context of the poem is a search for a temporal moment which must, as the author and the poem live on, recede and recede into the forgotten, as all moments do. Poems, on this theory of meaning, must always steadily grow less and less correctly known and knowable; they must dwindle in meaning and being toward a vanishing point. The best known and most valuable poem must be that written a moment ago and its best and only possible audience must be the author. But poems we know are not really like that ... Shakespeare has more meaning and value now than he had in his own day. There is a sense in which even Homer, though we construe his language with pain and are not sure how many persons he was, has more meaning and more value today than ever before": in Newton-DeMolina, ed., p. 138. Hirsch's invention of the meaning/significance binary is directly related to the problem of anachronism. His essay, "Three Dimensions of Hermeneutics," in Newton-DeMolina, ed., pp. 194–209, sees traditional hermeneutics as riven by the issue of the appropriateness of interpretations in a later language or theory and offers his binary as a solution, placing historical interpretations with meaning, others with significance. As I noted above (II.i, n. 30), Hirsch having left his followers with the rigid meaning/significance binary, kept moving in his thinking, especially in reflecting further on Heideggerian/Gadamerian hermeneutics, which he had briefly faced and then put aside in the earlier work (especially in "Three Dimensions"). His approach in the essays of 1983 and 1994, "Past Intentions" and "Transhistorical Intentions," interestingly accepts an evolutionist view of interpretation of intention, intention now broadly what could be possible for the author. He justifies changing readings of classics in each age as they fulfill their authors' broader intentions—to keep being meaningful to successive generations of readers who will apply (he says "allegorize") the text for their time. From this process of successive interpretations, all acceptable to this open-minded intentionalist, he excepts only cases of specifically de-

fined reference. Birnam Wood (my example) may move about in the play as much as it likes, but it can't be renamed Hyde Park by future interpreters. In practice, Hirsch's new view allows for classical texts (perhaps a result of his later interest in literacy) to live again in each generation and it really only excludes patent misappropriations, as in my example, or obvious anachronisms. He asks for respect for the author's spirit, but in this form this sounds like the mere ghost of intention. (Hirsch's idea of interpretation as allegory opens that concept too widely, I think, and treats allegory as a move from general to particular when it is usually the opposite.)

Not dissimilarly, Morse Peckham, also responding to Wimsatt and Beardsley, champions a modern hermeneutics that does not allow a "scruple of intention" to rule out new meanings, a process parallel to the growth of Christian doctrine by progressive acts of interpretation in Newman's thinking; any other procedure would be a kind of fundamentalism: Newton-DeMolina, ed., p. 150. On Newman's non-intentional, non-historical developmental hermeneutics see Anger, *Victorian Interpretation*, pp. 28–39.

Finally, Derrida, in a rare comment directly on hermeneutics, remarked that a text, product of an historical moment, "must efface in itself some stigma of singularity in order to outlast ... what it commemorates." In his odd attribution of agency to the text, it "absolves itself of its debt [to the original date] so that its utterance may ... make it readable and audible beyond its singularity" of its time: "Shibboleth," in Geoffrey H. Hartman and Sanford Budick, eds., *Midrash and Literature* (New Haven: Yale UP, 1986), pp. 318, 311. His thinking here is congruent with his insistence in "Signature Event Context" that written signs always break with context taken as the presences at the moment of writing and that their very repeatability absents them from their first use (see above, II.xvii, n.396).

418 A case raised by Beardsley, who seems simply wrong here. See discussion by Dutton, in Cascardi, ed., p. 205. The historical philology which triumphed in nineteenth-century debates over linguistics was a natural ally for historical hermeneutics (Anger, pp. 13 and 175, n. 28): language develops over time and meanings need to be recovered, hence students learn to use the *OED*. But earlier meanings fall into the same disturbing range of possible meanings as all words (see II.xi, above), even possibly including the direction that the word has taken since. And anti-intentionalists do not forswear philological knowledge, merely deny that one interpretation about an earlier meaning can dominate the interpretation of the text. Some might also follow Bakhtin in pointing out that most meanings of the moment, in terms of social use and nuance, are hopelessly lost with time.

419 Here again, Harris has the resolution to state the full conservative position: historical context gives us knowledge of author's intention which provides

the meaning (he sometimes uses "understanding," translated from Dilthey) to be opposed to mere significance (he often uses "symptomatic" from Grice). See *Literary Meaning*, esp. 102–25. An anachronism is not just the detail but any interpretive scheme not present in the writer's day, the usual suspects being psychological and Marxist.

Anger, *Victorian Interpretation*, p. 27, interestingly finds the nineteenth-century Oxford expert on Plato and commentator on religious hermeneutics, Benjamin Jowett, offering a similar distinction between "interpretations" and "applications": the former resting on the firm ground, in his traditional nineteenth-century hermeneutics, of author's intention, the latter mere modern extensions.

420 See Levinson, "Intention and Interpretation," in Iseminger, ed., pp. 221–56, who wishes interpretation to be constrained by a hypothetical idea of the limits of a typical audience of the day. One doesn't have to fall into Romantic ideas of individual genius to think writers should not be subject to such critical acts, after the fact, of conformity. Think of Leonardo the scientist if you don't want to credit anything new in his painting.

421 Perhaps a third major area of interpretations that seem to come from a specialized discipline external to literary study and hence thought of as eliciting new significances rather than meanings, mainly repressed now in favor of psychosexual or economic/social interpretive paradigms, are religious ones. These are more evidently based on rather universal broad conceptions of life and living, though they too can be highly technical. A Calvinist view of Homer isn't wrong because the concepts of Calvin would be inaccessible to Homer (there is a sense of predestination throughout the gods-driven conflict); it is unpersuasive (so far) because it doesn't well explain the detailed substance of this epic. Armstrong, p. 7, who oddly does not include religious interpretations, adds structuralist and Nietzschean (will to power hidden in the text) interpretive interests to what he calls archaeological hermeneutics, or hermeneutics of unmasking or reading by suspicion. I discuss our recent sexual and identity discourses below.

422 Shuttleworth differingly looks at issues of surveillance as master psychological categories—which she grounds in a selective reading of the psychological writing of Brontë's age. But these, useful indeed as a different foregrounding, clearly come from her own immersion in Foucauldian ideas of our time. My reading of the psychology, in a historical master-mind-of-the-century mode (*Charlotte Brontë and Sexuality*, 1984, also Cambridge UP) and hers (1996), in a look at more local discourses such as phrenology, both claim historical derivation for interpretations that in fact derive ultimately from the different foregroundings of our times. Helen Small's catalog of the varied views of nineteenth-century psychology shows that neither of us has done more than cluster, for purposes of interpretive

coherence, a few of the great and essentially incoherent mass of voices and opinions of the age: *Love's Madness* (Oxford: Clarendon, 1996).

423 Marie Bonaparte, *The Life and Work of Edgar Allan Poe: A Psycho-Analytic Interpretation*, trans. John Rodker (London: Hogarth, 1949), pp. 383–84.

424 For a summary of issues of same-sex desire in Brontë see Jin-Ok Kim, *Charlotte Brontë and Female Desire* (New York: Peter Lang, 2003).

425 Harris, p. 153, who is uncomfortable with just this view of feminist criticism that "we are now able to recognize an intended meaning not available to earlier readers."

426 Fetterley, *The Resisting Reader.*

427 Herbert Tucker, "Victorian Paranoia and the Stroke of the Contemporary," CUNY Victorian Conference on Victorian Poetry and its Modernities, May 3, 1996.

428 Cf. Naomi Schor: "interpretation has always already begun"; there is no originary place of interpretation: in Suleiman and Crosman, eds., p. 181.

429 I add the coda, imaginative and critical, for fear I may be labeled a mere indulger in the pleasures of literature—no bad thing in itself. But we also study literature to sharpen our critical understanding in general; and that is not fulfilled by isolating the past as an historical specimen; we need instead to bring our best thinking to bear on the texts of the past to see how that allows us to understand them more interestingly. I have just been arguing that this is what we necessarily do, even when we talk of objective history, historical specificity, knowing the past.

430 The cognitive psychologist makes this obvious but generally overlooked point about the nature of meaning: Kenneth J. Gergen, "The Communal Creation of Meaning," in Overton and Palermo, eds., pp. 19–39, who notes, p. 30, that even in ordinary social interaction it is the hearer who defines the meaning of what a speaker says—though there he may in turn redefine that meaning by an additional statement.

431 Catherine Belsey well puts this seductive appeal to the reader's desire for an illusory stability in her *Critical Practice* (London: Methuen, 1980), p. 55: the "correct reading" tries to install the reader as "transcendent subject addressed by an autonomous and authoritative author."

432 Jonathan Culler in Collini, ed., *Interpretation and Overinterpretation*, p. 109.

433 Bruns, "Intention, Authority, and Meaning," notes that interpretation puts all readers in the position of argument and justification: reading as interpretation is reading "for others": it is to participate in debate and attempt to persuade.

434 Again, note that I use hermeneutics as a term for the study of the debate over interpretation, not for the particular historical, intentional, or consciousness tradition associated with nineteenth-century hermeneutics. See II.xviii, n. 11, above.

435 *Contingencies of Value*, esp. pp. 24–29. Oddly Herrnstein Smith sees hermeneutics as necessarily attached to a prescriptive theory of interpretation, which she compares to a prescriptive theory of value, an axiology (p. 28). As in much twentieth-century hermeneutic discussion—especially that of Heidegger and his followers—hermeneutics is a discussion of interpretation beyond prescription, as it is in Rorty's discussions of interpretation. One can certainly speak of a pragmatic hermeneutics. It would involve a vision of successful interpretive arguments succeeding each other as time allows group and individual change. It becomes the theater of change, where different new perspectives vie with each other and the older, established ones in the emergence of acceptable new approaches, to be themselves superseded. The process is dynamic, unlike Fish's idea of communities (see III.v., below), because it is driven by individual contest for arguments that succeed in a changing world, not by mysteriously formed social totalities. I note that Herrnstein Smith, who seems to move from arguments over value to a history of value, is a good enough twentieth-century hermeneuticist to deny that this study could "yield an ultimately comprehensive, unified, and objective account of its subject; for to imagine it thus would be to repeat, only on a grander scale, elements of the raw positivism and naive scientism that have been responsible, in part, for both the exile of evaluation and the confinements of modern critical thinking"—a warning, I have been arguing, not sufficiently heeded in our historical turn. Herrnstein Smith does not seem to credit sufficiently good arguments over evaluation not based on foundationalist premises. Without such, the field of evaluation threatens to become merely a museum of once-live valuations.

Madison, p. 51, writing about post-Heideggerian hermeneutics, associates it with the Rortyian project, "the postmodern rejection of philosophy in the traditional metaphysical-epistemological sense of the term." Like Rorty, he sees interpretation always involved in a conversation about meaning, although with Gadamer he seems to hold onto a view that this can lead to a "decidable meaning" of the time. But Rorty's point would be that it remains debatable.

436 See my discussion of Knapp and Michaels, II.i, n. 20, above. Their use of neo-pragmatism as a return to history, reversing Rorty's reading of history (of epistemology) to argue in philosophy against epistemology, seems to fall into the trap Herrnstein Smith avoids, that is of failing to apply the same anti-foundationalist views to hermeneutics and historiography. I discuss Stanley Fish on intention in Appendix 2, and his theory of communities, never fully pragmatic in my view, in III.v, below.

437 Dasenbrock repeatedly makes this argument against the hidden grounding of the ungrounded in his critique of Rorty, Fish, Knapp and Michaels, and Smith. He identifies his position with similar critiques by recent analytic philosophers, especially Hilary Putnam. I find that his account, though

attractively open-minded, characterizes Rorty, in his approach to literature, too much as a social constructionist. In looking at the consequences of pragmatism, he confuses Fish's theories of community-driven interpretation with Rorty's quite different project, which is above all to try not to create a new dogma (such as that society exclusively makes us what we are and do) but to deprivilege those who claim a grounding. In this Rorty is pursuing the traditional goal of pragmatist thought, as Dasenbrock himself states it: "truth-claims cannot claim universal validity and need to be assessed on pragmatic grounds" (p. 252).

438 Dasenbrock, pp. 169–73, offers another argument worth consideration. This is one he locates in philosophers as diverse as Donald Davidson and Martha Nussbaum, that we need some place of truth, even if it can't be known to be reached, in order to maintain the serious aim of our enterprise. This may (or may not) be true in the search for scientific knowledge of the world, but hermeneutics can maintain its edge by seeking merely the best interpretive truth among those in the field (our legal system works at a serious level in such a context). Despite Dasenbrock's faith in it as the necessary goal (p. 172), author's intention seems a false goal, even a distorting and misleading goal, for such a pursuit. For writing, we ask, what does this mean, not the impossible and unuseful, what did he mean by this. As I have been arguing (II.vii and xviii and see III.v, below) I see no reason to imagine a monolith of culture or community of interpretation that blocks all independent thinking in the competitive process of quest for better meaning. It is in fact an engine of change.

439 Steven Mailloux notes that it is incorrect to say "that theory never has any consequences; at certain times in certain places it has very real rhetorical effects": *Rhetoric, Sophistry, Pragmatism* (Cambridge: Cambridge UP, 1995), p. 21. The anti-foundationalist's first business is arguing against theories of grounding, as Rorty has, not dismissing them off-handedly.

As I note in II.i, n. 21, Mailloux sometimes approaches the wholesale dismissal of hermeneutic discussions that characterizes the arguments of Knapp and Michaels. His agenda has focused on the rhetoric of arguments over interpretation in action in history, which very much include political and economic motivations. Yet his own point (above) is brought home by the immersion of these specific historical moments in ideological debates over hermeneutic theory. We must do interpretation ("Taking a position, making an interpretation, cannot be avoided": "Interpretation," in Lentricchia and McLaughlin, eds., p. 134) that will involve us in general interpretive arguments.

440 Fish makes a similar argument about the deferred end of pragmatism, *Doing What Comes Naturally*, p. 183.

441 On neopragmatism, see especially Richard Rorty's founding study, critiquing the long quest in Western philosophy for a certain epistemological foundation

to knowledge and more broadly critiquing all "attempts to eternalize a certain contemporary language-game, social practice, or self-image" by appeals to philosophical foundations: *Philosophy and the Mirror of Nature* (Princeton: Princeton UP, 1979), quotation, p. 10, and the collection of essays, *Consequences of Pragmatism (Essays: 1972–1980)* (Minneapolis: U of Minnesota P, 1982). (On his approaches to literary interpretation, see citations in II.xvi, n. 31, above.) One can parallel Rorty's view on epistemology, that no account of the nature of knowledge "can rely on a theory of representations which stand in privileged relations to reality" (*Philosophy and the Mirror of Nature*, p. 182), with a statement about hermeneutics: no account of the nature of knowledge of texts can rely on a theory of communication which stands in privileged relations to their meaning. I note above, II.i, n. 20, that Rorty did not accept the position on intentionality of Knapp and Michaels. See also, among many works in pragmatism and discussions of its development, Joseph Margolis, *Pragmatism Without Foundations: Reconciling Realism and Relativism* (Oxford: Basil Blackwell, 1986) and *The New Puzzle of Interpretation* (Chicago: U of Chicago P, 1992); Richard J. Bernstein, *Beyond Objectivism and Relativism* (Philadelphia: U of Pennsylvania P, 1983) and *The New Constellation: The Ethical-Political Horizons of Modernity/Postmodernity* (Cambridge: Polity Press, 1991); essays in Hiley, Bohman, and Shusterman, eds.; Cornel West, *The American Evasion of Philosophy: A Genealogy of Pragmatism* (Madison: U of Wisconsin P, 1989). West, philosophical pragmatist self-styled as "prophet pragmatist"—"a political form of cultural criticism" (p. 213)—demonstrates the same impatience to run with neopragmatism into identity, ethnic, political, social, and religious engagements—all, I should say, to me sympathetic—as literary pragmatists to jump into a new history. Indeed, his project is ultimately similar, a Foucauldian genealogy which jumps over problems of historiography that should direct pragmatist historical work (see esp. his pp. 208–9 and 223–26, where he does not criticize Foucault's historiography).

Among a number of discussions of literary theory from a pragmatist viewpoint, in addition to Herrnstein Smith and Stanley Fish, see especially Margolis (above); Richard Shusterman, *Pragmatist Aesthetics: Living Beauty, Rethinking Art* (Oxford: Blackwell, 1992); Steven Mailloux, "Introduction," *Rhetoric, Sophistry, Pragmatism*; and the collection of essays by various hands in all three subjects. Mailloux makes a good case for connecting neopragmatic discussion with revived interest in the sophistic traditions in philosophy and rhetoric. The latter involves a concern especially with rhetoric as argumentation rather than, as in de Man, tropes and figuration. The project of sophistry, as in Protagoras' much-attacked view of man as the measure of all things, was of course directly connected to the arts of persuasion that the sophists taught. Truth is not the grounded, foundational truth based on first principles or a First Principle but the truth that emerges in discussion, argument, persuasion. Like the sophistic rhetors, advocates of neopragmatism have been subject to accusations of encouraging dangerous relativism and impiety, opening avenues for mere dazzlement and charlatanism, throwing judgment from authorities to the crowd. Its partisans, with whom I am obviously sympathetic, see neopragmatism as honestly facing a universe that lacks absolute foundations, encouraging open debate and discussion as an heuristic for better thinking on subjects as they emerge, and situating truth-seeking activities in a necessary democratic context. Critics from right and left have attacked neopragmatism respectively for its radical chic and putative quietism. It refuses the caricature of frivolous anarchy, denies quietism, and rejects the assignment of mere liberalism. My own project here could be described as an attempt to free literary discussion and interpretation from foundationalist views of intention as pre-discursive intrusions on open argument, a false epistemological absolute troubling the living stream of interpretive discussion/debate/argument.

On specific discussion of intention by neopragmatists, see II.viii, n. 9, above.

442 Michel de Certeau notes, perhaps too optimistically, that weakening institutional controls (religious, political) allow the reader space against someone's conception of author/authority: "The creativity of the reader grows as the institution that controlled it declines": *The Practice of Everyday Life*, p. 172.

443 Also, oddly enough, with Hirsch "pure originalism risks turning our written inheritance into a dead letter": "Transhistorical Intentions," p. 62.

444 Rorty, *Consequences of Pragmatism*, pp. 173–74. It is no great deprecation of Rorty's significance as a major philosopher of our time to note how often his admirers give him only two cheers, often withholding the third for his complacency with the West, taken as a large amorphous tradition. Richard Shusterman finds even Rorty setting up a kind of rules of the pragmatic interpretation game, with private readings cordoned off from professional ones and newer professional modes preferred to older, established ones: see "Interpreting with Pragmatist Intentions," in Iseminger, ed., pp. 176–79.

My own hesitation is one that applies to my argument here as well, the old fear that a level playing field from which the intentionalist bully has been banished may allow play to be dominated by the "personal charisma" of the pragmatic sophist, the abuser of "language power": Stuart Sim, *Beyond Aesthetics: Confrontations with Poststructuralism and Postmodernism* (Toronto: U of Toronto P, 1992), pp. 93–94: quoted in Mailloux, *Rhetoric, Sophistry, Pragmatism*, pp. 19–20. Rhetorical persuasion, as a long history of skepticism about it suggests, can seem the victory of appeals to emotion or prejudice or be limited by the ethos of the audience. This seems very possible; but as with any abuse of open discussion, the solution is vigilance and better discussion, not reversion to authority. Aristotle saw rhetoric as a way of reaching the best truth possible in areas of discourse where only probable truth is possible. Arguments themselves are serious appeals to reason about the best version (in our cases, of interpretation), not merely appeals to emotion or prejudice (*Rhetoric* 1358a; 1404a, cited in Dasenbrock, p. 189). Certainly the identification of interpretation with rhetoric has the consequence of challenging successive interpretations to fit well with the material of the text.

445 Dasenbrock's interesting critique of conventionalism in thinking about truth in representations of reality seems not to the point when he carries it over to cultural conversations such as those on literary interpretation where, whatever our view of the controversy over scientific truth, the "truth claims" are relative and changing (see pp. 184–85). His critique of conventionalism as he finds it in Fish (the view that science or interpretation are created by a uniform social community that programs the individual) is more convincing. See III.v, below.

446 Noël Carroll, "Art, Intention and Conversation," in Iseminger, ed., p. 116, addresses this argument against intention as only an aesthetic one, about the richness of artwork to the consumer. My argument about the relevance of interpretive activity in so many areas beyond aesthetics should make it clear that I would strongly reject this characterization.

447 For instance, Dasenbrock, p. 156, rather trivially accuses Hillis Miller of a backslide to talking about Sophocles and George Eliot shortly after stating anti-intentionalist views.

448 Alexander Nehamas, "Writer, Text, Work, Author," in Irwin, ed., pp. 95–115, accepts Foucault's interrogation of the concept of author only to offer an even more ideal concept of author as the stabilizing concept (or presence) that allows us to interpret it as a work with a meaning. Wouldn't a title do better here? See the broader discussion of this idea of a concept of author in philosophical discussion, II.i, n. 30, above.

449 A point well made by Jean Corbett, *Representing Femininity: Middle-Class Subjectivity in Victorian and Edwardian Women's Autobiographies* (New York: Oxford, 1992), p. 46.

450 Dickens came close to this in putting his name generally on his magazines, *All the Year Round* and *Household Words,* and treating his authors like his writers, whom he could cajole and correct.

451 Nor am I comfortable with Matei Calinescu's metaphor of a game in which we make the author into our idea of the text: "Imagining or inventing the author is actually one of the most complicated and interesting aspects of the game": *Rereading*, p. 54. One thinks of poor Pip trying to construct his family from the writing styles on the gravestone inscriptions!

The issue of extension of proper names (what they refer to) has of course a very lively history in nineteenth- and twentieth-century analytic philosophy, where heavy hitters such as J.S. Mill, Gottlob Frege, Bertrand Russell, Ludwig Wittgenstein, Saul Kripke, and Hilary Putnam have argued whether names only refer to persons or extend to definite descriptions of persons named. If the latter, can they be changed or are they fixed by the first use? These gentlemen, dead or alive, will forgive me for my ordinary language and pragmatic approach. The weight of current opinion seems to follow Kripke in denying that proper names have any reference other than the person (Socrates refers to Socrates, not to his quality of wisdom: the proper name is not a disguised definition). Names do become descriptives in much literary and common use (Henry James as austere artist for art, Virginia Woolf, ditto). But they change with each new interpretive move (James as closeted homosexual, Woolf, ditto, and so on to James as pragmatist, Woolf as feminist, etc.). I would follow the Kripke position in saying that none of these associations can be taken as a permanent meaning of the name—even in common use. If names tend to be used to exemplify qualities ascribed to the writer, they are really functioning as shorthand for interpretive positions about a writer and are always subject to revision. Every interpretive move needs to put down these fictions; best after a revolution to be self-conscious and self-skeptical about use of names. As part of his advocacy of creating a pseudo-historical author (see II.i, 30), Gracia, "A Theory of the Author," in Irwin, ed. *The Death and Resurrection of the Author?*, pp. 182–85, realizes he must face the fact that his use of the name of the author is as a descriptor. He also grants that names, when used as descriptive words, may be used repressively. He is obliged to defend his position by arguing that repression can be good, as in procedures for surgeons. But we readers are *not* doing brain surgery and should prefer to find our own view of the text rather than start with a name that fossilizes someone else's interpretation.

452 Umberto Eco, whose early work got us thinking about the importance of the reader, seems especially gratuitous in using this idea of an author in name only—what he calls the Model Author—as a way of controlling the real reader's response into that of a Model Reader—which can only be his own preferred reading imputed to these two dummies he sets up before us. See *The Limits of Interpretation*, p. 59. Eco even admits he here reinscribes "the old and still valid hermeneutic circle." In his parallel argument in *Six Walks in the Fictional Woods* (Cambridge, MA: Harvard UP, 1994), p. 44, Eco even grants that the real author (his case is Nerval's *Sylvie*) may not have known the intricate art he was blundering into. Robert Scholes similarly evades the real issues over intention by focusing on the utility of naming a name in political critiques of texts. He implies that texts can only be made "other enough" for critique if we think of them in relation to an author. But this is wrong. We don't need to personify

a text to disagree with it and interpretation of a text independent of the author's name does not throw us into hermeneutic narcissism: "we will have turned all others into mirrors of ourselves": *Textual Power*, p. 39.

453 Gibbs's work, out of cognitive psychology and with a clear preference for intentional ways of thinking, nonetheless only asserts that people do tend to think of writing and other acts as intentional, on the model of pragmatic engagements with meaning in everyday life. Even he does not find intention necessary or conclusive for providing meanings; and he grants that other, non-Western, cultures look for intention less, or, upon reflection, not at all.

454 Nathan, in Iseminger, ed., pp. 196–97, nicely characterizes this shift as one from questions about the author to those about all of us—what would anyone mean by this? No simple answer but the debate can begin. Nathan's hypothetical author, however, is really a reader, or all readers in potential.

455 Again, see II.i, n. 20, above, on Knapp and Michaels. Irwin, *Intentionalist Interpretation*, insists that author's meaning exists or the text cannot. But he critiques Knapp and Michaels's assumption that we must think of author's meaning. His hermeneutics is normative: we focus on author's meaning as an ethical choice. Irwin goes on to propose an "urauthor," a monster half conceptual (what the author might be) and biographical: in practice one reader's interpretation with an aura of authority. See my discussion in II.1, n. 30, above.

456 *The Kristeva Reader*, ed. Toril Moi (New York: Columbia UP, 1986), p. 39. Foucault's term ("What Is an Author?" p. 210) to replace the author, "author function," seems not to have caught on and carries his specific take on cultural replacement of the author. I am less concerned than he to ignore real authors at their personal computers; I am more concerned here with the interpretive use of their presence. Wayne Booth's more established compromise, implied author, retains an unhelpful sense of texts as always consciously willed creations that can be best interpreted by the presumption that they are rhetorically organized to make specific points. Booth's shyness with texts that don't easily fit this pattern, e.g., Joyce's *Ulysses*, already suggests the limits of a label that works ill with other approaches to literature, e.g., psychoanalytic, Marxist, identity politics, and others where the salient pattern is not a rhetorical creation of the work's author.

457 I would cite here especially Stanley Fish's apparent inability to be more direct on the "vexed" subject. See discussion of his writings on Intention in Appendix 2: Stanley Fish's Intentions.

Pappas, "Authorship and Authority," in Irwin, ed., *The Death and Resurrection of the Author?*, discusses Foucault's unease with talk of the "work" as still implying a given meaning.

458 Su, p. 102, discusses the generally unexplored subject of agreement: "probably wider and more solid than people imagine." See II.i, which cites Holland on the subject.

459 Bruce Robbins, co-editor of *Social Text*, indicated in a MLA Convention discussion, Chicago, 1996, that the editorial board of the journal still did not find Alan Sokal's paper inappropriate, though the controversy and resultant scrutiny exposed some errors they had missed; i.e., the paper still resisted the author's stated intent. The article, "Transgressing the Boundaries: Toward a Transformative Hermeneutics of Quantum Gravity," appeared in numbers 46/47 (1996), 217–52. For a bibliography of debate on the article see Sokal's website <<http://www.physics.nyu.edu/faculty/sokal/>>.

460 My colleague was of course offering a version of a coded text, where the intention that the author (publicly here, as a polemical attention-getter; privately in braver offerings of subversively intended texts under repressive regimes) professes differs greatly from a likely uninformed reading. Dasenbrock, pp. 160–62, notes that such odd intentional issues are what Leo Strauss called "double-writing." The obvious problem with such writing is that, as here, one cannot simply reverse the meaning of a passable version of something conventional by saying that it was intended otherwise (try it after insulting someone in a bar-room!). Here too it is logical to trust the tale not the teller. That it may have been meant for a double reading by a privileged in-group (here the positivist side of a scientific community) is an interesting historical fact, but if the hoax was fully double writing, not necessarily persuasive. The double writer in a repressive political situation needs to be able persuasively to deny any such coded intention or forfeit freedom or life. Sokol needed such a good parody that it could pass the muster of the journal's board. As editors of a journal that publishes many cultural approaches to learned disciplines, I and my co-editor have been, ever since Sokol, even more vigilant, certainly not likely to let ourselves doze over a manuscript; but a perfect parody will certainly fool me. Authors often include a little explanation of what they intended, but when your professional reputation depends on it, you trust the work not the workman. Gibbs, pp. 206–10, discusses other cases of hoax writing.

461 Nathan in Iseminger, ed., p. 198, observes the paradox that the clearest intention of authors, that their work stand alone apart from them personally, is generally disregarded by intentionalists.

SECTION THREE*

REREADING READER THEORIES: INTERVENTIONS AND INTRUSIONS

I. INTRODUCTION

I have dwelt at such length on the grand old issues of literary intention because I believe the abandonment of this subject is indicative of a tendency in literary studies today to abandon the central business of interpretation. Turning from interpretation, no longer willing to keep vital the central theoretical issues that cluster on the controversy concerning intentionality, we slipped into New Historicism, thence into mere history; will we end up in antiquarianism and pure philology? Even vital new areas of concern—multiculturalism, postcolonialism, identity politics, gay and then queer studies, ecocriticism—seemed to need to have our natural interest in rereading texts from new points of view packaged in authoritative historical boxes. While other fields were debating whether they were left with only a turn to interpretation "all the way down," we, heirs to the great enterprise of interpretation, were fleeing it for history. From a sociological perspective this is understandable. Just as professors of literature had tried to associate themselves with the prestige of science in the structuralist movement of the 1970s, they now sought the more comfortable and secure chairs of fact, history and sociology. To our profession this seemed to offer the empowerment of special knowledge and professional expertise.

*Notes appear at the end of the section. Substantive notes are bolded.

We don't compete over the sharpness of our interpretations because we have privileged information guiding our insider opinions. But in the process of such empowerment we lose what is in fact our special power: declining the hurly-burly of open debate over interpretation, we find that literature ceases to matter to us—at least professionally speaking (maybe, like Dickens's Wemmick, we do it at home in our little castle)—and we may cease to matter to anyone. Soon literary studies may even be reorganized as the cut-price annex to the history department. This is a shame, because we actually have many new and interesting things to talk about, but we cut ourselves off from the reading of literature that really empowers our activity and discussions. As in the discussion of intention above, I profess I am not writing against literary history, old or new, or cultural studies, or sociology, certainly not against knowledge; my own work has very much participated, to my personal satisfaction, in the great expansion of knowledge about the worlds out of which literature comes and into which it is received. It is the decline of interpretation, its deflection into historical takes on context and intention, that I deplore.

In retrospect, that brand of reader theory called reader response from about 1970 to 1985 looks like the last broad consideration of interpretive activity. The theorists of that time cared about interpretation; they believed in the power of reading. During their debate over how reading works, they seemed to offer a grand panoply of new ways of reading and interpreting. Rather than turn against interpretation in the name of reading, in their arguments with each other they kept pushing the envelope of interpretation. Sometimes inadvertently and rather against their individual agendas, as a group they in effect kept suggesting more and more ways one can make meaning of a text in responding to it.

What happened? I have to conclude, after a good number of years of reflection, that literary critics were not up to the open-ended truth they found. The profession as a whole reacted, as professionals do in *Bleak House* or our academic house, against a truth that seemed to empower their clients (to try different interpretive approaches) while it disempowered them (from being supreme authorities on correct interpretation). Fortunately for them, New Historicism and Cultural Criticism, shaped by political interests and by deconstruction, opened a way back to what I must call the new expertise: no mere student could hope to do anything but bow (or say wow) before the special knowledge that their re-empowered mentors now brought to the text. And most of those mentors did history all the time. Theory was reduced to a limited view of deconstruction (the world as text) that provided a little-examined foundation for New Historicism. Hermeneutics, except by the occasional Gerald Bruns or Richard E. Palmer, was misapprehended as some kind of subjectivity and relegated to history as well—an event of German Romanticism.[1] Theory was said not to have consequences for interpretation in any case; but this large claim, after a flurry of publicity, was not much interrogated because interpretation, before the oncoming juggernaut of history, also appeared inconsequential. Meanwhile, nervous conservative opponents of theory in general were most specifically in favor of author's intention as a bulwark against the anarchy they saw washing over the academic citadels long after the profession had opted for the calm seas of historical knowledge; essentially, they saw their own way back to biography, old history, or New Criticism done without the disturbance of indeterminacy, political and personal perspectives, or even old-fashioned ambiguity.

One might have expected more fuss against this new direction from the most prominent reader-responsers themselves. Instead, the only complaints have come from prominent literary generalists who, distinguished indeed, deplore the demise of reading: Robert Alter, Harold Bloom, Denis Donoghue.[2] The best known reader-responsers themselves have had little to say: Fish has gone off to legal studies, where he has had a great deal to say; Iser does a kind of literary anthropology. Robert Scholes, as we shall see, has been a special case: from his own intervention in this area in the mid-1980s until his recent work on the crafty reader, he has opposed the openness of reader thinking to non-historical interpretation. Only Norman Holland has continued to study reading as a theoretical issue, bringing the discussion into cognitive as well as his earlier Freudian areas of inquiry.[3] Reader theory, as the broader interest in readers has been called,[4] is not dead, despite these appearances—as I will explore in my final fourth section—but it has by and large moved away from issues of interpretation, and it has lacked even the apparent coherence of a critical school.[5] Except for the important work on women readers, most of it back in the 1980s,[6] it has certainly not played an important part in the development of the present critical scene. If we trouble, as I have here, to go back and read reader theory from the heyday of reader response, one quickly grasps why this school (only apparently a school, in fact more a collection of self-appointed experts on reading) has failed so signally to defend reading and interpretation. As a group they may have opened the Pandora's box of multiple interpretations. But the odd fact is that very few of them seemed to think that their business was to open up texts to varied interpretation by varied readers, far less to the broad experience of a work of literature suggested by the term "response" with its promise of interest in individual difference, personal preferences and emotions, even spontaneity. More typically, each believed she or he had only to propound the correct theory of reading, and readers would henceforth read as they should. It is a little like someone coming up with a theory of the stock market and then feeling assured that everyone would behave properly according to the theory. I wouldn't put any money on it. What could have been a lively debate on the relative merits of different approaches became merely another set of attempts of critics to impose their approaches on everyone else: the only difference being that they now defined not what the author intended or the text meant but what the reader necessarily had to do with the work—by a readerly virtue which is of the nature of reading, Molière might have added.

One could compare the situation to the ironic one which prevailed during the wars of truth between religious sects in the sixteenth and seventeenth centuries. No one intended that a more tolerant view of all religious belief would be the end result of truly cutthroat attempts to force and persuade others that their sect was the correct one. That readers might be understood as having many ways they could approach and interpret a text was no part of the agenda of most of those players at the critical game of reader response. Only deconstruction, a reader-response fellow traveler as its predecessor structuralism had been,[7] seemed indeed to offer open-ended approaches to reading. Certainly, in the form of Derridean play with open signification it seemed to open endless possibility. But it too was offering only one kind of reading, that of endless possibility; it could not then accept a reader with a conclusive reading of a text from one point of view or another. This appears in more aggravated form, as I show below, in the brand of deconstruction sold under the de Man label, where endless signification is inverted into dead-end impossibilities of interpretation. All possibilities and no possibilities!

Reader-response critics and deconstructive readers alike seem themselves to have modeled and enacted the reaction against diversity and variety in reading approaches that the broader profession would quickly adopt. The polemical essays that follow explore some of these problems with some of the best thinkers in the first flourishing of reader theory. They are not offered as a comprehensive study of the movement but as a series of case studies in the reaction to the apparent freedom of this period by those close to its promise. As often in political revolutions, it was the sponsors themselves who were first to delimit or call halt to its utopian possibilities. Iser's work is seen to be open to a tolerent view of a variety of possible readings and interpretations, and indeed to the variety of experience of reading. But it teases him and his work to find such possibility in it: his reaction to such a view of his work was profoundly negative and intolerant. De Man's trap for readers follows. Finally, I explore the writing on reading of Robert Scholes, the structuralist who has at least consistently advocated reading, as other major figures such as Bloom and Donoghue have. Alas, he insists on a controlled single approach, much embedded in intentionality despite its openness to ideological issues. The reader will find that Stanley Fish, our lost leader, the critic who led us into the desert and left us there while he went on to legal studies and his students retreated to New Historicism, figures in all these accounts. A coda to this section, however, revisits the issue of communities of readers raised by Fish in order to contrast briefly its traditional model of culture as a non-intersecting mosaic of separate cultures to more recent ideas of multiculturalism, cultural mulattoism, border crossings, cosmopolitanism. How reader theory made its unfortunate peace with history—limiting itself mainly to reception studies and history of reading (useful outcomes in themselves)—will be one subject of my concluding fourth section; where also it has gone and may go, and whether it may yet re-open our studies to diversity of readings and real readers, will be another.

II. WHAT WAS TO FEAR IN THE WOLF-GANG IN SHEEP'S CLOTHING

I begin inevitably with apologies for two things: first for the rude play with people's names which infests this area of criticism and seems to give the last word to Derridean dissemination no matter who else is discussed. Derrida is perhaps still *de rigueur* in all theoretical discussion about the freedoms we really take as we actually read as individuals, very much my issue here. But still mother told me not to make personal allusions; I'm sorry, but my tale is one not of multiplying fishes and loaves but of Fishes and Wolves, and thereby hangs a tale of a wolf that let his hang in the water and got bitten. So my second apology is for bringing up that old nasty business, the wolf-hunt performed by one of our mightiest hunters before the lord of rhetoric and politically effective hard hits—now there, I've left the world of Fish-ermen and on to hunters at least. I allude of course to the well-known *Diacritics* article way back in 1981 with its too effective play on the dissemination of wolves, Stanley Fish's "Why No One's Afraid of Wolfgang Iser."[8] And I do apologize as I would to Bill Clinton if I had to mention how his tale wouldn't wash clean; for Fish's short polemic, vigorously argued, entirely comprehensible (on first reading, as Iser certainly is not), and hard-hitting in the way of Fish's political work in the real world of law and television, seems virtually to have cur-tailed Iser's theoretical position in the study of reading, much as the influence of his approach continues to be felt—and this despite Iser's own cleverly framed (even with stamps of little fish provided in the margins) reply in which he cited Oliver Goldsmith's remark to Johnson about little fish who talk like whales.[9]

The unlikely outcome of the battle of the fishes and the wolves left Iser virtually dethroned as co-pack leader in the jungle of reader theory by Fish's whale-sized witty bites—though Iser, a theoretical prospector shaking the dust of reader response from his feet, has since found interesting new terrain in what he calls literary anthropology, an attempt to think out the idea of humanness from the universals of fiction and imagination, a project that repositions rather than entirely abandons the reader.[10] The rhetorical success of "Why No One's Afraid of Wolfgang Iser," like Fish's general rhetorical brilliance, has had the unfortunate effect of leaving Fish as the major lasting icon among reader theorists; Fish has survived, though now generally busy with legal theory rather than reading, whereas this thriving area of theory has seemed to opt for early retirement. This may be useful for Fish, unfortunate for his opponent; but it is a pure loss for this area of thinking about the reader, what has been called broadly reader theory. As the literary profession turned widely from interpretation to historical studies, it left an appearance of closure: Fish had dealt with all these issues definitively and emerged victorious: end of story; end of reader response.[11] To return to Iser's first career as reader theorist at this point provides an opportunity to see the potential within this history for expansion and development rather than an empty sea where all the reader fry have been eaten up by the biggest fish with the biggest rhetorical bite. More significantly, a return to Iser will especially remind us of the broader view of what reading is and can be that has been opened up by reader theory. It runs very much against the tendency in literary studies since then to privilege authorities and professional historically and contextually grounded reading and to exclude all others. And in this salutary work of reader theory, Fish, the seemingly more radical figure, is at best ambivalent.

Doing what comes naturally for Fish, which I do not deplore but merely observe, was to see Iser as a threat; yes, he was a threat as the other big name in the field, but I don't mean such pragmatic matters, though he does note that Iser's books are the Hopkins best sellers of their time. I mean the way Fish's basic rhetorical strategy gives him away from the start: no one's afraid of Wolfgang Iser? No one? Who said we should be? Well relax and talk about it, Mr. Fish: your unstoppable rhetorical machine is clearly drawn up to stop some kind of threat: unstoppable but not unflappable. So what's to fear in Wolfgang Iser? For one, he is much too liberal in the way one speaks disapprovingly of liberal parents: he lets all positions win, both text and reader, spatial readings and temporal, objective and subjective, intention and significance (in Hirsch's senses of the distinction between author's meaning and a reader's own creation of significance), historical fixity and variability, literature as not mimetic/representational but also changing our view of real life. "The theory, in short, has something for everyone, and denies legitimacy to no one." This is pluralism with a scandal to clear thinking; and Fish, unlike Iser, puts a great premium on clear thinking. He ends the essay indeed accusing Iser of creativity: he has actually written not theory but theory as a novel: a baggy monster of many arguments that asks us, in true Iser style of reading, to fill the gaps.

So Fish fears the "pluralism" of Iser's "capacious and liberal" theorizing. So what to do? He finds a thing to do, which is to bring in the true anarchists to scare away such wishy-washy wolves from the pond of theory. Fish lists himself as among the truly feared ones in his opening, along with the likes of Derrida and de Man. That he isn't, but he does have one scare routine which he does well: Iser is wrong to speak of a text that lays down strategies for the reader's performance of the virtual object to be created in reading. All readings, as Fish has so often argued, are controlled by the reader's way of reading them; to speak of a strategy in the text is to miss that this is placed by the person (Iser as exemplary reader) who finds them and is as much an act of reading as the reading that then follows the strategy. Fish gives convincing examples from Iser in Fielding and Thackeray. And the scary result is that anything goes; no more dots to connect or gaps to fill in, no more half-way compromise between text and reader: the text is a blank canvas to write on or at least a carpet that can be organized in any number of patterns by the beholder.

Well we all know about that as what to fear in the wolf in fish's clothing. It scared and angered Scholes so much that he multiplied this silly insult by disseminated name to try to stop the dissemination of Fish's theory.[12] But it is of course Fish's usual tactic to convert this radical, even solipsistic view of individual subjectivities producing whatever meaning they wish wherever they look into a gesture that does nothing and therefore threatens nothing. What's to fear? "the brakes," he admits, "are off everywhere."[13] But in fact "the brakes are on everywhere." Fish's theory simply amounts to everyone uses the strategies they use to make the readings they use, or even more simply, people will keep doing what they do because that's what they do. Fish indeed repeats here a central arc of his career as reader theorist that we see strikingly in the making in the well-known essay on "Interpreting the *Variorum*."[14] There we experience more a sense of discovery, as Fish seems genuinely surprised by the motile force of his own logic. Certainly he includes almost as many incompatible positions as Iser, but Fish keeps revising his reading temporally rather than, as Iser does, recursively filling in gaps. The long history of battles over interpretation of cruxes in the Milton *Variorum Commentary* shows that these are places where the decision is in fact thrown on the reader, not on the definitive call of the editor. This initial (very interesting) practical criticism leads to reflections on meaning that embody the general approach of early Fish as a new kind of reader of texts: he seeks to answer not the question of what a text says but of what it does.

Here he begins by insisting that he doesn't seek in the text for the meaning, a process he stigmatizes as "positivist, holistic, and spatial," but rather looks on the reader's activities "not as leading to meaning, but as *having* meaning."[15] This Fish calls "experiential analysis," and as a form of reading, as Culler said, Fish reading as a Fishian reader,[16] it certainly offers Fish's reader an experience—as anyone who has been an experiential reader of Fish will testify. But, as is well known, when Fish now attempts to stand back from this madcap headlong process of temporal experiential reading, he is as rapidly led down a different path of theory. Early Fish sounds liberal—meaning permissive—in the sense he castigates Iser for later. He even sounds here a bit like Iser, with his talk of reading as "experiencing," of a "moving field of concerns, at once wholly present (not waiting for meaning but constituting meaning) and continually in the act of reconstituting itself," of talk even of a "sequence where a reader first structures the field he inhabits and then is asked to restructure it," even of a suggestion that a reader "filled in the form." He even speaks of reading as an "action of the mind" (compare Iser's title, *The Act of Reading*).[17]

But the kissing stops when Fish steps back from his act of reading to theorize the magic he does so well. As in so much early reader theory (Culler's thinking in *Structuralist Poetics* would be an especially good example), one feels the pressure of an anxiety about the Pandora's box that the shift from author or text to reader seems to threaten to open. It is alright that he careens around himself as an exemplary reader having the experience of his experience; but he wants us to know that this is not as unanchored as it seems. Indeed, his first recourse is to anchor it to intentionality and history, what the author intended in his time, which can only be experienced by someone like Fish who is well qualified in Milton studies, a fully "informed reader." No sooner is this cautious, institutionally oriented gesture made than Fish, as fast in theory as in his trip with a text, moves to another back-up position. Of course not all readings are informed or claim knowledge of the author's intention; so a broader view of the experience of reading opens up: we each take a trip on the reading railroad with a ticket of interpretive strategies pre-purchased for the occasion. So we are back at a limited kind of openness that sorts out scholarly men from the boys in the caboose. You ride, Fish implies, in your way in your kind of car, I in the stockholder's gilt pullman.[18] All of us ride with some strategy pre-prepared.

This solution, certainly offering a broader view of the matter, must still have left Fish anxious: a theory of "so many persons, so many strategies" offers clarity but threatens chaos: no breaks on that pluralistic love train. So in the final gesture that has become codified into his by-line on the subject by the time of the onslaught on Iser, he locates the strategies within stablilizing interpretive communities. The brakes are on, people are doing what they always do, sticking to the ways of interpretation of their own crowd; no chance of a new experience of the act of reading here. Fish is as fast and clear as Iser is, as Fish complains, cumbrous and incrementally repetitive. But if Fish, perhaps rightly, sees Iser building an elaborate structure to accommodate a variety of theoretical positions (to put this more politely than he does), we can see Fish moving swiftly across a number of incompatible positions in a kind of desperate quest to settle this matter, apply the brakes, stop the train. He argues in the process that intentionality is merely what we claim a reading we make has found, that all readings claim intentionality: the famous but muddy, intention "is verified by an interpretive act, and I would add, it is not verifiable in any other way.... intention is known when and only when it is recognized; it is recognized as soon as you decide about it; you decide about it as soon as you make a sense; and you make a sense (or so my model claims) as soon as you can."[19] The effect is an odd one, to go way out to the end in theory, to the social constructive position of communities apparently determining readers' experience (do they determine them or merely offer a kind of clubhouse for those of like mind?) while leaving intact the implication, established earlier, that Fish reading as a Fishian reader is the right club, knew the author and his aims, has been there as the insider (informed) reader.[20] Caviar for us, a mosaic fair of odd community booths for the general.[21]

I come now to what must be a more speculative part of my history if I continue to pressure the opening question: what was to fear in Iser that Fish denied the wolf in Wolfgang so vociferously? One can grant him a fastidious dislike for a complex compromise theoretical structure even as one sees signs of fast, makeshift and anxiety-driven work in Fish's own theoretical train, at least as he first cobbled it together and sent it down the rails. And I don't like to be in a position of asking Fish if he has stopped being anxious about Iser's theory when he only says he is unhappy with it. What clearly makes Fish anxious, and drives him famously out of doing reader-response criticism, reading as a Fishian critic, and into the theoretical work that, he claims, puts him among the feared new theorists, is a kind of aporia that opens up when he moves, under pressure of the rather old-fashioned ambiguities in the various readings of Milton cruxes (after all, this could be handled very easily in New Criticism as Milton's complex textual art of ambiguity) to imagine a Fishian reader who experiences true diversity in reading: can and does go in all directions suggested by editorial arguments over the meanings of the cruxes. This would seem to have suddenly raised the question of what indeed it was to read in his way. And that is just the point: reading in the way he had developed it was an exciting experience of what the text does, not what it says ("what it does is what it means")[22] but it was a special report on what the text did to him, so a version of reading in his way. Once the prospect of a horde of readers having their own experiences of the text opens up, it needs to be stopped, or at least contained, by some larger theory. And here one should note that while Fish moves to a radically monistic view of interpretation as what we do to texts (so no longer what they do to us), he also solidifies the subject of reading around just that: interpretation. Thereafter the troubling issue of experience, "experiential analysis," "recognizing experiential (that is, temporal) structures," all the matter of what texts do to us, can drop out. It is as if Fish the older looks back at the demonic work of Fish the younger and recognizes that he has lived by dangerous gods, okay for a very informed reader aware of a scholarly assessment of the author's intention as an ideal goal, but rather dangerous for the rest of humanity.

The dangerous gods are of course those that make Fish as a reader so exciting, the rendering of one man's act of reading, which seems to invite us too to a table of reader-response where anything goes as we react word by word to the effect of what comes next. If we read carefully, beyond the excitement of the temporal motion, we see Fish has always been much concerned with what Jane Tompkins has identified as the habitual twentieth-century, whether New Critical or reader theorists', focus on reading as interpretation of meaning: "although reader-oriented critics speak of the 'poem as event' and of 'literature as experience,' meaning is still for them the object of the critical act.[23] That is, I would add, an interpretation fairly narrowly cast as rendering a statement of what the text says or does. Tompkins includes Iser among the reader-oriented folk who do this along with Fish. But in many ways this is not a proper placing of Iser, whose roots are in the Continent and specifically in the phenomenology of Roman Ingarden's reader theory, much as he loosens and adjusts that tradition and does put it in touch with the rhetorical-interpretive aims of an American such as Wayne Booth.[24] Clearly these are not Fish's roots, but Poulet's thinking (to add fowl to our story of fish and flesh) was in the air in the United States late 1960s, especially thanks to Hillis Miller's Geneva School early criticism, which attracted a lot of attention by its own energy and sense of movement around the mental world of an author. It at least offered a path out of New Critical formalism. Fish reading as a Fishian reader seems blinded by his own insight into the way a text does things to him from seeing that he was opening an area beyond meaning and interpretation in which the reader's experience could mean something much more vague and potentially much more threatening to traditional English studies.

What that could be is clear enough in the work that is closer to fitting the term reader response, both Norman Holland's concern with the psychological path of a work within a reader's psyche (modelled on Freudian psychology) and especially the open-ended work of David Bleich, which encouraged a fully subjective response in the reader.[25] This last, which has worked strongly in the high-school class, and perhaps more strongly in the college class than is generally recognized,[26] opened up academic reading to all those activities that could not be called interpretation of meaning, which Tompkins suggests had been with literature in other centuries, as well as to a lot of other activities we all know we do when we read but have never talked about in the classroom. In this history of criticism, Fish has always seemed strangely bedded with such work under that messy term reader response, which needs more decisive retirement as too much about only one set of interests to represent the entire field of reader-oriented theory and criticism. While his theory, once formulated, can allow him to acknowledge that there are such communities of reader libertarians—not, strictly speaking, interpretive communities at all—these are doubtless not clubs he would care to join. He prefers to speak, when he speaks of way-out interpretation, of religious fanatics still focused on interpretation, not of such grateful read groupies.

So what's to fear in Iser may be the side of his work that even reminds Fish of his own early flirtation with the attractive power of conceptions of reading that have the potentially disruptive, transgressive capacity to allow things to happen to you that you don't expect. Iser is then one of us (though he is really a Konstanz school critic from a far land and alien philosophical tradition) who reminds us of our own walk on the wild side, on the dangerous edge, of response. And the danger was just that his theory seemed so respectable, is so plausible and liberal, even mainly cites familiar English texts as examples. Iser, we should remind ourselves, was not primarily concerned with meaning or interpretation. He was interested in a kind of production of the text, by rules laid down as strategies in the text, in the mind of the reader. This allows him to discuss many things we don't usually focus on in an interpretive classroom, especially the way we actually make the text seem to come alive in our minds. No one has failed to remark, as Fish remarks of course, that Iser is conservative in insisting on giving a good deal of authority to the text in the individual production of a reading act. Few I think have missed Iser's positioning of reading, through his phenomenological rather than experimental focus (one could have, people now have, asked individual readers how they in fact read a particular text; Bleich and Holland were already doing that when Iser was publishing in English) in a kind of virtual space (his term) that looks like a kind of idealization of his own reading experience (research is presumably done by sitting alone and making it up as you go along, then writing it up as a truth universally acknowledged).[27] But if these and other aspects of this work as theory may bother us as they did Fish, what remains at this distance is still a vital kind of imagination of the act of reading that makes us rethink the too easily circumscribed boundaries of reading.[28] And at the far reach of his theorizing Iser also comes dangerously near the dangerous interpretive work of deconstruction, as I will explain.

Iser's phenomenological underpinnings, never very influential in an Anglo-American context where Husserl and even Merleau-Ponty have seemed only weaker versions of a generally not very accessible idealist tradition, have been since the 1970s further weakened by the powerful skeptical critique mounted from within that tradition by, of course, Derrida.[29] But the tradition in which he developed and in which, despite the addition of an overlay of Austin's Speech Act theory as a way of explaining the work of the reader as a distanced version of speech-like communication, Iser primarily worked, is as helpful as a set of metaphors for the dynamic process of reading as it is unhelpful as an ultimate ground for argument. It does in large part, I think, explain the alien quality of his way of approaching reading to even an innovative and often disturbing theorist of reading such as Fish. Terry Eagleton has seen aesthetic theory in the idealist tradition as the one area where Western tendencies to separate mind from material conditions of human life have been countered by a project of organizing the *Lebenswelt* (the life-world, the world as lived), a "*detour* through sensation, experience, 'naivety' as Husserl calls it."[30] In phenomenology this way of thinking of the relation of an increasingly rarefied and isolated idea of pure mind to an increasingly inaccessible world of the material gives art and its explanation in aesthetics a central role, perhaps in part accounting for the reciprocal interest of phenomenological philosophers and literary theorists and critics. To critics in this tradition such as Ingarden or Iser, reading is not just a process of interpreting a text; it takes them to central issues of how our minds are able to relate, in the special virtual reality of art, to the outside world. (Iser's usually disregarded subtitle is certainly indicative of this central concern: A *Theory of Aesthetic Response*.) The overall project may still seem muddy; indeed Husserl was to conclude that the goal of organization of the life-world embodied in the aesthetic project was ultimately illusory. But this tradition certainly casts the act of reading, and it is the *act* of reading not the process or goals (as in interpretation) that Iser pursues, as a major event of the subject. The text is indeed a stimulus of the highest order that brings the reader's mental forces into full play. And these are not the usual reader's equipment of careful attention to details and well balanced judgment.

Reading is, first of all, an act of imagination. Iser's text is filled with pictorial comparisons, so one easily thinks of his scheme as a plan for turning novels into cinema. Certainly we are at the least asked to stage and perform the text in our heads, to make it come alive for ourselves as we read. We are reminded in this how much of the act of reading regularly escapes comment in the "institutional" setting of learning, to use the unfortunate term coined for English studies by the theorists of the 1970s. But that was then and this now still finds us relatively indifferent to the processes of reading that inevitably catch our attention most strongly when we actually sit down with a book.[31] But it is to Iser's credit too that he rarely settles for the limited parallel to visual experience. He makes us realize that we are trying to see Tom Jones in our mind as we read, but that our resistance to the film version is just that we fall from the dynamic cinema of imagination, where we can keep remaking Tom's appearance and character with each new suggestion or recursion, to a single settled reality. The imagination of even physical details in a work is an act of energetic multiplicity, not, as we might think if we thought much about this, one simple decision. And the imagination is much more than image making. Here Iser's recurrent idea of filling in the blanks (so easily reduced to a game of connecting the dots) is too reliant on a visual idea, along with the parallel one of drawing out constellations (no mere work of connect the dots, if you ever try it on a summer night). What need to be filled in in novels are often events, even more, complex ideas about human relations, politics, morality. Fish's frustration with the elaborate constructs that Iser's examples offer is perhaps a frustration with novel reading itself, which involves so many areas of experience and so often leaves information or its schematization open to speculation.[32]

Fish of course could have seen his own ever-adjusting, forward-flowing reading method most obviously in Iser's mad careening through those baggy monsters. It is of course what seemed most different and exciting in Fish's own practical criticism. And both in fact tend to see the text as doing its diachronic work upon a passive reader, as Fish's famous not-what-it-says-but-what-it-does formula suggests. The difference seems nuanced but important. Iser seems really interested in describing the way in which one reads in time, Fish more in describing the way in which he has read in time as a reading. Iser's readings are examples, Fish's exemplary. That we might be encouraged to think of reading as an event in time that will keep being different with each reading is central to Iser's focus on mental acts; by contrast Fish seeks to frame and solidify a reading by a new method. I contrast not to judge between them but to suggest how different, even in this area, Iser's phenomenological interest in the reading act itself is from academic concern with interpretation or communities of interpretation. Iser's complexity is once again a plus as well as a negative: messy theory, but an open-ended idea of how we read in time, driven to activity with the appearance of each new signifier demanding a signified, how we simultaneously recur and revise, moving forward and backward in continually competing mental gestures. The "simple" act of sitting there doing nothing but reading at least finds description that gives some idea of its intensity and complexity. Iser's model suggests reading as a kind of intense mental stimulation, a kind of storming of the brain in a series of hastily successive and superseding activities.

Yes, of course Fish is broadly right about the interpretations we make being those we bring (as Coleridge learned of nature),[33] but the real point is that interpretation, the settled point of view or configuration of the work (that spatial view that Fish worked so hard so long to keep out but that is certainly implied in his interpretive strategies and even more in the settled business of interpretive communities that always interpret the way they interpret) hardly seems adequate to describe the excitement of reading. Iser can hardly contain himself in his admiration of the complexity of it all; as such, he is a good refresher to us all, offering a kind of destructive medium or act(ual) reading into which we may immerse ourselves when we think we have reading or hermeneutics down to a system. He is not trying to describe a reading (exemplary or not), nor is he trying to report on actual readings, which would be a different, perhaps today more convenable approach to the same breadth of interest in reading's acts.[34] Iser's philosophical background allows him to write theory as a kind of essay in praise of the act of reading. If we take it that way, an "institutional" academic exercise of a more traditional sort, and don't fret, as Fish does, over the multiplicity of arguments and their necessary confusions, we can appreciate the central inspiration, to do justice to the larger contours of the reading act as a central mental activity.[35]

It is perhaps for this reason that Iser's best work in this area seems to me to be the little essay he contributed to the Suleiman and Crosman anthology on *The Reader in the Text*—a subject incidentally that he summarizes beautifully, though it is not a central concern of his work: "there are four main perspectives in narration: those of the narrator, the characters, the plot, and the fictitious reader. Although these may differ in order of importance, none of them on its own is identical to the meaning of the text, which is to be brought about by their constant intertwining through the reader in the reading process."[36] This seems to say concisely all that the other contributors, with much expense of theoretical spirit, seem to be able to marshall on the rather tedious subject of positions for the reader in the text, a subject really no different from a formalist look at "centers" or perspective points in the text.

Iser's little essay is like a little epic of reading, with most of the cumbrous theoretical apparatus of speech act and the rest set aside and the intense, almost Dionysian act of reading put front and center. The major theoretical nod is indeed to R.D. Laing on the virtually schizophrenic complexities of interpersonal interaction. How much more so in the non-present act of reading where the reader is necessarily alienated from the text! Of course I note that reference to "meaning" in the quotation above; but he clearly doesn't *mean* it in the way Fish or Tompkins use it to talk about our quest for interpretation as meaning. The essay resounds with language of active acts of reading, not spatial closure to meaning: blanks go off everywhere to startle the tourists; as in *Alice in Wonderland* everything is always turning into its opposite: segments become themes, themes become backgrounds, blanks and vacancies succeed each other as in a nightmare of an existentialist. The world is weird and wonderful, with decided sexual overtones;[37] there is always that "wandering viewpoint," the roving eye, that the reader brings into play everywhere, as in the now-vanished pre-AIDS singles bar; blanks trigger off the reader's involuntary response, and while he fumbles about trying so hard to bridge the gap, he finds textual segments "projecting themselves one upon another." Soon, as in Havelock Ellis's notion of tumescence/detumescence, "this relationship gives rise to a tension that has to be resolved."[38] Above all, this is a world where nothing stays the same; as in a nightmare of impressionism by G.K. Chesterton, backgrounds become foregrounds, all that data that was pushed back into the woods suddenly becomes the foregrounding trees. The pattern in the carpet comes and goes like a neon Cheshire cat. Each reading is a unique pattern itself like a Paterian moment of evanescent consciousness: "It can never be the same twice over."[39]

I believe my reader will welcome these, my acts of reading Iser on reading, though granted they are a throwback to a kind of impressionistic criticism popular when school-of-Geneva phenomenological looks at authors had their day. I think you will at least prefer this to a run through the familiar details of the theory once more; and perhaps at this distance the point is clear in a way both Iser and Fish (the practical critic) would understand: Iser's theory *does* a great deal to us in shaking up our usually passive and confined notions of the reading process. The complex of theory we find cobbled together, as Fish rightly notes, in oddly jointed segments, works especially well in this condensed form simply to dazzle us with the number of perspectives we can take on the so complex act of reading. So what it does to us is to leave us confused but, unless we have a special taste for tight argument in itself that therefore resists the entire experience, born again into reading as an act. And of course it ends with a miracle, a kind of city built to music, as the aesthetic object emerges, whirling and samite, from the mere of successive reader acts: a virtual reality in our brains as wonderful as anything we will find in cyberspace.

He emphatically does not mean to image the act of reading as a Grecian urn, all still, silent, and Greek, naked to our settled and closure-bringing gaze. It dances in the lights of our continuous waves of creation, truly like a cyber image made up only of continuous streams of energy on a magic electronic screen. Indeed Fish is right to sense that there is a machine in the aesthetic ghost of virtual space. Iser's infernal act-of-reading machine, a logical Rube Goldberg but a little wonder of the modern world of theory nonetheless, gets going and there is no stopping it. It gets us going and we keep going. Indeed, and this is what I promised earlier, there is good reason to see this as yet another of the postmodern machines, spinning us out of our own control and into ever new configurations. It is a deconstructive machine.

No sooner is one perspective achieved, one *Gestalt* as Iser terms it, though he means not so much a visual formation as a way of organizing the materials humming about into some order, than it fails and another snaps into place. Think of it perhaps as a scan button jammed on the TV. We construct only to deconstruct. The *Gestalt* is the closest Iser comes to something like our idea of interpretive meaning, an interpretation, perhaps around a prominent theme (yes we still do theme criticism, foregrounding what interests us and backgrounding the rest, only in the newer areas, multicultural themes, New Historical themes, queer themes, political themes). And here his point, like that of postmodernism generally, is that no one will save the text. You like *Jane Eyre* as about feminist assertion; I give you sexuality; you like that, our colleague will give you Brontë's world of death—and on and on. In any area of criticism, the machine keeps moving, just as it does in our attempts as an industry to stop the wheel of interpretation on our number. The machine goes on, grinding up all us pussycats of interpretation.

I submit that *that* is to fear in Wolfgang Iser and his gang of critics, talk as they may about high-school and college teaching to please the masses. Those sheep will be fed but may be fed on too. Iser's engine, more than his bite, is implacable and infernal. So I suggest we admit him, wolf, after all, though in Fish's sheep's clothing, baaing and protesting, to the dangerous critics hall of fame. I have disturbed the dust on the ashes of this controversy of another day because I think it tells us something about the evasion of the radical implications of reader theory by even those most identified with its major emergence under the name of reader response (a term not used by either Fish or Iser) on or about 1980. The most radical, Fish, seems constrained to restrain Iser. Iser himself, while stressing the relative freedom given to the reader in his, as opposed to Ingarden's, phenomenological reader theory, nonetheless—wolf in sheeps' clothing—evaded then and apparently keeps evading the radical implications of his approach. A version of this chapter presented at a conference on his influence elicited a wolf-howl: why am I attacking him so viciously, a mere sheep of a moderate, a-little-text-a-little-reader, critic in the Wayne Booth booth? I explained to the group that I was befriending, not attacking, but could understand, given Iser's reluctance to come out of grandmother's closet, that he might feel that with friends like me he would never want enemies! The interchange of wolves and fishes seems to have been a ritual that attracted attention to reader-response pyrotechnics while muting its primary force as a theoretical intervention.[40]

Finally, I concur with Fish's especial nervousness about how Iser's compromise between text and reader actually makes us mainly the helpless victim of a text-started machine that then spins out of either author or reader's control—and inside our poor minds![41] When Poulet spoke of reading as a possession by another he descended to rather uncomfortable talk about a parasite inside us.[42] In the same tradition, Iser gets going Dunderbeck's machine in our brains: we suffer mind control, body-snatching, all those nightmares from late nights on the other machine. Is it any wonder that Fish cried stop the train, let me off, back to human communities of interpretation? And preferred to try to dress up this wolf and his gang of dangerous reading activities in pastoral folly.

III. DE MAN'S NARRATIVE OF READING: NO EXIT—FOR OTHERS

Paul de Man was controversial as a "deconstructionist" in his life and of course for political reasons after his death. One does not usually think of him as part of the controversy, coming to a head in the early 1980s, over reading. I want here to insert his exacting discussion of literature and language into that debate, where I believe it belongs, though it appears as trasher, intent on ending rather than continuing the discussion. "It is impossible to read reading";[43] nonetheless, that is just what he tried to do. My aim in this approach to the still disturbing, still exciting reading approach of Paul de Man is not to box in (he did that deliberately himself very well!) or to limit the impact of a fine critic. Nor can we list here (to use a typical de Manian strategy) all the specific fineness/finesse of his reading approach.[44]

But I think it is a helpful step toward self-consciousness about contemporary reading to see what are the larger strategies and scenarios in his reading method. For he of all persons has taught us that critics always have a blindness to their own decisive commitments, even when they seem most clear eyed. It is no real criticism of such a fine mind, so caught up as well as responsive to the historical and intellectual perplexities of the mid-twentieth century, to say that he brings to his reading a set of contemporary, then even fashionable and now by no means simply exhausted and superseded, assumptions and preoccupations. My own further assumption is that such concerns will inevitably be narrativized, put into some tale that speaks the age and, more to my purpose here, directs his reading process. It is my own tribute to what de Man has taught us about the complexities of all apparent projection of values into objective narrative that I begin with the assumption that there will be a bifurcation, a city of two tales, one the typical tale of the mentality of the time, which we will find repeated endlessly as *the* story found in the work, the other a tale of the reading enterprise itself, an implicit one, harder to locate as it hides behind the apparent tales of the text.

Let us begin by looking not at the tale de Man himself tells but how his tale was read in his time by those sympathetic to his message. I take as a most conspicuous example Jonathan Culler's well-known redaction—what I consider Culler's best work, if also rather culminating work of that brave new world of early theory that Culler made available to us in such a lucid form. The work is his best perhaps because Culler was finally under pressure, feeling the influx of disrupting new influences that profoundly disturbed his own role as the distressing new force *par excellence* in the brief offensive campaign of structuralism and semiotics in the anglophone literary world. The two disturbing new radical-chic elements in the neighborhood of theory are very boldly inscribed in his book, a work explicitly on one of them, titled indeed *On Deconstruction*, but also occupied for a very long prefatory comment (83 pages!) with what had been called reader response but was obviously a more general interest in looking at all aspects of reading than the rather psychological (as in the work of Norman Holland) term "response" suggested. Culler wisely entitles his excursus, "Readers and Reading." Culler's earlier response to Holland's then prominent studies of readers' psychological response and to the portent of Fish had been almost a paranoid fear of things falling apart, mere anarchy set loose in the halls of academe. The language of the recent challenger of all orthodoxy is, on this subject, filled with defensive conservative talk of the need for professional readers and "the institution of literature." "The claims of schools and universities to offer literary training cannot lightly be dismissed. To believe that the whole institution of literary education is but a gigantic confidence trick, would strain even a determined credulity," says Culler.[45] Amen we add, and considerably jeopardize our next paycheck too. His first strategy, a terribly failing one though understandable in the times, is to use structuralism—itself in a great mind such as Roland Barthes very much interested in allowing space and play for the reader—to control and circumscribe the dangers of reader criticism, seen as a kind of Pandora's box. Yes, Culler grants, we have had many readings, as many even among "professional" readers as there have been professional readers. But these can be ordered and contained by higher-level universals that consolidate their apparent diversity: all readers seek unity in texts ("poems are supposed to cohere"); all readers seek out "binary oppositions as thematic devices" and explore the "tension" thus created![46]

Ouch: New Criticism redivivus. All *that* was just about to be changed by the other new kid on the block, the subject Culler had now taken up. And now readers seemed even more threatening as a deluge of criticism; and the typical one, to a not unsympathetic male critic (the white and the straight would come later but is very much to this point), seems feminist: reading as a woman. The case was very well chosen. We had already had good work by Judith Fetterley,[47] controversial at the time, and it has opened to more and more reflections on more and more kinds of reading as a woman (e.g., essays in

Elizabeth Flynn and Patrocinio P. Schweickart's good anthology).[48] Clearly there was a threat to be dealt with: reader theory, lost at first in the psychological-individual readings of Holland or in the exactingly myopic Mr. Magoo readings of Stanley Fish, or the easy deconstruction reading—connect and disconnect the dots—of the putatively unterrifying Wolfgang, was coming of age and getting political. (How political it could become would be apparent in the subsequent queer/political reading of readings by Ross Chambers.)[49] Denis Donoghue was then predicting, quite rightly, that all criticism was about to take a turn to the political. What apparently bothered Culler were the implications for mainstream canonical criticism of a union of political, othered perspectives and focus on readers' ability to make texts differently in the reading. And this was not a misunderstanding. Culler's half book on reading is one of the best things on the subject just because he sees focus on the reader not as a single new theory in the making to challenge structuralism or deconstruction but as a place of potential anarchy: Fish isn't reading as a new kind of theorist; he is reading in a certain mode, as a Fishian reader. But if there is a Fishian reading that Fish can choose or not choose to adopt as his reading, then the world can be filled with ever more strange readings, ethnic, sexual, third world, etc. Let them work on their own non-canonical texts; let them do new histories and cultural studies—where they will even abandon the old greats—but keep their hands off the traditional canon! How? Let's see if the destructive power of deconstruction, which blew Culler's own early interests out of the water so effectively, can be brought to bear on this crowd at the gates of the institution and the profession.

Who better for a demolition job than de Man himself? For Culler, he tells a reassuring tale to keep any *ancien régime* institutionalized: no exit that way! Culler takes on de Man therefore as friendly opponent whose tale says whoa to all this disruptive reader positioning and jostling. Reading, he finds de Man conveniently saying, is much harder than you think; you can't make the text do what you want because it does what *it* wants; and the tale it tells us when we read it is of its unreadability. Tell the folks outside to come back another day: the master is hard at work on the problem and finds it, well, problematic. Enter if you will but then the warning is clear: no exit. Now note grossly in this strategy what de Man himself repeats finely in his work (and Culler as always is a fine redactor). Begin with a tale found by reading: the text speaks of its unreadability; but note beyond the tale the narrative of the telling: de Man as inscribed in the tale is the victim of unreadability who, unlike those hordes out there, wisely accepts the inevitability of his victimhood. Texts do this to us. But the text of Culler's tale is rather opposite: de Man is the strong man, the/de Man brought in to stop a riot of reading. Like the God of Fitzgerald's Rubyáiyát who presides over his world of inaction, "he knows—

HE knows." His reading is the ultimate reading, a better universal than those old New Critical ones of unity and binaries under tension, a decisive and final reading that effectively stops all this threatening play with the penetralia of the profession.[50] The text is empowered against all readers: but power, as Marx if not Foucault would say, always comes from somewhere: in this case the Yale authority. And the old Yale taboo on affective reading—reading from the point of view of one's individual interest and feeling—is effectively renewed under New Criticism's successor, deconstruction. Let politics and every variety of new interest come; it will remain outside the interpretive inner circle.

Does this seem unfair, making a thoughtful study (Culler's) ultimately a political one in our profession that does certain things performatively with words, no matter how complex and fine? But surely, to turn from Culler on de Man to de Man himself, one wouldn't take offense with such a polemical critic as de Man, who virtually reinvented the art (I am also practicing here) of criticism of criticism. Nor, in suggesting that de Man had an investment in actually serving the function that Culler assigned to him, am I falling into vulgar polemicism of the kind we have had all too much of around de Man, of attacking the man.[51] All I will allow myself here is the (I hope humanly sympathetic) observation that it must have written a terrible lesson (even Kafka's *Strafkolonie*-like on his body), to have found at such an early age that there are severe political consequences for writing words that tell too clear tales. If his dismay and guilt were personal and individual (and, yes, hidden and unreadable by us now), his response to the difficult public history of his time was typical. He was indeed very much in tune with an intellectual generation—be they former supporters of Stalin or, like de Man, former fellow travelers of the right. All had learned the terrible destruction and misprision that commitment cast into words can bring. So de Man is not so alien among the Karl Poppers, committed to avoiding ideological commitment and clear meaning; nor so alien among the various F.O. Matthiessens who hid their earlier radical commitments in the Ivies, though with Matthiessen's more fragile temperament the crack perhaps led to his death rather than appearing after death. Certainly de Man was no outsider among the postwar European intellectuals—from French existentialists to British/North American logical positivists—who all agreed only on the absurdity of verbal philosophical ultimates. The brilliant young de Man found his own niche in United States criticism as a self-professed disciple of Empson, whose wonderful endless shopping lists of possible readings de Man early embraced as the attractive end of the dead end he found in the New Criticism which he practiced egregiously at Harvard before he emerged at Yale. Dead end, his term in that prefigurative early essay, is indeed indicative of where he was going.[52] For de Man chose to join the formalists; he was a New Critic, a Browerite, the best of Browerites, from the time of that early essay until his strong critical appearance in *Blindness and Insight*.

What brought him out of the New Critical chamber of maiden thought was not Derrida, whose Empson-like play of significations he, much to his credit, almost immediately recognized and applauded,[53] but the threat of a new political/social criticism in France.[54] These people, the very title tells us, are (like his earlier self perhaps?) blind to think that their insight can lead to political and thus potentially activating stories of reading. They were to be stopped, at least where it mattered in the free world, in North American criticism. And they pretty much were: Lukács, Blanchot, Binswanger, Poulet, such interesting figures but with the exception of Lukács's influence in Marxist theory and the seeding of a brief American critical interest by Poulet's school of Geneva work, not major influences in American criticism.[55] The polemical strategy, a familiar one because de Man continues to be well read and influential, is of course to show some insight in the many different blindnesses of political or otherwise engaged readings. The blindness is manifold; the insight is always the same: into unreadability. And when we look at this better tale it is always a tale of de Man's age, especially of his coming of age: a tale of failed communication, a tale of no exit to meaning, a tale of you can't get there (in interpretation) from here (in reading), a tale of the reader as Sisyphus, a tale of facing the void, a tale of looking into the cleavage at the heart of being.

I do not have the space (to evoke de Man's favorite rhetorical device once again), to go into the myriad subtleties and excellences of his reading of critics in that first major telltale tale of reading; nor can I do adequate justice to the readings of difficult scenes and journeys of readings in the later (1979) and often superb *Allegories of Reading*. There the difficulties of reading are first displayed by what at first may look like a typical reader-response strategy, reading of the positioned reader in the text. This is the famous scene of reading—Marcel reading in the garden house on that hot quiet summer day: producing of course not a reader position to guide our reading but an insight into the impossibility of reading and interpreting because of the unstable nature of metaphors/metonymies. Then we have readings of Hölderlin, Nietzsche, and Rousseau that produce discussion of the reasons for general unreadability in literature. Finally, in the sections on Rousseau, de Man looks directly at the idea of allegory of reading, finding in the chapter on *Julie* that all allegories of reading—in effect readings of reading—are "always allegories of the impossibility of reading."[56] Allegory is actually a secondary reading of tropes ("allegories are always allegories of metaphor"); when we read these readings, that is perform an allegory of the initial interpretation, an allegory of an allegory, we find that the metaphor fails to denominate or designate one meaning. The story of reading is thus again two stories: that of the blind reader who simply tries a first-order reading of tropes, handling quicksilver as if it could be molded into firm interpretive shape, producing a reading that he/she believes is stable but is actually only another text, an allegory unstable in its own tropic language; this is a reader ultimately lost in wandering errors for whom there is indeed no exit; his error will be most often to try to read an order, make connections, where there are only separate effects. De Man does not mention Iser but he seems almost explicitly to forbid the connections between separate items that Iser assumes are fundamental to reading or themes.[57] Second, there is the story of the second-order reader, the smart reader whose reading of reading, the allegory of reading, is actually a success story, a version of the wily Ulysses or the clever younger son Jack who finds the right way to get around the Cyclopean giant metaphor by declaring its interpreters' blindness. For this reader, the de Manian reader, all readings are unstable texts themselves; he/she reads an allegory—produces a narration—of reading itself, of its very instability.[58]

Perhaps I may be permitted my own allegorical reading of de Man's late and charmingly candid assessment of his own project in the Preface to *The Rhetoric of Romanticism*.[59] There he endearingly deconstructs his life's work in this field as merely fragments that do not form a consistent approach or history—while also casting skeptical cold water on contemporary hopes for a new history (caps or not, take your pick). The consistency he does find has been one of approach, and he sees the earlier essays as doing what he calls "rhetorical analysis," like Molière's Jourdain, before "such a thing existed by name." The phrase he uses, which de Man has taught us to scrutinize, is extraordinary: "the Yeats chapter entitled 'Image and Emblem,' however, as its title suggests, was already a rhetorical analysis of figural language *avant la lettre*, anticipating a mode that would later become predominant for me." I refer to the pleonastic "rhetorical analysis of figural language" (not to mention the additional play of a play of figural language before words). At this point in de Man's career we can ask and answer the question, what the devil is rhetorical analysis of figural language? De Man habitually reduces rhetoric to tropes so that the sentence really becomes double: a rhetorical analysis of rhetoric or even a troping of tropes. What is this activity, to return to my moutons of reading theory, but a form of reading which plays with tropes, in de Man's terms writes an allegory of allegories?

And here we must interrogate the idea of a free play. The freest play with tropes and figures that I know is that of de Man's own admired predecessor, the New Critic *par excellence* before the letter as de Man is after the letter, Empson. And even in Empson's riot of plays on possible meanings of tropes one knows that there is some method in his metaphor multiplying, even some reader's thumb on the scale. Like all of us who read, he has an interpretive ax to grind, only it is the proof of multiplication, looking for ambiguity, which in fact gives such distinctive multiplicity to his reading in *Seven Types of Ambiguity*.[60] In de Man's case the question of free play is especially poignant as it arises in a Preface where he admits his practical criticism seems to have no determining theme, tells no history. But his consolation is indeed the unifying theme of "figural language": "I have myself taken refuge in more theoretical inquiries into the problems of figural language." This is the kind of feint de Man loves to deconstruct; he seems to have left interpretation, the reading of Romanticism, where his work is mere brilliant fragments, for a theoretical rather than interpretive project. But he has already identified the project, as I have translated it, I hope fairly, as a troping of tropes; and this is theory that is really only more interpretation, more reading. So the conclusion must be that de Man's refuge is really a consistent kind of reading, a troping of tropes with a method, a process somewhat obfuscated by the special use he develops in the term allegory of reading—a reading of reading. Looked at as a form of reader theory, de Man's second order reading, his successful narration of a reading of reading, allegory of reading, *is* a reader position, one kind of habitual reader response insisting on intersecting, self-canceling moves as its organizing ideology.

When de Man made his deliberate intervention into theory of the early 1980s, he similarly obscured his position, which was really a theory of reading, as general theory. The resistance to theory of the title of this collection is actually a resistance to theorizing, in philosophy, aesthetics, politics, and literary interpretation, caused by reading as it should be done. In de Man's version of reader theory, reading of rhetoric or rhetorical reading prohibits all attempts to use texts for rhetorical (in the other sense of persuasive, the original source for de Man's selective version of rhetoric) purposes. What de Man calls "mere reading," reading of the rhetorical difficulties of the text itself before any totalizing gestures of interpretation, is both the real literary theory, the higher truth of literature, that everyone hopes to resist and the function of reading that resists empty theorizing and blind interpretive assurance.[61] Although no one saw him doing so at the time, and no one has identified him since specifically with the reader-response criticism of that day, de Man was weighing in heavily as a theorist of reading. And his message was that there was only one kind of reading. Here all attempts at clear reading of a meaning, all exits to interpretation, are blocked by the difficulties of the system of language itself. Grammar and logic are useless because they are always already rendered ambiguous by the rhetorical—here read tropic and figural—elements of language as found everywhere in texts.

De Man is careful not to reify the old New Critical binary of literary versus pragmatic texts, yet in the end he finds literariness more present in what have been traditionally received as literary texts.[62] Similarly, he is careful to distance himself from aesthetics, which he sees as a philosophical project aimed at harmonizing language with reference, as if words could sound out their relations to things they speak for.[63] De Man insists rather on the dissonance of language, as a system, from the reference, mimesis, or attempts at philosophical coherence of texts everywhere. His brand of deconstruction shows the impossibility, because of the rhetorical nature of language, of all such projects in making language mean definitively.

It is hard for a literary critic to resist de Man's resistance. We have all been well tuned by our New Critical heritage, universally still alive and well in literary pedagogy, to sense dissonance, ambiguity, double-voicedness. It is, at some close to zero-degree-level critical activity, what we do. And de Man does it superbly well. Even more than Derrida, he has taught a generation of readers to find the place in a text where the center will not hold, where the dark forces of rhetorical unclarity rush in to extinguish the bright headlights of intepretation, leaving us in the dark again. He is a critic's critic who looks over our shoulders and asks us sternly not just if we have taken account of how plural the text is (that is Barthes's more genial question) but if we have considered how that plurality creates deadly aporias everywhere, landmines to stop us in our tracks. Those who have only heard of the writing for *Le Soir* during the war and his unforthcomingness—to put it delicately—about that personal history during his later life in the United States can hardly understand how de Man has functioned as a literary conscience to us literary people, telling us not to sell the farm of literariness in our quests for political, identity, sexual, gender, historical meanings in literature or in our historical projects that may tempt us to put aside interpretation altogether. De Man's project of understanding how language works in texts is what we all do, or should be doing, whatever else we do. In his exceptionally intense and intricately articulated discussions of texts he has been the voice of the New Critical grandfathers who, dead and forgotten, are still the founders of our interpretive enterprise and who speak through him still: it's the text, stupids.[64]

But this is also to say that de Man's theory of reading, mere reading, must fall under some of the critiques so long established, against New Criticism. It does privilege a literary aspect of language, what he calls literariness.[65] The more play of trope and figure, as there is in poetry such as Baudelaire's, the more mere reading to do, and paradoxically, the more easily all other "totalizing" strategies of reading are stopped in their tracks. Second, it does privilege not aesthetics, which it disdains as a philosophical field, but the aesthetic. Like its parent New Criticism, it has its roots broadly in literary aestheticism and *l'art pour l'art* and in its readaptation in modernism. Analogies may be helpful here: de Man trained with Harry Levin and Reuben Brower at Harvard, Levin a major modernist expert in himself, Brower a self-proclaimed disciple of F.R. Leavis and I.A. Richards.[66] As a Romanticist de Man was splendid in penetrating ideologies of Romanticism, from Rousseau to Baudelaire to Yeats, in the interest of analysis of form and rhetoric. His interpretive method, in all its finesse and intricacy, is nonetheless always to show how the language of the text works, a criticism that New Criticism insisted on, though de Man has none of the implicit Romantic ideology of organic unity that had been so closely intertwined with New Criticism from its origins and that gave it such an interest in the unity of well-wrought urns. This was *analyse de texte* without any mastering ideology.[67]

Except what we find everywhere: a blind (in de Man's own sense of blind to implications and consequences) insistence on unreadability itself. It does not follow that the presence of wild cards or blown fuses of tropes in texts renders them generally uninterpretable.[68] De Man so well shows examples where semantic chaos erupts from rhetorical constructions that we easily miss the sleight of hand that generates examples into universals—especially as de Man is so persistently insistent. Even his major focus on metaphor as a central trope can be criticized as a half truth, stressing the way in which metaphor can disconnect readers from meanings by ambiguation rather than their productivity to interpretation.[69] It would be reasonable to conclude after reading de Man, as one does after reading Empson, that we must be very careful not to ignore these hard places where we cannot determine meaning because of tropic play. These are in fact more versions of ambiguity. But our usual process of interpretation when our eyes are thus wide open to such unclarities will be to argue one position or another in relation to whatever other organizing approaches we find arguable in the text. If we are reading Keats's "Fall of Hyperion" as a poem that we make best sense of as about poetic vocation, then we are going to prefer the reading of the title, which de Man ambiguates so thoroughly, as the fall of (the poem) *Hyperion* and perhaps its author in that difficult earlier attempt. De Man would tell us not to do this, but to rest in our inconclusiveness. It is interesting to consider on what terms we would be likely to prefer his approach. The answer would seem to be when the entire text appeared to us to be consumed in such tropical (or other kinds of) ambiguity and not otherwise. In such especially hard cases—some poems of Mallarmé, some hymns of Hölderlin, certain places in the Cantos (places in English), some poems of Ashbery—we may be persuaded that unreadability is what the poem is about.[70]

For all his excellence and intelligence, we are not likely to be persuaded in other cases. In the end, we will see de Man's approach not as the fundamental one based on an essential nature of language but as one approach, emphasizing certain formal aspects of a text, offering itself as a universal. For all its elegance and brilliance, de Man's approach is serving up the usual, a reading that follows the old hermeneutic circle, starting with one idea or theme and then finding it everywhere in the works, so read. It thus leaves the center, where de Man hoped to place it permanently, and joins the ring of possible interpretive focuses, where it will have to argue the case out on its merits for each work it tries to read. Unreadability, too, may be the wrong reading, blind to its own limits and to more productive or useful approaches. For all that de Man teaches us, we must resist his attempt to leave us with only one reading message, his allegory of reading itself, the self-referentiality of literature. And this, de Man's own exit to a grounded belief, a system about literature he offers with assurance, as we all know, forbids other interpretations, which are stopped at the no exit sign erected for all less self-aware readings. What hermeneutic system, arrived at the degree of de Man's mature elaboration, does not? In his Preface to *The Rhetoric of Romanticism,* which so nobly admits the blindness of his own insights into romanticism (which we know to be so useful) de Man would offer his theoretical work as his true insight: but here of course he is blind to the single-minded circle of his own reading system. For reader theory, de Man is finally an exemplary case of the inability to stop the proliferation of readings and reader approaches. He recedes from the position Culler would play him as, the ultimate backstop, to himself represent yet another, though certainly a profoundly interesting, reading preoccupation. And that in turn exists within the democracy of readers and reading released in the world by the demise, slow but inevitable, of the New Critical critical *pax Americana* and the brief scientistic life of structuralism.

I can still hear Brower's reading, so wonderful and feeling, with a sense of its serious and comic effect on the modern North American New Critically cultured reader, of Dryden's "Drawn to the dregs of a democracy." I imagine de Man had heard it too.

Practicum: Reading without an Exit: a Model de Manian Reader of Reading

Clayton Koelb's *Inventions of Reading: Rhetoric and the Literary Imagination*[71] is not as well known as de Man's books; but it is the work of a responsible comparativist with a base in German literature who has allowed himself to be drawn into thinking about interpretation in the wake of de Man's considerable project of defining reading as a function of rhetoric. As such it allows us to see the blocking difficulties that lie in the way of anyone who attempts to wield de Man's skeptical system of rhetoricity as a model of reading. Koelb has a major commitment to a number of interesting texts that he discusses, from Rabelais and Boccaccio to Goethe and Hawthorne to Kafka and Calvino, so that his work, unlike de Man's more polemical and theoretical writing, and despite a substantial meta-discussion of his approach, really aims at "working with" de Manian rhetorical reading. The premise is twofold: that de Man has a central insight, namely his awareness of the wild-card nature of rhetorical figures as places that de/re/con/fuse meaning in a text; Koelb follows him in making his study generally focused on reading as a problem of rhetoric, as with de Man defined in a restrictive way as the third part of rhetoric, *elocutio*, style, especially in both the use of figures and tropes; that de Man is a dangerous influence. This second premise comes to the surface in his conclusion, where he admits he finds in de Man the "darker side of rhetoric."[72] Though he grants there is in de Man a Barthesian side that celebrates "the prolific fertility of unlimited semiosis," he is mainly aware of rhetoric as an immutable, like death and taxes, "to which we are condemned." For someone who still aspires to offer expert readings of important texts, de Man's tragic plot of more insight, more blindness, seems negative thinking, "semiological negativity." The project of "working with" de Manian deconstruction as a way of sponsoring readings seems indeed to offer only one obvious path: de Manian deconstruction as reading. Koelb, like deconstructive disciples of de Man, is willing to grant that deconstruction exists, as a kind of place of ultimate negativity in reading: "that incompatible, perhaps mutually destructive readings of a single text are possible." His good book interests me here just because he wishes to do more with de Man, to find some exit to reading as interpretation.

The lesson would seem to be that one must think one's way beyond the shackles of a system of thought if one is to redirect its apparently compelling arguments. And this Koelb, like so many of the generation reading de Man (from which few of us are excluded; dull would we have to be not to have followed his brilliantly skeptical system!), has not wanted to do. This unwillingness is signed by a slip in his generally so perceptive text when it comes to Fish, a critic who has decisively not let himself be made a slave to anyone else's system (or even to his own earlier ones). Koelb quotes Fish on hating the isolation of sabbatical terms: "I run around and go out in the street and grab people: You want to hear about interpretation?"[73] Koelb uses this to characterize Fish as (like himself) someone who "cannot leave a text alone." But Fish wants to talk not about interpretations but interpretation: those matters of theory that don't go away and come up more aggressively and disturbingly the more one attempts to read.

Like so many thinkers about reading and readers, Koelb runs into difficulties deciding whether he is speaking generally of something in texts or in readers. His observations on the problem are candid and interesting: "If now I appear to advocate a kind of essentialism that understands rhetorical elements to be somehow 'in' texts, and then I turn around and suggest they are a matter of the reader's act of reading, it is because I really do mean both, since both are necessary for rhetorical construction to work: the rhetorical text and its reader cooperate in order to make rhetorical moments visible."[74] This read of his own work—in the preface that is inevitably a last word, perhaps written last—is attractive but really creates a balanced system where there are in reality only opposing ventures. His term rhetorical construction is central to one of his strategies; and it is of course created as a rhetorical term itself to try to limit the damage of de Manian deconstruction. One is disappointed to find it generally given a rather limiting meaning: the reading of a prior text constructed by the writer (not the reader) of the text under consideration. Koelb imagines the writer going through a kind of center of indifference in which he reads a prior text (of art or of a culture more generally, say in myth or folkways) deconstructively, finding in the rhetorical moments the possibility of de Manian negative semiosis. This has allowed the writer to read the prior text differently and thus to move through an eternal nay to the prior vision and on to his/her new eternal yea, the constructive reading that we may find in the new text. The model, subject of a fine interpretation by Koelb, is Goethe's *Iphigenia in Tauris*, which he reads as proposing, even discussing, its reconstruction of Euripides' limiting though tragic vision into a progressive Western humanism by insisting on a consistently different set of interpretations of tropic moments of possible difference/disagreement.

I want to return to this reading at the end but for now note only that it stymies de Manian negativity at the price of allowing the writer/text full control over his text: *he* may have all the space in the world to reread Euripides but for us there is none; and in a sense there is none for him either therefore; his reading of Euripides is bound to be not different readings but misreadings, the kind of creative misreadings that constitute Harold Bloom's own rather Manichean system of reading, where the best readers lack all imagination and the worst are filled with the passionate intensity of genius. Goethe may do this, the implication is, but we are not forced to do it with his text. Dangerous deconstruction has been kicked upstairs for use by literary professionals only, too dangerous for the rest of us who are thus spared its use. This of course leaves Koelb, like most intentionalist Hirschian readers, a little hung up over where the interpretation is located. It is not, he insists, a biographical, genetic explanation of the text: though in fact the reading creates a kind of allegory of the creation of the text as its reading, as Bloom's readings of misreadings also do (Koelb, I should be clear, takes little interest in Bloom's system despite their crossings here). Or Koelb sometimes comes close to offering his readings as models of how writers used tropes and figures (parts of *elocutio*) to create rhetorical machines for their audience (normally separate in *inventio*). But here he comes dangerously close to harnessing de Man's wild horses of rhetoric to Wayne Booth's dray of reader-controlling rhetoric. Like Booth, he is in fact falling into a pre-New Critical reading of a text as an interpretation that places the critic in the privileged position of author's spokesperson, building a reading on what he/she believes the author had in mind, checked against a contextual knowledge of biography and history. The critic is equated with the author, in the traditional intentionalist manner. Dangerous semiosis is contained by merely a sophisticated version of a historicist reading, which emerges smoothly in the summary vision of Goethean German humanism, which we all think we know somewhat and of which we easily credit Koelb with expert knowledge. Alas, he would thus seem a good candidate for a de Manian blindness as insight reading of his reading of Goethe!

I am not going to offer that here; the good reader of de Man may do his work for him with delight. I am more interested in his more typical reading approach that, going off in quite a different direction, keeps this book from reverting to a collection of well-informed historicist and intentionalist readings of major authors who use many rhetorical effects (again read tropical or figurative language, though Koelb is especially good in finding expansions of de Manian indeterminate moments in tropes other than metaphor—hyperbole, for instance—or in ambiguous speech acts). For all his anxieties about de Manian rhetorical negativity, Koelb shares with de Man a love of tropical/figurative intricacies; indeed his unfolding of varieties of what Empson rightly called ambiguities, even if that term has not been fashionable among deconstructors, is the best part of this work. But if Koelb has added some good models to Empsonian/de Manian exploration of ambiguity/rhetorical moments, he has also demonstrated the old Marxist adage that he who takes to bed a bourgeois wife will someday find himself on the middle-class side of the barricades. Koelb finds himself especially interested in texts by self-conscious writers who self-reflexively reveal their own contemplation of rhetorical (again, tropical and figurative) language. Indeed his book is filled with such clever folk—Rabelais, Büchner, Hoffman, Hawthorne, Hans Christian Andersen, Kafka, Nathalie Sarraute, Calvino—and offers good readings of these good reads about writing. But what have we here then? Not a new theory-inspired read but a repeat of de Manian thematics: readings about texts that speak to us of our preoccupation with reading, especially our preoccupation with rhetoricity as unreadable, or in Koelb's more moderate approach, ultimately indeterminate.[75]

Here Koelb believes the important interpretation the author gives us in the text is precisely his/her own awareness of the ambiguity of tropes and metaphors: shall we read them, for instance, literally or tropically? ("My love is a rose": I love roses? or Ms. X is rose-like?) What seems like Koelb's immersion in the destructive element of negative semiosis is here, as in de Man, a guaranteed reading: text, author, critic all agree that the main interpretive result is the ambiguities of living in a world in which tropic language offers ambiguities galore. But of course this is, as with de Man, just a particular critic's focus, one he shares with much modern literature of his *Zeitgeist* and one which tunnels its way through earlier works looking for compatible texts. Calvino's charming story "All at One Point"[76] makes my point. Koelb reads this story about what we were like in prelapsarian days when we were all packed together ultra-claustrophobically but warmly in our original universal black hole as a story about the distance and difference that come with enough space to separate tenor from vehicle in our rhetorical language. In his fascinating reading it is indeed that gap that opens up the universe as one large place of distance and difference. Well and fine; but this interpretive *Gestalt*, to use Iser's term, brings into focus this thematic at the expense of repressing others that will be as obvious to other readers who come to the story with other preoccupations. The obvious one of course is not literal and figurative meanings but social closeness and distance, which are the subjects of the figurative play in which everything really was once close as can be. The science-fantasy, played as Koelb rightly remarks, with great lightness, allows us the distance to look at the good and bad of closeness—what we all want and what we all fear—with a little distance that actually enacts the sense of not being able to hold onto a closeness that is desired but lost by that very desire (Mrs. Ph(i)Nk_0, promiscuous lover of many in such a torridly close zone, attempts to make some nice pasta to bring them all even closer emotionally, but this erring Eve succeeds only in accidentally exploding out the universe). This way of reading the story is of course one and only one of many possible routes through the tale. I don't wish here to argue one against the other, only to insist that focus on the text as talking about its textuality, its awareness of its own rhetorical structures as placing its own indecidability or difficulty at the center of its meaning, is by nature limiting even as it offers itself as comprehensive. Like de Man, Koelb seems to propose a final interpretation of the text as "really" talking about itself but in fact he only offers himself reading with one obsession that always finds its target, as all critical obsessions do: indeed he reads as a de Manian critic. Despite his intention of reading with de Man beyond de Man, he regresses to that black hole of interpretation.

Good as Koelb's examples are, excellent as his command of the intricacies of different kinds of figural/literal configuration is, his overall project here thus seems a negative experiment in avoiding de Manian negation while holding on to de Man's preoccupation with abstract analysis of the elocutionary effects of rhetoric. Either he is driven back into the kinds of traditional interpretations leveraged by historical context and speculations about intention that de Man especially opposed before he came to oppose more sophisticated operations of blindness; or he is forced into repeating de Man's own limited strategies for self-reflexive reading. The exit must be found by reconceiving the entire project, not by trying to put it to work. And here let me just return to the promising talk of the Preface: there we are encouraged to think that writers' constructive rhetorical reading may be similar to that of readers (for instance, readers of the writer). But in fact Koelb will not give up the fiction that he can read from the text a Hirschian meaning, the author's really intended text, so he can not take what seems the next step of allowing everyone a constructive reading that builds upon a prior deconstruction. That way, apparently, madness lies: but we have seen this is the natural way of what Bloom would call strong writers so why not allow it for strong readers. My point isn't to assert the romantic ideology of strong (and weak) imaginations but to note the disruptive and dynamic model for making new readings that this offers as against de Man's skeptical system of static and uniform readings/non-readings. The exit back to interpretive reading is through insight that constructs one set of readings out of the deconstructive, destructive semiosis of multiple possible meanings. Rhetorical (tropical, figurative) moments naturally get organized by a strong reader like Goethe to follow a master concern. Strong readers will as naturally find their own routes through Goethe's own work that reflect and restate their own concerns. And if figures and tropes don't have the same awesome function here as they did in de Man's system, they are useful places, not where the text speaks to us of our hopeless imprisonment but as places that offer, in Ross Chambers's useful adaption, room for maneuver. Since there is some unfairness in pressuring Koelb's book so heavily to make what is a general point about de Man, not a review of Koelb, I'll end noting that his brief very fine discussion of Nietzsche, which takes up where de Man left him (in rhetoric) offers something like this different view of reading as endlessly productive of new readings, even when we reread or read ourselves differently. For a philosopher that seems to Koelb okay; but aren't most of us in this discussion doctors of philosophy too who think by making strong acts of interpretation—just as the writers and philosophers do? And, of course, as real readers often have a reasonable mind to do.

IV. READING IN TEXTUAL POWER REREAD: THE BIG ONE THAT GOT AWAY

> Reading is transformational.... But this transformation cannot be executed however one wishes. It requires protocols of reading. Why not say it bluntly: I have not yet found any that satisfy me.
>
> Jacques Derrida, *Positions*

A revisit to Robert Scholes's interesting and even award-winning (Christian Gauss) survey of theory, *Textual Power: Literary Theory and the Teaching of English* (New Haven: Yale UP, 1985), offers a useful occasion to look in some detail at some of the larger issues raised by reader-oriented criticism. Scholes's book is especially impressive in his moderate attacks on what he calls hermetic criticism: deconstruction, social discourse theory, and postmodernism generally. He helpfully points out the metaphysical Continental idealist underpinnings to even this most skeptical set of Continental philosophical works, bringing down their excessive, really idealist claims for the dissociation of all language from reality (signifiers from referents) by appeal to the more universal skepticism (skeptical even of its own claims to ignorance) of the Anglo-American/Wittgensteinian tradition. His critique is moderate because he consistently acknowledges the power gained by a philosophy, whether Derrida's or Foucault's, that encourages us to see discourse and ideology everywhere tending to be imposed upon a text by cultural assumptions built into the very rhetorical structures of the textual tradition out of which the text is written. Language *is* about reality, has important connections to real referents, yet in some sense Scholes also grants the practical value of the premise that there is nothing not always already coded by cultural institutions, epistemes, discourses, and pre-texts—no *hors-texte.* Dealing with texts involves understanding the discursive and ideological premises built into their very language and structures.

The odd thing about Scholes's text as I now reread it—and it was a very influential one of its time—was that while nicely reeling in such truly big fish of the contemporary scene, Scholes has so much more trouble, really pulls and sweats and cusses over the line, with what he proposes to consider small fry by comparison—namely Fish, Bleich, and the rather variously sorted reader schools of the time. His prolonged verbal play at the gag line of Fish, over two rather ichthyo-obsessed and rather loosely angling chapters, is indeed evidence in his own rhetoric of his discomfort with the ideas of this school of scholarship, where he seems quite out of his element. His attempts to land the elegant and eloquent Stanley Fish by dismissing him as merely a master of "consummate rhetoric" (in the narrow sense of rhetoric as mere persuasion, Autolycan trickery and advertising) do not now seem persuasive. Fish has been a major proponent, then and since, of the reviving, serious meaning of rhetoric as a way of searching out truth in hard matters, and Scholes does not adequately confront the larger force of Fish's points but seems, unlike in the chapters on the whales of theory, mainly to make debating points and offer cavils.

The problem seems to be that Fish's kind of criticism is really too close to Scholes's own, enlightened structuralist views (enlightened precisely by post-structuralism). Fish's questions threaten to deconstruct the system of reading that Scholes propounds as his unquestioned premises in this book about other people's unquestioned premises. That this should be his own weak point suggests that premises about reading may be as fundamental, and as easily taken for granted—hidden essentialist beliefs (the "natural" way we all read)—as are philosophical (epistemological) premises about language and referents. Scholes's system of reading in this work is easy to state because it is presented so lucidly and well. He uses the great terms of the profession of interpretation—reading, interpretation, criticism—so that his system is bound to be memorable, or at least easy to remember. At the same time, by distributing these terms, he practices an open sleight of hand that limits and compartmentalizes their activity. What we have is really a kind of new formal sequence of interpretation, threefold rather than fourfold. In some sense his ontogeny of criticism also recapitulates its phylogeny. Reading, that mega-term in Fish's arsenal, is merely a kind of philology, reading the words and checking special meanings and history: what George Lyman Kittredge and B.J. Whiting used to do in the good old days of classroom instruction. Interpretation is a space for a structuralist's renewal of professions of faith. Codes, those mysterious essences of that tradition of pseudo-scientific criticism, click into place (note he doesn't say are applied by the reader, though structuralist criticism was always almost a reader criticism in this way) to reveal the meanings appropriate to the text. These are not any meanings from any code possessed by any reader or readerly group, though they are the codes of what Jonathan Culler, at the same awkward place in structuralism, called professional "literary competence."[77] They really allow, within the freer language of codes (which lets each structuralist reader in fact invent his own codes, as Barthes wonderfully and notoriously did with great panache in *S/Z*) the appearance of validity in E.D. Hirsch's conservative, historicist sense: a reconstruction of meaning as author (or was it the original audience?) would have coded it.[78]

Barthes was already on the edge of breaking with this compromise formation in his consciously arbitrary and experimental use of codes, whether in the direction of exploding different meanings in the text, à la post-structuralism, or in a freer use of codes as a reader system as he might have found it in the early, reader-empowering work of Umberto Eco.[79] But Scholes's book appeared after the fact of deluge and wished in a properly statesmanlike way to mediate between these new explosions of interpretation beyond historically valid meaning—deconstruction and the more dangerous enemy he turns to later, reader-oriented criticism—and traditional conservative modes of teaching and thinking in our profession. His project can be stated as how we can use the expansion of interpretation without being totally thrown off our traditional bearings as practical critics. To do so Scholes adds a third, quite separate act to his sets of interpretation, which he calls criticism. By this sanitary provision of a special sphere for its application, deconstruction can lie down peacefully with reading and interpretation, or to be more exact, with valid historical meaning. Especially the ferreting out of binary oppositions through deconstructive scrutiny of signifiers can allow us to identify discourse and ideology in the text (really in the interpretation of the text we have just completed by philological/historical and structuralist means). We can see the textual object as it really is and use it to interrogate ourselves as to our own positions. Thus we grow in self-understanding (or at least in self-proclamation as politically correct) by this cool evaluation of the text.

It is easy to see how Scholes has confined and controlled reading by laying down such a system of what I find it useful to call staged readings: prescribed, distinct activities in reading, one following the other. But he is perhaps only more candid than many theorists of interpretation, who, looked at from this point of view, are rather covertly presuming an ordered (usually also orderly) process of reading activity. Perhaps the best known would be E.D. Hirsch's distinction between meaning and significance. Meaning, offered as simply what the author meant, is, in terms of reading, a first-stage reading following assumptions about authorial intention and historical context. The second stage, presented as if it is merely another approach, but also made clearly secondary in value, is significance, which as a reading activity would be bringing to the text various approaches or knowledges. The important thing is that these not be promiscuously mixed.[80] Scholes would follow a very similar set of covert staged readings when he returned to systems of reading in *Protocols of Reading*; there readings are divided into centripetal and centrifugal, the first moving toward the text, the second away from it, but the primacy of the first is guaranteed by the way the distinction is created.[81]

Staged readings are obviously part of traditions, like those of reading in the Middle Ages, where levels of approaches to texts were commonly advocated, whether of different types of allegory or, as in Scholes, procedures of interpretation.[82] In Jewish tradition one can speak of Mishnah as communicating the traditional enactments simply and briefly. One could say Midrash gathers the traditional material from the written text according to certain rules. Finally, Talmud can be said to be the application of rules to new cases.[83] We are not surprised to find more recent conservative hermeneuticists doing the same. In the eighteenth century, the hermeneutic thinker Johann Martin Chladenius insisted on separating straightforward sense from application and digression.[84] Nor are we surprised, for instance, to find the neo-Aristotelian Chicago school of genre critics of the 1950s similarly wanting to constrain interpretation as working with interpretive details whereas criticism concerned itself with structural and generic wholes.[85] But staged readings are often hidden even in traditions and thinkers most closely associated with reader freedom. David Bleich, who has sponsored the rights of readers since the 1970s, nonetheless explains that reading must be a double process: first symbolize the text in one's mind, then resymbolize it as one's own.[86] Norman Holland, another critic devoted to listening to the individual reader, nonetheless formulates reading as a three stage event: taking in the material, sending it down into the unconscious, reinterpreting it as it emerges shaped by the reader's habitual identity. "The literant [read reader] creates meaning and feeling in one continuous and indivisible transaction."[87] But if anyone chose to meditate on the material without sending it down to the unconscious for reshaping he would be ruled out of order by these procedural rules.

Gerald Prince, another critic associated with reader theory, nonetheless uses Barthes's freeing system of a range of codes each capable of independent application to move back toward prescribed stages: the proairetic code offers a literal reading followed by application of the hermeneutic code for hidden meanings followed by use of the symbolic code for broader meanings imported by the reader.[88] No sooner did Umberto Eco, who can most properly be said to have begun the turn toward interest in the reader, begin to be nervous about the need to limit the reader's interpretation than he reverted to a bilevel staged reading in which naive reading is succeeded by interpretive reading.[89]

Even a more recent thinker on reading such as Peter Rabinowitz wishes to define the reading experience in a way that would limit any particular reading: in his opinion, we move from prior opinion before we read, to the experience itself, to the reworking of after reading. Specifically he finds, very much as does Scholes, reading moving from a judgment of author's intention to other levels of reading such as Freudian or political; like Scholes he sees the reader having to make an evaluation of the author's position in a political reading and then resisting it.[90] An interesting exception to such prescriptive views of staged readings is offered by Hillis Miller's *The Ethics of Reading*, when he discusses de Man's appearance of creating a staged system of reading. Although Miller is critiqued by Scholes for his generally positive view of de Man's system of reading,[91] Miller in fact has a reservation about de Man on just this issue of staging. He is uncomfortable to find that de Man resorts to a sequence and in apologizing for de Man he offers a suggestion worth considering: that this is an essentially fictional construction that should not be mistaken for the reality of interpretive reading. De Man's "ethicity" occurs "in the midst of an intricate sequence, the sequentiality of which is of course only a fiction, a convenience of thinking as a narrative what in fact always occurs in the tangle of an 'all at once' mixing tropological, allegorical, referential, ethical, political, and historical dimensions."[92] The point is a fine one, and for that reason alone I think obviously subject to suspicion: when are we to know that a staged reading is actually offered only as a useful fiction? Even if the author should think that this is what he or she is offering, how can she keep her readers from taking it as a controling system of reading? If, as I do, one finds Miller's description of the complex reality of reading persuasive, why would you wish to consider more orderly fictions? Suffice it to say that most theorists begin to offer such staged readings at precisely the point where they wish to constrain reading or, which is the same thing, where they fear allowing the reader too much freedom.

Now Fish and the very diverse reader-oriented criticism he is made to stand up for in Scholes's argument really can have no place in Scholes's system of staged reading; hence Fish is left until the end of the book to be disposed of. For Fish calls into question the possibility of such a rational way of reading altogether. Indeed, his challenge would be for Scholes to become self-conscious about what it means to read as a Scholesian threefold interpretive reader.[93] It is, in effect, to downgrade reading itself to almost a mechanical act, thus banishing any question about how text ceases to be text and becomes read; it is to insist on the primacy and correctness of an historical reading—and to insist that this is not just a goal of one kind of scholarship but an attainable reality—the thing as in fact it really is.[94] And it is to insist on a very dispassionate activation of the reader's own intellectual horizon and personal concerns in the text: they (the readers' views and interests) have no place in the reading/interpretation of the text, only in our dispassionate evaluation of it. This last point sounds like an opening for the dullest kind of moral/political criticism in which students who have had no real engagement with the power of the text in their interpretation (which has been by the historical book) are now encouraged to make abstract judgments of the Shakespeare was an imperialist, Dickens a Jew hater, T.S. Eliot a fascist variety.[95] (Shall we add other critical judgments such as that Shaw was a dirty atheist/communist and Tennessee Williams a degenerate? For politically incorrect people play this game too, indeed invented it.) Meanwhile the real power of the text, which in the case of a great piece of writing is to keep calling out new, passionate engagements from each generation of readers and each individual reader—not ideas and slogans to judge but a full experience against which to react—seems to be totally defused.

Scholes makes logical mincemeat of Fish's awkward, now much-adjusted concept of communities of readers; from his structuralist familiarity with this kind of code—after all, a code was always in fact somebody or some group's code, even if this reader side of structuralism was regularly denied because of structuralists' scientistic, universalist leanings—he can see that

Fish hopelessly mixes apples and oranges, large linguistic communities, smaller ideological or social or special knowledge communities. We can hear him thinking how could such an intelligent and persuasive critic be so fuzzy in his theory of interpretation as to try to propose such an incongruous category of interpretation; at best, the various communities would need to be compartmentalized, as Scholes did his critical categories, not just into separate "codes" but into three- or fourfold kinds of interpretation. But this is just Fish's larger point: that only a very mechanical, exceptionally rational kind of reading divides up and compartmentalizes what is most often a single act: the critical development of an interpretive act of reading, threefold in one. For Fish, the opening recognition of the text is simply that, a recognition of the mere fact that the words are there; to go further in first stage reading would actually import all kinds of more complicated interpretive moves under the guise of mere "philology" or contextual information.[96] While he eventually acknowledged that his earlier, well-known Fishian reading (reading word by word what a text does to us) had covert stages, he continues in his later, legal work, to affirm a unitary, unstaged reading: "I do not proceed in two steps, first processing the text at a basic level and then sorting text into pattern and meaning in accordance with some rule or calculus. Rather, the act of sorting is coextensive with the act of reading."[97]

Now what seems to trouble Scholes is that this kind of critical unitarianism opens all kinds of possible irrationalities in interpretation. There is Fish's class, who read a prior class's list of authors on the blackboard, as they have learned to read—as a revenant community of seventeenth-century readers. Here a good interpretive activity—to follow Scholes's own ideas—actually being encouraged by Fish reading seventeenth-century work as a seventeenth-century reader *might* have is mercilessly degraded by application to the wrong text! Or a fundamentalist baseball player jumps over the (boring) structuralist signs and rules of the game to impose his providentialist vision on it. Scholes reasonably tries to straighten these muddles out; but the readers would object to having their power, exercised in these texts of textbooks and baseball, so diminished. Why can't we read as seventeenth-century critics on one day and as Scholesian critics on another? If you want to look at the everyday rules and facts of baseball rather than revel in home runs read as God-acts, then I will simply remind you that God created the world and all in it, including this favorite game of His and its rules. (And if you talk to me about baseball history and Commissioners and rules I will simply remind you that he—the highest Commissioner of baseball—works in strange ways.) Fish's later, and more impressive theoretical writing has focused on the nature of truth. He insists it isn't a baseball game to be played by Scholes-given rules with clear strikeouts and foul balls. It is a game played by readers who show the power of their truth in the act of arguing over texts. Reading is what we find in texts given our entire leaning, disposition, ideology. It is a site of necessary controversy and it can't be cut to more regular proportions or stuck into controlling, sanitizing compartments.

Fish and Scholes are indeed almost too close to the same general community: well-trained historical critics very aware of the structured and x-fold interpretive games of the past. Scholes can appreciate Fish's learned and fine sense of the historical genesis and reception of the seventeenth-century text (didn't Scholes's structuralism cut its teeth on Spenser with equal historical accuracy for the sixteenth-century reading?) and wonder how he should wish to empower lesser readers. He should have seen the special power of Fish's practical work, where Fish, as Culler acutely remarked, read as a Fishian critic, a community of one very twentieth-century sensibility reading with a special closeness and time-of-the-text perspective that made his work seem like the only post-New Critical exciting interpretive game in town.[98] A broader perspective will remind us that we historians don't own literature, that poets (e.g., T.S. Eliot) do more to bring alive seventeenth-century texts than all the well-informed academic critics, just as Peter Brook and company kept Shakespeare's plays (those now often virtually incomprehensible texts) alive for the twentieth century by regularly outraging scholarly critics with their directors' theaters based on contemporary engagements with the text. A text can't be proclaimed as finally interpreted by anyone, no matter how learned. New dimensions do open up with each new horizon of each new generation, including even each new generation of historical critics who see the historical context anew, as a generation of imaginative cultural historians of literature did in the late twentieth century. Great texts survive and prosper in the wars of truth over interpretation, where no perspective has the last word.

One final point: Scholes wished correctly and fairly to allow the wolves of ideology and discourse analysis into the traditional sheepfold of criticism. No doubt, in the years before and after he wrote this book, they came deep into the barns and farmhouses themselves, so that for a while we English professors, the exemplary cash cows of the past, were now looked on by deans and other reverend figures of the university with deepest suspicion—far worse than sociologists! But this happened in a Fishian way, not a Scholesian way. The power of ideologies was tested and proved not by dull moments of dispassionate judgment but as new modes of reading. We read as feminist readers (of so many sorts), as gay, lesbian, or queer readers, as neo-Marxist readers, as third-world and other Other readers, as deconstructionist readers and, even when we didn't want to admit that it was merely another mode of reading, as New Historical readers; and we read not in compartments of reading, interpretation, criticism but in unified engagements with the entire text, from language to explicit ideology. Ideologies worked naturally to find a space for themselves in the rereading and reinterpretation of texts. They shaped our intellectual world—how we saw great texts—as they wished to shape our political and social world. And they of course demanded a rereading of the canon itself.

Scholes's work, with its entirely reasonable tone and approach, no doubt at the time an aromatic kind of oil from a well-lit lamp poured on troubled professional waters, impressed me but also provoked me when I went back to it to see what connection it had to the discussion of reading at the time. Just because it does not offer merely a conservative view of political and social issues, it seemed to suggest how the opening to multiple reading approaches might be corralled and restricted by professional interests and habits of mind. Ideological readers may have been generally tolerated, and especially out of concerns for gender, sexual, and ethnic sensitivities. But historically based approaches, often working through preferred stages of reading procedure and generally implying that there is only one intended and historically correct reading, have become once again, after the interest in readers, after the interest in political readings, the professional norm. Scholes's work—and his specific interest in reader theory continued not only with *Protocols of Reading* back then, where a twofold system of centripetal and centrifugal readings replaced the more hierarchical model of his earlier work, but right up to the recent and charming *The Crafty Reader*[99]—highlights the alternatives we face and that his earlier work debated: we can continue the opening to multiple readings and full engagement in interpretation that opened with the major interest in reading of the 1970s and 1980s, or we can retreat to limited historically or author-oriented readings that allow a moral frosting on the properly staged and prepared interpretation.

With great respect for Robert Scholes—who after all confronts these issues clearly where others merely sweep them under their heavy rugs of historical, archival work muttering something about reader-response criticism and the big questions of interpretation it reopened being merely an annoying nest of effete paradoxes and theoretical problems that can safely be ignored—I will choose open-ended, unchanneled reading experiences. Not ignorant or unthoughtful ones, merely those not already forced into professional molds and thus able to breathe with readers and with their changing interests. Rather than retreating into history and pre-packaged interpretations, we should become more and more self-conscious about the fact of various readings. Contrary to Fish's own segmentations of readers, we should realize that we are not stuck in some one community, as religious readers were in ages of unquestioned truths. We can cross borders of reading and try reading as an Other. We can read and reread. I won't predict some new compromise melting pot of different readings, which is in no way desirable and would ultimately act as a hegemonic viewpoint to inhibit the emergence of the next set of needful new readings. But I will give two cheers for a liberal critical world in which we engage and re-engage fully and freely with others' readings (including readings by mulitple Others) and our own. This would be my version of Scholes's reasonable openness to ideology in reading—open to the very way in which we read as the performance of our beliefs and politics and our engagements with those of other people.

V. THEORY POSTSCRIPT: COMMUNITIES AND SCHOOLS OF FISH

I feel obliged to comment, though I will be brief, on Fish's once (still?) influential notion of communities of interpretation. Fish got there because he came to see the fallacy of his original reader-response approach on a theoretical level. This exciting form of close reading, word by word, always asking not what a text meant but what it did to us the readers, really offered one reader and his responses as a normative reader for us all. And it took one mode of reading, forward in time, word by word, as a universal: one size fits all readings and readers. Realizing this mistake, which had been a fortunate fall in giving him the self-assurance to offer an exciting set of new readings of seventeenth-century literature, Fish needed a better conceptualization of the variety of reading approaches that he was forced to recognize; and he reached out for communities of interpretation as an idea. This he offered as a way of locating meaning in the social group from which readers emerged rather than in author, text, or individual reader.[100]

The subsequent controversy displayed the problem with the attractively simple view that interpretations were pre-formed by communities and given to individuals like programs capable of processing whatever data are fed into them. His theory is founded, as he readily acknowledges, on the premise of the "power of social institutional circumstances to establish norms of behavior."[101] The objections now seem both diverse and fairly obvious: how can change ever be possible if people are so well programmed with interpreting structures?[102] What to do with an individual in touch with two communities? Here Fish answered that there could be two interpreting programs. But, then, what cues one or the other? Is it possible to evade normal cues and plug in the "wrong" program? What keeps the individual from mixing programs creatively? What happens when cultural hybridity happens? Are border cultures cued to one or another interpretive program, or do the cultures somehow mix? If they do, then should we say that cultures are always mixing, thus always complicating programs of interpretation?[103]

Another set of problems with Fish's mosaic of cultures approach had to do with the whole question of program application. Fish's famous examples, the fundamentalist baseball player, his class on seventeenth-century interpretation, face problems rather close to their programs: God's will in the fall of a baseball; religious interpretation of random events (that list of names of contemporary linguists from his prior course still on the blackboard).[104] But real interpreters in the same traditions notoriously fall into conflict over hard points, difficult applications. The experience often then leads to interpretive moves that really act as creative adjustments of the tradition of interpretation. Communities of application (say strict versus loose interpretation of the United States Constitution) become new communities of interpretation. But doesn't this suggest what every graduate student knows, that the theory (here read interpretive tradition) that one brings to a text gets recut and refitted in the act of application. That is, Fish's idea of communities of interpretation doesn't just reify communities; it reifies interpretive traditions into simplistic recipes, and this not because Fish isn't aware of the forces in a community that shape interpretation as extensive and diffuse but because his unifying explanation of interpretation as in the community must tend to create a limiting model of interpretation to justify its ability to produce one kind of interpretation or another; otherwise the community would not offer more than versions of possible interpretations.

Here I can ask my reader to kindly perform the application of my arguments against cultural determinism (II.vii, above) to Fish's conception of community-controlling readings. Those arguments, I hope varied and nuanced enough in themselves, deprecate both reductions: culture is never one simple structure unfissured enough to provide universal systems of interpretation that all can apply identically; and cultures do not have the power to override all individual diversity or even innovation and creativity. There is always some play between the individual created by the culture and the individual recreating the culture.[105] One may grant that large systems of culture may have certain predispositions, without thereby being able to predict the interpretive positions of individuals in the culture.[106] Fish should have understood the instability and mutability of cultural forces and their systems of interpretation because he is an expert on the period of wars of truth in the seventeenth century, when changing and fragmenting religious cultures and their systems of interpretation were growing up everywhere. He seems rather to follow what they said, that their culture and ways to truth were immutable and worth dying for, rather than what they did, which was to keep changing and fragmenting, clashing and reconstructing themselves. Fish is right to see how often interpretive positions follow patterns in communities; but he sees only half the picture when he misses the place that individual argument, disagreement, even originality (there I dared to use the word) play in changes in communities over time. All is not change; but all is also not stasis.

Fish will answer that he disposed of all such objections to his theory's difficulty in accommodating change in his essay of that name.[107] I confess I find this essay of a thinker I admire a great deal too casuistic. The problem is that the initial premise, that community totally determines meaning, allows only one clear explanation of change: that we change only when something (say a natural shock) changes our culture, which changes us. Because he is committed to a reduction of individuals to the intellectual systems of their cultures, he is thwarted in the usual explanations of change, needing to reduce all new ideas, such as deconstruction, to adaptations of earlier ideas/predilections. The big picture that gets lost here, as also in the historically more sophisticated thinking of Foucault, is the old one of the individual's relation to history. Not only is it hard to say that Derrida, for instance, didn't contribute something unique to the discussion that had to do with the individuality of Derrida, mind and will (or Fish himself for that matter), but it is also hard to say that there weren't individual decisions made by those sufficiently impressed by his work to "convert" to deconstruction. History is shaped by *grands hommes* like Derrida, yet there would have been no deconstruction without the sum of innumerable biographies of lesser readers and thinkers. Fish's confusion is about determinism. Wishing to deny the concept of a Cartesian rational decision-maker within each of us, he ends up arguing a different point, that the individual is under the control of society's community of interpretation. The individual may not have some rational freedom but may be free to be moved by passion (conversion to deconstruction for love of a fair deconstructionist), by external event (conversion when an apple lands on his head and breaks apart), or even by striking evidence or a forceful argument. On the last, Fish goes to great lengths to indicate that this can only be the result of an individual already residing in a community that appreciates striking evidence or strong arguments. The Zulu might have had a much harder time muddying the faith of the seventeenth-century Dean of St. Paul's than the nineteenth-century Bishop of Natal, it is true. Yet the same arguments seemed ridiculous to many of the Bishop's contemporaries from the same tradition. Arguments can persuade; they can fail to persuade.[108] The causes are diverse and hard to determine; they are often biographic or accidental; suffice it to say that radical conversions do take place, sometimes for more, sometimes for less rational reasons.

Where Fish needs a modern example he often reaches for the most hermetically sealed and simplistic kinds of communities, those of our religious fundamentalists. Students of recent centuries can hardly evade the broad phenomenon of emerging cosmopolitanism within cultures and increasing hybridization at the edges of cultures. Individuals, as I have been arguing, may not be originating uncaused causes; they may even, to some God's eye or infinitely patient computer, be determined by various causes in all they do and think; but they certainly are able in practice, as self-aware subjectivities, to carry a variety of views, from a variety of positions or cultural histories, whether in their cuisine, their music, or their approaches to conceptual thinking. And they keep acting as if new combinations are what they do best, whether in East-West California restaurants, the jazz-classical hybrids of Gershwin, or the feminist-queer deconstruction of Judith Butler. Left to their own good young brains, graduate students will do the same with approaches to interpretation: as one of mine recently blended Lacan and Abraham and Torok with historical views of Victorian mourning ritual to interpret the palpable presence of absent fathers in Victorian novels and poems thematizing crypts and graveyards.[109] Theory purists may look only for students to get patriarchal theorists' views right ("getting it right"). The best new thinking will usually prove to be hybridization or recombinant reformulation of prior thinking. Again, these may not be acts of rational freedom (my former student doesn't appear irrational or unfree either) but they are originating activities of the individual who thus remakes a piece of the community.

There is a nest of ironies in Fish's over-reliance on community in theory. Such a *cul de sac* that his theory of communities seemed to threaten to throw him into is very much against Fish's own naturally argumentative nature. He has himself been such an individual voice as an interpreter, so ready to go where his latest light takes him; he so exemplifies the pragmatic and syncretic approaches that transverse, merge, and break down different fixed systems; he is himself much more the iconoclast than any kind of follower or stabilizer of traditional views; in sum, he is no community player. Ever his own community of one, Fish reading, as Culler remarked, as a Fishian critic, couldn't hold him; once identified with his community, he left it a ghost town of critical approach. His succeeding polemic on communities of interpretation, like so many of his controversies, takes the rhetorical form of one new-seeing maverick against a million conformists.

The mistake, as in so much theory, is to take the simplest case as exemplar and model for all cases. In the narrowest traditions there are at least attempts to impose an interpretive system on all sacred texts, perhaps on all texts. But these systems, if not extreme in our brief 200,000-year history (really only about 70,000 after our near extinction; and only about 5,000+ years of text—starting in the late fourth millennium BCE), are extremes to us who worry about reading apart from theological activity. We may talk end of subjectivity, but we reserve the right to talk something else next year. We are part of a community that everyone knows thinks it is special; and the university community *is* special in agreeing not to agree. Let religious fanatics and fanatical baseball players follow the interpretive dictates of their communities; ours have no human or cultural dictators, only Fishes who tell us we must do as they say we do, not as they do themselves.[110]

I dwell on the problems in Fish's theory of community because it offered another too simple way of heading off the utopian possibilities of the turn to reading of the early 1980s. Everything is interpretation, Fish himself argued; but don't worry, that is all determined by the community and allows no place for individual eccentricity, wildness, or anti-professorial behavior. The institution of literature that Culler worried about will not be harmed; when change comes it will be welcomed as the obvious truth of another time. One is tempted to add that we are in the best of all possible worlds because whatever is is right for those who believe it now, and everyone does and always will. Like his associates Walter Benn Michaels and Steven Knapp,[111] Fish enables a turn to history. Reader theory effectively ends with all power (of intrepretation) to the community that controls readers rather than in the readers. So we should study the social webs that determined the readers rather than worry about interpretation itself. But if meaning does not lie entirely in the community, this move fails and history becomes a part of what we may do, not its main concern. Theory may have consequences by persuading individuals to change their interpretive ways from those of their initial community and individuals may be persuaded of new interpretations of works of literature or even devise their own. Fish keeps insisting that theory has only political consequences but that it does have these. A more thoroughgoing neo-pragmatism would begin by seeing all argument as political, acts of persuasion that may always succeed in persuading individuals.[112] Fish's theory of communities effectively stops the reader-friendly drift of his earlier work which could easily have moved toward a Rortyan belief in persuasive argumentation as the only fixed thing in the game of interpretation.[113] Instead, he needs to stop individual persuasion by his constricting theory of community. It was alright when a party of one performed his new persuasive interpretative method in early Fish; but rather than admit others he found a way to stop the party entirely—referring readers on to those institutional professionals, the New Historians.[114]

NOTES: SECTION THREE

1 See II.xviii, n. 408.

2 See Harold Bloom, *How to Read and Why* (New York: Scribner, 2000); Denis Donoghue, *The Practice of Reading*; (New Haven: Yale UP, 1998) Robert Alter, *The Pleasures of Reading in an Ideological Age* (1989; rev. New York: Norton, 1996).

3 I have not said a great deal about the thinking, early and late, of Norman Holland, not because I disrespect or disagree with him but because I find his project plausible and well pursued, even if his particular focus is not my own. His early psychoanalytic look at readers (rather than the more common shrinking of authors) led him very early to look at real readers reading, a concern generally more of the late 1980s and 1990s than the 1970s: see esp. *Five Readers Reading* (New Haven: Yale UP, 1975). His relentless focus on deep emotional response to texts, however, seems to preclude other kinds of varied individual readerly activity. It is the focus of his psychoanalytic specialty and, like psychoanalysis, the *bête noire* of certain unself-aware persons. His work since then on the cognition of reading opens another, indeed, more empirical, area of exploration of individual reading. See his *The Critical I* (New York: Columbia UP, 1992).

4 A term suggested by Peter Rabinowitz, though I don't know if he was the first to use it, and somewhat in use for the range of thinking from issues of reader interpretation to the psychology, sociology, and history of reading. Reader response, still also in use, covers a more narrow set of issues and is identified with a period (ca. 1975–1985).

5 In fact, there has been a great deal of further exciting work, such as that of Matei Calinescu, Ross Chambers, Elizabeth Flynn, Robert Holub, Clayton Koelb (whose work I look at in III.iii, below), Steven Mailloux, Victor Nell, Peter Rabinowitz himself, and Michael Steig, to name some of the most prominent, all also quite different and little in touch with each other—as anyone who knows their work is aware. And there has been a good deal of work on history of reading, including Alberto Manguel's general history, and on reception history, both of course convenable to a history-oriented critical scene. I might cite Steig as being especially concerned with issues of individual interpretation. He follows David Bleich, a major force in reader response though never as prominent as Fish, Iser, or Holland, who also continues to work in the area. However, *The Double Perspective: Language, Literary, and Social Relations* (New York: Oxford UP, 1988) takes a very broad view of reading, writing, and society. Like Holland, he did look at individual reading styles and even advocated diversity of reading approaches.

6 I recur to the interestingly different work on women readers elsewhere in my discussion (see III.iii and ns. 47, 48) and also in my concluding Section Four—generally as a place of openness to reader diversity and individuality. One of my Broadview reviewers noted nonetheless the male lineup of this section. That made me more conscious of the ways in which many reader theorists subverted possibilities of diverse readings in order to reestablish their own readings—their versions of patriarchal authority offered as substitutions for what Toril Moi identified as the intentionalist establishment

of the "patriarchal practice of authority": *Sexual/Textual Politics: Feminist Literary Theory* (London: Methuen, 1985), pp. 62–63.

7 Jonathan Culler, Tzvetan Todorov, Gerald Prince, and Christine Brooke-Rose were among those claimed for reader response by the anthologies.

8 *Diacritics* 11 (Spring 1981): 2–13. Reprinted in *Doing What Comes Naturally: Change, Rhetoric, and the Practice of Theory in Literary and Legal Studies* (Durham: Duke UP, 1989), pp. 68–86.

9 Wolfgang Iser, "Talk like Whales: A Reply to Stanley Fish," *Diacritics* 11 (Fall 1981): 82–87.

10 See especially Wolfgang Iser, *The Fictive and the Imaginary: Charting Literary Anthropology* (Baltimore: Johns Hopkins, 1993); also his *Prospecting: From Reader Response to Literary Anthropology* (Baltimore: Johns Hopkins, 1989), where the final essay introduces the overall project. Despite a certain continuing interest in the reader in the new project, the *Prospecting* volume, with its brief section on reader response in opening, nonetheless gives the impression that the subject of reader response, as opposed to that particular quarrel, has been worked out and is now to be abandoned for a new lode.

11 By no means the case as, under the broader term, reader theory has continued in a sporadic but interesting way: see discussion in III.i and n. 5, above, and IV.i, below.

12 Robert Scholes, *Textual Power: Literary Theory and the Teaching of English* (New Haven: Yale UP, 1985); the culminating attack on Fish is 149–65, preceded by a chapter entitled "Is there a Fish in this Text," on Pound's ideas of reading.

13 Fish, *Doing What Comes Naturally*, p. 82.

14 Originally published in *Critical Inquiry* 2 (Spring 1976) 465–85; citations below are from *Reader-Response Criticism: From Formalism to Post-Structuralism*, ed. Jane P. Tompkins (Baltimore: Johns Hopkins UP, 1980).

15 "Interpreting the *Variorum*," p. 172.

16 Jonathan Culler, *On Deconstruction: Theory and Criticism after Structuralism* (Ithaca: Cornell UP, 1982), p. 66.

17 "Interpreting the *Variorum*," pp. 172–73.

18 Reed Way Dasenbrock, former student of Fish's, criticizes his conception of professional literary learning as a model of initiation into the approval of a special, learned community rather than a mutual dialogue of learning between teacher and student where there is not one single professional community approach: *Truth and Consequences* (University Park: Pennsylvania State UP, 2001), pp. 207–09. Fish's earlier, reader-response work on Milton was founded on an assumption that he had special access, through professional, historical training, to what the author (Milton) intended his original readers to respond to as a member of his own community. See his *Surprised by Sin: The Reader in* Paradise Lost (Basingstoke: Palgrave-Macmillan, 1967).

19 "Interpreting the *Variorum*," p. 176. I examine Fish's convoluted position on intention in Appendix 2.

20 For fuller discussion of Fish's theory of communities of interpretation see III.v, below.

21 Culler, *On Deconstruction*, p. 65, notes that Fish acknowledges he does readings to conform readers to his community, not to encourage variety or individuality of response. Fish reiterated this assertion of his own particular community values at a theoretically more interesting level in an essay, "Yet Once More," *Professional Correctness* (Oxford: Clarendon, 1995). There he insists that English is a professional community with its own code, its unspoken sense of the "the kind of thing we do around here" (p. 16)—for Fish the period expert very much a matter of historical contextual knowledge at play in interpretation. His antagonistic tone and sense that he will offend many actually in the profession indicates how restrictive and normative a community he considers this to be.

22 Stanley Fish, "Literature in the Reader: Affective Stylistics," in Tompkins, p. 75.

23 Jane Tompkins, "The Reader in History: the Changing Shape of Reader Response," in Tompkins, ed.; esp. pp. 201–06.

24 Roman Ingarden, *The Cognition of the Literary Work of Art* (Evanston: Northwestern UP, 1973) and *The Literary Work of Art* (Evanston: Northwestern UP, 1973). Iser critiques Ingarden in *The Act of Reading* (Baltimore: Johns Hopkins UP, 1978), pp. 170–79, for imposing a code for reading that gives most of the control to the text, leaving the reader to add only banal details. Paul Armstrong, *Conflicting Readings* (Chapel Hill: U of North Carolina P, 1990), p. 167, defends Iser from charges that he follows Ingarden in making the text the primary determinant of interpretation. Wayne C. Booth's development of the implied author in *The Rhetoric of Fiction* (Chicago: U of Chicago P), a work arguing for rhetoric (by an author working on a reader) as a way of thinking of fiction, was an obvious launching site for Iser's idea of an implied reader, also in a mode of rhetorical direction of reader by author, though with an area of reader freedom.

25 David Bleich, *Readings and Feelings: An Introduction to Subjective Criticism* (Urbana, IL: NCTE, 1975) and his more theoretical work of that period, *Subjective Criticism* (Baltimore: Johns Hopkins UP, 1978). For Norman Holland see *The Dynamics of Literary Response* (New York: Columbia, 1968), a work that models psychological responses, as well as *Five Readers Reading*, a work that investigates individual differences in readings correlated to psychological profiles; in both studies, reading is clearly tuned to emotional response, reading from the gut, rather than merely to interpretation for meaning.

26 See the testimony by mainly high-school teachers in Nicholas J. Karolides, ed., *Reader Response in the Classroom: Invoking and Interpreting Meaning in Literature* (New York: Longman, 1992), a work paying homage to Louise Rosenblatt's transactional thinking about reading but very open to varied

emotional and personal responses in the classroom. For university work based on such classrooms see Michael Steig, *Stories of Reading: Subjectivity and Literary Understanding* (Baltimore: Johns Hopkins UP, 1989), a work indebted to both Bleich and Holland.

27 Iser took offense at this statement (as perhaps with my raising again the business with Fish) in a presentation of a condensed version of this chapter at the MLA convention in Chicago, 1995. He noted the experimental work of some of his students in Salzburg and Italy. I let the assertion stand as there is no indication in his work that it was used to build his theory.

28 In his brief answer to Fish, "Talk like Whales," Iser especially opposed Fish's implication that his own approach by interpretive communities would eliminate the subjective experience of the reader. He focused almost exclusively on the issue, raised in an aggravated form by Fish's monism, of his own division of the terrain of reading into three parts, a given of words in a text, determinate interpretations, and indeterminate (gap filling etc.) ones. He re-asserted the existence of all three. His focus suggests especially clearly the issue between Iser and Fish, with Fish's stress on all reading as interpretation, Iser's on the experiential nature of reading as a personal aesthetic action.

In the "Interview" in *Prospecting*, p. 53, Iser denied Norman Holland's assertion that he was mainly concerned with meaning, as opposed to a variety of other kinds of reader activities. Iser explained that he wished to examine the process, before meaning, by which "the aesthetic object" is produced in the reader's mind. In this it begins in experience: the object "might simply be an experience—which of course initially it always will be." He concludes: "I should not want to identify the aesthetic object solely with meaning; had I wished to do so, I should scarcely have bothered to use two different terms."

29 See especially his relatively early (1967 in French) study *Speech and Phenomena, and Other Essays on Husserl's Theory of Signs*, trans. David B. Allison (Evanston, IL: Northwestern UP, 1973).

30 Terry Eagleton, *The Ideology of the Aesthetic* (Oxford: Blackwell, 1990), pp. 18–19.

31 Robert Montgomery calls attention in *Terms of Response: Language and Audience in Seventeenth and Eighteenth Century Theory* (University Park: Pennsylvania State UP, 1992), p. 8, to how eighteenth-century writers on reading saw it typically as an art of picturing in one's mind. He notes Edmund Burke's special position in this discussion in his Iser-like insistence that linguistic pictorialism is not stereotyped but varies by reader.

32 Iser has found warm advocates in students of narrative more broadly conceived: for instance, Karl Kroeber on storytelling as the art of knowing what to leave out to draw the reader in: *Retelling/Rereading* (New Brunswick:

Rutgers UP, 1992), pp. 19, 62; or Robert Sturges on medieval narratives that put upfront their gaps of knowledge and call for readers' judgment, as in *Chaucer's* Troilus: *Medieval Interpretation: Models of Reading in Literary Narrative, 1100–1500* (Carbondale: Southern Illinois UP, 1991), pp. 139–46.

33 This is especially true with Iser's best-known concept of gaps left by the text for reader fulfillment: the identification of something as a gap and the choice of gaps on which to focus are all interpretive moves that we bring to a text depending on our approach or ideological presuppositions (for later Fish read communities of interpretation).

34 There is a growing literature on this subject quite apart from the more idiosyncratic psychoanalytic studies of Norman Holland, including Holland's own more recent study more based on cognitive psychology: see *The Critical I.* In addition, there is useful information on reading at different stages in human development, well summarized by J.A. Appleyard, *Becoming a Reader: The Experience of Fiction from Childhood to Adulthood* (Cambridge: Cambridge UP, 1990). See also the attempts at scientific descriptions of reading in Alan Kennedy, *The Psychology of Reading* (London: Methuen, 1984) and in the variously successful essays in collecting hard data in Elaine F. Nardocchio, ed., *Reader Response to Literature: The Empirical Dimension* (New York: Mouton de Gruyter, 1992).

Iser later would speak of his work as a kind of model building, which very much fits my sense of his activity: "In devising a model of interaction between text and reader I have tried to conceptualize—in the idealized manner that is fundamental to model-building—basic acts of communication": "Interview," in *Prospecting*, p. 68. Interestingly, in answering Norman Holland's objection that empirical studies of real readers would offer a better approach to the subject of Iser's work, Iser did not see any incompatibility between his model-building and empirical work, even suggesting that his model was a heuristic, a scheme for developing empirical research, which could then be restructured on the basis of that evidence (*Prospecting*, pp. 49–50). Although the reply opened up the possibility of a healthy cross-fertilization of Continental theory building and Anglo-American empiricism, no collaboration or major redevelopment of Iser's theory on the basis of empirical evidence has emerged.

35 Alan Kennedy's study of *The Psychology of Reading*, p. 85, makes a similar distinction between defining a psychological process in reading and making a reading. Iser shares with Kennedy's attempt at an empirical study of reading psychology, interests in imaging in reading (p. 88) and in the need for successive moments of focus (Iser's *Gestalten*, p. 89).

36 Wolfgang Iser, "Interaction between Text and Reader," in Susan R. Suleiman and Inge Crosman, eds., p. 113. *The Reader in the Text* (Princeton: Princeton UP, 1980), Iser liked the essay well enough to reprint it himself in the brief reader response section of his *Prospecting*, pp. 31–41.

37 In his *The Act of Reading*, pp. 157–68, Iser even suggests that the text releases an inner self we don't know: a surprising moment of propinquity to Norman Holland's views of the text's interaction with the unconscious.

38 "Interaction between Text and Reader," p. 114.

39 *The Act of Reading*, p. 150. Terry Eagleton's *Literary Theory: An Introduction* (Minneapolis: U of Minnesota P, 1983), p. 181, accuses Iser, I think unfairly, of reifying a (presumably bourgeois) reader. While Iser fears total subjectivity (hence his insistence on the part played by the text) he also presents the reading experience as a dynamic production of varied, subjective states. See *The Act of Reading*, pp. 118, 123. Eagleton similarly is unfair to the vibrancy of Iser's conception in connecting his idea of *Gestalten* with Ingarden's much more text-controlled conception as a way to "pin down its anarchic polysemantic potential" (p. 81).

40 Interesting to note that Iser has often been accepted on his own, conservative, terms, accused as I note above of merely following Ingarden or by David Bleich of really offering a reader-controlling system based on his own reading, Iser reading as an Iserian critic: *The Double Perspective*, p. 17. By contrast, Tilottama Rajan makes a point similar to mine in comparing Schleiermacher to Iser: "in the reader-response theory of Wolfgang Iser, there is a reluctance to pursue the more radical implications of a phenomenological approach and abandon the idea of an implied author": *The Supplement of Reading: Figures of Understanding in Romantic Theory and Practice* (Ithaca: Cornell UP, 1990), p. 90.

41 I am afraid too I must concur with Fish on some of the central unclarities in theory here, especially the degree to which the system ultimately assumes an author's intentionality fulfilled by the reader's activity. My graduate seminar, after heated debate, confessed itself unable to determine if Iser's 1980 essay was asserting that there was one normal reader path of construction/deconstruction that programmed in the reader's whirling states or any number of successive different acts available to different readers or readings. Given my general reading of Iser's postmodernist leanings, I have chosen, somewhat arbitrarily, the latter.

42 In *The Act of Reading*, pp. 153-56, Iser in fact embraces Poulet's ideas of reading as an alien working within us.

43 *Allegories of Reading: Figural Language in Rousseau, Nietzsche, Rilke and Proust* (New Haven: Yale UP, 1979), p. 33. De Man himself sees reading as the central issue in theory. He briefly surveys what he calls "theories of reading" (p. 65) in *The Resistance to Theory* (Minneapolis: U of Minnesota P, 1986). He finds structuralist critics trying to, in effect, hardwire interpretation as if literature were reducible to grammar and logic. The same is true of the newer speech act critics. And hermeneutic critics (soon to be personified in the New

Historicism) try to establish an "historically determined meaning" (p. 18). In his broad use of "theories of reading" for critical issues of the time, de Man is clearly intervening as his own theorist of reading.

44 I came to Rodolphe Gasché's *The Wild Card of Reading: On Paul de Man* (Cambridge: Harvard UP, 1998) only after completing this essay early in this project (given originally as a paper at the Narrative Conference in April 1995). As I do, he takes an approach to reading as central to de Man's own project. I highly recommend his much more extensive and close analysis of de Man's conception of reading. Like mine, his main concern is neither with the politics of de Man's early collaborative writings nor with his once important sociological place in the American academy but with what he rightly identifies as the total idiosyncrasy of his reading project, which denies any kind of totalization, any progression beyond an incomprehensible singularity. Gasché explores and ultimately, like me, critiques de Man's wild card of reading as rhetoricity, though he exercises far closer attention than I can here, especially to de Man's difference from Derrida.

45 "Literary Competence," in Tompkins, ed., pp. 108–09—originally in *Structuralist Poetics* (Baltimore: Johns Hopkins UP, 1980), pp. 113–30.

46 Culler, "Literary Competence," in Tompkins, ed., pp. 113–14.

47 *The Resisting Reader* (Bloomington: Indiana UP, 1978).

48 *Gender and Reading* (Baltimore: John Hopkins UP, 1986). William Irwin, *Intentionalist Interpretation* (Westport: Greenwood, 1999), pp. 27–28, argues that the true friends of feminists are the intentionalists, who do not efface the woman as author. The case, however, is that the exciting feminist work in applied reader theory has been about freeing the woman as reader from patriarchal systems of enforced reading—immasculation as readers. Irwin follows the thinking of Cheryl Walker, "Feminist Literary Criticism and the Author," (1990), rep. in Irwin, ed., *The Death and Resurrection of the Author?* (Westport, CT: Greenwood, 2002), pp. 141–59. Walker cites many legitimate feminist concerns with underrecognized and marginalized women writers, including those from minority and third-world groups. These restorations, as well as the historical, biographical, and sociological interests they of course attract, are improperly set by Walker against issues of interpretation, oranges of gathered knowledge versus apples of interpretive discord. Nor are these issues irrelevant to interpretation, which they may cue. My argument, like that of Barthes and Foucault that Walker and Irwin oppose, is that such information does not dictate interpretive positions.

49 *Room for Maneuver: Reading (the) Oppositional (in) Narrative* (Chicago: Chicago UP, 1991). Unfortunately, this direction has not been much followed.

50 Culler doesn't explicitly formulate the implied relation between his long essay on reader response and the subject, deconstruction, of the rest of his

book. Yet it has to be a progression: deconstruction as a reading approach replaces reader response. Of course, deconstruction, in both de Manian and Derridean forms, tries to erase the reader. But it needs a shadowy reader to erase; it is in some sense parasitic on the concept of a reader—in de Man, for instance, one bound to go wrong. And it offers its own position, as I show here with de Man, as an alternative better reading. Kevin Jaszek suggested in an unpublished paper that despite deconstructions's denial of readers—it is about texts—its practices can be perceived retrospectively as a set of reader strategies. As with New Criticism, to which it is historically and intellectually aligned, it in effect performs a set of reading practices under the pretense that it merely speaks the text. As Fish also notes, "formal units are always a function of the interpretive model one brings to bear; they are not 'in' the text" ("Interpreting the *Variorum*," in Tompkins, ed., p. 176). Cf. Barbara Johnson's remark on Derrida: his "theory of writing turns out to have been, in fact, a theory of reading": "Writing," in Lentricchia and McLaughlin, ed's, *Critical Terms for Literary Study* (2nd ed.; Chicago: U of Chicago P, 1995) p. 45. See also my comment on G.B. Madison's critique of Derrida as omitting the reader, n. 33. below.

51 For discussions of de Man's early journalism during World War II in which, as a young man, he expressed certain Nazi ideas, see Werner Hamacher, Neil Hertz, and Thomas Keenan, eds., *Responses on Paul de Man's Wartime Journalism* (Lincoln: U of Nebraska P, 1989); also the article by Jacques Derrida, "Like the Sound of the Sea Deep Within a Shell: Paul de Man's War," *Critical Inquiry* 14 (Spring 1988): 591–652.

52 "The Dead-End of Formalist Criticism," *Blindness and Insight: Essays in the Rhetoric of Contemporary Criticism* (1971; 2nd ed., Minneapolis: U of Minnesota P, 1983), pp. 229–45. Essay originally published in French, 1954.

53 As Gasché very well shows, de Man's appropriation of deconstruction is very different from Derrida's, who sees possible multiplicity of meaning as offering places of entry that invite "productive readings, readings that not only weave new interpretative threads into it but compose so many rewritings of it as well": Gasché, p. 176; his chapter on Derrida's different mode of reading studies "Plato's Pharmacy," in Derrida's *Dissemination* (Chicago: U of Chicago P, 1981), pp. 61–171.

54 The commonly used revised edition with Wlad Godzich's Introduction mutes the political focus of the original 1971 book by the addition of so many other essays to the seven original chapters focused on critique of critics; the title of the first chapter, "Criticism and Crisis" is revealing: what crisis? One is tempted to supply, in light of the date, the political temptations of the Vietnam era and, in Europe, of 1968.

55 Lukács remains a major figure, of course, in Marxist theory; and so does Maurice Blanchot as an elusive French writer at times occupied with

political themes, generally accepted as important and translated—and now often connected to his friend Emmanuel Levinas—but nonetheless still not greatly read in the anglophone world; Ludwig Binswanger continues an important force in existential psychoanalysis; George Poulet, phenomenological critic, was important as a major school of Geneva critic when de Man wrote.

56 *Allegories of Reading*, p. 205.

57 See Gasché, pp. 33, 104, who sees de Man's approach breaking the text into mere idiosyncratic linguistic events, a "linguistic atomism." Gasché calls this apathetic rhetoric, rhetoric with no passion driving it anywhere.

58 Vincent B. Leitch, *Deconstructive Criticism: An Advanced Introduction* (New York: Columbia UP, 1983), p. 184, interestingly for my argument recognizes that what de Man considers first-order readings are in fact, as allegories, also diachronic narrations: "a textual plot of another text's tale." An allegory of reading is then just another narration of that first allegorical narration.

59 (New York: Columbia UP, 1984) pp. vii–lx.

60 I noted above (II.xii) that Empson sees ambiguity being produced by grammatical and logical as well as tropic doubleness, something de Man downplays even where it is present in his examples. De Man tends to structure logic and grammar in opposition to rhetoric, as he does in the discussion of the trivium in *The Resistance to Theory.*

61 Gasché's full discussion of "mere reading" as the explanation of how reading is a "wild card" in interpretation is exemplary: pp. 114–48, esp. 114–16. I have benefited from Deep Biswas's reading of my own text here. He perceptively questioned my conflation of de Man's reading of texts with his reading of critics. I would answer that I believe de Man does find rhetorical dead ends in both "literary" and critical texts, making his reading of them in that respect the same.

62 It is a tribute to de Man's general impressiveness as a thinker that this fundamental commitment has not been more regularly criticized as carrying forward into contemporary theory the old New Critical and generally formalist division of poetry and literary art from other, pragmatic, discourse. Before Empson or New Criticism, Victor Shklovsky's idea of dehabitualization included an aim of making "forms difficult, to increase the difficulty and length of perception": "Art as Technique" (1917), in *Russian Formalist Criticism: Four Essays*, trans. Lee T. Lemon and Marion J. Reis (Lincoln: U of Nebraska P, 1965), p. 12. The turn away from formalism has included rejection of the reader positioned as aesthete with an interest only in the play of the self-referential text: for instance Karl Kroeber's *Retelling/Rereading*; influenced by Bakhtin, he attacks the idea of modernism's aesthetic reader unconnected to the content of the text and argues that "Self-referential imaging threatens narrative's existence as social negotiation turning its process

into a product" (p. 177). De Man does read some philosphers, e.g., Rousseau, but in these cases to insist on their literariness.

63 Again, Gasché pursues this issue further, especially connecting de Man's theory to a critique of Kantian aesthetics: see pp. 96–103, 122–26, 187–89.

64 So this speaks to those still concerned with major texts—by whatever canon qualification—in their writing and teaching; obviously those focusing on cultural and social history, as in Cultural Studies, may be less responsive to this tradition. As I have said above in discussing New Historicism and Cultural Studies, I find such work, along with biography, entirely interesting. But it is obvious that I do hear the call of de Man's attention to language when dealing with interpretation of texts.

65 *The Resistance to Theory*, pp. 10, 17.

66 Forgive a good story: I was at a discussion in which Brower, asking a question, cited Richards as an authority—to be contradicted by a still strong voice from the back: "I never said that, Ben."

67 Mikhail Bakhtin has noted the easy relations, almost identity, between new interests in rhetoric (as we find them certainly in late de Man) and formalism (earlier, New Critical de Man, though Bakhtin is thinking within the context of Russian formalism): "in fact, the re-establishment of rhetoric, with all its rights, greatly strengthens the formalist position. Formalist rhetoric is a necessary addition to formalist poetics": *The Dialogic Imagination: Four Essays*, ed. Michael Holquist (Austin: U of Texas P, 1981), p. 267.

68 Tilottama Rajan's *The Supplement of Reading* (Ithaca: Cornell UP, 1990), a sophisticated study of romantic hermeneutic theory and its appearance in scenes of reading in Romantic texts, makes a similar point to mine about de Man's approach as a form of reading itself. She suggests that a writer such as Shelley could anticipate the possibility that scenes of reading could be deconstructed at "figural moments" (p. 10); but they are also open to readings as discourses, in Ricoeur's sense of a hermeneutic intersection of world, speaker, audience, and situation, in which a narration is created by the reader. From this point of view unreadability is merely another reading. Like mine (developed before I read her book), her argument ultimately criticizes the attempt to use figural analysis as a fundamental ground (or grounding quicksand) of interpretation.

A broader version of this issue is raised by G.B. Madison in his defense of Gadamerian hermeneutics against deconstruction, in his example that of Derrida's unlimited signification: *The Hermeneutics of Postmodernity* (Bloomington: Indiana UP, 1990), p. 114. His broad point is that post-Heideggerian hermeneutics parallels deconstruction in offering no ultimately firm location for interpretation; but that it also insists on the necessity of a reader for a text and of a decidable reading for that reader. Applied to de

Man this would argue that there is always a possible reading of tropes for the interpreter. On the other hand, de Man would offer a useful critique of Madison's, and to some degree Gadamer's, hope to enable "decidable meanings." They are decidable for the moment, deconstructable as blindness in another time. Obviously it is also a mistake to assume that a reading for one person in a time is going to be decidable for someone else of that time. On the definition and history of hermeneutics see II.xviii, n. ll, above.

69 De Man's deconstructive view of metaphor offers an especially radical view of the special qualities of figurative language, particularly that of the disseminative power of metaphor, long recognized in different ways before de Manian deconstruction. If Jakobson, for instance, gives metaphor a central place in his construction of language as one way by which the mind relates words (his well-known metaphor/metonymy distinction), he sees metaphor as a place for substitutions of individual similar words based on perceived similarities, not as a function where any word may be replaced by any other word. If a metaphor functions as a switching place in which two concepts interchange qualities (a red rose and my love, for instance) and in the process open up many possibilities of new meanings (my love has a red nose, I prefer to love roses and on and on as Empson could), this doesn't mean that those possibilities are in theory endless (we cannot conceive of them as investing a major portion of the lexicon, though we may extend our list in practice rather far), nor does it suspend usual ways in which we sort out preferred meanings by the context of our interpretation. A metaphor is not even unique as a place in a text open to multiple interpretations: merely a good place to demonstrate the ways in which interpretation of any detail of a text will be directed by the conception of the whole. Susan R. Horton, *Interpreting Interpreting: Interpreting Dickens's* Dombey (Baltimore: Johns Hopkins UP, 1979), especially pp. 1–21, usefully reviews the way in which the hermeneutic circle allows different interpreters to identify different units of a text at different levels of generality as the parts from which to construct or to reshape to conform to the whole they have already created. Her interpretive ladder (p. 69) would put de Man's concerns with the universal activity of figural language in any text at the highest, semiotic, level of generality for his units.

It is worth noting that a very different interpretation of metaphor's slipperiness, not as a place of no exit and unreadability but as a place of productive thinking has a long history, from the defenses made by classical rhetoricians against the Platonic tradition of distrust of metaphor as a corruption of non-philosophical, illogical language down to Paul Ricoeur's *The Rule of Metaphor*. Metaphor, as in the broader study of metaphor in the work of George Lakoff and his associates, "is a semantic tool for exploring new meanings." For him, the difficult interaction between reader and metaphor is not to be looked on as a benighted householder down in the basement facing a blown fuse with no way to get the lights back on. Rather the reader has a creative experience of facing a disorientation of thinking at the junction of a metaphor followed by his/her response to the challenge by a new, reorienting, conception. Far from being the place where literature as literature is distinguished from other discourse and thinking, figurative structures are at the heart of all thinking, both as the place of resistance to new thought (as in dead metaphors) and as the place of challenge and new thinking (as in a striking new figure bringing together hitherto unconnected ideas). The assumption here is of course that a reader makes a decision about the meaning he routes through the metaphor rather than rests with concluding that the decision is difficult—though as a reading in itself this de Manian reading of unreadability is also possible. See the fuller discussion of metaphor in II.xiii, above. There, drawing especially on Donald Davidson's conception of metaphor as a literal falsehood that demands some kind of solution, I argue that metaphor opens up a sufficient space of variety that it especially allows different readings by different readers—which is not the same as requiring a reading of unreadability.

70 Clayton Koelb, whom this essay looks at below as exemplary of attempts to apply de Man in practical criticism, looks at this puzzle in his *Incredulous Reader: Literature and the Function of Disbelief* (Ithaca: Cornell UP, 1984), where he seems genuinely unable to determine if the difficult works that he looks at—what he calls lethetic fiction, forgetful of the world we know—constitute a genre of unreadable works or whether they are only archetypical in their unreadability. They would all fit the genre I am suggesting, where, in Koelb's words, "the word has the power to function independently of the world" (p. 79).

71 Ithaca: Cornell UP, 1988.

72 Koelb, p. 250.

73 Koelb, p. 254.

74 Koelb, p. x.

75 The difference in the terms is worth noticing: "unreadability" is a roadblock that ends our attempt to go anywhere; "indeterminability," the preferred deconstructive critical term, simply allows us to keep wandering. See the discussion of indeterminacy by Gerald Graff, "Determinacy/Indeterminacy," in Lentricchia and McLaughlin, eds., pp. 163–76.

76 In the collection *Cosmicomics*, trans. from the Italian *Le Cosmocomiche* of 1965 by William Weaver (New York: Harcourt Brace Jovanovich, 1976).

77 "Literary Competence," in his *Structuralist Poetics*, pp. 113–30.

78 In making this move Scholes, pp. 39–47, goes over rather lightly some venerable and major questions of his century and perhaps all centuries about

intention, whether of the author or as defined by knowledge of his broader historical milieu. His argument seems to focus, as I note below, on the need for a decisive identity behind the text in order to allow us to stand up against it. In chapter 2 of his *Protocols of Reading* (New Haven: Yale UP, 1989), Scholes returned to the issue of intention more rigorously in his intercession in the debate, frequently focused on reading for intention, between Derrida and Searle reprinted in Derrida's *Limited Inc* (Evanston, IL: Northwestern UP, 1988). For full discussion of these issues see my Appendix 1. In his "Afterword" Derrida directly takes on the issue of hierarchy of reading levels: the term "doubling commentary" used in *Of Grammatology* is what in "a very classical and very elementary layer of reading most resembles what traditionally is called 'commentary,' even paraphrase" (p. 144). But he then denies that it can be separated from interpretation: "This paraphrastic moment ... is already an interpretive reading. This moment, this layer already concerns interpretations and semantic decisions which have nothing 'natural' or 'originary' about them" (p. 144).

79 *The Open Work,* trans. Anna Cancogni (Italian orig. 1962; Cambridge, MA: Harvard UP, 1989). See also essays republished in *The Role of the Reader: Explorations in the Semiotics of Texts* (Bloomington: Indiana UP, 1979).

80 E.D. Hirsch, *Validity in Interpretation* (New Haven: Yale UP, 1967), esp. pp. 62–64. Hirsch, p. 43, even calls for an initial, philological stage, much like Scholes's first stage. Alastair Fowler, following Hirsch in intentionalist approaches to genre, more explicitly argues that a stage (he calls it phase) of construction—of the specific historical genre of the work—precedes the phase of interpretation. That way, one is tempted to add, the cart is always kept clearly in front of the horse. See *Kinds of Literature* (Cambridge: Harvard UP, 1982), pp. 256–72. Wendell Harris, *Interpretive Acts* (New York: Oxford UP, 1988), uses a similar system of intrinsic (historical, intentional) readings followed by extrinsic (such as Freudian) readings that build on the first stage: p. 165. He implicitly adds a third, aesthetic stage: "such a mixture is natural since we read for meaning, significance, and aesthetic qualities at the same time." It is interesting that in this summary of what has clearly been a "builds upon" approach, he reverts, as if by accident, to an "all at once" view. Harris, *Literary Meaning* (New York: New York UP, 1996), places the same staging in an historical frame, contextual information establishing intention followed by evaluation and/or significance—in Hirsch's sense. For a fuller discussion of Hirsch's impressive development, see II.i, n. 30, above.

81 *Protocols of Reading,* pp. 7–8. This work, a more sophisticated treatment of issues in reading, offers less of an approach than the earlier one to how to read, despite these conceptions. I have chosen the earlier and more influential work in order to focus on the issue of staged reading.

82 Martin Irvine, *The Making of Textual Culture: 'Grammatica' and Literary Theory, 350–1100* (Cambridge: Cambridge UP, 1994), offers a broader history of the quite stable protocols for reading (*scientia interpretandi*) in the schools' *grammatica* of the late Roman, Dark Ages, and earlier medieval period, a four-stage system of construing, interpreting tropes and figures, correcting, and finally, as with Scholes, evaluating (*iudicium*). On the different, more specific stages of medieval allegorical interpretation, see discussion of allegory in II.xvi and n. 376, above.

83 This particular formulation, and of course there are many for such a major historical tradition, comes from George Eliot's studies: "Miscellanies," (holograph note book), Berg Collection, New York Public Library, fol. 108. Gerald Bruns, *Hermeneutics Ancient and Modern* (New Haven: Yale UP, 1992), pp. 104–23, stresses far more the practice of Midrash not as a rule-bound practice but as an open-ended communal exploration of what meaningfulness the text possesses.

84 See Peter Szondi, *Introduction to Literacy Hermeneutics* (Cambridge: Cambridge UP, 1995) p. 38. Szondi himself questions whether it is thus possible to have a half rationalist (certain meaning) and half historically relative meaning.

85 See the useful discussion in Vincent B. Leitch, *American Literary Criticism from the Thirties to the Eighties* (New York: Columbia UP, 1988), p. 69.

86 Tompkins, ed., p. 156.

87 In Suleiman and Crosman, eds., *The Reader in the Text*, p. 367.

88 Suleiman and Crosman, eds., p. 237.

89 Umberto Eco, *The Limits of Interpretation* (Bloomington: Indiana UP, 1990), pp. 54–55.

90 *Before Reading* (Ithaca: Cornell UP, 1987), pp. 30–31. Even closer to Scholes's is the formula of two-stage reading in Wayne C. Booth, *The Company We Keep: An Ethics of Fiction* (Berkeley: U of California P, 1988), p. 136: "I serve myself best, as reader, when I both honor an author's offering for what it is, in its full otherness from me, and take an active critical stance against what seem to me its errors or excesses."

91 *Protocols of Reading*, pp. 145–55.

92 *The Ethics of Reading* (New York: Columbia UP, 1987), p. 208.

93 Culler, *On Deconstruction*, usefully provides this format, indicating even Fish as reading, when he performed his amazing diachronic constantly revisionary interpretations, in a Fishian manner.

94 That this is a central issue, specifically a main bone of contention between neo-pragmatist views of interpretation and others, is suggested by how it emerges in a pragmatist critique of another pragmatic approach to interpretation. Richard Shusterman in Gary Iseminger, ed., *Intention and Interpretation* (Philadelphia: Temple UP, 1992) critiques Joseph Margolis's view of "robust

relativism" for not being robust enough on this issue (Margolis' essay, also in Iseminger, ed., pp. 41–50). Margolis wishes to keep description of literature (stage one) a fact while allowing interpretation to be relative; Shusterman would prefer interpretation all the way down: pp. 70–71.

95 Contrast the implications, only marginally assessed, of reading in a classic text on ideology such as Edward Said's *Orientalism* (New York: Pantheon, 1978). Said is clear that orientalism as a discourse has created a master mode of reading in which all that does not fit its discourse is washed out in the very first moment of reading; by contrast, his book shows us (sometimes forcing us to see implied orientalist reader positions in the texts he cites by bracketed guides to the rhetoric of Western superiority structured into every aspect of the language) that ideologically critical reading is very much a matter of philological and code levels, not merely a passive reflection after reading.

96 Fish, *Doing What Comes Naturally*, p. 184.

97 *There's No Such Thing as Free Speech* (New York: Oxford, 1994), p. 10. Fish's essay, "Introduction, or How I Stopped Worrying and Learned to Love Interpretation," *Is There a Text in This Class?* (Cambridge: Harvard UP, 1980), pp. 1–16, analyzes his own earlier procedure in seventeenth-century studies as a staged reading through levels: the temporal reading as a preliminary that all must do followed by a "second level" as an interpretive level. These roughly parallel Scholes's first two levels. Fish interestingly acknowledges that he thus avoided a unitary reading out of an Arnoldian fear of allowing his students to do what they like; even more interestingly, because not wholly clearly, he offers his invention of communities of interpretation as the immediate reaction to his loss of covertly staged readings as a bulwark against individual "subjectivity." Having released the reader from his system, he binds him/her into communities. This use of communities as a stay against subjectivity is reaffirmed even in the essay that troubled Scholes so much: "How to Recognize a Poem When You See One," in the same collection of essays, esp. pp. 331–36. See my fuller discussion of Fish's communities, III.v, below.

98 Fish perhaps would argue against Culler that he was recreating an historical reading, as in the broader imputation of sin to the reader in the overall approach to *Paradise Lost* (see III.ii, n. 18). Despite this larger strategy, the approach at the level of line-by-line reading seems to this reader of poetry historically more appropriate for a poetic world of fast changes of tone and perspective of Robert Lowell or John Ashbery; that is, it offers a peculiarly postmodern way of reading for the breaks, gaps, and recastings of the whole.

99 I have looked here at Scholes's work of the 1980s on a revisit to seminal discussions of reading. In his genial and good-sensical *The Crafty Reader* (New Haven: Yale UP, 2001), Scholes offers a cogent and well digested critique of the aestheticism of the New Critical pedagogy that still dominates college

classes ("Reading Poetry: A Lost Craft," pp. 1–75), though my own experience has been that poetry isn't much read (the problem he addresses) because it isn't much taught; those who studied with New Critics who began with poetry still tell me they read poetry. But Scholes's suggestion that we invite students to connect with poetry rather than worship well-wrought urns is very much to the point as are his suggestions for teaching and his examples. Connecting by reading continues to be for him, as it is in *Textual Power*, a staged business, with "primary level" philological and contextual work preceding or replacing "secondary level" "symbolic" and thematic. His examples, for instance Edna St. Vincent Millay's Sacco and Vanzetti poem, "Justice Denied," to which he tries to do justice against Allen Tate's dislike of it, stress the need for historical and biographical information. "Situate, situate" (p. 17) is the way he suggests to connect. As in *Textual Power*, there is room in this text-filled classroom to agree or disagree, feel with or against the poem, as the final-level activity but apparently not as the shaping force of the interpretive approach. We crafty readers work our way to a correct—and this has to be intentional—reading based on philological and biographical-historical work.

100 For a clear, concise statement of his project see Fish, *Doing What Comes Naturally*, p. 142.

101 *Is There a Text in this Class?*, p. 371. The initial essays developing this theory appear in this collection, esp. pp. 301–71. It is interesting that the first, title essay, here argues that meaning is in fact determined by context; by a kind of slur, Fish then recreates this as an argument for broader contexts of meaning in communities. His case is local and oral—the student who asks if there is a text in a colleague's class is using fairly straightforward oral communication with a direct social aim: to see if the instructor is a Fish-type critic. To generalize such a kind of communication to textual examples is, as I argue in the essay on intention (e.g., II.x and elsewhere), not necessarily legitimate.

102 Fish might object to the phrase "interpreting structures" as implying that cultures provide some kind of theory that guides interpretation. He means all the constraints that lead a person to generate or accept certain statements about a work—or about anything else. But this certainly includes the specific interpreting instructions of some religious communities, or indeed of some literary schools, as well as more diffuse and epistemic assumptions and ways of thinking or material constraints built into the culture. In attempting to maintain the original idea of communities, Fish slipped from specific systems of interpretation in religious practices or literary schools, where there are specific guides to interpretation, into a general argument of cultural determinism over the individual; hence my need to counter both here. Harris, whose arguments on intention I oppose in II above, here seems appropriately commonsensical: *Literary Meaning*, pp. 38, 42–46.

103 Fish looks briefly at this set of issues at the end of his Introduction to *Doing What Comes Naturally*, pp. 30–33. There he accepts the nuancing of his conception of communities of interpretation by the possibility of an individual existing simultaneously in many communities and even looks at the possibility of a leaking from one to another. Almost perversely, he summons this idea up only to refuse it in the name of denying freedom to the individual. But the issue isn't whether such "leaking" between communities would prevent people from doing what comes naturally (that is, for Fish, having necessarily to exist within the naturalized restraints of cultural systems), but whether the individual can at least mix such communal systems, whether in fact this isn't done naturally as well, thus allowing individuals to innovate creatively (which need not be some ultimate freedom, even, as many original people attest, a fortunate accident—but not one programmed already into the culture). Fish's mosaic model of culture seems already to smell of a dating of his time, when his broad culture, like the Europe much of it came from, seemed to oppose a simplistic melting-pot idea to a too static model of distinct cultures sticking to their own kind. Hybridity increasingly makes the new America and the new Europe; individuals are more original by their mixture of cultures; mosaic seems too static a metaphor; tectonic plates slide, crack, merge, re-emerge. See Dasenbrock's similar observations, p. 246.

John Frow notes that in the modern world the idea of community of interpretation works with groups quite different from traditional ones formed by ethnic, religious, or even class affinities: "Interpretive and evaluative traditions" exist in modern situations eclectically among the more traditional communities as products of education or high culture. See "Economies of Value," in Machor and Goldstein, eds., p. 301, from his *Cultural Studies and Cultural Values* (New York: Oxford, 1995). His attempts to posit a special "regime of value" of cultural intellectuals seems more problematic. It too would be fissured and unstable.

104 See his "Normal Circumstances, Literal Language ..." and "How to Recognize a Text When You See One," *Is There a Text in This Class?*, pp. 269–72, 332–37.

105 Dasenbrock, pp. 149–50, 179–85, 210–15, *et passim*, sees Fish's devolution of interpretation to communities as a version of a broader "conventionalism" in neopragmatism, deconstruction, and Kuhnian history of science. He sees them all as denying the ability of the individual to determine conclusions apart from the programs of the society. His argument is weakened by its tendency to homogenize all these strains of contemporary thought against which he poses contemporary analytic philosophy in the form of Hilary Putnam and Donald Davidson. Fish thinks there is only the stereotypical interpretation of one's community; Dasenbrock and conservatives attracted

back to intentionality argue that we can engage with the author as the other; my view is that we may explore the text because we are not simple products of communities and will disagree substantially and interestingly over texts in even the tightest communities, thus allowing change. Dasenbrock stresses Davidson's recognition of difference as an access to the other. I see it only as a recognition of the need for new strategies of interpretation beyond our present ones—not necessarily taking us to a settled place of truth.

106 As presented by Pierre Maranda, who applies Althusser not so much to determine individuals as to suggest a certain less flexible set of underlying semantic biases—the West, for instance, toward problem solving or toward the proposition that time is money: see "The Dialectic of Metaphor: An Anthropological Essay on Hermeneutics," in Suleiman and Crosman, eds., pp. 183–204.

107 *Doing What Comes Naturally*, pp. 141–60.

108 A theoretician of rhetoric, Arabella Lyon, makes a similar critique of Fish on change from the view of someone passionately believing (as Fish the public debater also seems to do) in the possibility of change through strong rhetorical persuasion: *Intentions: Negotiated, Contested, and Ignored* (University Park: Pennsylvania State UP, 1998), pp. 50–53.

109 Monica Young-Zook, "Cryptic Fathers: Paternal Loss in Victorian Literature," Diss. New York University, 2002. Appearing soon with Palgrave.

110 In this perspective it seems incoherent to talk of a person belonging to many communities when we are really looking at a shifting or cosmopolitan variety of opinions held by the same person; that is not the same as being a fundamentalist on Sunday and a scientist the rest of the week or a Catholic in religion and plain-sense constitutional lawyer in the Supreme Court. Fish seems here too dependent on the American religious-ethnic model of community.

111 See the discussion of their works on the inconsequence of theory in II.i, note 20, above.

112 Despite his theory of communities of interpretation, Fish often reverts in his later work to this kind of pragmatic move; in his legal work he observes that when interpretive approaches conflict, "It is true that there is nowhere to go, no locus of judgment to which disputants can appeal for an authoritative announcement. But this doesn't mean that they must throw up their hands or toss the dice; it means that they must argue, thrash it out, present bodies of evidence to one another and to relevant audience, try to change one another's mind": *There's No Such Thing as Free Speech*, p. 10.

113 On Rorty's approach to literary interpretation see II.xvi, n. 37.

114 On Fish's parallel constricting and often contradictory positions on intention see Appendix 2.

SECTION FOUR*

CONCLUSION AND WORK IN PROGRESS: READER THEORY MEETS REAL READERS

Major reader theorists of the reader-response heyday, as we have just seen, found varied ways to avoid becoming advocates of reading and interpretation. Students of reading themselves, they seem to have had no particular wish to empower their readers as independent agents capable of developing their own reading styles, their own interpretations. Fortunately people can read, even be enthusiastic for reading and think they find important insights or ways of being in what they read without benefit of literary clergy. My reader may well ask what happened to reader theory since the time of reader response. The answer is, on the whole, that it diminished to a branch of history, marching to the tune of the times against theory and interpretation. Christine Brooke-Rose once observed at a conference, in answer to Walter Benn Michaels's claim that history was now all, that there was a great wheel of critical fortune that ran from history to interpretation to theory and on and on. That may seem to be the case, and I certainly now hear peeps of interest in interpretation and even in form; requests that I tell stories to the critical grandchildren about the old days of New Criticism; laments that no one reads poetry, or knows how to read poetry, anymore. But the turn of the wheel from interpretation and (reader) theory seemed especially driven by a need to move away from a moment of open interpretive possibilities entirely unpleasing to a professional's ear. Just as in the real world no one is supposed to go to a play and develop an opinion and an interpretation apart from the professional

*Notes appear at the end of the section. Substantive notes are bolded.

newspaper critics—leave it to John Simon!—so no one can learn to interpret in the academic world. We will teach *our* interpretations, *our* ways of reading or ... we will teach history instead. And we can use our research time to know more and more cultural history (albeit often about less and less) so we can be more and more impressively professional.

Reader theorists have been no exception to this professional re-empowerment, and most have devoted themselves to histories of reading or of the book (fascinating material in itself)[1] and to histories of reception (also often very interesting, if sometimes somewhat naive in their historiography).[2] The spirit has, however, often been close to philological: did medieval readers cease to read aloud and, if so, what changed with such a change?[3] What can we know about the varying reception of Shakespeare over the centuries?[4] How was reading changing during the development of new and ever more extensive print cultures and text medias?[5] However, much of the most vital work, like that in New Historicism and Cultural Studies generally, has had a political or identity motivation: to recover a lost history of a minority or special group. The exemplary case has been reading as a woman, as I noted in my Introduction, which actually inspired a good deal of excellent criticism investigating the history.[6] In this field there had even been a lively discussion during the earlier period of reader-response criticism (approximately 1970-1985) in which different writers attempted to establish norms for "reading as a woman."[7] Interestingly, as Jonathan Culler brilliantly pointed out in his *On Deconstruction*, the debate led to some realization of the underlying issue.[8] Norms for reading—say the norm of the woman reader—seem always to break up, when interrogated sufficiently, into subcategories—hetero-women readers, lesbian readers—and these in turn break into smaller units—middle-class lesbian women, African-American hetero-women readers, and on and on. The history of reading becomes a story of the diversity of readers in each age.[9] Reading from a point of view eventually leads one to an acceptance of diverse points of view: where neither the reader-response critics nor the profession in general wished to end up. Study of English working-class readers becomes a justification and even championing of reading by a group often sneered at in critical high culture.[10] African-American readers reading become so many kinds of outlooks on African-American experience.[11] Gay readers become so many kinds of gay approaches to gayness, to life.[12] As readers we are all queer, all individual.[13] We are all, to use Barbara Herrnstein Smith's cute phrase, "noncanonical audiences."[14]

This seems to me a happy place for me/us to end up. Reader theory work since the era of reader response has been at its best in such explorations, though it has lacked any broad theorization. Perhaps the most resonant approach to such a theory has been offered by a very intelligent maven of Cultural Studies who has not been content just to try to know social and cultural history but has had opinions about it. In his explorations of the history of reading, Michel de Certeau has found in the reading habits of real readers a potent answer to ideologies that declare the subjection of the masses.[15] In such ideologies, the masses are necessarily led in their reading, whether by the various cultural professionals (read: priests, professors of literature, members of the French cultural bureaucracy, the Académie Française) or by the capitalist forces of mass control (read: advertising, mass book marketing, culture of the masses); or, we could add, by the determinism of their Fishian communities of interpretation.[16] By contrast, de Certeau looks for places where individuals find their own control, use reading as a place for exploration and self-determination. In the same way that John Fiske has shown participants in mass culture defeating attempts made by corporations to shape them as cultural consumers by reshaping mass phenomena—bluejeans, for instance—to their needs for individual expression,[17] de Certeau sees reading as a place where the individual has waged guerrilla warfare, often successfully, with the establishments of culture or capital (after Pierre Bourdieu, we could reformulate this as establishments of cultural capital or the capitalism of culture) who would regiment them to their aims.

A parallel if unconnected argument has been made by American explorations of real readers. In studies quite unmindful of each other, Janice Radway famously and Victor Nell, with less fanfare, have defended the special uses of their own to which consumers put their reading. In her study of a kind of club of female romance readers, Radway refused the view that they are being subjected to a commercial soft porn that hooks them on Harlequin paperbacks.[18] These Chicago housewives find their own way into the romances, taking from them what they need to go on with their unfulfilling married lives, fantasizing their blunt husbands into rather violent heroes who latterly unfold hearts of gold: keeping those marital hopes alive.

Nell looks more broadly at many of the uses adults make of their reading.[19] An advocate against professional guardians of reading, Nell shamelessly argues the virtues of junk reading: westerns, historical romances, science fiction, humor novels, and mysteries. As a class, such reading, which he describes as almost trance-like activity, has physiological and psychological benefits. Even physical tests of brainwaves and heartrate show the experience of being lost in a book is a positive one to the reading organism, bringing it to a pleasant level of arousal followed by ability to enjoy deep rest: an experience he directly compares to the kind of moderate domestic sex that has mainly positive effects and little risk of heart attack; or it may sound like such reading has all the virtues of recreational drugs without the dangers. The virtues depend upon the reader's reassuring sense of her "sovereignty" over the book, a work she has chosen and takes for her own purposes. The book makes us professionals think about our knee-jerk reactions to popular reading habits. I confess that I certainly prefer reading Nell's book to reading the mysteries he touts because Nell's not only amuses but makes me think, but that is the way I have found to read that pleases me (and I take it you too, reader, if you have come so far with me). Nell's readers take their reading as great gulps; they would hardly appreciate being forced to analyze detectives as a structuralist such as Tzvetan Todorov has. The point is the wise, simple one that gets overlooked by professional readers: that individuals find different kinds of reading and different styles of reading, following their interests and desires.

Even a study that needs to be criticized for too much norming and stereotyping of classes of readers, J.A. Appleyard's look at stages of reading in the developing child and adult, *Becoming a Reader*, by its very conception underlines the different uses of reading for different readers. His study can be faulted for offering an American model of different stages of childhood reading as universal, yet this only reinforces his larger point: readers vary by the interests and concerns of their age group; we have only to add that they may vary by their culture or by their own place in the culture.[20]

These and other writers on the subject of real readers open up a nonjudgmental assessment of the manner and uses of reading. Even less than the generation of reader-response critics, who shared an interest and a direction of inquiry but were in no way a school,[21] analysts of real readers have worked independently of each other. As it follows the logic of its inquiry, however, this work does suggest a vector: reader theory tends to drive us to recognize the validity of different interpretations, with only a pragmatic standard (how persuasive they are in fact) for judging between them in any particular group at any particular moment in a work's reception. And it tends toward a taxonomy only of individuals: so many readers, so many particular uses and practices of reading at that moment. In a critical age that has fled to history for the appearance of certainty and professional importance and that continues to privilege the critic's authority through appeals to history, or to the intention of the author, or to the text proclaimed by critical fiat to speak that intention single-voicedly, it has instead suggested that the final authority is the individual reader who reads for her own interest or needs. It neither discounts nor privileges professional readings, only clarifies them as readings for one particular purpose or another.[22] The new focus on what one historian of reading has called "uncritical reading" does, however, tend to call into question any settled idea of what a proper critical reading might be, showing its historical origins, implicit social and political values, and actual multiplicity—so many want-to-be hegemonic individual critical readings.[23]

The issue of agency, another much contested area of theoretical discussion during the turn to history, immediately arises in this work. Reader theorists in their incarnation as reader-response critics of the 1970s and early 1980s gave the reader more or less room for activity but in practice offered mainly their own norms for the reader's adoption. Their somewhat famous tendency to invent types of readers—super-readers, informed readers, implied readers, most recently crafty readers—revealed their inability to leave readers be, their real project of norming readers to a prescribed practice of reading.[24] Students of real readers almost by the nature of their inquiry bless their subjects with some agency. Their subjects are choosing to read, even if they are only medieval clerks being initiated into a pre-formed set of authorized reading approaches (authorized in the sense that authority has been manifested on the text, usurped the place of the author, claimed infallible understanding of its meaning, and will try to force it on all readers). Most have much more latitude to read what interests them or fulfills some need. Reading is something we do, rather than merely undergo. The thinking about readers of the 1970s and 1980s seemed a dangerous subject to pursue for those who wished to assert social construction over all subjectivity. At a meta-level, the traditional fear of reading of those trying to assert social control in repressive societies was recapitulated as a theory fear of theory about subjectivity. Stanley Fish even created theory to calm this fear: don't worry, everything will be as it is despite the theory. According to his theory one could hardly benefit even from such reassurance. We are what we are; take the views we already take. But if it is true that people are not free to be just anything, they are more free, in reacting to, reflecting on, and working over their reading, to choose among possibilities. If that is not individual agency at the purest level of philosophy or psychology,[25] it is agency—choice and feedback from that choice—as we are likely to know it. The cultural constructionist who says there is no choice is of course choosing to say that rather than something else. All philosophy always has been in favor of determinism, most experience against it. We need here only say that the development of work in reader studies and theory is an exploration in places of apparent subjectivity and agency. The conventional wisdom has seen these as places of relative development of enlightenment, of at least exposure to new ideas, to a more cosmopolitan viewpoint. And perhaps that was a wisdom not to be dropped too easily. The most ardent social constructionists do their work by reading, writing, and hoping to be read. If they may appeal, in the last analysis, to social causes, their historical work is about the flow of ideas and discourses, their changes and rearticulations, most often by print and reading.

I want to end this study of literary intention and reader theory not by attempting fully to take on such grand consequences of the somewhat haphazard but certainly vectored development of reader theory but by at least suggesting a piece of that much larger pattern as example. As I have already published this work and also make it available on my web site,[26] I will only take the space here to reflect on the conclusions I came to. A friend had asked me to contribute a piece on literary biography. When I thought about biography, it occurred to me that we all talk about authors (their lives of course); through an association with professional biographers, I also knew first hand how much they like to talk about their work as authors of biography. But the readers of biography had been regularly ignored. So I made the first, and as far as I can tell, the only study of what I called bioreaders, readers of biography, both in history and in our time. What I found, even to my surprise, was an incredible diversity of readers and reading goals. Even my hop, skip, and a jump through the extremely large subject of bioreaders in history revealed so many types of readers: those looking for scandal and gossip, others seeking moral or political instruction, still others wishing to find paragons after which they could fashion themselves, sometimes with focus on a moment of religious or secular conversion. In more recent ages, readers looked to biography to learn "human nature," to discover common humanity, warts, beauty marks, and all, to find and nurture their love for star figures, Byron or Clint. Some read biography to celebrate reticence and the decorous life, others to unmask hypocrisy, others to find, in the Neronian festival of creative ego transformation or addictive degeneration, vicarious release. My look at real readers alive and reading biography in large amounts at the millennium (perhaps to professional literary folks' chagrin, who are lucky to see one hundred copies of their books sold to real reading individuals and another three or four hundred deposited in research libraries) found amazing variety even at one moment in time: there were star and celebrity gazers, questers after group identity, sensation seekers, lovers of causes, from Central Park (Olmstead) to feminism (Eleanor Roosevelt), history or other buffs, specialist readers, and just now and then a lover of a particular biographer. Even on one biography, Sylvia Nasar's best-seller A *Beautiful Mind* (on John Forbes Nash, the brilliant economist who went mad), there was an incredible range of interests, from mad identification to an Economics dissertation student who admired the brevity of Nash's own twenty-seven page dissertation.[27]

My study left me, above all, sensitized to the ways in which not just readers' interests but their readings and interpretations of the works they read were shaped by their very different motivations or psychological needs. Some needed mastery of information, others friends and a life, others confirmation of their backgrounds, social or sexual identity, or career choice. What Janet Malcolm called "the transgressive nature of biography"[28] perhaps explains the attraction (as also in all other literature) of voyeur readers, kinky readers, projecting, and identifying readers. Any type of reader I could identify turned out to be not a single defined type but a grouping holding more diversity. This followed the pattern I have already identified in the development of reader theory, especially in the study of the woman reader. As I have suggested, reader theory generally moved to consideration of the woman reader as a first major step beyond normative definition of reading. The attempt of early writers to offer their own norms quickly ran into diversity of kinds of female, kinds of feminist reading.[29] Gendered reading of biography similarly varied. It might take the form of inspirational reading of biographies of Eleanor Roosevelt (an obsession of some readers, as I found) or Mother Teresa. But a reader might focus instead on a subject's devotion to women friends. Or the salient point in her life might seem to another to be the story of a woman who found her way out of an upper-class angel-in-the-mansion role to an effective life of action and impact on her time. Reading biography as a woman is not a pre-scripted activity. And the same would be true for reading as a man, say Ellmann's biography of Wilde: reading as a gay man, as a Christian conservative, as a bi-sexual framed, like Wilde himself, in a conventional heterosexual marriage with children, as a sympathetic but macho man (a latter day Frank Harris).

The general point I wish to make from my study of bioreaders should be clear enough. Obviously such taxonomies of real readers need have no ending: there are as many bioreader positions as there are individual bioreaders, and no taxidermist, far less taxonomist, would hope to stuff and mount them all. And they were stuffed birds, after all, because my first look at readers of biography was not able to do what a mighty nation of readers of bioreaders must try now to do: to go out and find, by survey and interview, what positions readers of biography occupy,[30] or to dig up, in records of reading and memoirs of reading experience the reader positions of past receptions. You may smile. But how significant such work among those generally ignored, sometimes scorned, readers can be is suggested by the broad impact of Janice Radway's study, discussed above, of a special group of about fifty real readers—housewives—that opened up an entirely new view of both the readers and the texts they read. For twenty-five years, biographers and pedagogues have dominated work about biography as a discipline. Research on real readers of biography is not just a gesture toward democratic vistas, a celebration of de Certeau's nomadic everyday reader, but also a way of trying to understand the complete process of biographical writing, which goes nowhere except to a real reader. Certainly the age of grand theory has issued in our postmodern age in which there should be no normative reading positions assigned a priori by what Culler used to call the Institution of literature (should we speak of the Institution of biography? should we have established an Academy of Proper and Accepted Readings of Biography?). Which is not to say that there should not be discussion about which readings are more effective for certain purposes for certain readers. One good way to promote that discussion is indeed to study the varieties of actual readers reading.[31] I trust that such study suggests a contemporary approach to reading that manifests the emergence of our skeptical, individual-centered focus from the theoretical quarrels over reading of twenty-five and thirty-five years ago.

I would love to be able to extend this example to other genres and to introduce you more broadly: to other groups of readers around some preferred kind of writing, science fiction, Civil War history, contemporary poetry, self-improvement, ethnic roots, gardening or cooking, united (as my bioreaders are) only in that preference but, in that, intensely bonded; to the varieties of learning readers, from children to pensioners, reading for a purpose connected to their position in the progression of individual life cycles; to the varieties of readers who read for pleasures, of so many sorts—licit to me, perhaps illicit, some of them, to you; to readers in history: individuals with their own aims but also connecting to the reading paths and concerns of their times, some even reading aloud in ways we would never be allowed to; to readers in sects, more properly Stanley Fish's communities of reading, though never as unchanging, uncontroversial or unidiosyncratically individual as Fish's major statements (as opposed to his later adjustments) would seem to suggest; to readers with a personal purpose, reading out of the genetic, biological or developmental biases of their psychic constitutions, often focusing, as Norman Holland's interests make all of his real readers seem to, on emotional or psycho-sexual issues;[32] to personal readers who find in reading allegories of their own personal passages (always rejected by the institutional readers; but what better motive, speaking broadly, would anyone not rewarded by degree or salary have for reading?); to those active readers who socialize their experience, in reading groups—a major phenomenon especially among mainly women in North America today (and other parts of the world?) that deserves study—or in performance, by voicing, singing, writing out, or acting their response; to decoding readers, readers with a passion or obsession, readers we love to hate unless the bee is in our own bonnet, in which case all becomes clear. And, yes, to professional readers: have we not all gotten some bee in our academic bonnets, generally used our special talents for special readings that, as Bourdieu would note, serve our professional goals by declaring passé some other bonneted specialist? and on and on until the next sage of interpretation has himself been deposed. It is an improving if sometimes melancholy sight to observe all those professional showmen setting up their special booths at our utopic fair of reading. Mainly we pass the new interpretations of others—such as writers or psychologists or anthropologists or sociologists or philosophers or political scientists or political groups—on to a cross-section of those learning readers; and, yes, occasionally we start an exciting new hare of our own—anxiety of influence, deconstruction (shared of course with some philosophers), feminism (shared with some political feminists), queer theory, identity discourses, postcolonialism, ecocriticism—and may even find that great mass of real readers out there beyond our usual persuasions and sanctions may take some interest in what we read for.

I suggest that such a vision of readers' utopia, which I only sketch out here as a preliminary and leave to you to call up in all its messiness and fullness of life, ought to be our only stabilizing model for reading and interpretation. So let it stand as the unseen center of my study. Let it stand with all its imaginable bumps and warts, an incomplete utopia of messy diversity. The point is that reading belongs to everyone and to no one. That the games will go on. And that we may equally well study the games or play the games. But we should never, like the schoolboy who breaks up the Monopoly board when he finds he is losing, shouting it belongs to him and he can do what he wants with it, try to use our authority to claim ownership of the game. Perhaps then we may even find ways to come down, we literary types, from our ivory towers and make better connections with the world of readers who we might serve and engage more and sneer at less: whether those teachers and students who do most of the work of developmental reading before students come to us, or the real world of diverse enthusiasts out there actually reading—despite our ritual disparagement of their "illiteracy." I always see millions of them in my mind's eye reading on the New York subway. I have never struck up a conversation with one of those real readers without coming away not only persuaded of the limitations of their knowledge but also reminded of the limits of my own.

Which leads to my final point: what this hermeneutics of real readers of biography cannot provide is just what might at this point quicken the pulses of earlier hermeneuts: the possibility of creating an objective science or structured system of knowledge of reading, present or past—the hope perhaps inspiring the recently developing work of this kind in history of reading and reception.[33] There is, alas, an infinite regression operating here that injects into any attempt at a final system a principle of uncertainty. Any study such as the one I have been outlining in this paper is itself an act of reading and thus built on the uncertain sands of a momentary set of social coordinates for reading that exists in my time, and another set, often overlapping, of my individual motivations and approaches to reading. So my readings, too—anyone's readings—are themselves a reading point of view, even when they strive for taxonomic completeness. They will never be complete and what is included and excluded will be part of the reading point of view. And the entire taxonomy will have its less salient bias in my—or your—direction. The reason for trying, as objectively as possible, to study others' reading practices, now or at an earlier time, may be—surprise ending—to understand our own a little better.

NOTES: SECTION FOUR

1 I list here and in n. 5 below general and period works in these emerging areas. I should also note that work on the history of the book, more broadly work on the material conditions of texts, has had mainly an independent life from that of history of reading, emerging from Cultural Studies interest in material conditions of culture. But, as Michael Warner has observed, the project centered on the "materiality of the text" needs to be connected to the broader study of reading and readers: "Uncritical Reading," in Jane Gallop, ed., *Polemic: Critical or Uncritical* (New York: Routledge, 2004), p. 33. Many of the studies from both points of view in fact already attempt connections from book history to reading history. The broadest study is Alberto Manguel, *A History of Reading* (London: Penguin, 1996). Other broad approaches include Guglielmo Cavallo and Roger Chartier, eds., *A History of Reading in the West* (Amherst: U of Massachusetts P, 1999); Roger Chartier, *Forms and Meanings: Texts, Performances, and Audiences from Codex to Computer* (Philadelphia: U of Pennsylvania P, 1995); James Raven, Helen Small, and Naomi Tadmor, eds., *The Practice and Representation of Reading in England* (Cambridge: Cambridge UP, 1996); and the broader look at versions of reading in Jonathan Boyarin, ed., *The Ethnography of Reading* (Berkeley: U of California P, 1993). Although Manguel's book is curiously not on their bibliography, Jame L. Machor and Philip Goldstein, *Reception Study* (New York: Routledge, 2001), offer a helpful list of books, pp. 365–69. They also reprint Robert Darnton's broad-reaching prospectus of scholarship in this area, "First Steps Toward a History of Reading," pp. 160–79. Darnton lectures on the subject; one hopes for a book. For broad studies of the history of the book and print culture see Roger Chartier, *The Order of Books: Readers, Authors and Libraries in Europe Between the Fourteenth and Eighteenth Centuries* (Stanford: Stanford UP, 1994); Roger Chartier, ed., *The Cultural Uses of Print in Early Modern France* (Princeton: Princeton UP, 1987); and Adrian Johns, *The Nature of the Book: Print and Knowledge in the Making* (Chicago: U of Chicago P, 1998)—another subject currently much written on. See n. 5 below for a brief list of period studies of reading and book history.

2 See II.vii, n. 168. Machor and Goldstein, eds., offer a collection of essays on reception of many periods and authors. Historical studies of reading in different periods cited in n. 5 below often include study of the reception of individual authors. See also Andrew Taylor, *Textual Situations: Three Medieval Manuscripts and Their Readers* (Philadelphia: U of Pennsylvania P, 2002); Isabel Hofmeyr, *The Portable Bunyan: A Transnational History of* The Pilgrim's Progress (Princeton: Princeton UP, 2004); Barbara Benedict, *Making the Modern Reader: Cultural Mediation in Early Modern Literary Anthologies* (Princeton: Princeton UP, 1996); H.J. Jackson, *Marginalia:*

readers Writing in Books (New Haven: Yale UP, 2001); and n. 4 below for some of the studies of reception of Shakespeare.

3 See Mary Carruthers, *The Book of Memory,* pp. 156–88; Joyce Coleman, *Public Reading and the Reading Public in Late Medieval England and France* (Cambridge: Cambridge UP, 1996), and Paul Saenger, "Silent Reading: Its Impact on Late Medieval Script and Society," *Viator: Medieval and Renaissance Studies* 13 (1982): 367–414, and his full study: *Space Between Words: The Origins of Silent Reading* (Stanford: Stanford UP, 1997).

4 For example, Gary Taylor's broad *Reinventing Shakespeare: A Cultural History from the Restoration to the Present* (New York: Weidenfeld & Nicolson, 1989) or the more tightly argued R.A. Foakes, *Hamlet Versus Lear: Cultural Politics and Shakespeare's Art* (Cambridge: Cambridge UP, 1993), and essays in Jean I. Marsden, ed., *The Appropriation of Shakespeare: Post-Renaissance Reconstructions of the Works and the Myth* (New York: St. Martins, 1992), to name only some general works.

5 An area of a good deal of recent work: to cite only a few period studies—roughly in chronological order of subject—in the period from early modernism to the twentieth century, see: Eugene Kintgen, *Reading in Tudor England* (Pittsburgh: U of Pittsburgh P, 1996); Elizabeth Spiller, *Science, Reading, and Renaissance Literature: The Art of Making Knowledge: 1580–1670* (Cambridge: Cambridge UP, 2004); Kevin Sharpe, *Reading Revolutions: The Politics of Reading in Early Modern England* (New Haven: Yale UP, 2000); Jennifer Anderson and Elizabeth Sauer, eds., *Books and Readers in Early Modern England* (Philadelphia: U of Pennsylvania P, 2002); Isabel Rivers, ed., *Books and Their Readers in Eighteenth-Century England* (Leicester: Leicester UP, 1982) and her later edition of *Books and their Readers in Eighteenth-Century England: New Essays* (New York: Continuum, 2003); Hugh Amory and David D. Hall, eds. *A History of the Book in America. Volume One: The Colonial Book in the Atlantic World* (Cambridge: Cambridge UP, 2000); R.K. Webb, *The British Working Class Reader, 1790–1840: Literary and Social Tension* (London: Allen Unwin, 1955); Jon Klancher, *The Making of the English Reading Audiences, 1790–1832* (Madison: U of Wisconsin P, 1987); William St. Clair, *The Reading Nation in the Romantic Period* (Cambridge: Cambridge UP, 2004); William Gilmore-Lehne, *Reading Becomes a Necessity of Life: Material and Cultural Life in Rural New England: 1780–1835* (Knoxville: U of Tennessee P, 1989); Ronald Zboray, *A Fictive People: Antebellum Economic Development and the American Reading Public* (New York: Oxford UP, 1993); James L. Machor, ed., *Readers in History: Nineteenth-Century American Literature and the Contexts of Response* (Baltimore: Johns Hopkins UP, 1993); David Trotter, *The Making of the Reader: Language and Subjectivity in Modern American,*

English, and Irish Poetry (New York: St. Martin's, 1984); James Smith Allen, *In the Public Eye: A History of Reading in Modern France, 1800–1940* (Princeton: Princeton UP, 1991); Molly Abel Travis, *Reading Cultures: The Construction of Readers in the Twentieth Century* (Carbondale: Southern Illinois UP, 1998).

6 See especially the full, if somewhat elaborately detailed, account by Kate Flint, *The Woman Reader: 1837–1914* (Oxford: Oxford UP, 1993), and Jacqueline Pearson, *Women's Reading in Britain, 1750–1835: A Dangerous Recreation* (Cambridge: Cambridge UP, 1999).

7 See especially essays in Elizabeth A. Flynn and Patrocinio P. Schweickart, eds., *Gender and Reading* (Baltimore: Johns Hopkins UP, 1986). Judith Fetterley, *The Resisting Reader* (Bloomington: Indiana UP, 1978), was the groundbreaking work in the area. As I note in III.iv above, this interest in different women readers, or identity readers generally, has been at least tolerated, as generally politically correct, whereas the opening of reading to individual variety has not been where the professional and literary world wanted to go.

8 (Ithaca: Cornell UP, 1982), pp. 43–64.

9 Tony Bennett, "Texts in History," in Machor and Goldstein, eds., p. 69, sees such work becoming a practice of reading in itself, "studying texts in the light of their readings, readings in their texts." Such an analysis would make the texts "hum and reverberate with (ideally) the full range of meanings and effects for which they have furnished a site"—of course a very large "ideally" and the humming would be that of the historian of reading who would interpret each reading in history for her/his readers.

10 See, for instance, Jonathan Rose's interesting recent study, *The Intellectual Life of the British Working Classes* (New Haven: Yale UP, 2002).

11 For instance, the African-American response to *Uncle Tom's Cabin*: see Marva Banks, "*Uncle Tom's Cabin* and Antebellum Black Response," in Machor, ed., *Readers in History*, pp. 209–27, and Elizabeth McHenry, "Forgotten Readers: African-American Literary Societies and the American Scene," in James P. Danky and Wayne A. Wiegand, eds., *Print Culture in a Diverse America* (Urbana: U of Illinois P, 1998), pp. 149–72—and her fuller study, *Forgotten Readers: Recovering the Lost History of African American Literary Societies* (Durham: Duke UP, 2002).

12 Paul Armstrong proposed a set of these criteria for critical consensus, which I find entirely reasonable but not sufficient to restrain the skeptical view of truth in interpretation that I maintain. He sees an interpreter's ability to explain more material in a text as one criterion. But, as Iser has shown, there always comes a time when details not easily included drive a wedge in that inclusiveness and open the way to a new *Gestalt*, with former foregrounded material now in the background; intersubjectivity, the capacity of an interpretation to persuade others, is also a reasonable criterion,

but it fails with different communities or times. It looked like we all agreed until "we" were other or changed. Finally, efficacy, the production of new discoveries, works well until it also falls into different interests of different readers. The hot and expanding idea of one time or place can be the dullest dead end of another. See Paul Armstrong, "The Conflict of Interpretations and the Limits of Pluralism," *PMLA* 98 (1983): 346–47.

13 Machor and Goldstein, eds, p. 157, debate Jonathan Rose's suggestion that reception history is of the reading of professional readers as opposed to that of common readers not reading as a profession: "Rereading the English Common Reader: A Preface to the History of Audiences," *Journal of the History of Ideas* 53 (1992): 51. Rose's point is that history of real audiences has not been a focus of reception history. My approach here suggests that focus on real readers in reception history leads research eventually to a broadened look at the variety of real readers.

14 *Contingencies of Value* (Cambridge: Harvard UP, 1988), p. 25.

15 See *The Practice of Everyday Life* (Berkeley: U of California P, 1984), pp. 165–76. See also the studies by Roger Chartier, cited in n. 1, above.

16 A view of mass reading that smells as much of American cultural ghettoization as de Certeau's does of French statism or of late captitalism. See III.v, above.

17 See John Fiske, *Understanding Popular Culture* (New York: Routledge, 1989); also his *Reading the Popular* (Boston: Unwin Hyman, 1989). Both de Certeau and Fiske can be critiqued, in turn, for mistaking individual acts of resistance for political or social insurgence. Seán Burke goes further and accuses advocates of freedom for the reader from systems of authority of a "sallow retreat" from real politics "to readerly empowerment": *The Death and Return of the Author* (Edinburgh: Edinburgh UP, 1998), p. 201. This seems to me overstated from the other side and indeed uninformed about the history of politics in the West. Battles over hermeneutics, religious, political, and even literary, are themselves a major part of political history in Western culture. Present and future battles very much add those over the media to traditional arguments over written texts (as both de Certeau and Fiske's discussions recognize); but if this is new, there has been no message from the ultimate Author that there will be a new age beyond interpretation. May that God help us if we all agree on one interpretation of a major text, from Koran and Bible, Freud and Marx, to political Constitutions! Finally, to argue that communities make all meaning for their constituents or that most interpretive arguments are blindly entered into by those who accept authority is to condescend to all persons in history except those in power, or those making these assertions, to whom alone readerly agency is thus attributed.

18 *Reading the Romance: Women, Patriarchy, and Popular Culture* (1984; rev. ed. Chapel Hill: U of North Carolina P, 1991).

19 *Lost in a Book: The Psychology of Reading for Pleasure* (New Haven: Yale UP, 1988).

20 *The Experience of Fiction From Childhood to Adulthood* (Cambridge: Cambridge UP, 1990). See also Carol Feldman, Jerome Bruner, David Kalmar, and Bobbi Renderer, "Plot, Plight, and Dramatism: Interpretation at Three Ages," in William F. Overton and David S. Palermo, eds., *The Nature and Ontogenesis of Meaning* (Hillsdale, NJ: Lawrence Erlbaum, 1994) pp. 255–77, who do note the need for cross-cultural studies.

21 Italian Umberto Eco is a semiologist—and of course a famed novelist. German Wolfgang Iser followed the phenomenological direction of his predecessor Roman Ingarden (see Ingarden's *The Cognition of the Literary Work of Art* and *The Literary Work of Art* both pub. Evanston: Northwestern UP, 1973). Fish was a close critic and an historical critic in the American traditions finding his way to neopragmatism. Holland was a psychoanalytic critic looking at readers instead of authors. Scholes was a narratologist and structuralist interested in his reader work of the 1980s in textual ideologies. Louise Rosenblatt was a professor of English Education.

22 After writing this, I was agreeably surprised to find a virtuoso traditional critic, Denis Donoghue, ending his look at *The Practice of Reading* (New Haven: Yale UP, 1998), pp. 122–23, quoting de Certeau on the "tactics, diversionary exercises, ruses" in which real readers engage.

23 Warner's essay, cited n. 1, above, thus very nicely deconstructs notions of an inevitable and unified proper critical reading as it poses a project, much as I am here, to investigate "uncritical" (really unprofessional or other-professional) readings of all sorts. He might connect his work with that of Bruns on the diversity of hermeneutics as well as with the diversity of reader work I note here (see II.xviii, n. 408, above). Warner, like Bruns, focuses his discussion on other kinds of religious reading while noting how little has been done in this area; he cites as an exception Paul Griffiths, *Religious Reading: The Place of Reading in the Practice of Religion* (New York: Oxford UP, 1999). Jason Halt, "The Marginal Life of the Author," in William Irwin, ed., *The Death and Resurrection of the Author?* (Westport: Greenwood, 2002), pp. 65–78, meditates on abandoning the search for authority in reading, finding, as I do, room for all kinds of professional readings but none with authority. As I argue in II.xix, interpretations win their way pragmatically, as persuasive in discussion of a text at a time and among a discussion group. I believe (*my* normative position) that discussion should not be reduced to one set of rules (as in some religious sects) or, as I have amply demonstrated (Section II), to claims for the authority of author's intent. See also, in the same collection of essays, Robert Stecker, "Apparent, Implied, and Postulated Authors," esp. p. 137, who rejects "critical monism."

24 A point made by Soon Peng Su, drawing on work by Katie Wales: *Lexical Ambiguity in Poetry* (London: Longman, 1994), p. 96.

25 I have no (conscious) desire to argue for a psychological coherence in readers that I have denied to authors; indeed, I find in Norman Holland's now rather neglected studies of the Freudian psychology of reading, along with Harold Bloom's special studies of the psychology of writers reading, much food for thought. The individual reader may be individual precisely because of his half-unconscious psychological motivations.

26 I have been a member and sometime co-director, for more than 28 years, of the Biography Seminar of professional biographers at NYU. The piece, "In Search of Real Bioreaders," also offered on my website in revised form, was originally requested by Fred Karl for his journal, *Biography and Source Studies* 5 (2003): 105–36. <<http://homepages.nyu.edu/~jrm4>>.

My neologism faces stiff competition with that of "bioreader" in the security systems world.

27 How do I know? I read what real readers had to say on Amazon and I talked to the booksellers in New York's Biography Bookstore, as well as checked in the records of Bowker's and book distributor Ingram's. I also consulted Biography (the television and affiliated magazine group). And all this was only for the diversity in contemporary United States readers.

28 Mary Rhiel and David Suchoff, eds., *The Seductions of Biography* (New York: Routledge, 1996), p. 134.

29 See my discussion above.

30 A project in analysis of real readers was projected by the Book Industry Study Group, but never achieved funding: information from the current director, Jeff Abraham (2004).

31 Michael Steig, *Stories of Reading* (Baltimore: Johns Hopkins UP, 1989), writes of how he teaches by asking his students to report and explain their personal responses to works they read. The book surprises us by showing how even seemingly very personal and idiosyncratic readings accrue interest and persuasiveness as they become generalized in group discussion.

32 On Holland see III.i and n. 3 above.

33 The development of these fields, which I applaud, naturally limits their susceptibility to a positivist attitude. The more we look into reception, even in the initial period, the more we are aware of diversity—unless we have our own blinders on from what we think the reception "must" have been; or unless we are blinded by our Foucauldian commitments to finding great universal epistemes unifying response in any period; or hamstrung by our Fishian commitments to individuals being determined by their "communities." I have discussed the limits of these totalizing views repeatedly in this study; see esp. II.vii, xviii on New Historicism and III.v on Fish's concepts of communities. Such historical work should open our eyes to reading diversity, not be done with eyes wide shut.

APPENDIX 1*

MORE ON SPEECH ACT THEORY AND INTENTION

Because I examine in II.x a defense of intention especially put forward by Harris—particularly in *Interpretive Acts: In Search of Meaning*—though Paul Grice continues to be cited in his later and more genial *Literary Meaning: Reclaiming the Study of Literature* and in the work of others, e.g., Patrick Swinden, *Literature and the Philosophy of Intention*, pp. 36–43—I feel obliged to observe the more complicated details of his system, which I find only obscure the basic problem with his approach and give an imaginary sense of solution. In doing so, I think it will be useful to reflect in more detail on the debates over literary use of Speech Act theory, which generally turn on the issue of determinacy and the belief in intention that usually goes with it. Harris works with the later Austin's concepts of perlocutionary intent (what the speech intends to do to us), which he finds uncertain because the effect does so often fail, and of illocutionary force, which he finds useful in defining possible categories of intention that the speaker had in mind.

His model case (p. 38), from Paul Grice, "Can you pass the salt" (an indirect speech act), shows how we solve a simple oral uncertainty by resolving that this is not a question (are we able?) but a request (pass the salt!); decisions among such implicatures are made by context and by application of Ockham's razor: don't take more complicated speech act explanations than are necessary to solve the problem given. These work well in contextual oral situations (we would be as silly to think we were being asked if our exercise routine now

*Full citations to appendices are in Works Cited.

has us able to lift whole salt shakers at single grabs as we would be to offer a verbal cavil to the state trooper who asks if we can pull over). But they are not *fool* proof. And even Harris admits they work increasingly less well when we move from speeches put in context in a work to judgments of narrator or author's implications. It is a typical move of his and other defenders of intention to dismiss such problems as special cases while focusing on the power of their own special cases offered as general arguments. The problems, of author's intention, of speaker's intention in lyric poetry, are precisely the problems where belief in intention is to be leaned upon to settle difficult interpretive disputes. A definitional sleight of hand, similar to the great Hirschian one that Harris adopts and expands in which intention (meaning) and interpretation (significance) are really only declared different, allows Harris here to adapt Charles Altieri's (in his thoughtful *Act and Quality: A Theory of Literary Meaning and Humanistic Understanding*, 1981) distinction between intention (about sentences), purpose (about larger sections of a text), and project (about the entire work) to seem to prove the effectiveness of intentions (which he wishes to apply broadly) while only having to demonstrate it for the easier, less important cases (see fuller discussion in II.viii and n. 14, above).

Speaking of intentions as projects, it is worth recalling here more broadly the original project of ordinary language philosophy as it results in Speech Act theory (and the coordinate work in theory of implicature of Grice), which offers us rather confused possible intentions to consider. Austin, like the later Wittgenstein of the *Philosophical Investigations* himself, emerges from the analytic tradition of British philosophy's quest for a special clarity in use of language, even though his insistence on looking at the performative dimension of ordinary language runs importantly against the grain of the neo-positivist linguistic turn in twentieth-century analytic philosophy that was inaugurated in different emphases by Gottlob Frege, Bertrand Russell, and the earlier Wittgenstein of the *Tractatus*, and continued in the work of the Vienna circle and in British and American logical positivism. This tradition wished, as Richard Rorty has broadly suggested in *Philosophy and the Mirror of Nature*, to replace Descartes's or Locke's epistemological concerns with finding a certain foundation for scientific truths with a purely linguistic clarity that wished philosophy to aspire to the condition of science and mathematics (indeed to be a higher science of the possibilities of clear knowledge in those areas). That project was itself deeply involved in finding various ways of declaring and fixing a relation between language and the external world that would ensure the stability of what scientific theories say about the external world; language, properly understood and pruned by the logicians, could offer an Archimedes' point from which to securely evaluate the world. And one way, though by no means the only one, proposed to do this was to focus on philosophical intentionality (aboutness as a way of thinking about meaning—see II.i, n. 3, above), a conception often invoked within the broader analytical tradition wherever the concept of mind was explored as a way to define meaning.

As Rorty has so lucidly summarized, this tradition has in many ways self-destructed as the problems of fitting language to objects have emerged, like antithetical Minervas, from their own hard-worked foreheads, especially in the work of later Wittgenstein on language as a limitless series of different games, W.V. Quine on the impossibility of choosing correct translations on the basis of empirical evidence (thus showing language not logically based on a mirroring relation to an external world—see "Translation and Meaning," in *Word & Object*, pp. 26–79), and Thomas Kuhn's demonstrations of the incommensurability of different scientific paradigms in their relation to some presumed external given world; instead he found the paradigms creating the worlds they described: in *The Structure of Scientific Revolutions*. In its place a neopragmatist such as Richard Rorty has suggested a return to Heideggerian acceptance of a hermeneutic situatedness of meaning, in which meaning is not fixable but always dependent on a fusion of horizons between an utterance/text and the listener/reader. He has been criticized, in turn, by philosophers closer to the analytic tradition, such as Hilary Putnam and Donald Davidson, who accept the broad critique of the earlier positivism but insist that argument such as Rorty delights in still implies an acceptance of a notion of truth (see the useful summary of this last turn in Reed Way Dasenbrock, *Truth and Consequences: Intentions, Conventions, and the New Thematics*, esp. pp. 43–55). I give this minimalist history of recent philosophy only as a way of indicating that there is no monolithic attitude toward meaning to which we benighted literary types should be introduced over there in the philosophical world where we can get our hash settled on the issue of our literary intentionality issues; they are, like us, in their usual disarray, as I have indicated in II.x above in noting the various theories of meaning currently in play.

For all their (later) Wittgensteinian extension of linguistic philosophy to the ordinary working of natural languages, Austin and Grice, or an American like Searle, are still rather close to the original dream of their tradition, to use logical clarity to render even everyday uses of language logical, fixable, and translucent. Michael Dummett indeed noted in 1978 how quickly the apparent interest in ordinary language and actual use was replaced in the theory by a quest for normative "general semantic concepts": *Truth and Other Enigmas*, p. 445. Like literary theorists impatient of unclarity (I think of Wayne Booth's insistence on author's rhetorical control of his/her text in *The Rhetoric of Fiction*), they seem naturally to gravitate not only to defining rules of speech but to a model that stresses utterer's (Grice's word) intention rather than hearer's (or reader's) interpretation as a way of stabilizing the play of language they investigate. In this they sometimes do tend to connect those normally quite different things, literary intention, as I have been discussing it, and the intention (aboutness) of the analytic philosophical tradition, which sometimes, as in John Searle, uses mental intentionality as a way to fix meaning. Searle, unlike Austin or Grice, who are more directly concerned with defining kinds and rules of speech acts, specifically follows his theory of Speech Act with one of (of course philosophical) intentionality in his book *Intentionality: An Essay in the Philosophy of Mind*. Hence Rorty speaks of Searle as a believer in an essentialist idea of humans having an "intrinsic intentionality" that escapes "recontextualization"—Rorty's term for understanding in any different way: "Inquiry as Recontextualization," p. 67.

Searle's larger project here could be said to be not only to fix statements to one meaning by a system of labeling as types of speech acts—and thus to deny the play of possible interpretations—but also to connect these to a system of mental intentionality. But it isn't clear that even he found this entire program possible. Frank W. Liedtke, "Representational Semantics and Illocutionary Acts," interestingly notes a split in Searle's earlier work on speech acts and later work on intentionality. In the later work, mental intentions are not presented as communications but as representations. They thus can be said to have truth conditions in the tradition of analytic philosophy; one suspects Searle had abandoned the hope that speech acts as a system of communication could assure that the determinate meanings would be received. Instead the emphasis is on a meaning judged only from the private point of view of the utterer. There speech act definitions would not have to be evaluated for their success in predicting reception by the speaker's audience—as they must be in literary intention. Richard F. Kitchener, "Semantic Naturalism: The Problem of Meaning and Naturalistic Psychology," p. 288, would place Grice also as a thinker moving from speaker's psychology to determinate meaning via speech acts. Quine, by contrast, would prefer to avoid a mentalist structure entirely, though he accepts its inevitable vocabulary in ordinary thinking: *Word and Object*, pp. 219–21. The utterences with illocutionary force can be seen, as Searle has also argued in that tradition, as voiced versions of mental intentions that express, rather than a proposition as in a locutionary speech act (I express an intentional mental state that has some external thing as its intentional object), some desire (I express a desiring mental state that has its intentional object in the real world: "can you pass the salt?"). The philosopher's business was then to clarify the rules that constrained and controlled the meanings of the utterer's words.

Coming from this direction there was little reason or inclination in these philosophers to explore the play of language that opens up further as illocutionary expressions become increasingly complex and implicatures begin to multiply: see D. Sperber and D. Wilson, *Relevance: Communication and Cognition*, p. 236; the focus was rather on explaining the clarity of simpler, conversational situations. Searle has written on fictional discourse and on metaphor (chapters in *Expression and Meaning: Studies in the Theory of Speech Acts*, pp. 58–116), but the direction of his work here remains reductive clarification rather than exploration of literary complexity: fictional discourse is pretend speech acts in which usual rules are lifted; metaphor is examined for rules to clarify and control its slippery tendency. Literary illocutionary utterances really need to be treated as a class of social performatives that invite a space for the readers' participation in a joint speech or writing act of thinking, imagining, proposing, essaying, or storytelling. "Once upon a time" needs to be expanded, not analyzed, into "will you join with me in imagining a time and a place like ours but different, about which we will be bound to have various desires and opinions." Searle, I should say, considers the idea of separate speech acts in fiction but rejects it as creating an entire new language; but here he needs to distinguish between those which merely pretend, to use his term, to be practical speech acts and those which refer specifically to the speech act of the creative activity. (For a critique of his treatment of fictional discourse see Anne Reboul, "The Logical Status of Fictional Discourse: What Searle's Speaker Can't Say to his Hearer.")

Mary Louise Pratt, in *Towards a Speech Act Theory of Literary Discourse*, does provide an expansion of Speech Act thinking, based on Grice's work on theory of implicature rather than directly on Austin, adapted to literary narratives as special speech acts—what she calls display texts. As noted above, Grice offers a set of maxims for conversation; these he defines as based on a Cooperative Principle: his aim being mainly to indicate the grounds on which good conversational communication takes place. Pratt however finds in his enumeration of the various failures in these, which he grants all have implicature as well, a fertile system for describing narration. Narrators, or speakers inside texts, may and often do break Grice's rules by violating or opting out from them, finding themselves in a clash of rules, or flouting one of the maxims. I find this a productive taxonomy for explaining effects of first-person (mainly her cases) narrative and their relation to what Booth would call the implied author's implicature. At the same time she too easily links this to a system of author intention so that she threatens to offer a kind of new model for narrative rhetoric: writers are supposedly willing to accept Grice's norms except for their regular flouting of them to make a point, usually about the narrator. They expect us to read their narrators/speakers for give-aways as to their failures to follow norms of proper and polite literary discourse, which thus characterize them. Inevitably this threatens to become a rigid generic system in which narrators' narratives are understood by their degree of variation from norms, presumably held by the authors behind the narrators' norms.

The problem with this thinking is that it is circular: it pretends to find the norms it imposes—compare with my discussion of genre in II.xvi. When the cases are fairly simple narrative games—the irony of the opening of *Pride and Prejudice*—we might easily accept that all readers are with the author in her irony over the truth universally acknowledged—although on second thought even here some doubt arises: maybe it is true to this society; maybe it is deliciously evocative of what everyone thinks but dares not say, rather than ironic. Who is being ironic if it is irony: the author/narrator at the expense of those who hold the truth or the author at the expense of the narrator? We could also grant that Milton's statement of intention, a speech act of justifying (the ways of God to men) is clear enough—not a hard case until we think how devil's party interpretations would have to see it as ironically as most of us see Austen's opening declaration. To them, God's ways are indeed mysterious and really need justifying.

When Pratt takes a large narrative stretch, as in her discussion of Camus's *L'Etranger*, she admits that many critics, and indeed even the author as self-critic, see Meursault's detached and simplified style as a new model for an adult view of the world, where she insists on reading it as a violation of "our adult one" (p. 188). One can always set up a group of norms for narrative or genres of narrative and provide useful observations by recording different texts' departures from them. But Pratt is seduced by Grice's quest for discursive standards and rules into applying her intelligent adaptation not as a critical approach but as a set of narrative truths universally acknowledged. These work pretty well for narratives in which we all follow a clever exposure of a limited narrator but work less well with narratives that offer more open alternatives of meaning—precisely those where her system will not allow us to specify an author position to establish one authorized meaning. It would not work well, for instance, with *Heart of Darkness* (is the lie the author's give-away that Marlow is corrupted by Kurtz?—some of my students think so), *The Trial* (*what* standards of normal discourse in Kafka's world?) or any kind of poetic narrative, which normally breaks all Grice's rules; nor is literature stopped before publication and rewritten by the institutional gatekeepers Pratt keeps summoning to keep the rules. It also would not even work for the more complicated lyric-narrative first-person dramatic monologues of Robert Browning. Defining the relative values to be assigned to narrator or character-speaker is always an interpretive move, never a foregone conclusion from some external observations about genre, nature of narrative, or conventions. A.J.

Close's earlier and simpler adaption of Austin (pp. 189–90) similarly conflates his own critical discussion about the nature of the speech act in question with a fairly established author's intention—it is the author's intention only because one believes one's critical opinion is correct and thus "authorized." In her revisit to Speech Act theory in 1986, "Ideology and Speech-Act Theory," Pratt herself came to critique the norm-making tendency of Grice's work as ideological more than descriptive, ignoring not only discourse behavior in other cultures but also much of the uncooperating speech that goes on in Western culture daily, uncommunicative to playful to downright antagonistic verbal relations—in which critique she specifically includes Searle as well. Although she then calls for exploration of infelicitous communication between author and reader in literature, she does not make such an exploration nor, evidently, abandon the dream of a poetics of author speech types. See also her earlier "The Ideology of Speech-Act Theory."

Wayne A. Davis, *Implicature: Intention, Convention, and Principle in the Failure of Gricean Theory*, has argued more broadly that Gricean conversational maxims are not universal psychosocial principles but only conventional, sometimes culture-specific, and historical in origin. His critique certainly highlights the degree to which Grice's maxims are only descriptive of what "rational" people may tend to do (p. 25) and not of what they may do. Davis sees implicature as something not assured in the language but depending on the speaker's intention; this means, for literature, that there are no codes for interpreting implications that we can follow with assurance to the best meaning. By the same token, as Davis notes, an audience may receive a speech, far more literature, in many ways (pp. 21–22); the origin of an implication in the speaker—if he is indeed clear—will not assure the audience of a fixed meaning.

It is interesting to find Grice himself bothered in his "Retrospective Epilogue" to his collected papers on language by the shadow of the hearer looming over his usual utterer: "it might be suggested that there is a certain arbitrariness in my taking a relativized meaning as tantamount to a speaker's meaning something *by* an utterance; there are other notions which might compete for this spot, in particular the notion of something's meaning something *to* a hearer. Why should the claims of 'meaning *to*,' that is of a passive or recipient's meaning, be inferior to those of 'meaning *by*' (that is, of acting or agent's meaning)?" Not surprisingly, Grice maintains his career-long position that "what words mean is a matter of what people [e.g., utterers] mean by them." Unlike Davis, he believes that meaning will be clear from the words as processed by the universal maxims. A hearer's position is defined by a correct analysis of utterer's intention such as Grice's logical study promotes: "a hearer is intended to recognize himself as intended to be the subject of a particular form of acceptance, and to take on such an acceptance for that reason [here mixing all three senses of intention, philosophical, literary and ordinary—as motivation of action]." See *Studies in the Ways of Words*, pp. 340, 352. As noted in II.x, Max Black does precisely criticize Grice's identification of meaning with intention, which he finds leads him to an infinite regress of explanations of special cases: "Meaning and Intention: An Examination of Grice's Views." His more cogent general criticism is that the approach is deeply circular, intention being justified as the right intention only by our identification of it as the meaning we accept, while the Grice "Formula" has sought to define meaning as intention. His argument, which I also recall in looking at Stanley Fish's ideas of intention (Appendix 2), concludes that intention is only the result of our ascription of meaning, thus in Grice's system assured only "tautologically," as an automatic naming (p. 274).

One way to avoid these problems in working with speech conventions in literary interpretation has been to isolate dialogue in literature and treat it independently. Often it will function as if it were real dialogue to be analyzed; but not always, as anyone who tried to apply it to the imagined dialogues of *Alice in Wonderland* would learn. More importantly, in interpretation of the work the dialogues cannot be isolated from the broader interpretive issues facing the text as a whole; this is merely to pretend one is doing a kind of interpretation when in fact the text is being made to donate its parts to linguistic science as if they were not necessary to the overall life of the work. For an example of this kind of work see D. Tannen, "Ordinary Conversation and Literary Discourse: Coherence and the Poetics of Repetition."

Although they do not follow Searle, Pratt, or my discussion here in stressing the issue of intention, Paul de Man and Stanley Fish each mounted cogent and broadly similar critiques of the attempt to stabilize meaning by using Speech Act theory. In de Man's modernized system of the trivium (logic, grammar, and rhetoric), Speech Act thinking is trying to extend grammar into an area of reading controlled by the less stable rhetoric, "a grammatization of the *trivium* at the expense of rhetoric": "For the characterization of the performative as sheer convention reduces it in effect to a grammatical code among others": *The Resistance to Theory*, p. 19. J. Hillis Miller, *Speech Acts in Literature*, pp. 140–54, traces de Man's long involvement with the question of how speech acts function in literature: from his earlier sense that they are necessarily unstable (Miller stresses the inevitable confusion between performatives and constatives—illocutionary and locutionary uses) and born to misfire to his later tendency to see speech acts as language speaking on its own. Stated in relation to intention, this is a view that meaning, such as it is in de Man, is cut off from intentionality. De Man's wish to see language as untethered from its author doubtless explains the tendency Miller notes in him to give a face and person to language itself. But even here language does not know its intention or, if it does, it is a deliberate trickster whose intentions we cannot guess: a view especially antithetical to the ordinary language philosophers and their literary disciples. Stanley Fish has similarly critiqued attempts at overreaching by Speech Act theory within his system of interpretive communities. He distinguishes illocutionary effects—predictable because they obtain within communities who share oral conventions—from perlocutionary effects—contingent and thus not predictable. Like de Man, he finds the effects of speech, how it is received, a matter of rhetoric, not philosophy; and, as I am here, he denies that the precedents of speech (for instance, the intentions of the speaker) can be inferred from speech acts: "it is not a psychology": "How to Do Things with Austin and Searle," *Is There a Text in the Class? The Authority of Interpretive Communities*, pp. 226–27, 244. Fish uses speech acts in an exemplary, interpretive way to classify kinds of speaking in his discussion of *Coriolanus* but then turns to reject uses of Speech Act theory that would attempt to make it "serve as an all purpose interpretive key" (p. 244). It is also worth repeating Graham Hough's incisive point (in Newton-DeMolina, ed., pp. 228–29) which suggests and undermines the utopian wish for easy critical certainty in this entire project, that speech act labels are too gross to be of use in describing overall literary effects.

Speech Act theory has also been critiqued on broadly similar grounds by philosophers as unlike as Jacques Derrida, French deconstructionist, and Donald Davidson, heir to Quine's empirical tradition. Derrida's critique of Austin's theory and his subsequent embroilment in debate with Searle is of course especially well known—his side was conveniently brought together in *Limited Inc* by editor Gerald Graff, which includes an "Afterword" responding to questions by Graff. The original critique of Austin, "Signature Event Context," pp. 1–23, a brilliant gem of a piece, appeared in 1971, but in English, translated by Jeffrey Mehlman and Samuel Weber, only in 1977 (in *Glyph*). It appeared again in the translation by Alan Bass of *Margins of Philosophy*. Graff reprints the Mehlman-Weber text. Its date and general occupation with questions of authorship, signature, and authority approach it to the equally seminal essays questioning author and authority in discourse of Barthes and Foucault of 1967 and 1969. Derrida insists in this essay and in the proliferating discussion answering Searle's defense of Austin ("Reiterating the Differences: A Reply to Derrida" published in *Glyph* 2 [1977]) in "Limited Inc" (also *Glyph* 2), and in the "Afterword" in response to Graff's questions, that Speech Act theory cannot define a stable meaning to statements if there are cases where such stability is conceivably not present (pp. 16, 89–92). And he insists that Austin himself has tried to exclude many forms of less determinant (infelicitous) statements as exceptions or special cases, including those famous "parasite" literary uses and other types of non-serious statements. But his critique is broader, based on differing views of interpretation generally. If speech acts can fail, then Speech Act theory must be said to be a philosophy of prescriptives rather than descriptives (p. 122), or, as he later states it, a moral philosophy, "a theory of right, or law, of political ethics or of politics as ethics" (p. 97).

Because Derrida is concerned with literary speech acts as much as the more pragmatic ones Austin looks at, and because he critiques Austin by setting forth an entire way of thinking about interpretation, it is easy to confuse his frequent discussion of intentionality with the issue of literary intention. Coming from the tradition of Husserl, he is in fact surprised Searle can discuss intention without reference to the tradition (p. 130). He himself takes a position on philosophic intention that seems appropriate to his historical situation as the very skeptical scion of the Continental Phenomenological tradition in philosophy. While he grants that pragmatists might just jettison the concept of intention as a way of speaking of the aboutness or meaningfulness of a statement (p. 128), he instead insists on the concept but also insists on its practical attenuation. In the early essay ("Signature Event Context") this is relatively straightforward and may even sound like author's intention in some of the forms it appears in our literary discussion: "The intention animating the utterance will never be through and through present to itself and to its content" (p. 18). Derrida's point would take us into his central philosophy of language, ideas of différance, dissemination, graft, or supplement: his major explorations of ways in which language is always less than "present to itself," always capable of meaning what it doesn't mean to mean. In this essay this leads Derrida to some statements on interpretation which brilliantly describe context as the unstable determinant of meaning, and itself ultimately a matter of value or politics.

While taking away none of his skepticism about language's stability, the later essay, "Limited Inc," and the "Afterword" pressure further the idea of intention. While it may seem linked in the first essay to everyday (literary) ideas of *vouloir dire*, what one wishes to say, it is here clearly about the concept of meaning in language itself. It exists as a "telos" toward plenitude of meaning which is never realized (p. 130). Although his discussion of context has seemed to border on it, he is not concerned with a psychology of author's meaning, with "pre-critical psychologism," with thinking that is "pre-Saussurian, phenomenologically" (p. 66). Intention is not "something separable, intrinsic, and 'behind' the expressions" (p. 66). It is the nature of language, its already "riven"-ness, that makes it never sufficient to give the stable meaning that Austin and Searle look for. Our process of "making-sense" of a statement is not adequate (is "incommensurate with") the "undertaking of intended meanings," not just because (as I have been arguing) we cannot know or decide what the speaker intended but because even if we could imagine a meaning behind a meaning, it too would be cloven, unstable (p. 72). Far from arguing for intention as a way of adjudicating literary interpretation, Derrida dismisses it out of hand. His fidelity to philosophical intention is itself a kind of fidelity to the possible meaningfulness of language (quite apart from its author). It amounts to an unwillingness to give up the possibility that words might have one meaning in face of his own intensely skeptical analyses of the instability of language—another set of arguments against the view that words infallibly direct us to their author's meaning.

Derrida himself grants that his concept of (philosophical) intention as a presence that is always in practice an absence is a difficult one: "I admit that this enigma grows increasingly obscure to me. It communicates with the greatest questions of being, of meaning and of the phenomenon of consciousness, of the relation of the object in general, of transcendence and of appearing *as such* . . . My frequenting of philosophers and phenomenologies of intentionality, beginning with that of Husserl, has only caused my uncertainty to increase, as well as my distrust of this work or of this figure, I hardly dare to say 'concept'" (p. 130). I explore this difficult place in Derrida's philosophical thinking here only because its presence in a text so helpful in issues of intepretation makes it easily confused with our debate on literary intention. And of course I find Derrida's critique of Austin and Searle as attempting to create a normative system of ordinary language entirely sympathetic. Seán Burke, *The Death and Return of the Author,* pp. 116–71, reads other, earlier, texts of Derrida as closer to acceptance of intentionality. He bases this especially on Derrida's major and rather more traditional (compared to his later work) exposition of deconstruction. There (e.g., *Of Grammatology,* "Plato's Pharmacy"), according to Burke he enacts a reading of an author to which he then opposes an alternate (read, deconstructive) reading; Burke sees this as acceptance of author's intention, which is then subverted. While this work is indeed less playful and in a sense closer to exposition of other philosophers than much of the later work, one could alternatively see Derrida as opposing not the author's intended reading as the standard reading designated under the name of Rousseau or Plato. Derrida does not see deconstruction as a bringing to light of unconscious intentions in the author and it would seem incoherent to argue that the author's intention was in some way to subvert himself; it is far more in the mode of Derrida's thinking to consider the contradiction as that of the philosophical tradition, of a certain way of using language to stage ideas, rather than of an authorial intention. (Burke makes a more interesting broad case against Derrida's claims that Western philosophy was indeed antithetical to writing.)

Finally, Miller, pp. 63–139, offers an intricate and eloquent discussion of Derrida on Speech Act theory, which sees him for all practical purposes denying that a writer's intention can control the context of the iteration's reception. But he offers a different explanation of Derrida's continued concern with these ideas after the debate with Searle. He interestingly sees Derrida's investment in debating Speech Act thinking with Searle not only as a rejection of the constraining and corrective premises of ordinary language philosophy but as central to his turn to a philosophy of ethical and political issues, where the very quality that makes speech acts unable to perform the stabilizing function Austin and Searle hoped for makes them central to a philosophy of affirmation. The instability allows deconstruction of authoritative statements and/but also allows the possibility of origination in ethics or politics. A speech act can create its context rather than being, as in Austin or Searle, controlled and stabilized by a context (p. 112). (Miller builds on this to reverse the usual order of intention: speech acts create the feelings that seem to create them: a premise that love language, for instance, creates the love it seems to demonstrate—which may not please lovers or their beloveds!)

Working in a very different philosophical tradition, Donald Davidson also moves to a broader cogent critique of attempts to arm Speech Act theory to create laws of semantics. His essay, "Communication and Convention," *Inquiries into Truth and Interpretation*, pp. 265–80, comes closest to a Wittgensteinian view (from a Quinean empiricist!) that there is no specifying in advance the possible meanings that can be generated with language. He denies that we have conventions that we all know which control our interpretation of what we hear or read. This goes to the heart of Grice's, and after him, Pratt's, attempts to establish norms for communication. Davidson insists on the non-connectedness of literal sentence meanings and the "ulterior purposes" of speakers or writers. An imperative sentence is correctly read grammatically as a command; but that will not mean that we must interpret the message as a sincere command; it may be a facetious hypothetical case (goe catch with child a mandrake root) or an insult (go jump in the lake): "I conclude that it is not an accidental feature of language that the ulterior purpose of an utterance and its literal meaning are independent, in the sense that the latter cannot be derived from the former: it is the essence of language. I call this feature of language the principle of the *autonomy of meaning*" (p. 274). Davidson's view of semantics as a matter of pragmatic individual interpretive theorizing and adjustment to each specific statement seems to me a far better description of interpretive activity than the Speech Act theorists' attempts to establish norms for reception of entire utterances, individual sentences, or even individual words—the three levels of arguments for convention as controlling semantics under "standard" conditions that Davidson opposes.

Here, and in conclusion, is perhaps the place to note Dasenbrock's attempt (esp. pp. 72–76), to format Davidson's thinking as an argument for intention.

The case is our handling of malapropisms in speech or writing. Davidson argues that, before we face such an anomaly, we adapt our thinking to the new circumstance by creating a nonce or "passing" theory that explains it in terms of the speaker's intention (intended to say). But this doesn't restore a Gricean certainty to utterances. We read in Sheridan's *The Rivals* Mrs. Malaprop's suggestions for education: "I would have her instructed in geometry, that she might know something of the contagious countries," and find those are easy: she must have *meant* geography and contiguous. But the continuation, "and likewise that she might reprehend the true meaning of what she is saying" leads us into a darker place than mere obvious substitutions. We all reprehend our true meanings and avoid what comprehension we can: that is, we now deal with a literary text that speaks to us in complicated ways that go beyond the easy solutions, on which we will not disagree, provided by "she really means" intentional interpretations. Such method in Mrs. Malaprop's mistakes, or Joyce's portmanteau neologisms, will allow a variety of nonce theories, no single intentional and correct interpretation. As always, the only answers provided by an appeal to intention are the simple answers. I should say that Dasenbrock applied Davidson correctly in seeing his theories as a challenge to a belief that we can't adopt new interpretions to new situations, that is, that we are bound into some approach given by our communities. He also grants (p. 73) that "passing" theories do not guarantee the interpretations they produce. I do not find that we need the hope to recover intentions as a motivation to work out a problem in a text. Raymond Gibbs, *Intentions in the Experience of Meaning*, p. 113, offers simpler versions of getting away with it as a recourse to intention when we find errors and correct for what they must mean. But we hardly need to imagine an intender in any meaningful way to correct a typo or a grammatical solecism.

(My reader who has come all the way to the end of this appendix will try to understand why most readers, unlike her- or himself, would prefer not to confront this fuller discussion of Speech Act theory and intention as a clotted node in the text itself.)

APPENDIX 2

STANLEY FISH'S INTENTIONS

Stanley Fish's famous variorum essay, where Fish comes early to the "vexed" subject, comes very close to saying that we call author's intention what we find in the text. But at the same time he leaves us free to conclude that this is not so much an ironic and correctable state of affairs as perhaps a necessary one: "Interpreting the *Variorum*," p. 176. When he returns to the issue (brilliantly, as in so much that he does) he expresses more directly that all interpretation necessarily ascribes intention, though his argument is based, as so much unclear thinking in this area is, on the oral, contextual case, the old "can you pass the salt" example so dear to more rigid intentionalists: *Doing What Comes Naturally*, p. 295. He goes on to insist that "even to think of a sentence is to think of its ... conditions that include a speaker, with an intention and a purpose in a situation" (p. 320). I can't agree. A written text published to the world contains no speaker and its situation keeps changing with each reception. (I should note that Fish is here using his distinctions for a purpose with which I am sympathetic, his attack on Richard Posner's narrow views of legal intention.) Here, as in his early work, Fish in the "vexed matter of intention" (p. 294) is uncomfortable saying that intention is *merely* a rhetorical way of enforcing an interpretation. David Bleich early offered a simpler version of Fish's own presentation of intention, seeing it as merely a category of an interpretive community: "only two readers who agree that there will be such a thing as an extractable author's intention will preserve this intention. The authority for such a perception lies only in the influence of that interpretive community which claims that perspective, which is its accepted way of making a sense of what it reads" (Tompkins, ed., p. 151).

I have noticed above (II.x) that Max Black's general argument against Grice's identification of speaker's intention as the location of meaning follows this path: "The relevant sense of 'intend' is no more intelligible than the notion of speaker's meaning it is supposed to elucidate, because it implicates the problematic notion of meaning. Given this circularity, the presence of intention in acts of communication is indeed assured, but only tautologically, as following from the definition of speaker's intentions in terms of meaning and not vice versa" ("Meaning and Intention," p. 264). Black uses virtually the same argument against the concept of intention that Fish uses to assert it; Fish considers a universal—his view that we can't think of meaning without thinking of intention—what Black finds merely a tautology created by a peculiar definition of meaning, where every meaning is called an intention. Both Bleich's and Black's formulations seem to fit the oddly evacuated notion of intention with which Fish works, as something we ascribe to an interpretation after we make it.

Fish's own highly successful career as a period critic has similarly given him an instinct for contextual reading that seems at odds with his general theory of interpretation. Interpretation of Renaissance poetry should "begin with and stay close to those materials and to the traditions (as historical as any) that has produced them." As with the parallel concept of intention, he gives an uncertain degree of force to historical context by arguing that we cannot think without history: "it is impossible *not* to historicize, impossible to conceive of an event or a text independently of some notion of its origin, genealogical affiliations, generic habitation etc." This reliance on a "context of primary intelligibility" (*There's No Such Thing as Free Speech*, pp. 26, 259) creates in effect an intentional bias and justification for interpretation when what is really happening is that the interpreter is taking from the context what cues to interpretation already seem useful to him/her in approaching the text. Fish is as unclear and unsettled on historical context as on intention, immediately trying to limit the force he gives it by arguing against history as "last instance" evidence (p. 259).

The troubling issue of intention seems only to draw Fish into more confusions in his legal work, where it is of course a powerfully politicized notion. In a review of Gregory Leyh's collection of essays, *Legal Hermeneutics*, reprinted as "Play of Surfaces: Theory and the Law," in *There's No Such Thing as Free Speech*, pp. 180–99, Fish takes on the anti-originalist legal hermeneutics of David Hoy that would argue that "linguistic processing can be done without attention to intention" (p. 183). Fish is throughout his argument clearly uncomfortable that his position against Hoy might seem to place him where it needs indeed place him, with those who argue for founder's intentions. He wishes as always to have his intention and not to have its effects, so his argument becomes again a rarefied one for the necessity of intentional thinking but opposes the weight that such thinking gives to any argument from intention. This seems to me an impossible position to argue and leaves Fish, in legal arguments, giving a kind of closet weight to founder's intention just as in literary arguments his position on intention gives pragmatic force to arguments from author, context, or history. Interestingly he begins from the premises of Steven Knapp and Walter Benn Michaels in their end-to-theory arguments (see II.i, n. 20) that all interpretations are based on "one style of interpretation—the intentional style," an assertion that already creates a kind of ghost of intention in a style. As that argument led in practice to a privileging of historical arguments in literary interpretation, so Fish finds it difficult to make credible his denials that his belief in intention in legal arguments will not undercut his anti-originalist positions. His attempts to evacuate intentionality of any operative force tend to reduce it to something like a belief in intention in the philosophical sense, an aboutness or direction of a statement. But such a belief in a definition of meaning as the aboutness of a statement is quite different from an argument which locates, as Fish's must seem to, meaning in the originator of the statement or the context out of which it came.

I think Fish, master rhetorician though he is, misunderstands the force of his position here, which would seem to test against the decided realities of legal interpretation the validity of the theory-doesn't-matter school. What premises one begins with, in literature as in law, will greatly affect the argument one credits. By positing a necessary place for meaning in even the most evacuated spaces of intention, Fish necessarily adds force to those who would interpret the constitution by recourse to their notions of framers' intentions. Fish's belief in the necessity of an "intentional style" seems an oddly idealist wedge, a kind of epistemology controlling his thinking, in such a generally pragmatist body of thinking. When he says "since meaning cannot be determined apart from (the prior and simultaneous) assigning of intention, everyone who is an interpreter is in the intention business, and there is no methodological cash value to declaring yourself (or even thinking yourself) to be an intentionalist because you couldn't be anything else" (p. 184), Fish seems not only to be declaring, unargued, a theory of meaning (bad philosophy) but also strategically underestimating the practical force of such a concession to authority, once admitted (bad rhetoric). Fish is merely conservative in his pragmatic effect, as he has been in encouraging New Historicist styles of interpretation, even when he then hastens to critique them as trying to close down interpretive possibilities. Not surprisingly, Fish even begins to argue that some interpretations not founded in intention are in fact merely playing with the text and thus not worthy of the name interpretation (equivalent here to meaning-making in E. D. Hirsch's privileged sense): "I do not think it should be called interpreting" (p. 185). I find both of Hoy's arguments cited by Fish not destroyed by Fish's a priorist assertion of intention as the originary form of meaning: that we can find intention in a non-intended effect, say a noise (an argument I develop above in my own way—II.viii. n. 1); and that hermeneutics (obviously some hermeneuticians, among whom I would include myself) "takes the question about the intended meaning as a secondary one that presupposes a prior understanding of 'meaning' in some other sense" (p. 183). That is, meaning as a concept is not dependent on the concept of intention, as it has not been in philosophical thinking, especially in pragmatism. (On the varied meanings of the term hermeneutics see II.xviii, n. 11.)

At the end of this review, Fish comes to admit the pragmatic weakness of his argument. Such distinctions as "originalism and non-originalism ... do name positions one can invoke strategically in the course of engaging in the practice of what I have called 'doing what comes naturally.' Although one cannot be a nonoriginalist and cannot avoid being an originalist, the announcement that you are or are not one or the other may be crucial to the effectiveness of what you are trying to do.... They carry a calculable rhetorical weight" (p. 192). In literary study they carry a weight because they empower interpretations that privilege biographical, contextual, and historical interpretive approaches over more general interpretive engines; and in doing so they have a force to reinstate Hirsch's old hierarchy of meaning and significance. Dasenbrock, *Truth and Consequences*, p. 289, n. 2, offers a list of Fish essays bearing on intention, including a few I don't discuss here.

WORKS CITED

Abraham, Kenneth S. "Statutory Interpretation and Literary Theory: Some Common Concerns of an Unlikely Pair." In Sanford Levinson and Steven Mailloux, eds., *Interpreting Law and Literature*. Evanston, IL: Northwestern UP, 1988., pp. 115–29.

Abraham, Nicholas, and Maria Torok. *The Wolf Man's Magic Word: A Cryptonymy*. Trans. Nicholas Rand. Foreword by Jacques Derrida. Minneapolis: U of Minnesota P, 1986, pp.436–51.

Abrams, M.H. "How to do Things with Texts." In Hazard Adams and Leroy Searle, eds., *Critical Theory Since 1965*. Tallahassee: Florida State UP, 1986, 99. 436–51.

Achebe, Chinua. "An Image of Africa." *Research in African Literatures* 9 (1978): 1–15.

Adriaens, Geert, and Steven L. Small. "Word Expert Parsing Revisited in a Cognitive Science Perspective." In Steven L. Small, G.W. Cottrell, and M. Tanenhaus, eds., *Lexical Ambiguity Resolution*. San Mateo: Morgan Kaufmann, 1988, pp. 13–44.

Ahmad, Aijaz. "Jameson's Rhetoric of Otherness and the 'National Allegory.'" *Social Text* 17 (Fall 1987): 3–25.

Allen, James Smith. *In the Public Eye: A History of Reading in Modern France, 1800–1940*. Princeton: Princeton UP, 1991.

Alter, Robert. *The Pleasures of Reading in an Ideological Age*. 1989; rev. New York: Norton, 1996.

Althusser, Louis. *For Marx*. Trans. Ben Brewster. New York: Random House, 1970.

—. "Ideology and Ideological State Apparatuses." In *Lenin and Philosophy*. Trans. Ben Brewster. New York: Monthly Review Press, 1971. pp. 127–86.

Altieri, Charles. *Act and Quality: A Theory of Literary Meaning and Humannistic Understanding*. Amherst: U of Massachusetts P, 1981.

—. *Subjective Agency: A Theory of First-Person Expressivity and its Social Implications*. Cambridge: Blackwell, 1994.

Amory, Hugh, and David D. Hall, eds., *A History of the Book in America. Volume One: The Colonial Book in the Atlantic World*. Cambridge: Cambridge UP, 2000.

Anderson, Amanda. *Tainted Souls and Painted Faces*. Ithaca: Cornell UP, 1993.

Anderson, Jennifer, and Elizabeth Sauer, eds., *Books and Readers in Early Modern England*. Philadelphia: U of Pennsylvania P, 2002.

Anger, Suzy. *Knowing the Past*. Ithaca: Cornell UP, 2001.

—. *Victorian Interpretation*. Ithaca: Cornell UP, 2005.

Anscombe, G.E. *Intention*. Ithaca: Cornell UP, 1963.

Appleyard, J.A. *Becoming a Reader: The Experience of Fiction from Childhood to Adulthood*. Cambridge: Cambridge UP, 1990.

Armstrong, Paul B. *Conflicting Readings: Variety and Validity in Interpretation*. Chapel Hill: U of North Carolina P, 1990.

—. "The Conflict of Interpretations and the Limits of Pluralism." *PMLA* 98 (1983): 341–52.

Austin, J.L. *How to do Things with Words*. Oxford: Oxford UP, 1962.

Backus, Margot Gayle. "Discourse and Silence in the Victorian Family Cell: Problems of Subjectivity in *The History of Sexuality: Vol. I*." *Victorian Literature and Culture* 24 (1996): 159–74.

Bailey, Jane Garrison. "The Act of Reading Allegory: Filling the Gap between Narrative and Interpretive Strategies." MLA Conference, Dec. 28, 1995.

Bakhtin, Mikhail. *The Dialogic Imagination: Four Essays*. Austin: U of Texas P, 1981.

—. *Problems of Dostoevsky's Poetics*. Minneapolis: U of Minnesota P, 1984.

—. *Speech Genres and Other Late Essays*. Austin: U of Texas P, 1986.

Bal, Mieke. *Lethal Love: Feminist Literary Readings of Biblical Love Stories*. Bloomington: Indiana UP, 1987.

Banks, Marva. "*Uncle Tom's Cabin* and Antebellum Black Response." In James L. Machor, ed., *Readers in History: Nineteenth Century American Literature and the Contexts of Response*. Baltimore: Johns Hopkins UP, 1993. pp. 209–27.

Barsalous, Lawrence, and Dorrit Billman. "Systematicity and Semantic Ambiguity." In David S. Gorfein, ed., *Resolving Semantic Ambiguity*. Berlin: Springer-Verlag, 1989.

Barthes, Roland. "The Death of the Author." *Image—Music—Text*. New York: Hill and Wang, 1977.

—. *The Pleasure of the Text*. New York: Hill and Wang, 1975.

—. *Roland Barthes by Roland Barthes*. New York: Hill and Wang, 1977.

—. *S/Z*. Trans. Richard Miller. New York: Hill and Wang, 1974.

Baxandall, Lee, and Stefan Morawski, eds. *Marx and Engels on Literature and Art*. St. Louis: Telos, 1973.

Beardsley, M.C. "The Authority of the Text." In Gary Iseminger, ed., *Intention and Interpretation*. Philadelphia: Temple UP, 1992. pp. 24–40.

—. "Intentions and Interpretations: A Fallacy Revived." In Michael J. Wreen and Donald M. Callen, eds., *The Aesthetic Point of View*. Ithaca: Cornell UP, 1982.

—. *The Possibility of Criticism*. Detroit: Wayne State UP, 1970.

Beaujour, Michael. "Genus Universum." *Glyph* 7. Baltimore: Johns Hopkins UP, 1980. pp. 15-31.

Beebee, Thomas O. *The Ideology of Genre: A Comparative Study of Generic Instability*. University Park: Pennsylvania State UP, 1994.

Behler, Ernst. *Klassische Ironie, romantische Ironie, tragische Ironie*. Darmstadt: Wissenschaftliche Buchgesellschaft, 1972.

Bell, William. "Victorian Paratexts." *Victorian Literature and Culture* 27 (1999): 327–35.

Belsey, Catherine. *Critical Practice*. London: Methuen, 1980.

Benedict, Barbara. *Making the Modern Reader: Cultural Mediation in Early Modern Literary Anthologies*. Princeton: Princeton UP, 1996.

Benjamin, Walter. *Illuminations*. Trans. Harry Zohn. New York: Schocken, 1969.

—. *Ursprung des deutschen Trauerspiels*; English as *The Origin of German Tragic Drama*. Trans. John Osborne. London: Verso, 1985.

Bersalous, Lawrence and Dorrit Billman, "Systematicity and Semantic Ambiguity," In David S. Gorfein, ed., *Resolving Semanitc Ambiguity*. New York: Springer-Verlag, 1989.

Bennett, Andrew, ed. *Readers and Reading*. London: Longman, 1995.

Bennett, Tony. "Texts in History: The Determinations of Readings and their Texts." In James L. Machor and Philip Goldstein, eds., *Reception Study: From Literary Theory to Cultural Studies*. New York: Routledge, 2001, pp. 61–74.

Bernstein, Richard J. *Beyond Objectivism and Relativism*. Philadelphia: U of Pennsylvania P, 1983.

—. *The New Constellation: The Ethical-Political Horizons of Modernity/Postmodernity*. Cambridge: Polity Press, 1991.

Bersani, Leo. *A Future for Astyanax*. Boston: Little Brown, 1976.

Bevir, Mark. "Objectivity in History." *History and Theory* 33 (Oct. 1994): 328–44.

Bishop, Lloyd. *Romantic Irony in French Literature from Diderot to Beckett*. Nashville: Vanderbilt UP, 1989.

Black, Max. "How Metaphors Work: A Reply to Donald Davidson." In Sheldon Sacks, ed., *On Metaphor*. Chicago: U of Chicago P, 1979. pp. 181–92.

—. "Meaning and Intention: An Examination of Grice's Views." *New Literary History* 4 (1973): 257–79.

—. *Models and Metaphors*. New York: Cornell UP, 1962.

Bleich, David. *The Double Perspective: Language, Literary, and Social Relations*. New York: Oxford UP, 1988.

—. *Readings and Feelings: An Introduction to Subjective Criticism*. Urbana, IL: NCTE, 1975.

—. *Subjective Criticism*. Baltimore: Johns Hopkins UP, 1978.

Bloom, Harold. *How to Read and Why*. New York: Scribner, 2000.

Bloom, Lois. "Meaning and Expression." In Willis F. Overton and David S. Palermo, eds., *The Nature and Ontogenesis of Meaning*. Hillsdale, NJ: Lawrence Erlbaum, 1994. pp. 215–35.

—. *The Transition from Infancy to Language: Acquiring the Power of Expression*. Cambridge: Cambridge UP, 1993.

Bonaparte, Marie. *The Life and Work of Edgar Allan Poe: A Psycho-Analytic Interpretation*. Trans. John Rodker. London: Hogarth, 1949.

Bonvillian, John D., and Francine G.P. Patterson. "Sign Language and the Development of Meaning in a Lowland Gorilla." In Charlotte Mandell and Allyssa McCabe, eds., *The Problem of Meaning: Behavioral and Cognitive Perspectives*. New York: Elsevier, 1997.

Booth, Wayne. *The Company We Keep: An Ethics of Fiction*. Berkeley: U of California P, 1988.

—. "Metaphor as Rhetoric: The Problem of Evaluation." In Sheldon Sacks, ed., *On Metaphor*. Chicago: U of Chicago P, 1979. pp. 47–70.

—. *A Rhetoric of Irony*. Chicago: U of Chicago P, 1974.

Bourdieu, Pierre. *Distinction*. Cambridge, MA: Harvard UP, 1984.

—. *The Field of Cultural Production: Essays on Art and Literature*, ed. Randal Johnson. New York: Columbia UP, 1993.

Bouson, J. Brooks. *The Empathic Reader: A Study of the Narcissistic Character and the Drama of the Self*. Amherst: U of Massachusetts P, 1989.

Bové, Paul A. "Discourse." In Frank Lentricchia and Thomas McLaughlin, eds., *Critical Terms for Literary Study*. Rev. ed. Chicago: U of Chicago P, 1995. pp. 50–65.

Boyarin, Jonathan, ed. *The Ethnography of Reading*. Berkeley: U of California P, 1993.

Bratman, Michael. *Intention, Plans, and Practical Reason*. Cambridge, MA: Harvard UP, 1987.

Brest, Paul. "The Misconceived Quest for the Original Understanding." In Sanford Levinson and Steven Mailloux, eds., *Interpreting Law and Literature*. Evanston, IL: Northwestern UP, 1988, pp. 69–96.

Brooks, Cleanth. "The Formalist Critic." *Kenyon Review* 13 (Winter 1951): 72–81.

Brown, Terrance. "Affective Dimensions of Meaning." In Willis F. Overton and David S. Palermo, eds., *The Nature and Ontogenesis of Meaning*. Hillsdale, NJ: Lawrence Erlbaum, 1994. pp. 167–90.

Brugman, Claudia, and George Lakoff. "Cognitive Topology and Lexical Networks." In Steven L. Small, G.W. Cottrell, and M. Tanenhaus, eds., *Lexical Ambiguity Resolution*. San Mateo: Morgan Kaufmann, 1988, pp. 477–508.

Bruns, Gerald. *Hermeneutics, Ancient & Modern*. New Haven: Yale UP, 1992.

—. "Intention, Authority, and Meaning." *Critical Inquiry* 7 (1980): 297–309.

Bubka, Andrea, and David S. Gorfein. "Resolving Semantic Ambiguity: An Introduction." In David S. Gorfein, ed., *Resolving Semantic Ambiguity*. New York: Springer-Verlag, 1989.

Burke, Seán. *The Death and Return of the Author: Criticism and Subjectivity in Barthes, Foucault and Derrida*. Edinburgh: Edinburgh UP, 1998.

Burkhardt, Armin. "Searle on Metaphor." In Armin Burkhardt, ed., *Speech Acts, Meaning and Intentions: Critical Approaches to the Philosophy of John R. Searle*. New York: Walter de Gruyter, 1990. pp. 303–35.

Calinescu, Matei. *Rereading*. New Haven: Yale UP, 1993.

Calvino, Italo. *Cosmicomics*. Trans. William Weaver. New York: Harcourt Brace Jovanovich, 1976.

Cambridge Dictionary of Philosophy. Cambridge: Cambridge UP, 1995.

Carr, E.H. *What is History?* London: Penguin, 1961.

Carroll, Nöel. "Art, Intention and Conversation." In Gary Iseminger, ed., *Intention and Interpretation*. Philadelphia: Temple UP, 1992. pp. 103–11.

Carruthers, Mary. *The Book of Memory: A Study of Memory in Medieval Culture*. Cambridge: Cambridge UP, 1990.

Cavallo, Guglielmo, and Roger Chartier, eds. *A History of Reading in the West*. Amherst: U of Massachusetts P, 1999.

Cavell, Stanley. *A Pitch of Philosophy: Autobiographical Exercises*. Cambridge, MA: Harvard UP, 1994.

Chambers, Ross. *Room for Maneuver: Reading (the) Oppositional (in) Narrative*. Chicago: Chicago UP, 1991.

Champigny, Robert. "Semantic Modes and Literary Genres." In Joseph P. Strelka, ed., *Theories of Literary Genre*. University Park: Pennsylvania State UP, 1978, pp. 94–111.

Chartier, Roger. *Forms and Meanings: Texts, Performances, and Audiences from Codex to Computer*. Philadelphia: U of Pennsylvania P, 1995.

—. "Leisure and Sociability: Reading Aloud in Early Modern Europe." In S. Zimmerman and R.F.E. Weissman, eds., *Urban Life in the Renaissance*. Newark: U of Delaware Press, 1989, pp. 103–21.

—. *The Order of Books: Readers, Authors and Libraries in Europe Between the Fourteenth and Eighteenth Centuries*. Stanford: Stanford UP, 1994.

—, ed. *The Cultural Uses of Print in Early Modern France*. Princeton: Princeton UP, 1987.

Chatman, Seymour. "The Structure of Narrative Transmission." In Roger Fowler, ed., *Style and Structure in Literature*. Oxford: Blackwell, 1975. pp. 213–57.
Cioffi, Frank. "Intention and Interpretation in Criticism." In David Newton-DeMolina, ed., *On Literary Intention*. Edinburgh: Edinburgh UP, 1976.
Close, A.J. "*Don Quixote* and the Intentionalist Fallacy." In David Newton-DeMolina, ed., *On Literary Intention*. Edinburgh: Edinburgh UP, 1976. pp. 174–93.
Cmiel, Kenneth. "After Objectivity: What Comes Next in History?" *American Literary History* 2 (Spring 1990): 170–81.
Coe, Richard, Lorelei Lingärd, and Tatiana Teslenko, eds. *The Rhetoric and Ideology of Genre*. Cresskill, NJ: Hampton Press, 2002.
Cohen, Ralph. "Generating Literary Histories" In Jeffrey N. Cox and Larry J. Reynolds, eds., *New Historical Literary Study*. Princeton: Princeton UP, 1993.
Colebrook, Claire. *Irony: The New Critical Idiom*. London: Routledge, 2004.
—. *New Literary Histories*. Manchester: Manchester UP, 1997.
Coleman, Joyce. *Public Reading and the Reading Public in Late Medieval England and France*. Cambridge: Cambridge UP, 1996.
Colie, Rosalie L. *The Resources of Kind: Genre-Theory in the Renaissance*. Berkeley: U of California P, 1973.
Collingwood, R.G. *The Idea of History*. Oxford: Oxford UP, 1945.
Collini, Stefan, ed. *Interpretation and Overinterpretation*. Cambridge: Cambridge UP, 1992.
Corbett, Mary Jean. *Representing Femininity: Middle-Class Subjectivity in Victorian and Edwardian Women's Autobiographies*. New York: Oxford UP, 1992.
Crawford, Mary, and Roger Chaffin. "The Reader's Construction of Meaning: Cognitive Research on Gender and Comprehension." In Elizabeth A. Flynn and Patrocinio P. Schweickart, eds., *Gender and Reading: Essays on Readers, Texts, and Contexts*. Baltimore: Johns Hopkins UP, 1986. pp. 3–30.
Crosman, Robert. "Do Readers Make Meaning?" In Susan R. Suleiman and Inge Crosman, eds., *The Reader in the Text: Essays on Audience and Interpretation*. Princeton: Princeton UP, 1980. pp. 149–64.
Culler, Jonathan. *On Deconstruction: Theory and Criticism after Structuralism*. Ithaca: Cornell UP, 1982.
—. "Literary Competence." In Jane P. Tompkins, ed., *Reader-Response Criticism*. Baltimore: Johns Hopkins UP, 1985.
—. *Literary Theory: A Very Short Introduction*. Oxford: Oxford UP, 1997.
—. *On Puns: The Foundation of Letters*. Oxford: Basil Blackwell, 1988.
—. *Structuralist Poetics: Structuralism, Linguistics and the Study of Literature*. Ithaca: Cornell UP, 1976.

Curtis, Gerald. "Shared Lines." In Carol Christ and John O. Jordan, eds., *Victorian Literature and the Victorian Visual Imagination*. Berkeley: U of California P, 1995, pp. 27–59.

Danneberg, Lutz, and Hans-Harald Müller. "On Justifying the Choice of Interpretive Theories." *The Journal of Aesthetics and Art Criticism* 43 (Autumn 1984): 7–16.

Dasenbrock, Reed Way. *Truth and Consequences: Intentions, Conventions, and the New Thematics*. University Park: Pennsylvania State UP, 2001.

Davidson, Donald. "Communication and Convention." *Inquiries into Truth and Interpretation*. Oxford: Clarendon, 1984, pp. 265–80.

—. "On the Very Idea of a Conceptual Scheme." *Inquiries into Truth and Interpretation*. Oxford: Clarendon, 1984. pp. 183–98.

—. "What Metaphors Mean." *Inquiries into Truth and Interpretation*. Oxford: Clarendon, 1984, pp. 245–64.

Davis, Wayne A. *Implicature: Intention, Convention, and Principle in the Failure of Gricean Theory*. Cambridge: Cambridge UP, 1998.

de Certeau, Michel. *The Practice of Everyday Life*. Trans. Steven S. Rendall. Berkeley: U of California P, 1984.

—. "Reading as Poaching." In Andrew Bennett, ed., *Readers and Reading*. London: Longman, 1995, pp. 150–63.

de Man, Paul. *Allegories of Reading: Figural Language in Rousseau, Nietzsche, Rilke, and Proust*. New Haven: Yale UP, 1979.

—. "The Concept of Irony." *Aesthetic Ideology*. Minneapolis: U of Minnesota P, 1996.

—. "The Dead-End of Formalist Criticism." *Blindness and Insight: Essays in the Rhetoric of Contemporary Criticism*. 1971; Minneapolis: U of Minnesota P, 1983, pp. 229–45.

—. "The Epistemology of Metaphor." In Sheldon Sacks, ed., *On Metaphor*. Chicago: U of Chicago P, 1978. pp. 11–28.

—. "Form and Intent in the American New Criticism." *Blindness and Insight: Essays in the Rhetoric of Contemporary Criticism*. 1971; Minneapolis: U of Minnesota P, 1983. pp. 20–35.

—. *The Resistance to Theory*. Minneapolis: U of Minnesota P, 1986.

—. *The Rhetoric of Romanticism*. New York: Columbia UP, 1984.

—. "The Rhetoric of Temporality." *Blindness and Insight: Essays in the Rhetoric of Contemporary Criticism*. 1971; Minneapolis: U of Minnesota P, 1983. pp. 187–228.

de Saussure, Ferdinand. *Course in General Linguistics*. New York: Philosophical Library, 1959.

Dennett, Daniel C. *The Intentional Stance*. Cambridge: MIT P, 1987.

Derrida, Jacques. "Des Tours de Babel." In Joseph Graham, ed., *Difference in Translation*. Ithaca: Cornell UP, 1985. pp. 165–249.

—. *Dissemination*. Trans. Barbara Johnson. Chicago: U of Chicago P, 1981.
—. *Of Grammatology*. Baltimore: Johns Hopkins UP, 1974.
—. *Limited Inc*. Evanston, IL: Northwestern, 1988.
—. "La loi du genre/The Law of Genre." *Glyph* 7. Baltimore: Johns Hopkins UP, 1980. pp. 176–232.
—. "Like the Sound of the Sea Deep Within a Shell: Paul de Man's War." *Critical Inquiry* 14 (Spring 1988): 591–652.
—. "Signature Event Context." *Margins of Philosophy*. Trans. Alan Bass. Chicago: U of Chicago P, 1982. pp. 307–30.
—. "Signature Event Context," "Limited Inc," and "Afterward," *Glyph* 2 (1977).
—. "Shibboleth." In Geoffrey H. Hartman and Sanford Budick, eds., *Midrash and Literature*. New Haven: Yale UP, 1986.
—. "Signature Event Context." *Margins of Philosophy*. Trans. Alan Bass. Chicago: U of Chicago P, 1982. pp. 307–30.
—. *Speech and Phenomena, and Other Essays on Husserl's Theory of Signs*. Trans. David B. Allison. Evanston, IL: Northwestern UP, 1973.
—. "Structure, Sign, and Play in the Discourses of the Human Sciences." *Writing and Difference*. Trans. Alan Bass. Chicago: U of Chicago P, 1978.
—. "White Mythology: Metaphor in the Text of Philosophy." *Margins of Philosophy*. Trans. Alan Bass. Chicago: U of Chicago P, 1982. pp. 207–71.
Dimock, Wai-Chee. "Feminism, New Historicism and the Reader." *American Literature* 63 (1991): 601–22.
Donoghue, Denis. *The Practice of Reading*. New Haven: Yale UP, 1998.
Dubrow, Heather. "The Audiences of Early Modern Secular Lyric, or, This Poem May Be Monitored for Quality Control." Paper delivered at New York University, April 14, 2005.
Duff, David, ed. *Modern Genre Theory*. Harlow: Longman, 2000.
Dummett, Michael. *Truth and Other Enigmas*. Cambridge, MA: Harvard UP, 1978.
Dupré, John. *The Disorder of Things: Metaphysical Foundations of the Disunity of Science*. Cambridge, MA: Harvard UP, 1993.
Dutton, Denis. "Why Intentionalism Won't Go Away." In Anthony J. Cascardi, ed., *Literature and the Question of Philosophy*. Baltimore: Johns Hopkins UP, 1987. pp. 192–209.
Eagleton, Terry. *Ideology: An Introduction*. London: Verso, 1991.
—. *The Ideology of the Aesthetic*. Oxford: Blackwell, 1990.
—. *Literary Theory: An Introduction*. Minneapolis: U of Minnesota P, 1983.
Eco, Umberto. *Interpretation and Overinterpretation*. Cambridge: Cambridge UP, 1992.
—. *The Limits of Interpretation*. 1990; Bloomington: Indiana UP, 1994.
—. *The Open Work*. Trans. Anna Cancogni. Italian orig. 1962; Cambridge, MA: Harvard UP, 1989.

—. *The Role of the Reader: Explorations in the Semiotics of Texts.* Bloomington: Indiana UP, 1979.
—. *Six Walks in the Fictional Woods.* Cambridge, MA: Harvard UP, 1994.
—. *A Theory of Semiotics.* Bloomington: Indiana UP, 1976.
Edelman, Gerald. *Bright Air, Brilliant Fire: On the Matter of the Mind.* London: Penguin, 1994.
Eliot, George. "Miscellanies" (holograph note book). Berg Collection, New York Public Library, fol. 108.
Ellis, John. *Against Deconstruction.* Princeton: Princeton UP, 1989.
Empson, William. *Seven Types of Ambiguity.* Rev. 1930; New York: New Directions, 1947.
Fass, Dan. "An Account of Coherence, Semantic Relations, Metonymy, and Lexical Ambiguity Resolution." In Steven L. Small, G. W. Cottrell, and M. Tanenhaus, eds., *Lexical Ambiguity Resolution.* San Mateo: Morgan Kaufmann, 1988. pp. 151–77.
—. *Processing Metonymy and Metaphor.* Greenwich, CT: Ablex, 1997.
Feldman, Carol, Jerome Bruner, David Kalmar, and Bobbi Renderer. "Plot, Plight, and Dramatism: Interpretation at Three Ages." In Willis F. Overton and David S. Palermo, eds., *The Nature and Ontogenesis of Meaning.* Hillsdale, NJ: Lawrence Erlbaum Associates, 1994. pp. 255–77.
Felman, Shoshana. *Jacques Lacan and the Adventure of Insight: Psychoanalysis in Contemporary Culture.* Cambridge, MA: Harvard UP, 1987.
Fetterley, Judith. *The Resisting Reader: A Feminist Approach to American Fiction.* Bloomington: Indiana UP, 1978.
Fish, Stanley. *Doing What Comes Naturally: Change, Rhetoric, and the Practice of Theory in Literary and Legal Studies.* Durham, NC: Duke UP, 1989.
—. "Interpreting the Variorum." In Jane P. Tompkins, ed., *Reader-Response Criticism.* Baltimore: Johns Hopkins UP, 1980. pp. 164–84.
—. *Is There a Text in This Class?: The Authority of Interpretive Communities.* Cambridge, MA: Harvard UP, 1980.
—. "Literature in the Reader: Affective Stylistics." In Jane P. Tompkins, ed., *Reader-Response Criticism.* Baltimore: Johns Hopkins UP, 1980. pp. 70–100.
—. *Surprised by Sin: The Reader in* Paradise Lost. 1967; rpt. Cambridge, MA: Harvard UP, 1998.
—. *There's No Such thing as Free Speech . . . And It's a Good Thing Too.* New York: Oxford UP, 1994.
—. "Why No One's Afraid of Wolfgang Iser." *Diacritics* 11 (Spring 1981): 2–13.
—. "Yet Once More." *Professional Correctness.* Oxford: Clarendon, 1995. pp. 1–18.
Fishelov, David. *Metaphors of Genre: The Role of Analogies in Genre Theory.* University Park: Pennsylvania State UP, 1993.

Fiske, John. "Popular Culture." Frank Lentricchia and Thomas McLaughlin, eds., *Critical Terms for Literary Study*. Rev. ed. Chicago: U of Chicago P, 1995. pp. 321–35.

—. *Reading the Popular*. Boston: Unwin Hyman, 1989.

—. *Understanding Popular Culture*. Boston, Unwin Hyman, 1989.

Fletcher, Angus. *Allegory: The Theory of a Symbolic Mode*. Ithaca: Cornell UP, 1964.

Flint, Kate. *The Woman Reader: 1837–1914*. Oxford: Oxford UP, 1993.

Flynn, Elizabeth A., and Patrocinio P. Schweickart, eds. *Gender and Reading: Essays on Readers, Texts, and Contexts*. Baltimore: Johns Hopkins UP, 1986.

Foakes, R.A. *Hamlet Versus Lear: Cultural Politics and Shakespeare's Art*. Cambridge: Cambridge UP, 1993.

Foucault, Michel. *Archaeology of Knowledge*. New York: Pantheon, 1972.

—. *The Order of Things: An Archaeology of the Human Sciences*. New York: Vintage, 1973.

—. "Truth and Power." *Power/Knowledge: Selected Interviews and Other Writings, 1972–77*. New York: Pantheon, 1980.

—. "What is an Author?" In James D. Faubion, ed., *Aesthetics, Method, and Epistemology*. New York: New Press, 1998. pp. 205–22.

Fowler, Alastair. "Intention Floreat." In David Newton-DeMolina, ed., *On Literary Intention*. Edinburgh: Edinburgh UP, 1976.

—. *Kinds of Literature: An Introduction to the Theory of Genres and Modes*. Cambridge, MA: Harvard UP, 1982.

Frank, Manfred. "The Infinite Text." *Glyph* 7. Baltimore: Johns Hopkins UP, 1980. pp. 70-101.

Freedgood, Elaine. *The Ideas in Things: Fugitive Meaning in the Victorian Novel*. Chicago: U of Chicago P, 2006.

Freud, Sigmund. *The Interpretation of Dreams*. New York: Basic Books, 1956.

—. *Jokes and their Relation to the Unconscious*. Trans. James Strachey. New York: Norton, 1960.

Freund, Elizabeth. *The Return of the Reader: Reader-Response Criticism*. London: Methuen, 1987.

Frow, John. *Cultural Studies and Cultural Value*. Oxford: Clarendon, 1995.

Frye, Northrop. *Anatomy of Criticism*. Princeton: Princeton UP, 1957.

Furst, Lilian R. *Fictions of Romantic Irony*. Cambridge, MA: Harvard UP, 1984.

Gadamer, Hans-Georg. *Reason in the Age of Science*. Cambridge: MIT Press, 1981.

—. *Truth and Method*. New York: Seabury, 1975.

Gagnier, Regenia. *Subjectivities: A History of Self-Representation in Britain, 1832–1920*. Oxford: Oxford UP, 1991.

Gallagher, Catherine, and Stephen Greenblatt. *Practicing New Historicism*. Chicago: U of Chicago P, 2000.

Gasché, Rodolphe. *The Wild Card of Reading: On Paul de Man*. Cambridge, MA: Harvard UP, 1998.

Genette, Gérard. *The Architext: An Introduction*. Berkeley: U of California P, 1992.

—. *Narrative Discourse: An Essay in Method*. Ithaca: Cornell UP, 1970.

—. *Paratexts: Thresholds of Interpretation*. Cambridge: Cambridge UP, 1997.

Gentner, Deidre, and Ilene M. France. "The Verb Mutability Effect: Studies of the Combinatorial Semantics of Nouns and Verbs." In Steven L. Small, G. W. Cottrell, and M. Tanenhaus, eds., *Lexical Ambiguity Resolution*. San Mateo: Morgan Kaufmann, 1988. pp. 343–82.

Gergen, Kenneth J. "The Communal Creation of Meaning." In Willis F. Overton and David S. Palermo, eds., *The Nature and Ontogenesis of Meaning*. Hillsdale, NJ: Lawrence Erlbaum, 1994. pp. 19–40.

Gibbs, Raymond. *Intentions in the Experience of Meaning*. Cambridge: Cambridge UP, 1999.

Gilmore-Lehne, William. *Reading Becomes a Necessity of Life: Material and Cultural Life in Rural New England: 1780–1835*. Knoxville: U of Tennessee P, 1989.

Goffman, Erving. *Frame Analysis*. Cambridge, MA: Harvard UP, 1974.

Goodman, Nelson. "Metaphors as Moonlighting." In Sheldon Sacks, ed., *On Metaphor*. Chicago: U of Chicago P, 1979. pp. 175–80.

Gracia, Jorge J.E. "A Theory of the Author." In William Irwin, ed., *The Death and Resurrection of the Author?* Westport: Greenwood P, 2002. pp. 161–90

—. *Texts: Ontological Status, Identity, Author, Audience*. Albany: SUNY P, 1996.

Graff, Gerald. "Determinacy/Indeterminacy." In Frank Lentricchia and Thomas McLaughlin, eds., *Critical Terms for Literary Study*. Rev. ed. Chicago: U of Chicago P, 1995. pp. 163–76

Gramsci, Antonio. *Selections from the Prison Notebooks*. Trans. Q. Hoare and G.N. Smith. New York: International, 1971.

Green, Georgia M. "Ambiguity Resolution and Discourse Interpretation." In Kees van Deemter and Stanley Peters, eds., *Semantic Ambiguity and Underspecification*. Stanford: CSLI Publications, 1996. pp. 1–26.

Greenblatt, Stephen. "Columbus Runs Aground." In Paola Bottalla and Michela Calderaro, eds., *Counting and Recounting: Measuring Inner and Outer Space in the Renaissance*. Trieste: Edizioni La Mongolfiera, 1995.

—. *Marvelous Possessions: The Wonder of the New World*. Oxford: Clarendon, 1988.

—. *Renaissance Self-Fashioning: From More to Shakespeare*. Chicago: U of Chicago P, 1980.

—. *Shakespearean Negotiations: The Circulation of Social Energy in Renaissance England*. Oxford: Clarendon, 1988.

Greenfield, Sayre N. *The Ends of Allegory*. Newark: U of Delaware P, 1998.

Green-Lewis, Jennifer. *Framing the Victorians*. Ithaca: Cornell UP, 1996.

—. "Landscape, Loss and Sexuality." *Victorian Studies* 39 (Spring 1996): 391–404.

Grice, Paul. *Studies in the Ways of Words*. Cambridge, MA: Harvard UP, 1989.

Griffiths, Paul. *Religious Reading: The Place of Reading in the Practice of Religion*. New York: Oxford UP, 1999.

Hamacher, Werner, Neil Hertz, and Thomas Keenan, eds. *Responses on Paul de Man's Wartime Journalism*. Lincoln: U of Nebraska P, 1989.

Hancher, Michael. "Dead Letters: Wills and Poems." In Sanford Levinson and Steven Mailloux, eds., *Interpreting Law and Literature*. Evanston, IL: Northwestern UP, 1988. pp. 101–14

—. "Three Kinds of Intention." *Modern Language Notes* 87 (1992): 827–51.

Hardin, Michael. *Playing the Reader: The Homoerotics of Self-Reflexive Fiction*. New York: Peter Lang, 2000.

Harries, Karsten. "The Many Uses of Metaphor." In Sheldon Sacks, ed., *On Metaphor*. Chicago: U of Chicago P, 1979. pp. 165–72.

Harris, Wendell. *Interpretive Acts: In Search of Meaning*. Oxford: Clarendon, 1988.

—. *Literary Meaning: Reclaiming the Study of Literature*. New York: NYU Press, 1996.

Hassett, Constance W. *The Elusive Self in the Poetry of Robert Browning*. Athens: Ohio UP, 1982.

Hermerén, Göran. "Allusions and Intentions." In Gary Iseminger, ed., *Intention and Interpretation*. Philadelphia: Temple UP, 1992. pp. 203–20.

Hernadi, Paul. *Beyond Genre: New Directions in Literary Classification*. Ithaca: Cornell UP, 1972.

Hesse, Mary. *Models and Analogies in Science*. London: Sheed and Ward, 1963.

Hirsch, E.D. *Aims of Interpretation*. Chicago: U of Chicago P, 1987.

—. "Past Intentions and Present Meanings." *Essays in Criticism* 33 (April 1983): 79-98.

—. "Three Dimensions of Hermeneutics." In David Newton-DeMolina, ed., *On Literary Intention*. Edinburgh: Edinburgh UP, 1976. pp. 194–209.

—. "Transhistorical Intentions and the Persistence of Allegory." *New Literary History* 25 (Summer 1994): 549–67.

—. *Validity in Interpretation*. New Haven: Yale UP, 1967.

Hoffman, Robert R. "Some Ambiguities in the Study of Ambiguity." In David S. Gorfein, ed., *Resolving Semantic Ambiguity*. New York: Springer-Verlag, 1989.

Hofmeyr, Isabel. *The Portable Bunyan: A Transnational History of* The Pilgrim's Progress. Princeton: Princeton UP, 2004.

Holbrook, Jennifer K., Kurt P. Eiselt, Edward H. Matthei and Richard H. Granger, Jr., "(Almost) Never Letting Go: Inference Retention During Text

Understanding." In Steven L. Small, G.W. Cottrell, and M. Tanenhaus, eds., *Lexical Ambiguity Resolution*. San Mateo: Morgan Kaufmann, 1988. pp. 383–40

Holland, Norman. *The Critical I*. New York: Columbia UP, 1992.

—. *The Dynamics of Literary Response*. New York: Oxford UP, 1968.

—. *Five Readers Reading*. New Haven: Yale UP, 1975.

Hollander, John. *Vision and Resonance: Two Senses of Poetic Form*. New York: Oxford UP, 1975.

Holt, Jason. "The Marginal Life of the Author." In William Irwin, ed., *The Death and Resurrection of the Author?* Westport, CT: Greenwood, 2002. pp. 65–78.

Horton, Susan R. *Interpreting Interpreting: Interpreting Dickens's* Dombey. Baltimore: Johns Hopkins UP, 1979.

Hough, Graham. "An Eighth Type of Ambiguity." In David Newton-DeMolina, ed., *On Literary Intention*. Edinburgh: Edinburgh UP, 1976.

Hoy, David Couzens. "Interpreting the Law: Hermeneutical and Poststructuralist Perspectives." In Sanford Levinson and Steven Mailloux, eds., *Interpreting Law and Literature*. Evanston, IL: Northwestern UP, 1988. pp. 319–38.

Huisman, Johannes A. "Generative Classification in Medieval Literature." In Joseph P. Strelka, ed., *Theories of Literary Genre*. University Park: Pennsylvania State UP, 1978.

Hutcheon, Linda. *Irony's Edge: The Theory and Politics of Irony*. New York: Routledge, 1994.

—. *A Theory of Parody: The Teachings of Twentieth-Century Art Forms*. New York: Methuen, 1985.

Iggers, Georg G. *Historiography in the Twentieth Century: From Scientific Objectivity to the Postmodern Challenge*. Hanover, NH: Wesleyan UP, 1997.

Ingarden, Roman. *The Cognition of the Literary Work of Art*. Trans. Ruth Ann Crowley and Kenneth Olson. Evanston, IL: Northwestern UP, 1973.

—. *The Literary Work of Art: An Investigation on the Borderlines of Ontology, Logic, and Theory of Literature*. Evanston, IL: Northwestern UP, 1973.

Irvine, Martin. *The Making of Textual Culture: 'Grammatica' and Literary Theory, 350–1100*. Cambridge: Cambridge UP, 1994.

Irwin, William, ed. *The Death and Resurrection of the Author?* Westport: Greenwood P, 2002.

—. *Intentionalist Interpretation: A Philosophical Explanation and Defense*. Westport, CT: Greenwood, 1999.

Iseminger, Gary, ed. *Intention and Interpretation*. Philadelphia: Temple UP, 1992.

Iser, Wolfgang. *The Act of Reading: A Theory of Aesthetic Response*. Baltimore: Johns Hopkins UP, 1978.

—. *The Fictive and the Imaginary: Charting Literary Anthropology*. Baltimore: Johns Hopkins UP, 1993.

—. *The Implied Reader*. Baltimore: Johns Hopkins UP, 1974.

—. "Interaction between Text and Reader." In Susan R. Suleiman and Inge Crosman, eds., *The Reader in the Text: Essays on Audience and Interpretation*. Princeton: Princeton UP, 1980. pp. 106–19.

—. *Prospecting: From Reader Response to Literary Anthropology*. Baltimore: Johns Hopkins UP, 1989.

—. "Talk like Whales: A Reply to Stanley Fish." *Diacritics* 11 (Fall 1981): 82–87.

Jackson, H.J. *Marginalia: Readers Writing in Books*. New Haven: Yale UP, 2001.

James, Henry. *The Art of the Novel*. New York: Scribner's Sons, 1934.

Jameson, Fredric. *The Political Unconscious: Narrative as a Socially Symbolic Act*. Ithaca: Cornell, 1981.

—. *Postmodernism. Or, The Cultural Logic of Late Capitalism*. Durham: Duke UP, 1991.

Jauss, Hans Robert. *Toward an Aesthetic of Reception*. Minneapolis: U of Minnesota P, 1982.

Jay, Gregory S. "Postmodernism in *The Wasteland*: Women, Mass Culture, and Others." In Kevin J.H. Dettmar, ed., *Rereading the New: A Backward Glance at Modernism*. Ann Arbor: U of Michigan P, 1992. pp. 221–48.

Johns, Adrian. *The Nature of the Book: Print and Knowledge in the Making*. Chicago: U of Chicago P, 1998.

Johnson, Barbara. "Writing." In Frank Lentricchia and Thomas McLaughlin, eds., *Critical Terms for Literary Study*. Rev. ed. Chicago: U of Chicago P, 1995. pp. 39–49.

Jordan, Glenn, and Chris Weedon. "Whose History is It?: Class, Cultural Democracy and Constructions of the Past." *Cultural Politics: Class, Gender, Race and the Postmodern World*. Oxford: Basil Blackwell, 1995. pp. 112–74.

Joseph, Jay. *The Gene Illusion: Genetic Research in Psychiatry and Psychology*. New York: Algora, 2004.

Juhl, P.D. *Interpretation: An Essay in the Philosophy of Literary Criticism*. Princeton: Princeton UP, 1980.

Kambouchner, Denis. "The Theory of Accidents." *Glyph* 7. Baltimore: Johns Hopkins UP, 1980. pp. 149–75.

Karolides, Nicholas J., ed. *Reader Response in the Classroom: Envoking and Interpreting Meaning in Literature*. Rev, Mahneck, NJ: Lawrence Erlbaum, 2000.

Kennedy, Alan. *The Psychology of Reading*. London: Methuen, 1984.

Kennedy, Ian H.C. "In Memoriam and the Tradition of Pastoral Elegy." *Victorian Poetry* 15 (1977): 351–66.

Kent, Thomas. *Interpretation and Genre: The Role of Generic Perception in the Study of Narrative Texts*. Lewisburg, PA: Bucknell UP, 1986.

Kermode, Frank. *The Genesis of Secrecy*. Cambridge, MA: Harvard UP, 1979.

Kim, Jin-Ok. *Charlotte Brontë and Female Desire*. New York: Peter Lang, 2003.

King, Laurie R. "Why a Mystery." 1996 Edgar Allan Poe Awards Supplement. *New York Times Magazine*, April 21, 1996. p. 2.

Kintgen, Eugene. *Reading in Tudor England*. Pittsburgh: U of Pittsburgh P, 1996.

Kitchener, Richard F. "Semantic Naturalism: The Problem of Meaning and Naturalistic Psychology." In Willis F. Overton and David S. Palermo, eds., *The Nature and Ontogenesis of Meaning*. Hillsdale, NJ: Lawrence Erlbaum, 1994. pp. 279–93.

Kittay, Eva Feder. *Metaphor*. Oxford: Oxford UP, 1987.

Kittler, Friedrich A. *Discourse Networks 1800/1900*. Stanford: Stanford UP, 1990.

Klancher, Jon. *The Making of the English Reading Audiences, 1790–1832*. Madison: U of Wisconsin P, 1987.

Kligerman, Karen Ruth. "The Ravishing Word: Modern Narrative and the Romantic Ode." Diss. New York University, 1998.

Knapp, Steven, and Walter Benn Michaels. "Against Theory." In W.J.T. Mitchell, ed., *Against Theory: Literary Studies and the New Pragmatism*. Chicago: U of Chicago P, 1985. pp. 11–30.

—. "Against Theory 2: Hermeneutics and Deconstruction." *Critical Inquiry* 14 (1987): 49–69.

—. "Literary Theory and its Discontents." *New Literary History* 24 (1994): 649–50.

Köberl, Johann. *The Indeterminacy of Beowulf*. Lanham, MD: U Press of America, 2002.

Koelb, Clayton. *The Incredulous Reader: Literature and the Function of Disbelief*. Ithaca: Cornell UP, 1984.

—. *Inventions of Reading: Rhetoric and the Literary Imagination*. Ithaca: Cornell UP, 1988.

Kofman, Sarah. *Nietzsche and Metaphor*. Trans. Duncan Large. Stanford: Stanford UP, 1993.

Krausz, Michael. "Intention and Interpretation: Hirsch and Margolis." In Gary Iseminger, ed., *Intention and Interpretation*. Philadelphia: Temple UP, 1992.

Kristeva, Julia. *The Kristeva Reader*. Ed. Toril Moi. New York: Columbia UP, 1986.

—. *Revolution in Poetic Language*. New York: Columbia UP, 1984.

Kroeber, Karl. *Retelling/Rereading: the Fate of Storytelling in Modern Times*. New Brunswick, NJ: Rutgers UP, 1992.

Kucich, John. "Confessions of a Convert: Strategies for Teaching Theory." In Dianne Sadoff and William E. Cain, eds., *Teaching Contemporary Theory to Undergraduates*. New York: MLA, 1994. pp. 45–56.

Kuhn, Thomas. *The Structure of Scientific Revolutions.* 2nd ed. Chicago: U of Chicago P, 1970.

Lacan, Jacques. *Ecrits: A Selection.* New York: Norton, 1977.

Lakoff, George. *Philosophy in the Flesh: The Embodied Mind and Its Challenge to Western Thought.* New York: Basic Books, 1999.

Lakoff, George, and Mark Johnson. *Metaphors We Live By.* Chicago: U of Chicago P, 1980.

Lanham, Richard A. *A Handlist of Rhetorical Terms.* 2nd ed. Berkeley: U of California P, 1991.

Latour, Bruno. *Science in Action.* Cambridge, MA: Harvard UP, 1987.

Leenhardt, Jacques. "Toward a Sociology of Reading." In Susan R. Suleiman and Inge Crosman, eds., *The Reader in the Text: Essays on Audience and Interpretation.* Princeton: Princeton UP, 1980.

Le Guern, Michel. *Sémantique de la métaphore et de la métonymie.* Paris: Larousse, 1973.

Leitch, Vincent B. *American Literary Criticism from the Thirties to the Eighties.* New York: Columbia UP, 1988.

—. *Deconstructive Criticism: An Advanced Introduction.* New York: Columbia UP, 1983.

Lentricchia, Frank. "Foucault's legacy—A New Historicism?" In H. Aram Veeser, ed., *The New Historicism.* New York: Routledge, 1989.

Levine, George, ed. *Aesthetics and Ideology.* New Brunswick, NJ: Rutgers UP, 1994.

Levinson, Jerrold. "Intention and Interpretation: A Last Look." In Gary Iseminger, ed., *Intention and Interpretation.* Philadelphia: Temple UP, 1992. pp. 221–56.

Levinson, Sanford, and Steven Mailloux, eds. *Interpreting Law and Literature.* Evanston, IL: Northwestern UP, 1988.

Lewis, Bernard. *The Middle East: 2000 Years of History from the Rise of Christianity to the Present Day.* London: Weidenfeld and Nichols, 1996.

Liedtke, Frank W. "Representational Semantics and Illocutionary Acts." In Armin Burkhardt, ed., *Speech Acts, Meaning and Intentions: Critical Approaches to the Philosophy of John R. Searle.* New York: Walter de Gruyter, 1990. pp. 194–209.

Lodge, David. *The Modes of Modern Writing: Metaphor, Metonymy, and the Typology of Modern Literature.* Ithaca: Cornell UP, 1977.

Lowell, Robert. "On 'Skunk Hour.'" In Thomas Parkinson, ed., *Robert Lowell: A Collection of Critical Essays.* Englewood Cliffs, NJ: Prentice-Hall, 1968.

Lowes, Livingston. *The Road to Xanadu.* Boston: Houghton Mifflin, 1927.

Lyas, Colin. "Wittgensteinian Intentions." In Gary Iseminger, ed., *Intention and Interpretation.* Philadelphia: Temple UP, 1992. pp. 132–57.

Lyon, Arabella. *Intentions: Negotiated, Contested, and Ignored.* University Park: Pennsylvania State UP, 1998.

Lyons, John. *Semantics: I and II.* Cambridge: Cambridge UP, 1977.

Lyons, William. *Approaches to Intentionality.* Oxford: Oxford UP, 1995.

Lyotard, Jean-François. *The Differend: Phrases in Dispute.* Minneapolis: U of Minnesota P, 1988.

Lytinen, Steven L. "Are Vague Words Ambiguous?" In Steven L. Small, G.W. Cottrell, and M. Tanenhaus, eds., *Lexical Ambiguity Resolution.* San Mateo: Morgan Kaufmann, 1988. pp. 109–28.

Maasen, Sabine, and Peter Weingart. *Metaphors and the Dynamics of Knowledge.* London: Routledge, 2000.

MacCaffrey, Isabel G. *Spenser's Allegory: The Anatomy of Imagination.* Princeton: Princeton UP, 1976.

Mac Cormac, Earl R. *A Cognitive Theory of Metaphor.* Cambridge MA: MIT P, 1988.

Macherey, Pierre. *A Theory of Literary Production.* Trans. Geoffrey Wall. 1978; London: Routledge, 1985.

Machor, James L., ed. *Readers in History: Nineteenth-Century American Literature and the Contexts of Response.* Baltimore: Johns Hopkins UP, 1993.

Machor, James L., and Philip Goldstein, eds. *Reception Study: From Literary Theory to Cultural Studies.* New York: Routledge, 2001.

Mackay, Laura. "'Midway Between Poetry and Doctrine': Marcel Proust, Samuel Beckett and Translation as Poetics." Diss. New York University, 2000.

MacQueen, John. *Allegory.* London: Methuen, 1970.

Madison, G.B. *The Hermeneutics of Postmodernity: Figures and Themes.* Bloomington: Indiana UP, 1990.

Madsen, Deborah L. *Rereading Allegory: A Narrative Approach to Genre.* New York: St. Martin's P, 1994.

Mailloux, Steven. "Interpretation and Rhetorical Hermeneutics." In James L. Machor and Philip Goldstein, eds., *Reception Study: From Literary Theory to Cultural Studies.* New York: Routledge, 2001. pp. 39–60.

—. *Reception Histories: Rhetoric, Pragmatism and American Cultural Politics.* Ithaca: Cornell UP, 1998.

—, ed. *Rhetorical Power.* Ithaca: Cornell UP, 1989.

—. *Rhetoric, Sophistry, Pragmatism.* Cambridge: Cambridge UP, 1995.

Malle, Bertram F., Louis J. Moses, and Dare A. Baldwin, eds. *Intentions and Intentionality: Foundations of Social Cognition.* Cambridge: MIT P, 2001.

Malmgren, Carl D. *Anatomy of Murder.* Bowling Green, OH: Bowling Green State UP, 2001.

Manguel, Alberto. *A History of Reading.* New York: Penguin, 1996.

Margolis, Joseph. *The New Puzzle of Interpretation.* Chicago: U of Chicago P, 1992.

—. *Pragmatism Without Foundations: Reconciling Realism and Relativism.* Oxford: Basil Blackwell, 1986.

—. "Robust Relativism." In Gary Iseminger, ed., *Intention and Interpretation.* Philadelphia: Temple UP, 1992. pp. 41–50.

Marino, Adrian. "Towards a Definition of Literary Genres." In Joseph P. Strelka, ed., *Theories of Literary Genre.* University Park: Pennsylvania State UP, 1978.

Marsden, Jean I., ed. *The Appropriation of Shakespeare: Post-Renaissance Reconstructions of the Works and the Myth.* New York: St. Martin's P, 1991.

Maynard, John. "The Bildungsroman." In Patrick Brantlinger and William B. Thesing, eds., *A Companion to the Victorian Novel.* Oxford: Blackwell, 2002. pp. 279–303.

—. *Charlotte Brontë and Sexuality.* Cambridge: Cambridge UP, 1984.

—. "In Search of Real Bioreaders." *Biography and Source Studies* 5 (2003): 105-36.

—. "Sex, Love, and Victorian Poetry." In Richard Cronin, Alison Chapman, and Antony H. Harrison, eds., *A Companion to Victorian Poetry.* Oxford: Blackwood, 2002. pp. 543–66.

—. *Victorian Discourses on Sexuality and Religion.* Cambridge: Cambridge UP, 1993.

McCabe, Allysa. "Narrative Threads of Metaphor." In Charlotte Mandell and Allysa McCabe, eds., *The Problem of Meaning: Behavioral and Cognitive Perspectives.* New York: Elsevier, 1997. pp. 347–76.

McGann, Jerome J. *Black Riders: The Visible Language of Modernism.* Princeton: Princeton UP, 1993.

—. *The Textual Condition.* Princeton: Princeton UP, 1991.

McHenry, Elizabeth. "Forgotten Readers: African-American Literary Societies and the American Scene." In James P. Danky and Wayne A. Wiegand, eds., *Print Culture in a Diverse America.* Urbana: U of Illinois P, 1998. pp. 149–72.

—. *Forgotten Readers: Recovering the Lost History of African American Literary Societies.* Durham, NC: Duke UP, 2002.

Meaney, Michael J. "Nature, Nurture and the Disunity of Knowledge." *Annals of the New York Academy of Sciences* 935 (2001): 50–61.

Mellor, Anne K. *English Romantic Irony.* Cambridge, MA: Harvard UP, 1980.

Michaels, Walter Benn. "The Interpreter's Self: Peirce on the Cartesian 'Subject.'" In Jane P. Tompkins, ed., *Reader-Response Criticism.* Baltimore: Johns Hopkins UP, 1980. pp. 185–200.

—. "The Shape of the Signifier." *Critical Inquiry* 27 (2001): 271–83.

Miller, J. Hillis. *Speech Acts in Literature.* Stanford: Stanford UP, 2001.

—. *Theory Now and Then.* London: Harvester Wheatsheaf, 1990.

Mills, Sara. *Discourse.* New York: Routledge, 1997.

Mineur, Anne-Marie, and Paul Buitelaar. "A Compositional Treatment of Polysemous Arguments in Categorical Grammar." In Kees van Deemter and Stanley Peters, eds., *Semantic Ambiguity and Underspecification*. Stanford: CSLI Publications, 1996. pp. 125–44.

Mistacco, Vicki. "The Theory and Practice of Reading Nouveaux Romans." In Susan R. Suleiman and Inge Crosman, eds., *The Reader in the Text: Essays on Audience and Interpretation*. Princeton: Princeton UP, 1980. pp. 371–400.

Mitchell, W.J.T., ed. *Against Theory: Literary Studies and the New Pragmatism*. Chicago: U of Chicago P, 1985.

Mitscherling, Jeff, Tanya DiTommaso, and Aref Nayed. *The Author's Intention*. Lanham, MD: Lexington Books, 2004.

Moi, Toril. *Sexual/Textual Politics: Feminist Literary Theory*. London: Methuen, 1985.

Montgomery, Robert. *Terms of Response: Language and Audience in Seventeenth and Eighteenth Century Theory*. University Park: Pennsylvania State UP, 1992.

Morson, Gary Saul. *Boundaries of Genre: Dostoevsky's* Diary of a Writer *and the Traditions of Literary Utopia*. Austin: U of Texas P, 1981.

Mueller-Vollmer, Kurt, ed. Introduction. *The Hermeneutics Reader*. New York: Continuum, 1985.

Munslow, Alun. *Deconstructing History*. London: Routledge, 1997.

Murphy, Tim. *Nietzsche, Metaphor, Religion*. Albany: SUNY UP, 2001.

Nardocchio, Elaine F., ed. *Reader Response to Literature: The Empirical Dimension*. New York: Mouton de Gruyter, 1992.

Nathan, Daniel O. "Irony, Metaphor, and the Problem of Intention." In Gary Iseminger, ed., *Intention and Interpretation*. Philadelphia: Temple UP, 1992. pp. 183–202.

Nehamas, Alexander. "Writer, Text, Work, Author." In William Irwin, ed., *The Death and Resurrection of the Author?* Westport: Greenwood P, 2002. pp. 95–115.

Nell, Victor. *Lost in a Book: The Psychology of Reading for Pleasure*. New Haven: Yale UP, 1988.

Neven, Sesardic. *Making Sense of Heritability*. Cambridge: Cambridge UP, 2005.

Newton-DeMolina, David, ed. *On Literary Intention*. Edinburgh: Edinburgh UP, 1976.

Ngai, Sianne. *Ugly Feelings*. Cambridge, MA: Harvard UP, 2005.

Nietzsche, Friedrich. "On Truth and Lies in an Extra-Moral Sense." *The Portable Nietzsche*. Ed. Walter Kaufmann. New York: Viking P, 1954.

Niranjana, Tejaswini. *Siting Translation: History, Post-Structuralism, and the Colonial Context*. Berkeley: U of California P, 1992.

North, Michael. "Authorship and Autography." *PMLA* 116 (2001): 1378–85.

Novick, Peter. *That Noble Dream: The 'Objectivity Question' and the American Historical Profession*. Cambridge: Cambridge UP, 1988.

Ogden, C.K., and I.A. Richards. *The Meaning of Meaning*. 1923; rpt. New York: Harcourt Brace, 1956.

Overton, Willis F. "Contexts of Meaning: The Computational and the Embodied Mind." In Willis F. Overton and David S. Palermo, eds., *The Nature and Ontogenesis of Meaning*. Hillsdale, NJ: Lawrence Erlbaum, 1994. pp. 1–18.

Overton, Willis F., and David S. Palermo, eds. *The Nature and Ontogenesis of Meaning*. Hillsdale, NJ: Lawrence Erlbaum, 1994.

Palmer, Richard E. *Hermeneutics: Interpretation Theory in Schleiermacher, Dilthey, Heidegger and Gadamer*. Evanston, IL: Northwestern UP, 1969.

Pappas, Nickolas. "Authorship and Authority." In William Irwin, ed., *The Death and Resurrection of the Author?* Westport, CT: Greenwood P, 2002. pp. 117–28.

Paré, Anthony. "Genre and Identity: Individuals, Institutions, and Ideology." In Richard Coe, Lorelei Lingard, and Tatiana Teslenko, eds., *The Rhetoric and Ideology of Genre*. Cresskill: Hampton Press, 2002. pp. 57–72.

Parisi, Domenico, and Cristiano Castelfranchi. "Disambiguation in a Lexically Based Sentence Understanding System." In Steven L. Small, G. W. Cottrell, and M. Tanenhaus, eds., *Lexical Ambiguity Resolution*. San Mateo: Morgan Kaufmann, 1988.

Parker, Hershel. "Lost Authority: Non-Sense, Skewed Meanings, and Intentionless Meanings." In W.J.T. Mitchell, ed., *Against Theory: Literary Studies and the New Pragmatism*. Chicago: U of Chicago P, 1985.

Passmore, J.A. "The Objectivity of History." *Philosophy* 33 (April 1958): 97–111.

Paterson, Lee. "Literary History." In Frank Lentricchia and Thomas McLaughlin, eds., *Critical Terms for Literary Study*. Rev. ed. Chicago: U of Chicago P, 1995. pp. 250–62.

Patterson, Annabel. "Intention." In Frank Lentricchia and Thomas McLaughlin, eds., *Critical Terms for Literary Study*. Rev. ed. Chicago: U of Chicago P, 1995.

Pearson, Jacqueline. *Women's Reading in Britain, 1750–1835: A Dangerous Recreation*. Cambridge: Cambridge UP, 1999.

Peckham, Morse. "The Intentional? Fallacy?" In David Newton-DeMolina, ed., *On Literary Intention*. Edinburgh: Edinburgh UP, 1976.

Peirce, Charles Sanders. *Collected Papers*. Eds. Charles Hartshorne and P. Weiss. Cambridge, MA: Harvard UP, 1931.

Piattelli-Palmarini, Massimo, and Carlo Cecchetto. "The Problem of Meaning in Generative Grammar." In Charlotte Mandell and Allyssa McCabe, eds., *The Problem of Meaning: Behavioral and Cognitive Perspectives*. New York: Elsevier, 1997. pp. 415–70.

Pinker, Steven. *The Blank Slate: The Modern Denial of Human Nature.* New York: Viking, 2002.

—. "Why Nature and Nurture Won't Go Away." *Daedalus* (Fall 2004): 5–17.

Plato. *The Dialogues of Plato.* Oxford: Clarendon, 1875.

Poesio, Massimo. "Semantic Ambiguity and Perceived Ambiguity." In Kees van Deemter and Stanley Peters, eds., *Semantic Ambiguity and Underspecification.* Stanford: CSLI Publications, 1996. pp. 159–202.

Poovey, Mary. *Uneven Developments: The Ideological Work of Gender in Mid-Victorian England.* Chicago: U of Chicago P, 1988.

Porter, Roy, ed. *Rewriting the Self: Histories from the Renaissance to the Present.* London: Routledge, 1997.

Prather, P.A., and David A. Swinney. "Lexical Processing and Ambiguity Resolution." In Steven L. Small, G.W. Cottrell, and M. Tanenhaus, eds., *Lexical Ambiguity Resolution.* San Mateo: Morgan Kaufmann, 1988. pp. 289–310.

Pratt, Mary Louise. "Ideology and Speech-Act Theory." *Poetics Today* 7 (1986): 59–72.

—. "The Ideology of Speech-Act Theory." *Centrum* n.s. 1 (1981): 5–18.

—. "Interpretive Strategies/Strategic Interpretations: On Anglo-American Reader Response Criticism." *Boundary* 2, 11 (1982–83): 201–31.

—. *Toward a Speech Act Theory of Literary Discourse.* Bloomington: Indiana UP, 1977.

Prince, Gerald. "Introduction to the Study of the Narratee." In Jane P. Tompkins, ed., *Reader-Response Criticism.* Baltimore: Johns Hopkins UP, 1985. pp. 7–25.

Putnam, Hilary. "The Meaning of 'Meaning'." In K. Gunderson, ed., *Language, Mind, and Knowledge.* Minneapolis: U of Minnesota P, 1975. pp. 131–93.

Quamen, Harvey N. "Unnatural Interbreeding: H. G. Wells's A *Modern Utopia* as Species and Genre." *Victorian Literature and Culture* 33 (2005): 67–84.

Quilligan, Maureen. *The Language of Allegory: Defining the Genre.* Ithaca: Cornell UP, 1979.

Quine, W.V. "A Postscript on Metaphor." In Sheldon Sacks, ed., *On Metaphor.* Chicago: U of Chicago P, 1979. pp. 159–60.

—. *Word and Object.* Cambridge: MIT Press, 1960.

Rabinowitz, Peter. *Before Reading: Narrative Conventions and the Politics of Interpretation.* Ithaca: Cornell UP, 1987.

—. "'What's Hecuba to Us?' The Audience's Experience of Literary Borrowing." In Susan R. Suleiman and Inge Crosman, eds., *The Reader in the Text: Essays on Audience and Interpretation.* Princeton: Princeton UP, 1980. pp. 241–63.

Radway, Janice. *Reading the Romance: Women, Patriarchy, and Popular Culture.* 1984; rev. ed. Chapel Hill: U of North Carolina P, 1991.

Rajan, Tilottama. *The Supplement of Reading: Figures of Understanding in Romantic Theory and Practice*. Ithaca: Cornell UP, 1990.

Raval, Suresh. "Intention and Contemporary Literary Theory." *The Journal of Aesthetics and Art Criticism* 38 (Spring 1980): 261–77.

Raven, James, Helen Small, and Naomi Tadmor, eds. *The Practice and Representation of Reading in England*. Cambridge: Cambridge UP, 1996.

Reboul, Anne. "The Logical Status of Fictional Discourse: What Searle's Speaker Can't Say to his Hearer." In Armin Burkhardt, ed., *Speech Acts, Meaning and Intentions: Critical Approaches to the Philosophy of John R. Searle*. New York: Walter de Gruyter, 1990. pp. 336–63.

Redpath, Theodore. "The Meaning of a Poem." In David Newton-DeMolina, ed., *On Literary Intention*. Edinburgh: Edinburgh UP, 1976.

Reichert, John. "Do Poets Ever Mean What They Say?" *New Literary History* 13 (Autumn 1981): 53-68.

—. *Making Sense of Literature*. Chicago: U of Chicago P, 1977.

—. "More than Kin and Less than Kind: The Limits of Genre Theory." In Joseph P. Strelka, ed., *Theories of Literary Genre*. University Park: Pennsylvania State UP, 1978. pp. 60–65.

Rhiel, Mary, and David Suchoff, eds. *The Seductions of Biography*. New York: Routledge, 1996.

Ricks, Christopher. *The Poems of Tennyson*. Berkeley: U of California P, 1987.

Ricoeur, Paul. "The Metaphorical Process as Cognition, Imagination, and Feeling." In Sheldon Sacks, ed., *On Metaphor*. Chicago: U of Chicago P, 1979. pp. 141–57.

—. *The Rule of Metaphor: Multi-disciplinary Studies of the Creation of Meaning in Language*. Toronto: U of Toronto P, 1978.

—. "La structure, le mot, et l'événement." *Le Conflit des interprétations*. Paris: Seuil, 1969.

—. *Time and Narrative*. Vol. 3. Chicago: U of Chicago P, 1988.

Ridley, Matt. *Nature Via Nurture: Genes, Experience, and What Makes Us Human*. London: Fourth Estate, 2003.

Rivers, Isabel, ed. *Books and Their Readers in Eighteenth-Century England*. Leicester: Leicester UP, 1982.

—. *Books and their Readers in Eighteenth-Century England: New Essays*. New York: Continuum, 2003.

Robbins, Ruth. *Subjectivity*. Basingstoke: Palgrave, 2005.

Rorty, Richard. *Consequences of Pragmatism (Essays: 1972–1980)*. Minneapolis: U of Minnesota P, 1982.

—. *Contingency, Irony and Solidarity*. Cambridge: Cambridge UP, 1989.

—. "Inquiry as Recontextualization: An Anti-Dualist Account of Interpretation." In David R. Hiley, James F. Bohman, and Richard Shusterman, eds.,

The Interpretive Turn: Philosophy, Science, Culture. Ithaca:. Cornell UP, 1991. pp. 59–80.

—. "Nineteenth-Century Idealism and Twentieth-Century Textualism." *Consequences of Pragmatism.* Minneapolis: U of Minnesota P, 1982. pp. 139–59.

—. *Philosophy and the Mirror of Nature.* Princeton: Princeton UP, 1979.

—. "Philosophy without Principles." In W.J.T. Mitchell, ed., *Against Theory: Literary Studies and the New Pragmatism.* Chicago: U of Chicago P, 1985. pp.132–38.

—. "The Pragmatist's Progress." In Stefan Collini, ed., *Interpretation and Overinterpretation.* Cambridge: Cambridge UP, 1992. pp. 89–108.

—. "Response to Simon Critchley." In C. Mouffe, ed., *Deconstruction and Pragmatism.* London: Routledge, 1996. pp. 41–48.

Rose, Jonathan. *The Intellectual Life of the British Working Classes.* New Haven: Yale UP, 2002.

—. "Rereading the English Common Reader: A Preface to the History of Audiences." *Journal of the History of Ideas* 53 (1992).

Rose, Margaret A. *Parody: Ancient, Modern, and Post-Modern.* Cambridge: Cambridge UP, 1993.

Rosmarin, Adena. "On the Theory of 'Against Theory.'" In W.J.T. Mitchell, ed., *Against Theory: Literary Studies and the New Pragmatism.* Chicago: U of Chicago P, 1985.

—. *The Power of Genre.* Minneapolis: U of Minnesota P, 1985.

Roth, Paul A. "Interpretation as Explanation." In David R. Hiley, James F. Bohman, and Richard Shusterman, eds., *The Interpretive Turn: Philosophy, Science, Culture.* Ithaca: Cornell UP, 1991. pp. 179–96.

Rouse, Joseph. "Interpretation in Natural and Human Science." In David R. Hiley, James F. Bohman, and Richard Shusterman, eds., *The Interpretive Turn: Philosophy, Science, Culture.* Ithaca: Cornell UP, 1991. pp. 42–56.

—. *Knowledge and Power: Towards a Political Philosophy of Science.* Ithaca: Cornell UP, 1987.

Rumbaugh, Duane M., and E. Sue Savage-Rumbaugh. "A Comparative Perspective on the Etiology of Meaning and Assaying Behaviors for Meaning." In Charlotte Mandell and Allyssa McCabe, eds., *The Problem of Meaning: Behavioral and Cognitive Perspectives.* New York: Elsevier, 1997. pp. 147–80.

Ruthven, K.K. *Critical Assumptions.* Cambridge: Cambridge UP, 1979.

Ryan, Michael. "Narcissus Autobiographer." *ELH* 43 (1976): 184–208.

Rylance, Rick. *Victorian Psychology and British Culture.* New York: Oxford UP, 2000.

Sacks, Sheldon, ed. *On Metaphor.* Chicago: U of Chicago P, 1979.

Saenger, Paul. "Silent Reading: Its Impact on Late Medieval Script and Society." *Viator: Medieval and Renaissance Studies* 13 (1982): 367–414.

—. *Space Between Words: The Origins of Silent Reading.* Stanford: Stanford UP, 1997.

Said, Edward. *Orientalism.* New York: Pantheon, 1978.

St. Clair, William. *The Reading Nation in the Romantic Period.* Cambridge: Cambridge UP, 2004.

Saville, Julia. *A Queer Chivalry: The Homoerotic Asceticism of Gerard Manley Hopkins.* Charlottesville: U of Virginia P, 2000.

Schaeffer, Jean-Marie. *Qu'est-ce qu'un genre littéraire.* Paris: Seuil, 1989.

Scheffler, Israel. *Beyond the Letter: A Philosophical Inquiry into Ambiguity, Vagueness and Metaphor in Language.* London: Routledge & Kegan Paul, 1979.

Schleiermacher, Friedrich. "Compendium of 1819." In Heinz Kimmerle, ed., *Hermeneutics: The Handwritten Manuscripts.* Missoula: U of Montana P, 1977.

Scholes, Robert. *The Crafty Reader.* New Haven: Yale UP, 2001.

—. *Protocols of Reading.* New Haven: Yale UP, 1989.

—. *Textual Power: Literary Theory and the Teaching of English.* New Haven: Yale UP, 1985.

Schur, Owen. *Victorian Pastoral: Tennyson, Hardy, and the Subversion of Forms.* Columbus: Ohio State UP, 1989.

Searle, John R. *Expression and Meaning: Studies in the Theory of Speech Acts.* Cambridge: Cambridge UP, 1979.

—. *Intentionality: An Essay in the Philosophy of Mind.* Cambridge: Cambridge UP, 1983.

—. "Reiterating the Differences: A Reply to Derrida." *Glyph* 2 (1977): 198–208.

—. *Speech Acts.* Cambridge: Cambridge UP, 1969.

—. "Literary Theory and its Discontents." *New Literary History* 25 (1994): 649–50.

Sharpe, Jenny. *Allegories of Empire.* Minneapolis: U of Minnesota P, 1993.

Sharpe, Kevin. *Reading Revolutions: The Politics of Reading in Early Modern England.* New Haven: Yale UP, 2000.

Shawcross, John. *Intentionality and the New Traditionalism: Some Liminal Means to Literary Revisionism.* University Park: Pennsylvania State UP, 1991.

Shklovsky, Victor. "Art as Technique." *Russian Formalist Criticism: Four Essays.* Trans., and eds., Lee T. Lemon and Marion J. Reis. Lincoln: U of Nebraska Press, 1965.

Shusterman, Richard. "Interpretation, Intention, and Truth." In Gary Iseminger, ed., *Intention and Interpretation.* Philadelphia: Temple UP, 1992. pp. 65–75.

—. *Pragmatist Aesthetics: Living Beauty, Rethinking Art.* Oxford: Blackwell, 1992.

Shuttleworth, Sally. *Charlotte Brontë and Victorian Psychology.* Cambridge: Cambridge UP, 1996.

Sim, Stuart. *Beyond Aesthetics: Confrontations with Poststructuralism and Postmodernism*. Toronto: U of Toronto P, 1992.

—. *Irony and Crisis: A Critical History of Postmodern Culture*. London: Icon P, 2002.

Simpson, Greg B. "Varieties of Ambiguity: What Are We Seeking." In David S. Gorfein, ed., *Resolving Semantic Ambiguity*. New York: Springer-Verlag, 1989.

Simpson, Greg B., and Curt Burgess. "Implications of Lexical Ambiguity Resolution for Word Recognition and Comprehension." In Steven L. Small, G. W. Cottrell, and M. Tanenhaus, eds., *Lexical Ambiguity Resolution*. San Mateo: Morgan Kaufmann, 1988.

Sinfield, Alan. "Cultural Materialism, Othello, and the Politics of Plausibility." *Faultlines: Cultural Materialism and the Politics of Dissident Reading*. Berkeley: U of California P, 1992. pp. 29–51.

Skinner, Quentin. "Motives, Intentions, and the Interpretation of Texts." In David Newton-DeMolina, ed., *On Literary Intention*. Edinburgh: Edinburgh UP, 1976. pp. 210–21.

Slinn, E. Warwick. *Browning and the Fictions of Identity*. Totowa, NJ: Barnes and Noble, 1982.

Small, Helen. *Love's Madness*. Oxford: Clarendon, 1996.

Smith, Barbara Herrnstein. "Actions, Fictions, and the Ethics of Interpretation." *Centrum* 3 (1975): 117–24.

—. *Contingencies of Value: Alternative Perspectives for Critical Theory*. Cambridge, MA: Harvard UP, 1988.

Smith, Laurence D. "Historical and Philosophical Foundations of the Problem of Meaning." In Charlotte Mandell and Allysa McCabe, eds., *The Problem of Meaning: Behavioral and Cognitive Perspectives*. New York: Elsevier, 1997. pp. 15–80.

Sokal, Alan. "Transgressing the Boundaries: Toward a Transformative Hermeneutics of Quantum Gravity." *Social Text* 46/47 (1996): 217–52.

Sparshott, F.E. "Criticism and Performance." In David Newton-DeMolina, ed., *On Literary Intention*. Edinburgh: Edinburgh UP, 1976.

Sperber, D., and D. Wilson. *Relevance: Communication and Cognition*. Oxford: Basil Blackwell, 1986.

Spiller, Elizabeth. *Science, Reading, and Renaissance Literature: The Art of Making Knowledge: 1580–1670*. Cambridge: Cambridge UP, 2004.

Stallybrass, Peter. "Shakespeare, the Individual, and the Text." In Lawrence Grossberg, Cary Nelson, and Paula Treichler, eds., *Cultural Studies*. New York: Routledge, 1992. pp. 593–610.

Stecker, Robert. "Apparent, Implied, and Postulated Authors." In William Irwin, ed., *The Death and Resurrection of the Author?* Westport, CT: Greenwood P, 2002. pp. 129–40.

Steig, Michael. *Stories of Reading: Subjectivity and Literary Understanding.* Baltimore: Johns Hopkins UP, 1989.

Stewart, Garrett. *Reading Voices: Literature and the Phonotext.* Berkeley: U of California P, 1990.

Strawson, P.F. "Intention and Convention in Speech Acts." *The Philosophical Review* 73 (Oct. 1964). pp. 439–60.

Sturges, Robert S. *Medieval Interpretation: Models of Reading in Literary Narrative, 1100–1500.* Carbondale: Southern Illinois UP, 1991.

Su, Soon Peng. *Lexical Ambiguity in Poetry.* London: Longman, 1994.

Swinden, Patrick. *Literature and the Philosophy of Intention.* New York: St. Martin's P, 1999.

Szondi, Peter. *Introduction to Literary Hermeneutics.* Trans. Martha Woodmansee. Cambridge: Cambridge UP, 1995.

Tannen, D. "Ordinary Conversation and Literary Discourse: Coherence and the Poetics of Repetition." In E.H. Bendix, ed., *The Uses of Linguistics.* New York: New York Academy of Sciences, 1990. pp. 15–32.

Taylor, Andrew. *Textual Situations: Three Medieval Manuscripts and Their Readers.* Philadelphia: U of Pennsyslvania P, 2002.

Taylor, Charles. "Interpretation and the Sciences of Man." *Philosophy and the Human Sciences.* Cambridge: Cambridge UP, 1985. pp. 15–57.

Taylor, Gary. *Reinventing Shakespeare: A Cultural History from the Restoration to the Present.* London: Weidenfeld & Nicolson, 1989.

Todorov, Tzvetan. *Genres in Discourse.* Cambridge: Cambridge UP, 1990.

Toker, Leona. "Ambiguities in Vladimir Nabokov's *Invitation to a Beheading.*" In Hans P. Braendlin, ed., *Ambiguities in Literature and Film.* Tallahassee: Florida State UP, 1982. pp. 95–103.

Tolhurst, William. "On What a Text Is and How It Means." *British Journal of Aesthetics* 19 (1979). pp. 3–14.

Tompkins, Jane P. "The Reader in History: the Changing Shape of Reader Response." In Jane P. Tompkins, ed., *Reader-Response Criticism.* Baltimore: Johns Hopkins UP, 1980. pp. 201–32.

Tompkins, Jane P., ed. *Reader-Response Criticism.* Baltimore: Johns Hopkins UP, 1985.

Travis, Molly Abel. *Reading Cultures: The Construction of Readers in the Twentieth Century.* Carbondale: Southern Illinois UP, 1998.

Trotter, David. *The Making of the Reader: Language and Subjectivity in Modern American, English, and Irish Poetry.* New York: St. Martins, 1984.

Tucker, Herbert. "Victorian Paranoia and the Stroke of the Contemporary." CUNY Victorian Conference on Victorian Poetry and its Modernities. May 3, 1996.

Tully, James, ed. *Meaning and Context Quentin Skinner and his Critics.* Princeton, Princeton UP, 1988.

Turner, Mark. "Design for a Theory of Meaning." In Willis F. Overton and David S. Palermo, eds., *The Nature and Ontogenesis of Meaning.* Hillsdale, NJ: Lawrence Erlbaum, 1994.

Tushnet, Mark. "Following the Rules Laid Down: A Critique of Interpretivism and Neutral Principles." In Sanford Levinson and Steven Mailloux, eds., *Interpreting Law and Literature.* Evanston, IL: Northwestern UP, 1988. pp. 193–214.

Tuve, Rosamond. *Allegorical Imagery: Some Mediaeval Books and their Posterity.* Princeton: Princeton UP, 1966.

van Deemter, Kees, and Stanley Peters, eds. *Semantic Ambiguity and Underspecification.* Stanford: CSLI Publications, 1996.

Vickers, Brian. *In Defence of Rhetoric.* Oxford: Clarendon, 1988.

Vrettos, Athena. *Somatic Fictions: Imagining Illness in Victorian Culture.* Stanford: Stanford UP, 1995.

Walker, Cheryl. "Feminist Literary Criticism and the Author." In William Irwin, ed., *The Death and Resurrection of the Author?* Westport, CT: Greenwood P, 2002. pp. 141–60.

Wallenstein, Barry, and Robert Burr. *Visions and Revisions: The Poet's Process.* 1971; rpt. Peterborough, ON: Broadview, 2002.

Warner, Michael. "Uncritical Reading." In Jane Gallop, ed., *Polemic: Critical or Uncritical.* New York: Routledge, 2004. pp. 13–38.

Watson, George. "The Literary Past." In David Newton-DeMolina, ed., *On Literary Intention.* Edinburgh: Edinburgh UP, 1976.

Webb, R.K. *The British Working Class Reader, 1790–1840: Literary and Social Tension.* London: Allen & Unwin, 1955.

Weimann, Robert. *Shakespeare and the Popular Tradition in the Theater: Studies in the Social Dimension of Dramatic Form and Function.* Baltimore: Johns Hopkins UP, 1978.

Weitz, Morris. *The Opening Mind: A Philosophical Study of Humanistic Concepts.* Chicago: U of Chicago P, 1977.

West, Cornel. *The American Evasion of Philosophy: A Genealogy of Pragmatism.* Madison: U of Wisconsin P, 1989.

Wheeler III, Samuel C. "True Figures: Metaphor, Social Relations, and the Sorites." In David R. Hiley, James F. Bohman, and Richard Shusterman, eds., *The Interpretive Turn: Philosophy, Science, Culture.* Ithaca: Cornell UP, 1991.

—. "Metaphor According to Davidson and de Man." In Reed Way Dasenbrock, ed., *Redrawing the Lines.* Minneapolis: U Minnesota P, 1989. pp. 116–39.

White, Hayden. *The Content of the Form: Narrative Discourse and Historical Representation.* Baltimore: Johns Hopkins UP, 1987.

—. *Metahistory: The Historical Imagination in Nineteenth-Century Europe.* Baltimore: Johns Hopkins UP, 1973.

—. *Tropics of Discourse*. Baltimore: Johns Hopkins UP, 1978.

Whitman, Jon. *Allegory: The Dynamics of an Ancient and Medieval Technique*. Oxford: Clarendon, 1987.

Whitney, Paul, and Matthew B. Clark. "Disambiguation and Cognitive Control." In David S. Gorfein, ed., *Resolving Semantic Ambiguity*. New York: Springer-Verlag, 1989.

Whyte, Lancelot Law. *The Unconscious Before Freud*. New York: Basic Books, 1960.

Williams, Carolyn. "Victorian Studies and Cultural Studies." *Victorian Literature and Culture* 27 (1999): 355–64.

Williams, Raymond. *Keywords: A Vocabulary of Culture and Society*. 1976; Hammersmith: Fontana Press, 1983.

Wimsatt, W.K. "Genesis: A Fallacy Revisited." In David Newton-DeMolina, ed., *On Literary Intention*. Edinburgh: Edinburgh UP, 1976.

Wimsatt, W.K., and M.C. Beardsley. "The Intentional Fallacy." In W.K. Wimsatt, ed., *The Verbal Icon: Studies in the Meaning of Poetry*. New York: Farrar Straus & Giroux, 1954. pp. 3–20.

Wittgenstein, Ludwig. *Philosophical Investigations*. New York: Macmillan, 1953.

Young-Zook, Monica. "Cryptic Fathers: Paternal Loss in Victorian Literature." Diss. New York University, 2003.

Žižek, Slavoj. *The Sublime Object of Ideology*. London: Verso, 1989.

Zboray, Ronald. *A Fictive People: Antebellum Economic Development and the American Reading Public*. New York: Oxford UP, 1993.

INDEX